PRESIDENTS

GEORGE WASHINGTON. ABRAHAM LINCOLN.

THE CAPITOL AT WASHINGTON, D.C.

ANDREW JACKSON. ANDREW JOHNSON.

Eng'd by J.C.Buttre, N.Y.

OF THE

UNITED STATES.

ENGRAVED EXPRESSLY FOR ABBOTT'S LIVES OF THE PRESIDENTS.

LIVES OF THE PRESIDENTS

OF

THE UNITED STATES OF AMERICA,

FROM WASHINGTON TO THE PRESENT TIME.

CONTAINING

A NARRATIVE OF THE MOST INTERESTING EVENTS IN THE
CAREER OF EACH PRESIDENT ; THUS CONSTITUTING
A GRAPHIC HISTORY OF THE UNITED STATES.

TO WHICH IS ADDED

𝔄 Chapter showing the Hundred Years' Progress of the Republic.

BY

JOHN S. C. ABBOTT AND RUSSELL H. CONWELL.

ILLUSTRATED WITH PORTRAITS OF ALL THE PRESIDENTS ENGRAVED ON STEEL,
PICTURES OF THEIR PRIVATE RESIDENCES, AND THIRTY OTHER WOOD
ENGRAVINGS OF THE MOST INTERESTING SCENES IN THEIR LIVES ;

TOGETHER WITH ILLUSTRATIONS OF THE CENTENNIAL JUBILEE.

SOLD ONLY BY DISTRIBUTING AGENTS.

PORTLAND, ME.:
H. HALLETT AND COMPANY.
1882.

PREFACE.

THERE are few persons who can read this record of the Lives of the Presidents of the United States without the conviction, that there is no other nation which can present a consecutive series of twenty rulers of equal excellence of character and administrative ability. Probably the least worthy of all our presidents would rank among the best of the kings whom the accident of birth has placed upon hereditary thrones; and not an individual has popular suffrage elevated to the presidential chair, whom one would think of ranking with those many royal monsters who have in turn disgraced all the courts of Europe. This record settles the question, that popular suffrage, in the choice of rulers, is a far safer reliance than hereditary descent.

With us, the freedom of the press is so unlimited, and political partisanship so intense, that few persons have been able to take really an impartial view of the characters of those who have been by one party so inordinately lauded, and by the other so intemperately assailed. But, as we now dispassionately review the past, most readers will probably find many old prejudices dispelled.

In writing these sketches, the authors have endeavored to be thoroughly impartial, and to place themselves in the position which the subject of the sketch occupied, so as to look from his stand-point upon the great questions which he was called to consider. John Adams and Thomas Jefferson were in political antagonism; but no man can read a true record of their lives, and not be convinced that both were inspired with the noblest zeal to promote the best interests of their country and of the human race.

The writers have not thought that impartiality requires that they should refrain from a frank expression of their own views. It is an essential part of biography, that faults as well as virtues should be honestly detailed. No man is perfect. There have certainly been errors and wrong-doings in the past administration of this government. It is not the duty of the impartial historical biographer to ignore such, or to gloss them over. They should be distinctly brought to light as instruction for the future.

The materials from which the writers have drawn these biographical sketches are very abundant. Whatever of merit they possess must consist mainly in the skill which may be exhibited in selecting from the great mass those incidents which will give one the most vivid conception of the individual. The writers have attempted, with much labor, to present a miniature likeness of each character which shall be faithful and striking. If they have failed, they can only say that they have honestly done their best. They have not deemed it expedient to incumber these pages with foot-notes, as most of the important facts here stated, it is believed, are unquestioned; and all will be found substantiated in the memoirs and works, more or less voluminous, of our Chief Magistrates, contained in most of our large libraries.

NOTE. — Since the principal portion of this book was written, the celebrated author, John S. C. Abbott, has passed on to his eternal home. But he will long live on, as one of earth's moral powers, in the hearts of thousands of sincere friends, and in the numerous thrilling volumes of history and biography which he has written.

RUSSELL H. CONWELL.

CONTENTS.

CHAPTER I.

GEORGE WASHINGTON.

CHAPTER VIII.

MARTIN VAN BUREN.

CHAPTER IX.

WILLIAM HENRY HARRISON.

CHAPTER X.

JOHN TYLER.

CHAPTER XI.

JAMES KNOX POLK.

CHAPTER XII.

ZACHARY TAYLOR.

CHAPTER XIII.

MILLARD FILLMORE.

CHAPTER XIV.

FRANKLIN PIERCE.

CHAPTER XV.

JAMES BUCHANAN.

CHAPTER XVI.

ABRAHAM LINCOLN.

CHAPTER XVII.

ANDREW JOHNSON.

CHAPTER XVIII.

ULYSSES S. GRANT.

CHAPTER XIX.

RUTHERFORD B. HAYES.

CHAPTER XX.

JAMES A. GARFIELD.

CHAPTER XXI.

CHESTER ALAN ARTHUR.

CHAPTER XXII.

ONE HUNDRED YEARS' PROGRESS.

LIST OF ILLUSTRATIONS.

STEEL–PLATE ILLUSTRATIONS.

WOOD–CUT ILLUSTRATIONS.

LIVES OF THE PRESIDENTS.

CHAPTER I.

GEORGE WASHINGTON.

Ancestry of Washington. — His Birth and Childhood. — Anecdotes. — The Youthful Engineer. — The Fairfax Family. — Life in the Wilderness. — War with the Indians. — Domestic Griefs. — The French War. — Washington's Heroism at Braddock's Defeat. — Scenes of Woe. — Marriage. — Inheritance of Mount Vernon. — Domestic Habits. — American Revolution. — Patriotism of Washington. — Appointed Commander-in-chief. — Expulsion of the British from Boston. — Battles of the Revolution. — Perplexities and Sufferings. — Spirit of Self-Sacrifice. — Alliance with France. — Capture of Cornwallis. — Attacks upon the Character of Washington. — The Tomahawk and Scalping-Knife. — Close of the War. — Washington chosen President. — His Retirement. — Peaceful Life at Mount Vernon. — Sickness and Death.

Two centuries ago Virginia was almost an unexplored wilderness; but even then the beautiful realm had obtained much renown from the sketches of chance tourists. The climate, the soil, the rivers, bays, mountains, valleys, all combined to render it one of the most attractive spots upon our globe. Two young brothers, of wealth, intelligence, and high moral principle, — Lawrence and John Washington, — were lured by these attractions to abandon their home in England's crowded isle, and seek their fortunes in this new world. They were both gentlemen. Lawrence was a fine scholar, a graduate of Oxford; John was an accomplished man of business.

After a dreary voyage of four months they entered that magnificent inland sea, Chesapeake Bay, and from that ascended the beautiful Potomac. It was a scene as of fairyland which was spread around them that bright summer morning, when their vessel, propelled by a favoring breeze, glided over the mirrored waters of that river which the name of Washington was subsequently to render so renowned. The unbroken forest in all its primeval grandeur swept sublimely over hill and valley. The birch canoes of the Indian, paddled by warriors in their picturesque attire of paint and feathers, glided buoyant as bubbles over the waves. Distance lent enchantment to the view of wigwam villages in sunny coves, with boys and girls frolicking on the beach and in the water.

The two brothers had purchased a large tract of land about fifty miles above the mouth of the river, and on its western banks. John built him a house, and married Miss Anne Pope. Years rolled on, of joys and griefs, of smiles and tears, of births and deaths; and the little drama, so trivial, so sublime, of that family life disappeared, engulfed in the fathomless sea of the ages. Augustine, the second son of John, who, like his father, was an energetic, wise, good man, remained in the paternal homestead, cultivating its broad acres. Life, if prolonged, is a tragedy always. Augustine's wife, Jane Butler, as lovely in character as she was beautiful in person, died, leaving in the house, darkened with grief, three little motherless children. The disconsolate father, in the course of years, found another mother for his bereaved household.

He was singularly fortunate in his choice. Mary Ball was everything that husband or child could desire. She was beautiful in person, intelligent, accomplished, energetic and prudent, and a warm-hearted Christian. Augustine and Mary were married on the 6th of March, 1730. On the 22d of February, 1732, they received into their arms their first-born child. Little did they dream, as they bore their babe to the baptismal font and called him *George Washington*, that that name was to become one of the most memorable in the annals of time. Explain it as we may, there is seldom a great and a good man to be found who has not had a good mother.

In this respect George Washington was very highly blessed. Both of his parents were patterns for a child to follow. The birthplace of George, though very secluded, was one of the most picturesque spots on the banks of the Potomac. His parents were wealthy for those times, and his home was blessed with all substantial comforts. A beautiful lawn, smooth and green, spread in gentle descent from the door-stone of their one-story cottage to the pebbly shore of the river, which here spread out into a magnificent breadth of nearly ten miles. On the eastern bank there extended, as far as the eye could reach, the forest-covered hills and vales of Maryland. A few islands contributed their charm to this view of surpassing loveliness. The smoke of Indian fires curled up from the forest, the flash from the paddle of the Indian canoe glanced over the waves, and occasionally the sails of the white man's ship were seen ascending the stream.

From earliest childhood George developed a very noble character. He had a vigorous constitution, a fine form, and great bodily strength. In childhood he was noted for frankness, fearlessness, and moral courage; and yet he was as far removed as possible from manifesting a quarrelsome spirit, or from displaying any of the airs of the bravado. He never tyrannized over others; and none in his peaceful, rural, virtuous home were found to attempt to tyrannize over him. We must not omit the story, though the world has it by heart, of his cutting the cherry-tree. His reply to his indignant father, whose impetuous nature was roused by the outrage, "Father, I cannot tell a lie, I cut the tree," was but the development in boyhood of the character of his manhood. The father was worthy of the child. "Come to my heart," said he, as he embraced him with flooded eyes. "I had rather lose a thousand trees than find falsehood in my son."

Man is born to mourn. After twelve happy years of union with Mary Ball, when George was but ten years of age, Augustine Washington died, leaving George and five other children fatherless. The grief-stricken mother was equal to the task thus imposed upon her. The confidence of her husband in her judgment and maternal love is indicated by the fact that he left the income of the entire property to her until her children should respectively come of age. Nobly she discharged the task thus imposed upon her. A nation's homage gathers around the memory of the mother of Washington. George never ceased to revere his mother. He attributed to the principles of probity and religion which she instilled into his mind much of his success during the eventful career through which Providence led him.

In the final division of the estate, the oldest son, Lawrence, the child of Jane Butler, inherited Mount Vernon, including twenty-five hundred acres of land. George received the paternal mansion, which was some distance farther down the river, with the broad acres surrounding it. The other children were also amply provided for.

Lady Washington, before her marriage, was regarded as one of the most beautiful girls in Virginia. Her figure was commanding, her features lovely, and her demeanor dignified and courtly. Life's severe discipline developed a character simple, sincere, grave, cheered with earnest and unostentatious piety. Her well-balanced mind gave her great influence over her noble son, which she retained until the hour of her death.

Mrs. Alexander Hamilton tells the story that, when George Washington was in the meridian of his fame, a very brilliant party was given in his honor at Fredericksburg, Va. When the church-bell rang the hour of nine, Lady Washington rose, and said, " Come, George, it is nine o'clock: it is time for us to go home." George, like a dutiful son, offered to his mother his arm, and they retired. We must not, however, fail to record that Mrs. Hamilton admits that, after George had seen his mother safely home, he returned to the party.

There was then, as now, in Virginia, great fondness for splendid horses. Lady Washington had a span of iron-grays, very spirited, and very beautiful. With much pride she sat at her window, and gazed upon the noble creatures feeding upon the lawn, and often gamboling like children at play. One of these fiery colts, though accustomed to the harness with his companion in the carriage, had never been broken to the saddle. Some young men, one day, companions of George, in a frolic endeavored to mount the fiery steed. It could not be done. George, who was then about thirteen years of age, approached, soothed the animal by caresses, and, watching his opportunity, leaped upon his back. The horse, half terrified, half indignant, plunged and reared, in the vain attempt to free himself of his rider, and then, with the speed of the winds, dashed over the fields. George, exultant, sat his horse like a centaur, gave him free rein, and, when he flagged, urged him on.

Fearless, ardent, imprudent, he forgot the nervous energy of the noble steed, and was not aware of the injury he was doing until the horse broke a blood-vessel, and dropped beneath him. Covered with foam, and gasping for breath, the poor creature almost immediately died. George was greatly alarmed, and hastened to his mother to tell her what he had done. Her calm and characteristic reply was, —

" My son, I forgive you, because you have had the courage to tell me the truth at once. Had you skulked away, I should have despised you."

There was a common school in the neighborhood, which George attended, and where he acquired the rudiments of a good English education. He was a diligent scholar, without developing any great intellectual brilliance. He possessed strong common sense and a remarkably well-balanced mind. There is now extant a manuscript in his plain, legible handwriting, in which, in those boyish days, he had carefully written out several forms of business papers, that he might be ready on any emergency, without embarrassment, to draw up correctly such documents. The manuscript contains promissory notes, bills of sale, land warrants, leases, deeds, and wills. His serious, devotional character was developed in those early years. Several hymns, expressing earnest religious sentiments, he had carefully transcribed. Another manuscript book, which he had evidently collated with great care and sedulously studied, contained a record of " Rules of Behavior in Company and in Conversation."

" The boy is father of the man." This lad of thirteen years, in his secluded rural home, was pondering the great mysteries of the present and the future life, and was, with careful study, cultivating his mind, his manners, and his heart. He could hardly have made better preparation for the career which was before him had some good angel whispered into his ear the immense responsibilities which were to be laid upon him, and the renown he was to acquire. It was this early training, to which he was undoubtedly in some degree stimulated by the mind of his mother, to which he was indebted for much of his subsequent success in life.

At sixteen years of age George, then a man in character, and almost a man in stature, left school. He excelled in mathematical studies, and had become familiar with the principles of geometry and trigonometry and of practical surveying. It was then his intention to become a civil engineer. At that time, in this new and rapidly-growing country, there was great demand for such services, and the employment was very lucrative. There were then in the colonies but few men who were proficients in those sciences. George Washington came from school an accomplished man. He had formed his character upon the right model. Everything he did he did well. If he wrote a letter, every word was as plain as print, with spelling, capitals, punctuation, all correct. His diagrams and tables were never scribbled off, but all executed with great beauty. These excellent habits, thus early formed, were retained through life.

Upon leaving school George went to spend a little time with his elder half-brother, Lawrence, at Mount Vernon. Then, as now, that was an enchanting spot. The house was situated upon a swell of land, commanding an extensive view of the Potomac and of the surrounding country. It was nearly one hundred miles above the birthplace of the two children and the home of George. About eight miles from Mount Vernon an English gentleman, Mr. William Fairfax, resided. He was rich, with highly cultivated mind and polished manners, and a model for imitation in all private and social virtues. Lawrence Washington had married one of his daughters. George became intimate with the family, and derived much advantage from his association with these ladies.

Lord Fairfax, a near relative of William, a man of large fortune and of romantic tastes, had been lured by the charms of this delightful region to purchase a vast territory, which extended far away, over the Blue Mountains, to an undefined distance in the interior. It was a property embracing rivers and mountains, forests and prairies, and wealth unexplored. Lord Fairfax was at that time visiting William. He was charmed with young Washington, his frankness, his intelligence, his manliness, his gentlemanly bearing, — a boy in years, a man in maturity of wisdom and character.

Lord Fairfax engaged this lad, then but one month over sixteen years of age, to explore and survey these pathless wilds, a large portion of which was then ranged only by wild beasts and savage men. It may be doubted whether a lad of his age ever before undertook a task so arduous. With a few attendants, the boy entered the wilderness. It was the month of March, cold and blustering. Snow still lingered on the tops of the mountains, and whitened the sunless ravines. The spring freshets had swollen the rivers. The Indians were friendly, hospitable, and willing to act as guides. Frontiersmen, a rough and fearless set of men, were scattered about among the openings in the wilderness.

Through these solitudes the heroic boy was to thread his way, now following the trail of the Indian, now floating in the birch canoe upon the silent rivers, and now climbing mountains or struggling through morasses which the foot of the white man had perhaps never yet pressed. Often the cabin of the settler afforded him shelter for a night. Frequently he slept in the open air, with his feet to the fire. Again, the wigwam of the Indian was hospitably open to receive him. It must have been a strange experience to this quiet, thoughtful, adventurous boy to find himself at midnight, in the forest, hundreds of miles from the haunts of civilization. The cry of the night-bird, the howl of the wolf, or perhaps the wailings of the storm, fell mournfully upon his ear. He gazed upon the brands flickering at his feet, on the ground-floor of the hut. The Indian warrior, his squaw, and the dusky papooses shared with him the fragrant hemlock couch. We have some extracts from the journal which he kept, which give us a vivid idea of the life he then led. Under date of March 15, 1748, he writes, —

"Worked hard till night, and then returned. After supper, we were lighted into a room; and I, not being so good a woodman as the rest, stripped myself very orderly, and went into the bed, as they call it, when, to my surprise, I found it to be nothing but a little straw matted together, without sheet or anything else, but only one threadbare blanket, with double its weight of vermin. I was glad to get up and put on my clothes, and lie as my companions did. Had we not been very tired, I am sure we should not have slept much that night. I made a promise to sleep so no more in a bed, choosing rather to sleep in the open air before a fire."

On the 2d of April he writes, "A blowing, rainy night. Our straw, upon which we were lying, took fire; but I was luckily preserved by one of our men awaking when it was in a flame. We have run off four lots this day."

The following extract from one of his letters, written at this time, develops his serious, thoughtful, noble character, and also the adventurous life into which he had plunged : —

"The receipt of your kind letter of the 2d instant afforded me unspeakable pleasure, as it convinces me that I am still in the memory of so worthy a friend, — a friendship I shall ever be proud of increasing. Yours gave me more pleasure, as I received it among barbarians and an uncouth set of people. Since you received my letter of October last, I have not slept above three or four nights in a bed; but, after walking a good deal all the day, I have lain down before the fire on a little hay, straw, fodder, or bear-skin, whichever was to be had, with man, wife, and children, like dogs and cats; and

WASHINGTON THE SURVEYOR IN A PERILOUS SITUATION.

happy is he who gets the berth nearest the fire. I have never had
my clothes off, but have lain and slept on them, except the few nights
I have been in Fredericksburg."

Such experiences rapidly develop and create character. George
returned from this tramp with all his manly energies consolidated
by toil, peril, and hardship. Though but seventeen years of age,
he was a responsible, self-reliant man. The State of Virginia now
employed him as public surveyor. For three years he was engaged
in these laborious duties, which introduced him to scenes of romance
and adventure, in which his calm, strong, well-regulated spirit found
a singular joy. We can hardly conceive of anything more attractive
than such a life must have been to a young man of poetic imagination. The Indian paddled him, in his fairy-like canoe, along the
river or over the lake. Now he stood, in the bright morning sunlight, upon the brow of the mountain, gazing over an interminable
expanse of majestic forests, where lakes slept, and streams glided,
and valleys opened in Eden-like beauty. Though he often, during

these three years, visited the home of his mother, his headquarters, if we may so speak, were with his brother at Mount Vernon, as this was much more accessible from his field of labor. Lord Fairfax, who, it is said, was the victim of a love disappointment, had built him a substantial stone mansion in the valley beyond the Blue Ridge, where he was living in a sort of baronial splendor, and where George Washington was an ever welcome guest.

At the age of nineteen George Washington was one of the prominent men of the State of Virginia. The Indiáns were now beginning to manifest a hostile spirit. There is between savage and civilized life an " irrepressible conflict." Where wild beasts range freely, offering food for the hunter, there cannot be highly cultivated fields. Where the hum of human industry is heard, with villages, churches, schools, and manufactories, there can be no forest left for buffaloes, bears, and deer. Civilization was rapidly supplanting barbarism, and the savages were alarmed. They kindled their council-fires; pondered the question of the encroachments of industry, education, and wealth ; and resolved, Satan-inspired, to sweep every vestige of civilization from the land, that this continent might remain a howling wilderness.

The war-whoop echoed through the forest, and the Indians lighted their torches and sharpened their scalping-knives and tomahawks in preparation for the great battle. Billows of flame and woe desolated the land. Yelling savages rushed at midnight upon the cabin of the remote settler. Husband, wife, children, were all speedily massacred, and their bodies were consumed in the fire which destroyed their dwellings. No tongue can tell the woes which ensued. The whole military force of Virginia was called into action to meet this terrible foe, emerging at will from the forest, striking its terrific blows, and then retiring to those depths of the wilderness where pursuit was unavailing. The State was divided into districts, over each of which a military commander was appointed with the title of major. The responsibilities of these majors were very great ; for, in the fearful emergency, they were necessarily intrusted with almost dictatorial powers.

George Washington, who, be it remembered, was but nineteen years of age, was one of these majors. With characteristic sagacity and energy, he applied himself to the study of the military art, familiarizing himself with strategy and tactics, making himself a

2

proficient in the manual exercise, and acquiring the accomplishments of a good swordsman. Ingredients of bitterness are mingled in every cup of life. Storm after storm sweeps the ocean. Lawrence Washington was attacked with a painful and fatal disease. With fraternal love, George accompanied him to the West Indies, hoping that tender nursing and a change of climate might save him. " May you die at home!" is one of the Oriental benedictions. The invalid continued to fail during the tour, and only reached home in time to die. Virtues, like vices, love company, and live in groups. The Washingtons were a noble race. Lawrence was the worthy brother of George, endeared to his friends by every attraction which can make home happy. He died at the age of thirty-four, leaving an infant child and a broken-hearted widow.

The grief of George was very bitter. The loss of such a brother, so noble, so loving, was irreparable. Lawrence had been to George as both father and brother. He left a large property. Mount Vernon was bequeathed to his infant daughter; and, should she die without heirs, it was to pass to George, who was the executor of the estate.

Virginia, on the west, is bounded for a distance of several hundred miles by the waters of the Ohio, *la belle rivière*, as the French appropriately named it. England had seized the coast of the North American continent; had peopled it with colonies, whose enterprising, migratory population were rapidly crowding back into the vast and unexplored interior. France, with much sagacity, had seized the two most magnificent rivers of our land, the St. Lawrence and the Mississippi. Each of these European kingdoms, then equally powerful, was jealous of the other. While England was pushing her possessions rapidly towards the centre of the continent, France, equally eager to seize the boundless treasure, was rushing up the St. Lawrence and the Mississippi, establishing military posts and trading depots, forming treaties with the Indian tribes, and claiming, by right of these explorations, all that vast valley of millions of square miles drained by the Mississippi and its tributaries, and by the St. Lawrence and its chain of lakes.

Instead of settling the question by some amicable compromise, both parties determined to fight. Probably both were equally arrogant and unrelenting in their demands. John Bull has never been famed for the spirit of conciliation, and France has never been wanting in ambition. While the wordy warfare was raging between the two powerful contestants, the Indians shrewdly sent a deputation to the Governor of Virginia, inquiring what portion of the country belonged to them, since England, as they expressed it, demanded all the land on one side of the river, and France all upon the other.

And now the dogs of war were let loose. France and England met, straining every nerve, upon the bloody arena. Both parties dragged the Indian tribes into the conflict. Woes ensued which can never be revealed until the judgment of the great day. Conflagration, massacre, outrage, filled all homes with consternation, and deluged the land in misery. The solitude of the wilderness was broken, as savage bands burst from the forest, with the hideous war-whoop, upon the cabin of the lonely settler. The shrieks of the father, the mother, and the maiden, as they suffered all which savage brutality could devise, swept like the moaning wind through the wilderness, and no one was left to tell the tale.

Just before hostilities commenced, the Governor of Virginia sent George Washington as a commissioner to remonstrate with the French against establishing their military posts upon the waters of the Ohio. To carry this remonstrance to the garrisons to which it was sent, it was necessary that he should traverse a wilderness for a distance of five hundred and sixty miles, where there was no path but the trail of the Indian, and no abode but the wigwam of the savage. In this undertaking, there were two objects in view. The ostensible one was to present the remonstrance; the real one was to ascertain the number, strength, and position of the French garrisons.

It was a perilous enterprise. There was danger of perishing in the wilderness. There was danger from the tomahawk of the savage. There was danger that the French might not allow the commissioner to return with information so valuable to their foes; and, in those rude times and regions, it was very easy so to arrange matters that the party could be plundered and massacred. No suitable person could be found to run these risks until George Washington volunteered his services. He was then but twenty years and six months of age. As Governor Dinwiddie, a sturdy old Scotchman, eagerly accepted the proffered service, he exclaimed, —

" Truly, you are a brave lad; and, if you play your cards well, you shall have no cause to repent your bargain."

Washington started from Williamsburg on this perilous expedition on the 14th of November, 1753. There is something very sublime in the calm courage with which he set out, well knowing that he was to pass through the region of hostile Indian tribes; and that it was their practice not merely to kill their prisoners, but to prolong their sufferings, as far as possible, through the most exquisite and diabolical tortures. He took with him but eight men, two of them being Indians. They soon passed the few sparse settlements which were springing up near the Atlantic coast, and plunged into the pathless forest. Winter was fast approaching, and its dismal gales wailed through the tree-tops. The early snow crowned the summits of the mountains, and the autumnal rains had swollen the brooks and the rivers.

Guided by the sagacity of the Indians, they threaded the forest until they reached the Monongahela, which, flowing from the south, unites with the Alleghany from the north, and forms the Ohio. Here they took a canoe, and in eight days paddled down the river to the mouth of the Alleghany, where Pittsburgh now stands. They then descended the Ohio, with an ever-vigilant eye, for a distance of a hundred and twenty miles, to the principal port of the French commandant. Having successfully accomplished thus much of his mission, and fearing that the Indians might of their own will, or instigated by the French, intercept his return, he started, with but one faithful companion, to make his way back through the wilderness on foot, with their packs on their backs and their guns in their hands. Washington's suspicions proved not to be groundless. Some Indians were put upon their trail by the French. Washington's familiarity with wilderness life and Indian strategy enabled him to elude them. One Indian, however, succeeded in joining them, and offered his services as a guide. Treacherously he led them from their path, hoping to lure them into some ambush, and striving, but in vain, with all the arts of Indian cunning, to get possession of Washington's gun.

At night, seeing them so much fatigued by their day's tramp that he thought that they could not possibly pursue him, he, at fifteen paces distant, fired at Washington, missed his aim, and sprang into the woods. He was caught. Washington's companion, Gist, was for dispatching him on the spot; but Washington, regarding the wretched savage but as the tool of others, insisted upon letting him go. They did so; and then, without rest and without a guide, pushed on through the long December night. When they reached the Alleghany River, opposite the present site of Pittsburgh, they found the banks of the river fringed with ice, and large blocks drifting furiously down the middle of the stream. All day long, with one poor hatchet, they toiled to build a raft. It was a frail affair. As they struggled upon it through the broken masses of ice, it threatened every moment to go to pieces.

In the middle of the stream, Washington's setting-pole became entangled, and he was thrown into the river where it was ten feet deep. He was saved from drowning by clinging to a log. At length they succeeded in reaching an island, where they passed a dismal night, their clothes frozen into coats of mail. The night was so cold that in the morning the river was frozen over, and they crossed upon the ice. Washington's journal of this tour was published in London, and attracted much attention, as it contained conclusive proof that the French would resist any attempts of the English to establish their settlements upon the Ohio. The Legislature of Virginia was in session at Williamsburg when Washington returned. Modestly, and unconscious that he would attract any attention, he went into the gallery to observe the proceedings. The speaker chanced to see him, and, rising, proposed that

" The thanks of this house be given to Major Washington, who now sits in the gallery, for the gallant manner in which he has executed the important trust lately reposed in him by his excellency the governor."

Every member of the house rose to his feet; and Washington was greeted with a simultaneous and enthusiastic burst of applause. Embarrassed by the unexpected honor, and unaccustomed to public speaking, the young hero endeavored in vain to give utterance to his thanks. The speaker of the house happily came to his rescue, saying, "Sit down, Major Washington: your modesty is alone equal to your merit."

Governor Dinwiddie, a reckless, headstrong man, instantly organized a force, with orders "to drive away, kill, or seize as prisoners, all persons, not the subjects of the king of Great Britain, who should attempt to take possession of the lands on the Ohio or any of its tributaries."

A regiment of about four hundred men was raised. Washington

was appointed colonel. His mission was to march again through the wilderness, and drive the French from the Ohio. Washington had selected the point at the junction of the Monongahela and the Alleghany for a fort. But the French anticipated him. As he was hurrying to this spot with his garrison, and with the tools to construct a fort, he was disappointed and alarmed to hear that the French were already at work, under skillful engineers, throwing up their ramparts upon the very spot which he had selected. A thousand men from Canada had descended the river in sixty bateaux and three hundred canoes. They had already eighteen pieces of cannon in position. Washington had arrived very near Fort Duquesne before he received these tidings. The thought of attacking the French in such overpowering numbers, and behind their ramparts, was madness. Retreat, in their exhausted state, back through the wilderness, was almost impossible. Besides, the French, through their spies, had kept a close watch upon them. Their Indian allies were on the march to intercept their retreat. Washington was then but twenty-two years of age. His sufferings, in view of the humiliating surrender of his whole force without striking a blow, must have been awful. He was ready for almost any act of desperation rather than to do this. As yet, there was no war declared. The nations were at peace; not a hostile gun had been fired. In building the fort on disputed territory, which was then in the hands of the French, the French had merely anticipated the English by a few days. It was said that Indian allies were marching against the English; but this was rumor merely. No such foe had appeared. There is some little diversity of statement in reference to what immediately followed; but, so far as can now be ascertained, the following appear to be the facts: —

The French say that they sent out M. Jumonville as a civil messenger to confer with the English respecting the object of their approach, as there was no declaration of war. Washington was informed that a party of French, from the fort, was on the march to attack him by surprise. Just then there came a night dark and stormy, with floods of rain. Washington took forty men, leaving the rest to guard the camp, and through the midnight tempest and gloom, guided by some friendly Indians, reached, just before daylight in the morning, the camp where Jumonville and his men were unsuspectingly sleeping. Washington, regarding them as foes who were on the march to strike him by surprise, fell instantly upon them. There was a short, fierce conflict. Jumonville and ten of his men were killed. A few escaped. The rest, twenty-five in number, were taken prisoners. The war was thus inaugurated, — a long, cruel, bloody war of seven years.

This occurrence created great excitement at the time, and Washington was very severely blamed; but, now that the passions of that day have passed, the French magnanimously concur in the general verdict, that the event must be regarded as an untoward accident. Nothing is more certain than that Washington would have shrunk from any dishonorable deed. The peculiar perplexity and peril in which the young soldier was placed shield his fame from tarnish.

But this act opened the drama of war with all its horrors. The French, apprised of the deed, and regarding it as one of the grossest of outrages (for Jumonville had really been sent as a peaceful messenger), immediately dispatched fifteen hundred men, French and Indians, to avenge the wrong. Washington could not retreat; neither could he fight such overwhelming numbers with any hope of success. Still he threw up such breastworks as could be hastily constructed, and, with less than four hundred men, fought for a whole day against the army which surrounded him. Starvation compelled him to capitulate. M. de Villers, the French commander, was generous. The Virginia troops were allowed to retire with everything in their possession except their artillery. Thus they returned unmolested to the settlements.

On the whole, Washington's character did not suffer from this adventure. That he should be able to secure such favorable terms of capitulation, and march back his little force through the wilderness, notwithstanding the lawless character of the Indians, who, in such formidable numbers, were marshaled against him, was considered evidence of both sagacity and military genius. Many of the wild frontiersmen, waifs from all lands, who had been gathered into the ranks of Washington's army, were coarse and wicked men. Washington, as a gentleman and a Christian, abhorred the vice of profane swearing, to which they were very much addicted. The following record from one of the orders of the day will explain itself: —

" Colonel Washington has observed that the men of his regiment are very profane and reprobate. He takes this opportunity to inform them of his great displeasure at such practices ; and assures them, that if they do not leave them off they shall be severely punished. The officers are desired, if they hear any man swear or make use of an oath or execration, to order the offender twenty-five lashes immediately, without a court-martial. For a second offense, he shall be more severely punished."

On another occasion, when commander-in-chief of the army struggling for our national independence, he invited a number of officers to dine with him. At the table one of the guests, in conversation, uttered an oath. Washington dropped his knife and fork as suddenly as if he had been struck a blow, and thus arrested the attention of the whole company. In very deliberate and solemn tones he then said, "I thought that I had invited only gentlemen to my table."

Early in the spring of 1755 General Braddock, a self-conceited, stubborn man, landed in Virginia with two regiments of regular troops from Great Britain. Arrogant in the pride of his technical military education, he despised alike Frenchmen, Indians, and colonists. With his force, Braddock started on a march through the wilderness for the reduction of Fort Duquesne. Washington accompanied him as volunteer aid. As he abandoned important domestic business, and received no remuneration whatever for his services, he must probably have been influenced by patriotism and the love of adventure. In a straggling line four miles in length, this army of two thousand men, totally unacquainted with Indian warfare, and thoroughly despising such barbaric foes, commenced its march, with ponderous artillery and a cumbrous baggage-train, through the forest, for the distant junction of the Alleghany and the Monongahela. Washington, who well knew the foe they were to encounter, was alarmed at this recklessness, and urged greater caution. The regular British general was not to be taught the art of war by a provincial colonel, who had never even seen the inside of a military school. Successfully they had threaded the wilderness, and on a beautiful summer's day they were exultingly marching along the banks of the Monongahela, when they entered a defile of rare picturesque beauty.

The majestic forest spread around in all directions. On each side of a sort of natural path there was a dense growth of underbrush, rising as high as the men's heads. It would seem as though some bad genius had formed the spot for an Indian ambush. Proudly the army straggled along, with laughter and song, with burnished muskets and polished cannon and silken banners. They were British troops, led by British regular officers. What had they to fear from cowardly Frenchmen or painted savages? It was one of those silent days, calm, serene, sunny, when all nature seems hushed and motionless, which Herbert has so graphically described: —

> " Sweet day, so still, so calm, so bright,
> The bridal of the earth and sky."

Suddenly, like the burst of thunder from the cloudless heavens, came the crash of musketry, and a tempest of lead swept through their astounded ranks. Crash followed crash in quick succession, before, behind, on the right, on the left. No foe was to be seen; yet every bullet accomplished its mission. The ground was soon covered with the dead, and with the wounded struggling in dying agonies. Amazement and consternation ran through the ranks. An unseen fire was assailing them. It was supernatural; it was ghostly. Braddock stood his ground with senseless, bull-dog courage, until he fell pierced by a bullet. After a short scene of confusion and horror, when nearly half of the army were slain, the remnant broke in wild disorder and fled. The ambush was entirely successful. Six hundred of these unseen assailants were Indians. They made the forest ring with their derision in scorn of the folly of Braddock.

Washington, through this awful scene, which he had been constantly anticipating, was perfectly collected, and, with the coolest courage, did everything which human sagacity could do to retrieve the disaster. Two horses were shot beneath him, and four bullets passed through his coat. It is one of the legends of the day, that an Indian sharpshooter declared that Washington bore a charmed life; that he took direct aim at him several times, at the distance of but a few paces, and that the bullets seemed either to vanish into air or to glance harmless from his body. Eight hundred of Braddock's army, including most of the officers, were now either dead or wounded.

Washington rallied around him the few provincials, upon whom Braddock had looked with contempt. Each man instantly placed himself behind a tree, according to the necessities of forest warfare.

As the Indians were bursting from their ambush, with tomahawk and scalping-knife, to complete the massacre, the unerring fire of these provincials checked them and drove them back. But for this the army would have been utterly destroyed. All Washington's endeavors to rally the British regulars were unavailing. Indignantly he writes, " They ran like sheep before the hounds." Panic-stricken, abandoning artillery and baggage, they continued their tumultuous retreat to the Atlantic coast. The provincials, in orderly march, protected them from pursuit. Braddock's defeat rang through the land as Washington's victory. The provincials, who in silent exasperation, submitting to military authority, had allowed themselves to be led into this valley of death, proclaimed far and wide the cautions which Washington had urged, and the heroism with which he had rescued the remnant of the army. After the lapse of eighty years, a seal of Washington, containing his initials, which had been shot from his person, was found upon the battle-field, and is at the present time in possession of one of the family.

The state of things in Virginia was now awful. The savages, exultant, having lapped blood, had all their wolfish natures roused to the most intense excitement. War was with them pastime, and the only field of renown. Advancing civilization, penetrating the forests, had scattered its villages and secluded farm-houses along a frontier of nearly four hundred miles. It is one of the mysteries of God's providential government, which no finite mind can fathom, that He could have allowed such horrors. No imagination can picture them. Midnight conflagration, torture and outrage in every form which fiends could devise, became the amusement of bands of howling savages, who came and went like the wind.

Fifteen hundred demons, calling themselves Indian braves, in gangs of sometimes but eight or ten, and again of several hundred, swept the frontier, making themselves merry with the shrieks of their victims, and showing no mercy to mothers or maidens or helpless infancy. The French made no attempt to pursue their advantage, but quietly retired to Fort Duquesne, there to await another assault, should the English decide to make one.

A force, nominally of two thousand men, but in reality of but about seven hundred, was raised, and placed under the command of Washington, to protect the scattered villages and dwellings of this vast frontier. For three years Washington consecrated all his energies to this arduous and holy enterprise. It would require a volume to record the wonderful and awful scenes through which he passed during these three years. In after-life, Washington could not endure to recall the spectacles of suffering which he witnessed, and which he could not alleviate. At the time, he wrote to the governor, —

"The supplicating tears of the women, and moving petitions of the men, melt me into such deadly sorrow, that I solemnly declare I could offer myself a willing sacrifice to the butchering enemy, could that contribute to the people's ease."

One day as Washington, with a small portion of his troops, was traversing a part of the frontier, he came upon a single log-house. It was in a little clearing which the settler had made by his axe, and which was surrounded on all sides by the forest. As they were approaching the clearing, they heard the sound of a gun. Apprehending some scene of violence and horror, they crept cautiously through the underbrush until they came in sight of the settler's cabin. Smoke was curling up through the roof, while a party of savages were rioting around, laden with plunder, and flourishing dripping scalps. Upon the appearance of the soldiers, the savages, with the fleetness of deer, dashed into the forest. Washington thus describes the scene which met their eyes : —

"On entering we saw a sight that, though we were familiar with blood and massacre, struck us, at least myself, with feelings more mournful than I had ever experienced before. On the bed, in one corner of the room, lay the body of a young woman, swimming in blood, with a gash in her forehead which almost separated the head into two parts. On her breast lay two little babes, apparently twins, less than a twelvemonth old, with their heads also cut open. Their innocent blood, which once flowed in the same veins, now mingled in one current again. I was inured to scenes of bloodshed and misery ; but this cut me to the soul. Never in my after-life did I raise my hand against a savage, without calling to mind the mother with her little twins, their heads cleft asunder."

Eagerly the soldiers followed in the trail of the savages. They had gone but a few steps ere they found a little boy and his father, who had been working in the fields, both dead and scalped. The father had been plowing, and the boy was driving the horse. When the father was shot down, the terrified boy had run some distance towards his home ere he was overtaken and murdered. Thus the whole family was swept away. Such were then the perils of life on the frontier. No home was safe. The inmates of every cabin were liable, at midnight, to be roused by the yell of the savage; and, while the torch was applied to the dwelling, the tomahawk would sink into the brain. Washington writes, —

" On leaving one spot for the protection of another point of exposure, the scene was often such as I shall never forget. The women and children clung round our knees, beseeching us to stay and protect them, and crying out to us, for God's sake, not to leave them to be butchered by the savages. A hundred times, I declare to Heaven, I would have laid down my life with pleasure, even under the tomahawk and scalping-knife, could I have insured the safety of those suffering people by the sacrifice."

In November, 1758, Fort Duquesne was wrested from the French, and the valley of the Ohio passed from their control forever. The Canadas soon after surrendered to Wolfe, and English supremacy was established upon this continent without a rival. Washington was now twenty-six years of age. The beautiful estate of Mount Vernon had descended to him by inheritance. On the 6th of January, 1759, he married Mrs. Martha Custis, a lady of great worth and beauty. Washington was already wealthy; and his wife brought with her, as her dower, a fortune of one hundred thousand dollars. After the marvelously tumultuous scenes of his youth, he retired with his bride and her two children to the lovely retreat of Mount Vernon, where he spent fifteen years of almost unalloyed happiness.

He enlarged the mansion, embellished the grounds, and by purchase made very considerable additions to his large estate. The stern discipline of life had subdued his passions. His habits were frugal, temperate, and methodical. His imposing mansion, the abode of a generous hospitality, was visited by the most distinguished men from all lands. Though a strict disciplinarian, he was a considerate and indulgent master. It was his invariable rule to retire to rest at nine o'clock, whether he had company or not. He rose at four o'clock in the morning. The religious interests of the little community around him deeply engaged his attention, and the gospel ministry received from him very efficient support. The following letter, which he wrote to a nephew who was chosen to the legislative assembly, contains admirable advice, and is an interesting development of his own character : —

" If you have a mind to command the attention of the house, speak seldom, but on important subjects. Make yourself perfectly master of the subject. Never exceed a decent warmth ; and submit your sentiments with diffidence. A dictatorial style, though it may carry conviction, is always accompanied with disgust."

At Mount Vernon Washington's occupation was that of a large planter, raising wheat and tobacco. The wheat was ground upon the estate, and shipped for sale. The tobacco was sent to England ; from which country then almost every article of domestic use was imported. This splendid estate consisted of eight thousand acres, four thousand of which were in tillage : the remainder was in wood or uncultivated land. During these serene years of peace and prosperity an appalling storm was gathering, which soon burst with fearful desolation over all the colonies.

We now come down to the notable year 1775. The British ministry, denying the colonists the rights of British subjects, insisted upon exercising the despotic power of imposing taxes upon the colonists, while withholding the right of representation. All American remonstrances were thrown back with scorn. Hireling soldiers were insultingly sent to enforce obedience to the mandates of the British crown. The Americans sprang to arms, called a Congress, and chose George Washington commander-in-chief. A more perilous post man never accepted. The whole population of the United States then did not exceed three millions ; being almost a million less than the present population of the single State of New York. England was the undisputed mistress of the seas, and the strongest military power upon the globe. The little handful of colonists, who stepped forth to meet this Goliah in deadly conflict, had neither fleet, army, military resources, nor supplies. The odds were so fearful that it seems now strange that any courage could have met the encounter.

Defeat to Washington would prove not merely ruin, but inevitably an ignominious death upon the scaffold. Sublimely he stepped forward from his home of opulence and domestic joy, and accepted all the responsibilities of the post. The green in Lexington had already been crimsoned with the blood of patriots, and the battle of Bunker's Hill had rolled its echoes through Christendom. To a friend in England Washington wrote, —

" The Americans will fight for their liberties and property. Unhappy it is, though, to reflect that a brother's sword has been sheathed in a brother's breast, and that the once happy and peaceful plains of America are either to be drenched in blood or to be inhabited by slaves. Strange alternative! But can a virtuous man hesitate in his choice?"

To the Congress which elected him commander-in-chief of the American forces, he replied, —

"I beg leave to assure the Congress, that, as no pecuniary consideration could have tempted me to accept this arduous employment at the expense of my domestic ease and happiness, I do not wish to make any profit from it. I will keep an exact account of my expenses. Those, I doubt not, they will discharge. That is all I desire."

To his wife, who was ever the object of his most respectful regard and tender affection, he wrote that it was his greatest affliction to be separated from her, but that duty called, and he must obey. He said that he could not decline the appointment without dishonoring his name, and sinking himself even in her esteem.

Twelve thousand British regulars were then intrenched on Bunker's Hill and in the streets of Boston. About fifteen thousand provincial militia, wretchedly armed, and without any discipline, occupied a line nearly twelve miles in extent, encircling, on the land side, Charlestown and Boston. The British war-ships held undisputed possession of the harbor. These veterans could, apparently with ease, at any time, pierce the thin patriot line.

It requires long discipline to transform a man, just taken from the endearments of home, into merely a part of that obedient, unquestioning machine called an army. A thousand trained soldiers are ever regarded as equal in military power to three or four times that number fresh from the pursuits of peaceful life. The British had opened fire at Lexington on the 19th of April, 1775. On the 2d of July Washington arrived in Cambridge and took command of the army. The ceremony took place under the elm-tree which still stands immortalized by the event. General Gage was commander of the British forces. He had been the friend of Washington during the seven years' war, and had fought by his side at the time of Braddock's defeat; and yet this General Gage seized every patriot upon whom he could lay his hands in Boston, and threw them all, without regard to station or rank, into loathsome dungeons. To General Washington's remonstrance against such barbarity, he returned the insolent reply, —

"My clemency is great in sparing the lives of those who, by the laws of the land, are destined to the *cord*. I recognize no difference of rank but that which the king confers."

Washington at first resolved to retaliate upon the English prisoners. But his generous nature recoiled from the inhumanity of punishing the innocent for the crimes of the guilty. He countermanded the order, directing that the prisoners should be treated with all the humanity consistent with their security. In the subsequent and more successful war which the British government waged against popular rights in Europe, they practiced the same inhumanity. The French prisoners were thrown into hulks, and perished miserably by thousands. Napoleon, like Washington, refused to retaliate upon the helpless captives in his hands for the infamous conduct of their government.

At length, after surmounting difficulties more than can be enumerated, Washington was prepared for decisive action. In a dark and stormy night of March he opened upon the foe in the city, from his encircling lines, as fierce a bombardment as his means would possibly allow. Under cover of this roar of the batteries and the midnight storm, he dispatched a large force of picked troops, with the utmost secrecy, to take possession of the Heights of Dorchester. There, during the hours of the night, the soldiers worked with the utmost diligence in throwing up breast-works which would protect them from the broadsides of the English fleet. Having established his batteries upon those heights, he commanded the harbor; and the English would be compelled to withdraw, or he would blow their fleet into the air.

In the early dawn of the morning, while the gale swept sheets of mist and floods of rain over earth and sea, the British admiral saw, to his consternation, that a fort bristling with cannon had sprung up during the night, almost over his head. He immediately opened upon the works the broadsides of all his ships; but the Americans, defiant of the storm of iron which fell around them, continued to pile their sand-bags, and to ply their shovels, until ramparts so strong rose around them that no cannonade could injure them. The British fleet was now at the mercy of Washington's batteries. In a spirit almost of desperation, the admiral ordered three thousand men in boats to land and take the heights at every hazard. God came to the aid of the colonists. The gale increased to such fury that not a boat could be launched. Before another day and night had passed the redoubt could defy any attack.

The situation of the two parties was now very singular. The British fleet was at the mercy of the Americans: Boston was at the mercy of the English. "If you fire upon the fleet," said General Howe, "I will burn the city." — "If you harm the city," said Washington, "I will sink your fleet." By a tacit understanding, the English were permitted to retire unharmed, if they left the city uninjured.

It was the morning of the 17th of March, 1776. The storm had passed away. The blue sky overarched the beleaguered city and the encamping armies. Washington sat upon his horse, serene and majestic, and contemplated in silent triumph, from the Heights of Dorchester, the evacuation of Boston. Every gun of his batteries was shotted and aimed at the hostile fleet. Every torch was lighted. The whole British army was crowded on board the ships. A fresh breeze from the west filled their sails; and the hostile armament, before the sun went down, had disappeared beyond the distant horizon of the sea. As the last boats, loaded to the gunwales with British soldiers, left the shore for the fleet, the exultant colonial army, with music and banners, marched over the Neck into the rejoicing city. It was a glorious victory, won by genius without the effusion of blood. Such another case, perhaps, history does not record. Washington, *without ammunition*, had maintained his post for six months within musket-shot of a powerful British army. During this time he had disbanded the small force of raw militia he at first had with him, and had recruited another army; and had then driven the enemy into his ships, and out into the sea.

The British, thus expelled from Boston, gathered their strength of fleets and armies for an attack upon New York. The Congress, assembled in Philadelphia, which at first sought only the redress of grievances, now resolved to strike for independence. A committee was appointed, of which Thomas Jefferson was chairman, to draft a Declaration. The committee presented this immortal document to Congress, and it was unanimously adopted. History has recorded no spectacle more sublime than that which was witnessed as the members of the Continental Congress came forward, each one in his

THE EVACUATION OF BOSTON
MARCH 17, 1776
ENGRAVED EXPRESSLY FOR ABEL

turn, to sign that paper, which would be his inevitable death-warrant should the arms of America fail. Not one faltered. Every individual pledged to this sacred cause " his life, his fortune, and his sacred honor." It was the 4th of July, 1776.

This Declaration was read from the steps of the State House in Philadelphia to an immense concourse, and it was received with bursts of enthusiasm. It was sent to General Washington to be communicated to the army, which he had now assembled in the vicinity of New York. The regiments were paraded to hear it read. It was greeted with tumultuous applause. The troops thus defiantly threw back the epithet of "rebellious colonists," and assumed the proud title of " The Army of the United States." General Washington, in an order of the day, thus alludes to this momentous occurrence : —

" The general hopes that this important event will serve as a fresh incentive to every officer and soldier to act with fidelity and courage, as knowing that now the peace and safety of his country depend, under God, solely on the success of our arms, and that he is now in the service of a state possessed of sufficient power to reward his merit, and advance him to the highest honors of a free country."

The latter part of June, just before the Declaration of Independence, two large British fleets, one from Halifax and the other direct from England, met at the mouth of the Bay of New York, and, disembarking quite a powerful army, took possession of Staten Island. Washington had assembled all his available military force to resist their advances. The British government regarded the leaders of the armies, and their supporters in Congress, as felons, doomed to the scaffold. They refused, consequently, to recognize any titles conferred by congressional authority.

General Howe sent a flag of truce, with a letter, directed to George Washington, Esq. The letter was returned unopened. As occasional intercourse between the generals of the two armies was of very great moment, to regulate questions respecting the treatment of prisoners and other matters, General Howe, notwithstanding this merited repulse, wrote again, but insultingly to the same address. Again the letter was returned unopened, and with the emphatic announcement, that the commander-in-chief of the American army could receive no communication from General Howe which did not recognize his military position. The British officer then sent a

3

letter insolently addressed to *George Washington, Esq., &c., &c., &c.* This letter was also refused. A communication was then sent to General George Washington.

Thus were the members of the British Cabinet in London disciplined into civility. General Howe frankly confessed that he had adopted this discourteous style of address simply to save himself from censure by the home government. Washington, writing to Congress upon this subject, says, —

"I would not, on any occasion, sacrifice essentials to punctilio; but, in this instance, I deemed it my duty to my country, and to my appointment, to insist upon that respect, which, in any other than a public view, I would willingly have waived."

General Washington, a gentleman and a Christian, was exceedingly pained by that vulgar and wicked habit of profane swearing which was so prevalent among the troops. We have already alluded to his abhorrence of this vice. In August, 1776, he issued the following notice to his army at New York: —

"The general is sorry to be informed that the foolish and profane practice of cursing and swearing, a vice hitherto little known in an American army, is growing into fashion. He hopes that the officers will, by example as well as by influence, endeavor to check it, and that both they and the men will reflect that we can have little hope of the blessing of Heaven on our aims if we insult it by our impiety and folly. Add to this, it is a vice so mean and low, without any temptation, that every man of sense and character detests and despises it."

Just before this he had written to Congress, earnestly soliciting chaplains for the army. In this plea he writes, "The blessing and protection of Heaven are at all times necessary, but especially so in times of public distress and danger. The general hopes and trusts that every officer and man will endeavor to live and act as becomes a Christian soldier."

By the middle of August the British had assembled, on Staten Island and at the mouth of the Hudson River, a force of nearly thirty thousand soldiers, with a numerous and well-equipped fleet. To oppose them Washington had about twelve thousand men, poorly armed, and quite unaccustomed to military discipline and to the hardships of the camp. A few regiments of American troops, about five thousand in number, were gathered near Brooklyn. A few thousand more were stationed at other points on Long Island. The English landed without opposition, fifteen thousand strong, and made a combined assault upon the Americans. The battle was short, but bloody. The Americans, overpowered, sullenly retired, leaving fifteen hundred of their number either dead or in the hands of the English. Washington witnessed this rout with the keenest anguish; for he could not detach any troops from New York to arrest the carnage.

To remain upon the island was certain destruction; to attempt to retreat was difficult and perilous in the extreme. The East River flowed deep and wide between the few troops on the island and their friends in New York. The British fleet had already weighed anchor, and was sailing up the Narrows to cut off their retreat. A vastly superior force of well-trained British troops, flushed with victory, pressed upon the rear of the dispirited colonists. Their situation seemed desperate.

Again Providence came to our aid. The wind died away to a perfect calm, so that the British fleet could not move. A dense fog was rolled in from the ocean, which settled down so thick upon land and river, that, with the gathering darkness of the night, one's outstretched hand could scarcely be seen. The English, strangers to the country, and fearing some surprise, could only stand upon the defensive. The Americans, familiar with every foot of the ground, improved the propitious moments with energies roused to their highest tension. Boats were rapidly collected; and, in the few hours of that black night, nine thousand men, with nearly all their artillery and military stores, were safely landed in New York. The transportation was conducted so secretly, with muffled oars and hushed voices, that though the Americans could hear the English at work with their pickaxes, and were even within hearing of the challenge of the hostile sentinels, the last boat had left the Long Island shore ere the retreat was suspected. God does not always help the " heavy battalions."

The British now presented themselves in such force, of both fleet and army, that Washington, with his feeble and dispirited band, was compelled to evacuate the city. A rash and headstrong man would have been goaded to desperation, and would have risked a general engagement, which, in all probability, would have secured our inevitable ruin. A man easily depressed by adversity would, in hours apparently so hopeless, have abandoned the cause. Washington wrote to Congress, —

" Our situation is truly distressing. The check our detachment received has dispirited too great a proportion of our troops, and filled their minds with apprehension and despair. The militia, instead of calling forth their utmost efforts to a brave and manly opposition in order to repair our losses, are dismayed, intractable, and impatient to return to their homes."

The American army was now in a deplorable condition. It had neither arms, ammunition, nor food. The soldiers were unpaid, almost mutinous, and in rags. There were thousands in the vicinity of New York who were in sympathy with the British ministry. Nearly all the government officials and their friends were on that side. A conspiracy was formed, in which a part of Washington's own guard was implicated, to seize him, and deliver him to that ignominious death to which the British crown had doomed him. We were then, not a nation, but merely a confederacy of independent colonies. There was no bond of union, no unity of counsel, no concentration of effort. Each colony furnished such resources as it found to be convenient, or withheld them at its sovereign pleasure. England's omnipotent fleet swept, unobstructed, ocean and river and bay. Her well-drilled armies, supplied with the most powerful weapons and strengthened with all abundance, tramped contemptuously over the land, scattering our militia before them, burning and destroying in all directions. General Howe, despising his foe, and confident that the colonists could present no effectual resistance to his powerful army, issued his proclamations, offering pardon to all who would bow the neck in unquestioning obedience to the dictation of the British king, excepting only Washington, Franklin, and a few others of the most illustrious of the patriots.

Washington was equal to the crisis. He saw that the only hope was to be found in avoiding an engagement, and in wearing out the resources of the enemy in protracted campaigns. To adopt this course required great moral courage and self-sacrifice. To rush madly into the conflict, and sell life as dearly as possible, required mere ordinary daring. Thousands could be found capable of this. Animal courage is the cheapest of all virtues. The most effeminate races on the globe, by a few months of suitable drilling, can be converted into heroic soldiers, laughing lead and iron and steel to scorn.

But to conduct an army persistently through campaigns of inevitable defeat ; ever to refuse a battle ; to meet the enemy only to retire before him ; to encounter silently the insults and scorn of the foe ; to be denounced by friends for incapacity and cowardice ; and, while at the head of a mere handful of ragged and unfurnished troops, to be compelled, in order to save that little handful from destruction, to allow the country as well as the enemy to believe that one has a splendid army, splendidly equipped, — this requires a degree of moral courage and an amount of heroic virtue, which, thus far in the history of this world, has been developed only in George Washington.

America had many able generals ; but it may be doubted whether there was another man on this continent who could have conducted the unequal struggle of the American Revolution to a successful issue. Washington slowly retired from New York to the Heights of Haarlem, with sleepless vigilance watching every movement of the foe, that he might take advantage of the slightest indiscretion. Here he threw up breastworks, which the enemy did not venture to attack. The British troops ascended the Hudson and the East River to assail Washington in his rear. A weary campaign of marches and counter-marches ensued, in which Washington, with scarcely the shadow of an army, sustained, in the midst of a constant succession of disasters, the apparently hopeless fortunes of his country. At one time General Reed in anguish exclaimed, —

" My God ! General Washington, how long shall we fly ? "

Serenely General Washington replied, " We shall retreat, if necessary, over every river of our country, and then over the mountains, where I will make a last stand against our enemies."

Washington crossed the Hudson into the Jerseys. The British pursued him. With consummate skill, he baffled all the efforts of the foe. With an army reduced to a freezing, starving band of but three thousand men, he retreated to Trenton. The British pressed exultantly on, deeming the conflict ended and the Revolution crushed. The Congress in Philadelphia, alarmed by the rapid approach of the foe, hastily adjourned to Baltimore. It was December, with its wintry gales and frozen ground and storms of sleet. The " strong battalions " of the foe tracked the patriots by the blood of their lacerated feet. With great difficulty Washington succeeded in crossing the Delaware in boats, just as the British army, in all its pride and power, with horsemen, infantrymen, banners, music, and ponderous artillery, arrived upon the banks of the stream. Nearly all of New Jersey was now in the hands of the British. They needed but to cross the river to take possession of Philadelphia. The ice was now so rapidly forming that they would soon be able to pass at any point without obstruction. The enemy, with apparently nothing to fear, relaxed his vigilance. The British officers, welcomed by the Tories in the large towns, were amusing themselves with feasting and dancing, until the blocks of ice, sweeping down the stream, should be consolidated into a firm foothold.

The night of the 25th of December, 1776, was very dark and intensely cold. A storm of wind and snow raged so violently that both man and beast were forced to seek shelter. The British officers and soldiers, considering the patriots utterly dispersed, and that a broad, deep, icy river flowed between them and the retreating American bands, gathered around the firesides. In the darkness of that wintry night, and amidst the conflict of its elements, Washington reembarked his troops to recross the Delaware, and to plunge with all his strength into the midst of the unsuspecting foe.

In this heroic deed there were combined the highest daring and prudence. Facing the storm, and forcing his boats through the floating blocks of ice, he succeeded, before daylight the next morning, in landing upon the opposite shore twenty-four hundred men and twenty pieces of cannon. The British were carelessly dispersed, not dreaming of danger. The Americans sprang upon the first body of the foe they met, and, after a short but bloody strife, scattered them, capturing a thousand prisoners and six cannon. Elated with this success, which astounded and humbled the foe, the American troops recrossed the river, and gained their encampment in safety. The British were so alarmed by this indication of vitality in the American army, that they retreated to Princeton, and Washington took possession of Trenton. Soon the foe, under Lord Cornwallis, having received large reinforcements, marched upon Trenton, confident that General Washington could no longer escape them. It was at the close of a bleak winter day that Cornwallis with his army appeared before the lines which Washington had thrown up around Trenton. Sir William Erskine urged the British commander to make an immediate attack. Cornwallis replied, —

" Our troops are hungry and weary. Washington and his tatterdemalions cannot escape ; for the ice of the Delaware will neither bear their weight nor admit the passage of their boats. To-morrow, at the break of day, I will attack them. The rising sun shall see the end of the rebellion."

The sun rose the next morning, cold but cloudless. In the night the American army had vanished. Solitude reigned along those lines which, the evening before, had been crowded with the ranks of war. Replenishing his camp-fires to deceive the enemy, at midnight, with the utmost precaution and precipitation, he evacuated his camp, and, by a circuitous route, fell upon the rear of the English at Princeton. The sun was just rising as Washington's troops plunged upon the foe in this totally unexpected onset. A hundred and sixty of the British were shot down, and three hundred were taken prisoners.

While this event was taking place at Princeton, Lord Cornwallis stood upon an eminence, gazing in astonishment upon the deserted and waning fires of the Americans. Quite bewildered, he pressed his hand to his brow, exclaiming, "Where can Washington be gone?" Just then the heavy booming of the battle at Princeton fell upon his ear. "There he is!" he added. "By Jove! Washington deserves to fight in the cause of his king." Cheered by this success, Washington led his handful of troops to the Heights of Morristown. There he intrenched them for winter-quarters. He, however, sent out frequent detachments, which so harassed the enemy that, in a short time, New Jersey was delivered from the presence of the foe. The country became somewhat animated by these achievements, and Congress roused itself to new energies.

Washington, as we have said, was an earnest Christian. When the army was in the environs of Morristown, N. J., the communion service was to be administered in the Presbyterian church of the village. General Washington called upon Rev. Dr. Jones, then pastor of the church, and said to him, " Doctor, I understand that the Lord's Supper is to be celebrated with you next Sunday. I would learn if it accords with the rules of your church to admit communicants of other denominations? "

"Certainly," was the reply. "Ours is not the Presbyterian table, general, but the Lord's table ; and we give the Lord's invitation to all his followers, of whatever name."

"I am glad of it," the general replied. "That is as it ought to be. But, as I was not quite sure of the fact, I thought I would ascertain it from yourself, as I propose to join with you on that occasion. Though a member of the Church of England, I have no exclusive partialities."

The doctor reassured him of a cordial welcome, and the general was found seated with the communicants next Sabbath.

During the remainder of the winter vigorous efforts were made in preparation for the opening of the spring campaign. The different States sent troops to join the army at Morristown. The people of France, in cordial sympathy with our cause, sent two vessels, containing twenty-four thousand muskets, to General Washington. Immense embarrassments were, however, continually experienced, from the fact that we were not a nation, but a mere conglomeration of independent States. Each State decided for itself the pay it would offer to the troops. Each State claimed the right to withhold any portion of its troops for its own security, however much they might be needed for the general service. It was these difficulties of the old confederacy which induced " the people of the United States " to form themselves into a *nation*, with certain clearly defined rights reserved for the individual States.

The sympathy excited in behalf of our cause in France was of invaluable service to us. The Marquis de Lafayette left his mansion of opulence, and his youthful bride, to peril his life in the cause of American independence. The British officers, harassed by Washington's sleepless vigilance, and yet unable to compel him or to lure him into a general engagement, ascended the Delaware in a fleet, with eighteen thousand soldiers, to capture Philadelphia. They landed near Elkton, at the head of Chesapeake Bay. Washington, with but eleven thousand men, marched to encounter them. The two hostile bodies met on the banks of the Brandywine. A bloody battle ensued. Lafayette was wounded. The Americans, overpowered, were compelled to retire. With unbroken ranks, and determination still unflinching, they retired upon Philadelphia.

Congress had now invested Washington with nearly dictatorial powers, and the whole country approved of the act. In Philadelphia the army was rapidly recruited; and before the British had recovered from the blows which they received at the Brandywine, Washington was again upon the march to meet them. It was so important to save Philadelphia from the enemy, that he resolved to hazard another battle. The two forces again met, about twenty-three miles from the city. Just as the battle commenced, a storm arose, so violent, and with such floods of rain, that neither army could long pursue the contest. Washington, after a short but severe engagement at Germantown, retired with his ammunition spoiled, and the British took possession of Philadelphia.

Congress precipitately adjourned to Lancaster, and thence to York. For eight months the English held the city. Various petty battles ensued, some of them quite sanguinary, but none leading to any important results. The Americans were, however, acquiring experience, and continually gaining new courage. The surrender of Burgoyne, which occurred about this time at Saratoga, rolled a surge of exultation through all the States.

Winter again came. The British were comfortably housed in Philadelphia, in the enjoyment of every luxury. Washington selected Valley Forge, about twenty miles from Philadelphia, as his secure retreat for winter-quarters. The soldiers commenced rearing their log-huts here the latter part of December. Each hut was fourteen feet by sixteen, and accommodated twelve soldiers. The encampment, which was well protected by earth-works, presented the aspect of a very picturesque city, with neatly arranged streets and avenues. Eleven thousand men here passed the winter of 1777 and 1778. It was a period of great discouragement and suffering. The army was destitute of food, clothing, arms, and powder, — in a state of destitution which Washington did not dare to proclaim abroad, lest the foe should rush upon him in his helplessness. The commander-in-chief was assailed with terrible severity for this inaction. Though Washington felt these reproaches keenly, he endured them all with that external imperturbability of spirit which so wonderfully characterized him throughout all the conflict. He wrote to Mr. Laurens, President of Congress, —

" My enemies take an ungenerous advantage of me. They know the delicacy of my situation, and that motives of policy deprive me of the defense I might otherwise make against their insidious attacks. They know I cannot combat their insinuations, however injurious, without disclosing secrets it is of the utmost moment to conceal. But why should I expect to be exempt from censure, the unfailing lot of an elevated station? Merit and talent, which I cannot pretend to rival, have ever been subject to it."

It was in this dark hour of our struggle that France generously came forward to our aid; recognizing our independence, entering into a friendly alliance with us, and sending both a fleet and an army to our support. But for this efficient assistance it is scarcely possible that our independence could then have been achieved. The tidings of the French alliance were received at Valley Forge with unutterable joy. The most dishonorable means were now taken by our enemies to paralyze the influence of Washington by destroying his reputation. A pamphlet was published in London, and scattered widely throughout the States, containing forged letters, purporting to be private letters from Washington to his wife, found in a portmanteau taken from a servant of Washington after the evacuation of Fort Lee.

The forgery was skillfully got up. The letters denounced Congress for madness in declaring independence, and contained many expressions, which, if true, proved Washington to be totally unfit to be in command of the American armies. But fortunately the reputation of the commander-in-chief was too firmly established in this country to be thus demolished. The British army now in New York and Philadelphia amounted to thirty thousand men. The whole American army did not exceed fifteen thousand. But the alliance with France gave us the assurance that reinforcements would soon come to our aid. The British, apprehensive that a French fleet might soon appear, and thus endanger the troops in Philadelphia, evacuated the city, and sent their heavy material of war to New York by water, while the troops commenced their march through New Jersey. The cold of winter had given place to the heat of summer.

Washington followed closely in the rear of the foe, watching for a chance to strike. The 28th of June, 1788, was a day of intense heat. Not a breath of air was stirring, while an unclouded sun poured down its blistering rays upon pursuers and pursued. The British troops were at Monmouth. The march of one more day would so unite them with the army in New York, that they would be safe from attack. Washington ordered an assault. General Lee, with five thousand men, was in the advance. Washington sent orders to him immediately to commence the onset, with the assurance that he would hasten to his support. As Washington was pressing eagerly forward, to his inexpressible chagrin he met

General Lee at the head of his troops, in full retreat. It is said that Washington, with great vehemence of manner and utterance, cried out, " General Lee, what means this ill-timed prudence?" The retreating general threw back the angry retort, " I know of no man blessed with a larger portion of that rascally virtue than your excellency."

It was no time for altercation. Washington turned to the men. They greeted him with cheers. At his command they wheeled about and charged the enemy. A sanguinary battle ensued, and the English were driven from the field. Night closed the scene. The colonists slept upon their arms, prepared to renew the battle in the morning. Washington, wrapping his cloak around him, threw himself upon the grass, and slept in the midst of his soldiers. When the morning dawned, no foe was to be seen. The British had retreated in the night to the Heights of Middletown. They left three hundred of their dead behind them. The Americans lost but sixty-nine. The British also lost one hundred in prisoners, and over six hundred had deserted from their ranks since they left Philadelphia. The English common soldiers had but little heart to fight against their brothers who were struggling for independence. At Middletown the British embarked on board their ships, and were conveyed to New York.

They had now inhumanly summoned the Indians to their aid. The tomahawk and the scalping-knife were mercilessly employed. Towns, villages, farm-houses, were burned, and their inhabitants — men, women, and children — were massacred by savages inspired with the fury of demons. The British ministry encouraged these atrocities. They said that rebellious America must be punished into submission; and that, in inflicting this punishment, it was right to make use of all the instruments which God and Nature had placed in their hands.

But it must not be forgotten that there were many noble Englishmen who espoused our cause. Some of the ablest men in both the House of Commons and the House of Lords, and thousands throughout England, were in cordial sympathy with the colonists struggling for their rights. Instead of adopting the execrable sentiment, " Our country, right or wrong," they acted upon that noble maxim, " Our country, — when right, to be kept right; when wrong, to be put right." Of these men, some pleaded for us at home, some aided us with their money and counsel, and some entered our ranks as officers and soldiers. Lord Chatham, in tones which echoed throughout the civilized world, exclaimed in the House of Lords, and at the very foot of the throne, " Were I an American, as I am an Englishman, I would never lay down my arms, — never, *never*, NEVER ! "

Another cold and cheerless winter came ; and the American army went into winter-quarters mainly at West Point, on the Hudson. The British remained within their lines at New York. They sent agents, however, to the Six Nations of Indians, to arm them against our defenseless frontier. These fierce savages, accompanied by Tory bands, perpetrated horrors too awful for recital. The massacres of Cherry Valley and of Wyoming were among the most awful of the tragedies which have ever been witnessed on this globe. The narrative of these fiendish deeds sent a thrill of horror through England as well as America. Four thousand men were sent by Washington into the wilderness, to arrest, if possible, these massacres. The savages, and their still more guilty allies, were driven to Niagara, where they were received into an English fortress.

The summer campaign opened with an indiscriminate devastation and plunder, pursued vigorously by the English. " A war of this sort," said Lord George Germain, " will probably induce the rebellious provinces to return to their allegiance." The British now concentrated their forces for an attack upon West Point, and to get the control of the upper waters of the Hudson. Washington detected and thwarted their plan. General Clinton, who was then in command of the British forces, exasperated by this discomfiture, commenced a more vigorous prosecution of a system of violence and plunder upon the defenseless towns and farm-houses of the Americans who were unprotected. The sky was reddened with wanton conflagration. Women and children were driven houseless into the fields. The flourishing towns of Fairfield and Norwalk, in Connecticut, were reduced to ashes.

While the enemy was thus ravaging that defenseless State, Washington planned an expedition against Stony Point, on the Hudson, which was held by the British. General Wayne conducted the enterprise, on the night of the 15th of July, with great gallantry and success. Sixty-three of the British were killed, five hundred and forty-three were taken prisoners, and all the military stores of the fortress captured. During this summer campaign the American army was never sufficiently strong to take the offensive. It was, however, incessantly employed striking blows upon the English wherever the eagle eye of Washington could discern an exposed spot.

The winter of 1779 set in early, and with unusual severity. The American army was in such a starving condition that Washington was compelled to make the utmost exertions to save his wasting band from annihilation. Incited by his urgent appeals, the colonies made new efforts to augment their forces for a more vigorous campaign in the spring. Cheering intelligence arrived that a land and naval force might soon be expected from our generous friends the French.

In July twelve vessels of war arrived from France, with arms, ammunition, and five thousand soldiers. This squadron was, however, immediately blockaded in Newport by a stronger British fleet; and another expedition, which was about to sail from Brest, in France, was effectually shut up in that port. The war still raged in detachments, widely spread; and conflagration, blood, and misery deluged our unhappy land.

These long years of war and woe filled many even of the most sanguine hearts with despair. Not a few true patriots deemed it madness for the colonies, impoverished as they now were, any longer to contend against the richest and most powerful monarchy upon the globe. General Arnold, who was at this time in command at West Point, saw no hope for his country. Believing the ship to be sinking, he ingloriously sought to take care of himself. He turned traitor, and offered to sell his fortress to the English. The treason was detected: but the traitor escaped; and the lamented André, who had been lured into the position of a spy, became the necessary victim of Arnold's crime.

Lord Cornwallis was now, with a well-provided army and an assisting navy, overrunning the two Carolinas. General Greene was sent, with all the force which Washington could spare, to watch and harass the invaders, and to furnish the inhabitants with all the protection in his power. Lafayette was in the vicinity of New York, with his eagle eye fixed upon the foe, ready to pounce upon any detachment which presented the slightest exposure. Washington was everywhere, with patriotism which never flagged, with hope which never failed, cheering the army, animating the inhabitants, rousing Congress, and guiding with his well-balanced mind both military and civil legislation. Thus the dreary summer of 1780 lingered away in our war-scathed land.

Again our heroic little army went into winter-quarters, mainly on the banks of the Hudson. As the spring of 1781 opened, the war was renewed. The British directed their chief attention to the South, which was far weaker than the North. Richmond, in Virginia, was laid in ashes; and a general system of devastation and plunder prevailed. The enemy ascended the Chesapeake and the Potomac with armed vessels. They landed at Mount Vernon. The manager of the estate, to save the mansion from pillage and flames, furnished the legalized robbers with abundance of supplies. Washington was much displeased. He wrote to his agent, —

" It would have been a less painful circumstance to me to have heard, that, in consequence of your non-compliance with their request, they had burned my house, and laid the plantation in ruins. You ought to have considered yourself as my representative, and should have reflected on the bad example of communicating with the enemy, and making a voluntary offer of refreshments to them, with a view to prevent a conflagration."

The prospects of the country were still very dark. On the 1st of of May, 1781, Washington wrote, " Instead of magazines filled with provisions, we have a scanty pittance scattered here and there in the different States. Instead of arsenals well supplied, they are poorly provided, and the workmen all leaving. Instead of having field-equipage in readiness, the quartermaster-general is but now applying to the several States to supply these things. Instead of having the regiments completed, scarce any State has, at this hour, an eighth part of its quota in the field; and there is little prospect of their ever getting more than half. In a word, instead of having everything in readiness to take the field, we have nothing. Instead of having the prospect of a glorious offensive campaign, we have a gloomy and bewildering defensive one, unless we should receive a powerful aid of ships, land-troops, and money from our generous allies."

The army had in fact, about this time, dwindled away to three thousand; and the paper-money issued by Congress, with which the troops were paid, had become almost entirely valueless. Lord Cornwallis was now at Yorktown, in Virginia, but a few miles from Chesapeake Bay. There was no force in his vicinity seriously to annoy him. Washington resolved, in conjunction with our allies from France, to make a bold movement for his capture. He succeeded in deceiving the English into the belief that he was making great preparations for the siege of New York. Thus they were prevented from rendering any aid to Yorktown.

By rapid marches Washington hastened to encircle the foe. Early in September Lord Cornwallis, as he arose one morning, was amazed to see, in the rays of the morning sun, the heights around him gleaming with the bayonets and the batteries of the Americans. At about the same hour the French fleet appeared, in invincible strength, before the harbor. Cornwallis was caught. There was no escape; there was no retreat. Neither by land nor by sea could he obtain any supplies. Shot and shell soon began to fall thickly into his despairing lines. Famine stared him in the face. After a few days of hopeless conflict, on the 19th of October, 1781, he was compelled to surrender. Seven thousand British veterans laid down their arms to the victors. One hundred and sixty pieces of cannon, with corresponding military stores, graced the triumph. Without the assistance of our generous allies the French, we could not have gained this victory. Let not our gratitude be stinted or cold.

When the British soldiers were marching from their intrenchments to lay down their arms, Washington thus addressed his troops: " My brave fellows, let no sensation of satisfaction for the triumphs you have gained induce you to insult your fallen enemy. Let no shouting, no clamorous huzzaing, increase their mortification. Posterity will huzza for us."

This glorious capture roused hope and vigor all over the country. The British Cabinet became disheartened by our indomitable perseverance. The darkness of the long night was passing away. The day after the capitulation, Washington devoutly issued the following order to the army: —

" Divine service is to be performed to-morrow in the several brigades and divisions. The commander-in-chief earnestly recommends that the troops not on duty should universally attend, with that seriousness of deportment and gratitude of heart which the recognition of such reiterated and astonishing interpositions of Providence demands of us."

The joyful tidings reached Philadelphia at midnight. A watchman traversed the streets, shouting at intervals, " Past twelve o'clock, and a pleasant morning. Cornwallis is taken ! "

These words rang upon the ear almost like the trump which wakes the dead. Candles were lighted ; windows thrown up ; figures in night-robes and night-caps bent eagerly out to catch the thrilling sound ; shouts were raised ; citizens rushed into the streets, half clad, — they wept ; they laughed. The news flew upon the wings of the wind, nobody can tell how ; and the shout of an enfranchised people rose, like a roar of thunder, from our whole land. With France for an ally, and with such a victory, the question was now settled, and forever, that republican America would never again yield to the aristocratic government of England.

Though the fury of the storm was over, the billows of war had not yet subsided. Washington, late in November, 1781, again retired to winter-quarters. He urged Congress to make preparations for the vigorous prosecution of the war in the spring, as the most effectual means of securing a speedy and an honorable peace. The conviction was now so general that the war was nearly at an end, that with difficulty ten thousand men were marshaled in the camp. The army, disheartened by the apparent inefficiency of Congress, — for Congress had really but very little power, being then only a collection of delegates from independent States, — very emphatically expressed the wish that Washington would assume the supreme command of the government, and organize the country into a constitutional kingdom, with himself at the head.

But Washington was a republican. He believed that the people of this country, trained in the science of legislation, religious in their habits, and intelligent, were abundantly capable of governing themselves. He repelled the suggestion promptly, and almost indignantly.

Early in May the British Cabinet opened negotiations for peace. Hostilities were, by each party, tacitly laid aside. Negotiations were protracted in Paris during the summer and the ensuing winter. Washington had established his headquarters at Newburg, on the Hudson, and was busy in consolidating the interests of our divided and distracted country. A government of republican liberty, and yet of efficiency, was to be organized ; and its construction required the highest energies of every thinking mind.

It was also necessary to keep the army ever ready for battle; for a new conflict might at any moment break out. Thus the summer and winter of 1782 passed away.

The snow was still lingering in the laps of the Highlands when the joyful tidings arrived that a treaty of peace had been signed at Paris. The intelligence was communicated to the American army on the 19th of April, 1783, — just eight years from the day when the conflict was commenced on the Common at Lexington. England had for eight years deluged this land with blood and woe. Thousands had perished on the gory field of battle; thousands had been beggared; thousands had been made widows and orphans, and doomed to a life-long wretchedness. It was the fearful price which America paid for independence.

Late in November the British evacuated New York, entered their ships, and sailed for their distant island. Washington, marching from West Point, entered the city as our vanquished foes departed. It was a joyful day, and no untoward incident marred its festivities. America was free and independent. Washington was the savior of his country.

And now the day arrived when Washington was to take leave of his companions in arms, to retire to his beloved retreat at Mount Vernon. The affecting interview took place on the 4th of December. Washington, with a flushed cheek and a swimming eye, entered the room where the principal officers of his army were assembled. His voice trembled with emotion as he said, —

" With a heart full of love and gratitude, I now take leave of you. I most devoutly wish that your latter days may be as prosperous and happy as your former ones have been glorious and honorable. I cannot come to each of you to take my leave, but shall be obliged if each of you will come and take me by the hand."

All unaccustomed as Washington was to exhibit emotion, he was now quite overcome. Tears blinded his eyes, and he could say no more. One after another, these heroic men silently grasped his hand in this last parting. Not a word was spoken. It was a scene of those invisible strugglings of the spirit which the pencil cannot picture, and which words cannot describe. Washington traveled slowly towards his beloved home at Mount Vernon, from which he had so long been absent. In every city and village through which he passed, he was greeted with love and veneration. At Annapolis

4

he met the Continental Congress, where he was to resign his commission. It was the 23d of December, 1783. All the members of Congress, and a large concourse of spectators, were present. His address was closed with the following words : —

"Having now finished the work assigned me I retire from the great theatre of action, and bidding an affectionate farewell to this august body, under whose orders I have so long acted, I here offer my commission, and take my leave of all the employments of public life."

MOUNT VERNON.

The next day he returned to Mount Vernon. The following extract from a letter which he then wrote to Lafayette reveals those gentle and domestic traits of character which had been somewhat veiled by the stern duties of his military career : —

"At length I am become a private citizen : and under the shadow of my own vine and fig-tree, free from the bustle of a camp and the busy scenes of public life, I am solacing myself with those tranquil enjoyments, of which the soldier, who is ever in pursuit of fame ; the statesman, whose watchful days and sleepless nights are spent in devising schemes to promote the welfare of his own, perhaps the ruin of other countries, as if this globe were insufficient for us all ; and the courtier, who is always watching the countenance of his prince, in hopes of catching a gracious smile, — can have very little conception. Envious of none, I am determined to be pleased with all. And this, my dear friend, being the order for my march, I will move gently down the stream of life until I sleep with my fathers."

The great problem which now engrossed all minds was the consolidation of the thirteen States of America in some way which should secure to the States certain reserved rights of local administration, while a nation should be formed, with a general government which could exert the energies of centralized power, and thus take its stand, the equal in efficiency, with the renowned kingdoms and empires of earth. The old confederacy, which was merely a conglomeration of independent States, had developed such utter weakness, that all thoughts were turned to the organization of a government upon a different principle.

To this subject Washington, who had suffered so intensely from the inefficiency of the Continental Congress, devoted his most anxious attention. A convention was called to deliberate upon this momentous question. It assembled at Philadelphia in the year 1787. Washington was sent a delegate from Virginia, and, by unanimous vote, was placed in the president's chair. The result was the present Constitution of the United States ; which, rejecting a mere confederacy of independent States, created a nation from the people of all the States, with supreme powers for all the purposes of a general government, and leaving with the States, as state governments leave with the towns, those minor questions of local law in which the integrity of the nation was not involved. The Constitution of the United States is, in the judgment of the millions of the American people, the most sagacious document which has ever emanated from uninspired minds. It has created the strongest government upon this globe. It has made the United States of America what they now are. The world must look at the fruit, and wonder and admire.

It is stated in the Madison Papers, that, in the convention which framed our Constitution, it was proposed that the title of the President of the United States should be *His Excellency;* but the Committee of Style and Arrangement negatived this, and reported in favor of the simple title of *President of the United States.* It has been said that this was done at the instance of Dr. Franklin, who, when the question was under discussion, sarcastically proposed to insert immediately after " His Excellency " the words, " And the Vice-President shall be styled, *His most superfluous Highness.*"

There were some provisions in the compromises of the Constitution from which the heart and mind of Washington recoiled. He had fought for human liberty, — to give to the masses of the people those rights of which aristocratic usurpation had so long defrauded them. " All men are born free and equal " was the motto of the banner under which he had rallied his strength. Equal rights, under the law, for all men, was the corner-stone of that American democracy which Washington, Adams, and Jefferson wished to establish ; but there was a spirit of aristocracy, of exclusive rights for peculiar classes and races, which infused its poison into the Constitution, and which subsequently worked out its natural fruit of woe and death. Alluding to the unfortunate compromise which this spirit insisted upon, in reference to slavery and the colored people, Washington wrote, —

" There are some things in this new form, I will readily acknowledge, which never did, and I am persuaded never will, obtain my cordial approbation. But I did then conceive, and do now most firmly believe, that, in the aggregate, it is the best constitution that can be obtained at the epoch, and that this, or a dissolution, awaits our choice, and is the only alternative."

Upon the adoption of the Constitution all eyes were turned to Washington as chief magistrate. By the unanimous voice of the electors he was chosen the first President of the United States. There was probably scarcely a dissentient voice in the nation. New York was then the seat of government. As Washington left Mount Vernon for the metropolis to assume these new duties of toil and care, we find recorded in his journal, —

"About ten o'clock I bade adieu to Mount Vernon, to private life, and to domestic felicity ; and, with a mind oppressed with more anxious and painful sensations than I have words to express, set out for New York, with the best disposition to render service to my country in obedience to its call, but with less hopes of answering its expectations."

Washington was inaugurated President of the United States on the 30th of April, 1789. He remained in the presidential chair two terms of four years each. At the close of his illustrious administration, in the year 1796, he again retired to the peaceful shades of Mount Vernon, bequeathing to his grateful countrymen the rich legacy of his Farewell Address. The admiration with which these parting counsels were received never will wane. Soon after Washington's return to his beloved retreat at Mount Vernon he wrote a letter to a friend, in which he described the manner in which he passed his time. He rose with the sun, and first made preparations for the business of the day.

"By the time I have accomplished these matters," he adds, "breakfast is ready. This being over, I mount my horse, and ride round my farms, which employs me until it is time to dress for dinner, at which I rarely miss to see strange faces, come, as they say, out of respect to me. And how different is this from having a few friends at the social board! The usual time of sitting at table, a walk, and tea, bring me within the dawn of candle-light; previous to which, if not prevented by company, I resolve that, as soon as the glimmering taper supplies the place of the great luminary, I will retire to my writing-table, and acknowledge the letters I have received. Having given you this history of a day, it will serve for a year."

The following anecdotes have been related, illustrative of President Washington's habits of punctuality. Whenever he assigned to meet Congress at noon, he seldom failed of passing the door of the hall when the clock struck twelve. His dining-hour was at four o'clock, when he always sat down to his table, whether his guests were assembled or not, merely allowing five minutes for the variation of time-pieces. To those who came late, he remarked, "Gentlemen, we are punctual here: my cook never asks whether the company has arrived, but whether the hour has."

When visiting Boston, in 1789, he appointed eight o'clock in the morning as the hour when he would set out for Salem; and, while the Old South clock was striking eight, he was mounting his saddle. The company of cavalry which had volunteered to escort him, not anticipating this punctuality, did not overtake him until he had reached Charles River Bridge. As the troops came hurrying up, the President said to their commander with a good-natured smile,

" Major, I thought you had been too long in my family not to know when it was eight o'clock."

Captain Pease had purchased a beautiful span of horses, which he wished to sell to the President. The President appointed five o'clock in the morning to examine them at his stable. The captain arrived with his span at quarter past five. He was told by the groom that the President was there at five o'clock, but was then gone to attend to other engagements. The President's time was wholly preoccupied for several days, so that Captain Pease had to remain a whole week in Philadelphia before he could get another opportunity to exhibit his span.

Washington, having inherited a large landed estate in Virginia, was, as a matter of course, a slaveholder. The whole number which he held at the time of his death was one hundred and twenty-four. The system met his strong disapproval. In 1786 he wrote to Robert Morris, saying, " There is no man living who wishes more sincerely than I do to see a plan adopted for the abolition of slavery."

Lafayette, that true friend of popular rights, was extremely anxious to free our country from the reproach which slavery brought upon it. Washington wrote to him in 1788, " The scheme, my dear marquis, which you propose as a precedent to encourage the emancipation of the black people of this country from the state of bondage in which they are held, is a striking evidence of the state of your heart. I shall be happy to join you in so laudable a work."

'In his last will and testament, he inscribed these noble words: " Upon the decease of my wife, it is my will and desire that all the slaves which I hold in my own right shall receive their freedom. To emancipate them during her life would, though earnestly wished by me, be attended with such insuperable difficulties, on account of their mixture by marriage with the dower negroes, as to excite the most painful sensation if not disagreeable consequences, from the latter, while both descriptions are in the occupancy of the same proprietor; it not being in my power, under the tenure by which the dower negroes are held, to manumit them."

Long before this he had recorded his resolve: " I never mean, unless some particular circumstances should compel me to it, to possess another slave by purchase ; it being among my first wishes to see some plan adopted by which slavery in this country may be abolished by law."

Mrs. Washington immediately after her husband's death, learning from his will that the only obstacle to the immediate emancipation of the slaves was her right of dower, immediately relinquished that right, and the slaves were at once emancipated.

The 12th of December, 1799, was chill and damp. Washington, however, took his usual round on horseback to his farms, and returned late in the afternoon, wet with sleet, and shivering with cold. Though the snow was clinging to his hair behind when he came in, he sat down to dinner without changing his dress. The next day three inches of snow whitened the ground, and the sky was clouded. Washington, feeling that he had taken cold, remained by the fireside during the morning. As it cleared up in the afternoon he went out to superintend some work upon the lawn. He was then hoarse, and the hoarseness increased as night came on. He, however, took no remedy for it, saying, "I never take anything to carry off a cold. Let it go as it came."

He passed the evening as usual, reading the papers, answering letters, and conversing with his family. About two o'clock the next morning, Saturday, the 14th, he awoke in an ague-chill, and was seriously unwell. At sunrise his physician, Dr. Craig, who resided at Alexandria, was sent for. In the mean time he was bled by one of his overseers, but with no relief, as he rapidly grew worse. Dr. Craig reached Mount Vernon at eleven o'clock, and immediately bled his patient again, but without effect. Two consulting physicians arrived during the day ; and, as the difficulty in breathing and swallowing rapidly increased, venesection was again attempted. It is evident that Washington then considered his case doubtful. He examined his will, and destroyed some papers which he did not wish to have preserved.

His sufferings from inflammation of the throat and struggling for breath, as the afternoon wore away, became quite severe. Still he retained his mental faculties unimpaired, and spoke briefly of his approaching death and burial. About four o'clock in the afternoon he said to Dr. Craig, "I die hard ; but I am not afraid to go. I believed, from my first attack, that I should not survive it: my breath cannot last long." About six o'clock, his physician asked him if he would sit up in his bed. He held out his hands, and was raised up on his pillow, when he said, "I feel that I am going. I thank you for your attentions. You had better not take any more trouble about me, but let me go off quietly. I cannot last long."

He then sank back upon his pillow, and made several unavailing attempts to speak intelligibly. About ten o'clock he said, " I am just going. Have me decently buried, and do not let my body be put into the vault until three days after I am dead. Do you understand me ? " To the reply, " Yes, sir," he remarked, " It is well." These were the last words he uttered. Soon after this he gently expired, in the sixty-eighth year of his age.

At the moment of his death Mrs. Washington sat in silent grief at the foot of his bed. " Is he gone ? " she asked, in a firm and collected voice. The physician, unable to speak, gave a silent signal of assent. " 'T is well," she added, in the same untremulous utterance. " All is now over. I shall soon follow him. I have no more trials to pass through."

On the 18th his remains were deposited in the tomb at Mount Vernon, where they now repose, enshrined in a nation's love : and his fame will forever, as now, fill the world.

CHAPTER II.

JOHN ADAMS.

JOHN ADAMS was born in the present town of Quincy, then a portion of Braintree, on the 30th of October, 1735. His father's elder brother, Joseph, had been educated at Harvard, and was, for upwards of sixty years, minister of a Congregational church at Newington, N. H. The father of John Adams was a farmer of moderate means, a worthy, industrious man, toiling early and late for the very frugal support which such labor could furnish his family. The fact that he was a deacon of the church attests the esteem in which he was held by the community. Like most Christian fathers, he was anxious to give his son a collegiate education, hoping that he would become a minister of the gospel.

But, like most boys, John Adams was not fond of his books. In the bright, sunny morning of his boyhood in Braintree, with the primeval forest waving around, the sunlight sleeping upon the meadows, the sparkling brooks alive with trout, and the ocean rolling in its grandeur before him, out-door life seemed far more attractive than the seclusion of the study, and the apparent monotony of life in the midst of books. When he was about fourteen years of age his father said to him, " My son, it is time for you to decide respecting your future occupation in life. What business do you wish to follow ? "

" I wish to be a farmer," the energetic boy replied.

" Very well," said the judicious father ; " it is time now for you to commence your life-work. You must give up play, and enter upon that steady, hard work without which no farmer can get a living." The next morning, at an early hour, John was with his hoe alone in the field. He worked all the morning till noon; came home to his dinner; returned to the field; worked all the afternoon till night. As he hoed, he thought. The blue sky was above him; but there was also a blazing, scorching sun. The forest waved around. He would have enjoyed wandering through it with his gun; but that was boy's play which he had given up, not farmer's work upon which he had entered. Work, work, work, was now to him life's doom; and forest, brook, and ocean strangely lost their charms.

In the evening he said to his father, with some considerable hesitation, " Father, I have been thinking to-day, and have concluded that I should like to try my books." His father offered no objections, and was willing to make every effort in his power to indulge his son in his choice, if he were determined to devote all his energies to the acquisition of an education. There was a very good school in the town, and John laid aside his hoe for his grammar. He entered Harvard College at the age of sixteen, and graduated in 1755, highly esteemed for integrity, energy, and ability. He must have struggled with small means; for his father found it necessary to add to his labors as a farmer the occupation of a shoemaker, to meet the expenses of his household. When John graduated at twenty years of age, he was considered as having received his full share of the small paternal patrimony; and, with his education as his only capital, he went out to take his place in the conflicts of this stormy world. The first thing the young graduate needed was money. He obtained the situation of instructor in one of the public schools in Worcester. While teaching school he also studied law. All thoughts of the ministerial profession were soon abandoned.

This was a period of great political excitement. France and England were then engaged in their great seven years' struggle for the mastery over this continent. Braddock had just suffered his ignoble defeat. A young Virginian by the name of George Washington, who had saved Braddock's army, was then beginning to be known. The colonies were in great peril. The question, whether French or English influence was to dominate on this continent, was trembling in the balance. A large number of the young men of the colonies were called to the camp, and the great theme engrossed every mind. At this time John Adams wrote a very remarkable letter to a friend, in which, with almost prophetic vision, he described the future greatness of this country, — a prophecy which time has more than fulfilled.

To these engrossing themes young Adams consecrated all the enthusiasm of his nature. He thought, he talked, he wrote. He hesitated whether to give himself to law, to politics, or to the army. Could he have obtained a troop of horse, or a company of foot, he declares that he should infallibly have been a soldier.

For two years John Adams remained in Worcester, then a town of but a few hundred inhabitants, teaching a public school and studying law. He was a very earnest student. His journal proves that, inspired by a noble ambition, he consecrated his time, with great moral courage and self-denial, to intellectual culture. Speaking of the profligate lives of some of the young men around him, he writes, —

" What pleasure can a young gentleman, who is capable of thinking, take in playing cards? It gratifies none of the senses. It can entertain the mind only by hushing its clamors. Cards, backgammon, etc., are the great antidotes to reflection, to thinking. What learning and sense are we to expect from young gentlemen in whom a fondness for cards, etc., outgrows and chokes the desire of knowledge? "

When but twenty-two years of age he returned to his native town of Braintree, and, opening a law office, devoted himself to study with renewed vigor. Soon after this his father died ; and he continued to reside with his mother and a brother, who had taken the farm. His native powers of mind and untiring devotion to his profession caused him to rise rapidly in public esteem. In October, 1764, he married Miss Abigail Smith, daughter of Rev. William Smith, pastor of the church in Weymouth. She was a lady of very rare endowments of person and of mind, and, by the force of her character, contributed not a little to her husband's celebrity. The British government was now commencing that career of aggressions upon the rights of the colonists which aroused the most determined resistance, and which led to that cruel war which resulted in the independence of the colonies. An order was issued by the British crown imposing taxes upon certain goods, and authorizing an indiscriminate search to find goods which might have evaded the tax. The legality of the law was contested before the

Superior Court. James Otis was engaged by the merchants to argue their cause against this encroachment of arbitrary power. With consummate ability he performed his task. John Adams was a delighted listener.

" Otis," he wrote, " was a flame of fire. With a promptitude of classical allusion, a depth of research, a rapid summary of historical events and dates, a profusion of legal authorities, and a prophetic glance of his eyes into futurity, he hurried away all before him. *American independence was then and there born.* Every man of an immensely crowded audience appeared to me to go away, as I did, ready to take up arms."

A literary club was about this time formed of prominent gentlemen of the bar, which met once a week in a small social circle, at each other's houses, to discuss subjects of popular interest. Mr. Adams read an essay upon the state of affairs, which was published in the journals, republished in England, and which attracted great attention. The friends of the colonists in England pronounced it " one of the very best productions ever seen from North America."

The memorable Stamp Act was now issued ; and Adams, gathering up his strength to resist these encroachments, entered with all the ardor of his soul into political life. He drew up a series of resolutions, remonstrating against the Stamp Act, which were adopted at a public meeting of the citizens at Braintree, and which were subsequently adopted, word for word, by more than forty towns in the State. Popular commotion prevented the landing of the Stamp Act papers. This stopped all legal processes and closed the courts. The town of Boston sent a petition to the governor that the courts might be reopened. Jeremy Gridley, James Otis, and John Adams were chosen to argue the cause of the petitioners before the governor and council. Mr. Gridley urged upon the council the great distress which the closing of the courts was causing. Mr. Otis argued that this distress fully warranted them to open the courts while the question was being referred to the authorities beyond the sea ; but John Adams boldly took the ground that the Stamp Act was an assumption of arbitrary power, violating both the English Constitution and the charter of the province. It is said that this was the first direct denial of the unlimited right of Parliament over the colonies.

Soon after this the Stamp Act was repealed. Mr. Adams now

entered upon a distinguished political career. A press-gang from a king's ship in the harbor of Boston seized a young American by the name of Ansell Nickerson. The intrepid sailor thrust a harpoon through the heart of Lieutenant Panton, the leader of the gang. He was tried for murder. John Adams defended him. He argued that the *usage* of impressment had never extended to the colonies; that the attempt to impress Nickerson was unlawful; that his act of killing his assailant was justifiable homicide. The hero was acquitted, and the principle was established, that the infamous royal prerogative of impressment could have no existence in the code of colonial law.

To suppress the spirit of independence, daily becoming more manifest among the people, the British crown sent two regiments of soldiers to Boston. A more obnoxious menace could not have been devised. The populace insulted the soldiers: the soldiers retaliated with insolence and threats.

On the 5th of March, 1770, a small party of soldiers, thus assailed, fired upon the crowd in State Street, Boston, killing and wounding several. Mutual exasperation was now roused almost to frenzy. The captain and six soldiers were arrested and tried for murder. Very nobly, and with moral courage rarely equaled, John Adams and Josiah Quincy undertook the task of their defense. They encountered unmeasured obloquy. They were stigmatized as deserters from the cause of popular liberty, and the bribed advocates of tyranny. But both of these ardent patriots had witnessed with alarm the rise of mob violence, and they felt deeply that there was no tyranny so dreadful as that of anarchy. Better it was, a thousand fold, to be under the domination of the worst of England's kings than that of a lawless mob.

An immense and excited auditory was present at the trial. The first sentence with which John Adams opened his defense produced an electrical effect upon the court and the crowd. It was as follows: —

"May it please your honors, and you, gentlemen of the jury, I am for the prisoners at the bar, and shall apologize for it only in the words of the Marquis Beccaria: 'If I can be the instrument of preserving one life, his blessing and tears of transport shall be a sufficient consolation to me for the contempt of all mankind.'"

Captain Preston and the soldiers were acquitted, excepting two, who were found guilty of manslaughter, and received a very slight punishment. Though Boston instituted an annual commemoration of the massacre, Mr. Adams's popularity suffered so little that he was elected by the citizens of Boston, to which place he had removed, as one of their representatives to the colonial Legislature. Governor Hutchinson, though a native of the province, was a man of great energy and of insatiable ambition. Anxious to secure the royal favor, upon which he was dependent for his office, he gave all his influence in favor of the demands of the crown. In all these measures John Adams was recognized as one of his most formidable antagonists. In 1772 Mr. Adams, finding his health failing from his incessant application to business, returned to his more secluded home at Braintree.

The energetic remonstrances of the colonists against taxation without representation, and their determination not to submit to the wrong, had induced the repeal of the tax upon all articles except tea. This led to organizations all over the land to abandon the use of tea. Large shipments were made to Boston. The consignees endeavored to send it back. The crown officers in the custom-house refused a clearance. On the evening of the 15th of December a band of men, disguised as Indians, boarded the vessels, hoisted the chests upon the deck, and emptied their contents into the sea.

Under the circumstances this was a deed of sublime daring, being the first open act of rebellion. The crown, exasperated, punished Boston by sending armed ships to close the port. This was a deadly blow to the heroic little town. The other colonies sympathized nobly with Massachusetts. Combinations were formed to refuse all importations from Great Britain. A General Congress was convened in Philadelphia, 1774, to make common cause against the powerful foe. John Adams was one of the five delegates sent from Massachusetts to the Continental Congress. He was entreated by a friend, the king's attorney-general, not to accept his appointment as a delegate to the Congress. " Great Britain," said the attorney-general, " has determined on her system. Her power is irresistible, and will be destructive to you, and to all those who shall persevere in opposition to her designs."

The heroic reply of John Adams was, " I know that Great Britain has determined on her system; and that very determination determines me on mine. You know that I have been constant and uniform in my opposition to her measures. The die is now cast. I have passed the Rubicon. Sink or swim, live or die, survive or perish, with my country, is my fixed, unalterable determination."

Few comprehended more fully than Mr. Adams the sublimity of the crisis which was impending. He wrote at this time in his journal, —

"I wander alone, and ponder; I muse, I mope, I ruminate; I am often in reveries and brown studies. The objects before me are too grand and multifarious for my comprehension. We have not men fit for the times. We are deficient in genius, in education, in travel, in fortune, in everything. I feel unutterable anxiety. God grant us wisdom and fortitude! Should the opposition be suppressed, should this country submit, what infamy and ruin! God forbid! Death in any form is less terrible."

He was not blind to the danger of incurring the vengeance of the British government. He wrote to James Warren, "There is one ugly reflection. Brutus and Cassius were conquered and slain. Hampden died in the field; Sidney, on the scaffold."

Mr. Adams was strongly attached to his friend Mr. Sewall, who remonstrated with him against his patriotic course, and who was disposed to espouse the cause of the king. On bidding him adieu, Mr. Adams said, "I see we must part; and with a bleeding heart I say, I fear forever: but you may depend upon it, this adieu is the sharpest thorn upon which I ever set my foot."

The Colonial Congress commenced its session at Philadelphia the 5th of September, 1774, when Mr. Adams took his seat. He was speedily placed on several of the most important committees. The general desire then was merely for a redress of grievances. Very few wished to break away from the British crown. George Washington was one of the Virginia delegation. He doubted whether the British Cabinet, in its arrogance, would relinquish its insane attempt to deprive the colonists of their liberties; but Richard Henry Lee, another of the Virginia delegation, said to Mr. Adams, —

"We shall infallibly carry all our points. You will be completely relieved. All the offensive acts will be repealed. The army and fleet will be recalled, and England will give up her foolish project."

Much as Mr. Adams might have desired this to be true, his sagacity led him to concur in the judgment of George Washington. This Congress, by its ability and heroism, rendered its memory immortal. Lord Chatham said, —

"I have studied and admired the free states of antiquity, the master-spirits. of the world; but for solidity of reason, force of sagacity, and wisdom of conclusion, no body of men can take the precedence of this Continental Congress."

At this time the idea of independence was extremely unpopular in Pennsylvania and in all the Middle States. Virginia was the most populous State in the Union; and its representatives, proud of the ancient dominion, not without a show of reason, deemed it their right to take the lead in all important measures. A Virginian was appointed commander-in-chief. A Virginian wrote the Declaration of Independence; a Virginian moved its adoption by Congress. Mr. Adams says of the Massachusetts delegation, —

"We were all suspected of having independence in view. 'Now,' said they, 'you must not utter the word "independence," nor give the least hint or insinuation of the idea, either in Congress or in private conversation: if you do, we are undone.' "

It was soon rumored throughout Philadelphia that John Adams was for independence. The Quakers and the gentlemen of property took the alarm. Adams " was sent to Coventry," and was avoided like a leper. With a saddened yet imperial spirit, borne down, yet not crushed, by the weight of his anxieties and unpopularity, almost in solitude, for a time he walked the streets of Philadelphia. It would have been well for him could he have blended a little more of the *suaviter in modo* with the *fortiter in re.*

The British crown, with utter infatuation, pursued its reckless course. In April, 1775, the war of the Revolution was opened, as brave men were shot down by English soldiery upon the green at Lexington. Boston was placed under martial law. All its citizens were imprisoned within the lines of the British fleet and army which encompassed the city. The inhabitants were plunged into the deepest distress. On the 10th day of May the Congress again assembled in Philadelphia. Mrs. Adams kept her husband minutely informed of all the events occurring in Boston and its vicinity. About the middle of May, one Sabbath morning, Mrs. Adams was roused from sleep by the ringing of alarm-bells, the firing of cannon, and the beating of drums. She immediately sent a courier to Boston, and found everything in great confusion. Three vessels of war had left the harbor, manifestly on some hostile mission, and were sailing along the shores of Massachusetts Bay, approaching Braintree or

Weymouth. Men, women, and children were flying in all directions. The sick were placed in beds on carts, and hurried to a place of safety. The report was that three hundred soldiers had landed, and were marching up into the town of Braintree. Men seized their guns, and came flocking from their farms, until two thousand were collected.

It soon turned out that the hostile expedition had landed on Grape Island to seize a large quantity of hay which was stored there. The

RESIDENCE OF JOHN ADAMS.

impetuous colonists soon mustered two vessels, jumped on board, and put off for the island. The British, seeing them coming, decamped. Our men landed, and set fire to the hay, about eighty tons. Mrs. Adams, in giving an account of this, writes, —

Our house has been, upon this alarm, in the same scene of confusion that it was upon the former; soldiers coming in for lodging, for breakfast, for supper, for drink. Sometimes refugees from Boston, tired and fatigued, seek an asylum for a day, a night, a week. You can hardly imagine how we live.

5

The battle of Bunker's Hill was fought on the 17th of June, 1775. The next afternoon, which was Sunday, Mrs. Adams wrote to her husband, —

" The day, perhaps the decisive day, is come, on which the fate of America depends. My bursting heart must find vent at my pen. I have just heard that our dear friend Dr. Warren is no more, but fell gloriously fighting for his country ; saying, ' Better to die honorably in the field than ignominiously hang upon the gallows.'

" Charlestown is laid in ashes. The battle began upon our intrenchments upon Bunker's Hill, Saturday morning, about three o'clock, and has not ceased yet ; and it is now three o'clock, Sabbath afternoon. The constant roar of the cannon is so distressing, that we cannot either eat, drink, or sleep."

These scenes had aroused the country around Boston to the very highest pitch of excitement. The farmers had come rushing in from all the adjoining towns with rifles, shot-guns, pitch-forks, and any other weapons of offense or defense which they could grasp. Thus a motley mass of heroic men, without efficient arms, supplies, powder, or discipline, amounting to some fourteen thousand, were surrounding Boston, which was held by about eight thousand British regulars, supported by a powerful fleet.

The first thing now to be done by Congress was to choose a commander-in-chief for this army. The New England delegation were almost unanimous in favor of General Ward, then at the head of the army in Massachusetts. Mr. Adams alone dissented, and urged the appointment of George Washington, a delegate from Virginia, but little known out of his own State. Through the powerful influence of John Adams, Washington was nominated and elected. He was chosen without an opposing voice. A powerful fleet, said to contain twenty-eight thousand seamen and fifty-five thousand land troops, was now crossing the ocean for our enslavement. It would seem impossible, to human vision, that such a force could then be resisted. Our destruction seemed sure. Goliah was striding down upon David, and all onlookers expected to see the stripling tossed upon the giant's spear high into the air.

Washington hastened to Massachusetts to take command of the army. Five days after his appointment Thomas Jefferson made his appearance upon the floor of Congress. A strong friendship immediately sprang up between Adams and Jefferson, which, with a short interruption, continued for the remainder of their lives. After a brief adjournment, Congress met again in September. The battle was still raging about Boston; and the British, with free ingress and egress by their fleet, were plundering and burning, and committing every kind of atrocity in all directions. John Adams presented and carried the decisive resolution, that, in view of the aggressions and demands of England, "it is necessary that the exercise of every kind of authority under said crown should be totally suppressed." Having thus prepared the way, a few weeks after, on the 7th of June, 1776, Richard Henry Lee of Virginia offered the memorable resolution, which John Adams seconded, —

"That these United States are, and of right ought to be, free and independent."

A committee was then appointed to draught a Declaration of Independence. It consisted of Jefferson, Adams, Franklin, Sherman, and Livingston. Jefferson and Adams were appointed, by the rest, a sub-committee to draw up the Declaration. At Mr. Adams's earnest request Mr. Jefferson prepared that immortal document, which embodies the fundamental principles of all human rights. At this time Mr. Adams wrote to a friend, —

"I am engaged in constant business, — from seven to ten in the morning in committee, from ten to five in Congress, and from six to ten again in committee. Our assembly is scarcely numerous enough for the business. Everybody is engaged all day in Congress, and all the morning and evening in committees."

Jefferson wrote of his illustrious colleague, "The great pillar of support to the Declaration of Independence, and its ablest advocate and champion on the floor of the house, was John Adams. He was our Colossus. Not graceful, not always fluent, he yet came out with a power, both of thought and expression, which moved us from our seats."

Mr. Jefferson, though so able with his pen, had little skill in debate, and was no public speaker. That which he wrote in the silence of his closet, John Adams defended in the stormy hall of Congress. When Adams and Jefferson met to draw up the Declaration of Independence, each urged the other to make the draft. Mr. Adams closed the friendly contention by saying, —

"I will not do it : you must. There are three good reasons why you should. First, you are a Virginian ; and Virginia should take the lead in this business. Second, I am obnoxious, suspected, unpopular : you are the reverse. Third, you can write ten times better than I can." " Well," Jefferson replied, " if you insist upon it, I will do as well as I can."

On the 4th of July, 1776, the Declaration of Independence was adopted by Congress, and signed by each of its members. This was one of the boldest acts in the records of time. Every man who affixed his signature to that paper thus cast the glove of mortal defiance at the foot of the most majestic power on this globe. The scene was one upon which the genius of both pen and pencil has been lavished. In its grandeur it stands forth as one of the most sublime of earthly acts. Of the fifty-five who signed that declaration, there was not probably one who would deny that its most earnest advocate, and its most eloquent defender, was John Adams.

The day after the achievement of this momentous event, Mr. Adams wrote to his wife as follows : —

" Yesterday the greatest question was decided that was ever debated in America; and greater, perhaps, never was or will be decided among men. A resolution was passed, without one dissenting colony, ' That these United States are, and of right ought to be, free and independent States.' The day is passed. The 4th of July, 1776, will be a memorable epoch in the history of America. I am apt to believe it will be celebrated by succeeding generations as the great anniversary festival. It ought to be commemorated, as the day of deliverance, by solemn acts of devotion to Almighty God. It ought to be solemnized with pomps, shows, games, sports, guns, bells, bonfires, and illuminations, from one end of the continent to the other, from this time forward forever. You will think me transported with enthusiasm; but I am not. I am well aware of the toil and blood and treasure that it will cost to maintain this Declaration, and support and defend these States ; yet, through all the gloom, I can see that the end is worth more than all the means, and that posterity will triumph, though you and I may rue, which I hope we shall not."

A few weeks before this, early in March, Washington had taken possession of Dorchester Heights, and had driven the British out of Boston. Mrs. Adams, in a letter to her husband, under date of March 4, writes, —

" I have just returned from Penn's Hill, where I have been sitting to hear the amazing roar of cannon, and from whence I could see every shell that was thrown. The sound, I think, is one of the grandest in nature, and is of the true species of the sublime." The next morning, she adds to her letter, " I went to bed about twelve, and rose again a little after one. I could no more sleep than if I had been in the engagement : the rattling of the windows, the jar of the house, the continual roar of twenty-four pounders, and the bursting of shells, give us such ideas, and realize a scene to us of which we could form scarcely any conception. I hear we got possession of Dorchester Hill last night ; four thousand men upon it to-day : lost but one man. The ships are all drawn round the town. To-night we shall realize a more terrible scene still. I sometimes think I cannot stand it. I wish myself with you out of hearing, as I cannot assist them."

In August a British army, landing from their fleet, under Lord Howe, overran Long Island, defeating the American army, which only escaped destruction by retreating in a dark and foggy night to the main-land. Howe imagined that the discouragement of this defeat would induce the Americans to listen to terms of submission. He therefore requested an interview with some of the leading members of Congress. John Adams was not in favor of the conference. He was well assured that England would present no terms to which America could accede. A committee, however, was appointed to treat with the British general, consisting of Adams, Franklin, and Rutledge.

On Monday, September 9, 1776, the delegates set out to meet General Howe on Staten Island. Franklin and Rutledge took chairs, — a vehicle for but one person. Mr. Adams rode on horseback. The first night they lodged at an inn in New Brunswick, which was so crowded that Franklin and Adams had to take one bed in a chamber but little larger than the bed, with no chimney, and but one window. The window was open ; and Mr. Adams, who was quite an invalid, wished to shut it. "Oh !" said Franklin, "don't shut the window : we shall be suffocated." Mr. Adams replied, that he was afraid of the evening air. Dr. Franklin answered, " The air within this chamber will soon be, and indeed is now, worse than that without doors. Come, open the window, and come to bed, and I will convince you." Mr. Adams opened the window, and leaped into bed. He writes, —

" The doctor then began an harangue upon air and cold, and respiration and perspiration, with which I was so much amused that
I soon feel asleep, and left him and his philosophy together: but I
believe that they were equally sound and insensible within a few
minutes after me; for the last words I heard were pronounced as if
he were more than half asleep. I remember little of the lecture,
except that the human body, by respiration and perspiration, de-
stroys a gallon of air in a minute, that two such persons as were
now in that chamber would consume all the air in it in an hour or
two; that, in breathing over and over again the matter thrown off
by the lungs and the skin, we should imbibe the real cause of colds,
not from abroad, but from within."

The next morning they proceeded on their journey. When they
came to the water's edge, they met an officer whom General Howe
had sent as a hostage for their safe return. Mr. Adams said to
Dr. Franklin, " that it would be childish to depend on such a pledge,
and that he preferred to trust entirely to the honor of General
Howe. They therefore took the officer back to Staten Island with
them in his lordship's barge. As they approached the shore, Lord
Howe came down upon the beach to meet them. Seeing the officer
in their company, he said, —

" Gentlemen, you pay me a high compliment, and you may depend upon it that I will consider it the most sacred of things."

They walked up to the house between a line of guards, who ma-
nœuvred and handled their muskets in the most approved style of
military etiquette. The house, which was " dirty as a stable," was
carpeted with a sprinkling of moss and green sprigs, so that it looked
picturesquely beautiful. After a slight, cold repast, they entered
upon business. Lord Howe remarked that his powers enabled him
to confer with any private gentlemen of influence in the colonies,
and that he could only confer with them in that character. John
Adams, with his characteristic straightforward bluntness, replied, —

" We came, sir, but to listen to your propositions. You may
view us in any light you please, except that of British subjects.
We shall consider ourselves in no other character than that in which
we were placed by order of Congress."

His lordship, who had only permission to offer pardon to the
leaders of the Revolution, with a few exceptions, if the States would
return to their allegiance to the king, anxious to conciliate the dele-

gation, was profuse in expressions of gratitude to the State of Massachusetts for erecting in Westminster Abbey a monument to his brother, Lord Howe, who was killed in the French war. He said that his affection for America was, on that account, so strong, that he felt for America as for a brother; and that, if America should fall, he should lament it like the loss of a brother. Dr. Franklin, with an easy air, bowed and smiled, and replied, with all that grace and suavity which marked him as one of the most accomplished of diplomatists, —

" My lord, we will do our utmost endeavors to save your lordship that mortification."

Mr. Adams, in his account of the interview, remarks that his lordship appeared to feel this with much sensibility. But with Mr. Adams's remark, to which we have referred, he was evidently not a little nettled; for, turning to Dr. Franklin and Mr. Rutledge, he said, with much gravity and solemnity, " Mr. Adams is a decided character."

This was the darkest period of the conflict. Our affairs looked so gloomy that even the most sanguine were disheartened. Many were exceedingly dissatisfied with that *prudence* of General Washington which alone saved us from destruction. Many were anxious to displace him. It has been said that Mr. Adams was one of this number. He denies it peremptorily.

The advance of the enemy towards Philadelphia had rendered it necessary for Congress to adjourn to Baltimore. It was in those days a long and tedious journey from Boston to that " far-away country," as Mrs. Adams called it. Mr. Adams, in his journal, gives an account of a horseback ride which he took in January, 1777, from Boston, to attend a session of Congress in that distant city.

He rode across the State of Connecticut to Fishkill on the Hudson, and ascended the banks of the river to Poughkeepsie, where he was able to cross upon the ice. He then rode down the western banks to New Windsor, five miles below Newburg. Then he struck across the country to Easton in Pennsylvania. He passed through Sussex County in New Jersey, the stronghold of the Tories, but encountered no insult, as the firm attitude of the patriots overawed them. It took him three weeks of excessive fatigue to accomplish this journey. One can now go to California in one third that time, and with far less discomfort. Alluding to the weary ride, he writes, "The weather has been sometimes bitterly cold, sometimes warm, sometimes rainy, and sometimes snowy, and the roads abominably hard and rough; so that this journey has been the most tedious I ever attempted."

The number of members assembled in Congress had become quite small, often falling as low as twenty-three. The labors of these men have never been properly appreciated. Their peril was about as great as that of those who met the foe in the field, and their toils scarcely less severe. The imperfections of the old confederation were very palpable to the sagacious mind of John Adams. Mr. Marchant, one of the delegates, relates the following characteristic anecdote: —

"The articles of confederation being completed, the members, by rotation, were called upon to place their signatures to them. This being concluded, a pause and perfect calm succeeded. Mr. Adams sat and appeared full of thought. He rose: 'Mr. President.' His cane slipped through his thumb and forefinger, with a quick tap upon the floor; his eyes rolled upwards; his brows were raised to their full arch. 'This business, sir, that has taken up so much of our time, seems to be finished; but, sir, I now, upon this floor, venture to predict, that before ten years the confederation, like a rope of sand, will be found inadequate to the purpose, and its dissolution will take place. Heaven grant that wisdom and experience may avert what we then have most to fear!'"

The confederacy proved, as Mr. Adams predicted, a failure. It was a mere league of States, each reserving all effective powers to itself, and conferring upon Congress but the shadow of a sovereignty.

Dr. Gordon gives the following testimony to Mr. Adams's influence: "I never can think we shall finally fail of success while Heaven continues to the Congress the life and abilities of Mr. John Adams. He is equal to the controversy in all its stages. He stood upon the shoulders of the whole Congress when reconciliation was the wish of all America. He was equally conspicuous in cutting the knot which tied us to Great Britain. In a word, I deliver to you the opinion of every man in the house when I add, that he possesses the clearest head and firmest heart of any man in Congress."

The energy with which he was inspired and the confidence reposed in him may be inferred from the fact that he was a member of ninety committees and chairman of twenty-five. Until November, 1777, Mr. Adams was assiduous in his attendance upon Congress, devoting himself with tireless diligence to his public duties.

In November, 1777, Mr. Adams was appointed a delegate to France, to take the place of Silas Deane, who had been recalled, and to coöperate with Benjamin Franklin and Arthur Lee, who were then in Paris, in the endeavor to obtain assistance in arms and money from the French government. This was a severe trial to his patriotism, as it separated him from his home, compelled him to cross the ocean in winter, and exposed him to imminent peril of capture by the British cruisers. Anxiously he pondered the question. He was a man of ardent affections; and it was hard to be separated from his family, consisting of a wife and four children. The news of his appointment was known by the British, and they had a large fleet in Newport, R. I., which would undoubtedly be employed to intercept him. Capture would lodge him in Newgate. He would be tried in England for treason, and Mr. Adams had no doubt that they would proceed to execute him. But, on the other hand, our country was in extremest peril. It was clear that, without the aid of some friendly European power, our feeble armies must be crushed. France was the only nation from which there was the slightest hope that aid could be obtained. Mr. Adams had done, perhaps, more than any other man to induce the colonies to declare their independence. As was to be expected of the man, he adopted the heroic resolve to run all the risks.

" My wife," he writes, " who had always encouraged and animated me in all the antecedent dangers and perplexities, did not fail me on this occasion. After much agitation of mind, and a thousand reverses unnecessary to be detailed, I resolved to devote my family and my life to the cause, accepted the appointment, and made preparation for the voyage."

It was several months before a frigate could be got ready. On a cold day in February, 1778, a wintry wind roughening Massachusetts Bay, Mr. Adams took a sad leave of his wife and three children, and accompanied by his son, John Quincy, then a lad of but ten years of age, was rowed out to the frigate Boston, riding at anchor at some distance from the shore. The voyage was stormy, uncomfortable, and eventful. When five days out, on the 15th of

February, three large English frigates were seen, probably cruising for the Boston. They gave chase. Two of them were soon run out of sight. The third, a better sailer, continued the pursuit. Arrangements were made for a desperate fight. Mr. Adams urged them to contend to the last extremity.

" My motives," he writes, " were more urgent than theirs ; for it will be easily believed that it would have been more eligible for me to be killed on board the Boston, or sunk to the bottom in her, than to be taken prisoner."

Mr. Adams sat at the cabin-windows, watching the frowning enemy gaining very rapidly upon them, when suddenly the black clouds of a rising tempest gathered in the skies. The wind rose to a gale. The clouds hastened the approach of the darkness of the night, in which the ships lost sight of each other; and when the morning dawned the British frigate was nowhere to be seen, while the ocean was tossed by a hurricane.

On the 14th of March another sail hove in sight. Trusting that it might prove a prize which they would be able to take, they gave chase, and it was soon overtaken and captured. Mr. Sprague, in his Eulogy of Adams and Jefferson, relates the following anecdote of this engagement. Captain Tucker begged Mr. Adams to retire to a place of safety below. Soon after, as the balls of the hostile ship were flying over their heads, Captain Tucker saw Mr. Adams on deck with a musket in his hand, fighting as a common marine. In the excitement of the moment he rushed up to his illustrious passenger, exclaiming, " Why are you here, sir ? I am commanded to carry you safely to Europe, and I will do it ; " and, seizing him in his arms, he forcibly carried him from the scene of danger.

They took the prize, and a prize indeed it was. It proved to be a letter of marque, the Martha, Captain McIntosh, of fourteen guns, with a cargo insured in London for seventy-two thousand pounds. The captured vessel was sent to Boston. Captain McIntosh, who was kept on board the Boston, was a very intelligent, gentlemanly man, and held much friendly conversation with Mr. Adams. On the evening of the 15th of March, as they were approaching the French coast, Mr. Adams was sitting in the cabin, when Captain McIntosh came down, and, addressing him with great solemnity, said, —

" Mr. Adams, this ship will be captured by my countrymen in

less than half an hour. Two large British men-of-war are bearing directly down upon us, and are just by. You will hear from them, I warrant you, in six minutes. Let me take the liberty to say to you, that I feel for you more than for any one else. I have always liked you since I came on board, and have always ascribed to you the good treatment which I have received. You may depend upon it, all the good service I can render you with my countrymen shall be done with pleasure."

This was indeed startling intelligence. Mr. Adams, who had heard an uncommon trampling upon deck, only responded with a silent bow, and, taking his hat, ascended the cabin-stairs. It was a bright moonlight evening, and there were the two ships already within musket-shot. They could see everything, — even the men on board. All expected every moment to be hailed, or perhaps to be saluted with a broadside. But the two ships passed without speaking a word. "I stood upon deck," writes Mr. Adams, "till they had got so far off as to remove all apprehension of danger from them. Whether they were two American frigates, which had been about that time in France, we never knew. We had no inclination to inquire about their business or destination, and were very happy that they discovered so little curiosity about ours."

On the morning of March 30th they made Bordeaux Lighthouse, and ran safely into the river. Mr. Adams was charmed with the appearance of La Belle France. The sight of land, cattle, villages, farm-houses, women and children, after so long and dreary a voyage, gave indescribable pleasure. There was a French ship in the stream ; and Mr. Adams and his son were invited to a very elegant entertainment, served up in style to which they had been quite unaccustomed in their frugal provincial home. They there learned that Dr. Franklin, who had been received by Louis XVI. with great pomp, and who, from his courtesy of manners, affability, and aptness in paying compliments, was admirably adapted to impress the French mind, had already succeeded in concluding a treaty with France.

Indeed, it is probably fortunate that Mr. Adams did not arrive any sooner. He was not at all at home in French diplomacy. While Franklin was greatly admired and caressed, Mr. Adams was decidedly unpopular in the Parisian court. His virtues and his defects were those of a blunt, straightforward, unpolished Englishman. In Paris he met with David Hartley, a member of the British House of Commons. They came together like two icebergs. Mr. Hartley, on his return to London, said to Sir John Temple and others, " Your Mr. Adams, that you represent as a man of such good sense, — he may have that; but he is the most ungracious man I ever saw."

Mr. Adams's first interview with the President of the Parliament of Bordeaux was alike characteristic of the affable Frenchman and the bluff Yankee. The premier received him not only respectfully and politely, but with affection which was even tender.

"I am charmed," said he, " to see you. I have long felt for you a brother's love. I have trembled for you in the great perils through which you have passed. You have encountered many dangers and sufferings in the cause of liberty; and I have sympathized with you in them all, for I have suffered in that cause myself."

All this was in accordance with national courtesy, and was as sincere as are the usual salutations of social life. It was by no means hypocrisy: it was only politeness. Dr. Franklin would have responded in a similar strain, and the two friends would have separated, charmed with each other. We learn how Mr. Adams received these cordial advances by the following ungracious entry in his journal: —

" Mr. Bondfield had to interpret all this effusion of compliments. I thought it never would come to an end; but it did: and I concluded, upon the whole, there was a form of sincerity in it, decorated, and almost suffocated, with French compliments."

Mr. Adams and his little son, John Quincy, reached Paris on the 8th of April, after land-travel of five hundred miles. As the ambassador of the infant colonies struggling for independence, Mr. Adams was received by both court and people with the utmost kindness. In his journal he records, " The attention to me which has been shown, from my first landing in France, by the people in authority of all ranks, and by the principal merchants, and, since my arrival in Paris, by the ministers of state and others of the first consideration, has been very remarkable."

Mr. Adams could not speak French, which was almost a fatal obstacle to his success as a courtier. He says that Dr. Franklin could not speak it grammatically; but, at all events, Dr. Franklin succeeded in speaking it so well as to charm all with whom he conversed, and his polite auditors averred that his pronunciation was truly Parisian. He was an exceedingly gallant old gentleman of seventy, possessed of extraordinary tact in paying compliments.

In a sketch of his colleagues, Mr. Adams writes of Dr. Franklin, —

"That he was a great genius, a great wit, a great humorist, a great satirist, a great politician, is certain. That he was a great philosopher, a great moralist, a great statesman, is more questionable." On the other hand, Dr. Franklin writes of his colleague, "Mr. Adams is always an honest man, often a wise one ; but he is sometimes completely out of his senses."

Mr. Adams was an earnest, methodical business man. He was disgusted at the loose way in which he found business conducted by his colleagues. There was not a minute-book, letter-book, or account-book to be produced. He undertook a vigorous reform, bought some blank books, declined invitations to dine, and bowed down to the hard work of acquiring the French language. He became unduly suspicious of the designs of France. One day he was crossing the court of the palace of Versailles with his colleague, Mr. Lee, and the Count de Vergennes. They passed and exchanged bows with the distinguished general, Marshal Maillebois. "That is a great general," said Mr. Lee. "I wish," responded the count, "that he had the command with you." This was a very natural remark, when we had then no generals of distinction in our country, and when even many of our own most devoted patriots were distrusting Washington. Mr. Adams thus comments on these words :

"This escape was, in my mind, a confirmation strong of the design at court of getting the whole command of America into their own hands. My feelings on this occasion were kept to myself ; but my reflection was, "I will be buried in the ocean, or in any other manner sacrificed, before I will voluntarily put on the chains of France, when I am struggling to throw off those of Great Britain."

Mr. Adams's earnest patriotism induced him to practice the most rigid economy while abroad, that Congress might be put to as little expense as possible. The treaty of alliance with France was already formed before his arrival ; and, soon finding that there was but little for him to do in Paris, he resolved that he had rather run the gauntlet through all the British men-of-war, and all the storms of the ocean on a return, than remain where he was.

His journal shows that he was entirely devoted to the business of his mission, — an unwearied, self-sacrificing patriot. It also shows that he was deficient in certain qualities essential to success in the court of Versailles, and that he was daily becoming more alienated from his colleagues, and especially from Dr. Franklin, the supremacy of whose influence could not be concealed. Under these circumstances, and in consequence of representations from both Franklin and Adams, Congress decided to make Dr. Franklin sole minister at the court of France. Mr. Lee was dispatched to Madrid; but for Mr. Adams no provision was made. This oversight was simply owing to the harassed and distracted condition of Congress at that time. Thus doomed to idleness, and uncertain respecting duty, his situation was exceedingly painful. "I cannot," he wrote, "eat pensions and sinecures: they would stick in my throat."

On the 17th of June, 1779, he embarked on board the French frigate Sensible, and arrived safely in Boston with his son on the 2d of August, after an absence of seventeen months.

For such a man as Mr. Adams, in such stirring times, there was no such thing as rest. Immediately upon his arrival at Braintree he was chosen to represent the town in the state convention then held at Cambridge. At the same time he prepared an elaborate review of the state of the different nations in Europe, so far as it might have a bearing on the interests of the United States. The controversies between the individual members of the foreign delegation had agitated Congress and the country. There were many who were in favor of recalling Dr. Franklin; but his popularity with the French court, and especially with the minister, Count de Vergennes, defeated this measure. There was a long and bitter conflict in Congress respecting the appointment of commissioners to the foreign courts.

In September, 1779, Mr. Adams was chosen again to go to Paris, there to hold himself in readiness to negotiate a treaty of peace and of commerce with Great Britain so soon as the British Cabinet might be found willing to listen to such proposals. The Chevalier de la Luzerne, the French minister, who had accompanied Mr. Adams to America, wrote him a very polite note, congratulating him upon his appointment, and offering him a passage in the return French frigate. M. Marbois had been so much impressed with the distinguished talents of Mr. Adams's son, John Quincy, that he sent his father a special injunction to carry him back, that he might profit by the advantages of a European education.

On the 13th of November, 1779, Mr. Adams was again on board the Sensible, outward bound. The voyage was dismal; and the ship having sprung a leak, and being in danger of foundering, they were compelled to make the first European port, which was that of Ferrol, in Spain. In midwinter Mr. Adams crossed the Pyrenees, and reached Paris on the 5th of February, 1780. He was to remain in the French capital until an opportunity should present itself to open negotiations with Great Britain. The Count de Vergennes assumed, and very properly, that France, our powerful ally, should be specially consulted upon any terms which were to be presented to the British Cabinet; and that it would be manifestly unjust, under the circumstances, for the United States to negotiate a separate peace with Great Britain without the approval of the French nation. On the other hand, Mr. Adams very properly assumed that the United States had not placed their destinies in the hands of France, so as to lose all their independent power, and to be bound, like a slave, to obey the behests of a master. Here came the split, distrust, alienation, mutual repugnance.

There were two motives which influenced France to enter into the American alliance. One was a strong popular sympathy in our cause, as patriots struggling for liberty: the other was a national dislike to England, and a desire to humble that uncompromising power, and so to secure the friendship of America as to obtain a favorable commercial treaty. Mr. Adams acted upon the principle that sympathy with Americans, as victims of oppression, had no influence whatever with France; that the French government, in its alliance, was influenced by pure and undiluted selfishness. Dr. Franklin did not sympathize in these views, and did not give Mr. Adams his moral support. Much annoyed, Mr. Adams at length decided to go to Holland. In taking his departure, he wrote a letter to the Count de Vergennes, which did but increase the alienation. The count was so indignant that he sent to the Congress at Philadelphia, soliciting the recall of the commissions which had been intrusted to Mr. Adams.

In Holland he was eminently useful, negotiating important loans and forming important commercial treaties. In his bold measures here he assumed much responsibility, for which he was commended by Congress. In this brief sketch it is impossible to do full justice to these complicated negotiations. The Count de Vergennes apprehended Mr. Adams might propose terms to Great Britain unfavorable to the interests of France. Mr. Adams apprehended that the count would insist upon terms of peace so favorable to French commerce as to cripple the commercial intercourse of the United States with England and the other nations of Europe. Both had reason for their fears.

Mr. Adams ever regarded, and justly, his mission to Holland as the greatest success of his life. Through his very great efforts, sagaciously conducted, he was at length received as the accredited minister of the United States, and recognized as a member of the *corps diplomatique* at the Hague. On the very day that he was thus received by the States-General, he proposed a treaty of amity and commerce ; and on the 7th of October, 1782, had the pleasure of announcing the second alliance entered into by the United States as a sovereign power. The glory of this great event belongs undeniably to John Adams. It was deemed so important that two medals were engraved in Holland in its commemoration. "Monsieur," said a French gentleman to Mr. Adams on his return to Paris, "you are the Washington of negotiation." Mr. Adams was highly gratified by the compliments which were lavished upon him; but he intimates that Dr. Franklin would die of jealousy should he hear them.

The alliance with Holland was a great victory, — no less important in its bearing upon the war than the surrender of Cornwallis, which occurred about the same time. The conflict in the Cabinet was as arduous as that in the field. The British ministry now began to manifest some disposition to negotiate. In October, 1782, Mr. Adams returned to Paris. Private emissaries had been sent to the continent from London to ascertain who the Americans were who were authorized to treat, and what was the extent of their powers. In anticipation of this event, Congress had appointed a commission, consisting of Adams, Franklin, H. Laurens, Jay, and Jefferson, with full authority to negotiate a treaty of peace.

The alienation between Mr. Adams and the French court was well known ; and an agent was sent by Lord North to sound him upon the possibility of a separate truce, abandoning France. A meaner act we could not have been guilty of than to have acceded to this proposal. England, exasperated against the nation which had rescued us from her grasp, was anxious, by detaching us from the conflict, to wreak her whole vengeance upon our generous ally. This was just what Count de Vergennes had apprehended. Mr. Adams consented to meet this emissary at Amsterdam on the 20th of March; though he wisely attached the condition, that a witness should be present at the interview, and that he should be permitted to communicate all that should pass to both Dr. Franklin and the Count de Vergennes, who were in cordial sympathy with each other. These conditions so embarrassed Digges, the British envoy, that his mission was an entire failure. France, Spain, and Holland were now all, with more or less of zeal, combined with the United States against England. The British Cabinet made a covert effort for a separate pacification with France, which was also unsuccessful.

After a vast amount of diplomatic manœuvring, a definite treaty of peace with England was signed at Paris on the 21st of January, 1783. The reaction from the excitement, toil, and anxiety through which Mr. Adams had passed, threw him into a fever. He occupied the Hôtel du Roi, in the Place du Carrousel. It was a thoroughfare over whose pavements a constant stream of carriages was rolling, with a noise like thunder, incessantly for twenty-one hours out of the twenty-four. Burning with fever, he found sleep impossible. His friends despaired of his recovery.

The sufferings of Mrs. Adams, in this long separation from her husband, were very severe. A nobler woman never breathed. She deserves from a nation's gratitude a monument equally high and massive with that of her illustrious companion. When asked, after Mr. Adams had been absent three years, " Had you known that Mr. Adams would have remained so long abroad, would you have consented that he should have gone ? " she replied, after a moment's hesitation, —

" If I had known that Mr. Adams could have effected what he has done, I would not only have submitted to the absence I have endured, painful as it has been, but I would not have opposed it, even though three years more should be added to the number. I feel a pleasure in being able to sacrifice my selfish passions to the general good, and in imitating the example which has taught me

6

to consider myself and family but as the small dust of the balance when compared with the great community."

As soon as Mr. Adams could be removed he was taken to Auteuil, where he enjoyed the pure air and silence of the country. But recovery was very slow. Feeble, emaciated, languid, his friends advised him to go to England to drink the waters of Bath. On Monday, the 20th of October, he set out, with his son and one servant, for London. While Mr. Adams was in England, still drooping and desponding, he received dispatches urging the indispensable neces-

JOHN ADAMS THE AMBASSADOR.

sity of his repairing immediately to Amsterdam to negotiate another loan.

"It was winter," writes Mr. Adams. "My health was very delicate. A journey to Holland, at that season, would very probably put an end to my labors. I scarcely saw a possibility of surviving it. Nevertheless, no man knows what he can bear till he tries. A few moments' reflection determined me."

Mr. Adams and his son repaired to the coast; spent three days in a miserable inn, waiting for a wind; were tossed upon sickening billows three days, beating against a wintry gale; were driven to the Island of Goeree, and landed on a desolate shore; walked five miles over ice and snow to a wretched town; hired a farmer's cart, the only vehicle which could be obtained, without cushions or springs; rattled over the deep ruts of the frozen ground twelve miles, till they reached a ferry to cross over to the main-land; found all the boats on the other side; waited at the ferry several days; hired, at a great price, an ice-boat to take them over; were rowed in the water till they came to the ice; then the sailors, eight in number, dragged the boat upon the ice, and pushed it along while the passengers walked. When they came to a spot where the ice was thin, and the boat broke through, they all jumped in again. Were all day, and until late at night, making the passage, embarking and disembarking many times. Wet, chilled, exhausted, reached the shore; could find no carriage; hired a peasant's wagon to take them to Brielle, and there obtained conveyance through intense cold to the Hague, where Mr. Adams succeeded in raising another loan, and saved the credit of his country. There is other heroism besides that which is exhibited on the bloody field, and there are other battles besides those which are fought with powder and bullets.

Mr. Adams writes in his journal, " I had ridden on horseback often to Congress, over roads and across ferries, of which the present generation have no idea; and once, in 1777, in the dead of winter, from Braintree to Baltimore, five hundred miles, on a trotting horse. I had been three days in the Gulf Stream, in 1778, in a furious hurricane, and a storm of thunder and lightning, which struck down our men upon deck and cracked our mainmast; when the oldest officers and stoutest seamen stood aghast, at their last prayers, dreading every moment that a butt would start, and all perish. I had crossed the Atlantic, in 1779, in a leaky ship, with perhaps four hundred men on board, who were scarcely able, with two large pumps going all the twenty-four hours, to keep water from filling the hold; in hourly danger, for twenty days together, of foundering at sea. I had passed the mountains in Spain, in the winter, among ice and snow, partly on mule-back and partly on foot. Yet I never suffered so much in any of these situations as in that jaunt from Bath to Amsterdam, in January, 1784. Nor did any of these adventures ever do such lasting injury to my health. I never got over it till my return home in 1788."

While in England Mr. Adams had enjoyed the intense gratification of hearing George III., from his throne, announce to Parliament that he had concluded a treaty of peace, in which he recognized the independence of the United States. While in Holland Frederick II. of Prussia made overtures to Mr. Adams for a treaty of commerce. At the same time Mr. Adams received a new commission, authorizing him to act with Franklin and Jefferson to negotiate treaties of commerce with any of the foreign powers. As it was evident that his residence abroad was to be extended, he wrote to Mrs. Adams to join him with the residue of their family. The happy reunion took place in the summer of 1784; and they selected for their residence a quiet retreat at Auteuil, near Paris. And now came probably the happiest period of Mr. Adams's life. His wife, his eldest son, John Quincy, then rising into a youth of great promise, and his daughter, whose beauty and accomplishments made her justly the pride of both father and mother, were with him.

Mrs. Adams, in her letters, gives a very graphic account of her life at Auteuil. The village was four miles from Paris. The house was very large, and coldly elegant, with mirrors and waxed floors, but destitute of comfort. It was situated near the celebrated park called the Woods of Boulogne, where Mr. Adams, whose health required that he should take much exercise, walked several hours every day. The walls were lined with magnificent mirrors; but there was not a carpet in the house, nor a table better than an oak board. A servant polished the floors each morning with a brush buckled to one of his feet. The expenses of housekeeping were found to be enormous. A heavy tax was imposed upon everything. All articles of domestic use were about thirty per cent higher than in Boston. It was absolutely necessary to keep a coach; and the coachman and horses cost fifteen guineas a month. The social customs of the country rendered it indispensable that they should keep seven servants. Their expenses were so heavy that it required all Mrs. Adams's remarkable financial skill to save them from pecuniary ruin. The humble style in which they were compelled to live, compared with the splendor in which all the other foreign ministers indulged, must have been no small trial. Mr. Jay was compelled to resign his office, as he found that he could not support himself upon his salary.

On the 24th of February, 1785, peace with England having been proclaimed, Congress appointed Mr. Adams envoy to the court of St. James. He crossed the Channel to assume these new arduous and delicate responsibilities. He was now to meet, face to face, the King of England, who had so long regarded him as a traitor, and against whose despotic power he had assisted the nation so successfully to contend. Mr. Adams, in his dispatch to Mr. Jay, then secretary of foreign affairs, has left an interesting account of his first public reception.

He rode to court, by invitation of Lord Carmarthen, in his coach. In the ante-chamber he found the room full of ministers of state, generals, bishops, and all sorts of courtiers, each waiting his turn for an audience. He was soon conducted into the king's closet, where he was left alone with the king and his secretary of state. Mr. Adams, according to the court etiquette upon which he had carefully informed himself, made three low bows, — one at the door, another when he made a couple of steps, and the third when he stood before the king. He then, in a voice tremulous with the emotion which the scene was calculated to inspire, addressed his majesty in the following words : —

" Sire, the United States of America have appointed me their minister plenipotentiary to your majesty, and have directed me to deliver to your majesty this letter, which contains the evidence of it. It is in obedience to their express commands that I have the honor to assure your majesty of their unanimous disposition and desire to cultivate the most friendly and liberal intercourse between your majesty's subjects and their citizens, and of their best wishes for your majesty's health and for that of the royal family.

" The appointment of a minister from the United States to your majesty's court will form an epoch in the history of England and America. I think myself more fortunate than all my fellow-citizens in having the distinguished honor to be the first to stand in your majesty's royal presence in a diplomatic character ; and I shall esteem myself the happiest of men if I can be instrumental in recommending my country more and more to your majesty's royal benevolence, and of restoring the entire esteem, confidence, and affection, or, in better words, the old good-nature and the old harmony between people, who, though separated by an ocean and under different governments, have the same language, a similar religion, and kindred blood. I beg your majesty's permission to add, that although I have sometimes before been intrusted by my country, it was never, in my whole life, in a manner so agreeable to myself."

The king listened to this address in evident emotion. He seemed not a little agitated; for to his proud spirit it was an hour of deep humiliation. With a voice even more tremulous than that with which Mr. Adams had spoken, he replied: —

"Sir, the circumstances of this audience are so extraordinary, the language you have now held is so extremely proper, and the feelings you have discovered so justly adapted to the occasion, that I must say that I not only receive with pleasure the assurance of the friendly disposition of the people of the United States, but that I am very glad that the choice has fallen upon you as their minister. But I wish you, sir, to believe, and that it may be understood in America, that I have done nothing in the late contest, but what I thought myself indispensably bound to do by the duty which I owed to my people. I will be frank with you. I was the last to conform to the separation; but the separation having been made, and having become inevitable, I have always said, as I say now, that I would be the first to meet the friendship of the United States as an independent power. The moment I see such sentiments and language as yours prevail, and a disposition to give this country the preference, that moment I shall say, Let the circumstances of language, religion, and blood have their full effect."

This formality being over, the king asked Mr. Adams if he came last from France. Upon receiving an affirmative reply, he smiled, and, assuming an air of familiarity, said, "There is an opinion among some people that you are not the most attached, of all your countrymen, to the manners of France." This perhaps explains the reason why the king had said, "I am glad that the choice has fallen upon you," and throws light upon the suggestion he had ventured to throw out, that we should manifest "a disposition to give this country the preference." But for the aid of our ally we should inevitably have been crushed by the British armies. Yet Mr. Adams, regarding those efforts as purely selfish, was not disposed to manifest the slightest gratitude. He was, however, a little embarrassed by the king's allusion to his want of attachment to France, and replied, "That opinion, sir, is not mistaken. I must avow to your majesty, I have no attachment but to my own country." The king instantly responded, "An honest man will never have any other."

Mr. Adams's situation in London was more painful even than in Paris. He was met there only with haughtiness and ill-will. Everywhere he encountered cold civility, supercilious indifference. His literary labors in London were of much service to his country, as he published "A Defense of the American Constitution," in three volumes, which displayed much ability, and exerted a powerful influence. As Great Britain did not condescend to appoint a minister to the United States, and as Mr. Adams felt that he was accomplishing but little, he solicited permission to return to his own country, and reached his rural home in Braintree, from which he had so long been absent, in June of 1788.

When some persons accused Mr. Adams of being covertly in favor of monarchical institutions, Mr. Jefferson replied, "Gentlemen, you do not know that man. There is not upon this earth a more perfectly honest man than John Adams. It is not in his nature to meditate anything which he would not publish to the world. I know him well; and I repeat, that a more honest man never issued from the hands of his Creator."

Five years after the accomplishment of our independence, it was found, to the very bitter disappointment of many, that there was not so much prosperity, neither was order so well established, as in colonial days, while matters were manifestly growing worse. There was no common principle harmonizing the action of the different States. We were not a nation. We had no national sense of honor. It was necessary to organize the federal government anew. The success of the Revolution had afforded the United States, as Washington said, "the opportunity of becoming a respectable nation."

Fifty-five delegates were appointed by the various States of the confederacy to frame a Constitution for the United States of America. They met in Independence Hall, in Philadelphia, where the Declaration of Independence had been signed. The Constitution which they drew up was accepted by the States, and we became a nation. George Washington was unanimously chosen President for four years; and John Adams, rendered illustrious by his signal services at home and abroad, was chosen Vice-President.

The first Congress under the Constitution met in New York on the 4th of March, 1789. The City Hall, which stood at the corner of Wall and Nassau streets, where the Custom House now stands, had been remodeled for their accommodation, and had received the name of Federal Hall. The first business, after the organization of the two houses, was to count the votes for President and Vice-President. Mr. Adams was the first to receive the official information of his election. At ten o'clock on the morning of the 12th of April, he left his residence in Braintree, and was escorted by a troop of horse to Boston. He was received with the ringing of bells, the firing of cannon, and the shouts of an immense concourse of people. His journey to New York was a continued ovation. At Hartford the manufacturers presented him with a piece of broadcloth for a suit of clothes, and the corporation of New Haven presented him with the freedom of the city. The West-Chester Light Horse escorted him from the Connecticut line to King's Bridge, where he was met by a cavalcade of the heads of departments, a large number of members of Congress, military officers and private citizens, in carriages and on horseback, who conducted him through the swarming streets to the house of John Jay, in the lower part of the city. The President's mansion was the house since known as Bunker's Hotel, near the Bowling Green. Mr. Adams occupied a very beautiful residence at Richmond Hill.

The question at this time was very warmly agitated in Congress and throughout the country respecting the permanent location of the seat of government. In 1783 the old Continental Congress adjourned from Philadelphia to Princeton, where it occupied for a time the halls of the college. Thence it adjourned to New York, where it assembled in the spring of 1785. The question of the seat of government was brought before the convention for forming the Constitution, which was assembled in Philadelphia. The eastern States were in favor of New York. Pennsylvania pleaded for the banks of the Delaware. The more southern States advocated the banks of the Potomac.

It was urged in favor of New York, that " honesty was in fashion " there, and that there was no city in the world so celebrated " for the orderly and decent behavior of its inhabitants." On the other hand, Dr. Rush wrote, " I rejoice in the prospect of Congress leaving New York. It is a sink of political vice. Do as you please, but tear Congress away from New York in any way." The South Carolinians objected to Philadelphia on account of the Quakers, who,

they said, "were eternally dogging Southern members about with
their schemes of emancipation." This question, which was connected
with another respecting the assumption of state debts, threatened
to "dissolve the Union." One morning Jefferson met Hamilton
on Broadway; and for an hour they walked up and down the
crowded pavement, discussing the agitating theme. In conclusion,
Jefferson proposed that Hamilton should dine with him the next
evening, promising to invite a few other influential friends to talk
the matter over. "It is impossible," said Jefferson, "that reasonable men, consulting together coolly, can fail, by some mutual
sacrifices of opinion, to form a compromise which is to save the
Union."

By uniting the two questions of the location of the Capitol and
the assumption of the state debts, a compromise was effected. It
was agreed that the government should be permanently established
on the Potomac, at a place called Conogocheague, now the District
of Columbia; that ten years should be allowed for the erection of
the necessary buildings for the accommodation of the government;
and that, in the mean time, Philadelphia should be the metropoli-
tan city. The people of New York were greatly vexed. Robert
Morris, senator from Pennsylvania, was quite influential in accomplishing this result. He concluded that if the public offices were
once opened in Philadelphia they would continue there, and that
Conogocheague would be forgotten. But for the influence of Washington it is not improbable that this might have been the case.

The irritation of New York received graphic expression in a cari-
cature which was posted throughout the city. It represented Robert Morris marching off with Federal Hall upon his shoulders. Its
windows were crowded with members of both houses eagerly looking out, some encouraging, others anathematizing, the stout Pennsylvania senator as he bore away the prize. The devil stood grin-
ning upon the roof of Paulus Hook Ferry House, beckoning in a
patronizing way to Mr. Morris, and saying, "This way, Bobby;
this way."

Mrs. Adams superintended the removal of their effects to Philadelphia. She thus describes her new residence at Bush Hill:
"Though there remains neither bush nor shrub upon it, and very
few trees except the pine grove behind it, yet Bush Hill is a very
beautiful place; but the grand and the sublime I left at Richmond
Hill."

For a long time Congress was not at all pleased with the change, and bitter were the complaints which were unceasingly uttered. But at length the murmurs subsided, and were lost in the excitement of politics and the gayeties of the republican court. The winter presented a continual succession of balls, dinner-parties, and similar festivities. "I should spend a very dissipated winter," Mrs. Adams writes, " if I were to accept one half the invitations I receive, particularly to the routs, or tea and cards." In the midst of this external gayety, Congress was tossed by angry passions and stormy debates. Both Washington and Adams were assailed with intensest bitterness. Both were accused of monarchical tendencies, and of fondness for the pomp and pageantry of royalty. The Democratic party was now rapidly rising into controlling power. Still both Washington and Adams were reëlected, and again on the 4th of March, 1793, took the oaths of office.

There was certainly then a degree of ceremony observed, reflecting somewhat the pageantry of European courts, which has not since been continued. President Washington every fine day walked out. Two aids always accompanied him, who were kept at a respectful distance, never engaging in conversation. He had three very splendid carriages. He drove to church with two horses, into the the country with four, and six magnificent cream-colored chargers drew him to the Senate. His servants wore a livery of white trimmed with scarlet or orange. Both Washington and Adams were "gentlemen of the old school," reserved and somewhat stately in courtesy. An eye-witness describes the scene presented as Washington opened a session of Congress. An immense crowd filled the street through which he was to pass. As he left his carriage, he ascended the steps of the edifice, and paused upon the upper platform. " There he stood for a moment, distinctly seen by everybody. He stood in all his civic dignity and moral grandeur, erect, serene, majestic. His costume was a full suit of black velvet; his hair, in itself blanched by time, powdered to snowy whiteness, a dress sword at his side, and his hat held in his hand. Thus he stood in silence; and what moments those were! Throughout the dense crowd profound stillness reigned. Not a word was heard, not a breath. Palpitations took the place of sounds. It was a feeling infinitely beyond that which vents itself in shouts. Every heart was full. In vain would any tongue have spoken. All were gazing in mute, unutterable admiration. Every eye was riveted on that form, — the greatest, purest, most exalted of mortals."

Just about this time that moral earthquake, the French Revolution, shook the continent of Europe. Mr. Adams felt no sympathy with the French people in this struggle; for he had no confidence in their power of self-government, and utterly abhorred the atheistic character of those *philosophers*, who, in his judgment, inaugurated the movement. He wrote to Dr. Price, —

"I know that encyclopedists and economists, Diderot and D'Alembert, Voltaire and Rousseau, have contributed to this event more than Sidney, Locke, or Hoadly, — perhaps more than the American Revolution; and I own to you, I know not what to make of a republic of thirty million atheists."

On the other hand, Jefferson's sympathies were strongly enlisted in behalf of the French people, struggling to throw off the yoke of intolerable despotism. Hence originated the alienation between these two distinguished men. Washington at first hailed the French Revolution with hope; but as its disorders became more developed he leaned more strongly to the views of Mr. Adams. Two very powerful parties were thus soon organized. Adams was at the head of the one whose sympathies were with England. Jefferson led the other in sympathy with France.

England proclaimed war against the French republicans; played the tyrant over weaker nations upon the ocean; and, despising our feeble navy, insulted and harassed our commerce. This conduct swept increasingly the current of popular feeling towards Mr. Jefferson and his party. Upon the retirement of Washington, at the close of his second presidential term, there was a very hotly contested election; and Mr. Adams, by a slender majority, was chosen President; and Thomas Jefferson, Vice-President.

Weary of the cares of state, and longing to return to his loved home at Mount Vernon, Washington gladly transferred the sceptre to the hands of his successor. Henry VII. said of his son, who was eager for the crown, "Alas! he little knows what a heap of cares and sorrows he snatcheth at." John Adams found indeed, as even Washington had found before him, the crown of empire to be a crown of thorns. On the 4th of March, 1797, at Philadelphia, John Adams was inaugurated President of the United States. At an early hour in the morning, Chestnut Street, in the vicinity of

Congress Hall, was densely crowded. The hall itself was thronged, many of the members surrendering their seats to the ladies. Mr. Jefferson first took the oath as Vice-President. At twelve o'clock Washington entered the hall, followed in a few moments by Mr. Adams. They were both received with enthusiasm. As soon as the oath had been administered, Mr. Adams pronounced his inaugural. At the close of the ceremony Washington retired, followed by a tumultuous throng, eager to catch a last look of the object of their veneration. Mr. Adams had but just reached his residence when President Washington called upon him, and cordially congratulated him with wishes for his happy, successful, and honorable administration.

These were stormy days, and it required great wisdom safely to navigate the ship of state. That Mr. Adams's administration was conscientious, patriotic, and able, will now be universally conceded. In the then divided state of the public mind, an archangel could not have conciliated the hostile parties. The excitement which the French Revolution created in this country, as the community ranged themselves on the side of England or of France, was intense. For four years Mr. Adams struggled through almost a constant tempest of assaults. He was never truly a popular man. The party arrayed against him, with the Vice-President at its head, was powerful in numbers, and still more powerful in ability. He was not a man of conciliatory manners or of winning speech. After four years of harassment, which must have been the four least happy years of his life, he was mortified by losing a reëlection. Jefferson was chosen President; Aaron Burr, Vice-President; and John Adams was left to return to his farm at Quincy. His chagrin was great, so great as to lead him to the lamentable mistake of refusing to remain in Philadelphia to witness the inauguration of his successful rival.

There had ensued a breach in the friendship of these illustrious men which was not closed for thirteen years. But it is the duty of the historian to record that there was never a more pure and conscientious administration in this country than that of John Adams. Posterity has given its verdict in approval of nearly all his measures. In almost every conflict, it is now admitted that he was in the right, and his opponents in the wrong. Though the treatment he had received wounded him deeply, and he keenly felt the failure of his reëlection, it was not without some emotions of gladness that he laid aside the cares of state to seek refuge in the quiet retreat of his home at Braintree.

It was on the 4th of March, 1801, that Mr. Adams retired to private life, after uninterrupted devotion to the public service for twenty-six years, — service as arduous, as self-sacrificing, as devoted, as ever fell to the lot of any man. During these long years of anxiety and toil, in which he was laying, broad and deep, the foundations of an empire destined to be the greatest upon which the sun has ever shone, he had received from his impoverished country but a meagre support. The only privilege he carried with him into his retirement was that of franking his letters, and receiving them free from postage, for the remainder of his life.

He had barely sufficient property to give him needful comforts during his declining years. Party spirit then ran so high that obloquy pursued him even into his retreat. Many hours were imbittered by the attacks which were made upon him. Clouds of social grief, which at times darken over every family, threw their shades upon the homestead at Quincy.

About the time of Mr. Adams's retirement, his eldest son, who was married and settled in New York, suddenly died, leaving as a legacy to his father's care a wife and two infant children. He then spoke of this event as the deepest affliction of his life. Almost forgotten in his secluded retreat, he found the transition painful from his life of excitement, agitation, and the most intense intellectual activity, to one of repose, amounting almost to stagnation. He was then sixty-six years of age. A quarter of a century still remained to him before he died. He generally avoided all public gatherings, and took but little part in political questions, devoting his time mainly to the cultivation of his farm. When England, looking contemptuously upon our feeble navy, persisted in perpetrating the outrage of searching American ships wherever they might be found, and dragging from them any sailors who might be designated by any pert lieutenant as British subjects, both John Adams and his son, John Quincy, nobly supported the policy of Mr. Jefferson in resenting these outrages. It now seems strange that a single man could be found in all America willing to submit to such insolence. But Mr. Adams was for this bitterly accused of being recreant to his life-long principles, and of joining the party who were charged with seeking an excuse for dragging our country into a war against England, that we might thus aid France.

On this occasion John Adams, for the first time since his retirement, broke silence, and drew up a very able paper, exposing the atrocity of the British pretensions. It was one of the shrewd observations of Napoleon, that it is not safe to judge of what a nation will do from what it is for the interest of that nation to do, as peoples are governed far more by their passions than by their supposed interests. England, actuated by haughty and imbittered feelings, plunged into her second war with America. Mr. Adams had been associated with a party hostile to France, and in favor of submission to the British pretensions. In advocating resistance, he was regarded as abandoning his old friends, and with bitter animosity was he assailed.[1]

Years rolled on. The treaty of Ghent brought peace with England. Jefferson's two terms of service expired. Madison and Monroe came and went; and still the sage of Quincy remained, approaching his ninetieth year. In 1813 their only daughter, who was not very happily married, died, after a long and painful sickness. In 1818, when Mr. Adams was eighty-two years of age, his noble wife, who had shared with him the joys and griefs of more than half a century, died at the age of seventy-four. The event threw over him a shade of sadness which never disappeared. A gentleman who visited Quincy a year or two before her death gave a description of the interview. Mr. Adams was, in bodily strength, very infirm, tottering and shaking with age; but his mind seemed as vigorous, and his heart as young, as ever. There was a boy's joyousness and elasticity in his hearty laugh. He joked, was full of fun, and talked about everybody and everything with the utmost freedom and *abandon*. His knowledge seemed to his visitor boundless; for he was equally at home upon whatever subject might be introduced. Nothing could be more entertaining than his conversation, it was so replete with anecdote and lively sallies of wit.

While thus conversing, Mrs. Adams came in, — a tall and stately lady of rather formal address. "A cap of exquisite lace surrounded features still exhibiting intellect and energy. Her dress was snowy white, and there was that immaculate neatness in her appearance

---

[1] It is not impossible that some of these statements may be disputed; but incontrovertible evidence will be found to sustain them in the *Life and Times of John Adams.*

which gives to age almost the sweetness of youth. With less warmth of manner and sociableness than Mr. Adams, she was sufficiently gracious, and her occasional remarks betrayed intellectual vigor and strong sense. The guest went away, feeling that he should never again behold such living specimens of the 'great old.' "

While his drooping frame and feeble step and dimmed eye showed the ravages of years, his mind retained its wonted vigor. He read until his vision failed, and was then read to, many hours every day. He loved, in conversation with his friends, to recall the scenes of his younger years, and to fight his battles over again. His son, John Quincy, rose to distinction, and occupied high posts of honor at home and abroad. In 1825 his parental pride was gratified, and his parental heart gladdened, in the elevation of his son to the chair which the father had honored as President of the United States. When John Quincy Adams received a note from Rufus King, informing him of his election, he inclosed it to his father, with the following lines from his own pen, under date of February 9, 1825 : —

MY DEAR AND HONORED FATHER, — The inclosed note from Mr. King will inform you of the event of this day ; upon which I can only offer *you* my congratulations, and ask your blessing and prayers. Your affectionate and dutiful son,

JOHN QUINCY ADAMS.

John Adams was now ninety years of age. His enfeebled powers indicated that his end was drawing nigh. The 4th of July, 1826, came. The nation had made arrangements for a more than usually brilliant celebration of that anniversary. Adams and Jefferson still lived. It was hoped that they might be brought together, at some favored spot, as the nation's guests. It would indeed have been a touching spectacle to have seen these venerable men, after a separation of twenty-five years, again clasp each other's hands, and exchange congratulations in view of the prosperity and power of the nation which they had done so much to form.

But, as the time drew near, it was evident that neither of them could bear a journey. On Friday morning, the 30th of June, a gentleman called upon Mr. Adams to obtain a toast to be presented on the 4th of July at the celebration in Quincy. "I give you," said he, " *Independence forever.*"

He was now rapidly declining. On the morning of the 4th his physician judged that he would scarcely survive the day. There was the ringing of bells, the exultant music of martial bands, the thunders of artillery from ships and forts, from hills and valleys, echoing all over our land, as rejoicing millions welcomed the natal day of the nation. Mr. Adams, upon his dying couch, listened to these sounds of joy with silent emotion. " Do you know what day it is ? " some one inquired. " Oh, yes ! " he replied : " it is the glorious 4th of July. God bless it ! God bless you all ! It is a great and glorious day." " Thomas Jefferson," he murmured at a later hour to himself, " still survives." These were his last words. But he was mistaken. An hour or two before the spirit of Jefferson had taken its flight. The sands of his own long and memorable life were now run out, and gently he passed away into that sleep from which there is no earthly waking.

Mr. Adams was a man of rather cold courtesy of manners, of powerful intellect, of incorruptible integrity. It was one defect in his character, that he was deficient in those genial, sympathetic, brotherly graces which bind heart to heart. Wherever he appeared, he commanded respect : seldom did he win love. His neighbors called him the " Duke of Braintree." But, through all time, he must occupy a conspicuous position in the history of this country. It is not easy to find any other name to which America is more indebted for those institutions which constitute its power and its glory than that of John Adams.

PRESIDENTS

JOHN ADAMS

WHITE HOUSE — WASHINGTON

OF THE
UNITED STATES.

CHAPTER III.

THOMAS JEFFERSON.

Birth and Childhood. — College Life. — A Law Student. — Earnest Scholarship. — Marriage. — Estate at Monticello. — Interest in Public Affairs. — Action in the Continental Congress. — Governor of Virginia. — Death of his Wife. — His Grief. — Letters to his Children. — Minister to France. — His Popularity. — Political Views. — Scientific Accuracy. — Interest in the French Revolution. — Returns to America. — The Two Parties, Federal and Democratic. — Secretary of State. — Monarchical Sentiments. — Letters. — Correspondence with John Adams. — Alexander Hamilton. — Weary of Office. — Vice-President. — President. — Inaugural. — Stormy Administration. — Life in Retirement. — Scenes at Monticello. — Death.

THE ancestors of Thomas Jefferson are said to have been of Welsh origin, emigrating from the vicinity of Mount Snowdon.

MONTICELLO, — RESIDENCE OF THOMAS JEFFERSON.

But little is known of them. Peter Jefferson, the father of Thomas, was a man of handsome property and of considerable culture. He

7

married Jane Randolph, a young lady of nineteen, of opulent parentage, born in London, and accustomed to the refinements of life. Mr. Peter Jefferson, from his worth of character and mental attainments, acquired considerable local distinction, and was at one time professor of mathematics in William and Mary College.

Peter, with his young bride, took an estate of fourteen hundred acres upon the slopes of the Blue Ridge, in what is now called Albemarle County, and in the vicinity of the present town of Charlottesville. The plantation was called Shadwell, from the name of the parish in London where his wife was born. His home was literally hewn out of the wilderness. There were but few white settlers within many miles of the mansion, which consisted of a spacious story and a half cottage-house. A wide hall and four large rooms occupied the lower floor. Above these there were good chambers and a spacious garret. Two huge outside chimneys contributed to the picturesque aspect of the mansion. It was delightfully situated upon a gentle swell of land upon the slopes of the Blue Ridge, and commanded a sublime prospect of far-reaching mountains and forests.

Here Thomas was born, the oldest child of his parents, on the 2d of April, 1743. When he was fourteen years of age his father died, leaving a widow and eight children. We know but very little about these parents. Mr. Jefferson seldom alluded to them. His most distinguished biographer says, "He was singularly shy in speaking or writing of matters of family history." It is only known of his mother, that she was a beautiful and accomplished lady, an admirable housekeeper, a good letter-writer, with a great fund of humor. Mr. Jefferson used to mention as his earliest recollection that of being carried by a slave on a pillow on horseback, when he was but two years of age, in one of the journeys of the family.

His father and mother belonged to the Church of England. Thomas was naturally of a serious, pensive, reflective turn of mind. From the time he was five years of age he was kept diligently at school under the best teachers. He was a general favorite with both teachers and scholars; his singular amiability winning the love of the one, and his close application to study and remarkable proficiency securing the affection and esteem of the other. It is not usual for a young man to be fond both of mathematics and classics; but young Jefferson was alike devoted to each of these branches of learning. He has often been heard to say, that if he were left to decide between the pleasure derived from the classical education which his father had given him and the large estate which he inherited, he should have decided in favor of the former.

In the year 1760 he entered William and Mary College. He was then seventeen years of age, and entered an advanced class. Williamsburg was then the seat of the Colonial Court, and it was the abode of fashion and splendor. Young Jefferson lived in college somewhat expensively, keeping fine horses, and much caressed by gay society. Still he was earnestly devoted to his studies, and irreproachable in his morals.

It is strange that he was not ruined. In the second year of his college course, moved by some unexplained inward impulse, he discarded his horses, society, and even his favorite violin, to which he had previously given much time. He often devoted fifteen hours a day to hard study; allowing himself for exercise only a run in the evening twilight of a mile out of the city, and back again. He thus attained very high intellectual culture, alike excelling in philosophy and the languages. The most difficult Latin and Greek authors he read with facility. A more finished scholar has seldom gone forth from collegiate halls; and there was not to be found, perhaps, in all Virginia, a more pure-minded, upright, gentlemanly young man.

Immediately upon leaving college he entered the law office of Mr. Wythe, one of the most distinguished lawyers of the State. Mr. Jefferson was then not twenty-one years of age. But there was something in his culture, his commanding character, and his dignified yet courteous deportment, which gave him position with men far his seniors in age and his superiors in rank. The English governor of the colony, Francis Fauquier, was a man of great elegance of manners, whose mansion was the home of a very generous hospitality. He had three especial friends who often met, forming a select circle at his table. These were the eminent counselor, George Wythe; Dr. Small, a Scotch clergyman, one of the most distinguished professors in the college; and Thomas Jefferson. It is said that that polish of manners which distinguished Mr. Jefferson through life was acquired in this society.

In the law office he continued his habits of intense application to study. In the winter he rose punctually at five o'clock. In the summer, as soon as, in the first gray of the morning, he could discern the hands of the clock in his room, he sprang from his bed. At nine o'clock in summer he retired; at ten o'clock in winter. His vacations at Shadwell consisted only of a change of place: there was no abatement of study. His politeness to all shielded him from incivility, and he never became engaged in any personal rencounter. Gambling he so thoroughly detested that he never learned to distinguish one card from another. Ardent spirits he never drank, tobacco in any form he never used, and he was never heard to utter an oath.

He was fond of music, and had studied it both practically and as a science. Architecture, painting, and sculpture had attracted so much of his attention that he was esteemed one of the best of critics in the fine arts. The accurate knowledge he had acquired of French was of immense use to him in his subsequent diplomatic labors. He read Spanish, and could both write and speak the Italian. The Anglo-Saxon he studied as the root of the English, regarding it as an important element in legal philology. Thus furnished, he went forth to act his part in life's great conflict.

While a student at law he heard Patrick Henry, who had suddenly burst forth as Virginia's most eloquent orator, make one of his spirit-moving speeches against the Stamp Act. It produced an impression upon Jefferson's mind which was never effaced. In 1767 he entered upon the practice of the law. His thoroughly disciplined mind, ample stores of knowledge, and polished address, were rapidly raising him to distinction, when the outbreak of the Revolution caused the general abandonment of the courts of justice, and introduced him to loftier spheres of responsibility, and to action in an arena upon which the eyes of the civilized world were concentrated.

Jefferson, though so able with his pen, was not distinguished as a public speaker. He seldom ventured to take any part in debate. Still, wherever he appeared, he produced a profound impression as a deep thinker, an accurate reasoner, and a man of enlarged and statesman-like views.

He had been but a short time admitted to the bar ere he was chosen by his fellow-citizens to a seat in the Legislature of Virginia. This was in 1769. Jefferson was then the largest slaveholder in the house. It is a remarkable evidence of his foresight his moral courage, and the love of liberty which then inspired him, that he introduced a bill empowering slaveholders to manumit their slaves if they wished to do so. Slavery caught the alarm. The proposition was rejected by an overwhelming vote.

In 1770 Mr. Jefferson's house at Shadwell was burned to the ground; and his valuable library, consisting of two thousand volumes, disappeared in the flames. He was absent from home at the time. A slave came to him with the appalling news. "But were none of my books saved?" exclaimed Mr. Jefferson. "None," was the reply; and then the face of the music-loving negro grew radiant as he added, "But, massa, we saved the fiddle." In after years, when the grief of the irreparable loss was somewhat assuaged, Mr. Jefferson was in the habit of relating this anecdote with much glee.

He had inherited an estate of nearly two thousand acres of land, which he soon increased to five thousand acres. His income from this land, tilled by about fifty slaves, and from his practice at the bar, amounted to five thousand dollars a year, — a large sum in those times.

In 1772 he married Mrs. Martha Skelton, a very beautiful, wealthy, and highly accomplished young widow. She brought to him, as her munificent dowry, forty thousand acres of land, and one hundred and thirty-five slaves. He thus became one of the largest slaveholders in Virginia: and yet he labored with all his energies for the abolition of slavery; declaring the institution to be a curse to the master, a curse to the slave, and an offense in the sight of God.

Upon Mr. Jefferson's large estate at Shadwell there was a majestic swell of land called Monticello, which commanded a prospect of wonderful extent and beauty. This spot Mr. Jefferson selected for his new home; and here he reared a mansion of modest yet elegant architecture, which, next to Mount Vernon, became the most distinguished resort in our land. His wedding, which took place at the house of John Wayles, the father of the bride, who resided at a seat called "The Forest," in Charles City County, was celebrated with much splendor. It was a long ride in their carriage, along the alley of the James, to their secluded home among the mountains of Albemarle County. It was the month of January. As they drew near the hills, the ground was whitened with snow, which increased in depth as they advanced. until, when in the evening they were entering the mountains, they found the road so obstructed that they were compelled to leave their carriage at a dilapidated house and mount their horses. It was a cold winter's night. The snow was two feet deep along the mountain track which they were now threading. Late at night, shivering and weary, they reached the summit of the hill, nearly six hundred feet above the level of the stream at its base.

Here a gloomy reception awaited them. There were no lights in the house : all the fires were out. The slaves were soundly asleep in their cabins. But youth and prosperity and love could convert this " horrible dreariness " into an occasion of mirth and fun and laughter.

With his large estates, and his retinue of servants, Mr. Jefferson could afford to indulge in the luxury of magnificent horses. He usually kept half a dozen high-blooded brood-mares. He was very particular about his saddle-horse. It is said that, when quite a young man, if there was a spot on the horse, when led out, which would soil a linen handkerchief, the groom was sure of a severe reprimand.

There was, about this time, a British vessel, the Gaspee, stationed in Narragansett Bay to enforce the revenue laws. The insolence of its officers had led, in June, 1772, to its being decoyed aground, and burned. The British government retaliated by passing a law that the willful destruction of the least thing belonging to the navy should be punishable with death. At the same time a court of inquiry was sent over to try those implicated in the Gaspee affair, or to send them to England for trial should they choose to do so.

Some very spirited resolutions were immediately drawn up by Thomas Jefferson, appointing a standing committee to obtain the earliest intelligence of all proceedings in England with regard to the colonies, and by communicating this knowledge, in correspondence with the sister colonies, to prepare for united action in opposing any infringement of colonial rights. This was the intent of the resolutions. They were so skillfully worded that even the moderate party could not refuse to vote for them. But the then governor, the Earl of Dunmore, manifested his displeasure by immediately dissolving the house. The committee, however, met the next day, sent a copy of the resolutions to the other colonies, and requested them to appoint a committee to correspond with the Virginia committee. Though Massachusetts had two years before made a similar movement, for some unexplained reason the measure did not go into action; and Jefferson is justly entitled to the honor of having put into operation the "Committees of Correspondence," which afterwards became so potent in resisting the encroachments of the British crown.

When the British Cabinet, in 1774, enacted the Boston Port Bill, shutting up the harbor, and thus dooming Boston to ruin, Mr. Jefferson and a few of his associates met, and, as a measure to rouse the people of all the colonies to sympathetic action with Massachusetts, drew up some resolutions, appointing a day of fasting and prayer "to implore Heaven to avert from us the evil of civil war, to inspire us with firmness in support of our rights, and to turn the hearts of the king and Parliament to moderation and justice." Mr. Nichols, a man of grave and religious character, moved the resolutions, and they were adopted without opposition. The governor was so irritated that he dissolved the house, declaring that the measure "was a high reflection upon his majesty and the Parliament of Great Britain."

The members of the Colonial Court, after the dissolution, met in association, received into their number several clergymen and private citizens, denounced the course of England, declared it unpatriotic to purchase any of the articles which she had taxed, avowed that they considered an attack on one colony an attack on all, and recommended a *General Annual Congress*. This was in the spring of 1774. Thomas Jefferson, Patrick Henry, and the two Lees, were the active agents in this important movement. The clergy entered into the measures with earnest patriotism. The day of prayer was almost universally observed with appropriate discourses. Mr. Jefferson writes, "The effect of the day through the whole colony was like a shock of electricity, arousing every man, and placing him erect and solidly on his centre."

Mr. Jefferson was now very thoroughly aroused; and he was busy with voice and pen in the assertion that the American colonies had a right to govern themselves through their own legislatures. He wrote a pamphlet entitled "A Summary View of the Rights of British America." It attracted so much attention that it was published in several editions in England. The British had now unsheathed

the sword at Lexington, and Jefferson was in favor of decisive measures. His pen was ever active, and every line that came from it
was marked with power.

At the meeting of the second convention of Virginia, in March,
1775, the resolution was adopted, earnestly advocated by Jefferson,
to put the colony into a state of defense by embodying, arming, and
disciplining a sufficient number of men. George Washington and
Thomas Jefferson were on the committee to carry these resolutions
into effect.

On the 11th of June, 1775, Mr. Jefferson left Williamsburg to
take his seat in the Colonial Congress at Philadelphia. He traveled
in a phaeton, leading two spare horses, and was ten days in making
a journey which can now be accomplished in as many hours. The
roads were so intricate and unfrequented, that at times he had to
hire guides. Congress had been in session six weeks when he arrived; and he was the youngest member in the body but one. His
reputation as a writer had preceded him; and he immediately took
a conspicuous stand, though he seldom spoke. John Adams, in his
autobiography, alluding to the favorable impression which Mr. Jefferson made, writes, —

" Though a silent member in Congress, he was so prompt, frank,
explicit, and decisive upon committees and in conversation (not
even Samuel Adams was more so), that he soon seized upon my
heart."

Blunt, brave-hearted, magnanimous John Adams could not brook
opposition, and he was ever involved in quarrels. The impetuous
fiery debater is, of course, more exposed to this than the careful
writer who ponders the significance of every word. The native
suavity of Jefferson, his modesty, and the frankness and force with
which he expressed his views, captivated his opponents. It is said
that he had not an enemy in Congress. In five days after he had
taken his seat he was appointed on a committee to prepare an
address on the causes of taking up arms. The production was
mainly from his pen. It was one of the most popular documents
ever written, and was greeted with enthusiasm from the pulpit and
in the market-place. It was read at the head of the armies amidst
the booming of cannon and the huzzas of the soldiers. Yet Thomas
Jefferson suffered the reputation of the authorship to rest with one
of his associates on the committee all his life long. It was only

after the death of both Jefferson and Dickinson that the real author of the document was publicly known. These traits of character which are thus developed, one after another, surely indicate a very noble and extraordinary man. It is a remarkable fact, that decided as he was in his views, never in the slightest degree a trimmer, he won the confidence and the affection both of the most radical men of the progressive party and the most cautious of the conservatives. John Adams on the one side, and John Dickinson on the other, were warm personal friends of Thomas Jefferson.

Soon after this, on the 22d of July, a committee, consisting of Benjamin Franklin, Thomas Jefferson, John Adams, and Richard H. Lee, were appointed to report on Lord North's "conciliatory proposition." Jefferson, the youngest member in the house, was chosen by these illustrious colleagues to draft the paper.

Even as late as the autumn of 1775 Mr. Jefferson was hoping for reconciliation with England. In a letter to Mr. Randolph, who had sided with the British, and was about to sail for England, he wrote, —

" I am sincerely one of those who still wish for reunion with the parent country ; and would rather be in dependence on Great Britain, properly limited, than on any nation upon earth, or than on no nation. But I am one of those, too, who, rather than submit to the rights of legislating for us assumed by the British Parliament, and which late experience has shown they will so cruelly exercise, would lend my hand to sink the whole island in the ocean."

Three months after this, roused by the ferocity which the British ministry were displaying, he wrote to the same man, then in England, in tones of almost prophetic solemnity and indignation :—

" Believe me, dear sir, there is not in the British empire a man who more cordially loves a union with Great Britain than I do : but, by the God that made me, I will cease to exist before I yield to a connection on such terms as the British Parliament propose ; and in this I think I speak the sentiments of America."

At length the hour came for drafting the "Declaration of Independence." The responsible task was committed to the pen of Jefferson. Franklin and Adams suggested a few verbal corrections before it was submitted to Congress. The immortal document was presented to the Congress on the 28th of June, 1776, and was adopted and signed on the 4th of July. The Declaration passed a

fiery ordeal of criticism.   For three days the debate continued.
Mr. Jefferson opened not his lips.   " John Adams," it has been
said, " was the great champion of the Declaration on the floor, fighting fearlessly for every word of it, and with a power to which a
mind masculine and impassioned in its conceptions, a will of torrent-
like force, a heroism which only glared forth· more luridly at the
approach of danger, and a patriotism whose burning throb was
rather akin to the feeling of a parent fighting over his offspring
than to the colder sentiment of tamer minds, lent resistless sway."

The comic and the tragic, the sublime and the ridiculous, are
ever blended in this world.   One may search all the ages to find a
more solemn, momentous event than the signing of the Declaration
of Independence.   It was accompanied with prayer to Almighty
God.   Silence pervaded the room as one after another affixed his
name to that document, which brought down upon him the implaca-
ble hate of the mightiest power upon the globe, and which doomed
him inevitably to the scaffold, should the feeble colonies fail in the
unequal struggle.   In the midst of this scene, Benjamin Harrison,
a Virginia grandee of immense corpulence, weighing something like
a third of a ton, looked down upon Mr. Gerry, a small, fragile,
slender man, whom a breath of wind would almost blow away, and
remarked, with a characteristic chuckle, —

" Gerry, when the *hanging comes*, I shall have the advantage.
You 'll kick in the air half an hour after it is all over with me."

The colonies were now independent *States*.   Jefferson resigned
for a time his seat in Congress to aid in organizing the government
of Virginia.   Here we first meet in public with a young man —
James Madison — of refined culture, of polished address, of keen
powers of reasoning, of spotless purity of character, with whose
name the future of the nation became intimately blended.

In 1779 Mr. Jefferson was chosen governor of Virginia.   He was
then thirty-six years of age.   The British were now preparing to
strike their heaviest blows upon Georgia and the Carolinas.   Establishing themselves in those thinly populated States, they intended thence to march resistlessly towards the North.   A proclamation was also issued declaring the intention of Great Britain to
devastate the colonies as utterly as possible, that, in the event of the
success of the Revolution, they might prove valueless to France,
who had become our ally.   When Jefferson took the chair of state,

Georgia had fallen helpless into the hands of the foe; South Carolina was invaded, and Charleston threatened; the savages on the Ohio and the Mississippi, provided with British arms, and often led by British officers, were perpetrating horrid outrages on our frontiers.

In these trying hours, Mr. Jefferson, with all the energies of his mind and heart, sustained General Washington, ever ready to sacrifice all local interests for the general cause. At one time the British officer, Tarleton, sent a secret expedition to Monticello to capture the governor. Scarcely five minutes elapsed, after the hurried escape of Mr. Jefferson and his family, ere his mansion was in the possession of the British troops. Mr. Jefferson had a plantation at Elk Hill, opposite Elk Island, on the James River. A detachment of the army of Cornwallis, in their march north from the Carolinas, seized it. The foe destroyed all his crops, burnt his barns and fences, drove off the cattle, seized the serviceable horses, cut the throats of the colts, and left the whole plantation a smouldering, blackened waste. Twenty-seven slaves were also carried off. " Had he carried off the slaves," says Jefferson with characteristic magnanimity, " to give them freedom, he would have done right." A large number of these slaves died of putrid fever, then raging in the British camp. Of all this Mr. Jefferson never uttered a complaint.

In September, 1776, Congress had chosen Franklin, Jefferson, and Silas Deane commissioners to negotiate treaties of alliance and commerce with France. Jefferson declined the appointment, as he deemed it necessary that he should remain at home to assist in the organization of the state government of Virginia. As governor, he had rendered invaluable service to the common cause. He was now, in June, 1781, again appointed to coöperate with Adams, Franklin, Jay, and Laurens in Europe, as ministers plenipotentiary to treat for peace; but the exceedingly delicate state of Mrs. Jefferson's health, who had suffered terribly from anxiety, exposure, and grief, and who was so frail that it would have been the extreme of cruelty to expose her and her two surviving children to the peril of capture by British ships then covering the ocean, or to leave her at home separated from her husband, while Tarleton, with savage ferocity, was sweeping the State in all directions, rendered it clearly his duty again to decline.

About this time he was thrown from his horse, and quite seriously injured. This accident, and the sickness of his wife, confined him to his secluded forest home for several months. He improved the hours in writing his celebrated " Notes on Virginia." The work attracted much attention, was republished in England and France, and introduced his name favorably to the philosophers of the Continent. It is still a perplexing question how it was possible for Mr. Jefferson, in those days when Virginia was in many parts almost an unexplored wilderness, ranged by Indians, with scarcely any roads, to have obtained the vast amount of minute and accurate information which he has presented in these Notes. The whole is written in a glowing style of pure and undefiled English, which often soars to the eloquent.

But man is born to mourn. In every life there come days which are " cold and dark and dreary." It was now the latter part of the year 1781. Jefferson, like Washington, was excessively sensitive to reproach; while at the same time both of these illustrious men possessed that noble nature which induced them to persevere in the course which seemed to be right, notwithstanding all the sufferings which calumny could heap upon them. A party rose in Virginia, dissatisfied with the course Jefferson had pursued in his attempt to repel the invaders of the State. They tried to drive him from his office, crush his reputation, and raise a dictator to occupy his place. The indignity pierced him to the quick. He was too proud to enter upon a defense of himself. His wife, one of the most lovely and loving of Christian ladies, and to whom he was attached with a romance of affection never exceeded, was sinking away in lingering death. There was no hope of her recovery. The double calamity of a pitiless storm of vituperation out of doors, and a dying wife within, so affected his spirits that he resolved to retire from public life, and to spend the remainder of his days in the quietude of his desolated home. It was indeed a gloomy day which was now settling down around him.

He had been pursued like a felon, from place to place, by the British soldiery. His property had been wantonly and brutally destroyed. Many of his slaves whom he loved, and whose freedom he was laboring to secure, had perished miserably. He was suffering from severe personal injuries caused by the fall from his horse. His wife was dying, and his good name was fiercely assailed.

Mrs. Jefferson was a Christian, a loving disciple of the Redeemer.

But there were no cheering Christian hopes to sustain the sinking heart of her husband ; for he had many doubts respecting the truth of Christianity. He must often have exclaimed in anguish of spirit, " Oh that I could believe ! " The poison of skepticism had been early instilled into his nature ; and in these hours of earthly gloom he had no faith, no hope, to support him. Happy is he, who, in such seasons of sorrow, can by faith hear a Saviour's voice whispering to him, " Let not your heart be troubled." Beautifully has Jefferson's biographer, Mr. Randall, said, in describing these scenes, —

" The faithful daughter of the Church had no dread of the hereafter ; but she yearned to remain with her husband with that yearning which seems to have power to retard even the approaches of death. Her eyes were rested on him, ever followed him. When he spoke, no other sound could reach her ear or attract her attention. When she waked from slumber, she looked momentarily alarmed and distressed, and even appeared to be frightened, if the customary form was not bending over her, the customary look upon her."

For weeks Mr. Jefferson sat lovingly, but with a crushed heart, at that bedside. Unfeeling letters were sent to him, accusing him of weakness, of unfaithfulness to duty, in thus secluding himself at home, and urging him again to come forth to life's great battle. For four months Jefferson was never beyond the call of his dying wife. No woman could have proved a more tender nurse. He seemed unwilling that any one else should administer to her medicine and drink. When not at her bedside, he was writing in a closet which opened at the head of her bed. She died on the 6th of September, 1782. Who can imagine the anguish which a warm-hearted man must feel in witnessing the death of a wife whom he loved almost to adoration, and unsustained by that hope of reunion in heaven which a belief in Christianity confers ? His distress was so terrible that his friends were compelled to lead him from the room, almost in a state of insensibility, before the scene was closed. With difficulty they conveyed him into the library. He fainted entirely away, and remained so long insensible that it was feared he never would recover. His eldest daughter, Mrs. Randolph, writes, —

" The violence of his emotion, when almost by stealth I entered his room at night, to this day I dare not trust myself to describe. He kept his room three weeks, and I was never a moment from his side. He walked almost incessantly night and day ; only lying down occasionally, when nature was completely exhausted, on a pallet which had been brought in during his long fainting-fit. When at last he left his room, he rode out; and from that time he was incessantly on horseback, rambling about the mountain, in the least frequented roads, and just as often through the woods. In those melancholy rambles, I was his constant companion; a solitary witness to many violent bursts of grief, the remembrance of which has consecrated particular scenes of that lost home beyond the power of time to obliterate."

The inscription which the philosopher, uncheered by Christian faith, placed upon the gravestone of his companion, one cannot but read with sadness. It was a quotation, in Greek, from the "Iliad," of the apostrophe of Achilles over the dead body of Hector. The lines are thus freely translated by Pope: —

> "If, in the melancholy shades below,
> The flames of friends and lovers cease to glow,
> Yet mine shall sacred last; mine, undecayed,
> Burn on through death, and animate my shade."

Without the light which Christianity gives, death is, indeed, the king of terrors, and the grave retains its victory. Forty-four years after the death of Mrs. Jefferson there were found in a secret drawer in a private cabinet, to which he frequently resorted, locks of hair, and various other little souvenirs of his wife, with words of endearment upon the envelopes. He never married again. This tenderness of affection in this man of imperial mind and inflexible resolve is one of the most marked traits of his character.

The English ministry were now getting tired of the war. The opposition in Parliament had succeeded in carrying a resolution on the 4th of March, 1782, "That all those who should advise, or by any means attempt, the further prosecution of offensive war in America, should be considered as enemies to their king and country." This popular decision overcame the obstinacy of the king, and he was compelled to make overtures for peace. Mr. Jefferson was reappointed on the 12th of November by Congress, unanimously, and without a single adverse remark, minister plenipotentiary to negotiate a treaty.

Alluding to this, he writes to a friend, "Your letter found me a little emerging from the stupor of mind which had rendered me as dead to the world as she whose loss occasioned it. Before that event, my scheme of life had been determined. I had folded myself in the arms of retirement, and rested all prospects of future happiness on domestic and literary objects. In this state of mind an appointment from Congress found me, requiring me to cross the Atlantic."

There were various and complicated obstacles in the way of his departure; while, in the mean time, the treaty of peace was effected, and it became unnecessary for him to go upon that mission. Those who had assailed him had withdrawn their accusations, and legislative enactment had done justice to his career. He was again elected to Congress. At this period he wrote many affectionate letters to his daughters, who were then at school. These letters reveal the heart of a watchful and loving father. Martha, who was at school at Annapolis, had been disturbed by some predictions respecting the speedy end of the world. He writes to her, —

"As to preparations for that event, the best way for you is to be always prepared for it. The only way to be so is never to do or say a bad thing. If ever you are about to say anything amiss, or to do anything wrong, consider beforehand. You will feel something within you which will tell you it is wrong, and ought not to be said or done. This is your conscience, and be sure to obey. Our Maker has given us all this faithful internal monitor; and, if you always obey it, you will always be prepared for the end of the world, or for a much more certain event, — which is death. This must happen to all. It puts an end to the world as to us; and the way to be ready for it is never to do a wrong act."

Her sainted Christian mother would have added to this most excellent advice, "And, my dear child, pray night and morning to your heavenly Father that He will help you to do right, and to resist temptation to do wrong. And, when you feel your own unworthiness, do not be disheartened. God is a loving father. He has given his Son to die for us; and, sinners as we all are, we can be forgiven if we repent, and trust in him."

In March, 1784, Mr. Jefferson was appointed on a committee to draft a plan for the government of that immense region called the Northwestern Territory. The draft is still preserved in his handwriting in Washington. True to his unwavering principle of devotion to the rights of humanity, he inscribed in the ordinance the provision, "That, after the year 1800 of the Christian era, there shall be neither slavery nor involuntary servitude in any of the said States, otherwise than in punishmnt of crimes whereof the party shall have been duly convicted to have been personally guilty." This clause was stricken out by motion of Mr. Spaight of North Carolina, seconded by Mr. Read of South Carolina.

Mr. Jefferson had wonderful power of winning men to his opinions, while he scrupulously avoided all controversy. The following extract from a letter to his grandson brings clearly to light this trait in his character : —

"In stating prudential rules for our government in society, I must not omit the important one of never entering into dispute or argument with another. I never yet saw an instance of one of two disputants convincing the other by argument. I have seen many of them getting warm, becoming rude, and shooting one another. Conviction is the effect of our own dispassionate reasoning, either in solitude or weighing within ourselves dispassionately what we hear from others, standing uncommitted in argument ourselves. It was one of the rules, which, above all others, made Dr. Franklin the most amiable of men in society, 'never to contradict anybody.' "

Jefferson was by nature a gentleman, — affable, genial, courteous, considerate to the poor. Thus he was a great favorite with all who knew him. Stormy as were the times in which he lived, he never got into a personal altercation with any one, never gave or received a challenge, and was never known to encounter a personal insult.

In May, 1784, Congress appointed Mr. Jefferson to act as minister plenipotentiary with Mr. Adams and Dr. Franklin in negotiating treaties of commerce with foreign nations. Leaving two daughters with their maternal aunt, one six years of age and the other a frail babe of two years, who soon died, he took his eldest daughter Martha with him, and sailed for Europe on the 5th of July from Boston. After a delightful voyage he reached Paris on the 6th of August. Here he placed his daughter at school, and, meeting his colleagues at Passy, engaged vigorously with them in accomplishing the object of his mission. Dr. Franklin, now aged and infirm, obtained permission to return home from his embassy to France. His genial character, combined with his illustrious merit, had won the love of the French people ; and he was unboundedly popular with both peasant and prince. Such attention were lavished upon him in his journey from Paris to the coast, that it was almost an ovation. It was, indeed, a delicate matter to step into the position which had been occupied by one so enthusiastically admired. Few men could have done this so gracefully as did Jefferson.

"You replace M. Franklin, I hear," said the celebrated French minister, the Count de Vergennes. "I *succeed* him," was the prompt reply: "no man can *replace* him."

The French officers who had served in America had carried back glowing reports of Mr. Jefferson, as the accomplished gentleman, the brilliant scholar and philosopher, and the profound statesman. One of his noble visitors, the Count Chastellux, had written a graphic account of his elegant mountain-home, amidst the sublime solitudes of the Alleghanies, where, from his veranda, he looked down upon countless leagues of the primeval forest, and where the republican senator administered the rites of hospitality with grace which would have adorned the saloons of Versailles. Jefferson and Franklin were kindred spirits. They were both on the most friendly terms with the French minister.

"I found the Count de Vergennes," writes Mr. Jefferson, "as frank, as honorable, as easy of access to reason, as any man with whom I had ever done business."

Even Mr. Adams's dogmatic spirit was mollified by the urbanity of his colleague, and the most sincere attachment existed between them. Mrs. Adams, who stood upon the highest platform of moral excellence, and who was a keen judge of character, was charmed with Mr. Jefferson, and wrote to her sister that he was "the chosen of the earth."

His saloon was ever crowded with the choicest society of Paris. If any distinguished stranger came to the gay metropolis, he was sure to find his way to the hotel of the American ambassador. No foreign minister, with the exception of Franklin, was ever so caressed before. The gentleness and refinement of French manners possessed great charms for one of his delicate and sensitive nature. "Here," he wrote, "it seems that a man might pass his life without encountering a single rudeness."

Still he was very much opposed to Americans going to Europe for an education. He said that they were in danger of acquiring fondness for European luxury and dissipation, and would look

8

with contempt upon the simplicity of their own country; that they would be fascinated by the privileges enjoyed by the aristocracy; that they would lose that perfect command of their own language which can never be acquired if neglected during the period between fifteen and twenty years of age. "It appears to me, then," he says, "that an American coming to Europe for education loses in his knowledge, in his morals, in his health, in his habits, and in his happiness."

Mr. Jefferson occupied in Paris a very fine house on the Champs Élysées; he had also taken some rooms in the Carthusian monastery on Mount Calvary. When business pressed him, he would retire, and bury himself for a time in the unbroken solitude of this retreat. He was deeply impressed with the degradation and oppression of the great mass of the French people; and his detestation of the execrable government under which France groaned increased every day. As he pondered the misery into which twenty millions of people were plunged through that terrible despotism which had been the slow growth of ages, and which placed all the wealth, honor, and power of the realm in the hands of a few noble families, he often expressed the conviction, which was ever after the first article in his political creed, that our liberties could never be safe unless they were placed in the hands of the masses of the people, and those people were well educated.

In France, he found universally kind and respectful feelings towards our country. The philosophers and all the thinkers were charmed with the new era of republican liberty which we had introduced; and even the court, gratified that we had been the instrument of humbling the intolerable arrogance of Great Britain, was ever ready to greet with words of most cordial welcome the representatives of the United States. There never has been a story more falsely told, never a perversion of history more thorough, than the usual representations which have been made of the French Revolution,— the most sublime conflict, the most wonderful tragedy, of all the ages. The combined despotic courts of Europe endeavored to crush the people in their despairing struggle to shake off the fetters which had eaten through the flesh to the bone; and then, having fastened the fetters on again and riveted them anew, the hireling advocates of these despotisms gave their own base version of the story to the world.

In the despairing hours of this conflict the French people were at times driven to such frenzy as to lose all self-control. The spirit with which they were assailed maddened them. "Kings and queens," wrote an Austrian princess, "should no more heed the clamors of the people than the moon heeds the barking of dogs." The sympathies of Jefferson were always with the people struggling for popular rights; never with those struggling to crush those rights. In March, 1786, he went to London with Mr. Adams to negotiate a treaty of commerce. His sensitive nature keenly felt the insulting coldness of his reception. "On my presentation as usual to the king and queen," he writes, "it was impossible for anything to be more ungracious than their notice of Mr. Adams and myself." Speaking of the delicacy of his mental organization, the Hon. Mr. Coles of Philadelphia, a life-long friend of Jefferson, writes, "He not only could never enter on any freedom in manners or conversation himself, but any approach to a *broad* one in his presence made him literally blush like a boy."

His sympathies with France were increased by the conviction, which he never hesitated to avow, that, but for the aid which we derived from that country, we never could have gained our independence. In a letter written about this time, he gives the following as his estimate of the character of his illustrious colleague, John Adams: —

"You know the opinion I formerly entertained of my friend Mr. Adams. A seven months' intimacy with him here, and as many weeks in London, have given me opportunities of studying him closely. He is vain, irritable, and a bad calculator of the force and probable effect of the motives which govern men. This is all the ill which can possibly be said of him. He is as disinterested as the Being who made him. He is profound in his views, and accurate in his judgment, except where knowledge of the world is necessary to found judgment. He is so amiable, that I pronounce you will love him if ever you become acquainted with him. He would be, as he was, a great man in Congress."

Jefferson was present at the opening of the Assembly of Notables, at Versailles, on the 22d of February, 1787. Soon after, he wrote to Lafayette, "Keeping the good model of your neighboring country before your eyes, you may yet get on, step by step, towards a good constitution. Though that model is not perfect, as it would unite more suffrages than any new one which could be proposed, it is better to make that the object. If every advance is to be purchased by filling the royal coffers with gold, it will be gold well employed."

This was the plan of Lafayette and his coadjutors to establish popular rights in France under a monarchy framed on the model of the British Constitution. Jefferson agreed with these men in their wish to maintain the monarchical form of government, as the best *for them.* But he would surround it with republican institutions. He had great influence with all the patriot leaders, and was frequently consulted by them in their most important measures. While engaged in these matters of national interest, he wrote to his daughters, and watched over them with truly feminine tenderness. He was a mother as well as a father to them. His letters were filled with affection, and entered into the most minute details of the practical rules of life. To his daughter, who wished to incur some slight debt, he wrote, —

" This is a departure from that rule which I wish to see you governed by through your whole life, — of never buying anything which you have not money in your pocket to pay for. Be assured that it gives much more pain to the mind to be in debt, than to do without any article whatever which we may seem to want."

It is the concurrent testimony of his children and grandchildren, that, in all his domestic relations, he was one of the most amiable of men ; never speaking a harsh word, never manifesting sullenness or anger or irritation. His daughter Martha, one of the most accomplished of ladies, writes, " Never, never did I witness a particle of injustice in my father. Never have I heard him say a word, or seen him do an act, which I, at the time or afterwards, regretted. We venerated him as something wiser and better than other men. He seemed to know everything, — even the thoughts of our minds, and all our untold wishes. We wondered that we did not fear him ; and yet we did not, any more than we did companions of our own age." In all their joys, in all their griefs, these motherless girls ran to their father. Never was there a more beautiful exhibition of the parental tie.

All the honors which Mr. Jefferson received seemed to produce no change in the simplicity of his republican tastes. To one of the friends of his early years he wrote at this time, —

"There are minds which can be pleased by honors and prefer-ments; but I see nothing in them but envy and enmity. It is only necessary to possess them to know how little they contribute to happiness, or rather how hostile they are to it. I had rather be shut up in a very modest cottage with my books, my family, and a few old friends, dining on simple bacon, and letting the world roll on as it liked, than to occupy the most splendid post which any hu-man power can give."

And now the king's troops, with clattering cavalry and lumber-ing artillery, came pouring into the streets of Paris to crush the patriots. No reform was to be permitted, no constitution to be allowed. The cry of perishing millions, ragged, starving, was to be answered with the sword, the musket, and the cannon. Mr. Jeffer-son, in his carriage, chanced to witness the first collision between the royal troops and the people in the Place of Louis XV. It is difficult to turn away from the sublime and tremendous scenes which now ensued; but this brief sketch compels us to omit them all. The demolition of the Bastille; the rush of Paris upon Ver-sailles; the capture of the king and queen, and their transportation to the Tuileries; the attempted flight, arrest, trial, imprisonment, execution, — where is there to be found another such drama in the annals of time? Jefferson thought, that, could the weak but kind-hearted king have been left to himself, he would in good faith have accepted and carried out the contemplated reforms.

Amidst these stormy scenes the National Assembly conferred the unprecedented compliment upon Mr. Jefferson of inviting him to attend and assist in their deliberations; but he felt constrained to decline the honor, as his sense of delicacy would not allow him to take such a part in the internal transactions of a country to whose court he was a recognized ambassador. One day he received a note from Lafayette, informing him that he should bring a party of six or eight friends to ask a dinner of him the next day. They came, — Lafayette, and seven of the leading patriots, the representatives of different parties in the Assembly. The cloth being removed, after dinner, Lafayette introduced the object of the meeting, re-marking that it was necessary to combine their energies, or all was lost. The conference continued for six hours, — from four in the afternoon until ten at night: "During which time," writes Jeffer-son, "I was a silent witness to a coolness and candor of argument unusual in the conflicts of political opinion, to a logical reasoning and chaste eloquence, disfigured by no gaudy tinsel of rhetoric or declamation, and truly worthy of being placed in parallel with the finest dialogues of antiquity as handed to us by Xenophon, by Plato and Cicero." They agreed upon a single legislature, giving the king a veto.

Mr. Jefferson, considering his relation to the court, was placed in a very embarrassing situation in having such a conference thus held at his house. With his characteristic frankness, he promptly.decided what to do. The next morning he waited on Count Montmorin, the minister of the king, and explained to him just how it had happened. The minister very courteously replied that he already knew everything that had passed; and that, instead of taking umbrage at the use thus made of his house, he would be glad to have Mr. Jefferson assist at all such conferences, being sure that his influence would tend to moderate the warmer spirits, and to promote only salutary reform.

Soon after this Mr. Jefferson returned to America. As we have mentioned, his departed wife had been a member of the Episcopal Church. Her eldest daughter, Martha, had all her moral and religious feelings educated in that direction. Her father never uttered a word to lead his children to suppose that he had any doubts respecting Christianity. He attended the Episcopal Church with them, and devoutly took part in the responses. In France, Mr. Jefferson had placed his daughters at school in a convent. Martha, a serious, thoughtful, reverential girl, of fine mind and heart, became very deeply impressed with the seclusion, the devotion, the serene life, of Panthemont. Having one of those sensitive natures peculiarly susceptible to such influences, and dreaming of finding freedom in the cell of the nun from the frivolities, turmoil, and temptations of life, she wrote to her father for permission to remain in the convent, and to dedicate herself to the duties of a religious life.

A few days passed, and there was no answer. Then her father's carriage rolled up to the door of the convent. Martha, trembling, and with palpitating heart, advanced to meet him. He greeted her with almost more than his wonted cordiality and affection, held a short private interview with the abbess, and informed his daughters that he had come to take them away. The carriage rolled from the door, and their days in the convent were ended. Martha, tall, graceful, beautiful, accomplished, was introduced to society, and became the ornament of her father's saloons; and never was there the slightest allusion made, by word or letter, to her desire to enter the convent. In after years, she spoke, with a heart full of gratitude, of her father's judicious course on the occasion. Her wish was not a deep religious conviction: it was merely the transient emotion of a romantic girl.

This was in April, 1789. Jefferson had not expected to remain so long in Europe. He was now anxious to return with his daughters to his own country. We have spoken of the two parties then rising in the United States, one of which would rather favor England in commercial and legislative policy: the other would favor France. John Adams was a distinguished representative of the English party. He scouted the idea that we owed any gratitude to France for her intervention in our behalf. Jefferson was prominently of the French party. In the following terms he expresses his views upon this subject, in a letter to Mr. James Madison. Speaking of the National Assembly in France, he says, —

" It is impossible to desire better dispositions toward us than prevail in this Assembly. Our proceedings have been viewed as a model for them on every occasion. I am sorry, that, in the moment of such a disposition, anything should come from us to check it. The placing them on a mere footing with the English will have this effect. When, of two nations, the one has engaged herself in a ruinous war for us ; has spent her blood and money to save us ; has opened her bosom to us in peace, and received us almost on the footing of her own citizens ; while the other has moved heaven, earth, and hell to exterminate us in war ; has insulted us in all her councils in peace ; shut her doors to us in every port where her interests would permit it; libeled us in foreign nations ; endeavored to poison them against the reception of our most precious commodities, — to place these two nations on a footing is to give a great deal more to one than to the other, if the maxim be true, that, to make unequal quantities equal, you must add more to one than to the other."

Having obtained leave of absence, Jefferson left Paris, to return to America, on the 23d of September, 1789. His numerous friends gathered around him on his departure, with the warmest demonstrations of admiration and love.   It was supposed that he was leaving but for a short visit home.   Had it been known that his departure was to be final, his unbounded popularity would have conferred upon him no less imposing demonstrations than those which had been lavished upon Benjamin Franklin.

After the usual vicissitudes of a sea-voyage, Mr. Jefferson and his daughters landed at Norfolk in December.   There were no stages

JEFFERSON'S RETURN TO MONTICELLO.

there in those days.   They set out in a private carriage, borrowing horses of their friends, for Monticello; which they reached on the 23d of December.   They loitered on the way, making several friendly visits.   Two or three days before reaching home, Mr. Jefferson sent an express to his overseer to have his house made ready for his reception.   The news spread like wildfire through the negro-huts, clustered at several points over the immense plantation.   The slaves begged for a holiday to receive their master.   The whole number, men, women, and children, at an early hour, dressed in their best, were straggling along towards the foot of the mountain to meet the carriage about two miles from the mansion.

After waiting several hours, a coach, drawn by four horses, was seen approaching. The negroes raised a shout, and in a moment were surrounding the carriage. In spite of the entreaties of their master, — probably not very earnestly given, — they detached the horses, and, some dragging, some pushing, and all shouting at the top of their lungs, whirled the coach along until they reached the lawn in front of the house. As, in the midst of the wild uproar, Mr. Jefferson stepped from the carriage, a network of black, sinewy arms grasped him ; and, with resounding triumph, he was borne up the steps and into his home.

With instinctive delicacy, " the crowd then respectfully broke apart for the young ladies ; and as the stately, graceful Martha and the little fairy-like Maria advanced between the dark lines, shouts rent the sky, and many a curly-headed urchin was held aloft to catch a look at what their mothers and sisters were already firmly persuaded could not be paralleled in the Ancient Dominion."

Mr. Jefferson was, from beginning to end, an ardent admirer and warm supporter of Washington ; and the esteem was reciprocal. Immediately upon his return from France, Washington wrote to him in the most flattering terms, urging upon him a seat in his Cabinet as Secretary of State. After some conference he accepted the appointment. Martha, having forgotten her disposition to be a nun, was married on the 23d of February, 1790, to a very splendid young man, — Colonel Thomas M. Randolph. A few days after the wedding, on the 1st of March, Mr. Jefferson set out for New York, which was then the seat of government. He went by way of Richmond and Alexandria. The roads were horrible. At the latter place he took a stage, sending his carriage round by water, and leading his horses. Through snow and mud, their speed seldom exceeded three or four miles an hour by day, and one mile an hour by night. A fortnight, of great fatigue, was consumed in the journey. Occasionally Jefferson relieved the monotony of the dreary ride by mounting his led saddle-horse. At Philadelphia he called upon his friend Benjamin Franklin, then in his last illness.

The American Revolution did not originate in hostility to a monarchical form of government, but in resisting the oppressions which that government was inflicting upon the American people. Consequently, many persons, who were most active in the Revolution, would have been very willing to see an independent monarchy established here. But Mr. Jefferson had seen so much of the pernicious influence of kings and courts in Europe that he had become an intense republican. Upon his arrival in New York he was much surprised at the freedom with which many persons advocated a monarchical government. He writes, —

"I cannot describe the wonder and mortification with which the table conversation filled me. Politics were the chief topic; and a preference of a kingly over a republican government was evidently the favorite sentiment. An apostate I could not be, nor yet a hypocrite; and I found myself, for the most part, the only advocate on the republican side of the question, unless among the guests there chanced to be some member of that party from the legislative houses."

Washington was constitutionally, and by all the habits of his life, averse to extremes. He was a sincere republican, and, being thoroughly national in his affections, kept as far as possible aloof from parties; sacredly administering the government in accordance with the Constitution which he revered. In the great conflict which has ensued, neither party has ventured very loudly to claim him. It cannot, however, be denied, that, with the Federalists, he felt the need of a little more strength in the national government to meet the emergencies which the growing wealth, population, and power of the nation would eventually introduce. The great pressure which Adams and his friends had foreseen came when our civil war was ushered in. The government, struggling for very existence, instinctively grasped those powers which were found to be essential to its preservation; scarcely stopping to ask whether the act were authorized by the Constitution or not.

On the 1st of September Mr. Jefferson set out for his home in his private carriage. He took Mr. Madison with him. They stopped at Mount Vernon, and spent a few days with President Washington. His letters to his daughters, during his six months' absence in New York, are truly beautiful as developments of parental solicitude and love. To Maria he writes, who was then but twelve years of age, —

"Tell me whether you see the sun rise every day; how many

pages a day you read in 'Don Quixote,' — how far you are advanced in him; whether you repeat a grammar-lesson every day; what else you read; how many hours a day you sew; whether you have an opportunity of continuing your music; whether you know how to make a pudding yet, to cut out a beef-steak, to sow spinach, or to set a hen. Be good, my dear, as I have always found you; never be angry with anybody, nor speak hard of them; try to let everybody's faults be forgotten, as you would wish yours to be; take more pleasure in giving what is best to another than in having it yourself; and then all the world will love you, and I more than all the world. If your sister is with you kiss her, and tell her how much I love her also."

Mr. Jefferson remained at Monticello, in a delighted reunion with his loved and loving children, until the 8th of November, when his official duties called him back to New York. Mr. Madison again took a seat in his carriage, and again they paid the President a short visit at Mount Vernon.

John Adams was then Vice-President; Alexander Hamilton, Secretary of the Treasury. The favorable opinion which both these illustrious men entertained of the English Constitution was well known. Mr. Jefferson states, that at a small dinner-party which he gave early in 1791, both Adams and Hamilton being present, Mr. Adams said, speaking of the British Constitution, " Purge that constitution of its corruption, and give to its popular branch equality of representation, and it will be the most perfect constitution ever devised by the wit of man." Mr. Hamilton, after a moment's pause, said, " Purge it of its corruption, and give to its popular branch equality of representation, and it will become an impracticable government. As it stands at present, with all its supposed defects, it is the most perfect government which ever existed." " This," says Mr. Jefferson, " was assuredly the exact line which separated the political creeds of these two gentlemen. The one was for two hereditary branches, and an honest elective one; the other, for an hereditary king, with a house of lords and commons corrupted to his will, and standing between him and the people."

In the later years of his life Mr. Jefferson gave it as his opinion, that, though Mr. Adams had been originally a republican, the glare of royalty and nobility which he had witnessed in England had made him believe their fascination a necessary ingredient in government.

To throw light upon the political rupture which subsequently took place between Mr. Jefferson and Mr. Adams, the following extract from one of Mr. Jefferson's letters, under date of May 8, 1791, will be read with interest : —

" I am afraid the indiscretion of a printer has committed me with my friend Mr. Adams, for whom, as one of the most honest and disinterested men alive, I have a cordial esteem, increased by long habits of concurrence of opinion in the days of his republicanism ; and, even since his apostasy to hereditary monarchy and nobility, we differ as friends should do."

Two months after this Mr. Jefferson wrote a very friendly letter to Mr. Adams, in which he alludes to the difference which he supposed existed between them in reference to government. Assuming that both of these illustrious men were perfectly frank and honest, knowing that they were most intimately acquainted with each other, and had been so for years, discussing publicly and privately, on the floor of Congress and in committees, every conceivable point of national polity, and remembering that the slight estrangement which had now arisen originated in the fact that Mr. Adams had published a pamphlet expressing political views which Mr. Jefferson deemed so erroneous that he wished to have an English pamphlet, written by Thomas Paine, republished as an answer to them, we read with no little surprise Mr. Adams's reply, in which he says, —

" You observe, ' That you and I differ in our ideas of the best form of government is well known to us both.' But, my dear sir, you will give me leave to say that I do not know this. I know not what your idea is of the best form of government. You and I have never had a serious conversation together, that I can recollect, concerning the nature of government. The very transient hints that have ever passed between us have been jocular and superficial, without ever coming to an explanation. If you suppose that I have, or ever had, a design or desire of attempting to introduce a government of king, lords, and commons, or, in other words, an hereditary executive or an hereditary senate, either into the government of the United States or that of any individual state, you are wholly mistaken."

In pondering this remarkable statement, there is a possible solution of its apparent difficulty in the supposition, that while Mr. Adams considered the British Constitution, if purged as he had proposed, the best that had ever existed, he had still no idea whatever of attempting to make our Constitution give place to it. It has also been suggested, that, from the peculiarity of Mr. Adams's mind, he did not regard anything in the light of political disquisition which did not embrace at least a folio or two.

The flame of partisan feeling began now to burn more and more intensely throughout the whole length and breadth of the United States. Lafayette, in France, was then at the head of the patriot army struggling against the despotisms of Europe, with the hope, daily becoming more faint, of establishing popular rights in his native land. Mr. Jefferson wrote to him under date of June 16, 1792, —

" Behold you, then, my dear friend, at the head of a great army, establishing the liberties of your country against a foreign enemy. May Heaven favor your cause, and make you the channel through which it may pour its favors ! While you are extirpating the monster *aristocracy*, and pulling out the teeth and fangs of its associate *monarchy*, a contrary tendency is discovered in some here. A sect has shown itself among us, who declare that they espoused our new Constitution, not as a good and sufficient thing in itself, but only as a step to an English Constitution, — the only thing good and sufficient in itself in their eyes. It is happy for us that these are preachers without followers, and that our people are firm and constant in their republican purity. You will wonder to be told that it is from the eastward chiefly that these champions for a king, lords, and commons come."

President Washington watched with great anxiety the rising storm, and did all he could to quell its fury. His Cabinet was divided. General Hamilton, Secretary of the Treasury, was leader of the so-called Federal party. Mr. Jefferson, Secretary of State, was leader of the Republican party. On the 30th of September, 1792, as he was going from Monticello to the seat of government, he stopped, as usual, at Mount Vernon, and spent a night with President Washington. Mr. Jefferson makes the following record in his note-book of this interview, which shows conclusively that President Washington did not agree with Mr. Jefferson in his belief that there was a strong monarchical party in this country : —

" The President," he writes, " expressed his concern at the differences which he found to subsist between the Secretary of the Treasury and myself, of which, he said, he had not been aware. He knew, indeed, that there was a marked difference in our political sentiments; but he had never suspected it had gone so far in producing a personal difference, and he wished he could be the mediator to put an end to it; that he thought it important to preserve the check of my opinions in the administration, in order to keep things in their proper channel, and prevent them from going too far; *that, as to the idea of transforming this government into a monarchy, he did not believe there were ten men in the United States, whose opinions were worth attention, who entertained such a thought.*"

Some important financial measures which were proposed by Mr. Hamilton, Mr. Jefferson violently opposed. They were, however, sustained by the Cabinet, adopted by both houses of the legislature, and approved by the President. The enemies of Mr. Jefferson now pressed him with the charge of indelicacy in holding office under a government whose leading measures he opposed. Bitter was the warfare waged between the two hostile secretaries. We now and then catch a glimpse of Washington in this bitter strife, endeavoring, like an angel of peace, to lay the storm. Hamilton accused Jefferson of lauding the Constitution in public, while in private he had admitted that it contained those imperfections *of want of power* which Hamilton laid to its charge. This accusation was so seriously made, that Mr. Jefferson sent a document to the President to disprove it, containing numerous extracts from his private and confidential correspondence. The President replied, under date of October 18, 1792, —

"I did not require the evidence of the extracts which you inclosed to me to convince me of your attachment to the Constitution of the United States, or your disposition to promote the general welfare of this country; but I regret, deeply regret, the difference in opinions which has arisen, and divided you and another principal officer of the government; and I wish devoutly there could be an accommodation of them by mutual yieldings. I will frankly and solemnly declare, that I believe the views of both of you to be pure and well meant, and that experience only will decide with respect to the salutariness of the measures which are the subjects of dispute. I am persuaded that there is no discordance in your views. I have a great, a sincere esteem and regard for you both and ardently wish that some line could be marked out by which both of you could walk."

The President seems to have been in accord with Mr. Jefferson in his views of the importance of maintaining cordial relations with France. Both England and Spain were then making encroachments upon us, very menacing in their aspect. The President, in a conversation with Mr. Jefferson, on the 27th of December, 1792, urged the necessity of making sure of the alliance with France in the event of a rupture with either of these powers. " There is no nation," said he, " on whom we can rely at all times, but France." This had long been one of the fundamental principles of Mr. Jefferson's policy. Upon the election of President Washington to his second term of office, Mr. Jefferson wished to retire from the Cabinet. Dissatisfaction with the measures of the government was doubtless a leading cause. At the earnest solicitation, however, of the President, he consented to remain in his position, which was daily becoming more uncomfortable, until the last of July, when he again sent in his resignation.

But still again President Washington so earnestly entreated him to remain, that, very reluctantly, he consented to continue in office until the close of the year. In the following extracts from a letter to James Madison, it will be seen how irksome the duties of his office had become to him : —

" I have now been in the public service four and twenty years; one half of which has been spent in total occupation with their affairs, and absence from my own. I have served my tour, then. The motion of my blood no longer keeps time with the tumult of the world. It leads me to seek happiness in the lap and love of my family ; in the society of my neighbors and my books ; in the wholesome occupation of my farm and my affairs; in an interest or affection in every bud that opens, in every breath that blows around me ; in an entire freedom of rest, of motion, of thought ; owing account to myself alone of my hours and actions.

" What must be the principle of that calculation which should balance against these the circumstances of my present existence ? — worn down with labors from morning to night, and day to day ; knowing them as fruitless to others as they are vexatious to myself ; committed singly in desperate and eternal contest against a host, who are systematically undermining the public liberty and prosperity ; even the rare hours of relaxation sacrificed to the society of persons in the same intentions, of whose hatred I am conscious, even in those moments of conviviality when the heart wishes most to open itself to the effusions of friendship and confidence ; cut off from my family and friends ; my affairs abandoned to chaos and derangement ; in short, giving everything I love in exchange for everything I hate ; and all this without a single gratification in possession or prospect, in present enjoyment or future wish."

In the following terms, the President, on the 1st of January, 1794, accepted Mr. Jefferson's final resignation : " I received yesterday, with sincere regret, your resignation of the office of Secretary of State. Since it has been impossible to prevail upon you to forego any longer the indulgence of your desire for private life, the event, however anxious I am to avert it, must be submitted to ; but I cannot suffer you to leave your station without assuring you that the opinion which I had formed of your integrity and talents, and which dictated your original nomination, has been confirmed by the fullest experience, and that both have been eminently displayed in the discharge of your duty."

On the 5th of January Mr. Jefferson, with his fragile, beautiful daughter Maria, left Philadelphia for his loved retreat at Monticello. On the 16th he reached home. So utterly weary was he of public affairs, that he endeavored to forget them entirely. Four months after this, in May, he wrote to John Adams, then Vice-President, " I do not take a single newspaper, nor read one a month. I feel myself infinitely the happier for it." His landed estate at this time consisted of ten thousand six hundred and forty-seven acres. He had sold a considerable portion to pay off some debts with which his wife's patrimony was incumbered. His slaves amounted to one hundred and fifty-four. From the lawn at Monticello he could look down upon six thousand of his broad acres, spread out magnificently before him. He had thirty-four horses, five mules, two hundred and forty-nine cattle, three hundred and ninety hogs. Such an estate as this will not take care of itself ; and he found, through his long absence from home, his fields exhausted, and his affairs in confusion. Nine months passed away in entire devotion to the cares of the farm, and in enjoying the endearments of his children and his grandchildren. President Washington then made another endeavor to call him back to the Cabinet. In reply, Mr. Jefferson wrote to the Secretary of State, through whom the application came, —

" No circumstances, my dear sir, will ever more tempt me to engage in anything public. I thought myself perfectly fixed in this determination when I left Philadelphia; but every day and hour since has added to its inflexibility. It is a great pleasure to me to retain the esteem and approbation of the President; and this forms the only ground of any reluctance at being unable to comply with every wish of his."

Every day the political horizon was growing more stormy. All Europe was in the blaze of war. England, the most powerful monarchy on the globe, was straining every nerve to crush the French Revolution. The haughty course which the British government pursued towards the United States had exasperated even the placid Washington. He wrote to General Hamilton on the 31st of August, 1794, —

" By these high-handed measures of that government, and the outrageous and insulting conduct of its officers, it would seem next to impossible to keep peace between the United States and Great Britain."

Even John Adams became roused. Two years after, he wrote, in reference to the cool treatment which his son, John Quincy Adams, had received in England, " I am glad of it; for I would not have my son go as far as Mr. Jay, and affirm the friendly disposition of that country to this. I know better. I know their jealousy, envy, hatred, and revenge, covered under pretended contempt." Jefferson's slumbering energies were electrified : he subscribed for a newspaper, wrote fiery letters, and by his conversational eloquence moved all who approached him.

A new presidential election came on. John Adams was the Federal candidate; Thomas Jefferson, the Republican. It does not appear that Mr. Jefferson was at all solicitous of being elected. Indeed, he wrote to Mr. Madison, " There is nothing I so anxiously hope as that my name may come out either second or third ; as the last would leave me at home the whole of the year, and the other two thirds of it." Alluding to the possibility that " the representatives may be divided," he makes the remarkable declaration, of the sincerity of which no one who knows the man can doubt, " This is a difficulty from which the Constitution has provided no issue. It is both my duty and inclination, therefore, to relieve the embarrassment, should it happen ; and, in that case, I pray you, and au-

9

thorize you fully, to solicit on my behalf that Mr. Adams may be preferred.   He has always been my senior from the commencement of our public life; and, the expression of the public will being equal, this circumstance ought to give him the preference."

As the result of the election, Mr. Adams became President; and Mr. Jefferson, Vice-President.   This rendered it necessary for him to leave Monticello for a few months each year to attend the sessions of Congress.   His numerous letters to his children show how weary he had become of party strife, with what reluctance he left his home, with what joy he returned to it.   His correspondence is full of such expressions as the following: "I ought oftener, my dear Martha, to receive your letters, for the very great pleasure they give me, and especially when they express your affection for me; for though I cannot doubt, yet they are among those truths which, not doubted, we love to hear repeated.   Here, too, they serve like gleams of light to cheer a dreary scene, where envy, hatred, malice, revenge, and all the worst passions of men are marshaled to make one another as miserable as possible.   I turn from this with pleasure to contrast it with your fireside, where the single evening I passed at it was worth ages here."

Again he writes to Maria, from Philadelphia, on the 1st of January, 1797, "Without an object here which is not alien to me, and barren of every delight, I turn to your situation with pleasure, in the midst of a good family which loves you, and merits all your love."   It is a melancholy reflection that such enmities should have sprung up between men, and imbittered all their intercourse, who were alike true patriots, who were sincerely and earnestly seeking the good of their common country, and who only differed, and that conscientiously, respecting the best measures to be adopted for the national welfare.

In June, 1800, Congress moved from Philadelphia to Washington.   The new seat of government, literally hewn out of the wilderness, was a dreary place.   Though for twelve years workmen had been employed in that lonely, uninhabited, out-of-the-way spot, in putting up the public buildings, there was nothing as yet finished; and vast piles of stone and brick and mortar were scattered at great distances from each other, with swamps or forests or sand-banks intervening.   Transient huts were sprinkled about for the workmen.   The Capitol was built on a large swell of land; and a mile and a half from it was the unfinished "President's House," with literally a mud-road between. No arrangements had been made for lodging or boarding the members of Congress.

Mrs. John Adams, who had seen the residences of royalty in Europe, — Buckingham Palace, Versailles, and the Tuileries, — gives an amusing account of their entrance upon the splendors of the "White House." In trying to find Washington from Baltimore, they got lost in the woods. After driving for some time, bewildered in forest paths, they chanced to come upon a black man, whom they hired to guide them through the forest. "The house," she writes, "is upon a grand and superb scale, requiring about thirty servants to attend, and keep the apartments in proper order, and perform the necessary business of the house and stables. The lighting the apartments, from the kitchen to parlors and chambers, is a tax indeed; and the fires we are obliged to keep, to secure us from daily agues, is another very cheering comfort. To assist us in this great castle, and render less attendance necessary, bells are wholly wanting, not a single one being hung through the whole house; and promises are all you can obtain. This is so great an inconvenience, that I know not what to do or how to do. If they will put me up some bells, and let me have wood enough to keep fires, I design to be pleased. I could content myself almost anywhere three months; but, surrounded with forests, can you believe that wood is not to be had, because people cannot be found to cut and cart it?"

The four years of Mr. Jefferson's Vice-Presidency passed joylessly away, while the storm of partisan strife between Federalist and Republican was ever growing hotter. General Hamilton, who was a great power in those days, became as much alienated from Mr. Adams as from Mr. Jefferson. There was a split in the Federal party. A new presidential election came on. Mr. Jefferson was chosen President; and Aaron Burr, Vice-President.

The news of the election of Jefferson was received in most parts of the Union with the liveliest demonstrations of joy. He was the leader of the successful and rapidly increasing party. His friends were found in every city and village in our land. They had been taught to believe that the triumph of the opposite party would be the triumph of aristocratic privilege and of civil and religious despotism. On the other hand, many of the Federalists turned pale when the tidings reached them that Thomas Jefferson was President of the United States. Both the pulpit and the press had taught them that he was the incarnation of all evil, — an infidel, an atheist, a scoffer of all things sacred, a Jacobin, breathing threatenings and slaughter. There is no exaggeration in this statement, strong as it is.

The following is an extract from Jefferson's inaugural. Nobler words were never uttered by one assuming power. That he was sincere in the utterance, and that the measures of his administration were in conformity with the principles here laid down, nearly every man will now admit.

" About to enter, fellow-citizens, on the exercise of duties which comprehend everything dear and valuable to you, it is proper that you should understand what I deem the essential principles of our government, and consequently those which ought to shape its administration. I will compress them within the narrowest compass they will bear, stating the general principle, but not all its limitations.

" Equal and exact justice to all men, of whatever state or persuasion, religious or political; peace, commerce, and honest friend ship with all nations, entangling alliances with none; the support of the state governments in all of their rights, as the most competent administrations for our domestic concerns, and the surest bul warks against ante-republican tendencies; the preservation of the general government in its whole constitutional vigor, as the sheet-anchor of our peace at home, and safety abroad; a jealous care of the right of election by the people, — a mild and safe corrective of abuses, which are topped by the sword of revolution where peaceable remedies are unprovided; absolute acquiescence in the decisions of the majority, — the vital principle of republics, from which there is no appeal but to force, the vital principle and immediate parent of despotism; a well-disciplined militia, — our best reliance in peace, and for the first moments of war, till regulars may relieve them; the supremacy of the civil over the military authority; economy in the public expense, that labor may be lightly burdened; the honest payment of our debts, and sacred preservation of the public faith; encouragement of agriculture, and of commerce as its handmaid; the diffusion of information, and the arraignment of all abuses at the bar of public reason; freedom of religion; freedom of the press; freedom of person, under the protection of the habeas corpus, and trial by juries impartially selected, — these principles form the bright constellation which has gone before us, and guided our steps through an age of revolution and reformation."

He closes with the following words: "And may that Infinite Power which rules the destinies of the universe lead our councils to what is best, and give them a favorable issue for your peace and prosperity!"

Jefferson was exceedingly simple in his taste, having a morbid dislike of all that court etiquette which had disgusted him so much in Europe. Washington rode to the halls of Congress in state, drawn by six cream-colored horses. For some unexplained reason, on the morning of his inauguration, Jefferson rode on horseback to he Capitol in a dress of plain cloth, without guard or servant, dismounted without assistance, and fastened the bridle of his horse to the fence. This certainly looks like the affectation of simplicity. It may be suggested, in excuse, that Mr. Jefferson had allowed his mind to become so thoroughly imbued with the conviction that our government was drifting towards monarchy and aristocracy, that he felt bound, in his official character, to set the example of extreme democratic simplicity.

In this spirit he abolished levees, which, though he did not so intend it, was a movement in an aristocratic direction; for the levee threw the presidential mansion open to the most humble of the people. By its abolition none could enter the White House but those who were specially invited. The invitations to dine were no longer given in the name of the "President of the United States," as Washington and Adams had given them, but in the name of "Thomas Jefferson." His views upon this subject may be inferred from the following remarks which he made upon the character of Washington. After speaking of him in the highest terms of eulogy, as one of the greatest and best men this world has ever known, he writes, —

"I do believe that General Washington had not a firm confidence in the durability of our government. He was naturally distrustful of men, and inclined to gloomy apprehensions; and I was ever persuaded that a belief that we must at length end in something like a British Constitution had some weight in his adoption of the ceremonies of levees, birthdays, pompous meetings with Congress, and other forms of the same character, calculated to prepare us gradually for a change which he believed possible, and to let it come on with as little shock as might be to the public mind."

Mr. Jefferson and his eldest grandson were one day riding in a carriage together. They met a slave, who respectfully took off his hat, and bowed. The President, according to his invariable custom, returned the salutation by raising his hat. The young man paid no attention to the negro's act of civility. Mr. Jefferson, after a few moments' pause, turned a reproachful eye to him, and said, " Thomas, do you permit a slave to be more of a gentleman than yourself ? "

On another occasion he was riding on horseback, accompanied by two young men, from Monticello to Charlottesville. They found Moore's Creek so swollen by a sudden shower that the water was up to the saddle-girths. A man, with a saddle on his shoulders, was standing upon the bank. He looked at the young men as they rode through the stream, and said nothing ; but turning to Mr. Jefferson, he asked permission to mount the croup behind him to be carried across. The President reined his horse up to a stone, and carried the man across. The countryman then dismounted, and trudged along the dusty road. Soon a party in the rear, who had witnessed the operation, came up. One inquired, " What made you let the young men pass, and ask the old gentleman to carry you over the creek ? " The backwoodsman replied, in the broad patois of his region, " Wal, if you want to know, I 'll tell you. I reckon a man carries ' Yes ' or ' No ' in his face. The young chaps' faces said ' No ; ' the old 'un's, Yes.' " " It is n't every one," the other replied, " that would have asked the President of the United States for a ride behind him." " What," said the man, "you don't say that was Tom Jefferson, do you ? " Then, pausing a moment, he added, " Wal, he 's a fine old fellow, any way. What will Polly say when I tell her I have rid behind Jefferson ? She 'll say I voted for the right man."

The political principles of the Jeffersonian party now swept the country, and Mr. Jefferson swayed an influence which was never exceeded by Washington himself. Louisiana, under which name was then included the whole territory west of the Mississippi to the Pacific, was purchased of France, under his administration, in the year 1803, for fifteen millions of dollars. He was now smitten by another domestic grief. In the year 1804 his beautiful daughter Maria, whom he so tenderly loved, sank into the grave, leaving her babe behind her. His eldest daughter, Martha, says, speaking of her father's suffering under this terrible grief, —

" I found him with the Bible in his hands. He who has been so often and so harshly accused of unbelief, — he, in his hour of intense affliction, sought and found consolation in the sacred volume. The comforter was there for his true heart and devout spirit, even though his faith might not be what the world calls orthodox."

Mr. Jefferson writes, in response to a letter of condolence from a friend, " My loss is great indeed. Others may lose of their abundance; but I, of my want, have lost even the half of all I had. My evening prospects now hang on the slender thread of a single life. Perhaps I may be destined to see even this last chord of parental affection broken. The hope with which I had looked forward to the moment, when, resigning public cares to younger hands, I was to retire to that domestic comfort from which the last great step is to be taken, is fearfully blighted.

" We have, however, the traveler's consolation. Every step shortens the distance we have to go. The end of our journey is in sight, — the bed whereon we are to rest and to rise in the midst of the friends we have lost. ' We sorrow not, then, as others who have no hope,' but look forward to the day which joins us to the great majority. But, whatever is to be our destiny, wisdom as well as duty dictates that we should acquiesce in the will of Him whose it is to give and take away, and be content in the enjoyment of those who are still permitted to be with us."

Another presidential election came in 1804. Mr. Jefferson was reëlected President with wonderful unanimity; and George Clinton, Vice-President. Jefferson was sixty-two years of age, when, on the 4th of March, 1805, he entered upon his second term of office. Our relations with England were daily becoming more complicated from the British demand of the right to stop any of our ships, whether belonging to either the commercial or naval marine, and to take from them any sailors whom they felt disposed to claim as British subjects. The United States frigate Chesapeake, of thirty-eight guns, was fired upon, on the 22d of June, 1807, by the British man-of-war Leopard, of fifty-six guns; and after a loss of three men killed and ten wounded, including Commodore Barron, the Chesapeake, which was not in a condition to return a single shot, surrendered. Four men were then taken by the British officer from the frigate, three of whom were Americans. This outrage, which occurred but a few leagues out from Hampton Roads, created intense excitement. The President dispatched a vessel to England to demand reparation for the insult; while, at the same time, he issued a proclamation forbidding the waters of the United States to all British vessels of war unless in distress or bearing dispatches. Captain Douglass, who was at that time in command of a British squadron of three men-of-war at Norfolk, paid no attention to this proclamation, but wrote an insolent letter to the mayor, saying that the Americans could have peace or war, just as they desired. In a letter to Lafayette upon this subject, the President wrote, —

"Never, since the battle of Lexington, have I seen this country in such a state of exasperation as at present; and even that did not produce such unanimity. The Federalists themselves coalesce with us as to the object, although they will return to their old trade of condemning every step we take towards obtaining it."

The course England pursued rendered it certain that war could not be avoided. Mr. Jefferson humanely did everything in his power to prevent the Indians from taking any part in it whatever. The British, on the contrary, were endeavoring to rouse them to deluge the frontiers in blood. England, who was engaged in the endeavor to crush Napoleon and reinstate the Bourbons, had resolved, at whatever hazard of war with America, to replenish her navy by seizing any British-born subjects, wherever she could find them in the marine of the United States. Any young lieutenant, protected by the guns of a British man-of-war, would step on board any of our ships, and, claiming whoever he pleased as British subjects, would impress them to fight against France. In this way, according to the official returns, more than twelve hundred *Americans* were dragged from our ships. Strange as it may now seem, the measures of government to redress these wrongs were virulently opposed. Notwithstanding the strength and influence of the opposition to Mr. Jefferson's administration, he was sustained by the general voice of the nation.

Amidst all these cares, the President manifested the most affectionate interest in the welfare of his family. On the 24th of November, 1808, he wrote a letter to his grandson, who was absent from home at school, from which we make the following extracts, —

"Your situation at such a distance from us cannot but give us all great anxieties for you; but thrown on a wide world, among entire strangers, without a friend or guardian to advise, so young too, and with so little experience of mankind, your dangers are great, and still your safety must rest on yourself. A determination never to do what is wrong, prudence, and good humor, will go far towards securing for you the estimation of the world.

" When I recollect that at fourteen years of age the whole care and direction of myself was thrown on myself entirely, without a relation or friend qualified to advise or guide me, and recollect the various sorts of bad company with which I associated from time to time, I am astonished that I did not turn off with some of them, and become as worthless to society as they were. I had the good fortune to become acquainted very early with some characters of very high standing, and to feel the incessant wish that I could ever become what they were. Under temptations and difficulties, I would ask myself, ' What would Dr. Small, Mr. Wythe, Peyton Randolph, do in this situation? What course in it will insure me their approbation ? '

" From the circumstances of my position, I was often thrown into the society of horse-racers, card-players, fox-hunters, scientific and professional men, and of dignified men; and many a time have I asked myself, in the enthusiastic moment of the death of a fox, the victory of a favorite horse, the issue of a question eloquently argued at the bar or in the great council of the nation, ' Well, which of these kinds of reputation should I prefer, — that of a horse-jockey, a fox-hunter, an orator, or the honest advocate of my country's rights ? ' Be assured, my dear Jefferson, that these little returns into ourselves, this self-catechizing habit, is not trifling nor useless, but leads to the prudent selection and steady pursuit of what is right."

In the year 1808 Mr. Jefferson closed his second term of office, and James Madison succeeded him as President of the United States. In the following terms the retiring President expresses to a friend his feelings upon surrendering the cares of office : —

" Within a few days I retire to my family, my books, and farms; and, having gained the harbor myself, I shall look on my friends, still buffeting the storm, with anxiety indeed, but not with envy. Never did a prisoner, released from his chains, feel such relief as I shall on shaking off the shackles of power. Nature intended me for the tranquil pursuits of science by rendering them my supreme delight; but the enormities of the times in which I have lived have forced me to take a part in resisting them, and to commit myself on the boisterous ocean of political passions. I thank God for the opportunity of retiring from them without censure, and carrying with me the most consoling proofs of public approbation."

President Jefferson, after remaining in Washington to see his successor and bosom friend inaugurated, left for Monticello. Between them, after Mr. Jefferson's retirement, a free and confidential correspondence was kept up respecting the measures of government. Their intellectual traits were very similar, while their tastes and political principles were quite the same. Jefferson's subsequent life at Monticello was very similar to that of Washington at Mount Vernon. A kinder master never lived. On no account would he allow his slaves to be overworked. His mornings he devoted to his numerous correspondence; from breakfast to dinner he was in the shops and over the farms; from dinner to dark he devoted to recreation and friends; from dark to early bedtime he read. He was particularly interested in young men, advising them as to their course of reading. Several came, and took up their residence in the neighboring town of Charlottesville, that they might avail themselves of his library, which was ever open for their use.

From a series of untoward events, which we have not space here to record, Mr. Jefferson became deeply involved in debt, so that it was necessary for him to sell a large portion of his estate. Still, in the year 1809, he owned about ten thousand acres of land, a valuable mansion, richly furnished, with a large and costly library. His vast plantation, cut up into several farms, was well stocked. His slaves numbered two hundred. The value of the whole property was about two hundred thousand dollars, His debts were then but about twenty thousand dollars. But it is to be remembered that this property was productive only so far as the land could be worked. Of the two hundred slaves, one hundred were either children too young, or the aged too infirm, to be of much service. Of the one hundred who remained, some were mechanics, and a large number were employed as house-servants. Mr. Jefferson was profuse in his hospitality. Whole families came in their coaches with their horses, — fathers and mothers, boys and girls, babies and nurses, — and remained three or even six months. One family of six persons came from Europe, and made a visit of ten months.

After a short tour they returned, and remained six months longer. Every day brought its contingent of guests. A gentleman who was often present says, —

"People of wealth, fashion, men in office, professional men, military and civil, lawyers, doctors, Protestant clergymen, Catholic priests, members of Congress, foreign ministers, missionaries, Indian agents, tourists, travelers, artists, strangers, friends, came, some from affection and respect, some from curiosity, some to give or receive advice or instruction, and some from idleness. Life at Monticello, for years, resembled that at a fashionable watering-place. Mr. Jefferson always made his appearance at the breakfast-table : his guests were then left to amuse themselves as they pleased until dinner-time. They walked, talked, read, made excursions with the ladies, or hunted in the woods: some sought the retirement of the splendid library ; others, the social enjoyments of the drawing-room ; while others retired to the quiet of their own chambers, or to a solitary stroll down the mountain-side."

Such hospitality would speedily consume a larger fortune than Mr. Jefferson possessed. He had a favorite servant, Wormley, who, with the utmost fidelity, watched over the interests of his master. Mr. Jefferson had three carriage-houses, each of which would hold a four-horse coach. These carriage-houses were for the accommodation of his friends, who came with their loaded coaches, drawn by four horses, to visit him. Some time after Mr. Jefferson's death a gentleman at Monticello asked Wormley how often those carriage-houses were all filled in Mr. Jefferson's time. He replied, "Every night, sir, in summer; and we commonly had two or three carriages besides under that tree," pointing to a large tree in the vicinity. "It must have taken," the gentleman added, "all hands to have taken care of your visitors." "Yes," the faithful old slave replied, "and the whole farm to feed them."

Mr. Jefferson's daughter, Mrs. Randolph, was the presiding lady of this immense establishment. The domestic service required thirty-seven house-servants. Mrs. Randolph, upon being asked what was the greatest number of guests she had ever entertained any one night, replied, "she believed fifty."

In the winter Mr. Jefferson had some little repose from the crowd of visitors. He then enjoyed, in the highest possible degree, all that is endearing in domestic life. It is impossible to describe the love with which he was cherished by his grandchildren.   One of them writes, in a letter overflowing with the gushing of a loving heart, " My Bible came from him, my Shakespeare, my first writing-table, my first handsome writing-desk, my first Leghorn hat, my first silk dress: what, in short, of all my treasures did *not* come from him?   My sisters, according to their wants and tastes, were equally thought of, equally provided for.   Our grandfather seemed to read our hearts, to see our individual wishes, to be our good genius, to wave the fairy wand to brighten our young lives by his goodness and his gifts."

Another writes, " I cannot describe the feelings of veneration, admiration, and love, that existed in my heart towards him.   I looked on him as a being too great and good for my comprehension ; and yet I felt no fear to approach him, and be taught by him some of the childish sports I delighted in.   Not one of us, in our wildest moods, ever placed a foot on one of the garden-beds, for that would violate one of his rules ; and yet I never heard him utter a harsh word to one of us, or speak in a raised tone of voice, or use a threat."

In 1812 a perfect reconciliation took place between Mr. Adams and Mr. Jefferson ; the latter very handsomely and magnanimously making the first advances.   This friendship, which was kept up by a constant interchange of letters, continued unabated until their death, — on the same day, and almost at the same hour.

After Mr. Jefferson had passed his threescore years and ten, he wrote to Mr. Adams in the following *philosophic* strain, which, as usual, leaves us in the dark in reference to his religious faith : —

" You ask if I would live my seventy, or rather seventy-three, years over again.   To which I say, ' Yea.'   I think, with you, that it is a good world, on the whole : that it has been framed on a principle of benevolence ; and that more pleasure than pain is dealt out to us.

" There is a ripeness of time for death, regarding others as well as ourselves, when it is reasonable we should drop off, and make room for another growth.   When we have lived our generation out, we should not wish to encroach on another.   I enjoy good health ; I am happy in what is around me: yet I assure you I am ripe to leave all this day, this year, this hour."   In a letter to Mr. Adams, dated January, 1817, we find the remark, " Perhaps, however, one of the elements of future felicity is to be a constant and unimpassioned view of what is passing here." In the same letter, he says, that, in reply to the question of one respecting his religious faith, he answered, "Say nothing of my religion : it is known to my God and myself alone."

Mr. Jefferson was ever ready to express his views frankly upon all subjects of science, philosophy, and politics. It is certainly remarkable that such a man was not willing to express his views upon a subject more important than all others, — the eternal well-being of man. Again, he writes to Mr. John Adams in a strain which throws interesting light upon his occupation at that time, " Forty-three volumes read in one year, and twelve of them quarto. Dear sir, how I envy you ! Half a dozen of octavos in that space of time are as much as I am allowed. I can read by candle-light only, and stealing long hours from my rest. From sunrise to one or two o'clock, and often from dinner to dark, I am drudging at the writing-table : and all this to answer letters in which neither interest nor inclination on my part enters, and often from persons whose names I have never before heard ; yet, writing civilly, it is hard to refuse them civil answers." He had the curiosity to count the letters received for one year, — a fair average ; and they amounted to one thousand two hundred and sixty-seven. At his death he had *copies* of sixteen thousand letters which he had written ; and he had twenty-five thousand letters on file which he had received.

In November, 1818, Mrs. John Adams died ; and President Jefferson wrote the following beautiful letter of condolence to her husband : —

" The public papers, my dear friend, announce the fatal event of which your letter of October the 20th had given me ominous foreboding. Tried myself in the school of affliction by the loss of every form of connection which can rive the human heart, I know well and feel what you have lost, what you have suffered, are suffering, and have yet to endure. The same trials have taught me, that, for ills so immeasurable, time and silence are the only medicine. I will not, therefore, by useless condolences, open afresh the sluices of your grief ; nor, although mingling sincerely my tears with yours, will I say a word more, where words are vain, but that it is some comfort to us both that the term is not very distant at which we are to deposit in the same cerement our sorrows and suffering bodies, and

to ascend in essence to an ecstatic meeting with the friends we
have loved and lost, and whom we shall still love, and never lose
again. God bless you, and support you under your heavy affliction!"

In a letter dated March 21, 1819, he writes to Dr. Vine Utley,
"I never go to bed without an hour or half an hour's previous reading of something moral whereon to ruminate in the intervals of
sleep." The book from which he oftenest read was a collection
which he had made by cutting such passages from the evangelists as
came directly from the lips of the Saviour. These he arranged in a
blank-book. Jefferson writes to a friend, "A more beautiful or
precious morsel of ethics I have never seen: it is a document in
proof that *I* am a *real Christian;* that is to say, a disciple of the
doctrines of Jesus." This book Mr. Jefferson prepared evidently
with great care. It is a very full compend of the teachings of our
Saviour. It was entitled "The Philosophy of Jesus of Nazareth."
He also prepared a second volume, which he had bound in morocco,
in a handsome octavo volume, and which he labeled on the back,
"Morals of Jesus." It is a little remarkable that Mr. Jefferson
should have made these collections so secretly that none of the
members of his family knew even of the existence of the books until
after his death. One would have supposed that he would have considered these teachings valuable for his children and his grandchildren as well as for himself. Indeed, we are informed that he conferred with some friends upon the expediency of printing them in
several Indian dialects for the instruction of the Indians.

He devoted much attention to the establishment of the university
at Charlottesville. Having no religious faith which he was willing
to avow, he was not willing that any religious faith whatever should
be taught in the university as a part of its course of instruction.
This establishment, in a Christian land, of an institution for the
education of youth, where the relation existing between man and his
Maker was entirely ignored, raised a general cry of disapproval
throughout the whole country. It left a stigma upon the reputation
of Mr. Jefferson in the minds of Christian people, which can never
be effaced. He endeavored to abate the censure by suggesting that
the various denominations of Christians might establish schools, if
they wished, in the vicinity of the university; and the students, if
they wished, could attend their religious instructions.

The year 1826 opened gloomily upon Mr. Jefferson. He was very infirm, and embarrassed by debts, from which he could see but little hope of extrication. The indorsement for a friend had placed upon him an additional twenty thousand dollars of debt. To be old and poor is one of the greatest of earthly calamities. He applied to the Legislature for permission to dispose of a large portion of his property by lottery, hoping thus to realize a sum sufficient to pay his debts, and to leave enough to give him a competence for his few remaining days. Though bitterly opposed to all gambling, he argued, in support of his petition, that lotteries were not immoral. The university at Charlottesville, which was regarded almost exclusively as Mr. Jefferson's institution, had cost vastly more than had been anticipated. The members of the Legislature had become weary of making grants; and, just as Mr. Jefferson sent in his petition for a lottery, they had, by a very decisive vote, refused an application for an additional grant of money for the university. Mortified and saddened, and anxious for the future, he wrote to a friend, that, if the Legislature would grant him the indulgence he solicited, —

"I can save the house of Monticello and a farm adjoining to end my days in, and bury my bones; if not, I must sell house and all here, and carry my family to Bedford, where I have not even a log hut to put my head into."

At the same time he wrote to his eldest grandson in a strain of dignity and of sorrow which no one can read but with sympathy. The letter was dated February 8, 1826. " I duly received your affectionate letter of the 3d, and perceive there are greater doubts than I had apprehended whether the Legislature will indulge my request to them. It is a part of my mortification to perceive that I had so far overvalued myself as to have counted on it with too much confidence. I see, in the failure of this hope, a deadly blast of all my peace of mind during my remaining days. You kindly encourage me to keep up my spirits; but, oppressed with disease, debility, age, and embarrassed affairs, this is difficult. For myself, I should not regard a prostration of fortune; but I am overwhelmed at the prospect in which I leave my family. My dear and beloved daughter, the cherished companion of my early life, and nurse of my age, and her children, rendered as dear to me as if my own, from their having lived with me from their cradle, left in a comfortless situation, hold up to me nothing but future gloom; and I should not care if life were to end with the line I am writing, were it not that, in the unhappy state of mind which your father's misfortunes have brought upon him, I may yet be of some avail to the family."

To Mr. Jefferson's great gratification, the lottery bill passed. But, all over the country, friends. who appreciated the priceless value of the services which he had rendered our nation, began to send to him tokens of their love. The mayor of New York, Philip Hone, sent him, collected from a few friends, eight thousand five hundred dollars ; from Philadelphia, five thousand dollars were sent; from Baltimore, three thousand dollars ; and one or two thousand more were sent from other sources. These testimonials, like sunshine breaking through the clouds, dispelled the gloom which had been so deeply gathering around his declining day. Very rapidly he was now sinking. His steps became so feeble that with difficulty he could totter about the house.

His very eloquent and truthful biographer, Henry S. Randall, says that the Bible was one of the principal books, which, with the Greek philosophers, occupied his last reading. " The majesty of Æschylus, the ripe art of Sophocles, the exhaustless invention of Euripides, now came back to him in more than their pristine grandeur and beauty ; and in the Bible he found flights of sublimity more magnificent than in these, coupled with a philosophy to which the Grecian was imperfect, narrow, and base. No sentiment did he express oftener than his contempt for all moral systems compared with that of Christ."

There was something peculiarly gentle and touching in his whole demeanor. His good-night kiss, his loving embrace, his childlike simplicity and tenderness, often brought tears to the eyes of those whose privilege it was to minister to his wants. It was evident that he was conscious that the hour of his departure was at hand. He was exceedingly careful to avoid making any trouble, and was far more watchful for the comfort of those around him than for his own. His passage was very slow down into the vale of death. To one who expressed the opinion that he seemed a little better, he replied, —

" Do not imagine for a moment that I feel the smallest solicitude about the result. I am like an old watch, with a pinion worn ou here and a wheel there, until it can go no longer."

He manifested no desire to depart, no cheerful hope of the future and no dread. Looking up to the doctor, he said calmly, " A fev hours more, and it will all be over." Hearing the name of the minister of the Episcopal Church which he attended, who had called, he said, " I have no objection to see him as a kind and good neighbor." His friends inferred from this that he did not wish to see him as a minister of Jesus Christ. Very truly and charitably he said, in reference to the anathemas which had been hurled upon him, that his enemies had never known *him ;* that they had created an imaginary being, whom they had clothed with imaginary attributes, and to whom they had given his name ; and that it was this creature of their imagination whom they had so virulently assailed.

On Monday evening, the 3d of July, he awoke about ten o'clock from troubled sieep, and, thinking it morning, remarked, " This is the 4th of July." Immediately he sank away again into slumber. As the night passed slowly away, all saw that he was sinking in death. There was silence in the death-chamber. The mysterious separation of the soul from the body was painlessly taking place. At ten minutes before one o'clock, at noon, of July 4, 1826, the last breath left the body. It was a day of darkness and rain when the remains were borne to their burial. The Rev. Mr. Hatch, the clergyman of the parish, whom Mr. Jefferson highly esteemed, read the burial service of the Episcopal Church.

In conclusion, let me give an abstract of a sketch of his character, as given by his grandson, Thomas Jefferson Randolph, who was the companion of his life, and who was thirty-four years of age when Mr. Jefferson died. He writes, —

" My mother was his eldest, and, for the last twenty years of his life, his only child. She lived with him from her birth to his death. I was more intimate with him than with any man I have ever known. His character invited such intimacy. Soft and feminine in his affections to his family, he entered into and sympathized with all their feelings, winning them to paths of virture by the soothing gentleness of his manner. While he lived, and since, I have reviewed with severe scrutiny those interviews ; and I must say, that I never heard from him the expression of one thought, feeling, or sentiment, inconsistent with the highest moral standard, or the purest Christian charity in the largest sense. His moral character was of the highest order, founded upon the purest and sternest models of antiquity, softened, chastened, and developed

10

by the influence of the all-pervading benevolence of the doctrines of Christ, which he had intensely and admiringly studied.

"In his contemplative moments, his mind turned to religion, which he studied thoroughly. He had seen and read much of the abuses and perversions of Christianity: he abhorred those abuses and their authors, and denounced them without reserve. He was regular in his attendance on church, taking his prayer-book with him. He drew the plan of the Episcopal Church at Charlottesville, was one of the largest contributors to its erection, and contributed regularly to the support of its minister. I paid, after his death, his subscription of two hundred dollars to the erection of the Presbyterian church in the same village. A gentleman of some distinction calling upon him, and expressing his disbelief in the truths of the Bible, his reply was, 'Then, sir, you have studied it to little purpose.'

"He was guilty of no profanity himself, and did not tolerate it in others. He detested impiety; and his favorite quotation for his young friends, as the basis of their morals, was the fifteenth Psalm of David. He did not permit cards in his house: he knew no game with them. His family, by whom he was surrounded, and who saw him in all the unguarded privacy of private life, believed him to be the purest of men. The beauty of his character was exhibited in the bosom of his family, where he delighted to indulge in all the fervor and delicacy of feminine feeling. Before he lost his taste for the violin, in winter evenings he would play on it, having his grandchildren dancing around him. In summer, he would station them for their little races on the lawn, give the signal for the start, be the arbiter of the contest, and award the prizes.

"In his person he was neat in the extreme. In early life, his dress, equipage, and appointments were fastidiously appropriate to his rank. When at Paris, Philadelphia, and Washington, his furniture, table, servants, equipage, and the *tout ensemble* of his establishment, were deemed highly appropiate to the position he held. He was a gentleman everywhere. His habits were regular and systematic. He rose always at dawn. He said in his last illness that the sun had not caught him in bed for fifty years. He never drank ardent spirits or strong wines. Such was his aversion to ardent spirits, that when, in his last illness, his physician wished him to use brandy as an astringent, he could not induce him to take it strong enough."

After Mr. Jefferson's death the lottery plan was abandoned. The lands were sold; and after the disposal of the whole property, the proceeds not being sufficient to pay the debts, the executor met the balance from his own purse. As soon as it was known that his only child was thus left without any independent provision, the legislatures of South Carolina and Louisiana generously voted her ten thousand dollars each.

As time dispels the mists of prejudice, the fame of Thomas Jefferson will shine with ever-increasing lustre; and he must, in all the future, occupy one of the most conspicuous niches in the temple of American worthies.

CHAPTER IV.

JAMES MADISON.

THE name of James Madison is inseparably connected with most of the important events in that heroic period of our country during

MONTPELIER, — RESIDENCE OF JAMES MADISON.

which the foundations of this great republic were laid. The Madison family were among the earliest emigrants to this New World landing upon the shores of the Chesapeake but fifteen years after the settlement at Jamestown.

The father of James Madison was an opulent planter, residing upon a very fine estate called "Montpelier," in Orange County, Va. The mansion was situated in the midst of scenery highly picturesque and romantic, on the west side of Southwest Mountain, at the foot of the Blue Ridge. It was but twenty-five miles from the home of Jefferson at Monticello. The closest personal and political attachment existed between these illustrious men, from their early youth until death.

James Madison was born on the 5th of March, 1751. He was blessed with excellent parents; both father and mother being persons of intelligence and of great moral worth. The best society of Virginia often visited at their hospitable mansion; and thus, from early life, Mr. Madison was accustomed to those refinements which subsequently lent such a charm to his character. His sobriety and dignity of demeanor were such, that it has been said of him, that "he never was a boy."

James was the eldest of a family of seven children, — four sons and three daughters, — all of whom attained maturity, and passed through life esteemed and beloved. His early education was conducted mostly at home, under a private tutor. He was naturally intellectual in his tastes, and, with but little fondness for rough, out-of-door sports, consecrated himself with unusual vigor to study. Even when a boy, he had made very considerable proficiency in the Greek, Latin, French, and Spanish languages. In the year 1769, at the age of eighteen, he was sent to Princeton College in New Jersey, of which the illustrious Dr. Witherspoon was then president. Here he applied himself to study with the most imprudent zeal, allowing himself, for months, but three hours' sleep out of the twenty-four. His health thus became so seriously impaired that he never recovered any vigor of constitution. He graduated in 1771, at the age of twenty, with a feeble body, with a character of the utmost purity, and with a mind highly disciplined, and richly stored with all the learning which embellished and gave efficiency to his subsequent career.

Returning to Virginia, he commenced the study of law, and a course of extensive and systematic reading. This educational course, the spirit of the times in which he lived, and the society with which he associated, all combined to inspire him with a strong love of liberty, and to train him for his life-work of a statesman. Being naturally of a religious turn of mind, and his frail health leading him to think that his life was not to be long, he directed especial attention to theological studies. Endowed with a mind singularly free from passion and prejudice, and with almost unequaled powers of reasoning, he weighed all the arguments for and against revealed religion, until his faith became so established as never to be shaken.

The Church of England was then the established church in Virginia, invested with all the prerogatives and immunities which it enjoyed in the father-land. All were alike taxed to support its clergy. There was no religious liberty. Mr. Madison first appears before the public, associated with Mr. Jefferson, as the opponent of this intolerance. The battle was a fierce one. The foes of intolerance were denounced as the enemies of Christianity; but liberty triumphed, and religious freedom was established in Virginia.

In the spring of 1776, when twenty-six years of age, he was elected member of the Virginia Convention to frame the Constitution of the State. Being one of the youngest members of the house, naturally diffident, and having no ambitious aspirings to push him forward, he took but little part in the public debates. Like Jefferson, his main strength lay in his conversational influence and in his pen. Real ability and worth cannot long be concealed. Every day, almost unconsciously to himself, he was gaining influence and position. The next year, 1777, he was a candidate for the General Assembly. He refused to treat the whisky-loving voters, and consequently lost his election; but those who had witnessed the talents, energy, and public spirit of the modest young man, enlisted themselves in his behalf, and he was appointed a member of the Executive Council.

Both Patrick Henry and Thomas Jefferson were governors of Virginia while Mr. Madison remained member of the council; and their appreciation of his intellectual, social, and moral worth, contributed not a little to his subsequent eminence. In the year 1780 he was elected a member of the Continental Congress. Here he met the most illustrious men in our land, and he was immediately assigned to one of the most conspicuous positions among them. Mr. Jefferson says of him, in allusion to the study and experience through which he had already passed, —

" Trained in these successive schools, he acquired a habit of self-possession which placed at ready command the rich resources of his luminous and discriminating mind and of his extensive information, and rendered him the first of every assembly afterwards of which he became a member. Never wandering from his subject into vain declamation, but pursuing it closely in language pure, classical, and copious ; soothing always the feelings of his adversaries by civilities and softness of expression, — he rose to the eminent station which he held in the great National Convention of 1787 ; and in that of Virginia, which followed, he sustained the new Constitution in all its parts, bearing off the palm against the logic of George Mason and the fervid declamation of Patrick Henry. With these consummate powers were united a pure and spotless virtue, which no calumny has ever attempted to sully. Of the power and polish of his pen, and of the wisdom of his administration in the highest office of the nation, I need say nothing. They have spoken, and will forever speak, for themselves."

Every American citizen must reflect with pride upon the fact that he can point to a series of rulers over these United States such as no other nation on earth can boast of. Let any intelligent reader glance at the catalogue of kings of England, France, Spain, — rulers who have attained the supreme power by hereditary descent, — and compare them with the presidents which the elective franchise has given to this country, and even prejudice the most unbending will be compelled to admit that popular choice is far more unerring in the selection of rulers than the chances of birth. Every monarchy in Europe has had upon the throne men as worthless as earth has ever seen. America has not had a single President who has not been a man of moral and social excellence, who was not in heart a true patriot, and who did not honestly, though perhaps at times with mistaken policy, seek the promotion of the best interests of his country.

For three years Mr. Madison continued in Congress, one of its most active and influential members. In the year 1784, his term having expired, he was elected a member of the Virginia Legislature. Here he was the earnest supporter of every wise and liberal measure. He advocated the revision of the old statutes, the abrogation of entail and primogeniture, and the establishment of perfect religious freedom. His " Memorial and Remonstrance " against a general assessment for the support of religion is considered one of the ablest papers which emanated from his pen. It settled the question of the entire separation of church and state in Virginia.

He still continued, in the midst of all these responsibilities, to prosecute with much energy his legal and literary studies. It was never his wish to enter upon the practice of the law ; and, in a letter to Mr. Randolph in 1785, he says, " Another of my wishes is, to depend as little as possible on the labor of slaves." The following extract from a letter of Mr. Jefferson, from Annapolis, to Mr. Madison, under date of February 20, 1794, gives a pleasing picture of the friendship then and ever existing between Jefferson, Madison, and Monroe : —

" I hope you have found access to my library. I beg you to make free use of it. The steward is living there now, and, of course, will always be in the way. Monroe is buying land almost adjoining me : Short will do the same. What would I not give could you fall into the circle ! With such a society, I could once more venture home, and lay myself up for the residue of life, quitting all its contentions, which grow daily more and more insupportable.

" Think of it. To render it practicable, only requires you to think it so. Life is of no value but as it brings us gratifications. Among the most valuable of these is rational society. It informs the mind, sweetens the temper, cheers our spirits, and restores health. There is a little farm of one hundred and forty acres adjoining me, and within two miles, all of good land, though old, with a small, indifferent house upon it ; the whole worth not more than two hundred and fifty pounds. Such a one might be a farm of experiment, and support a little table and household. Once more, think of it, and adieu."

There was a vein of pleasantry pervading the character of Mr. Madison, which ever rendered him to his friends one of the most agreeable of companions. No man felt more deeply than Mr. Madison the utter inefficiency of the old confederacy, with no national government, with no power to form treaties which would be binding or to enforce law. There was not any State more prominent than Virginia in the declaration that an efficient national government must be formed. In January, 1786, Mr. Madison carried a resolution through the General Assembly of Virginia, inviting the other States to appoint commissioners to meet in convention at Annapolis to discuss this subject. Five States only were represented. The convention, however, issued another call, drawn up by Mr. Madison, urging all the States to send their delegates to Philadelphia, in May, 1787, to draft a Constitution for the United States, to take the place of that confederate league which the sagacity of John Adams had foretold must prove a failure.

The delegates met at the time appointed. Every State but Rhode Island was represented. George Washington was chosen president of the convention; and the present Constitution of the United States was then and there formed.

When Charles X. was driven from France, and Louis Philippe was invited to take the throne, Lafayette took his hand as they stood upon a balcony of the Hôtel de Ville in Paris, while swarming thousands were gathered around, and said, —

" You know that I am a republican, and that I regard the Constitution of the United States as the most perfect that has ever existed."

" I think as you do," replied Louis Philippe. " It is impossible to pass two years in the United States, as I have done, and not be of that opinion. But do you think that, in the present state of France, a republican government can be sustained here ? "

" No," said Lafayette; " that which is necessary for France is a throne, surrounded by republican institutions: all must be republican."

When we consider the speakers and the occasion, we must regard this as the highest compliment ever paid to the Constitution of the United States ; and our nation owes a debt of gratitude which can never be paid, not only to the founders of this Constitution, but also to those heroic soldiers of our land, who on the field of battle, and with their blood, have defended it when treason would have trampled it in the dust.

There was, perhaps, no mind and no pen more active in framing this immortal document than the mind and the pen of James Madison. Mr. Jefferson pays the following beautiful tribute to his character and ability : —

" I have known him from 1779, when he first came into the public councils, and, after three and thirty years' trial, I can say conscientiously, that I do not know in the world a man of purer integrity, more dispassionate, disinterested, and devoted to genuine republicanism; nor could I, in the whole scope of America and Europe, point out an abler head."

There were two parties to be reconciled in forming the Constitution. The Federal party were in favor of making the *central government* strong, investing it with such powers that we should be a compact and united nation; while they still would give the state governments full authority in all local matters. The Republican party would make the *state governments* strong, reserving for them all rights excepting those which it was absolutely necessary to surrender to the central power at Washington. The Constitution, as formed, was a very harmonious blending of these two apparently antagonistic principles. Neither party was fully satisfied with the results. The Federalists would have given the central government more power: the Republicans would have given the state governments more power. And, from that time to this, that point has been prominent in the conflict of parties.

Washington and John Adams strongly inclined to the Federal side; Jefferson, to the Republican side. " Mr. Madison," writes George Washington, " thinks an individual independence of the States utterly irreconcilable with their aggregate sovereignty, and that a consolidation of the whole into one simple republic would be as inexpedient as it is unattainable. He therefore proposes a middle ground, which may at once support a due supremacy of the national authority, and not exclude the local authorities whenever they can be subordinately useful."

During the discussion of these great questions, the views of the Federal party were urged in a series of letters, which then attained the celebrity which they have ever since held. These letters were signed *The Federalist.* General Hamilton was the principal writer, though several papers were furnished by Mr. Madison and Mr. Jay.

Some were in favor of electing the President and the members of the Senate for life, or during good behavior, as with our judges. Others wished that the President might be reëlected every four years, like a Polish king; and that he might thus, should the people choose, by continual reëlections, become a life-long ruler. Others urged that he should serve but one term, and be forever after ineligible. It has become a matter of *custom* only, that no President shall continue in office more than two terms. In the convention

Mr. Madison and General Washington almost invariably coincided in opinion. At length the Constitution was formed, and was adopted by a vote of eighty-nine to seventy-nine. It was then to be presented to the several States for acceptance. Very great solicitude was felt. Should it be rejected we should be left but a conglomeration of independent States, with but little power at home, a ̶ ̶ ̶ ̶ respect abroad. Mr. Madison was selected by the convention to draw up an address to the people of the United States, expounding the principles of the Constitution and urging its adoption.

In every State there was a battle between the friends and the foes of the new Constitution; but at length it triumphed over all opposition, and went into effect in 1789. In Virginia it encountered very formidable hostility; but Mr. Madison's brilliant statesmanship and persuasive powers secured its unconditional ratification, notwithstanding it was opposed by the brilliant rhetoric of Patrick Henry and the stern logic of George Mason. He was soon after elected a member of the House of Representatives in the First Congress, which then met in the old City Hall in New York, at the corner of Wall and Nassau streets. Here he found himself drifting to the side of the Republican party in nearly all its measures; and yet so courteous was he in his manners, so conciliatory in tone, and so undeniably conscientious in his convictions, that he retained the affection and confidence of his former friends.

Upon Mr. Jefferson's return from France, President Washington earnestly solicited Mr. Madison to accept that mission; but he firmly declined the appointment, and also the office of Secretary of State, which was urged upon him. He had gradually become so identified with the Republican party in his principles, that he felt that he could not harmoniously coöperate with the majority of Washington's Cabinet. In 1772 Mr. Madison was the avowed leader of the Republican party in Congress. He sympathized with Mr. Jefferson in his foreign policy, gratefully cherishing the remembrance of French intervention in our behalf, and advocating with all his powers of voice and pen a retaliatory policy towards the conduct of Great Britain.

When President Washington was about to retire from his second term of office in 1797, it was the wish of many that Mr. Madison should be the candidate of the Republican party. Mr. Jefferson wrote, —

"There is not another person in the United States, with whom, being placed at the helm of our affairs, my mind would be so completely at rest for the fortune of our political bark."

But Mr. Madison would not consent. His term in Congress had now expired, and he returned from New York to his beautiful retreat at Montpelier. While in Congress, he had met, in the gay society of New York, a young widow of remarkable powers of fascination, — Mrs. Todd. Her maiden name was Dolly Paine. She was born in North Carolina, of Quaker parents, and had been educated in the strictest rules of that sect. When but eighteen years of age she married a young lawyer, and moved to Philadelphia, where she was introduced to brilliant scenes of fashionable life. She speedily laid aside the dress and the address of the Quakeress, and became one of the most fascinating ladies who has embellished our republican court. In New York, after the death of her husband, she was the belle of the season, and was surrounded with admirers. Mr. Madison won the prize. They were married in 1794. He was then forty-three years of age.

He had previously met with a serious disappointment in his affections. Some years before, in Philadelphia, he had become ardently attached to Miss Floyd, of New York, the accomplished daughter of one of the signers of the Declaration of Independence. For some unexplained reason, the attachment, which seemed to be mutual, was broken off, to the great grief of Mr. Madison.

The companion whom Mr. Madison had secured at this late hour of life proved invaluable. She was, in person and character, queenly. As graceful as Josephine, with a heart overflowing with kindness, endowed with wonderful powers of conversation, persuasion, and entertainment, and with a face whose frankness and winning smiles at sight won all hearts, she contributed greatly to the popularity and power of her husband in the elevated sphere through which he afterwards moved.

As, in the case of Napoleon, all who wished for special favors felt safe if they could secure the advocacy of Josephine; so it was found, that, through Mrs. Madison, one could ever obtain the readiest access to the heart of her distinguished husband. She was a true and sympathizing friend of all who were in sorrow. Mr. Catlin, the renowned delineator of Indian life, when a young man, just after his marriage, was in Virginia, in the vicinity of Mr. Madison' home, endeavoring to earn a living by painting portraits. He was poor, a stranger, in a cheerless inn, and his young wife was taken sick with the intermittent fever. Their situation was desolate indeed. But soon a lady of wonderfully prepossessing appearance and manners entered he chamber, apologized gracefully for the intrusion, introduced herself as Mrs. Madison, and, taking off bonnet and shawl, sat down by the bedside of the sick one, cheered her with words of hope, administered the medicines, and from that hour, with a sister's tenderness, watched over her, and supplied her with comforts and luxuries, until she was quite recovered.

In Washington, she was the life of society. A group of the young were ever gathered around her. If there were any diffident, timid young girl just making her appearance, she was sure to find in Mrs. Madison a supporting and encouraging friend. Probably no lady has thus far occupied so prominent a position in the very peculiar society which has constituted our republican court as Mrs. Madison.

At Montpelier, in this brief season of retirement from the cares of office, Mr. Madison was in the enjoyment of almost every blessing earth can confer. His opulence enabled him to indulge in unbounded hospitality, and his celebrity drew to his mansion distinguished guests from all lands. Mr. Madison, though a vein of pleasantry was intertwined with his nature, was naturally reserved and formal. Mrs. Madison was the charm and the life of every social circle in which she appeared. The happy and harmonious household was truly blessed by the presence of the widowed mothers of both Mr. and Mrs. Madison, and two orphan sisters of Mrs. Madison. Prosperity, love, distinction, all lent their charms to gild the scenes of this favored Virginian home.

At the time when Mr. Madison retired from Congress, the condition of our country was very critical. The Jacobinical Directory in France, which Napoleon afterwards overthrew, was fast sundering the ties of gratitude which bound us to that nation; and England, proud mistress of the seas, despising our infant navy, was treating us with indignities which America would not *now* submit to for a single hour. The Federalists had far more dread of France than of England, and were inclined to combine with England to arrest the progress of the French Revolution. They called the Republicans Jacobins. Party spirit ran so high, that, in many parts of the country, all social intercourse between Federalists and Republicans was broken up: even the children of the opposing parties were not allowed freely to associate with each other. The wildest tales were circulated through the country, that the French Jacobins were coming over to coöperate with the Republicans, and overthrow our government. It is scarcely possible for the people of the present day to realize the frenzy of that delirium.

Under its influence, in the early days of Mr. John Adams's administration, two acts were passed, called " Alien and Sedition Laws." By these laws the President was authorized, in case of war, made or threatened, to imprison, banish, or place under bonds, at his discretion, any natives or subjects of the hostile power not actually naturalized; and also it was decreed that any one who should unlawfully conspire to oppose any measure of the United States government should be punished, on legal conviction, by fine not exceeding five thousand dollars, or by imprisonment not exceeding five years.

It was generally understood that these acts were aimed at the Republican party, who were in sympathy with that equality of rights which the French Revolution was struggling to introduce and who were opposing bitterly, and sometimes with measures of doubtful legality, the administration of our government. These laws were vehemently denounced. They contributed greatly to John Adams's unpopularity. To add to the excitement, a bill was introduced into the Senate of the United States by Mr. Lloyd, of Maryland, which passed to a second reading by a vote of fourteen to eight, declaring the people of France to be enemies of the United States, and adherence to them, or giving them aid and comfort, punishable with death.

Mr. Jefferson was so roused by these measures that he drew up some resolutions, the authorship of which was for many years kept secret, but which were adopted by the Legislature of Kentucky, so determined in their character that his enemies have charged him with advocating nullification and violent resistance. Mr. Madison, though repudiating everything like nullification, drew up resolutions, which were carried by a large majority through the Virginia Legislature, denouncing the acts with great severity. The legislatures of other States, however, warmly supported the acts as both constitutional and needful. Mr. Madison's writings upon this subject are by all admitted to exhibit masterly vigor; and, in their advocacy of a "strict construction" of the Constitution, they became the text-book of his party.

But the storm passed away. The Alien and Sedition Laws were repealed. John Adams lost his reëlection. Thomas Jefferson was chosen President in 1801, and the Republicans came into power. The new President immediately appointed his friend, Mr. Madison, Secretary of State. With great ability he discharged the duties of this onerous and responsible office during the whole eight years of Mr. Jefferson's administration. This summoned him from his happy home in Virginia to Washington.

As Mr. Jefferson was a widower, and neither of his daughters could be often with him, Mrs. Madison usually presided over the festivities of the White House ; and as her husband succeeded Mr. Jefferson, holding his office for two terms, this very remarkable woman was, in reality, the mistress of the presidential mansion for sixteen years. The White House, our republican palace, was then a very shabby affair. The building, but half completed, stood in a pasture of old oaks, surrounded by rough masses of stone and piles of lumber, and other accumulations of unsightly materials. It was, indeed, solitary and alone, looking far more like an abandoned ruin than a rising palace.

Far away in the distance stood the Capitol Hill, surrounded by groves, forests, and wide-spreading plains, with a few houses or huts scattered here and there at most unsocial distances. The crowd which flocked to Washington from our widely extended and rapidly increasing country came with all their provincial peculiarities. It was a motley throng, But wonderful harmony pervaded Mr. Jefferson's Cabinet. "We were," he writes, "one family." The stately forms of etiquette which were congenial to the tastes of Presidents Washington and Adams were now laid aside, and the simplicity of private life reigned in the presidential mansion.

Mr. Madison being entirely engrossed by the cares of his office, all the duties of social life developed upon his accomplished wife. Never were such responsibilities more ably and delightfully discharged. Every visitor left her with the impression of having been the object of peculiar attention as an especial favorite. She never forgot a face or a name. The most bitter foes of her husband and the administration were received with the frankly proffered hand

and the cordial smile of welcome. This was not policy merely: it was the resistless outflowing of her own loving nature. Her house was plainly furnished; her dress, though elegant, simple; and the influence of this gentle woman, in allaying the bitterness of party rancor, became a great and salutary power in the nation.

Mr. Madison's correspondence, while Secretary of State, with foreign ambassadors and our ministers at foreign courts, constitute a very important part of the history of President Jefferson's administration. There is not any nation which can exhibit a more able series of state papers than came from his pen.

It is the genius of our country to reject pompous titles: we have laid them aside with the powdered wigs and scarlet coats of other days. But no other land can exhibit a more brilliant catalogue of truly great men, — of Nature's noblemen. Washington, Adams, Jefferson, Madison, and a host of others in the galaxy of American worthies, have a fame more durable than sculptured marble, or molten brass, or monumental granite. Theirs is a nobility not of hereditary descent, and mouldy parchments, and unearned laurels, but a nobility of heroic achievement, which shall be recognized through all the ages, and, like the untitled stars, shall shine forever.

As the term of Mr. Jefferson's Presidency drew near its close, party rancor was roused to the utmost in the strife to elect his successor. It was like a death-grapple between the two great parties, the Federal and the Republican. Mr. Madison was not an emotional man. He stood, like the peak of Teneriffe in a storm, undisturbed by the howl of the gale and the dash of the wave. Strong in honesty which he knew to be unimpeachable, he contemplated, in imperturbable serenity, assaults of the press which would have driven many men frantic. Mrs. Madison, in accordance with her husband's wishes, continued to exercise the rites of hospitality without regard to party politics. The chiefs of the different parties met in her parlor, and all alike shared in the smiles and kindly greetings which made that parlor so attractive.

The unintelligent are easily deceived by tinsel. Even in our land where education was so generally diffused, the barbers of Washington judged of the merits of great men by the length of their cue and the amount of powder on their hair. The morning after Mr. Madison was nominated for President, a barber in Washington, addressing a senator whom he was shaving, said, —

"Surely this country is doomed to disgrace and ruin. What Presidents we might have, sir! Just look at Daggett of Connecticut, and Stockton of New Jersey! What cues they have got, sir! as big as your wrist, and powdered every day, like real gentlemen as they are. Such men would confer dignity on the station. But this little Jim Madison, with a cue no bigger than a pipestem, sir, — it is enough to make a man forswear his country!"

Out of one hundred and seventy-five electoral votes, Mr. Madison received one hundred and twenty-two, and with this handsome majority took his seat as President on the 4th of March, 1809. The encroachments of England had brought us to the verge of war. British orders in council destroyed our commerce, and our flag was exposed to constant insult. The British minister, Mr. Erskine, who was disposed to be conciliatory, was recalled, and a Mr. Jackson, a man of insolent address, was sent to occupy his place. He became so unbearable that the Secretary of State was directed to hold no further communication with him, and the British government was requested to withdraw him. This was done; but no one was sent in his place. Congress, in its extreme displeasure, passed a resolution declaring the official communications of Mr. Jackson as having been highly indecorous and insolent, approving the conduct of the executive in requesting his recall, and passing an act of non-intercourse with both England and France, — with the latter power in consequence of the Berlin and Milan decrees. Napoleon immediately revoked those decrees, sending word to our government that they had not been issued out of any unfriendly feeling to us, but as a necessary measure of retaliation against the atrocious orders in council which England had issued.

The act of non-intercourse now remained in full force against England alone. Mr. Madison was a man of peace. Scholarly in his tastes, retiring in his disposition, war had no charms for him. But the meekest spirit can be roused. It makes one's blood boil, even now, to think of an American ship brought to, upon the ocean, by the guns of an English cruiser. A young lieutenant steps on board, and orders the crew to be paraded before him. With great nonchalance, he selects any number whom he may please to designate as British subjects, orders them down the ship's side into his boat, and places them on the gun-deck of his man-of-war, to fight, by compulsion, the battles of England. This right of search and

11

impressment no efforts of our government could induce the British Cabinet to relinquish.

There was a popular meeting held in the city of New York on the 26th of April, 1806, when the resolution was unanimously passed, "That the suffering foreign armed ships to station themselves off our harbor, and there to stop, search, and capture our vessels, to impress, wound, and murder our citizens, is a gross and criminal neglect of the highest duties of government; and that an

BRITISH RIGHT OF SEARCH.

administration which patiently permits the same is not entitled to the confidence of a brave and free people."

Where resistance was attempted, the impressment was conducted with unsparing severity. The cudgel and the cutlass were freely used. Those who refused to submit were scourged, placed in irons, and scourged again on the raw wounds until they succumbed. It was proved by official records that more than a thousand American citizens were thus torn from home and friends, many of whom were compelled for years to man British guns, and were thus forced when the war between the United States and England was opened, to fight against their own flag. No government could be worthy of respect which would not at least attempt to protect its citizens from such outrages.

The following case illustrates that of hundreds. Hiram Thayer was born in Greenwich, Conn. He was a young man of sobriety, industry, high moral worth, and was greatly endeared to his friends. He was impressed in 1803, with barbarity which would have disgraced an Algerine courser. For five years, in the war which England was then waging against France, he was compelled to serve the British cannon. In 1805 he was transferred on board the British frigate Statira. In reply to his remonstrances he was told that, if he were not submissive and obedient, "he should be tied to the mast, and shot at like a dog." He contrived to get a letter to his father. His friends exerted themselves to the utmost to obtain his release. General Lyman, the American consul at London, applied to the Lords Commissioners in vain for his discharge. Certificates of his nativity were exhibited from the selectmen, town-clerk, and parish minister of his native town.

Still he was held in British slavery all through our second war with England, compelled to fight against his own countrymen. On the 14th of March, 1814, Commodore Decatur sent the father, under a flag of truce, on board the Statira, which was then one of the British blockading squadron off New London. Commodore Decatur sent with the flag a note to Captain Capel of the Statira, saying "that he felt persuaded that the application of the father, furnished as he was with conclusive evidence of the nativity and identity of his son, would induce an immediate order for his discharge." The interview between the father and the son, after eleven years of separation, was most affecting. There was not a doubt in the mind of a single British officer of Hiram Thayer's being an American citizen; but they refused to release him, alleging simply that they had no authority to do so. The unhappy man was still detained in this slavery, as atrocious as ever disgraced a Cuban plantation. Not long after this he fell overboard and was drowned. A trunk containing portions of his clothing were the only memorials of their loved son which were ever returned to his afflicted parents.

On the 18th of June, 1812, President Madison gave his approval to an act of Congress declaring war against Great Britain. Notwithstanding the bitter hostility of the Federal party to the war, the country in general approved; and Mr. Madison, on the 4th of March, 1813, was reëlected by a large majority, and entered upon his second term of office. This is not the place to describe the various adventures of this war on the land and on the water. Our infant navy then laid the foundations of its renown in grappling with the most formidable power which ever swept the seas. The contest commenced in earnest by the appearance of a British fleet, early in February, 1813, in Chesapeake Bay, declaring nearly the whole coast of the United States under blockade.

The Emperor of Russia offered his services as mediator. America accepted; England refused. A British force of five thousand men landed on the banks of the Patuxent River, near its entrance into Chesapeake Bay, and marched rapidly by way of Bladensburg upon Washington. There was no sufficient force in the vicinity to resist them. General Winder was in command of a few regular troops and some regiments of militia.

The straggling little city of Washington was thrown into consternation. The cannon of the brief conflict at Bladensburg echoed through the streets of the metropolis. The whole population fled from the city. The President, leaving Mrs. Madison in the White House, with her carriage drawn up at the door to await his speedy return, hurried to meet the officers in a council of war. He met our troops utterly routed, and could not go back without danger of being captured. She writes to her sister under date of Wednesday, August 12, 1814, twelve o'clock at noon, —

"Since sunrise I have been turning my spy-glass in every direction, and watching with unwearied anxiety, hoping to discern the near approach of my dear husband and his friends; but, alas! I can descry only groups of military wandering in all directions, as if there was a lack of arms or of spirit to fight for their own firesides.

"*Three o'clock.* — Will you believe it, my sister? we have had a battle, or skirmish, near Bladensburg, and I am still here within sound of the cannon. Mr. Madison comes not: may God protect him! Two messengers, covered with dust, came to bid me fly; but I wait for him. At this late hour a wagon has been procured. I have had it filled with the plate and the most valuable portable articles belonging to the house. Whether it will reach its destination

— the Bank of Maryland, — or fall into the hands of British soldiery, events must determine."

But a few hours elapsed ere the presidential mansion, the Capitol, and all the public buildings in Washington, were in flames. A few months after this great humiliation, the British made an attempt upon New Orleans. They were repulsed by General Jackson with great slaughter. Napoleon was now overpowered. The allied despots were triumphant, and, assembled in congress at Vienna, were partitioning out the reënslaved nations of Europe between them. Their one great object was so to divide Europe that the people should not again have the opportunity to rise against the old *régimes* of tyranny. Truthfully does "The British Quarterly" say, —

"The treaties of Vienna of 1815, though the most desperate efforts have been made by the English diplomatists to embalm them as monuments of political wisdom, are fast becoming as dead as those of Westphalia. In fact, they should be got under ground with all possible dispatch ; for no compacts so worthless, so wicked, so utterly subversive of the rights of humanity, are to be found in the annals of nations."

England was the leading power in this Congress. The British Cabinet, flushed with victory, was never more arrogant than then. England was now prepared to turn her whole immense armament against our country. We were sadly divided among ourselves. The New England States were so hostile to the war as seriously to embarrass the government. Never was our country enveloped in deeper gloom. Commissioners had been sent to Ghent to obtain peace with the British crown, if it could possibly be obtained on any reasonable terms.

About noon of the 13th of February, 1815, a strange rumor was found floating through Washington, — that a treaty of peace had been signed at Ghent. Gathering strength as it flew, the whole city was soon in a state of the most intense excitement. Whence came the story, no one could satisfactorily tell. At length, after diligent inquiring, it appeared that a private express had rapidly passed through the city, bearing the important tidings to merchants in the South. Still it was but a rumor. Mr. Gales, editor of "The National Intelligencer," anxious to obtain some reliable information upon an event so momentous, called upon President Madison.

He found him sitting alone, in the dusk of the evening, apparently pondering the prodigious change which the news, if true, would produce in public affairs.

The President, always affable, never excited, was inclined to credit the report. He knew that mercantile zeal might outrun political ardor. His manner was so composed, his spirits so tranquil and unruffled, that one not acquainted with his perfect power over himself might have supposed it a matter of much indifference to him whether the report were true or false.

Information then, when there were neither railroads nor telegraph wires, traveled slowly. It was not until late in the afternoon of the next day that a coach, drawn by four foaming horses, came thundering down Pennsylvania Avenue, with official communication of the glad tidings. What pen can describe the excitement of that hour, as cheers burst from all lips? The drawing-room at the President's mansion was speedily thronged. Mrs. Madison was there, radiant with joy, the President being absent with his Cabinet. In a moment, to use the expressive phrase of John Adams, the country had passed from "gloom to glory."

No one rejoiced more heartily than did President Madison. It had been with the utmost reluctance that he had been forced into a war. England did not relinquish her *claim* of the "right of search;" but, as there was peace in Europe, there was no longer any motive to continue the practice. It was, of course, inexpedient for the United States to persist in the war for a mere abstraction. It is safe to say that Great Britain will never again undertake to drag a man from the protecting folds of the stars and stripes. Americans of all coming ages will revere the memory of James Madison for resisting such wrongs. "I am an American citizen" will henceforth be an argument which will command the respect of the world.

On the 4th of March, 1817, his second term of office expired, and he resigned the presidential chair to his friend James Monroe. Happy in his honorable release from the cares of state, he retired to the leisure and repose of his beautiful retreat at Montpelier. He was within a day's ride of Monticello, and was thus, in the estimation of a Virginian, a near neighbor of Mr. Jefferson. Here, in his paternal home, embosomed among the hills, a victor in life's stern battle, he passed peacefully the remainder of his days.

The mansion was large and commodious, situated at the base of a high and wooded hill. A fine garden behind the house, and a spacious lawn in front, contributed their embellishments to the rural scene, where over countless acres the undulating expanse was covered with the primeval forest. The venerable mother of Mr. Madison still resided with her son, the object of his unceasing and most affectionate attentions. One wing of the mansion was appropriated to her.

" By only opening a door," writes a visitor, " the observer passed from the elegances, refinements, and gayeties of modern life into all that was venerable, respectable, and dignified in gone-by days ; from the airy apartments, windows opening to the ground, hung with light silken drapery, French furniture, light fancy chairs, gay carpets, to the solid and heavy carved and polished mahogany furniture darkened by age, the thick, rich curtains, and other more comfortable adjustments, of our great-grandfathers'. times."

Mr. Madison's health was delicate. He was much beloved by his neighbors and friends ; and, though his union had not been blessed with children, his accomplished and amiable wife was ever to him a source of the greatest happiness. Nineteen years of life still remained to him. He seldom left his home, though he took much interest in the agricultural prosperity of the country, and very cordially coöperated with President Jefferson in watching over the affairs of the university at Charlottesville.

In 1829 he consented to become a member of the convention at Richmond to revise the Constitution of the State. Small in stature, slender and delicate in form, with a countenance full of intelligence, and expressive alike of mildness and dignity, he attracted the attention of all who attended the convention, and was treated with the utmost deference. He seldom addressed the assembly, though he always appeared self-possessed, and watched with unflagging interest the progress of every measure. Though the convention sat for sixteen weeks, he spoke but twice ; but when he did speak, the whole house paused to listen. His voice was feeble, though the enunciation was very distinct. One of the reporters — Mr. Stansbury — relates the following anecdote of the last speech he made. Having carefully written out the speech, he sent the manuscript to President Madison for his revision.

" The next day, as there was a great call for it, and the report had not been returned for publication, I sent my son with a respectful note, requesting the manuscript. My son was a lad of about sixteen, whom I had taken with me to act as amanuensis. On delivering my note, he was received with the utmost politeness, and requested to come up to Mr. Madison's chamber, and wait while he ran his eye over the paper, as company had, until that moment, prevented his attending to it. He did so; and Mr. Madison sat down, pen in hand, to correct the report. The lad stood near him, so that his eye fell on the paper. Coming to a certain sentence in the speech, Mr. Madison struck out a word, and substituted another; but hesitated, and, not feeling quite satisfied with the second word, drew his pen through it also.

"My son was young, ignorant of the world, and unconscious of the solecism of which he was about to be guilty, when, in all simplicity, he *suggested a word.* Yes, he ventured, boy that he was, to suggest to James Madison an improvement in his own speech! Probably no other individual then living would have taken such a liberty. But the sage, instead of regarding such an intrusion with a frown, raised his eyes to the boy's face with a pleased surprise, and said, ' Thank you, sir; it is the very word,' and immediately inserted it. I saw him the next day, and he mentioned the circumstance, with a compliment on the young critic."

On the 28th of June, 1836, Mr. Madison, then eighty-five years of age, fell asleep in death. His memory is embalmed in a nation's veneration and gratitude. Like all public men, exposed to much obloquy in his political life, that obloquy has now so passed away that we can scarcely believe that it ever existed. In a glowing tribute to his memory, uttered by the venerable ex-President, John Quincy Adams, the following words, eloquent in their truthfulness, were uttered : —

"Of that band of benefactors of the human race, the founders of the Constitution of the United States, James Madison is the last who has gone to his reward. Their glorious work has survived them all. They have transmitted the precious bond to us, now entirely a succeeding generation to them. May it never cease to be a voice of admonition to us, of our duty to transmit the inheritance unimpaired to our children of the rising age!"

Mrs. Madison survived her husband thirteen years, and died on the 12th of July, 1849, in the eighty-second year of her age. She was one of the most remarkable women our country has produced; and it is fitting that her memory should descend to posterity in company with that of the companion of her life.

CHAPTER V.

JAMES MONROE.

Parentage and Birth. — Education. — Enters the Army. — A Legislator. — A Senator. — Political Views. — Mission to France. — Bonaparte. — Purchase of Louisiana. — Unfriendliness of England. — Prospective Greatness of America. — Washington's Views of the French Revolution. — Colonel Monroe Governor. — Secretary both of War and of State. — Elected to the Presidency. — Northern Tour. — Purchase of Florida. — Sympathy with Revolutionary Soldiers. — The Monroe Doctrine. — Retirement and Death.

MANY years ago there was a hotly contested election in Virginia, when two young men, James Madison and James Monroe, were rival.

RESIDENCE OF JAMES MONROE.

candidates for some local office. The friends of both parties were exhausting their energies to bring every voter to the polls. A very infirm and aged man was transported from a considerable distance, in a wagon, by the friends of Mr. Madison. As he was sitting in the building, waiting for his opportunity to vote, the name of James Monroe struck his half-paralyzed ear. He started up, and inquired if James Monroe was the son of the man of that name who some years ago lived and died in the province. Upon being told that he was the grandson of that person, the old man exclaimed with emotion, —

" Then I shall vote for James Monroe. His grandfather befriended me when I first came into the country, fed me and clothed me, and I lived in his house. I do not know James Madison. I shall vote for James Monroe."

Virtues seem to be often hereditary. That same spirit of benevolence which prompted the grandfather to feed and clothe and shelter the child of want descended to his children and his children's children. The Monroe family were among the first who emigrated to this country, and selected their home in what is now Westmoreland County, Va., — that beautiful expanse of fertile land which is spread out on the western banks of the Potomac. They were the near neighbors of the Washington family ; and being the owners of a large estate, were in comparative opulence.

James Monroe, who became fifth President of the United States, was born upon his father's plantation on the 28th of April, 1758. At that time Virginia presented an aspect somewhat resembling feudal Europe in the Middle Ages. Here and there, in wide dispersion, were to be seen the aristocratic mansions of the planters, while near by were clustered the cheerless hovels of the poor and debased laborers. There were intelligence, culture, luxury, in the saloons of the master; debasement, ignorance, barbarism, in the cabins of the slaves.

James Monroe, in childhood, like all his predecessors thus far in the presidential chair, enjoyed all the advantages of education which the country could then afford. He was early sent to a very fine classical school, and at the age of sixteen entered William and Mary College. It was his intention to study law. But the cloud of the great Revolution which sundered the colonies from the mother-country was gathering blackness ; and young Monroe, an earnest, impetuous, vigorous youth, whose blood coursed fiercely through his veins, could not resist his impatience to become an active partici-pator in the scenes which were opening.

In 1776, when he had been in college but two years, the Declaration of Independence was adopted, and our feeble militia, without arms or ammunition or clothing, were struggling against the trained armies of England. James Monroe left college, hastened to General Washington's headquarters at New York, and enrolled himself as a cadet in the army.

It was one of the gloomiest hours in our history. The British were sweeping all before them. Our disheartened troops were deserting in great numbers; and the Tories, favoring the cause of England, were daily becoming more boastful and defiant. But James Monroe belonged to the class of the indomitable. With courage which never faltered, he took his place in the ranks. Firmly yet sadly he shared in the melancholy retreat from Harlem Heights and White Plains, and accompanied the dispirited army as it fled before its foes through New Jersey. In four months after the Declaration of Independence, the patriots had been beaten in seven battles.

At Trenton, Lieutenant Monroe so distinguished himself, receiving a wound in his shoulder, that he was promoted to a captaincy. Upon recovering from his wound, he was invited to act as aide to Lord Sterling; and in that capacity he took an active part in the battles of Brandywine, Germantown, and Monmouth. At Germantown he stood by the side of Lafayette when the French marquis received his wound. General Washington, who had formed a high idea of young Monroe's abilities, sent him to Virginia to raise a new regiment, of which he was to be colonel; but so exhausted was Virginia at that time, that the effort proved unsuccessful. He, however, received his commission.

Finding no opportunity to enter the army as a commissioned officer, he returned to his original plan of studying law, and entered the office of Thomas Jefferson, who was then Governor of Virginia. Mr. Jefferson had a large and admirable library, and inspired his pupil with zeal for study. He developed a very noble character, frank, manly, sincere. Abounding with kindliness of feeling, and scorning everything ignoble, he won the love of all who knew him. Mr. Jefferson said of him, —

"James Monroe is so perfectly honest, that if his soul were turned inside out there would not be found a spot on it."

In 1782, when but twenty-three years of age, he was elected to the Assembly of Virginia, and was also appointed a member of the Executive Council. The next year he was chosen delegate to the Continental Congress for a term of three years. He was present at Annapolis when Washington surrendered his commission of commander-in-chief. Young as Colonel Monroe was, he proved himself in Congress a very efficient man of business.

With Washington, Jefferson, and Madison, he felt deeply the inefficiency of the old Articles of Confederation, and urged the formation of a new Constitution, which should invest the central government with something like national power. Influenced by these views, he introduced a resolution that Congress should be empowered to regulate trade, and to lay an impost duty of five per cent. The resolution was referred to a committee of which he was chairman. The report, and the discussion which rose upon it, led to the convention of five States at Annapolis, and the subsequent general convention at Philadelphia, which, in 1787, drafted the Constitution of the United States.

At this time there was a controversy between New York and Massachusetts in reference to their boundaries. The high esteem in which Colonel Monroe was held is indicated by the fact that he was appointed one of the judges to decide the controversy. While in New York attending Congress, he formed a matrimonial connection with Miss Kortright, a young lady distinguished alike for her beauty and her accomplishments. For nearly fifty years this happy union continued unbroken, a source of almost unalloyed happiness to both of the parties. In London and in Paris, as in her own country, Mrs. Monroe won admiration and affection by the loveliness of her person, the brilliancy of her intellect, and the amiability of her character.

Returning to Virginia, Colonel Monroe commenced the practice of law at Fredericksburg. He was almost immediately elected to a seat in the state Legislature; and the next year he was chosen a member of the Virginia Convention, which was assembled to decide upon the acceptance or rejection of the Constitution which had been drawn up at Philadelphia, and was now submitted to the several States. Deeply as he felt the imperfections of the old confederacy, he was opposed to the new Constitution, thinking, with many others of the Republican party, that it gave too much power to the central government, and not enough to the individual States. Still he retained the esteem of his friends, who were its warm supporters, and who, notwithstanding his opposition, secured its adoption. In 1789 he became a member of the United States Senate, which office he held acceptably to his constituents, and with honor to himself, for four years. Every month the line of distinction between the two great parties which divided the nation, the Federal and the Republican, was growing more distinct. The two prominent ideas which now separated them were, that the Republican party was in sympathy with France, and was also in favor of such a strict construction of the Constitution as to give the central government as little power and the state governments as much power as the Constitution would warrant. The Federalists sympathized with England, and were in favor of a liberal construction of the Constitution, which would give as much power to the central government as that document could possibly authorize.

Mr. Monroe, having opposed the Constitution as not leaving enough power with the States, of course became more and more identified with the Republican party. Thus he found himself in cordial coöperation with Jefferson and Madison. The great Republican party became the dominant power which ruled the land. But we can imagine the shades of John Adams and Alexander Hamilton rising from their graves in the midst of our awful civil war, and exclaiming, sadly yet triumphantly, " Did we not tell you so? Has it not been that very doctrine of state sovereignty which has plunged our land into this conflict? and have you not found it necessary, that you might save the country from destruction, to arm the Constitution with those very powers which we were so anxious to stamp upon it ? "

The leading Federalists and Republicans were alike noble men, consecrating all their energies to the good of the nation. Two more honest men or more pure patriots than John Adams the Federalist, and James Monroe the Republican, never breathed. In building up this majestic nation, which is destined to eclipse all Grecian and Assyrian greatness, the combination of their antagonisms was needed to create the right equilibrium. And yet each, in his day, was denounced as almost a demon. Let this consideration, hereafter, allay the bitterness of party strife.

George Washington was then President. England had espoused the cause of the Bourbons against the principles of the French Revolution. All Europe was drawn into the conflict. We were feeble, and far away. President Washington issued a proclamation of neutrality between these contending powers. France had helped us in the struggle for our liberties. All the despotisms of Europe were now combined to prevent the French from escaping from tyranny a thousand-fold worse than that which we had endured. Colonel Monroe, more magnanimous than prudent, was anxious that, at whatever hazard, we should help our old allies in their extremity. It was the impulse of a generous and a noble nature. He violently opposed the President's proclamation as ungrateful and wanting in magnanimity.

Washington, who could appreciate such a character, developed his calm, serene, almost divine greatness, by appointing that very James Monroe who was denouncing the policy of the government, as the minister of that government to the republic of France. He was directed by Washington to express to the French people our warmest sympathy, communicating to them corresponding resolves approved by the President, and adopted by both houses of Congress.

Mr. Monroe was welcomed by the National Convention in France with the most enthusiastic demonstrations of respect and affection. He was publicly introduced to that body, and received the embrace of the president, Merlin de Douay, after having been addressed in a speech glowing with congratulations, and with expressions of desire that harmony might ever exist between the two countries. The flags of the two republics were intertwined in the hall of the convention. Mr. Monroe presented the American colors, and received those of France in return. The course which he pursued in Paris was so annoying to England, and to the friends of England in this country, that, near the close of Washington's administration, Mr. Monroe was recalled.

Mr. Pickering, Secretary of State, who was a fanatical hater of France, and proportionably an adulator of England, sent an angry dispatch to Mr. Monroe, charging him with "expressing a solicitude for the welfare of the French republic in a style too warm and affectionate, by which we were likely to give offense to other countries, particularly to England."

In reply to this, Mr. Monroe states in his "View" the instructions he received from Washington, which are interesting as showing the personal feelings of Washington towards France. He writes, —

"My instructions enjoined it on me to use my utmost endeavors to inspire the French government with perfect confidence in the solicitude which the President felt for the success of the French Revolution; of his preference of France to all other nations, as the friend and ally of the United States; of the grateful sense which we still retained for the important services that were rendered us by France in the course of our Revolution; and to declare in explicit terms, that although neutrality was the lot we preferred, yet, in case we embarked in the war, it would be on her side, and against her enemies, be they who they might."

In 1796 President Washington addressed the French minister in the following words: "My best wishes are irresistibly excited, whensoever, in any country, I see an oppressed nation unfurl the banner of freedom; but, above all, the events of the French Revolution have produced the deepest solicitude as well as the highest admiration. To call your nation brave, were to pronounce but common praise. Wonderful people! Ages to come will read with astonishment your brilliant exploits. In delivering to you these sentiments, I express not my feelings only, but those of my fellow-citizens, in relation to the commencement, the progress, and the issue of the French Revolution."

All despotic Europe combined against the enfranchised nation. In the frenzy of the unequal fight, France was plunged into anarchy; from which she was rescued by Napoleon, into whose imperial arms, in her dire necessity, she had cast herself. And then all despotic Europe turned its arms against that one man. He was crushed. The unfurled banner of "Equal Rights," which he had so grandly borne aloft, was trampled in the dust; and subjugated France again bowed her neck to the old feudal tyranny.

While Mr. Monroe was our minister in France, Mr. Jay, with strong English proclivities, was our ambassador at the court of St. James. He was ever ready to enter into a commercial treaty which would favor that country at the expense of our old ally. Mr. Jay, with other men of his party, scouting the idea that any thanks were due to France for the aid she had rendered us in the Revolution, and was not disposed to discriminate in the least in her favor. Hence there was intense antagonism between Colonel Monroe and Mr. Jay.

Colonel Monroe, after his return, wrote a book of four hundred pages, entitled "A View of the Conduct of the Executive in Foreign Affairs." In this work he very ably advocated his side of the question ; but, with magnanimity characteristic of the man, he recorded a warm tribute to the patriotism, ability, and spotless integrity of John Jay ; and, in subsequent years, he expressed in warmest terms his perfect veneration for the character of George Washington.

Shortly after his return to this country, Colonel Monroe was elected Governor of Virginia, and held that office for three years, — the period limited by the Constitution. In the year 1802 it was announced that Spain had ceded to France that vast territory, extending from the Mississippi to the Pacific, which was called Louisiana. Napoleon, then at the head of the armies of revolutionary France, with " Liberté, Fraternité, Égalité," inscribed on their banners, was trampling down those despots who had banded together to force back the execrated old *régime* of the Bourbons upon the emancipated empire. Most of our knowledge of what was transpiring on the continent of Europe came to us through the English press. Never had a story been more falsely told than that press had narrated, — the struggle of the French people for equal rights, in the revolution and in the establishment of the empire.

The name of Bonaparte became a terror throughout the United States. Mothers frightened their disobedient children with the threat that Bonaparte would get them. It was proclaimed that the conqueror of Europe had only reserved us as his last victim ; that, taking possession of this vast territory of Louisiana, and landing upon it countless legions of his triumphant veterans, he would sweep the country from New Orleans to Canada, establish his empire here, and trample our liberties in the dust. The writer of this well remembers his terror, when a child, in contemplation of this invasion by that Napoleonic monster whom we had been taught to regard as the embodiment of all evil.

Mr. Livingston was then our minister to France. He drew up a very able memorial to the First Consul, arguing that it would be for the true interest of both countries that France should cede the province of Louisiana to the United States. It was so manifest that the United States must have the control of the mouths of the Mississippi, through which alone the most majestic valley on our globe could have access to the ocean, that our most sagacious statesmen felt assured that, if we could not obtain this province by treaty, it would inevitably involve us erelong in war.

Mr. Jefferson was then President. He was beloved in France. The memory of James Monroe was cherished there with universal respect and affection. He was accordingly sent to coöperate with Chancellor Livingston to endeavor to obtain by treaty, if possible, this vast possession. Their united efforts were successful. For the comparatively small sum of fifteen millions of dollars, though a very large one for us in those days, "the entire territory of Orleans, and district of Louisiana," were added to the United States. It has been truly said that this was probably the largest transfer of real estate which was ever made since Adam was presented with the fee-simple of Paradise. The country thus obtained was in extent equal to the whole previous territory of the Union. It is universally admitted that Mr. Monroe's influence was very prominent in this measure, and he ever regarded it as the most important of his public services. We have now such a territory in magnitude, and adaptation to human wants, as no other nation on this globe ever possessed.

From France Mr. Monroe went to England to obtain from that government some recognition of our rights as neutrals, and to remonstrate against those odious impressments of our seamen which were fast rousing the indignation of the country to the highest pitch. But England was unrelenting. He then went to Spain, by way of Paris, where he saw Napoleon crowned. In Spain he endeavored, though unavailingly, to adjust a controversy which had arisen respecting the eastern boundary of the territory, which that government had ceded to France, and France to us. Napoleon, in his cession, had copied the same words which Spain had used in conveying the territory to France.

Our relations with England were daily becoming more menacing. We would not willingly revive old griefs to perpetuate animosities: we would gladly have past wrongs forgotten, that kindly sympathies may pervade the whole human brotherhood. But it is the duty of the biographer and the historian to hold up the errors of the past as a warning for the future. There is not a nation on this globe, savage or civilized, which regards with cordial friendship the British government. For the last half-century England has been the leading power among the nations. Her demeanor has been arrogant, haughty, and overbearing. The powerful have been repelled by her proud assumptions, and the weak have been trampled upon in undisguised contempt. England is no longer the leading power in the world, and there are none who mourn to see her shorn of her strength.

Let America take warning. It is as important that a nation should have the good will of all surrounding powers as that an individual should be loved by his neighbors. Let us be courteous, obliging, and unselfish in our intercourse with the strong, and sympathetic, gentle, and helping to the weak: Let us try to prove the world's great benefactor, the friend and comforter of our brother man everywhere struggling beneath the heavy burden of life.

England, despising our feeble navy, forbade our trading with France ; and seized and confiscated mercilessly our merchant-ships bound to any port in France or Spain, wherever her cruisers could arrest them. Mr. Monroe again returned to England, almost in the character of a suppliant; for our government was extremely averse to adopt any measures which could lead to war. The administration was even taunted with the declaration, that it " could not be kicked into a war." No redress could be obtained. Mr. Monroe returned to this country, bearing with him a treaty which was so very unsatisfactory that the President was not willing to submit it to the Senate. Plundered merchants and ruined shipowners poured in upon Congress petitions and remonstrances, and there was a cry throughout the land that that government was recreant to its trust which did not protect its citizens from outrage.

At this time Mr. Monroe, at the age of forty-eight, returned to his quiet home in Virginia, and with his wife and children, and an ample competence from his paternal estate, enjoyed a few years of domestic repose.

In the year 1809 Mr. Jefferson's second term of office expired. Many of the Republican party were anxious to nominate James Monroe as his successor. The majority were in favor of Mr. Madison. Mr. Jefferson also favored Mr. Madison, as being the more moderate man, and the more likely to carry the votes of the whole party. Mr. Monroe withdrew his name, and was soon after chosen a second time Governor of Virginia. He soon resigned that office to accept the position of Secretary of State, offered him by President Madison. The correspondence which he then carried on with the British government demonstrated that there was no hope of any peaceful adjustment of our difficulties with the Cabinet of St. James. War was consequently declared in June, 1812. Immediately after the sack of Washington, the Secretary of War resigned ; and Mr. Monroe, at the earnest request of Mr. Madison, assumed the additional duties of the War Department, without resigning his office of Secretary of State. It has been confidently stated, that, had Colonel Monroe's energy been in the War Department a few months earlier, the disaster at Washington would not have occurred.

The duties now devolving upon Mr. Monroe were extremely arduous. Ten thousand men, picked from the veteran armies of England, were sent, with a powerful fleet, to New Orleans, to acquire possession of the mouths of the Mississippi. Our finances were in the most deplorable condition. The treasury was exhausted, and our credit gone ; and yet it was necessary to make the most vigorous preparations to meet the foe. In this crisis James Monroe, the Secretary of War, with virtue unsurpassed in Greek or Roman story, stepped forward, and pledged his own individual credit as subsidiary to that of the nation, and thus succeeded in placing the city of New Orleans in such a posture of defense that it was enabled successfully to repel the invader.

Mr. Monroe was truly the armor-bearer of President Madison, and the most efficient business man in his Cabinet. His energy, in his double capacity of Secretary both of State and War, pervaded all the departments of the country. With the most singular unselfishness, regardless both of his private interests and his political popularity, he advocated every measure which in his judgment would aid in securing the triumph of his country. He proposed to increase the army to a hundred thousand men, — a measure which he deemed absolutely necessary to save us from ignominious defeat, but which, at the same time, he knew would render his name so unpopular as to preclude the possibility of his being a successful candidate for the Presidency. He conversed freely with his friends upon the subject, and calmly decided to renounce all thoughts of the presidential chair, while he urged that conscription which would enter every dwelling in search of a soldier.

The happy result of the conference at Ghent in securing peace rendered the increase of the army unnecessary; but it is not too much to say, that James Monroe placed in the hands of Andrew

Jackson the weapon with which he beat off the foe at New Orleans. Upon the return of peace Mr. Monroe resigned the Department of War, devoting himself exclusively to the duties of the Secretary of State. These he continued to discharge until the close of President Madison's administration, with zeal which never abated, and with an ardor of self-devotion which made him almost forgetful of the claims of fortune, health, or life.

Mr. Madison's second term of office expired in March, 1817; and Mr. Monroe, thoroughly acquainted with all the affairs of the nation, and perfectly versed in all the duties before him, succeeded to the Presidency. He was the candidate of the Republican party, now taking the name of Democratic Republican; and was chosen by a large majority. There seemed to be for a time a lull in party strife. Mr. Monroe was a man of ability, at home in all statesman-like duties, more familiar than perhaps any other person with our internal and foreign relations: he was a man of unblemished character, of honesty of purpose, and purity of patriotism which no man could question. A better choice could not have been made. His inaugural was conciliatory, and pleased all. The Constitution which he had opposed, wishing merely to introduce some amendments before it was adopted, he now admitted to be nearly perfect.

It has been said, happy is that nation which has no history; for history is but a record of revolutions and battles. There is but little to be recorded during the eight years in which President Monroe was at the head of the administration of our government. They were years of prosperity and peace. In forming his Cabinet, Mr. Monroe placed the Department of State in the hands of John Quincy Adams. Florida was purchased of Spain for five millions of dollars, by the exercise of that power which Mr. Monroe, in his inexperienced days, had been so reluctant to confer upon the general government.

In June of 1817 President Monroe took a very extensive journey through the States, visiting all the fortifications. He was every-where received with enthusiasm. He was conveyed up the Delaware from Wilmington to the navy-yard in Philadelphia in a barge of the Franklin (seventy-four). The barge was lined and trimmed with crimson velvet, and rowed by sixteen oarsmen, dressed in scarlet vests, white sleeves and trousers. The President wore a dark-blue coat, buff vest, doeskin buff-colored breeches, and top boots, with a military cocked-hat of the fashion of the Revolution, and a black ribbon cockade. His route led him through New York, New Haven, Hartford, and Springfield, to Boston. His reception in Boston was very imposing. A cavalcade of citizens met him on the Neck, and escorted him through the principal streets of the city to rooms sumptuously prepared for his reception in the Exchange Coffee House. Salutes were fired from Dorchester Heights, the Common, and the forts in the harbor. State Street was brilliantly

THE BARGE.

decorated; and the crowd which was gathered in the commercial emporium of New England was greater than had ever been seen there since the visit of Washington.

From Boston he passed through New Hampshire and Vermont to Plattsburg in New York, and thence continued his journey to Ogdensburg, Sackett's Harbor, and Detroit, returning to Washington the latter part of September. His long and fatiguing tour, which then occupied four months, could now be easily performed in three weeks.

When President Monroe was a young man of eighteen, he was wounded at the battle of Trenton. Passing through Hanover, N. H., in this tour, he called upon the widow of President Wheelock of Dartmouth College, who, when a young lady at her father's house, had with her own hands prepared the bandages with which the surgeon had dressed the wound. In pensive memory of the past, the care-worn statesman and the bereaved widow exchanged their sympathetic greetings, and then separated, not again to meet on this earth.

All along his route President Monroe met his old companions in arms, many of whom were impoverished. One friend he found whom he had known as a young, scholarly, accomplished officer, and who had contributed lavishly of his fortune to feed and clothe the soldiers of his regiment, but whose threadbare garments too plainly bespoke the poverty which had come with his gray hairs. The President was deeply moved, and, on his retiring, spoke with great warmth of the neglect of our country in making provision for the wants of those who had shed their blood for our independence. On his return to Washington he exerted himself in securing a pension law to cheer the declining years of these fast-disappearing veterans.

In 1821 President Monroe was reëlected, with scarcely any opposition. Out of 232 electoral votes, Mr. Monroe had 231. The slavery question, which subsequently assumed such formidable dimensions, threatening to whelm the whole Union in ruins, now began to make its appearance. The State of Missouri, which had been carved out of that immense territory which we had purchased of France, applied for admission to the Union with a slavery constitution. There were not a few who foresaw the evils impending. In the long and warm debate which ensued, Mr. Lourie of Maryland said, —

"Sir, if the alternative be, as gentlemen broadly intimate, a dissolution of the Union, or the extension of slavery over this whole western country, I, for one, will choose the former. I do not say this lightly. I am aware that the idea is a dreadful one. The choice is a dreadful one. Either side of the alternative fills my mind with horror. I have not, however, yet despaired of the Republic." .

After the debate of a week, it was decided that Missouri could not be admitted into the Union with slavery. The question was at length settled by a compromise, proposed by Henry Clay. Missouri was admitted with slavery on the 10th of May, 1821; and slavery was prohibited over all the territory ceded by France, north of thirty-six degrees, thirty minutes, north latitude.

The famous "Monroe Doctrine," of which so much has recently been said, originated in this way: In the year 1823 it was rumored that the Holy Alliance was about to interfere to prevent the establishment of republican liberty in the European colonies in South America. President Monroe wrote to his old friend Thomas Jefferson, then the sage of Monticello, for advice in the emergency. In the reply, under date of October 24th, Mr. Jefferson writes upon the supposition that our attempt to resist this European movement might lead to war, —

"Its object is to introduce and establish the American system of keeping out of our land all foreign powers; of never permitting those of Europe to intermeddle with the affairs of our nation. It is to maintain our own principle, not to depart from it."

A few weeks after this, on the 2d of December, 1823, President Monroe sent a message to Congress, declaring it to be the policy of this government not to entangle ourselves with the broils of Europe, and not to allow Europe to interfere with affairs of nations on the American continents; and the doctrine was announced, that any attempt on the part of the European powers "to extend their system to any portion of this hemisphere would be regarded by the United States as dangerous to our peace and safety."

On the 4th of March, 1825, Mr. Monroe, surrendering the presidential chair to his Secretary of State, John Quincy Adams, retired, with the universal respect of the nation, to his private residence at Oak Hill, in Loudoun County, Va. His time had been so entirely consecrated to the country, that he had neglected his own pecuniary interests, and was deeply involved in debt. In devotion to his duties, he had engaged "in labors outlasting the daily circuit of the sun, and outwatching the vigils of the night." The welfare of the country — the whole country — had ever been the one prominent thought in his mind. If we allow the panorama of his life to pass rapidly before us, we see him, just emerging from boyhood, weltering in blood on the field of Trenton; then, still a youth, he is seated among the sages of the land, forming the laws; then he moves with power which commands attention and respect in the courts of Britain, France, and Spain, defending the rights of his country; then his native State raises him to the highest honor in her gift, and twice places in his hand the sceptre of gubernatorial power; again we behold him successfully forging the thunderbolts of war with which to repel invasion, while at the same time he conducts our diplomatic correspondence, and frames our foreign policy, with jealous and often hostile nations; and again we see him, by the almost unanimous voice of his countrymen, placed in the highest post of honor the nation could offer, — the Presidency of the United States; and then, with dignity, he retires to a humble home, a poor man in worldly wealth, but rich in all those excellences which can ennoble humanity.

For many years Mrs. Monroe was in such feeble health that she rarely appeared in public. In 1830 Mr. Monroe took up his residence with his son-in-law in New York, where he died on the 4th of July, 1831, at the age of seventy-three years. The citizens of New York conducted his obsequies with pageants more imposing than had ever been witnessed there before. Our country will ever cherish his memory with pride, gratefully enrolling his name in the list of its benefactors, pronouncing him the worthy successor of the illustrious men who had preceded him in the presidential chair.

CHAPTER VI.

JOHN QUINCY ADAMS.

Birth and Childhood. — Education in Europe. — Private Secretary. — Enters Harvard College. — Studies Law — Minister to the Netherlands. — Commendation of Washington. — Other Missions. — Return to America. — Elected to the Massachusetts Senate. — To the National House of Representatives. — Alienation of the Federalists. — Professor of Rhetoric. — Mission to Russia. — Anecdote of Alexander. — Treaty of Ghent. — Secretary of State. — President. — Unscrupulous Opposition. — Retirement. — Returned to the House of Representatives. — Signal Services. — Public Appreciation. — Death.

JOHN QUINCY ADAMS, the sixth President of the United States, was born in the rural home of his honored father, John Adams, in

RESIDENCE OF JOHN QUINCY ADAMS.

Quincy, Mass., on the 11th of July, 1767. His mother, a woman of exalted worth, watched over his childhood during the almost constant absence of his father. At the village school he commenced his education, giving at an early period indications of superior mental endowments. When but eight years of age he stood with his mother upon an eminence, listening to the booming of the great battle on Bunker's Hill, and gazing upon the smoke and flame billowing up from the conflagration of Charlestown. Often, during the siege of Boston, he watched the shells thrown day and night by the combatants.

When but eleven years old he took a tearful adieu of his mother and was rowed out in a small boat to a ship anchored in the bay, to sail with his father for Europe, through a fleet of hostile British cruisers. The bright, animated boy spent a year and a half in Paris, where his father was associated with Franklin and Lee as minister plenipotentiary. His intelligence attracted the notice of these distinguished men, and he received from them flattering marks of attention.

Mr. John Adams had scarcely returned to this country in 1779 ere he was again sent abroad, empowered to negotiate a treaty of peace with England, whenever England should be disposed to end the war. Again John Quincy accompanied his father. On this voyage he commenced a diary, noting down the remarkable events of each day; which practice he continued, with but few interruptions, until his death. With his active mind ever alert, he journeyed, with his father from Ferrol in Spain, where the frigate landed, to Paris. Here he applied himself with great diligence, for six months, to study; then accompanied his father to Holland, where he entered, first a school in Amsterdam, and then the University of Leyden. About a year from this time, in 1781, when the manly boy was but fourteen years of age, he was selected by Mr. Dana, our minister to the Russian court, as his private secretary.

In this school of incessant labor and of ennobling culture he spent fourteen months, and then returned to Holland through Sweden, Denmark, Hamburg, and Bremen. This long journey he took alone, in the winter, when in his sixteenth year. Again he resumed his studies, under a private tutor, at the Hague. Thence, in the spring of 1782, he accompanied his father to Paris, traveling leisurely, and forming acquaintance with the most distinguished men on the Continent; examining architectual remains, galleries of paintings, and all renowned works of art. At Paris he again became the associate of the most illustrious men of all lands in the contemplation of the loftiest temporal themes which can engross the human mind.   After a short visit to England, he returned to Paris, and consecrated all his energies to study until May, 1785, when he returned to America, leaving his father our ambassador at the court of St. James.   To a brilliant young man of eighteen, who had seen much of the world, and who was familiar with the etiquette of courts, a residence with his father in London, under such circumstances, must have been extremely attractive; but, with judgment very rare in one of his age, he preferred to return to America to complete his education in an American college.   He wished then to study law, that, with an honorable profession, he might be able to obtain an independent support.

The advancement which he had already made in education was such that in 1786 he entered the junior class in Harvard University.   His character, attainments, and devotion to study secured alike the respect of his classmates and the faculty, and he graduated with the second honor of his class.   The oration he delivered on this occasion upon the " Importance of Public Faith to the Well-being of a Community," was published; an event very rare in this or in any other land.

Upon leaving college, at the age of twenty, he studied law for three years with the Hon. Theophilus Parsons, in Newburyport. In 1790 he opened a law office in Boston.   The profession was crowded with able men, and the fees were small.   The first year he had no clients; but not a moment was lost, as his eager mind traversed the fields of all knowledge.   The second year passed away; still no clients; and still he was dependent upon his parents for support.   Anxiously he entered upon the third year.   He had learned to labor and to wait.   The reward now came, — a reward richly merited by the purity of his character, the loftiness of his principles, and his intense application to every study which would aid him to act well his part in life.   Clients began to enter his office; and before the close of the year he was so crowded with business that all solicitude respecting a support was at an end.

When Great Britain commenced war against France, in 1793, to arrest the progress of the French Revolution, Mr. Adams wrote some articles, urging entire neutrality on the part of the United States. The view was not a popular one.   Many felt that as France had helped us, we were bound to help France. But President Washington coincided with Mr. Adams, and issued his proclamation of neutrality. His writings at this time in the Boston journals attracted national attention, and gave him so high a reputation for talent, and familiarity with our diplomatic relations, that in June, 1794, he, being then but twenty-seven years of age, was appointed by Washington resident minister at the Netherlands.

Sailing from Boston in July, he reached London in October, where he was immediately admitted to the deliberations of Messrs. Jay and Pinckney, assisting them in negotiating a commercial treaty with Great Britain. After thus spending a fortnight in London, he proceeded to the Hague, where he arrived just after Holland was taken possession of by the French under Pichegru. The French gathered around Mr. Adams, as the representative of a nation which had just successfully passed through that struggle for liberty in which they were then engaged.

In the agitated state of Europe, swept by the great armies struggling for and against "equal rights for all men," there was but little that a peaceful ambassador could then accomplish; but being one of the most methodical and laborious of men, he devoted himself to official duties, the claims of society, reading the ancient classics, and familiarizing himself with the languages of modern Europe. Every hour had its assigned duty. Every night he reviewed what he had done for the day; and at the close of every month and every year he subjected his conduct to rigorous retrospection.

In July, 1797, he left the Hague to go to Portugal as minister plenipotentiary. Washington at this time wrote to his father, John Adams, —

"Without intending to compliment the father or the mother, or to censure any others, I give it as my decided opinion, that Mr. Adams is the most valuable character which we have abroad; and there remains no doubt in my mind that he will prove himself the ablest of all our diplomatic corps."

On his way to Portugal, upon his arrival in London, he met with dispatches directing him to the court of Berlin, but requesting him to remain in London until he should receive his instructions. While waiting he was married to an American lady to whom he had been previously engaged, — Miss Louisa Catharine Johnson, daughter of Mr. Joshua Johnson, American consul in London; a lady endowed with that beauty and those accomplishments which eminently fitted her to move in the elevated sphere for which she was destined.

Mr. Adams was very reluctant to accept the mission to Berlin, as it was an appointment made by his father, who had succeeded Washington in the presidential chair. But his father wrote to him, informing him of the earnest wish of Washington that the country might not lose the benefit of his familiarity with the European courts. To his mother, John Quincy wrote, in reply, —

"I know with what delight your truly maternal heart has received every testimonial of Washington's favorable voice. It is among the most precious gratifications of my life to reflect upon the pleasure which my conduct has given to my parents. How much, my dear mother, is required of me to support and justify such a judgment as that which you have copied into your letter!"

He reached Berlin with his wife in November, 1797, where he remained until July, 1799, when, having fulfilled all the purposes of his mission, he solicited his recall. In the mean time he traveled extensively through the German States, writing a series of letters which were subsequently published. As soon as permission came for his return, he embarked, and reached the United States in September, 1801.

Soon after his return, in 1802, he was chosen to the Senate of Massachusetts from Boston, and then was elected senator of the United States for six years from the 4th of March, 1804. Alike the friend of Washington and Jefferson, with cordial commendations from them both, he was in an admirable position to take an independent stand, unbiased by partisan prejudices. His reputation, his ability, and his experience, placed him immediately among the most prominent and influential members of that body. In every measure which his judgment approved, he cordially supported Mr. Jefferson's administration. Especially did he sustain the government in its measures of resistance to the encroachments of England, destroying our commerce and insulting our flag. There was no man in America more familiar with the arrogance of the British court upon these points, and no one more resolved to present a firm resistance.

This course, so truly patriotic, and which scarcely a voice will now be found to condemn, alienated from him the Federal party dominant in Boston, and subjected him to censure. In 1805 he was chosen professor of rhetoric in Harvard College ; and this indefatigable man, in addition to his senatorial duties, entered vigorously upon a course of preparatory studies, reviewing his classics, and searching the literature of Europe for materials for his lectures. The lectures he thus prepared were subsequently published, and constitute enduring memorials of his genius and his industry.

On the 22d of June, 1807, an event occurred to which we have referred, and to which it is necessary to allude more particularly.

On the 7th of June, 1807, the United States frigate Chesapeake proceeded to sea from Norfolk. The British man-of-war Leopard, knowing that she was to sail, had preceded her by a few hours, keeping advantage of the weather-gauge. As soon as the Chesapeake was fairly out to sea, the Leopard came down upon her, hailed her, and said she had dispatches to send on board. Commodore Barron of the Chesapeake answered the hail, and said that he would receive a boat. A British lieutenant came on board, and presented an order from the British admiral, which stated that he had reason to believe that there were four British subjects among the seamen of the Chesapeake, and ordered Commodore Barron to muster the crew that he might select them.

The commodore refused. As soon as informed of this by the return of the boat's crew, the Leopard commenced firing upon the Chesapeake, and for fifteen minutes continued pouring in her broadsides, though the Chesapeake was in such a condition, thus taken by surprise, as not to be able to answer by a single gun. Three men were killed, and Commodore Barron and nine others wounded. The Chesapeake's flag was struck. The English captain refused to receive her as a prize, but took four men from the crew, whom he claimed as Englishmen. One of these soon after died ; one he hung as a deserter ; the two others were eventually returned to the Chesapeake as Americans.

This outrage roused general indignation. A meeting was called at the State House in Boston. But few Federalists attended. Mr. Adams presented resolutions, which were unanimously adopted. His father, the ex-President, acted with him in this movement. For this they were both denounced as apostates from the Federal party. President Jefferson called a special meeting of Congress to act upon this affair. Mr. Adams earnestly supported the measures of Mr. Jefferson's Cabinet, when it proposed, in response to this outrage, that —

" No British armed vessel shall be permitted to enter the harbors and waters under the jurisdiction of the United States, except when forced in by distress, by the dangers of the sea, or when charged with public dispatches, or coming as a public packet."

John Quincy Adams, in a letter to James Otis, dated March, 1808, writes, " Examine the official returns from the Department of State. They give the names of between four and five thousand men impressed since the commencement of the present war, of which *not one fifth part were British subjects*. I hazard little in saying that more than three fourths were native Americans. If it be said that some of these men, though appearing on the face of the returns American citizens, were really British subjects, and had fraudulently procured their protections, I reply, that this number must be far exceeded by the cases of citizens impressed which never reach the Department of State. The American consul in London estimates the number of impressments during the war at *three times* the amount of the names returned." Thus England dragged from our ships *fifteen thousand men*, whom she claimed as her subjects, and forced into her men-of-war to fight her battles. There was no trial by a court to substantiate a claim. Neither Tripoli nor Algiers ever perpetrated a grosser outrage.

Mr. Adams, averring that the course the administration proposed was the only safe one for the country, became upon this point separated from his Federal friends, and allied to the administration ; and his services were recognized with gratitude by Mr. Jefferson. The Legislature of Massachusetts gave such unequivocal indication of their displeasure with Mr. Adams, that he addressed to them a letter, stating that he deemed it his duty to support the administration in those measures which to him seemed essential to the dignity and safety of the country ; but, as the Legislature had disapproved of his course, he resigned his seat, that they might have an opportunity to place in the Senate of the United States a member whose views would be more consonant with those which they entertained.

James Lloyd was immediately chosen to fill the place thus vacated by one whose renown filled two hemispheres. Mr. Adams returned to his professorship, not only neglected and avoided by his old friends, but assailed by them with the bitterest invectives. From this weight of obloquy he had no relief but in the approval of his own conscience, and his anticipation of that verdict which posterity has already rendered.

In 1809 Madison succeeded Jefferson in the presidential chair; and he immediately nominated John Quincy Adams minister to St. Petersburg. Washington had declared that Mr. Adams was the ablest of the diplomatic corps, and that he must not think of retiring from that service. Stung by the treatment he had received from the Federalists in Boston, Mr. Adams abandoned the Federal party, and allied himself earnestly with Mr. Madison in his administration.

Resigning his professorship, he embarked at Boston with Mrs. Adams and their youngest son in August, 1809, and, after a stormy passage, reached St. Petersburg on the 23d of October. Twice their ship, which was a merchantman, was stopped and searched by British cruisers; and, but for Mr. Adams's firmness and thorough acquaintance with the law of nations, the ship would not have been permitted to continue to its port of destination.

He was received by the Emperor Alexander alone in his cabinet, and a warm attachment immediately sprang up between those illustrious men; and thus was laid the foundations of that friendship which binds the two nations together to the present day. I have before spoken of the arrogance assumed by the British government in the days of its power, which has alienated from that government the sympathies of all nations. I have spoken of this as a warning to America, now that we are stepping forward to be the leading nation upon the globe. The following anecdote will illustrate this sentiment: —

A short time ago a small party of American military officers were traveling upon the Danube. They met a party of Russian officers. The Russians gave them very manifestly the cold shoulder, so repelling the slightest advances as to indicate emphatically that they desired no acquaintance whatever. After thus traveling together for half a day, one of the Russian officers overheard a remark which led him to step forward, and inquire, " Gentlemen, may I take the liberty to ask if you are Americans ? " " We are," was the response. Instantly they were surrounded with all cordial greetings. " We beg your pardon," said one; " we beg your pardon : but we thought you were English, and we all hate the English."

Mrs. Adams became a great favorite with the imperial family. The emperor, influenced by the kindliness with which he regarded our minister and his family, tendered to the British government the offer of his mediation in the war which soon after broke out between Great Britain and America. Though England declined the mediation, she felt constrained by the offer to propose to treat directly. Thus peace was effected.

The Danish government had sequestered much American property in the ports of Holstein. Upon an intimation from Mr. Adams, the emperor sent word to that government that it would be gratifying to him if the American property could be restored as soon as possible. The request was immediately granted. The foreign ministers at the Russian court were generally living in the greatest magnificence; but Mr. Adams received so small a salary that he was compelled to practice the most rigid economy. He was expected to attend the splendid entertainments of others, but could give none in return. One morning, as he was out walking, he met the emperor, who came cordially up to him, and, clasping his hand, said, —

" Why, Mr. Adams, it is a hundred years since I have seen you! " After some common observations, he inquired, " Do you intend to take a house in the country this summer? "

" No," Mr. Adams replied: " I had that intention for some time, but have given it up."

" And why? " inquired the emperor. Then, observing a little hesitation in Mr. Adams's manner, he relieved him from his embarrassment by saying in perfect good humor, and with a smile, " Perhaps it is from considerations of finance."

" Those considerations are often very important," Mr. Adams replied. " You are right," rejoined the emperor: " it is always necessary to proportion one's expenses to one's receipts."

While in Russia Mr. Adams was an intense student. He devoted his attention to the language and history of Russia; to the Chinese trade; to the European system of weights, measures, and coins; to the climate, and astronomical observations; while he kept up a familiar acquaintance with the Greek and Latin classics. In all the universities of Europe a more accomplished scholar could scarcely be found. All through life the Bible constituted an important part of his studies. It was his rule every day to read five chapters. He also read with great attention the works of the most eminent the-

13

ologians. With this eagerness in the pursuit of knowledge, it is not surprising that he should write to a friend, —

"I feel nothing like the tediousness of time. I suffer nothing like *ennui*. Time is too short for me rather than too long. If the day was forty-eight hours, instead of twenty-four, I could employ them all, if I had but eyes and hands to read and write."

In 1811 President Madison nominated Mr. Adams to a seat on the bench of the Supreme Court of the United States; but he declined the appointment. As England had consented, in response to the Russian offer of mediation, to treat for peace, Mr. Adams was appointed, with Mr. Gallatin and Mr. Bayard, to conduct the negotiations. The commissioners met at Ghent. Mr. Adams took the leading part. The Marquis of Wellesley, in commenting upon the treaty which was then entered into, said in the British House of Lords, —

"In my opinion, the American commissioners have shown the most astonishing superiority over the English during the whole of the correspondence."

From Ghent Mr. Adams went to Paris, where he chanced to be when the Emperor Napoleon returned from Elba and again took possession of the Tuileries. Mrs. Adams joined him here; and they proceeded together to London, he having been appointed minister to the British court. He arrived in London on the 25th of May, 1815.

Taking up his residence in the country, about nine miles from London, he again resumed his vigorous habits of study, while attending energetically to his diplomatic duties, and receiving the attentions which his official station and his renown caused to be lavished upon him. Both Mr. and Mrs. Adams were honored with a private audience with the queen, and were present at the marriage of the Princess Charlotte with Leopold. The most eminent men of all classes sought Mr. Adams's acquaintance. He had an interview with Mr. Canning, "in which the illustrious statesman," says Mr. Adams, "seemed desirous to make up by an excess of civility for the feelings he had so constantly manifested against us."

On the 4th of March, 1817, Mr. Monroe took the presidential chair, and immediately appointed Mr. Adams Secretary of State. Taking leave of his numerous friends in public and private life in Europe, he sailed in June, 1817, for the United States. On the

18th of August he again crossed the threshold of his home in Quincy, and, after an absence of eight years, received the embraces of his venerable father and mother, whom he found in perfect health. After a short visit home, he repaired to Washington, and entered upon his new duties, as thoroughly prepared for them, in ability, education, and experience, as one could be. During the eight years of Mr. Monroe's administration, Mr. Adams continued Secretary of State. Few will now contradict the assertion, that the duties of that office were never more ably discharged. Probably the most important measure which Mr. Adams conducted was the purchase of Florida from Spain for five million dollars.

Some time before the close of Mr. Monroe's second term of office, new candidates began to be presented for the presidency. The friends of Mr. Adams brought forward his name, urging in his favor the unblemished purity of his character, his abilities and acquirements, the distinguished services he had rendered his country, and his extraordinary familiarity with all our foreign and domestic relations.

It was an exciting campaign. Party spirit was never more bitter. Two hundred and sixty-one electoral votes were cast. Andrew Jackson received ninety-nine; John Quincy Adams, eighty-four; William H. Crawford, forty-one; Henry Clay, thirty-seven. As there was no choice by the people, the question went to the House of Representatives. Mr. Clay gave the vote of Kentucky to Mr. Adams, and he was elected.

The friends of all the disappointed candidates now combined in a venomous and persistent assault upon Mr. Adams. There is nothing more disgraceful in the past history of our country than the abuse which was poured, in one uninterrupted stream, upon this high-minded, upright, patriotic man. There never was an administration more pure in principles, more conscientiously devoted to the best interests of the country, than that of John Quincy Adams; and never, perhaps, was there an administration more unscrupulously and outrageously assailed. It throws a shade over one's hopes of humanity thus to see patriotism of the most exalted character hunted down as though it were the vilest treason. Mr. Adams, with a mind enlarged by familiarity with all the governments of Europe, and with affections glowing with love for his own country, took his seat in the presidential chair, resolved not to know any partisanship, but only to consult for the interests of the whole republic. He refused to dismiss any man from office for his political views. Under his government, no man suffered for his political opinions. If he were a faithful officer, that was enough. Bitter must have been Mr. Adams's disappointment to find that the nation could not appreciate such nobility of character and conduct. The four years that he occupied the presidential chair must have been years of anguish, imbittered by the reflection, that could he have stooped to the partisanship of dismissing from office every one who did not vote for him, and of filling every post at his disposal with those who would pledge themselves intensely to his support, he might perhaps have fought off his enemies, and have secured a reelection. Virtue does not always, in this world, triumph.

Mr. Adams, in his public manners, was cold and repulsive; though it is said that with his personal friends he was at times very genial. In his public receptions and official intercourse he often appeared " with a formal coldness, that froze like the approach to an iceberg." This chilling address very seriously detracted from his popularity. When the result of the election which placed Mr. Adams in the presidential chair was known, the rival candidates, and especially their friends, experienced disappointment amounting to anguish. Mr. Cobb, one of the warmest partisans of Mr. Crawford, was afraid to call upon him with the announcement of his defeat. He shrank from witnessing the shock of his chief's disappointment. General Jackson was indignant, and he nursed his wrath in secret, while, externally, he appeared unconcerned and cheerful. A few days after the event, Mr. Cobb wrote to his friends, —

" The presidential election is over, and you will have heard the result. The clouds were black, and portentous of storms of no ordinary character. They broke in one horrid burst, and straight dispelled. Everything here is silent. The victors have no cause to rejoice. There was not a single window lighted on the occasion. A few free negroes shouted, ' Huzza for Mr. Adams ! ' but they were not joined even by the cringing populace of this place. The disappointed submit in sullen silence. The friends of Jackson grumbled, at first, like the rumbling of distant thunder ; but the old man himself submitted without a change of countenance. Mr. Crawford's friends changed not their looks. They command universal respect. Crawford will return home, and we must do the best we can with him. Should he and our friends wish that he should again go into the Senate, the way shall be open for him. I am sick and tired of everything here, and wish for nothing so much as private life. My ambition is dead."

The evening after the election Mr. Monroe held a presidential levee. All Washington crowded to the White House, eager to pay homage to the rising sun. Mr. S. G. Goodrich happened to be present, and with his graphic pen has described the scene : —

" I shall pass over," he writes, " other individuals present, only noting an incident which respects the two persons in the assembly, who, most of all others, engrossed the thoughts of the visitors, — Mr. Adams the elect, General Jackson the defeated. It chanced in the course of the evening that these two persons, involved in the throng, approached each other from opposite directions, yet without knowing it. Suddenly, as they were almost together, the persons around, seeing what was to happen, by a sort of instinct stepped aside, and left them face to face. Mr. Adams was by himself : General Jackson had a large, handsome lady on his arm. They looked at each other for a moment; and then General Jackson moved forward, and, reaching out his long arm, said, ' How do you do, Mr. Adams ? I give you my left hand ; for the right, as you see, is devoted to the fair. I hope you are very well, sir.' All this was gallantly and heartily said and done. Mr. Adams took the general's hand, and said, with chilling coldness, ' Very well, sir ; I hope General Jackson is well.'

" It was curious to see the Western planter, the Indian fighter, the stern soldier, who had written his country's glory in the blood of the enemy at New Orleans, genial and gracious in the midst of a court ; while the old courtier and diplomat was stiff, rigid, cold as a statue. It was all the more remarkable from the fact, that, four hours before, the former had been defeated, and the latter was the victor, in a struggle for one of the highest objects of human ambition. The personal character of these two individuals was, in fact, well expressed in that chance-meeting, — the gallantry, the frankness, the heartiness, of the one, which captivated all ; the coldness, the distance, the self-concentration, of the other, which repelled all."

No one can read the impartial record of John Quincy Adams's administration without admitting that a more noble example of uncompromising integrity can scarcely be found. It was stated publicly that Mr. Adams's administration was to be put down, " though it be as pure as the angels which stand at the right hand of the throne of God." Not a few of the active participants in those scenes lived to regret the course they pursued. Some years after, Mr. Warren R. Davis of South Carolina, turning to Mr. Adams, then a member of the House of Representatives, said, —

" Well do I remember the enthusiastic zeal with which we reproached the administration of that gentleman, and the ardor and vehemence with which we labored to bring in another. For the share I had in those transactions, — and it was not a small one, — *I hope God will forgive me ; for I never shall forgive myself.*"

Mr. Adams was, to a very remarkable degree, abstemious and temperate in his habits ; always rising early, and taking much exercise. When at his home in Quincy, he has been known to walk seven miles to Boston before breakfast. In Washington, it was said that he was the first man up in the city, lighting his own fire, and applying himself to work in his library often long before the dawn. He was an expert swimmer, and was exceedingly fond of bathing ; and was in the habit in the summer, every morning, of plunging into the Potomac with all the sportiveness of a boy. He sometimes made the journey from Quincy to Washington on horseback, accompanied by a single attendant.

On the 4th of March, 1829, Mr. Adams retired from the presidency, and was succeeded by Andrew Jackson. John C. Calhoun was elected Vice-President. The slavery question now began to assume portentous magnitude. Mr. Adams returned to Quincy and to his studies, which he pursued with unabated zeal. But he was not long permitted to remain in retirement. In November, 1830, he was elected representative to Congress. He thus recognized the Roman principle, that it is honorable for the general of yesterday to act as corporal to-day, if by so doing he can render service to his country. Deep as are the obligations of our republic to John Quincy Adams for his services as ambassador, as Secretary of State, and as President, in his capacity as legislator in the House of Representatives he conferred benefits upon our land which eclipsed all the rest, and which can never be overestimated.

For seventeen years, until his death, he occupied the post of representative, towering above all his peers, ever ready to do brave battle for freedom, and winning the title of " the old man eloquent."

Upon taking his seat in the house, he announced that he should hold himself bound to no party. Probably there was never a member of the house more devoted to his duties. He was usually the first in his place in the morning, and the last to leave his seat in the evening. Not a measure could be brought forward, and escape his scrutiny. The battle which Mr. Adams fought, almost singly, against the proslavery party in the government, was sublime in its moral daring and heroism. For persisting in presenting petitions for the abolition of slavery, he was threatened with indictment by the grand jury, with expulsion from the house, with assassination; but no threats could intimidate him, and his final triumph was complete.

On one occasion Mr. Adams presented a petition, signed by several women, against the annexation of Texas for the purpose of cutting it up into slave States. Mr. Howard of Maryland said that these women discredited not only themselves, but their section of the country, by turning from their domestic duties to the conflicts of political life.

"Are women," exclaimed Mr. Adams, "to have no opinions or actions on subjects relating to the general welfare? Where did the gentleman get this principle? Did he find it in sacred history, — in the language of Miriam the prophetess, in one of the noblest and most sublime songs of triumph that ever met the human eye or ear? Did the gentleman never hear of Deborah, to whom the children of Israel came up for judgment? Has he forgotten the deed of Jael, who slew the dreaded enemy of her country? Has he forgotten Esther, who by her *petition* saved her people and her country?

"To go from sacred history to profane, does the gentleman there find it 'discreditable' for women to take an interest in political affairs? Has he forgotten the Spartan mother, who said to her son, when going out to battle, 'My son, come back to me *with* thy shield, or *upon* thy shield?' Does he not remember Cloelia and her hundred companions, who swam across the river, under a shower of darts escaping from Porsena? Has he forgotten Cornelia, the mother of the Gracchi? Does he not remember Portia, the wife of Brutus and the daughter of Cato?

"To come to later periods, what says the history of our Anglo-Saxon ancestors? To say nothing of Boadicea, the British heroine in the time of the Cæsars, what name is more illustrious than that of Elizabeth ? Or, if he will go to the Continent, will he not find the names of Maria Theresa of Hungary, of the two Catharines of Russia, and of Isabella of Castille, the patroness of Columbus. Did she bring ' discredit' on her sex by mingling in politics ? "

In this glowing strain, he silenced and overwhelmed his antagonists. Congress, yielding to the proslavery spirit of the South, passed a resolve in January, 1837, "that all petitions relating to slavery, without being printed or referred, shall be laid on the table, and no action shall be had thereon." Some of the proslavery party forged a petition, as if from slaves, to see if Mr. Adams would dare to present it.

On the 6th of February, 1837, Mr. Adams rose with this forged petition in his hand, and said, "I hold a paper purporting to come from slaves. I wish to know if such a paper comes within the order of the house respecting petitions."

The strange sensitiveness of the house upon this subject may be inferred from the fact, that a storm of indignation was instantly roused. Waddy Thompson of South Carolina, Charles E. Haynes of Georgia, Dixon H. Lewis of Alabama, sprang to the floor, presenting resolutions, " that John Quincy Adams, by attempting to present a petition purporting to be from slaves, has been guilty of gross disrespect to the house, and that he be instantly brought to the bar to receive the severe censure of the speaker."

Never were assailants more thoroughly discomfited. "Mr. Speaker," said Mr. Adams, "to prevent the consumption of time, I ask the gentlemen to modify their resolution a little, so that, when I come to the bar of the house, I may not, by a word, put an end to it. *I did not present the petition.* I said that I had a paper purporting to be a petition from slaves ; and I asked the speaker whether he considered such a paper as included in the general order of the house, that all petitions relating to slavery should be laid upon the table. I intended to take the decision of the speaker before I went one step toward presenting that petition. This is the *fact*.

"I adhere to the right of petition. Where is your law which says the mean, the low, the degraded, shall be deprived of the right of petition ? Petition is supplication, entreaty, prayer. Where is the degree of vice or immorality which shall deprive the citizen of the right to supplicate for a boon, or to pray for mercy ? Where is such a law to be found? It does not belong to the most abject despotism. There is no absolute monarch on earth, who is not compelled, by the constitution of his country, to receive the petitions of his people, whosoever they may be. The Sultan of Constantinople cannot walk the streets, and refuse to receive petitions from the meanest and vilest in the land. The right of petition belongs to all; and, so far from refusing to present a petition because it might come from those low in the estimation of the world, it would be an additional incentive, if such an incentive were wanting."

After a debate of extreme bitterness, running through four days, only twenty votes could be found to cast any censure upon Mr. Adams. There was perhaps never a fiercer battle fought in legislative halls than Mr. Adams waged, for nearly a score of years, with the partisans of slavery in Congress. In every encounter he came off victor. We have not space, in this brief sketch, to refer to his labors to secure a right appropriation for the Smithsonian Fund of half a million of dollars. At the age of seventy-four he appeared in the Supreme Court of the United States, after an absence from that court of thirty years, to plead the cause of a few friendless negroes, the Amistad captives, who, with their own strong arms, had freed themselves from the man-stealers. His effort was crowned with complete success; and the poor Africans, abundantly furnished with the implements of civilized life, were returned to the homes from which they had been so ruthlessly torn.

In 1839 Congress was for a time seriously disorganized in consequence of two delegations appearing from New Jersey, each claiming the election. By usage, the clerk of the preceding Congress, on the first assembling, acts as chairman until a speaker is chosen. When, in calling the roll, the clerk came to New Jersey, he stated that, as the five seats of the members from that State were contested, he should pass over those names. A violent debate ensued. For four days there was anarchy, and it was found impossible to organize the house. Mr. Adams, during all this scene of confusion, sat quietly engaged in writing, apparently taking no interest in the debate, but, like a sagacious general on the battlefield, watching intently for the moment when he could effectually make a movement.

On the morning of the fourth day, the clerk again commenced calling the roll. When he reached New Jersey, he again repeated, "as these seats are contested," when Mr. Adams sprang to the floor, and in clear, shrill tones, which penetrated every portion of the house, cried out, —

"I rise to interrupt the clerk."

A multitude of voices shouted, "Hear him! hear him! — hear John Quincy Adams!"

In an instant, there was profound silence. Every eye was riveted upon that venerable old man, whose years and honors, and purity of character, commanded the respect of the bitterest of his foes. For a moment he paused; and there was such stillness that the fall of a sheet of paper might have been heard. Then, in those tones of intensity which ever arrested the attention of the house, he said, —

"It was not my intention to take any part in these extraordinary proceedings. I had hoped that this house would succeed in organizing itself. This is not the time or place to discuss the merits of conflicting claimants: that subject belongs to the House of Representatives. What a spectacle we here present! We do not and cannot organize; and why? Because the clerk of this house — the mere clerk, whom we create, whom we employ — usurps the *throne*, and sets us, the vicegerents of the whole American people, at defiance. And what is this clerk of yours? Is he to suspend, by his mere negative, the functions of government, and put an end to this Congress. He refuses to call the roll. It is in your power to compel him to call it, if he will not do it voluntarily."

Here he was interrupted by a member, who stated that the clerk could not be compelled to call the roll, as he would resign rather than do so.

"Well sir, let him resign," continued Mr. Adams, "and we may possibly discover some way by which we can get along without the aid of his all-powerful talent, learning, and genius. If we cannot organize in any other way, if this clerk of yours will not consent to our discharging the trust confided to us by our constituents, then let us imitate the example of the Virginia House of Burgesses, which, when the colonial Governor Dinwiddie ordered it to disperse, refused to obey the imperious and insulting mandate, and like men" —

Here there was such a burst of applause from the whole house, that, for a moment, his voice was drowned. Cheer upon cheer rose, shaking the walls of the Capitol. As soon as he could again be heard, he submitted a motion, requiring the clerk to call the roll. "How shall the question be put?" The voice of Mr. Adams was heard rising above the tumult, as he cried out, "I intend to put the question myself!"

Another burst of applause followed; when Mr. Barnwell Rhett of South Carolina leaped upon one of the desks, and shouted, "I move that the Hon. John Quincy Adams take the chair of the speaker of the house, and officiate as presiding officer till the house

JOHN QUINCY ADAMS IN THE HOUSE OF REPRESENTATIVES.

be organized by the election of its constitutional officers. As many as are agreed to this will say 'Ay!'"

One universal, thundering "Ay!" came back in response. Mr. Adams was conducted to the chair, and the house was organized. Mr. Wise of Virginia, soon after addressing him, said, —

"Sir, I regard it as the proudest hour of your life; and if, when you shall be gathered to your fathers, I were asked to select the words which, in my judgment, are best calculated to give at once the character of the man, I would inscribe upon your tomb this sentence, 'I will put the question myself.'"

In January, 1842, Mr. Adams presented a petition from forty-five citizens of Haverhill, Mass., praying for the peaceable dissolution of the Union. The proslavery party in Congress, who were then plotting the destruction of the government, were roused to a pretense of commotion such as even our stormy hall of legislation has rarely witnessed. They met in caucus, and, finding that they probably would not be able to *expel* Mr. Adams from the house, drew up a series of resolutions, which, if adopted, would inflict upon him disgrace equivalent to expulsion. Mr. Adams had presented the petition, which was most respectfully worded, and had moved that it be referred to a committee instructed to report an answer, showing the reasons why the prayer ought not to be granted.

It was the 25th of January. The whole body of the proslavery party came crowding together into the house, prepared to crush Mr. Adams forever. One of their number, Thomas F. Marshall of Kentucky, was appointed to read the resolutions, which accused Mr. Adams of high treason, of having insulted the government, and of meriting expulsion; but for which deserved punishment, the house, in its great mercy, would substitute its severest censure. With the assumption of a very solemn and magisterial air, there being breathless silence in the imposing audience, Mr. Marshall hurled the carefully prepared anathemas at his victim. Mr. Adams stood alone, the whole proslavery party madly against him.

As soon as the resolutions were read, every eye being fixed upon him, up rose that bold old man, whose scattered locks were whitened by seventy-five years; and casting a withering glance in the direction of his assailants, in a clear, shrill tone, tremulous with suppressed emotion, he said, —

"In reply to this audacious, atrocious charge of high treason, I call for the reading of the first paragraph of the Declaration of Independence. Read it, read it! and see what that says of the right of a people to reform, to change, and to dissolve their government."

The attitude, the manner, the tone, the words; the venerable old man, with flashing eye and flushed cheek, and whose very form seemed to expand under the inspiration of the occasion, — all presented a scene overawing in its sublimity. There was breathless silence as that paragraph was read, in defense of whose principles our fathers had pledged their lives, their fortunes, and their sacred honor. It was a proud hour to Mr. Adams, as they were all compelled to listen to the words, —

" That, to secure these rights, governments are instituted among men, deriving their just powers from the consent of the governed, and that, whenever any form of government becomes destructive of those ends, it is the right of the people to alter or abolish it, and to institute new government, laying its foundations on such principles, and organizing its powers in such form, as shall seem most likely to effect their safety and happiness."

That one sentence baffled and routed the foe. The heroic old man looked around upon the audience, and thundered out, " Read that again?" It was again read. Then, in a few fiery, logical words, he stated his defense in terms which even prejudiced minds could not resist. His discomfited assailants made sundry attempts to rally. After a conflict of eleven days they gave up vanquished, and their resolution was ignominiously laid upon the table.

It is pleasant to see that such heroism is eventually appreciated. In the summer of 1843 Mr. Adams took a tour through western New York. His journey was a perfect ovation. In all the leading cities he was received with the highest marks of consideration. The whole mass of the people rose to confer honor upon the man who had battled so nobly for human rights, and whose public and private character was without a stain. The greeting which he received at Buffalo was such as that city had never before conferred upon any man. The national flag was floating from every masthead. The streets were thronged with the multitude, who greeted with bursts of applause the renowned patriot and statesman as soon as he appeared. The Hon. Millard Fillmore, subsequently President of the United States, welcomed him in the following words: —

"You see here assembled the people of our infant city, without distinction of party, sex, age, or condition, — all, all, anxiously vying with each other to show their respect and esteem for your public and private worth. Here are gathered, in this vast multitude of what must appear to you strange faces, thousands whose hearts have vibrated to the chord of sympathy which your speeches have touched. Here is reflecting age and ardent youth and lisping childhood, to all of whom your venerated name is dear as household words, — all anxious to feast their eyes by a sight of that extraordinary and venerable man, that *old man eloquent*, upon whose lips Wisdom has distilled her choicest nectar. Here you see them all, and read in their eager and joy-gladdened countenances and brightly beaming eyes, a welcome, a thrice-told, heartfelt, soul-stirring welcome, to the man whom they delight to honor."

In January, 1846, when seventy-eight years of age, he took part in the great debate on the Oregon question, displaying intellectual vigor, and an extent and accuracy of acquaintance with the subject, which excited great admiration. At the close of the session, on the 17th of November, he had an attack of paralysis while walking in the streets of Boston. He, however, so far recovered, that he soon resumed his official duties in Washington. As he entered the house on the 16th of February, 1847, for the first time since his illness, every member instinctively rose in token of respect; and by two members he was formally conducted to his seat. After this, though constantly present, he took but little part in the debates.

It has been said of President Adams, that when his body was bent and his hair silvered by the lapse of fourscore years, yielding to the simple faith of a little child, he was accustomed to repeat every night, before he slept, the prayer which his mother taught him in his infant years. There is great moral beauty in the aspect of the venerable, world-worn statesman, folding his hands and closing his eyes, as he repeated, in the simplicity and sincerity of childhood, the words, —

> " Now I lay me down to sleep,
> I pray the Lord my soul to keep:
> If I should die before I wake,
> I pray the Lord my soul to take."

On the 21st of February, 1848, he rose on the floor of Congress, with a paper in his hand, to address the speaker. Suddenly he fell, again stricken by paralysis, and was caught in the arms of those around him. For a time he was senseless, as he was conveyed to a sofa in the rotunda. With reviving consciousness he opened his eyes, looked calmly around, and said, *"This is the end of earth;"* then, after a moment's pause, he added, *"I am content."* These were his last words. His family were summoned to his side; and in the apartment of the speaker of the house, beneath the dome of the Capitol, — the theatre of his labors and his triumphs, — he soon breathed his last.

The voices of denunciation were now hushed, and all parties united in tributes of honor to one of the purest patriots, and one of the most distinguished statesmen, America has produced.

CHAPTER VII.

ANDREW JACKSON.

Birth and Education. — A Bad Boy. — Keeps School. — Studies Law. — Emigrates. — Frontier Life. — Low Tastes. — A Representative. — Senator. — Judge. — Shop-keeper. — Major-General. — Quarrels and Duels. — Marriage and its Romance. — Fight with the Bentons. — War with the Indians. — Defense of New Orleans. — Passion and Violence. — President of the United States. — Administration. — Retirement. — Conversion. — Religious Character. — Death.

" PAINT me as I am," said Cromwell to the young artist. There were lights and shades in the character of Andrew Jackson, and

HERMITAGE, — RESIDENCE OF ANDREW JACKSON.

the world wishes to know him as he was. One hundred years ago, in 1765, an Irishman of Scotch descent, extremely poor, emigrated, with his wife and two infant children, from the North of Ireland to South Carolina. George III. had then been five years on his throne. The old French war, which gave Canada to England, had just ended. The humble emigrants had no money to purchase land. They, however, landing at Charleston, penetrated the wild interior, in a northwest direction, a hundred and sixty miles, and built their log hut on a branch of the Catawba River, called Waxhaw Creek, formerly the seat of the Waxhaw Indians. They were on the boundary-line between the Carolinas.

The lonely settlers in this wilderness of pines had reared their cabin, cleared an opening in the forest, and raised one crop, when the husband and father fell sick and died. Mrs. Jackson, with her two little boys, and just on the eve of again becoming a mother, was thus left in utter destitution. Not far from the cabin of the deceased there was a room built of logs, called a church. The corpse was taken in a wagon; the widow and her two children sat by its side; and in a field near by the body was buried, no one can now tell where.

The grief-stricken widow did not return to her desolated home. There was nothing to draw her there. From the grave she drove a few miles to the cabin of Mr. McKenney, who had married her sister, and who lived across the border, in North Carolina. There, in that lonely log hut, in the extreme of penury, with a few friendly women to come to her aid, she, within a few days, gave birth to Andrew Jackson, the child whose fame as a man has filled the civilized world. It was the 15th of March, 1767. A few lines tell this story. But where is the pencil or the pen which can delineate its true pathos? — the cabin, the pain-crushed, heart-stricken mother, the clotheless babe, the coarse fare, the penury, the wild surroundings, and the cheerlessness with which the dark future opened before the widow and the orphans.

Could some good angel then have opened to that Christian mother (for she was a true Christian of the Presbyterian faith) the future career of her son, — his renown, his influence, his conversion to Christ, his triumphant death, and that honor, glory, and immortality to which we trust he has attained in the spirit-land, — she might have smiled through her anguish, and exclaimed, " These light afflictions are indeed but for a moment, and work out for us a far more exceeding and eternal weight of glory." Mother and child have long ago met in heaven, and earthly griefs are gone forever.

Three weeks after the birth of Andrew, the widow, leaving her eldest little boy with Mr. McKenney, went with the babe and the other child a distance of two miles to the cabin of another brother-in-law, Mr. Crawford, whose wife was an invalid. Here Mrs. Jackson remained with her children for ten years, receiving the hospitality of her kind brother, and repaying it, as far as possible, by that hard work of washing, mending, and cooking which is inseparable from frontier life.

Andrew, or Andy as he was universally called, grew up a very rough, rude, turbulent boy. His features were coarse, his form ungainly; and there was but very little in his character, made visible, which was attractive. A companion said of him, "Andy is the only bully I ever knew who was not a coward." A mother's prayers must have been ascending earnestly for him; for even then, in her utter penury, she was endeavoring to devise some way by which she could educate him for the Christian ministry.

When five or six years of age he was sent to what was called a school, in a wretched log pen about twenty feet square. Here he learned to read tolerably well. Spelling was an art which he never attained. He learned to write in characters which those skillful in hieroglyphics could read. He also became somewhat familiar with the four fundamental rules of arithmetic. This seems to be about the substance of all the school education he ever received.

He grew up to be a tall, lank boy, with coarse hair and freckled cheeks, with bare feet dangling from trousers too short for him, very fond of athletic sports, running, boxing, wrestling. He was generous to the younger and weaker boys, but very irascible and overbearing with his equals and superiors. He was profane, marvelously profane, — a vice in which he surpassed all other men, and which clung to him until, after the age of threescore years, he learned of Christ to "swear not at all."

The character of his mother he revered; and it was not until after her death that his predominant vices gained full strength. Through some unknown influence, he imbibed such a reverence for the character of woman, and such firm principles of purity, that in that respect he was without reproach.

When nine years of age the Declaration of Independence was signed. The billows of war soon swept down into the Carolinas, bringing terror, blood, and desolation to the humble cabins of the

14

Waxhaw.   More intense was the animosity, and more bitter the strife, between the patriot and the Tory, than between the armies which were facing each other in the field.   As Tarleton and his dragoons came thundering along, the older brother, Hugh, not yet eighteen years of age, rode with a volunteer company to meet him, and died of heat and exhaustion at the battle of Stono.

With three hundred horsemen, Tarleton surprised a detachment of militia at the Waxhaw settlement, killed one hundred and thirteen, wounded one hundred and fifty, and captured or put to flight all the rest.   The old log meeting-house was used as a hospital. Mrs. Jackson was unwearied in nursing the wounded soldiers. Andrew, a boy of thirteen, and his brother, assisted their mother in these works of mercy.   Andrew at times expressed the most intense desire to avenge their wounds and his brother's death.

In August, 1780, the victorious army of Cornwallis rushed upon Waxhaw; and Mrs. Jackson, with her two boys, fled before them. Andrew was placed in the family of Mrs. Wilson, in Charlotte, where he paid for his board by being a servant of all work.   Here his rage against the British found vent in forming various kinds of weapons, which he would swing, expressing the delight it would give him thus to beat the British down.   He remained in this place for about six months, and then the family returned to their ravaged home at Waxhaw.   Andrew was now fourteen, tall as a man, but slender and weak from his rapid growth.   Terrible was the maddened strife in that neighborhood between Whig and Tory.   A band of Tories made a midnight attack upon the house of a Whig.   Andrew Jackson was there as one of the guard.   Quite a little battle ensued, in which he behaved gallantly, and the Tories were repulsed.   This was the first time he took part in active service.   Cornwallis sent a body of dragoons to aid the Tories.   They surrounded the patriots, routed them with slaughter, and Andrew and his brother were taken prisoners.   A British officer ordered him to brush his mud-spattered boots.   "I am a prisoner of war, not your servant," was the reply of the dauntless boy.

The brute drew his sword, and aimed a desperate blow at the head of the helpless young prisoner.   Andrew raised his hand, and thus received two fearful gashes, — one upon his hand, and the other upon his head.   The officer then turned to his brother Robert with the same demand.   He also refused, and received a blow from the keen-edged sabre, which quite disabled him, and which probably soon after caused his death.

The two wounded boys, one fourteen and the other sixteen, with twenty other prisoners, were hurried off to Camden in South Carolina, forty miles distant, where the British were in strength. Their brutal captors allowed them no food or water by the way, and would not even permit them to drink from the streams they forded. At Camden they were thrown into a contracted inclosure, without beds, medical attendance, or any means of dressing their wounds. Their supply of food was scanty and bad. Days and nights of misery passed away. The small-pox, in its most loathsome form, broke out. The dying and the dead were all together. Mrs. Jackson, hearing of the sufferings of her boys, hastened to their relief.

There was resistless energy in a mother's love. She succeeded in obtaining the release of her sons by exchange, and gazed horror-stricken upon their wan and wasted frames. Having obtained two horses, she placed Robert, who was too weak to stand, or even to sit in his saddle, upon one, where he was held in his seat by some of the returning prisoners. Mrs. Jackson rode the other. Andrew, bareheaded, barefooted, clothed in rags, sick even then with the small-pox, and so weak that he could scarcely drag one limb after the other, toiled painfully behind. Thus they made their journey through the wilderness for forty miles, — from Camden back to Waxhaw.

Before this sad family reached their home, a drenching rain-storm set in. The mother at length got her sons, both sick of small-pox, home and to bed. In two days Robert was dead, and Andrew apparently dying in the wildest ravings of delirium. The strength of his constitution triumphed; and, after months of languor, he regained health and strength.

As he was getting better, his mother heard the cry of anguish from the prisoners whom the British held in Charleston, among whom were the sons of her sisters. She hastened to their relief, was attacked by fever, died, and was buried where her grave could never afterwards be found. A small bundle of the clothing which she wore was the only memorial of his mother which was returned to her orphan boy. Thus Andrew Jackson, when fourteen years of age, was left alone in the world, without father, mother, sister, or brother, and without one dollar which he could call his own.

Before Andrew had fully recovered his strength, he entered a shop to learn the trade of a saddler, and for six months labored diligently in this calling. But gradually, as health returned, he became more and more a wild, reckless, lawless boy. He drank, gambled, fought cocks, and was regarded as about the worst character that could anywhere be found. In December, 1782, the British having evacuated Charleston, Andrew, who by some means had come into possession of a fine horse, mounted him, and rode through the wilderness to Charleston. Having no money, he soon ran up a long bill at the tavern. One evening, as he was strolling the streets, he entered a gambling-house, and was challenged to stake his horse against two hundred dollars. He won. With this money he settled his bill, mounted his horse, and rode home through the solitary pine-barrens, reflecting not very pleasantly upon the past, and forming plans for the future.

He now turned school-master. A school in a log hut in those wilds was a very humble institution. Andrew Jackson could teach the alphabet, perhaps the multiplication-table; and, as he was a very bold boy, it is not impossible that he might have adventured to teach handwriting. And now he began to think of a profession, and decided to study law. With a very slender purse, and on the back of a very fine horse, he set out for Salisbury, N. C., a distance of about seventy-five miles, where he entered the law office of Mr. McCay. Andrew was then eighteen years of age. Here he remained for two years, professedly studying law. He is still vividly remembered in the traditions of Salisbury, which traditions say, —

"Andrew Jackson was the most roaring, rollicking, game-cocking, horse-racing, card-playing, mischievous fellow that ever lived in Salisbury. He did not trouble the law-books much. He was more in the stable than in the office. He was the head of all the rowdies hereabouts."

Andrew was now, at the age of twenty, a tall young man, standing six feet and an inch in his stockings. He was very slender, but remarkably dignified and graceful in his manners, an exquisite horseman, and developing, amidst his loathsome profanity and multiform vices, a vein of rare magnanimity. His temper was fiery in the extreme; but it was said of him, that no man knew better than Andrew Jackson when to get angry, and when not. He was fond of all rough adventures, wild riding, camping out; loved a horse passionately; and, though sagacious and prudent, was bold in facing danger. The experience through which he had passed in the Revolution had made him a very stanch republican.

He had now got his profession. Again mounting his horse, he rode to Martinsville, N. C., where it seems that he spent a year as a clerk in a country store, waiting for an opportunity to open an office somewhere. The whole of that region which we now call Tennessee was then almost an unexplored wilderness, called Washington County, N. C. It was ranged by bands of Indians, who had been so outraged by vagabonds among the whites that they had become bitterly hostile. Ravaged by Indian wars, it became a burden to North Carolina, and was ceded to Congress. There was a small settlement of pioneers, five hundred miles west of the summit of the Alleghanies, near the present site of Nashville, on the banks of the Cumberland. Jonesborough was another small settlement in East Tennessee, near the western base of the Alleghanies. The intervening space was a wilderness, which could only be traversed by parties well guarded, to repel attacks to which they were constantly exposed.

Andrew Jackson was appointed public prosecutor for the remote district of Nashville. It was an office of little honor, small emolument, and great peril. Few men could be found to accept it. Early in the spring of 1788 Jackson joined a party of emigrants, who rendezvoused at Morgantown, the last frontier settlement in North Carolina. They were all mounted on horseback, with their baggage on pack-horses. In double file, the long cavalcade crossed the mountains by an Indian trail, which had widened into a road. Each night they camped in the open air. The journey of a few days brought them, without adventure, to Jonesborough, where there was a small settlement of about sixty log huts. They were now to enter the wilderness, which, for a distance of over two hundred miles, was filled with hostile bands of savages. There they waited several weeks for the arrival of other parties of emigrants, and for a guard from Nashville to escort them. Nearly one hundred composed the cavalcade, which included many women and children.

One night, after a march of thirty-six hours, with only a halt of one short hour, they encamped at a point which was thought to be the most safe in the midst of the most perilous part of the journey.

The women and children at an early hour, in utter exhaustion, had crept into their little tents. The men, with their blankets wrapped around them, were sleeping under the shelter of logs, with their feet toward the fire. The sentinels, with their muskets, were silently and sleepily standing on the watch. Andrew Jackson had retired a little apart from the rest, and sitting upon the ground, with his back against a tree, was smoking a corn-cob pipe. Lost in silent musing, at ten o'clock, just as he was beginning to fall asleep, his attention was arrested by the various notes of the owls hooting in the forest around him. Just then he was startled by a louder hoot than usual very near the camp. Instantly suspicion flashed upon his mind.

Grasping his rifle, and with all his faculties on the alert, he crept along to where a friend was sleeping, and startled him with the announcement, "There are Indians all around us! I have heard them in every direction! They mean to attack us before daybreak!"

The experienced woodsmen were aroused. They listened, and were fully confirmed in the same suspicion. Silently they broke up their camp, and, with the utmost caution, resumed their march. An hour after they had left, a party of hunters came, and occupied the spot. Before the day dawned, the Indians sprang from their ambush upon them, and all but one were killed. Andrew Jackson's sagacity had saved his party.

Late in October, 1788, this long train of emigrants reached Nashville. They took with them the exciting news that the new Constitution had been accepted by a majority of the States, and that George Washington would undoubtedly be elected the first President. It was estimated that then, in this outpost of civilization, there were scattered, in logs huts clustered along the banks of the Cumberland, about five thousand souls. The Indians were so active in their hostilities that it was not safe for any one to live far from the stockade. Every man took his rifle with him to the field. Children could not go out to gather berries unless accompanied by a guard.

Nashville had its aristocracy. Mrs. Donelson belonged to one of the first families. She was the widow of Colonel John Donelson, and lived in a cabin of hewn logs, the most commodious dwelling in the place. She had a beautiful, mirth-loving daughter, who had married a very uncongenial Kentuckian, Lewis Robards, of whom but little that is good can be said. She and her husband lived with her widowed mother, and Andrew Jackson was received into the family as a boarder. It was an attractive home for him. Of the gay and lively Mrs. Robards it is said that she was then the best story-teller, the best dancer, the sprightliest companion, the most dashing horsewoman, in the western country.

And now Andrew Jackson commenced vigorously the practice of law. It was an important part of his business to collect debts. It required nerve. Many desperate men carried pistols and knives. There were some disputed claims to adjust. A court-house in that country, at that time, consisted of a hut of unhewn logs, without floor, door, or window. Long journeys through the wilderness were necessary to reach the distant cabins where the courts were held. During the first seven years of his residence in those wilds, he traversed the almost pathless forest between Nashville and Jonesborough, a distance of two hundred miles, twenty-two times. Hostile Indians were constantly on the watch, and a man was liable at any moment to be shot down in his own field. Andrew Jackson was just the man for this service, — a wild, rough, daring backwoodsman. He sometimes camped in the woods for twenty successive nights, not daring to shoot a deer, or to kindle a fire, lest he should attract the attention of some roving band of savages.

One night, after dark, he came to a creek, swollen by the rains to a roaring torrent. It was pitch-dark, and the rain was falling in floods. He could not ford the stream; he dared not light a fire; it was not safe to let his horse move about to browse. He took off the saddle, placed it at the foot of a tree, and sat upon it; wrapped his blanket over his shoulders; held his bridle in one hand, and his rifle in the other; and thus, drenched with rain, and listening to the wail of the storm and the rush of the torrent, waited the dawn. He then mounted his horse, swam the creek, and proceeded on his journey.

"You see how near," Andrew Jackson once said, "I can graze danger!" Daily he was making hair-breadth escapes. He seemed to bear a charmed life. Boldly, alone, or with few companions, he traversed the forests, encountering all perils, and triumphing over all.

Mrs. Robards and her husband lived unhappily together. He

was jealous of her, but, in the judgment of all acquainted with the facts, without any cause. Before Mr. Jackson's arrival, he had once, from his jealous disposition, separated from her. Andrew Jackson was an exceedingly polite, gallant, fascinating man with ladies. Captain Robards became jealous of Jackson, and treated Mrs. Robards with great cruelty. Jackson decided, in consequence, to leave the house, but determined first to have a little conversation with Mr. Robards. He found the man abusive and unrelenting; and Mr. Jackson, offering to meet him in a duel if he desired it, retired from the family, and took board in another place. Soon after this, Mr. and Mrs. Robards separated. The affair caused Andrew Jackson great uneasiness; for though he knew that the parties had separated once before, and though conscious of innocence, he found himself to be the unfortunate cause of the present scandal. It was rumored that Captain Robards, who had gone to Kentucky, was about to return. A friend of Andrew Jackson, subsequently Judge Overton, who was then his intimate companion, writes, that, perceiving Mr. Jackson to be much depressed, he inquired the cause. The reply was, —

"I am the most unhappy of men, in having innocently and unintentionally been the cause of the loss of peace and happiness of Mrs. Robards, whom I believe to be a fine woman."

To escape from the persecutions of her husband, she decided to go to Natchez with the family of an elderly gentleman, Colonel Stark. As there was great danger from the Indians, Colonel Stark entreated Mr. Jackson to accompany them as a guard. He did so, and returned to Nashville. This was in the spring of 1791.

Captain Robards applied to the Legislature of Virginia for a bill of divorce. It was granted by an act of the Legislature, *provided that the Supreme Court should adjudge that there was cause for such divorce*. Robards laid aside this act, and did nothing about it for two years. Virginia was far away. The transmission of intelligence was very slow. It was announced in Nashville that Robards had obtained a divorce. This was universally believed. No one doubted it. Mrs. Robards believed it: Andrew Jackson believed it. Influenced by this belief, Andrew Jackson and Rachel Robards were married in the fall of 1791. No one acquainted thoroughly with the parties and the facts doubted of the purity of the connection.

Two years after this, Mr. and Mrs. Jackson learned, to their great surprise, that Robards had just obtained a divorce in one of the courts of Kentucky, and that the act of the Virginia Legislature was not final, but conditional. Thus Mr. Jackson had, in reality, been married for two years to another man's wife, though neither he nor Mrs. Jackson had been guilty of the slightest intentional wrong. To remedy the irregularity as far as possible, a new license was obtained, and the marriage ceremony was again performed.

It proved to be a marriage of rare felicity. Probably there never was a more affectionate union. However rough Mr. Jackson might have been abroad, he was always gentle and tender at home; and through all the vicissitudes of their lives, he treated Mrs. Jackson with the most chivalric attentions. He was always very sensitive upon the question of his marriage. No one could breathe a word which reflected a suspicion upon the purity of this affair but at the risk of pistol-shot instantly through his brain.

The country was rapidly prospering. The Indians were quelled, and thousands of emigrants were pouring into the inviting territory. Mr. Jackson, purchasing large tracts of land, and selling lots to settlers, was becoming rich. The following anecdote, which he related when President, sheds light upon his own character and upon the times. A friend in Washington was expecting to be assailed in the streets by a political opponent: —

"Now," said the general to him, "if any man attacks you, I know how you'll fight him with that big black stick of yours. You'll aim right for his head. Well, sir, ten chances to one he will ward it off; and, if you *do* hit him, you won't bring him down. No, sir" (taking the stick into his own hands); "you hold the stick so, and punch him in the stomach, and you'll drop him. I'll tell you how I found that out.

"When I was a young man, practicing law in Tennessee, there was a big, bullying fellow that wanted to pick a quarrel with me, and so trod on my toes. Supposing it accidental, I said nothing. Soon after, he did it again; and I began to suspect his object. In a few minutes he came by a third time, pushing against me violently, and evidently meaning fight. He was a man of immense size, — one of the very biggest men I ever saw. As quick as a flash, I snatched a small rail from the top of the fence, and gave him the point of it full in the stomach. Sir, it doubled him up. He fell at my feet, and I stamped on him. Soon he got up *savage*, and was about to fly at me like a tiger. The bystanders made as though they would interfere. Says I, ' Gentlemen, stand back, give me room, that 's all I ask, and I 'll manage him.' With that I stood ready, with the rail pointed. He gave me *one* look, and turned away a whipped man, and feeling like one. So, sir, I say to you, if any villain assaults you, give him the *pint* in his belly."

In these wild regions, and among these rough frontiersmen, such pluck gave a man an enviable reputation. Jackson was always ready for a fight. An opposing lawyer ridiculed some position he had taken. He tore a blank leaf from a law-book, wrote a peremptory challenge, and handed it to his opponent. They met that evening in a glen, exchanged shots, which did not hit, shook hands, and became friends again.

Jackson loved cock-fighting. He kept chickens for that purpose. When, upon one occasion, one of his chickens, after being struck down, revived, and by a lucky stroke killed his antagonist, Jackson, turning to a companion, exclaimed, delighted, " There is the greatest emblem of bravery on earth! Bonaparte is not braver!"

In January, 1796, the Territory of Tennessee then containing nearly eighty thousand inhabitants, the people met in convention at Knoxville to frame a constitution. Five were sent from each of the eleven counties. Andrew Jackson was one of the delegates from Davidson County. They met in a shabby building in a grove outside of the city. It was fitted up for the occasion at an expense of twelve dollars and sixty-two cents. The members were entitled to two dollars and a half a day. They voted to receive but a dollar and a half, that the other dollar might go to the payment of secretary, printer, and door-keeper, etc. A constitution was formed, which was regarded as very democratic; and in June, 1796, Tennessee became the sixteenth State in the Union.

The new State was entitled to but one member in the national House of Representatives. Andrew Jackson was chosen that member. Mounting his horse, he rode to Philadelphia, where Congress then held its sessions, — a distance of eight hundred miles. Albert Gallatin thus describes the first appearance of the Hon. Andrew Jackson in the House : —

" A tall, lank, uncouth-looking personage, with locks of hair hanging over his face, and a cue down his back, tied with an eelskin, his dress singular, his manners and deportment those of a rough backwoodsman."

Jackson was an earnest advocate of the Democratic party. Jefferson was his idol. He admired Bonaparte, loved France, and hated England. As Mr. Jackson took his seat, General Washington, whose second term of service was then expiring, delivered his last speech to Congress. A committee drew up a complimentary address in reply. Andrew Jackson did not approve of the address, and was one of twelve who voted against it. He was not willing to say that General Washington's administration had been "wise, firm, and patriotic."

Tennessee had fitted out an expedition against the Indians, contrary to the policy of the government. A resolution was introduced that the national government should pay the expenses. Jackson advocated it. It was carried. This rendered Mr. Jackson very popular in Tennessee. A vacancy chanced soon after to occur in the Senate, and Andrew Jackson was chosen United States Senator by the State of Tennessee. John Adams was then President; Thomas Jefferson, Vice-President.

Many years after this, when Mr. Jefferson had retired from the presidential chair, and Andrew Jackson was candidate for the presidency, Daniel Webster spent some days at the romantic home of the sage of Monticello. He represents Mr. Jefferson as saying, —

"I feel much alarmed at the prospect of seeing General Jackson President. He is one of the most unfit men I know of for such a place. He has very little respect for law or constitutions, and is, in fact, an able military chief. His passions are terrible. When I was president of the Senate he was senator; and he could never speak on account of the rashness of his feelings. I have seen him attempt it repeatedly, and as often choke with rage. His passions are no doubt cooler now. He has been much tried since I knew him; but he is a dangerous man."

In 1798 Mr. Jackson returned to Tennessee and resigned his seat in the Senate. Soon after he was chosen judge of the Supreme Court of that State, with a salary of six hundred dollars. This office he held for six years. It is said that his decisions, though sometimes ungrammatical, were generally right.

When Senator Jackson was one of the judges of the Supreme Court of Tennessee, John Sevier was governor of the State. There had been some altercation between them; and Jackson had challenged Sevier to a duel, which Sevier had declined. They met one day in the streets of Knoxville in a very unfriendly mood. In the conversation which ensued, Judge Jackson alluded to the services which he had rendered the State. "Services!" exclaimed the governor; "I know of none except a trip to Natchez with another man's wife." "Great God!" cried out Judge Jackson, "do you mention her sacred name?" He immediately drew a pistol and fired. The governor returned the shot. The bullets whistled through the crowded streets of Knoxville. Bystanders separated them.

Soon after, Judge Jackson, when traveling with a friend, Dr. Vandyke, met upon the road Governor Sevier, with his son. The judge immediately drew his pistol and ordered the governor to defend himself. The governor leaped from his horse, and the frightened animal ran away. Young Sevier drew upon Jackson; Dr. Vandyke drew upon Sevier. Some chance travelers came up and stopped the fray.

The quarrel between the judge and the governor enlisted partisans on either side; and several scenes of clamor and violence occurred, which we have not space to record. Judge Jackson did not enjoy his seat upon the bench, and renounced the dignity in the summer of 1804. About this time he was chosen major-general of militia, and lost the title of judge in that of general. When he retired from the senate chamber, it seems that he had decided to try his fortune through trade. He purchased a stock of goods in Philadelphia, sent them to Pittsburgh by wagon, down the Ohio to Louisville in flat-boats, thence by wagons or pack-horses to Nashville, where he opened a store.

He lived about thirteen miles from Nashville, on a tract of land of several thousand acres, mostly uncultivated. He used a small block-house for his store, from a narrow window of which he sold goods to the Indians. As he had an assistant, his office as judge did not materially interfere with this business. The general tended store, sent goods, and, it is said, occasionally negroes, down the Mississippi. As to slavery, born in the midst of it, the idea never seemed to enter his mind that it could be wrong. He became eventually an extensive slave-owner; but he was one of the most humane and gentle of masters. At a horse-race, where General Jackson brought forward his favorite horse Truxton, and where the stakes on either side were two thousand dollars, the general became involved in a quarrel with a young man by the name of Swann. He refused to accept the challenge of Swann, who was a young lawyer just from Virginia, upon the ground that he was not a gentleman; but beat him with his bludgeon. It was a very disgraceful quarrel.

This led to another difficulty, with Mr. Charles Dickenson, who was also a lawyer, and a dealer in country produce. Jackson challenged him to a duel, and insisted upon an immediate fight. The meeting was appointed at a day's ride from Nashville, at seven o'clock in the morning of Friday, May 30, 1806. The parties were to stand facing each other, twenty-four feet apart, with pistols down. At the word "Fire!" they were to discharge their pistols as soon as they pleased.

Dickenson had a young and beautiful wife and an infant child, and was said to have been a very amiable man. As he stole from the side of his wife and child early on Thursday morning, stating that he had business which called him to Kentucky, he kissed her, saying, "Good-by, darling! I shall be *sure* to be at home to-morrow night." Meeting a gay party of his friends, they rode off in the highest spirits. Dickenson was a sure shot. He could strike a dollar with his bullet, and even cut a string, at the distance of twenty-four feet. General Jackson and his party followed. The two parties spent the night at houses about two miles from each other.

The next morning they met in a grove. Dickenson got the first fire. His aim was unerring; but the ball broke a rib, and glanced, leaving a bad but not dangerous wound. Jackson then took deliberate aim. Dickenson, appalled by the certain death which awaited him, recoiled a step or two. "Back to the *mark*, sir!" shouted Jackson's second. The unhappy man took his stand. Again Jackson raised his pistol with calm, determined aim, and pulled the trigger. The pistol did not go off. He examined it, and found that it had stopped at half-cock. Readjusting it, he again, unrelentingly, took cool aim, and fired. Dickenson reeled, and fell. The ball had passed through his body, just above the hips. Jackson and his party retired from the field, leaving the dying man in the hands of his friends. All day long he suffered agony which extorted shrieks from him, and in the evening died. The next day, his frantic wife, hurrying to his relief, met a wagon conveying back to Nashville his remains. Dickenson was convivial in his tastes, a great favorite in Nashville, and his untimely death excited profound sympathy. For a time this affair greatly injured General Jackson's popularity. The verdict then was, and continues to be, that General Jackson was outrageously wrong. If he subsequently felt any remorse, he never revealed it to any one but to God.

General Jackson at this time resided in a very humble house on what was called "The Hermitage Farm." It consisted of one room on the lower floor, and two above. There was no ceiling. A trap-door in the middle of the floor opened into a hole for storage.

THE DUEL.

There was another smaller cabin near by, connected by a covered passage. General Jackson's rustic taste was amply satisfied with these accommodations. He desired nothing better. Subsequently, when to gratify his wife he built the comfortable house called "The Hermitage," these two buildings were converted into negro cabins. The general was proverbial for his hospitality, and the low as well as the high were equally welcome. Aaron Burr made the general a visit of five days. On his return from New Orleans he made another visit to the Hermitage Farm of eight days. He writes, —

" For a week, I have been lounging at the house of General Jackson, once a lawyer, afterwards a judge, now a planter; a man of intelligence, and one of those frank, ardent souls whom I love to meet."

Gradually General Jackson began to suspect Burr of designs of dismembering the Union, and establishing a Southern empire, of which New Orleans was to be the capital, and Aaron Burr the sovereign. He communicated his suspicions to the government, and offered his services. Subsequently he formed the opinion that Burr was innocent of any traitorous designs, and earnestly defended him, and became alienated from Jefferson and his administration. General Jackson now withdrew from commercial pursuits, which he had not found very profitable, and devoted himself to the culture of his plantation. His home was a very happy one. Mrs. Jackson was an excellent manager, and one of the most cheerful and entertaining of companions. She had a strong mind, much intelligence, but very little culture. They had no children, but adopted one of the twin sons, but a few days old, of one of Mrs. Jackson's sisters. This boy became the pride, the joy, the hope, of the general's life. Soon after, he received another little nephew into his family, whom he nurtured and educated. It is said (and the assertion is well substantiated) that this wonderfully irascible man was never *impatient* even with wife, children, or servants.

One day, when traveling alone, he met two burly wagoners, who ordered him to get out of his carriage and dance for them. Feigning simplicity, he said that he could not dance without his slippers, which were in his trunk. They told him to get them. Opening his trunk, he took out his pistols; and then, with eyes glaring like fireballs, and with such oaths as few men ever heard before, approached them, saying, —

"Now, you infernal villains, you shall dance for me! Dance, dance!" There was death in his eye and in his tone. They danced until the general was satisfied, and he then dismissed them with a moral lecture which they probably never forgot.

When the war of 1812 with Great Britain commenced, Madison occupied the presidential chair. Aaron Burr sent word to the President that there was an unknown man in the West, Andrew Jackson, who would do credit to a commission if one were conferred upon him. Just at that time General Jackson offered his services and those of twenty-five hundred volunteers. His offer was accepted, and the troops were assembled at Nashville.

As the British were hourly expected to make an attack upon New Orleans, where General Wilkinson was in command, he was ordered to descend the river with fifteen hundred troops to the aid of Wilkinson. As General Jackson hated the commandant at New Orleans, and expected a " difficulty," he took with him his dueling pistols and powder.

The expedition reached Natchez; and after a delay of several weeks there, without accomplishing anything, the men were ordered back to their homes. But the energy General Jackson had displayed, and his entire devotion to the comfort of his soldiers, won him golden opinions; and he became the most popular man in the State. It was in this expedition that his *toughness* gave him the nickname of " Old Hickory."

A young friend of General Jackson, by the name of William Carroll, challenged Jesse Benton, a younger brother of Colonel Thomas H. Benton, to a duel. Andrew Jackson, then forty-six years of age, somewhat reluctantly acted as second to Carroll. Both parties were wounded, young Benton quite severely. This roused the indignation of Colonel Thomas H. Benton, who had conferred some signal favors upon General Jackson; and, in his rage, he made such remarks as passionate men were accustomed to make in those days and in that region. The general, hearing of these remarks, swore " by the Eternal " that he would horsewhip Benton. Learning that Benton was in Nashville, he rode into the city, and with pistols in his pocket, a small sword at his side, and a whip in his hand, went to the City Hotel, accompanied by a friend. Colonel Benton was at the front-door, with his brother Jesse near. Jackson advanced upon him with his whip, exclaiming, —

" Now, you d——d rascal, I am going to punish you! Defend yourself! "

Benton clapped his hand into his breast-pocket as if feeling for a pistol. Jackson instantly drew a pistol, and presented it at the breast of his antagonist. Benton stepped back through the hall towards the door at the other end, Jackson following closely. Jesse Benton, seeing his brother's peril, fired at Jackson. The pistol was loaded with two balls and a slug. The slug struck his left shoulder, shattering it horribly. The ball buried itself in his arm, where it remained for twenty years. Jackson fell heavily and helplessly to the floor, bleeding profusely. His friend, Colonel Coffee, rushed upon Colonel Benton, fired his pistol, and missed. He then clubbed his pistol, and was just about to strike the colonel over the head, when Benton tripped, and fell back over some stairs behind him which he had not observed, and rolled to the bottom. Coffee now turned his attention to his wounded friend. But another actor immediately appeared. Stokely Hays, a nephew of General Jackson, and a man of gigantic strength and stature, rushed upon Jesse Benton. With gleaming knives, they had a rough-and-tumble fight. Blood flowed freely. Bystanders interfered, and separated them.

Faint with loss of blood, Jackson was carried to the Nashville Inn, a short distance; and the Bentons remained in possession of the field. Jackson's wounds were very severe. While he was lingering, haggard and wan, upon a bed of suffering, news came that the Indians, who had combined under Tecumseh, from Florida to the Lakes, to exterminate the white settlers, were committing the most awful ravages. Decisive action became necessary. General Jackson, with his fractured bones just beginning to heal, his arm in a sling, and unable to mount his horse without assistance, gave his amazing energies to the raising of an army to rendezvous at Fayetteville, on the borders of Alabama, on the 4th of October, 1813.

The varied incidents of the war which ensued cannot here be described. On the bloody field of Talluschatches, where the whole of a band of one hundred and eighty Indian warriors met with their death, an Indian babe was found clinging to the bosom of its dead mother. Jackson urged some of the Indian women, who were captives, to give it nourishment. They refused, saying, " All his relations are dead : kill him too." The general took the child to his own tent, nursed it with sugar and water, sent it to the Hermitage, and brought the child up as a son, giving him the name of Lincoyer. He grew up a finely formed young man, but died of consumption at the age of seventeen.

A narrative of the heroism of the troops, their sufferings and their achievements, would fill pages. On one occasion a starving soldier approached the general, begging for food. " I will divide with you my own food," said he, and, drawing a few acorns from his pocket, presented them to the man, saying, " This is all the fare I have." Mutinies arose in the camp, one after another, which General Jackson, almost by his own single energies, vanquished. The discouragement and embarrassments he encountered were terrible. In the severe chastisement of the Indians at Talladega; in the struggle with his own starving troops at Fort Strother; in his twelve days' excursion, culminating in the routing of the Indians at Enotochopco, — there was as high a display of energy and sagacity as has, perhaps, ever been recorded.

The Indians were numerous and desperate. The battles were fierce and bloody. The settlers in that remote wilderness were entirely dependent upon their crops for the support of their families. Absence in seed-time or harvest exposed wives and children to starvation. It was exceedingly difficult to hire men even for six months' military service. Two hundred young men volunteered for a three-months' campaign. The contract was written and signed. General Roberts had enlisted these men. He marched them to within a short distance of Fort Strother, and then halted them, and rode forward to get a promise from General Jackson to receive them for the short service for which they had enlisted.

The wrath of the general was roused. He would not hear of their serving for less than six months. The men heard of it, and immediately started for their homes. Awful were the oaths of the enraged general. Every available man was sent after them to arrest them as deserters. He needed the men so much, that, while he swore that he would shoot them as deserters if they did not return, he assured them that they should be pardoned, and received into service on the terms upon which they had enlisted, if they would come back.

Thus assured, they again rendezvoused at Fayetteville. Here a man who was anxious to retire engaged another young man, not quite eighteen years of age, John Wood, to serve as his substitute. John the more readily assented to this as he had an elder brother in the company. They were now marched to Fort Strother.

A few days after this, on a cold, rainy morning in February, John Wood was on guard. Wet, chilled, and hungry, he obtained permission to go to his tent to get a blanket. His comrades had left his breakfast for him; and, while he was hastily eating it, an officer came along, and reproved him sharply for the bones and other litter which were strewn about. John went on eating. The officer, in the coarse, insulting language of the camp, ordered him to pick up the bones. John replied, probably not very respectfully, that he was on guard, and had permission to leave his post but for a few moments, to which he must immediately return. A loud altercation ensued. The officer ordered the bystanders to arrest Wood. He seized his gun, and swore that he would shoot the first man who should attempt to touch him.

General Jackson heard that a man was mutinying, and came rushing from his tent like an enraged maniac. Wood was put in irons. General Jackson was about to start upon a very important enterprise. There was but little subordination in the army. He thought it time to make an example. He had been struggling against mutiny for three months, and his patience was exhausted. John, sitting upon a log in the forest, a mere boy, knowing nothing of military life, having been but a month in service, was condemned to die. General Jackson was urged to pardon him, or, at least, to mitigate the sentence, in consideration of his youth, and of his aged parents, of whom he was the main-stay. The general replied that he was sorry for his parents; but the boy was a mutineer, and must die.

The whole army was drawn up to witness the execution. A general order was read, in which it was asserted that Wood had been a *deserter* as well as a mutineer. A deserter he certainly was not; for he did not join the company until after the flight and its rendezvous at Fayetteville. No one has ever read this story without a deep feeling of sympathy for John Wood.

The Creek Indians had established a strong fort on one of the bends of the Tallapoosa River, near the centre of Alabama, about fifty miles below Fort Strother. With an army of two thousand men, General Jackson traversed the pathless wilderness in a march of eleven days. He reached their fort, called Tohopeka, or Horseshoe, on the 27th of March, 1814. The bend of the river inclosed nearly one hundred acres of tangled forest and wild ravine. Across the narrow neck the Indians had constructed a formidable breastwork of logs and brush. Here nine hundred warriors, with an ample supply of arms and ammunition, were assembled.

The fort was stormed. The fight was utterly desperate. Not an Indian would accept of quarter. When bleeding and dying, they would fight those who endeavored to spare their lives. From ten in the morning until dark the battle raged. The carnage was awful

and revolting.   Some threw themselves into the river ; but the unerring bullet struck their heads as they swam.   Nearly every one
of the nine hundred warriors was killed.   A few probably, in the
night, swam the river and escaped.   This ended the war.   The
power of the Creeks was broken forever.   This bold plunge into
the wilderness, with its terrific slaughter, so appalled the savages,
that the haggard remnants of the bands came to the camp, begging
for peace.

General Jackson returned a conqueror.   No one but those who
know from experience what are the horrors of Indian warfare — the
midnight yell of the savage, the torch, the tomahawk, the carnage,
the torture — can appreciate the gratitude with which this deliverer
of the frontiers was received as he journeyed homewards.   A cavalcade of the citizens of Nashville flocked to meet him.   With loudest
acclaim they conducted him to the court-house.   All past enmities
were forgotten, and every tongue spoke his praise.

This closing of the Creek war enabled us to concentrate our
militia upon the British, who were the allies of the Indians.   No
man of less resolute will than General Jackson could have conducted
this Indian campaign to so successful an issue.   Immediately, on
the 31st of May, Jackson was appointed major-general in the army
of the United States.   This gave him an income of between six and
seven thousand dollars a year, and made him, for those times, a rich
man.   Through the whole Indian campaign he suffered terribly
from the wounds and debility occasioned by his senseless feud with
Colonel Benton.   He was pale and haggard and pain-worn, often
enduring the extreme of agony.   Not many men, suffering as he
did, would have been out of the sick chamber.   As one of the results of the Creek war, the Creeks were compelled to cede to the
United States government nearly the whole of the territory now
embraced in the State of Alabama.

Napoleon had now fallen ; the Bourbons were restored ; and the
English, flushed with victory, with a splendid army, and a still more
splendid navy of more than a thousand vessels, were free to concentrate all their energies against this infant republic.   The Federalists
were glad that Napoleon was overthrown ; the Republicans generally
mourned.   Andrew Jackson was a Republican, and a great admirer
of Napoleon.

Immediately upon the fall of Napoleon, the British Cabinet decided to gather up its strength to strike America a crushing blow. It was their plan to take New Orleans, lay all our seaport towns in ashes, annihilate our navy, and, by holding the Atlantic, the Mississippi, and the Lakes, to imprison us in our forests. The British were at Pensacola and Appalachicola, dispensing arms to the Indians in that region, and preparing for their grand naval and land expedition to New Orleans. Florida then belonged to Spain, an ally of England; and the British Cabinet doubted not its ability to wrest from us Louisiana, which we had purchased of France. Most of the hostile Indians, flying from the tremendous blows which General Jackson had dealt out to them, had also taken refuge in Florida. Jackson, far away in the wilderness, was left to act almost without instructions. He decided to take the responsibility, and assumed the independence of a sovereign.

Late in August, with an army of two thousand men, on a rushing march, General Jackson traversed the wilderness from which he had driven out the Creeks, and reached Mobile, then an insignificant hamlet of one hundred and fifty houses, and took possession of a dilapidated rampart, called Fort Bowyer, at Mobile Point. A British fleet came from Pensacola, landed a force upon the beach, anchored near the little fort, and from both ship and shore commenced a furious assault. The battle was long and doubtful. At length, one of the ships was blown up, and the rest of the force retired in utter discomfiture.

The whole South and West were fully aroused to meet and repel the foe. By the 1st of November General Jackson had in Mobile an army of four thousand men. His wrath against the Spaniards had no limits; and he resolved to march upon Pensacola, where the Spaniards were sheltering our foes, and, as he expressed it, "rout out the English." Regardless of the rights of Spain, he advanced upon Pensacola, stormed the town, took possession of every fort, and drove the British fleet out to sea. But where had the fleet gone? This question General Jackson asked with great anxiety. Fearing for Mobile, he put his force in rapid motion to return. On the 3d of November he left Mobile, and on the 11th got back again, having marched nearly two hundred miles, and achieved a great victory. Many, at that time, condemned him for the invasion of Florida; but the final verdict has been clearly in his favor.

Garrisoning Mobile, he moved his troops to New Orleans, a distance of a hundred and seventy miles. General Jackson himself was so feeble that he could ride but seventeen miles a day. He reached New Orleans the 1st of December. New Orleans contained then twenty thousand inhabitants. There was plunder enough of cotton and sugar stored in the city to make the expedition of the British, if successful, very profitable. The following description has been given of General Jackson, as, accompanied by his staff alone, he entered the city: —

" The chief of the party, which was composed of five or six persons, was a tall, gaunt man, of very erect carriage, with a countenance full of stern decision and fearless energy, but furrowed with care and anxiety. His complexion was sallow and unhealthy, his hair was iron gray, and his body thin and emaciated, like that of one who had just recovered from a lingering and painful sickness. But the fierce glare of his bright and hawk-like eye betrayed a soul and spirit which triumphed over all the infirmities of the body. His dress was simple, and nearly threadbare. A small leather cap protected his head, and a short Spanish blue cloak his body ; whilst his feet and legs were incased in high dragoon-boots, long ignorant of polish or blacking, which reached to the knees. In age he appeared to have passed about forty-five winters."

In some mysterious way General Jackson had acquired the manners of the most polished and accomplished gentleman. There was something in his presence which charmed every one, in the saloon as well as in the camp. Always self-possessed, there were dignity and courtliness, united with affability, in his address, which would have rendered him conspicuous as a gentleman, even in the court of Louis XIV.

Every available man in New Orleans was immediately brought into service. The battle of New Orleans, which soon ensued, was, in reality, a very arduous campaign. A British fleet of sixty ships, many of them of the first class, and which had obtained renown in the naval conflicts of Trafalgar and the Nile, was assembled in a spacious bay on the western end of the Island of Jamaica. This fleet, which carried a thousand cannon, was manned by nearly nine thousand soldiers and marines, and transported a land force of ten thousand veteran soldiers, fresh from the wars of Europe, and flushed with victory over Napoleon. The fleet entered Lake Borgne. It was the 10th of December, 1814. There were five small cutters in the lake, which were soon overpowered by the immense force of the foe. The fleet now ran along to the western extremity of the lake, and landed the troops at the mouth of the Bayou Bienvenue. The shallow water would not allow the large ships to approach near the land; but sixteen hundred troops were speedily put on shore by the boats but eight miles from New Orleans. Unaware how feeble the force General Jackson had at his disposal, they did not deem it prudent to move upon the city until they had greatly increased their numbers. This delay probably saved New Orleans.

The British troops commenced landing on the 16th. The process was very slow and tedious; and it was not until the 22d that they were prepared to move forward. Thus far it had been uncertain by what direction they would advance upon the city. As soon as General Jackson heard of their line of approach he advanced to meet them. He had placed the city under martial law. Every available man, horse, mule, ox, had been called into requisition. The two armed schooners were stationed in the river. Fort St. Philip was strengthened, to prevent the British fleet, which was impelled by wind alone, from ascending the river.

At two o'clock in the afternoon on the 23d, General Jackson learned that the foe, marching from Lake Borgne, were within nine miles of the city. He immediately collected his motley force of young farmers and mechanics, about two thousand in number, and marched to meet them. He fell upon them impetuously in a night attack, checked their progress, and drove them back towards their landing-place. The British, surprised by the fury of the assault, waited for reinforcements, which came up in large numbers during the night.

In the mean time General Jackson, with that indomitable energy, that fiery impetuosity in which he surpassed all living men, fell back with his men to a point about four miles down the river from New Orleans, and commenced cutting a ditch, and throwing up a line of breastworks from the river across the plain, which was about a mile in width, to the impassable swamp. Every man and boy in the city was put to the work. The general was everywhere. His zeal inspired all. He seemed neither to eat nor sleep. It is said that for five days and four nights he was without sleep. Two precious days the British allowed him, while they were laboriously bringing up their reinforcements of men, ammunition, provisions, and guns.

General Jackson had two sloops of war in the river, which annoyed the foe terribly. It is but a narrow strip of land which lines the turbid Mississippi. It was only along this strip that the foe could advance. They were on the eastern banks, and were exposed unsheltered to the fire of these vessels. The levee, rising some fifteen feet from the plain, alone prevented the inundation of the ground where the British forces were collecting. On their right, as they looked up the stream, the swamp shut them in; while the swift, turbid, deep river was on their left. On the 25th Sir E. Packenham reached the British camp, bringing with him a powerful battery. He planted it near the levee in the night, opened fire in the morning, blew one of the vessels into the air, and drove the other out of range of his guns. He was the nephew of the Duke of Wellington. But Andrew Jackson was in spirit the duke himself, expanded and intensified.

Packenham, on the 28th, pushed his veteran battalions forward on a reconnoissance, and to sweep, if possible, like a Mississippi flood, over General Jackson's frail and unfinished breastwork. In the construction of his ditch and earthworks, he could scoop up the earth only to the depth of three feet before he came to the water. It was a brilliant morning, the 28th of December. Jackson, with an old borrowed telescope in his hand, was on the watch. The solid columns of red-coats came on, in military array, as beautiful as awe-inspiring. The artillery led, heralding the advance with a shower of Congreve-rockets, round shot, and shell. The muskets of the infantry flashed like mirrors in the light of the morning sun. The Britons were in high glee. It was absurd to suppose that a few thousand raw militia could resist the veterans who had conquered the armies of Napoleon.

General Jackson had not quite three thousand men behind his breastwork; but every one had imbibed the spirit of his chieftain. There were eight thousand veteran soldiers marching upon them. For a few hours there were the tumult, the horror, the carnage of a battle; and then the British host seemed to have melted away. Panting, bleeding, with shattered ranks, leaving their dead behind them, again they retreated.

Another week passed away. Both parties exerted almost superhuman energy in preparing for the renewal of the strife. General Jackson had made his arrangements, if defeated, to retire to the

BATTLE OF NEW ORLEANS.

JANUARY 8th 1815.

ENGRAVED EXPRESSLY FOR MARTIN'S LIVES OF THE PRESIDENTS.

Drawn by H. Billings

city, fire it, and, amidst its flames, to fight with desperation ; slowly falling back to some strong position on the river banks, and, by cutting off the supplies of the foe, compel him to depart.

The British now decided to advance upon the American lines by regular approaches. For three days they remained in their encampment two miles below our breastworks, but in open view. They brought from their ships heavy cannon, and other needful supplies. Thus passed the three last days of the year. The banks of the river were lined with sentinels, and watch-boats patroled the majestic stream. The British had brought forward twenty eighteen-pounders and ten twenty-fours.

The night of the 31st of December was very dark. In its gloom one half of the British army advanced within three hundred yards of our front, and, under cover of a heavy cannonade on their right, commenced throwing up a chain of works. The next morning was Sunday, the first day of the new year. It dawned through a fog so dense that no man could be seen at a distance of twenty yards. Suddenly, at ten o'clock, like the uprolling of a curtain at a theatre, the fog lifted ; and the whole plain, glittering with all the pageantry of war, was opened to view. Instantly the British batteries commenced their fire upon the American lines.

Within ten minutes one hundred balls struck the house which General Jackson had occupied as his headquarters. The reply from the American lines was prompt, and such a storm of war was opened as never before had been witnessed upon this continent. Fifty pieces of cannon were discharged, each from two to three times a minute ; and, as there was not a breath of air, the plain was soon so covered with smoke that nothing could be seen but an impenetrable cloud, blazing and bellowing with volcanic flash and roar. After an hour and a half of such work the guns became so hot that they could no longer be loaded.

As the smoke rolled away the British batteries were seen totally destroyed ; the soldiers who had manned them were running to the rear ; and the British army, which had been drawn up to advance upon our works, were hiding behind the ramparts which they had thrown up. Again the British were defeated. Annoyed by the terrible fire which was opened upon them by our artillerists and sharpshooters, they were compelled to fall back to their former position. This was the third battle, not including the gunboat fight, of the campaign. It was on this occasion only that cotton bales were used. They were found valueless, and were thrown aside, as the cannon-balls knocked them about, or set them on fire.

What the enemy would next attempt was now the great question. Four days passed away with no decisive movements on either side. The British were, however, evidently preparing for another advance. No words can describe the efforts made by our army to prepare for the next movement of the foe, whatever it might be. On Friday, the 6th, General Jackson became assured that the enemy was preparing to attack him on both sides of the river.

We cannot here describe the preparations made for the attack and for the repulse. At half an hour before dawn, Sunday morning, January 8, 1815, a rocket from the hostile lines gave the signal for the attack. In two solid columns, the British advanced upon our ramparts, which were bristling with infantry and artillery, and behind which General Jackson had now collected an army of about four thousand men, all inspired with the zeal of their commander. On both sides of the river the blood-red billows of battle rolled and broke.

Our men were well protected. With bare bosoms, the British marched upon the embankment, from which there was poured forth an incessant storm of bullets, balls, and shells, which no flesh and blood could stand. It was one of the most awful scenes of slaughter which was ever witnessed. Every bullet accomplished its mission, spending its force in the bodies of those who were insanely driven forward to inevitable death. Two hundred men were cut down by one discharge of a thirty-two-pounder, loaded to the muzzle with musket-balls, and poured into the head of a column at the distance of but a few yards. Regiments vanished, a British officer said, " as if the earth had opened and swallowed them up." The American line looked like a row of fiery furnaces. General Jackson walked slowly along his ranks, cheering his men, and saying, —

" Stand to your guns ! Don't waste your ammunition ! See that every shot tells ! Let us finish the business to-day ! "

Two hours passed, and the work was done, — effectually done. As the smoke lifted, the whole proud array had disappeared. The ground was so covered with the dying and the dead, that, for a quarter of a mile in front, one might walk upon their bodies ; and, far away in the distance, the retreating lines of the foe were to be seen. On both sides of the river the enemy was repulsed.

The British had about nine thousand in the engagement, and we but about four thousand. Their loss in killed and wounded was two thousand six hundred, while ours was but thirteen. Thus ended the great battle of New Orleans. For ten days after the battle the British remained in their encampment, continually annoyed by our artillerists and sharpshooters, until at length through great difficulties they effected their escape to their ships.

In those days intelligence traveled so slowly, that it was not until the 4th of February that tidings of the victory reached Washington. The whole country blazed with illuminations, and rang with rejoicings. Ten days after this, news of the Treaty of Ghent was received, which treaty had been signed before the bloody battle of New Orleans took place. General Jackson was not a man of tender sympathies. Inexorable in discipline, soon after this, on the 21st, at Mobile, he ordered six militia-men to be shot for mutiny. It is a sad story. They were honest, well-meaning men, who probably had no intention of doing wrong. Some of them were true Christians, and they supposed that their term of service had really expired. No one can read the story of their death without anguish ; and it required all the glory of the victory at New Orleans to obliterate the memory of the execution at Mobile.

Rumors of the Treaty of Ghent reached New Orleans in March, and were published by one of the New Orleans editors. General Jackson, deeming such an announcement injudicious, ordered the editor to retract. He refused, and was arrested. Judge Hall, to vindicate the supremacy of the civil authority, issued a writ of *habeas corpus.* The general arrested the judge, and sent him out of his lines. Soon intelligence of peace was received. The judge returned, and, by virtue of his office, fined the general a thousand dollars. The people of New Orleans, adoring their deliverer, were indignant, and wished to pay the fine for him. The general refused their offer, and paid it himself.

He now returned to Nashville, and honors were poured in upon him without number. He still retained his command of the southern division of the army. The Seminole Indians in Florida were committing outrages upon our frontiers. General Jackson gathered an army of over two thousand men, and, regardless of treaties, marched into Florida, punished the Indians severely, attacked a Spanish post, shot by court-martial a Scotchman, and hung an

Englishman accused of inciting the Indians to insurrection. His energy, and disregard of treaties and the forms of law, were denounced by one party, and commended by another. He was, however, sustained by Congress and the President; and, after the purchase of Florida from Spain, General Jackson was appointed governor of the newly acquired territory. The powers with which he was invested were so great, that he said, upon assuming the command, —

" I am clothed with powers that no one under a republic ought to possess, and which, I trust, will never again be given to any man."

For some reason he soon became tired of his office, and, resigning it, again retired to his farm and his extremely humble home in Tennessee. His name soon began to be brought forward as that of a candidate for the presidency of the United States. In the autumn of 1823 he was elected, by the Tennessee Legislature, United States senator. In the stormy electoral canvass of 1824, which resulted in the choice of John Quincy Adams by the House of Representatives, General Jackson received a larger number of electoral votes than either of his competitors. The Democratic party now with great unanimity fixed upon him to succeed Mr. Adams. In the campaign of 1828 he was triumphantly elected President of the United States. In 1829, just before he assumed the reins of government, he met with the most terrible affliction of his life in the death of his wife, whom he had loved with devotion which has perhaps never been surpassed. From the shock of her death he never recovered.

He ever afterwards appeared like a changed man. He became subdued in spirit, and, except when his terrible temper had been greatly aroused, seldom used profane language. It is said that every night afterwards, until his own death, he read a prayer from his wife's prayer-book, with her miniature likeness before him. With frankness characteristic of his nature, he expressed his deep conviction of the necessity of vital godliness, and his hope and intention to become a Christian before he should die.

His administration was one of the most memorable in the annals of our country; applauded by one party, condemned by the other. No man had more bitter enemies or warmer friends. It is, however, undeniable, that many of the acts of his administration, which were at the time most unsparingly denounced, are now generally commended. Every year the judgment of the whole community is settling into the conviction, that, with all his glaring faults of character, he was a true patriot, honestly seeking the good of his country. With the masses of the people, Andrew Jackson was the most popular President, with possibly the exceptions of Washington and Lincoln, who ever occupied the presidential chair. At the expiration of his two terms of office, he retired, in 1837, to the Hermitage, resigning his office at Washington to his warm friend and able supporter, Martin Van Buren.

The remains of his much-loved wife were reposing in the humble graveyard near his house. The evening of his stormy life had come. Hours of reflection were forced upon him. The sublimities of the world beyond the grave had ever overawed his soul. There was a series of religious meetings of several days' continuance. General Jackson devoutly attended them all. The last sermon was on Saturday afternoon, upon God's interposition among the affairs of men. General Jackson went home, intensely impressed with a sense of ingratitude and sin. He passed the night walking the floor of his chamber in anguish and in prayer. In the morning he announced to his family his full conviction that he had repented of his sins, and, through faith in Christ, had obtained forgiveness. That day the sacrament of the Lord's Supper was to be administered. With his customary decision of character, he sent for the elders of the church, informed them of the new life upon which he believed he had entered, and expressed the desire that very day to make a profession of his faith in Christ, and to partake of the emblems of his body broken for us, and his blood shed for our sins. It was a solemn scene which was that morning witnessed in that rural church, almost buried in the forests of Tennessee. The warworn veteran, with bronzed face and frosted hair, knelt with the humility of a little child before the altar, in acceptance of pardon through an atoning Saviour, and was baptized in the name of the Father, and of the Son, and of the Holy Ghost. The prayers of his Christian mother were now answered.

His subsequent life was that of the Christian who is conscious that his sins are forgiven, but who is conscious, also, that he has yet many remaining infirmities. Family prayer was immediately established in his dwelling, which General Jackson himself conducted, however numerous might be his guests. Scott's Family Bible he read through twice before he died. The household servants were all called in to partake in the devotions. At one of the meetings of the church General Jackson was nominated a "ruling elder."

"No," he replied. "The Bible says, 'Be not hasty in the laying on of hands.' I am too young in the church for such an office. My countrymen have given me high honors; but I should esteem the office of ruling elder in the Church of Christ a far higher honor than any I have received."

His sufferings from sickness during the last years of his life were dreadful; but he bore them with the greatest fortitude, never uttering a complaining word. Still, at times, the gleams of his impetuous soul would flash forth. "What would you have done with Calhoun and the other nullifiers, if they had kept on?" asked Dr. Edgar one day.

The old general half rose from his bed, and with flashing eye, and great vehemence of manner, said, "I would have hung them, sir, as high as Haman. They should have been a terror to traitors for all time; and posterity would have pronounced it the best act of my life."

On Sunday, May 24, 1845, he partook of the communion. "Death," said he, "has no terrors for me. When I have suffered sufficiently, the Lord will take me to himself; but what are my sufferings compared with those of the blessed Saviour who died on the accursed tree for me? Mine are nothing."

Still he lingered in the extreme of weakness and of suffering. On Sunday morning, June the 8th, it was seen that his last hour had come. He assembled all his family around him, and, in the most affecting manner, took leave of each one. "He then," writes one who was present, "delivered one of the most impressive lectures on the subject of religion that I have ever heard. He spoke for nearly half an hour, and apparently with the power of inspiration." The servants had all been called in. In conclusion, he said, "My dear children and friends and servants, I hope and trust to meet you all in heaven, both white and black." The last words he repeated, turning his eyes tenderly towards the slaves clustered around. For some time he remained apparently in a state of stupor. At length his adopted son took his hand, and said, "Father, do you know me?"

"Yes," he replied, "I know you. Where is my daughter, and

Marian? God will take care of you for me. I am my God's. I belong to Him. I go but a short time before you; and I want to meet you all, white and black, in heaven."

The slaves, men, women, and children, who crowded the piazza, looking in at the windows, sobbed loudly. Turning to them, their dying master said, —

" What is the matter with my dear children? Have I alarmed you? Oh! do not cry, and we will all meet in heaven."

Soon after this he suddenly, and without a struggle, ceased to breathe. Two days after he was placed in a grave by the side of his wife. He had often said, " Heaven will be no heaven to me if I do not meet my wife there." For miles around the people flocked to the burial. It was estimated that three thousand were assembled upon the lawn in front of the house. A favorite psalm of the departed was sung, —

> " Why should we start, and fear to die?
> What timorous worms we mortals are ! "

A sermon was preached from the text, " These are they which came out of great tribulation, and have washed their robes, and made them white in the blood of the Lamb."

The brief sketch which we have given of this remarkable man must leave the impression upon every mind that he possessed great virtues and great defects. He was the first President America had chosen who was not a man of intelligence, of culture, and of experienced statesmanship. Though intense in his prejudices, and slow to listen to the voice of reason, and though many of his actions were fearfully unjust, few will now deny that he was honest in his purposes, and sincerely patriotic.

Mr. Parton, in his admirable Life of Jackson, says very truly, " His ignorance of law, history, politics, science, — of every thing which he who governs a country ought to know, — was extreme. Mr. Trist remembers hearing a member of the general's family say that General Jackson did not believe the world was round. His ignorance was a wall round about him, high and impenetrable. He was imprisoned in his ignorance, and sometimes raged around his little dim inclosure like a tiger in his den." It is said that, when he was elected President of the United States, he had never read a book through except " The Vicar of Wakefield." The honorary degree of LL. D. was conferred upon him in 1833 by Harvard University.

Chief Justice Taney, at the time of his death, paid the following beautiful tribute to his memory : —

" The whole civilized world already knows how bountifully he was endowed by Providence with those high gifts which qualified him to lead, both as a soldier and as a statesman. But those only who were around him in hours of anxious deliberation, when great and mighty interests were at stake, and who were also with him in the retired scenes of domestic life, in the midst of his family and friends, can fully appreciate his innate love of justice, his hatred of oppression in every shape it could assume, his magnanimity, his entire freedom from any feeling of personal hostility to his political opponents, and his constant and unvarying kindness and gentleness to his friends."

CHAPTER VIII.

MARTIN VAN BUREN.

Birth and Childhood. — Studies Law. — Talents and Industry. — Political Principles. — Success as a Lawyer and Politician. — Aids in the Election of Jackson. — Secretary of State. — Mrs. Eaton. — Resigns his Secretaryship. — Minister to England. — Rejected by the Senate. — Attains the Vice-Presidency. — Patronage of General Jackson. — Chosen President. Retirement and Declining Years.

THERE is but little in the life of Martin Van Buren of romantic interest. He fought no battles, engaged in no wild adventures.

RESIDENCE OF MARTIN VAN BUREN.

Though his life was stormy in political and intellectual conflicts, and he gained many signal victories, his days passed uneventful in those incidents which give zest to biography. His ancestors, as his name indicates, were of Dutch origin, and were among the earliest

16

emigrants from Holland to the banks of the Hudson. His father was a farmer, residing in the old town of Kinderhook. His mother, also of Dutch lineage, was a woman of superior intelligence and of exemplary piety. Martin, their eldest son, was born on the 5th of December, 1782.

He was decidedly a precocious boy, developing unusual activity, vigor, and strength of mind. At the age of fourteen he had finished his academic studies in his native village, and commenced the study of the law. As he had not a collegiate education, seven years of study in a law office were required of him before he could be admitted to the bar. Inspired with a lofty ambition, and conscious of his powers, he pursued his studies with indefatigable industry. After spending six years in an office in his native village, he went to the city of New York, and prosecuted his studies for the seventh year under the tuition of William P. Van Ness, who subsequently obtained celebrity as the second of Burr in his duel with Hamilton.

Martin Van Buren's father was a tavern-keeper, as well as a farmer; a man of imperturbable good nature, and a very decided Democrat. His son inherited from him both his *bonhomie* and his political principles. It is said of the son, that, all through life, he was ever ready to greet his most bitter opponent with an open hand and a friendly smile. Burr was in the most brilliant period of his career when the young law student first made his acquaintance. There was a certain congeniality of spirit between them which promoted friendship. Martin, then a young man of twenty, was very handsome, and was endowed with shining abilities; and one can apparently see in his after-life the influence which the seductive and commanding mind of Burr exerted upon his youthful nature. In one respect, indeed, they were different: Mr. Van Buren was ever a man of irreproachable morality.

In 1803 Mr. Van Buren, then twenty-one years of age, commenced the practice of law in his native village. The great conflict between the Federal and Republican parties was then at its height. It has often been necessary in the previous sketches to allude to the principles which separated the two parties. Washington and John Adams considered our great danger to consist in not giving the *Central* government sufficient power: the Democratic party, on the contrary, under the leadership of Jefferson, thought that our danger consisted in not giving the *State* governments sufficient power.

In August, 1786, George Washington wrote to Jay, "We have probably had too good an opinion of human nature in forming our confederacy. I do not conceive that we can long exist as a nation, without having centralized somewhere a power which will pervade the whole Union in as energetic a manner as the authority of the state governments extends over the several States."

Mr. Van Buren was, from the beginning, a politician. He had, perhaps, imbibed that spirit while listening to the many discussions which had been carried on in his father's bar-room. He was in cordial sympathy with Jefferson, and earnestly and eloquently espoused the cause of State Rights; though, at that time, the Federal party held the supremacy, both in his town and State. Though ever taking an active part in politics, he devoted himself with great assiduity to the duties of a village lawyer, and rose rapidly in his profession.

His success and increasing reputation led him, after six years of practice, to remove to Hudson, the shire-town of his county. Here he spent seven years, constantly gaining strength by contending in the courts with some of the ablest men who have adorned the bar of his State. The heroic example of John Quincy Adams, in retaining in office every faithful man, without regard to his political preferences, had been thoroughly repudiated under the administration of General Jackson. The unfortunate principle was now fully established, that "to the victors belong the spoils." Still this principle, to which Mr. Van Buren gave his adherence, was not devoid of inconveniences. When, subsequently, he attained power which placed vast patronage in his hands, he was heard to say, —

"I prefer an office which has no patronage. When I give a man an office I offend his disappointed competitors and their friends. Nor am I certain of gaining a friend in the man I appoint; for, in all probability, he expected something better."

Just before leaving Kinderhook for Hudson, Mr. Van Buren married a lady alike distinguished for beauty and accomplishments. After twelve short years she sank into the grave, the victim of consumption, leaving her husband and four sons to weep over her loss. For twenty-five years Mr. Van Buren was an earnest, successful, assiduous lawyer. The record of those years is barren in items of public interest. The political affairs of the State of New York, with which he was constantly intermingled, were in an entangled condition which no mortal would now undertake to unravel. In 1812, when thirty years of age, he was chosen to the state Senate, and gave his strenuous support to Mr. Madison's administration. In 1815 he was appointed attorney-general; and the next year moved to Albany, the capital of the State. Here he cordially supported the administration of Mr. Madison; and yet he voted for Clinton, in opposition to Madison, at his second election. Soon after this, we again find him the unrelenting opponent of Clinton.

While he was acknowledged as one of the most prominent leaders of the Democratic party, he had the moral courage to avow that true democracy did not require that "universal suffrage" which admits the vile, the degraded, the ignorant, to the right of governing the State. In true consistency with his democratic principles, he contended that while the path leading to the privilege of voting should be open to every man without distinction, no one should be invested with that sacred prerogative unless he were in some degree qualified for it by intelligence, virtue, and some property interest in the welfare of the State. He contended that "universal suffrage" with the motley mass who crowd the garrets and cellars of New York would render the elections a curse rather than a blessing, and would drive all respectable people from the polls.

Mr. Van Buren cannot, perhaps, be accused of inconsistency in his political life; and yet, in endeavoring to trace out his career amidst the mazes of party politics, one is reminded of the attempt to follow with the eye the mounted aide of a general amidst the smoke, tumult, and uproar of the field of battle, now moving in one direction, now in another, and yet ever in accordance with some well-established plan.

In 1818 there was a great split in the Democratic party in New York; and Mr. Van Buren took the lead in organizing that portion of the party called the "Albany Regency," which is said to have swayed the destinies of the State for a quarter of a century. In 1821 he was elected a member of the United States Senate; and in the same year he took a seat in the convention to revise the Constitution of his native State. His course in this convention secured the approval of men of all parties. No one could doubt the singleness of his endeavors to promote the interests of all classes in the community. In the Senate of the United States he rose at once to a conspicuous position as an active and useful legislator; acting always, however, in sympathy with the Republican, or Democratic party.

In 1827, John Quincy Adams being then in the presidential chair, Mr. Van Buren was reëlected to the Senate. He had been from the beginning a determined opposer of the administration, adopting the State-Rights view in opposition to what was deemed the Federal proclivities of Mr. Adams. In his letter accepting the senatorship, in accordance with his character as a strict "constructionist," he said, —

" It shall be my constant and zealous endeavor to protect the remaining rights reserved to the States by the Federal Constitution, to restore those of which they have been divested by construction, and to promote the interest and honor of our common country."

Soon after this, in 1828, he was chosen Governor of the State of New York, and accordingly resigned his seat in the Senate. Probably no one in the United States contributed so much towards ejecting John Quincy Adams from the presidential chair, and placing in it Andrew Jackson, as did Martin Van Buren. Whether entitled to the reputation or not, he certainly was regarded throughout the United States as one of the most skilful, sagacious, and cunning of manœuvrers. It was supposed that no one knew so well as he how to touch the secret springs of action ; how to pull all the wires to put his machinery in motion ; and how to organize a political army which would, secretly and stealthily, accomplish the most gigantic results. By these powers, it is said that he outwitted Mr. Adams, Mr. Clay, Mr. Webster, and secured results which few thought then could be accomplished. In the spring of 1827 Mr. Webster had no doubt that Mr. Adams's administration would be sustained. He wrote to Jeremiah Mason, —

" A survey of the whole ground leads me to believe confidently in Mr. Adams's reëlection. I set down New England, New Jersey, the greater part of Maryland, and perhaps all Delaware, Ohio, Kentucky, Indiana, Missouri, and Louisiana, for him. We must then get votes enough in New York to choose him, and, I think, cannot fail of this."

At the appointed hour Mr. Van Buren opened his masked batteries. Mines were sprung all over the United States. The battle raged with fury which had scarcely ever been equaled. The names of Adams and Jackson rang out upon every breeze : each was represented as an angel, each a demon. There was not an aristocratic crime which John Quincy Adams had not committed, no democratic atrocity of which Andrew Jackson had not been guilty.

At length the electoral votes were cast. General Jackson received one hundred and seventy-eight; Mr. Adams, eighty-three. General Jackson immediately offered the post of Secretary of State to Mr. Van Buren; a tribute, as he said, " to his acknowledged talents and public services, and in accordance with the wishes of the Republican party throughout the Union."

Scarcely had General Jackson taken his seat in the presidential chair, ere there arose one of the most singular difficulties which ever distracted the government of a nation. There was a tavern-keeper in Washington who had a pretty, vivacious, free-and-easy daughter, by the name of Peg O'Neil. Peg may have been a very virtuous girl ; but she was so intimate with all her father's guests, so unreserved in conversation and manners, and withal so fascinating, that her reputation was not unblemished. General Jackson, when senator in 1823, had boarded with the old man, and had become acquainted with his pretty daughter. Miss O'Neil, however, eventually married a purser in the United States navy, by the name of Timberlake. He was, of course, much of the time absent from home. Major John H. Eaton, a senator from Tennessee, took board at O'Neil's tavern, and became very much fascinated by the beautiful and witty Mrs. Timberlake. Report was busy with the fair fame of them both ; and the lady, whether justly or unjustly, acquired a very unenviable reputation. Her husband one day, in a fit of melancholy, while in the Mediterranean, committed suicide ; and Major Eaton immediately after married her. This event took place soon after General Jackson's election to the presidency.

Major Eaton was a friend of General Jackson, and was appointed by him Secretary of War. The ladies of the other members of the Cabinet were in great trouble. How could they receive Peg O'Neil (now Mrs. Eaton), with her sullied reputation, into their social circles ? They conferred together, and resolved that they would not do it. General Jackson, mindful of his own past troubles in that line, and assuming, with all the force of his impetuous nature, that Mrs. Eaton was a traduced and virtuous woman, resolved that she should be received as an honored member of the republican court. Several of the members of the Cabinet were married, and these gentlemen sympathized with their wives. The Cabinet was divided. The conflict roused all the tremendous energies of General Jackson's soul.

Mr. Van Buren had neither wife nor daughter. He was one of the most pliant, politic, and courteous of men. It was one of the fundamental principles of his life, never to give offense, and never to appear to notice an injury. He was ever polite, alike to saint and sinner, to friend and enemy. Not unconscious of the gratification it would afford General Jackson, he called upon Mrs. Eaton, made parties for her, and treated her with the most marked respect. His great abilities had already secured the confidence of the President, which this policy tended only to increase. Those familiar with the state of things at Washington soon perceived that Martin Van Buren had become a great power, and that he was on the high road to any degree of elevation he might desire.

The boundless popularity of General Jackson rendered it probable that any one whom he might suggest as his successor would obtain the election. Not one year had elapsed after General Jackson had assumed the reins of government, ere he avowed to his friends his intention to do everything in his power to secure the presidency for Mr. Van Buren. About this time the President was taken very sick. He therefore wrote a letter, carefully worded, to be published in case he should die, expressive of his wishes. In this letter he says, —

" Permit me here to say of Mr. Van Buren, that I have found him everything I could desire him to be, and believe him not only deserving my confidence, but the confidence of the nation. Instead of his being selfish and intriguing, as has been represented by his opponents, I have ever found him frank, open, candid, and manly. As a counselor, he is able and prudent, republican in his principles, and one of the most pleasant men to do business with I ever saw. He is well qualified to fill the highest office in the gift of the people, who in him will find a true friend, and safe depositary of their rights and liberty."

For two years this Mrs. Eaton conflict raged bitterly. Foreign ministers and their wives were drawn into the troubled arena. Mr. Van Buren, however, succeeded in so governing his own actions, as to be ever increasing in strength. Daniel Webster wrote, early in the year 1831, —

"Mr. Van Buren has evidently, at this moment, quite the lead in influence and importance. He controls all the pages on the back stairs, and flatters what seems at present the 'Aaron's serpent' among the President's desires, — a settled purpose of making out the lady, of whom so much has been said, a person of reputation. It is odd enough, but too evident to be doubted, that the consequence of this dispute in the social and fashionable world is producing great political effects, and may very probably determine who shall be successor to the present Chief Magistrate."

In the division of the Cabinet, there were, for Mrs. Eaton, Mr. Van Buren, Major Eaton, Mr. Barry, and the President; against her, Mr. Ingham, Mr. Branch, Mr. Berrien, and the Vice-President, Calhoun. This latter personage now hated Van Buren with perfect hatred. The President so loved him, that he was accustomed to address him with endearing epithets; speaking of him to others as Van, and calling him, to his face, Matty. At length the President resolved to introduce harmony into his Cabinet by the unprecedented measure of dismissing them all, and organizing the Cabinet anew. This was to be accomplished by having those who were in sympathy with him resign, and receive rich offices elsewhere. If the others took the hint, and resigned also, well and good; if not, they were to be dismissed. Mr. Van Buren sent in his resignation, and immediately was appointed minister to the court of St. James.

All this redounded to the reputation of Mr. Van Buren; and more and more he was regarded as the great magician, whose wand possessed almost supernatural power. Upon returning to New York, he met with a triumphant reception, and, early in the autumn of 1831, sailed for London. Soon after his arrival there, Congress again met. It was necessary that the Senate should ratify his appointment. Messrs. Calhoun, Clay, and Webster appeared prominently as his opponents, accusing him of such a spirit of narrow partisanship as to unfit him to be the representative of our whole country. He was accused of being the originator of the system of removing from office every incumbent, however able and faithful, who did not advocate the principles of the party in power. It was during the discussion upon this question that Governor Marcy of New York, in defending the system of party removals, uttered the memorable words, —

" It may be, sir, that the politicians of New York are not so fastidious as some gentlemen are as to disclosing the principles on which they act. They boldly preach what they practice. When they are contending for victory, they avow their intention of enjoying the fruits of it. If they are defeated, they expect to retire from office ; if they are successful, they claim, as a matter of right, the advantages of success. They see nothing wrong in the rule, that to the victor belong the spoils of the enemy."

In this hour, when Mr. Van Buren was so bitterly assailed, Governor Forsyth of Georgia paid the following beautiful tribute to his character : —

" Long known to me as a politician and a man ; acting together in the hour of political adversity, when we had lost all but our honor ; a witness of his movements when elevated to power, and in possession of the confidence of the Chief Magistrate and of the great majority of the people, — I have never witnessed aught in Mr. Van Buren which requires concealment, palliation, or coloring ; never anything to lessen his character as a patriot or a man ; nothing which he might not desire to see exposed to the scrutiny of every member of this body, with the calm confidence of unsullied integrity. He is called an artful man, a giant of artifice, a wily magician. Those ignorant of his unrivaled knowledge of human character, his power of penetrating into the designs and defeating the purposes of his adversaries, seeing his rapid advance to power and public confidence, impute to *art* what is the natural result of those simple causes. Extraordinary talent ; untiring industry ; incessant vigilance ; the happiest temper, which success cannot corrupt, nor disappointment sour, — these are the sources of his unexampled success, the magic arts, the artifices of intrigue, to which only he has resorted in his eventful life. Those who envy his success may learn wisdom from his example."

Mr. Van Buren's rejection by the Senate must have been to him a great mortification. When the news reached London, it was proclaimed in all the journals of the city. That evening Prince Talleyrand, the French minister, gave a party. Mr. Van Buren was present, as calm, social, and smiling as if floating on the full tide of prosperity. He returned to America, apparently untroubled ; was nominated for Vice-President, in the place of Calhoun, at the reelection of President Jackson ; and with smiles for all, and frowns for none, went to take his place at the head of that Senate which had refused to confirm his nomination as ambassador.

Mr. Calhoun supposed that Mr. Van Buren's rejection by the Senate would prove his political death, and is reported to have said triumphantly, "It will kill him, sir, — kill him dead. He will never kick, sir, — never kick." This rejection roused all the zeal of President Jackson in behalf of his repudiated favorite ; and this, probably more than any other cause, secured his elevation to the chair of the Chief Executive. On the 20th of May, 1836, Mr. Van Buren received the Democratic nomination to succeed General Jackson as President of the United States. He was elected by a handsome majority, to the great delight of the retiring President. "Leaving New York out of the canvass," says Mr. Parton, "the election of Mr. Van Buren to the presidency was as much the act of General Jackson as though the Constitution had conferred upon him the power to appoint a successor."

It was one of the most brilliant days of spring, when the long procession which accompanied Mr. Van Buren to his inauguration passed through Pennsylvania Avenue. A small volunteer corps escorted the President elect as he rode in a phaeton drawn by four grays. General Jackson accompanied his friend, and both rode uncovered. As they alighted from the carriage at the foot of the steps, and ascended through the dense and moving mass, the tall head of the old chieftain, with his bristling hair, towered above all the rest, and attracted every eye. The day was calm, and the air elastic. Twenty thousand people were there assembled. As Mr. Van Buren delivered his inaugural address, his clear voice, in its distinct articulation, reached every ear.

The policy of the government had been so distinctly marked out by General Jackson, and Mr. Van Buren had so distinctly avowed his intention of following in the footsteps of his illustrious predecessor, that there was no call for the introduction of any new acts, or for any change in the administration.

Mr. Van Buren had scarcely taken his seat in the presidential chair, when a financial panic, almost unprecedented in its disastrous results, swept the land. Many attributed this to the war which General Jackson had waged upon the banks, and to his endeavor to secure an almost exclusive specie currency. Nearly every bank in the country was compelled to suspend specie payment, and ruin pervaded all our great cities. Not less than two hundred and fifty houses failed in New York in three weeks. All public works were brought to a stand, and there was a general state of dismay. At the same time we were involved in an inglorious war with the Seminole Indians in Florida, which reflected no honor upon our arms. The slavery question was rising in portentous magnitude, introducing agitation, rage, and mob violence in almost every city and village of the land.

BURNING OF THE CAROLINE.

There was an insurrection in Canada against the British government, which came near involving us in a war with that nation. A party of Canadian insurgents had rendezvoused on Navy Island, in the Niagara River, opposite the village called Fort Schlosser, on the American side. A small steamboat, called The Caroline, which was suspected of having carried ammunition and supplies to the insurgents, was moored to the American shore. The British commander, regardless of territorial rights, sent an armed force across the river, attacked the steamer, killed several of her defenders, applied the torch to the boat, and sent it in flames over the Falls of Niagara. The circumstance called forth a long and angry correspondence with the British government; and, in the exasperations of the hour, we barely escaped war.

About the same time there also arose a contest between Maine and Great Britain respecting boundary-lines; and there was the angry mustering of hosts, in preparation for battle. With all these troubles on his hands, the four years which Mr. Van Buren spent in the White House must have been years of anxiety and toil. Still, he was anxious for a reëlection. General Jackson did everything in his power to aid him. But public sentiment was now setting so strongly against the administration, that the Whig candidate, William Henry Harrison, was chosen President, and Mr. Van Buren was permitted to retire to the seclusion of Kinderhook.

He had ever been a prudent man, of frugal habits, and, living within his income, had now fortunately a competence for his declining years. His unblemished character, his commanding abilities, his unquestioned patriotism, and the distinguished positions which he had occupied in the government of the country, secured to him, not only the homage of his party, but the respect of the whole community. It was on the 4th of March, 1841, that Van Buren retired from the presidency. From his fine estate at Lindenwald he still exerted a powerful influence upon the politics of the country. In 1844 his friends made strenuous efforts to have him renominated for the presidency. The proslavery portion of the Democratic party, however, carried the day; and James K. Polk of Tennessee received the nomination. Again, in 1848, the Free-soil Democrats brought forward his name for the presidency. Three hundred thousand votes were cast in his favor. General Taylor, however, the Whig candidate, was the choice of the people. From this time until his death, on the 24th of July, 1862, at the age of eighty years, he resided at Lindenwald, a gentleman of leisure, of culture, and of wealth; enjoying, in a healthy, vigorous old age, probably far more happiness than he had before experienced amidst the stormy scenes of his active life. He was surrounded by friends, and his own cheerful disposition gilded every hour. Martin Van Buren was a great and good man; and no one will question his right to a high position among those who have been the successors of Washington in the occupancy of the presidential chair.

CHAPTER IX.

WILLIAM HENRY HARRISON.

Birth and Ancestry. — Enters United States Army. — Is promoted. — Resigns his Commission. — Sent to Congress. — Governor of Indiana Territory. — His Scrupulous Integrity. — Indian Troubles. — Battle of Tippecanoe. — War with Great Britain. — Governor Harrison's Perplexities and Labors. — The British repulsed. — Tecumseh slain. — False Accusations. — Speech in Congress. — Reply to Randolph. — Letter to President Bolivar. — Temperance Principles. — Views respecting Slavery. — Duelling. — Elected President. — Death.

WILLIAM HENRY HARRISON was born in Virginia, on the banks of the James River, at a place called Berkeley, February 9, 1773.

RESIDENCE OF WILLIAM HENRY HARRISON.

His father, Benjamin Harrison, was in comparatively opulent circumstances, and was one of the most distinguished men of his day.

He was an intimate friend of George Washington, was early elected a member of the Continental Congress, and was conspicuous among the patriots of Virginia in resisting the encroachments of the British crown. In the celebrated Congress of 1775, Benjamin Harrison and John Hancock were both candidates for the office of speaker. Mr. Harrison at once yielded to the illustrious patriot from the Bay State; and, seeing that Mr. Hancock modestly hesitated to take the chair, Mr. Harrison, who was a very portly man, and of gigantic strength, with characteristic good nature and playfulness seized Mr. Hancock in his athletic arms, and carried him, as though he were a child, to the seat of honor. Then turning around, with his honest, beaming face, he said to his amused associates, —

"Gentlemen, we will show Mother Britain how little we care for her by making a Massachusetts man our President, whom she has excluded from pardon by a public proclamation."

Like most men of large stature, Mr. Harrison was full of fun, and never liked to lose an opportunity for a joke. He was one of the signers of the Declaration of Independence; and he it was who made the ludicrous remark about "hanging" to Elbridge Gerry, to which we have referred in the life of Jefferson.

Mr. Harrison was subsequently chosen Governor of Virginia, and was twice reëlected. His son William Henry, of course, enjoyed in childhood all the advantages which wealth and intellectual and cultivated society could give. Having received a thorough common-school education, he entered Hampden Sidney College, where he graduated with honor soon after the death of his father. He then repaired to Philadelphia to study medicine under the instruction of Dr. Rush and the guardianship of Robert Morris, both of whom were, with his father, signers of the Declaration of Independence.

George Washington was then President of the United States. The Indians were committing fearful ravages on our northwestern frontier. For the protection of the settlers, General St. Clair was stationed, with a considerable military force, at Fort Washington, on the far-away waters of the then almost unexplored Ohio, near the spot where the thronged streets of Cincinnati are now spread out. Young Harrison, either lured by the love of adventure or moved by the sufferings of families exposed to the most horrible outrages, abandoned his medical studies, and, notwithstanding the remonstrances of his friends, entered the army, having obtained a commission of ensign from President Washington. He was then nineteen years of age.

The hostile Indians, who had originally been roused against us during the war of the Revolution by the government of Great Britain, were spread over that vast wilderness now occupied by the States of Ohio, Indiana, and Illinois. They could bring many thousand warriors into the field, who had been supplied with ammunition and arms by the British authorities in Canada. Just before young Harrison received his commission, General St. Clair, advancing into the wilderness with fourteen hundred men, was attacked by the Indians near the head waters of the Wabash, and utterly routed, with a loss of five hundred and thirty killed, and three hundred and sixty wounded. This awful defeat had spread consternation throughout the whole frontier.

Winter was setting in. Young Harrison, in form and strength, was frail; and many of his friends, thinking he would be unable to endure the hardships of a winter campaign, urged him to resign his commission. He, however, rejected this advice, and, crossing the country on foot to Pittsburgh, descended the Ohio to Fort Washington. The first duty assigned him was to take command of a train of pack-horses bound to Fort Hamilton, on the Miami River, about forty miles from Fort Washington. It was a very arduous and perilous service; but it was so well performed as to command the especial commendation of General St. Clair. A veteran frontiersman said of the young soldier, —

"I would as soon have thought of putting my wife into the service as this boy; but I have been out with him, and find those smooth cheeks are on a wise head, and that slight frame is almost as tough as my own weather-beaten carcass."

Intemperance was at that time, as it ever has been, the bane of the army; but young Harrison, inspired by some good impulse, adopted the principles of a thorough temperance man, to which he adhered throughout his whole life. This enabled him to bear hardships and endure privations under which others sank to an early grave.

Soon he was promoted to the rank of lieutenant, and joined the army which Washington had placed under the command of General Wayne to prosecute more vigorously the war with the Indians. The new general who succeeded St. Clair had acquired, by his reckless daring, the title of "Mad Anthony." On the 28th of November, 1792, General Wayne, with an army of about three thousand non-commissioned officers and privates, descended the Ohio from Pittsburgh, a distance of twenty-two miles, and encamped for the winter. In the spring he conveyed his troops in boats down the river to Fort Washington. Here Lieutenant Harrison joined the "Legion," as Wayne's army was called. His soldierly qualities immediately attracted the attention and secured the confidence of his commander-in chief.

Several months were lost in waiting for supplies before the army could move. In October they advanced to a post which they called Greenville, about eighty miles due north. Here the army encamped for the winter. A strong detachment was sent some twenty miles farther north, to occupy the ground where St. Clair was defeated, to bury the remains of the dead, and to establish there a strong post, which they named Fort Recovery. In this enterprise Lieutenant Harrison is mentioned as having rendered conspicuous service.

The Indians, in the early spring, attacked the fort with the greatest determination. They were, however, repulsed in repeated assaults, and at length retired, having lost a large portion of their band.

General Wayne then advanced with his whole army some sixty miles north to the junction of the Auglaize and Maumee rivers, where he constructed a strong fort. On the 20th of August, as he was continuing his march down the Maumee, he encountered the Indians in great force, lying in ambush. Their numbers were estimated at two thousand. A bloody battle ensued, in which both parties fought with the utmost desperation. The savages were driven howling into the woods, their villages were burned, and their cornfields destroyed. This signal discomfiture broke their spirit, and they implored peace. Again Lieutenant Harrison signalized himself, and obtained from his commanding officer the following commendation : —

"Lieutenant Harrison was in the foremost front of the hottest battle. His person was exposed from the commencement to the close of the action. Wherever duty called, he hastened, regardless of danger, and, by his efforts and example, contributed as much to secure the fortunes of the day as any other officer subordinate to the commander-in-chief."

Lieutenant Harrison was promoted to the rank of captain, and was placed in command at Fort Washington. The British military posts in the Northwest were about this time surrendered to the national government, and Captain Harrison was employed in occupying them and in supplying them with provisions and military stores. While thus employed he married a daughter of John Cleves Symmes, one of the frontiersmen who had established a thriving settlement on the banks of the Maumee.

In 1797 Captain Harrison, then twenty-four years of age, resigned his commission in the army, and was appointed secretary of the Northwestern Territory, and *ex officio* lieutenant-governor, General St. Clair being then governor of the Territory. At that time the law in reference to the disposal of the public lands was such that no one could purchase in tracts less than four thousand acres. This inured to the benefit of the rich speculator; and the poor settler could only purchase at second hand, and at a greatly advanced price. Mr. Harrison, in the face of violent opposition, succeeded in obtaining so much of a modification of this unjust law, that the land was sold in alternate tracts of six hundred and forty and three hundred and twenty acres. The Northwestern Territory was then entitled to one delegate in Congress, and Captain Harrison was chosen to fill that office.

In the spring of 1800 the Northwestern Territory was divided by Congress into two portions. The eastern portion, comprising the region now embraced in the State of Ohio, was called "The Territory northwest of the Ohio." The western portion, which included what is now called Indiana, Illinois, and Wisconsin, was called "The Indiana Territory." William Henry Harrison, then twenty-seven years of age, was appointed by John Adams Governor of the Indiana Territory, and immediately after, also Governor of Upper Louisiana. He was thus the ruler over almost as extensive a realm as any sovereign upon the globe. He was Superintendent of Indian Affairs, and was invested with powers nearly dictatorial over the now rapidly-increasing white population. The ability and fidelity with which he discharged these responsible duties may be inferred from the fact that he was four times appointed to this office, — first by John Adams, twice by Thomas Jefferson, and afterwards by President Madison.

When he commenced his administration there were but three

17

white settlements in that almost boundless region, now crowded with cities, and resounding with all the tumult of wealth and traffic. One of these settlements was on the Ohio, nearly opposite Louisville; one at Vincennes, on the Wabash; and the third a French settlement.

Governor Harrison discharged his arduous duties with such manifest justice, that no one ventured to question his integrity. During his administration, he effected thirteen treaties with the Indians, by which the United States acquired sixty millions of acres of land. Governor Harrison was sole commissioner, and every treaty he formed received the sanction of the President and Senate of the United States. He had ample opportunities to enrich himself; for he could confirm grants of land to individuals, his sole signature giving a title which could not be questioned: but he never held a single acre by a title emanating from himself. The frontiers of civilization are always occupied by a lawless class of vagabonds, who shrink from no outrages: these men abused the Indians in every way which passion or interest could dictate. In a communication to the government, July, 1801, Governor Harrison says, —

"All these injuries the Indians have hitherto borne with astonishing patience. But though they discover no disposition to make war upon the United States, I am confident that most of the tribes would eagerly seize any favorable opportunity for that purpose; and should the United States be at war with any European nations who are known to the Indians, there would probably be a combination of more than nine tenths of the northern tribes against us, unless some means are made use of to conciliate them."

Mr. Jefferson was now President, and humanely made great exertions to protect the Indians, and to induce them to abandon their wild hunting-life, and to devote themselves to the cultivation of the land. In 1804 Governor Harrison obtained a cession from the Indians of all the land between the Illinois River and the Mississippi.

A territorial legislature was soon organized for the rapidly-increasing population, over which the governor presided with that dignity, courtesy, and unswerving integrity which secured to him universal respect. By nature he had much kindness of heart; and his affability of manners, and his tact in meeting all varieties of human character, rendered him greatly beloved. His magnanimous devotion to the public interest was such that he several times appointed decided political opponents to offices of trust which he deemed them eminently fitted to fill. He was so cautious to avoid the appearance of evil, that he would not keep the public money on hand, but always made his payments by drafts upon Washington. It has been said that no man ever disbursed so large an amount of public treasure with so little difficulty in adjusting his accounts.

For twelve years he was Governor of the Territory of Indiana. A wealthy foreigner, by the name of M'Intosh, loudly accused the governor of having defrauded the Indians in the treaty of Fort Wayne. The governor demanded investigation in a court of justice; and not only was he triumphantly acquitted, but the jury brought in a verdict against M'Intosh for damages to the amount of four thousand dollars. Governor Harrison, having thus obtained the perfect vindication of his character, distributed one third of the sum to the orphan children of those who had died in battle, and restored the remainder to M'Intosh himself.

The proprietor of the land upon which the city of St. Louis now stands offered him nearly half of the whole town for a merely nominal sum if he would assist in building up the place. So nice was his sense of honor, that he declined the offer, lest it might be said that he had used his official station to promote his private interests. In a few years that property was worth millions. A large tract of land near Cincinnati had been sold, in the early settlement of the country, under an execution against the original proprietor, for a very small sum. At length, after the property had become immensely valuable, it was found that, by some defective proceedings in the court, the sale was not valid, and the legal title was vested in Mrs. Harrison and another individual, as heirs at law. The lofty spirit of integrity which animated General Harrison led him instantly to discriminate between a *legal* and an *equitable* title. He obtained the consent of the co-heir, and immediately relinquished the whole property to the purchasers. These incidents surely reveal a character of very unusual magnanimity, disinterestedness, and generosity.

The vast wilderness over which Governor Harrison reigned was filled, as we have mentioned, with many tribes of Indians. About the year 1806, two extraordinary men, twin brothers, of the Shawnese tribe, rose up among them. One of these was called Tecumseh, or " The Crouching Panther ; " the other, Olliwacheca, or " The

Prophet." Tecumseh was not only an Indian warrior, but a man of great sagacity, far-reaching foresight, and indomitable perseverance in any enterprise in which he might engage. He was inspired with the highest enthusiasm, and had long regarded with dread and with hatred the encroachment of the whites upon the hunting-grounds of his fathers. His brother, the Prophet, was an orator, who could sway the feelings of the untutored Indian as the gale tossed the tree-tops beneath which they dwelt.

But the Prophet was not merely an orator: he was, in the superstitious minds of the Indians, invested with the superhuman dignity of a medicine-man, or a magician. With an enthusiasm unsurpassed by Peter the Hermit rousing Europe to the crusades, he went from tribe to tribe, assuming that he was specially sent by the Great Spirit. In the name of his divine Master, he commanded them to abandon all those innovations which had been introduced through the white man, to return to the customs of their fathers, and to combine together for the extermination of the pale-faces. In co-operation with him, his heroic brother Tecumseh traversed thousands of miles of the forest, visiting the remoter tribes, announcing to them the divine mission of his brother, and seeking to enlist their co-operation. No discouragements chilled the zeal of these extraordinary and determined men. They probably wrought themselves up to the full conviction that they were commissioned by the Great Spirit.

The Prophet had occasionally protracted meetings for exhortation and prayer, in which, through successive days, he plied all the arts of devotion and persuasion to fire the hearts of his followers. Two years were thus employed by these two brothers.

In the summer of 1808 the Prophet established his encampment on the banks of the Tippecanoe, a tributary of the Upper Wabash. The measures of Tecumseh and the Prophet, in organizing this formidable conspiracy, had been conducted as secretly as possible but the suspicions of the government began to be aroused. To allay these suspicions, the Prophet visited Governor Harrison, and, in an exceedingly insidious and plausible speech, stated that he had no designs whatever of rousing his people to hostilities; that he sought only their moral and religious improvement.

A large number of the Indians accompanied him. He often preached to them in the presence of the governor; and his two great topics were the evils of war and of whisky-drinking. His power over them had become so great that by no persuasions of the whites could one of his followers be induced to take a drop of intoxicating drink. Still rumors were continually reaching Governor Harrison that the Indians were making extensive preparations for hostilities.

In his earnest solicitude to learn the facts in the case, he sent urgent invitations for both Tecumseh and the Prophet to visit him. Tecumseh at length came to Vincennes in proud array, with four hundred plumed warriors completely armed. A council was holden on the 12th of August, 1809. The governor was quite unprepared for the appearance of a host so formidable. Assuming, however, that all was friendly, he met the proud chieftain, whom we call a savage, to deliberate upon the state of affairs. The governor was attended by the judges of the Supreme Court, a few army officers, and a number of citizens. A small body-guard, consisting merely of a sergeant and twelve men, were drawn up at a little distance. Tecumseh still affirmed, in a very dignified speech which he made to the governor, that he had no intention of making war : but he very boldly declared that it was his intention and endeavor to combine all the tribes for the purpose of putting a stop to all further encroachments by the whites ; that not another acre of land should be ceded to them without the consent of all the tribes ; and that those chiefs who had recently made treaties by which they had disposed of lands to the United States should all be put to death.

This statement led to indignant remonstrance on the part of Governor Harrison. As he was speaking, Tecumseh interrupted him, and in angry tones, and with violent gesticulations, declared that he had cheated the Indians. Immediately his warriors, who were squatted upon the grass around, sprang to their feet, and began to brandish their war-clubs in the most threatening manner. Governor Harrison rose from his arm-chair, and drew his sword. The army officers gathered around him. The citizens seized brick-bats, and such other weapons as they could lay their hands on ; and the guard came rushing forward, ready to open fire upon the Indians.

But Governor Harrison calmly ordered them not to fire. Then, turning to Tecumseh, he told him that he should hold no more communication with him, but that, as he had come under protection of the council-fire, he might depart unharmed. Tecumseh and his companions retired to their encampment. That night the militia of Vincennes were under arms, every moment expecting an attack. The night, however, passed without any alarm. In the morning Tecumseh called upon the governor, expressed regret for his conduct the day before, and reiterated his declaration that he had no hostile intentions, but was still firm in his position that no more land should be ceded to the whites without the consent of the chiefs of all the tribes; and that the treaty which a few of the

HARRISON'S INTERVIEW WITH TECUMSEH.

chiefs had recently entered into with the governor at Fort Wayne, he and his confederate tribes would regard as null and void.

Soon after this, Governor Harrison, anxious to conciliate, visited Tecumseh at his camp on the Tippecanoe River, a branch of the Upper Wabash, some two hundred miles above Vincennes. He was politely received by the Indian chieftain; but he was informed, in language courteous but decided, that, though the Indians were very unwilling to go to war with the United States, they were determined that the land recently ceded should not be given up, and that no other treaty should ever be made without the consent of all the tribes. This was ridiculously assuming that all the land on the continent belonged to the Indians in common, and that tribes on the St. Lawrence could not enter into a treaty without the consent of tribes upon the Gulf.

Months rolled on, while Tecumseh and the Prophet were busy in their hostile preparations. Marauding bands of Indians, whom they professed to be unable to control, were perpetrating innumerable annoyances. Horses were stolen, houses plundered, and the frontier settlements, which had now become quite numerous, were thrown into a state of great alarm. Tecumseh set out on a journey to enlist the southern Indians in his confederacy. The posture of affairs became so threatening, that it was decided that the governor should visit the Prophet's town with an armed force, to observe what was going on, and to overawe by an exhibition of power, but to avoid hostilities if possible. Nearly a thousand troops were collected for this enterprise at Fort Harrison, on the Wabash, about sixty miles above Vincennes.

The army commenced its march on the 28th of October, 1812. Conscious of the bravery and sagacity of their enemies, they moved in two bands, on each side of the Indian trail, over the prairies, in such order that they could instantly be formed into line of battle, or thrown into a hollow square. Their route led them along the east bank of the Wabash, through an open prairie country. Early in November they approached the valley of the Tippecanoe, and encamped within ten miles of the Prophet's town. The next morning, the 5th, as they resumed their march, several parties of Indians were seen prowling about; but they evaded all attempts at communication, replying only to such endeavors with defiant and insulting gestures. When they had arrived within three miles of the town, three Indians of rank made their appearance, and inquired why Governor Harrison was approaching them in so hostile an attitude. After a short conference, arrangements were made for a meeting the next day, to agree upon terms of peace.

But Governor Harrison was too well acquainted with the Indian character to be deceived by such protestations. Selecting a favorable spot for his night's encampment, he took every precaution against surprise. His troops were posted in a hollow square, and slept upon their arms. Each corps was ordered, in case of an attack, to maintain its position at every hazard, until relieved. The dragoons were placed in the centre, and were directed, should there be any alarm, immediately to parade, dismounted, and hold themselves in readiness to relieve the point assailed. The most minute arrangements were given to meet every conceivable contingency.

The troops threw themselves upon the ground for rest; but every man had his accoutrements on, his loaded musket by his side, and his bayonet fixed. The wakeful governor, between three and four o'clock in the morning, had risen, and was sitting in conversation with his aides by the embers of a waning fire. It was a chill, cloudy morning, with a drizzling rain. In the darkness the Indians had crept as near as possible, and just then, with a savage yell, rushed, with all the desperation which superstition and passion most highly inflamed could give, upon the left flank of the little army. The savages had been amply provided with guns and ammunition by the English. Their war-whoop was accompanied with an incessant shower of bullets.

The camp-fires were instantly extinguished, as the light aided the Indians in their aim. With hideous yells, the Indian bands rushed on, not doubting a speedy and an entire victory. But General Harrison's troops stood as immovable as the rocks around them until the day dawned: they then made a simultaneous charge with the bayonet, and swept everything before them. The wretched Indians found the predictions of their Prophet utterly false; for the bullets and the bayonets of the white man pierced their bodies with appalling slaughter. The Prophet was present to witness this terrible defeat of his picked braves. The Indians, even when most reckless, were careful to conceal themselves as much as possible behind trees and rocks; consequently, in most of their battles, they lost but few in killed and wounded: but in this case, when they fled to the swamp, they left sixty-one dead upon the field, and one hundred and twenty bleeding and helpless.

Though the victory was entire, the loss of the Americans was fully equal to that of the Indians.

General Harrison was exposed like all his men. One bullet passed through the rim of his hat; another struck his saddle, and, glancing, hit his thigh; a third severely wounded the horse on which he rode. His coolness and good generalship were so conspicuous as to add greatly to his reputation; and subsequently the battle of Tippecanoe became a watchword to inspire the zeal of those who were elevating him to the presidency of the United States. After burying the dead and taking care of the wounded, they burned the Indian town, and destroyed everything which could aid the savages in their future hostilities, and returned to Vincennes.

Tecumseh was then far away in the South, endeavoring to rouse the Indians there. But the tribes in the Northwest, disappointed by the false predictions of the Prophet, and disheartened by their defeat, began to send deputies to Vincennes to secure peace. Soon, however, Tecumseh returned; our second war with Great Britain commenced; and the savages were drawn into an alliance with the English, and were animated to renew hostilities with more desperation than ever before.

Governor Harrison had now all his energies tasked to the utmost. The British, descending from the Canadas, were of themselves a very formidable force; but with their savage allies, rushing like wolves from the forest, searching out every remote farm-house, burning, plundering, scalping, torturing, the wide frontier was plunged into a state of consternation which even the most vivid imagination can but faintly conceive. The war-whoop was resounding everywhere through the solitudes of the forest. The horizon was illuminated with the conflagration of the cabins of the settlers. General Hull had made the ignominious surrender of his forces at Detroit. Under these despairing circumstances, Governor Harrison was appointed by President Madison commander-in-chief of the Northwestern army, with orders to retake Detroit, and to protect the frontiers.

To meet the emergency, he was invested with almost unlimited authority. His army was to be collected from widely dispersed cabins, where the women and the children would thus be left unprotected. His men were entirely ignorant of discipline. His officers were inexperienced. There was then neither railroad nor steamboat; and almost everything for the supply of the army had to be transported over the wildest, roughest roads, from the Atlantic States. To reach Detroit, it was necessary for him to traverse a swampy forest, two hundred miles in extent, without roads; and the wilderness was ranged by the prowling Indian, ever liable to burst upon him from his ambush. At Detroit he would encounter the trained soldiers of England, veterans of a hundred battles, under leaders of renown, and aided by ferocious bands of savages, amply supplied with the most deadly weapons of war. The English had also quite a fleet which commanded the waters of Lake Erie.

It would be difficult to place a man in a situation demanding more energy, sagacity, and courage; but General Harrison was found equal to the position, and nobly and triumphantly did he meet all the responsibilities. A minute account of his adventures, his midnight marches, his bloody conflicts, his sufferings from storms of sleet and snow, from famine, sickness, exposure, destitution, would fill volumes. The renown of such a man as General Harrison is not cheaply gained. It is purchased at a great price. The government, as we have mentioned, invested him with almost absolute power; but, with all his tireless energy, never did he in the slightest degree abuse that trust.

He was a man of winning address, of a gentle and affectionate spirit, and possessed native powers of persuasive eloquence which were very rare. A scene is described at one of their encampments which will illustrate many others. The little army was groping through the forest, on the banks of the Auglaize. Night came on, dark, stormy, and with sheets of rain. The low ground was soon flooded. They had no axes, could build no fires; and, as they had got ahead of their baggage, they had no food. Some took their saddles, and sat upon them; others found logs; others stood in the water, and leaned against the trunks of trees. Thus they passed the miserable night. General Harrison shared all these discomforts with his men. As he sat in the pouring rain, wrapped in his cloak, with his staff around him, he called upon one of his officers, who had a fine voice, to sing a humorous Irish song, with the chorus, —

> "Now's the time for mirth and glee:
> Sing and laugh and dance with me."

The troops joined in the refrain; and thus, in that black night of storm and flood, the forest echoed with sounds of merriment.

General Harrison had succeeded in raising a force of about six thousand men. He soon became satisfied that Detroit could be taken only in a winter-campaign, when the vast morasses, being frozen, could be traversed by the army. His right wing was rendezvoused at Sandusky. About eight hundred men, under General Winchester, marched to the mouth of the River Raisin, where they

were attacked, routed, and compelled to surrender. All the wounded
were massacred by the Indians. Dreadful was the suffering that this
disaster caused; and it was a long time before it could be known
who were prisoners, and who had fallen beneath the bloody knives
of the savages. This unfortunate expedition had been undertaken
without the knowledge of General Harrison. Having heard of the
movement, he did everything in his power, but in vain, to avert
the disastrous results. Nine hundred of the most promising young
men of the Northwest were lost in this melancholy adventure. This
was the latter part of January, 1813. General Harrison, who had
now received the appointment of major-general in the United States
army, found it necessary to go into winter-quarters; though he fitted
out three expeditions against the Indians, one only of which proved
successful.

The government at length, urged by General Harrison, prepared
for the construction of a fleet to command the waters of the lake.
General Harrison had an unstable body of men at Fort Meigs; the
enlistments being for short periods, and it being impossible to hold
the men after the term of service had expired. The most arduous
of General Harrison's labors were his almost superhuman exertions
to raise an army. In August of 1814, the British, with their
savage allies, appeared before Sandusky, which was protected by
Fort Stephenson. They approached by their vessels along the lake,
and also, with a land force, through the forest, followed by their
howling allies. They were, however, after a stern battle, handsomely repulsed. On the 10th of September, Commodore Perry,
with his gallant squadron, met the British fleet, and, at the close
of an heroic struggle, had the pleasure of announcing that they
were ours. General Harrison was now prepared to carry the war
home to the enemy. He crossed the lake, took possession of Sandwich, the British retreating before him, and then sent a brigade
across the strait, which seized Detroit. The British retreated up
the Thames, pursued by the Americans. Proctor led the British
forces, and Tecumseh led his savage allies. The foe made a stand
on the banks of the Thames. The battle was short and decisive.
Our dragoons rode impetuously over the ranks of the British, and
compelled an almost instantaneous surrender. The Indians continued the fight a little longer, but were at length dispersed, leaving their chief, Tecumseh, dead upon the field. All the stores of
the British army fell into the hands of the victors.

General Harrison won the love of his soldiers by always sharing with them their fatigue. His whole baggage, while pursuing the foe up the Thames, was carried in a valise; and his bedding consisted of a single blanket lashed over his saddle. Thirty-five British officers, his prisoners of war, supped with him after the battle. The only fare he could give them was beef roasted before the fire, without bread or salt.

This great victory gave peace to the Northwestern frontier; and General Harrison decided to send a large portion of his force to Niagara, to assist in repelling the foe, who were concentrating there. Fifteen hundred men were transported by the fleet to Buffalo, which they reached on the 24th of October, 1814.

In consequence of some want of harmony with the Secretary of War, General Harrison resigned his commission, much to the regret of President Madison: he, however, still continued to be employed in the service of his country. He was appointed to treat with the Indian tribes; and he conducted the negotiations so skillfully as to secure the approbation both of the Indians and of the United States government. In 1816 General Harrison was chosen a member of the national House of Representatives to represent the District of Ohio. It was not possible that a man who had occupied posts so responsible, who had often thwarted the attempted frauds of government contractors, and who had defended the weak against the powerful, should not have some bitter enemies. In the contest which preceded his election to Congress, he had been accused of corruption in respect to the commissariat of the army. Immediately upon taking his seat, he called for an investigation of the charge. A committee was appointed: his vindication was triumphant; and a high compliment was paid to his patriotism, disinterestedness, and devotion to the public service. For these services a gold medal was presented to him, with the thanks of Congress.

In Congress he proved an active member; and, whenever he spoke, it was with a force of reason, and power of eloquence, which arrested the attention of all the members. When the celebrated debate came up respecting the conduct of General Jackson during the Seminole war, he eloquently supported the resolutions of censure, while he paid a noble tribute to the patriotism and good intentions of the reckless and law-defying general. In the splendid speech which he made upon this occasion, which was alike replete with eloquence, true philosophy, and the most exalted patriotism, he said, —

"I am sure, sir, that it is not the intention of any gentleman upon this floor to rob General Jackson of a single ray of glory; much less to wound his feelings, or injure his reputation. If the resolutions pass, I would address him thus : ' In the performance of a sacred duty, imposed by their construction of the Constitution, the representatives of the people have found it necessary to disapprove of a single act of your brilliant career. They have done it in the full conviction, that the hero who has guarded her rights in the field will bow with reverence to the civil institutions of his country; that he has admitted as his creed, that the character of the soldier can never be complete without eternal reverence to the character of the citizen. Go, gallant chief, and bear with you the gratitude of your country ; go, under the full conviction, that, as her glory is identified with yours, she has nothing more dear to her than her laws, nothing more sacred than her Constitution. Even an unintentional error shall be sanctified to her service. It will teach posterity that the government which could disapprove the conduct of a Marcellus will have the fortitude to crush the vices of a Marius.' "

General Jackson was not a man to bear the slightest opposition. These noble sentiments, as uttered by General Harrison, he never forgot or forgave.

In 1819 Harrison was elected to the Senate of Ohio ; and in 1824, as one of the presidential electors of that State, he gave his vote for Henry Clay, and in the same year was chosen to the Senate of the United States. The half-crazed John Randolph made one of his characteristic attacks, virulent and senseless, accusing him of being a black-cockade Federalist, and of associating with gentlemen of that party. Mr. Harrison rose, and, with that dignified and attractive eloquence which he had at his command, said, —

"I am seriously charged with the heinous offense of associating with Federal gentlemen. I plead guilty. I respected the Revolutionary services of President John Adams, and have paid him that courtesy which was due to him as a man and as Chief Magistrate. I have also associated with such men as John Marshall and James A. Bayard. Is the acknowledgment of such guilt to throw me out of the pale of political salvation ?

" On the other hand, I am on intimate terms with Mr. Jefferson, Mr. Gallatin, and the whole Virginia delegation, among whom I have many kinsmen and dear friends. These were my principal associates in Philadelphia, in whose mess I have often met the gentleman who is now my accuser, and with whom I have spent some of the happiest hours of my life. It is not in my nature to be a violent or proscriptive partisan ; but I have given a firm support to the Republican administrations of Jefferson, Madison, and Monroe. I hope the senator from Virginia is answered."

In the latter part of the year 1828, President John Quincy Adams appointed General Harrison minister plenipotentiary to the Republic of Colombia; but General Jackson, immediately after his inauguration in 1829, implacably recalled him. While he was in Colombia, the proposition was agitated of laying aside the Constitution, and investing Bolivar with the dictatorship. General Harrison addressed a letter to Bolivar, who was his personal friend, entreating him not to accede to this arrangement. This document was written with so much elegance of diction, such glowing eloquence, and such enlightened statesmanship, as to secure the admiration of every one who read it.

A few sentences only can we quote as specimens of the whole : —

" A successful warrior is no longer regarded as entitled to the first place in the temple of fame. In this enlightened age, the hero of the field, and the successful leader of armies, may, for the moment, attract attention ; but it is such as will be bestowed upon the passing meteor, whose blaze is no longer remembered when it is no longer seen. To be esteemed eminently great, it is necessary to be eminently good. The qualities of the hero and the general must be devoted to the advantage of mankind before he will be permitted to assume the title of their benefactor. If the fame of our Washington depended upon his military achievements, would the common consent of the world allow him the preëminence he possesses ? The victories at Trenton, Monmouth, and York, brilliant as they were, exhibiting, as they certainly did, the highest grade of military talents, are scarcely thought of. The source of the veneration and esteem which are entertained for his character by every class of politicians — the monarchist and aristocrat, as well as the republican — is to be found in his undeviating and exclusive devotedness to his country. No selfish consideration was ever suffered to intrude itself into his mind. General, the course which he pursued is open to you ; and it depends upon yourself to attain the eminence which he has reached before you."

Upon General Harrison's return from Colombia to the United States, he retired to his farm at North Bend, on the Ohio, and in the enjoyment of a humble competency, devoted himself to the peaceful pursuits of agriculture. With true Roman dignity, he accepted the office of clerk to the court of Hamilton County, as a means of adding to his limited income. In 1831 he was chosen to give the annual discourse before the agricultural society of that county.

General Harrison had once owned a distillery ; but, perceiving the sad effects of whisky upon the surrounding population, he promptly abandoned the business, at a very considerable pecuniary sacrifice. In his very admirable address, he, with great fervor and eloquence, entreats his brother-farmers not to convert their corn into that poison which was found so deadly both to the body and to the soul. " I speak more freely," said he, " of the practice of converting the material of the staff of life into an article which is so destructive of health and happiness, because in that way I have sinned myself ; but in that way I shall sin no more."

The subject of slavery was at this time fearfully agitating our land. General Harrison, though very decidedly opposed to any interference on the part of the general government with slavery as it existed in the States, was still the warm friend of universal freedom. In replying to the accusation of being friendly to slavery, he said, —

" From my earliest youth, and to the present moment, I have been the ardent friend of human liberty. At the age of eighteen, I became a member of an abolition society established at Richmond, Va., the object of which was to ameliorate the condition of slaves, and procure their freedom by every legal means. The obligations which I then came under I have faithfully performed. I have been the means of liberating many slaves, but never placed one in bondage. I was the first person to introduce into Congress the proposition, that all the country above Missouri should never have slavery admitted into it."

Again, the high Christian integrity of this noble man is developed in the reply to a letter from a gentleman wishing to know his views upon the subject of dueling. The whole letter was admirable, and was one of the most effective attacks upon that absurd and barbarous system that has ever been made. In conclusion, he says, —

"In relation to my present sentiments, a sense of higher obligations than human laws or human opinions can impose has determined me never on any occasion to accept a challenge, or seek redress for a personal injury, by a resort to the laws which compose the code of honor."

In 1836 the friends of General Harrison brought him forward as a candidate for the presidency. Mr. Van Buren was the administration candidate, supported by the almost omnipotent influence of General Jackson. The opposition party could not unite, and four candidates were brought forward ; but the canvass disclosed the popularity of General Harrison, as he received seventy-three electoral votes without any general concert among his friends. The Democratic party triumphed over their disorganized opponents and Mr. Van Buren was chosen President.

At the close of Mr. Van Buren's four years of service, he was renominated by his party, and William Henry Harrison was unanimously nominated by the Whigs, by a convention in which twenty-three out of the twenty-six States were represented. John Tyler of Virginia was nominated for the Vice-Presidency. The contest, as usual, was very animated. General Jackson gave all his influence to prevent General Harrison's election ; but his triumph was signal. He received two hundred and thirty-four electoral votes, leaving but sixty for Mr. Van Buren. He was then sixty-seven years of age. It may be doubted if any of his predecessors had taken the presidential chair better prepared for its responsibilities, in ability, education, experience, and immaculate integrity, than was William Henry Harrison.

His passage from his plain home to the Capitol presented a constant succession of brilliant pageants and enthusiastic greetings.

A vast concourse attended his inauguration. His address on the occasion was in accordance with his antecedents, and gave great satisfaction ; expressing the fear that we were in danger of placing too much power in the hands of the President, and declaring his intention of exercising the powers intrusted to him with great moderation.

The Cabinet which he formed, with Daniel Webster at its head as Secretary of State, was one of the most brilliant with which any

President had ever been surrounded. Never were the prospects of an administration more flattering, or the hopes of the country more sanguine. In the midst of these bright and joyous prospects, General Harrison was seized by a pleurisy fever, and after a few days of violent sickness died on the 4th of April, just one short month after his inauguration. In the delirium of his sickness, as if aware that death was approaching, and fancying that he was addressing his successor, he said, —

"Sir, I wish you to understand the principles of the government: I wish them carried out. I ask nothing more."

These were his last words. His death was universally regarded as one of the greatest of national calamities. The nation mourned with unfeigned grief. Never, then, since the death of Washington, were there throughout our land such demonstrations of sorrow. A careful scrutiny of his character and life must give him a high position in the affection and the esteem of every intelligent mind. Not one single spot can be found to sully the brightness of his fame; and through all the ages Americans will pronounce with love and reverence the name of William Henry Harrison.

18

CHAPTER X.

JOHN TYLER.

His Parentage. — Education and Scholarship. — Early Distinction. — Success at the Bar and in Political Life. — Democratic Principles — Course in the Senate. — Elected Vice-President. — Accession to the Presidency. — False Position, and Embarrassments. — Retirement from Office. — Joins in the Rebellion. — Death.

JOHN TYLER was the favored child of affluence and high social position. His father possessed large landed estates in Virginia and was one of the most distinguished men of his day; filling the offices of

RESIDENCE OF JOHN TYLER.

speaker of the House of Delegates, judge of the Supreme Court, and governor of the State. John was born in Charles City County, Va., the 29th of March, 1790. He enjoyed, in his youthful years, all the advantages which wealth and parental distinction could confer. At the early age of twelve he entered William and Mary College; and graduated, with much honor, when but seventeen years old. His commencement address upon "Female Education" was pronounced to be a very masterly performance. After graduating, he devoted himself with great assiduity to the study of the law, partly with his father and partly with Edmund Randolph, one of the most distinguished lawyers of Virginia.

At nineteen years of age he commenced the practice of the law. His success was rapid and astonishing. It is said that three months had not elapsed ere there was scarcely a case on the docket of the court in which he was not retained. When but twenty-one years of age he was almost unanimously elected to a seat in the state Legislature. He connected himself with the Democratic party, and warmly advocated the measures of Jefferson and Madison. For five successive years he was elected to the Legislature, receiving nearly the unanimous vote of his county.

Sympathizing cordially with the administration in the second war with England, when the British were ravaging the shores of Chesapeake Bay, he exerted himself strenuously to raise a military force to resist them. When but twenty-six years of age he was elected a member of Congress. Here he acted earnestly and ably with the Democratic party, opposing a national bank, internal improvements by the general government, a protective tariff, and advocating a strict construction of the Constitution, and the most careful vigilance over State Rights. His labors in Congress were so arduous, that, before the close of his second term, he found it necessary to resign, and retire to his estate in Charles City County to recruit his health.

He, however, soon after consented to take his seat in the state Legislature, where his influence was powerful in promoting public works of great utility. Many of his speeches developed statesmanlike views, and powers of eloquence of a high order. With a reputation thus constantly increasing, he was chosen by a very large majority of votes, in 1825, governor of his native State,— a high honor; for Virginia had many able men to be competitors for the prize. His administration was signally a successful one. He urged forward internal improvements, strove to remove sectional jealousies, and did much to rouse the people to an appreciation of their own interests. His popularity secured his reëlection.

John Randolph, a brilliant, erratic, half-crazed man, then represented Virginia in the Senate of the United States. A portion of the Democratic party was displeased with Mr. Randolph's wayward course, and brought forward John Tyler as his opponent; considering him the only man in Virginia of sufficient popularity to succeed against the renowned orator of Roanoke. Mr. Tyler was the victor; and, in taking his seat in the Senate, he said to his Democratic constituents, —

"The principles on which I have acted, without abandonment in any one instance, for the last sixteen years, in Congress, and in the legislative hall of this State, will be the principles by which I shall regulate my future political life."

John Quincy Adams was then President of the United States, having been placed in that office by the Whigs. Mr. Tyler immediately upon his election declared, in a public letter, his uncompromising hostility to the principles of Mr. Adams's administration.

" In his message to Congress," wrote Mr. Tyler, " I saw an almost total disregard of the federative principle, a more latitudinarian construction of the Constitution than has ever before been insisted on. From the moment of seeing that message, all who have known anything of me have known that I stood distinctly opposed to this administration."

In accordance with these professions, upon taking his seat in the Senate, he joined the ranks of the opposition. He opposed the tariff; he spoke against and voted against the bank, as unconstitutional; he strenuously opposed all restrictions upon slavery, resisted all projects of internal improvements by the general government, and avowed his sympathy with Mr. Calhoun's views of nullification; he declared that General Jackson, by his opposition to the nullifiers, had abandoned the principles of the Democratic party. Such was Mr. Tyler's record in Congress, — a record in perfect accordance with the principles which he had always avowed.

Perhaps there was never hate more unrelenting than that with which John C. Calhoun and Andrew Jackson regarded each other. Mr. Tyler was in sympathy with Mr. Calhoun; voted with him; and it thus happened that Mr. Tyler was found in opposition to Jackson's administration. This hostility to Jackson caused Mr. Tyler's retirement from the Senate, after his election to a second term. The Legislature of Virginia passed resolutions calling upon their Senators in Congress to vote to *expunge* from the journal of the Senate a vote censuring General Jackson for his usurpation of power in removing the deposits of public money from the United States bank, and placing them in state banks.   Mr. Tyler had cordially approved of this censure, avowing his convictions that General Jackson had usurped powers which the Constitution did not confer upon him.   He had also very emphatically expressed his belief that it was the duty of the representative to obey the directions of his constituents.   Under these circumstances he felt constrained to resign his seat.

Returning to Virginia, he resumed the practice of his profession. There was a split in the Democratic party.   His friends still regarded him as a true Jeffersonian, gave him a public dinner, and showered compliments upon him.   He had now attained the age of forty-six.   His career had been very brilliant.   In consequence of his devotion to public business, his private affairs had fallen into some disorder; and it was not without satisfaction that he resumed the practice of the law, and devoted himself to the culture of his plantation.

Soon after this he removed to Williamsburg, for the better education of his children; and again took his seat in the Legislature of Virginia.   He had thus far belonged very decidedly to the Calhoun or States-Rights party.   The complications of party in this country are inexplicable.   There have been so many diverse and clashing interests, the same name being often used in different sections to represent almost antagonistic principles, that one need not be surprised to find Mr. Tyler, without any change of views, taking the name of a Southern Whig, still opposing the tariff, the bank, and advocating, to the fullest extent, State Rights.   He was still what the North would call a Democrat.

By the Southern Whigs he was sent to the national convention at Harrisburg to nominate a President in 1839.   The majority of votes was given to General Harrison, a genuine Whig, much to the disappointment of the South, who wished for Henry Clay.   To conciliate the Southern Whigs, and to secure their vote, the convention then nominated John Tyler for Vice-President.   It was well known that he was not in sympathy with the Whig party in the North: but the Vice-President has but very little power in the government; his main and almost only duty being to preside over the meetings of the Senate. Thus it happened that a Whig President, and, in reality, a Democratic Vice-President, were chosen.

In 1841 Mr. Tyler was inaugurated Vice-President of the United States. In one short month from that time President Harrison died, and Mr. Tyler thus found himself, to his own surprise and that of the whole nation, an occupant of the presidential chair. This was a new test of the stability of our institutions, as it was the first time in the history of our country that such an event had occurred. Mr. Tyler was at his home in Williamsburg when he received the unexpected tidings of the death of President Harrison. He hastened to Washington, and, on the 6th of April, was inaugurated into his high and responsible office. He was placed in a position of exceeding delicacy and difficulty. All his life long he had been opposed to the main principles of the party which had brought him into power. He had ever been a consistent, honest man, with an unblemished record. General Harrison had selected a Whig Cabinet. Should he retain them, and thus surround himself with counselors whose views were antagonistic to his own? or, on the other hand, should he turn against the party which had elected him, and select a Cabinet in harmony with himself, and which would oppose all those views which the Whigs deemed essential to the public welfare? This was his fearful dilemma.

President Tyler deserves more charity than he has received. He issued an address to the people, carefully worded, which gave general satisfaction. He invited the Cabinet which President Harrison had selected to retain their seats. He recommended a day of fasting and prayer, that God would guide and bless us.

The Whigs carried through Congress a bill for the incorporation of the fiscal bank of the United States. The President, after ten days' delay, returned it with his veto. He suggested, however, that he would approve of a bill drawn up upon such a plan as he proposed. Such a bill was accordingly prepared, and privately submitted to him. He gave it his approval. It was passed without alteration, and he sent it back with his veto. Here commenced the open rupture. It is said that Mr. Tyler was provoked to this measure by a published letter from the Hon. John M. Botts, a distinguished Virginia Whig, containing the following sentences, which severely touched the pride of the President: —

" Captain Tyler is making a desperate effort to set himself up with the *Locofocos :* but he 'll be headed yet ; and I regret to say that it will end badly for him. He will be an object of execration with both parties, — with the one, for vetoing our bill, which was bad enough ; with the other, for signing a worse one : but he is hardly entitled to sympathy. You 'll get a bank bill, but one that will serve only to fasten him, and to which no stock will be sub- scribed ; and when he finds out that he is not wiser in banking than all the rest of the world, we may get a better."

The opposition now exultingly received the President into their arms. The party which elected him denounced him bitterly. All the members of his Cabinet, excepting Mr. Webster, resigned. The Whigs of Congress, both the Senate and the House, held a meeting, and issued an address to the people of the United States, proclaim- ing that all political alliance between the Whigs and President Tyler was at an end.

Still the President attempted to conciliate. He appointed a new Cabinet of distinguished Whigs and Conservatives, carefully leaving out all strong party men. Though opposed to a protective tariff, he gave his sanction to a tariff bill which passed Congress. Thus he placed himself in a position in which he found that he could claim the support of neither party. The Democrats had a majority in the House ; the Whigs, in the Senate. Mr. Webster soon found it necessary to resign, forced out by the pressure of his Whig friends.

Thus the four years of Mr. Tyler's unfortunate administration passed sadly away. No one was satisfied. The land was filled with murmurs and vituperation. Whigs and Democrats alike assailed him. More and more, however, he brought himself into sympathy with his old friends the Democrats, until, at the close of his term, he gave his whole influence to the support of Mr. Polk, the Demo- cratic candidate, for his successor. Several very important measures were adopted during his administration. Situated as he was, it is more than can be expected of human nature that he should, in all cases, have acted in the wisest manner ; but it will probably be the verdict of all candid men, in a careful review of his career, that John Tyler was placed in a position of such exceeding difficulty, that he could not pursue any course which would not expose him to the most severe denunciation.

Mr. Tyler earnestly and eloquently opposed any protective tariff. In glowing periods he depicted the abounding prosperity of the

North, and the dilapidation and decay of the South. The fact no one could deny, that the North was bounding forward in the most brilliant career of prosperity, while the South presented a general aspect of paralysis and desolation. "The protective tariff," said Mr. Tyler, "is the cause of our calamities and our decay. We buy dear, and sell cheap. That is the simple secret. The tariff raises the price of all we buy, and diminishes the demands for our products abroad by diminishing the power of foreign nations to buy them."

The reply to this cannot be better given than in the words of Mr. Parton, in his "Life of Andrew Jackson:" "The Southern system — be it wrong or be it right, be it wise or be it unwise — is one that does not attract emigrants; and the Northern system does. That is the great cause. From the hour when Columbus sprang, exulting, upon these Western shores, the great interest of America has been emigration. That country of the New World has prospered most which has attracted the greatest number of the best emigrants by affording them the best chance to attain the sole object of emigration, — the improvement of their condition; and that portion of that country has outstripped the rest which offered to emigrants the most promising field of labor. For a MAN, view him in what light you may, is the most precious thing in the world: he is wealth in its most concentrated form. A stalwart, virtuous, skillful, thoughtful man, progenitor of an endless line of such, planted in our Western wilds to hew out home and fortune with his own glorious and beautiful right hand and heart, is worth, to the State that wins him, a thousand times his weight in Kohinoor. Such have poured into the Northern States, in an abounding flood, these fifty years. Behold what they have wrought!

"Such emigrants go to the South in inconsiderable numbers, partly because from infancy they learn to loathe the very name of slavery. They sicken at the thought of it. They shrink from contact with it. They take Wesley's characterization of it in the most literal acceptation of the words, and esteem it the SUM of all villainies, — that solely possible crime which includes in its single self all the wrong that man can wreak on man. Whether they are right or whether they are wrong in so thinking, is not a question here. They think so; and, if they did not, they would not go in great numbers to the South, because it does not afford to a man with six

children and a hundred dollars the immediate opportunities for profitable and congenial labor which the North affords. On the prairies,
in the forests of the North, the struggling emigrant finds himself surrounded by neighbors whose condition, antecedents, prospects, social
standing, are all similar to his own. There is no great proprietor
to overtop him. There is no slave with whom he has to compete.
He forgets that there is any such thing as a graduated social scale,
and feels, that, by virtue of his manhood alone, he stands on a level
with the best."

It has been well said, that nothing is ever settled in this world
until it is settled right. There can be no peace, and no abiding
prosperity, until the brotherhood of man is recognized. True democracy demands *impartial suffrage and equal rights for all;* and
if anything be certain this is certain, — that *true democracy* will
never rest content until this shall be attained. Whoever, therefore,
places himself in opposition to this fundamental principle of true
democracy, does but perpetuate conflict, and postpone the long-
looked-for hour when the bitter strife of parties shall cease. It is
in vain for the demon of aristocracy and of exclusive privilege to
clothe itself in the garb of *democracy* and assume its sacred name.
The masses cannot long be thus deceived, and those defrauded of
their rights *will not* acquiesce unresistingly.

It is not slavery alone which saps the foundations of public prosperity: it is any attempt to keep any portion of the people ignorant and degraded, and deprived of privileges conferred upon others
no more deserving. This was the political vice of John Tyler and
his associates. They strained every nerve to keep millions of their
fellow-countrymen in the South in a state of the most abject ser-
vility, ignorance, and degradation ; and then, as they looked around
upon the general aspect of rags, impoverishment, and degradation
in the South, and contrasted it with the beauty and wealth and
power of those States in the North where every man was encouraged
to feel himself a *man*, and to educate to the highest possible degree
his children, and to surround his home with every embellishment
which taste and industry could create, they refused to admit the
true cause for the difference.

In a beautiful strain of philosophic truth, the Hon. Mr. Dallas
said in the Senate of the United States, in a debate upon this subject in 1862, " The lights of science and the improvements of art,

which vivify and accelerate elsewhere, cannot penetrate, or, if they do, penetrate with dilatory inefficiency, among the operatives of the South. They are merely instinctive and passive. While the intellectual industry of other parts of this country springs elastically forward at every fresh impulse, and manual labor is propelled and redoubled by countless inventions, machines, and contrivances, instantly understood and at once exercised, the South remains stationary, inaccessible to such encouraging and invigorating aids. Nor is it possible to be blind to the moral effects of this species of labor upon those freemen among whom it exists. A disrelish for humble and hardy occupation, a pride adverse to drudgery and toil, a dread that to partake in the employments allotted to color may be accompanied also by its degradation, are natural and inevitable.

"When, in fact, the senator from South Carolina asserts that 'slaves are too improvident, too incapable of that minute, constant, delicate attention, and that persevering industry, which are essential to the success of manufacturing establishments,' he himself admits the defect in the condition of Southern labor by which the progress of his favorite section must be retarded. He admits an inability to keep pace with the rest of the world. He admits an inherent weakness, — a weakness neither engendered nor aggravated by the tariff."

These views, now that slavery is dead, are as practically important as ever; for they do conclusively show that it is one of the first principles of political economy that there should not be fostered in any community a servile and degraded class; that it should be the first endeavor of the state to inspire every individual, without a single exception, with the ambition to make the most of himself, intellectually, physically, and morally, that he possibly can. Every facility should be presented which wisdom can devise to promote this elevation of the whole community. Everywhere a poor, ignorant, degraded family is an element of weakness and impoverishment. But Mr. Tyler, from the beginning to the end of his career, was the earnest advocate of slavery, — of its perpetuation and extension.

On the 4th of March, 1845, he retired from the harassments of office, to the regret of neither party, and probably to his own unspeakable relief. His first wife, Miss Letitia Christian, died in Washington in 1842, and in June, 1844, President Tyler was again married, at New York, to Miss Julia Gardiner, a young lady of many personal and intellectual accomplishments.

The remainder of his days Mr. Tyler passed mainly in retirement at his beautiful home, — Sherwood Forest, Charles City County, Va. A polished gentleman in his manners, richly furnished with information from books and experience in the world, and possessing brilliant powers of conversation, his family circle was the scene of unusual attractions. With sufficient means for the exercise of a generous hospitality, he might have enjoyed a serene old age with the few friends who gathered around him, were it not for the storms of civil war which his own principles and policy had helped to introduce.

When the great Rebellion rose, which the State-Rights and nullifying doctrines of Mr. John C. Calhoun had inaugurated, President Tyler renounced his allegiance to the United States, and joined the Confederates. He was chosen a member of their Congress; and while engaged in active measures to destroy, by force of arms, the government over which he had once presided, he was taken sick and, after a short illness, died. There were but few to weep over his grave, excepting his own family, to whom he was much endeared, and the limited circle of his personal friends. His last hours must have been gloomy; for he could not conceal from himself that the doctrines which he had advocated were imperiling the very existence of the nation. Unfortunately for his memory, the name of John Tyler must forever be associated with all the misery and crime of that terrible Rebellion whose cause he openly espoused. It is with sorrow that history records that a President of the United States died while defending the flag of rebellion, which was arrayed in deadly warfare against that national banner which he had so often sworn to protect.

CHAPTER XI.

JAMES KNOX POLK.

Ancestry of Mr. Polk. — His Early Distinction. — His Success as a Lawyer. — Political Life.
— Long Service in Congress. — Speaker in the House. — Governor of Tennessee. — Anec-
dote. — Political Views. — Texas Annexation. — Candidate for the Presidency. — Mexican
War. — Its Object and Results. — Retirement. — Sickness. — Death.

NEAR the southwestern frontier of North Carolina, on the eastern
banks of the Catawba, there is a region now called the County of
Mecklenburg.   In this remote, almost unexplored wilderness, a small

RESIDENCE OF JAMES K. POLK.

settlement was commenced by the Scotch-Irish in the year 1735.
Among these settlers there were two brothers by the name of Polk.
Both of them were men of much excellence of character and of ex-

tensive influence. Early in the spring of 1775 news reached those distant settlers beneath the primeval forests of the atrocities which the crown of Great Britain was perpetrating against the liberties of this country in Massachusetts. There were several public meetings held to discuss these wrongs.

At length, Colonel Thomas Polk, the elder of these brothers, " well known and well acquainted in the surrounding counties, a man of great excellence and merited popularity," was empowered to call a convention of the representatives of the people. Colonel Polk issued his summons ; and there was a convention in Charlotte, the shire-town of the county, held on the 19th of May, 1775. About forty of the principal citizens of the county of Mecklenburg were present as delegates. At this meeting, the announcement was made, that the first blood of the Revolution had been shed in Lexington, Mass. The excitement was intense. Anxious deliberations were protracted late into the night, and resumed the next morning. People were, in the mean time, rapidly gathering in large numbers. Resolutions were at length adopted unanimously, which were read from the court-house steps by Colonel Polk, declaring that " we, the citizens of Mecklenburg County, do hereby dissolve the political bands which have connected us to the mother country, and hereby absolve ourselves from all allegiance to the British crown ; and that we do hereby declare ourselves a free and independent people."

This heroic and extraordinary declaration of independence was unquestionably the first that was made. Colonel Thomas Polk, and his brother Ezekiel, who resided then across the border, in South Carolina, were among the most prominent men in this movement. In the course of the war which ensued, Lord Cornwallis established his headquarters at Charlotte, which he called the hot-bed of rebellion, and the hornet's nest. But little more is known respecting Ezekiel Polk, who was the grandfather of James Knox Polk, the eleventh President of the United States. He left a son, Samuel, who married Jane Knox. Samuel Polk was a plain, unpretending farmer. James was the eldest son of a family of six sons and four daughters. He was born in Mecklenburg County, N. C., on the 2d of November, 1795.

In the year 1806, with his wife and children, and soon after followed by most of the members of the Polk family, Samuel Polk emigrated some two or three hundred miles farther west to the rich valley of the Duck River.   Here in the midst of the wilderness, in a region which was subsequently called Maury County, they reared their log huts, and established their new home.   In the hard toil of a new farm in the wilderness, James K. Polk spent the early years of his childhood and his youth.   His father, adding the pursuits of a surveyor to that of a farmer, gradually increased in wealth until he became one of the leading men of the region.   His mother was a superior woman, of strong common sense and earnest piety.   Young James often accompanied his father on his surveying tours, and was frequently absent from home for weeks together, climbing the mountains, threading the defiles, exposed to all the vicissitudes of the weather, and not a little in peril from hostile Indians.   To a boy of reflective spirit, there is much in such a life to bring out all there is noble in his nature.

Very early in life James developed a taste for reading, and expressed the strongest desire to obtain a liberal education.   His mother's training had rendered him methodical in his habits, had taught him punctuality and industry, and had inspired him with lofty principles of morality.   James, in the common schools, rapidly became a proficient in all the common branches of an English education.   His health was frail, and his father, fearing that he might not be able to endure a sedentary life, got a situation for him behind the counter, hoping to fit him for commercial pursuits.

This was to James a bitter disappointment.   He had no taste for these duties, and his daily tasks were irksome in the extreme.   He remained in this uncongenial occupation but a few weeks, when, at his earnest solicitation, his father removed him, and made arrangements for him to prosecute his studies.   Soon after, he sent him to Murfreesborough Academy.   This was in 1813.   With ardor which could scarcely be surpassed, he pressed forward in his studies, and in less than two and a half years, in the autumn of 1815, entered the sophomore class in the University of North Carolina, at Chapel Hill.   Here he was one of the most exemplary of scholars, so punctual in every exercise, never allowing himself to be absent from a recitation or a religious service, that one of the wags of the college, when he wished to aver the absolute certainty of anything, was in the habit of saying, " It is as certain as that Polk will get up at the first call."

To every branch of a solid and an accomplished education he alike devoted his energies. He graduated in 1818 with the highest honors, being deemed the best scholar of his class, both in mathematics and the classics. He was then twenty-three years of age. Mr. Polk's health was at that time much impaired by the assiduity with which he had prosecuted his studies. After a short season of relaxation he went to Nashville, and entered the office of Felix Grundy to study law. Mr. Grundy was a man of national fame, not only standing at the head of the bar in Nashville, but having also distinguished himself on the floor of Congress. Here Mr. Polk renewed his acquaintance with Andrew Jackson, who resided on his plantation, the Hermitage, but a few miles from Nashville. They had probably been slightly acquainted before. When Mrs. Jackson, with her two orphan boys, fled before the army of Cornwallis, she took refuge in Mecklenburg County, and for some time resided with the neighbors of Mr. Polk's father.

As soon as he had finished his legal studies, and been admitted to the bar, he returned to Columbia, the shire-town of Maury County, and opened an office. His success was rapid. Very seldom has any young man commenced the practice of the law more thoroughly prepared to meet all of its responsibilities. With rich stores of information, all his faculties well disciplined, and with habits of close and accurate reasoning, he rapidly gained business, and won fame.

Mr. Polk's father was a Jeffersonian Republican, and James K. Polk ever adhered to the same political faith. He was a popular public speaker, and was constantly called upon to address the meetings of his party friends. His skill as a speaker was such, that he was popularly called the Napoleon of the stump. He was a man of unblemished morals, genial and courteous in his bearing, and with that sympathetic nature in the joys and griefs of others which ever gave him troops of friends. There is scarcely any investment which a man can make in this world so profitable as pleasant words and friendly smiles, provided always that those words and smiles come honestly from the heart. In 1823 Mr. Polk was elected to the Legislature of Tennessee. Here he gave his strong influence towards the election of his friend, Andrew Jackson, to the presidency of the United States. He also procured the passage of a law designed to prevent dueling. From principle he was utterly opposed to the practice, and it required no little moral courage for one in those rude times and regions to attempt the abrogation of that so-called "code of honor," obedience to which was deemed essential to the character of a chivalric gentleman.

Mr. Polk, as a "strict constructionist," did not think that the Constitution empowered the general government to carry on a system of internal improvements in the States ; but, with Mr. Monroe, he deemed it important that the government should have that power, and wished to have the Constitution amended that it might be conferred. Subsequently, however, with most of the Southern gentlemen, he became alarmed lest the general government should become so strong as to undertake to interfere with slavery. He therefore gave all his influence to strengthen the state governments, and to check the growth of the central power.

In January, 1824, Mr. Polk married Miss Sarah Childress of Rutherford County, Tenn. His bride was altogether worthy of him, — a lady of beauty and of culture. Had some one then whispered to him that he was destined to become President of the United States, and that he should select for his companion one who would adorn that distinguished station, he could not have made a more fitting choice. The following anecdote is related of Mrs. Polk, when, in 1848, she was lady of the White House. It should be remembered that Mr. Polk was a Democrat, and Mr. Clay a Whig, and that they had been rival candidates for the presidency. There was quite a brilliant dinner-party at the President's. Henry Clay, as one of the most distinguished guests, was honored with a seat near Mrs. Polk, who as usual, by her courteous and affable manner, won the admiration of all her guests.

During the entertainment Mr. Clay turned to her, and said, in those winning tones so peculiar to him, —

"Madam, I must say, that in my travels, wherever I have been, in all companies and among all parties, I have heard but one opinion of you. All agree in commending, in the highest terms, your excellent administration of the domestic affairs of the White House. But," continued he, looking towards her husband, "as for that young gentleman there, I cannot say as much. There is some little difference of opinion in regard to the policy of *his* course."

"Indeed," said Mrs. Polk, "I am glad to hear that *my* administration is popular ; and, in return for your compliment, I will say, that, if the country should elect a Whig next fall, I know of no one whose elevation would please me more than that of Henry Clay. And I will assure you of one thing : if you do have occasion to occupy the White House on the 4th of March next, it shall be surrendered to you in perfect order from garret to cellar."

" Thank you, thank you ! " exclaimed Mr. Clay ; " I am certain that "— No more could be heard, such a burst of laughter followed Mrs. Polk's happy repartee. In the fall of 1825 Mr. Polk was chosen a member of Congress. The satisfaction which he gave to his constituents may be inferred from the fact, that for fourteen successive years, until 1839, he was continued in that office. He then voluntarily withdrew, only that he might accept the gubernatorial chair of his native State. In Congress he was a laborious member, a frequent and a popular speaker. He was always in his seat, always courteous ; and whenever he spoke, it was always to the point, and without any ambitious rhetorical display. Mr. Polk was the warm friend of General Jackson, who had been defeated in the electoral contest by John Quincy Adams. This latter gentleman had just taken his seat in the presidential chair when Mr. Polk took his seat in the House of Representatives. He immediately united himself with the opponents of Mr. Adams, and was soon regarded as the leader of the Jackson party in the house.

The four years of Mr. Adams's administration passed away, and General Jackson took the presidential chair. Mr. Polk had now become a man of great influence in Congress, and was chairman of its most important committee, — that of Ways and Means. Eloquently he sustained General Jackson in all of his measures, — in his hostility to internal improvements, to the bank, to the tariff. The eight years of General Jackson's administration ended, and the powers he had wielded passed into the hands of Martin Van Buren ; and still Mr. Polk remained in the house, the advocate of that type of democracy which those distinguished men upheld.

During five sessions of Congress Mr. Polk was speaker of the house. Strong passions were roused, and stormy scenes were witnessed; but Mr. Polk performed his arduous duties to very general satisfaction, and a unanimous vote of thanks to him was passed by the house as he withdrew on the 4th of March, 1839. In his closing address, he said, —

" When I look back to the period when I first took my seat in this house, and then look around me for those who were at that

19

time my associates here, I find but few, very few, remaining. But five members who were here with me fourteen years ago continue to be members of this body. My service here has been constant and laborious. I can perhaps say what few others, if any, can, — that 1 have not failed to attend the daily sittings of this house a single day since I have been a member of it, save on a single occasion, when prevented for a short time by indisposition. In my intercourse with the members of this body, when I occupied a place upon the floor, though occasionally engaged in debates upon interesting public questions and of an exciting character, it is a source of unmingled gratification to me to recur to the fact, that on no occasion was there the slightest personal or unpleasant collision with any of its members."

In accordance with Southern usage, Mr. Polk, as candidate for governor, canvassed the State. He was elected by a large majority, and on the 14th of October, 1839, took the oath of office at Nashville. In 1841 his term of office expired, and he was again the candidate of the Democratic party. But in the mean time a wonderful political revolution had swept over the whole country. Martin Van Buren had lost his reëlection, and General Harrison had been called triumphantly to the presidential chair. In Tennessee the Whig ticket had been carried by over twelve thousand majority. Under these circumstances the success of Mr. Polk was hopeless. Still he canvassed the State with his Whig competitor, Mr. Jones, traveling in the most friendly manner together, often in the same carriage, and, it is said, at one time sleeping in the same bed. Mr. Jones obtained the election by three thousand majority. Again, in 1843, the same gentlemen were competitors for the governorship, and again Mr. Polk was defeated.

And now the question of the annexation of Texas to our country agitated fearfully the whole land. It was a plan which originated with the advocates of slavery, that they might get territory to cut up into slave States, to counterbalance the free States which were being formed in the Northwest. Texas was a province of Mexico. We were on friendly terms with that puny and distracted republic, and could find no plausible occasion to pick a quarrel with it. The territory we coveted was in extent equal to the whole empire of France, and could be divided into six first-class States. The following plan was adopted to gain the prize : —

There was a wild, eccentric frontiersman by the name of Sam Houston, who had abandoned civilization, and for six years had lived among the Indians, adopting their habits. He was a man of very considerable native ability. In his character there was a singular blending of good and bad qualities. He had so far commended himself to the Cherokee Indians that they had chosen him as one of their chiefs. This man gathered a pretty numerous band of lawless adventurers, and entered Texas to wrest it from Mexico as a private speculation. The plan was distinctly announced ; and from all parts of the country there was a very extensive emigration to those wide and fertile plains of those who were in sympathy with the movement. They went strongly armed, and with abundant supplies furnished them from the South.

These men, settlers in Texas, in 1836 called a convention, issued a declaration of independence, formed a constitution establishing perpetual slavery, and chose their intrepid leader, Sam Houston, their governor. A short, bloody, merciless war ensued. The Mexicans were utterly repulsed. Population from the United States rapidly flowed in. It was manifest to every one that Mexico could never regain her lost province. The first step was triumphantly accomplished. A few months after this the second step was taken, and Congress acknowledged the independence of Texas. The Texans then sent an envoy to Washington, proposing the annexation of Texas to the American Union.

The friends of slavery generally were in favor of the movement. Mr. Benton said that nine slave States could be carved out of the majestic domain, each nearly equal to the State of New York. Most of the foes of slavery extension were opposed to the measure of annexation. Mr. Webster said, —

"Slavery in this country stands where the Constitution left it. I have taken an oath to support the Constitution, and I mean to abide by it. I shall do nothing to carry the power of the general government within the just bounds of the States. I shall do nothing to interfere with the domestic institutions of the South, and the government of the United States have no right to interfere therewith. But that is a very different thing from not interfering to prevent the extension of slavery by adding a large slave country to this. Texas is likely to be a slaveholding country ; and I frankly avow my unwillingness to do anything that shall extend the slavery of the

African race on this continent, or add another slaveholding State to this Union."

Thus the question of the annexation of Texas became national. Mr. Polk, as the avowed champion of annexation, became the presidential candidate of the proslavery wing of the Democratic party, and Dallas their candidate for the vice-presidency. He was elected by a majority in the popular vote of about forty thousand. In January, 1845, he left his home in Tennessee for Washington, having first had a long private interview with General Jackson at the Hermitage. As he was ascending the Ohio River in a steamboat at one of the landings, a plain, farmer-like looking man, in his working-dress, pressed through the crowd, and, taking Mr. Polk's hand, said, —

"How do you do, colonel? I am glad to see you. I am a strong Democrat, and did all I could for you. I am the father of twenty-six children, who were all for *Polk, Dallas, and Texas.*"

On the 4th of March, 1845, Mr. Polk was inaugurated President of the United States. The verdict of the country in favor of annexation exerted its influence upon Congress; and the last act of the administration of President Tyler was to affix his signature to a joint resolution of Congress, passed on the 3d of March, approving of the annexation of Texas to the American Union. As Mexico still claimed Texas as one of her provinces, the Mexican minister, Almonte, immediately demanded his passports, and left the country, declaring the act of annexation to be an act hostile to Mexico. But Mexico was poor, feeble, and distracted, — a very feeble foe for this great republic to encounter. It would have been folly for her to attempt to strike a blow. She could only protest.

In his first message President Polk urged that Texas should immediately, by act of Congress, be received into the Union on the same footing with the other States. In the mean time General Taylor was sent with an army into Texas to hold the country. He was sent first to the Nueces, which the Mexicans said was the western boundary of Texas. Then he was sent nearly two hundred miles farther west, to the Rio Grande, where he erected batteries which commanded the Mexican city of Matamoras, which was situated on the western banks.

The anticipated collision soon took place. We had pushed forward our army nearly two hundred miles, to the extreme western frontier of the disputed territory ; had erected our batteries so as to command the Mexican city of Matamoras, on the opposite banks ; had placed our troops in such a position that lawless violence was sure to provoke retaliation ; and then, as soon as the Mexican troops crossed the river, and a conflict ensued, President Polk announced to the country that war with Mexico existed.

" Now, Mexico," he said, " has passed the boundary of the United States, has invaded our territory, and shed American blood on American soil. She has proclaimed that hostilities have commenced, and that the two nations are at war. As war exists, notwithstanding our efforts to avoid it, — exists by the act of Mexico herself, — we are called upon by every consideration of duty and patriotism to vindicate with decision the honor, rights, and interests of our country."

The war was pushed forward by Mr. Polk's administration with great vigor. General Taylor, whose army was first called one of "observation," then of " occupation," then of " invasion," was sent forward to Monterey. The feeble Mexicans in every encounter were hopelessly and awfully slaughtered. The day of judgment alone can reveal the misery which was caused. It was by the ingenuity of Mr. Polk's administration that the war was brought on. Mr. Webster said, —

" I believe that, if the question had been put to Congress before the march of the armies and their actual conflict, not ten votes could have been obtained in either house for the war with Mexico under the existing state of things."

" To the victors belong the spoils." Mexico was prostrate before us. Her capital was in our hands. We now consented to peace upon the condition that Mexico should surrender to us, in addition to Texas, all of New Mexico, and all of Upper and Lower California. This new demand embraced, *exclusive of Texas*, eight hundred thousand square miles. This was an extent of territory equal to nine States of the size of New York. Thus slavery was securing eighteen majestic States to be added to the Union. There were some Americans who thought this all right : there were others who thought it all wrong.

Mr. Polk's administration called for a grant of three millions of dollars, to be judiciously expended among the Mexicans to induce them voluntarily to make this surrender. There was a split in the

Democratic party; and some of the Northern Democrats succeeded in attaching to this appropriation what was called the " Wilmot Proviso," in these words: —

" Provided always that there shall be neither slavery nor involuntary servitude in any territory on the continent of America which shall hereafter be acquired or annexed to the United States by virtue of this appropriation, or in any other manner whatsoever, except for crimes whereof the party shall have been duly convicted."

This was called also the *Thomas Jefferson Proviso*, as its language was copied from the ordinance originally drafted by him for the government of the Northwestern Territory. This restriction struck Mr. Polk and his friends with consternation. They did not wish to annex one single acre more of land, unless it could add to the area of slavery. The excitement which pervaded the Southern mind was violent in the extreme. Passionate speeches were made. Fiery resolutions were drafted by legislatures of the slaveholding States. The " dissolution of the Union " was threatened. Under the influence of the threat, the proviso was reconsidered and rejected.

At last peace was made. We had wrested from Mexico territory equal, it has been estimated, to four times the empire of France, and five times that of Spain. In the prosecution of this war we expended twenty thousand lives, and more than a hundred million of dollars. Of this money, fifteen millions were paid to Mexico.

> " God moves in a mysterious way
> His wonders to perform."

Scarcely twenty years elapsed ere the whole of this vast region was consecrated to freedom. Gold was discovered in California. Northern emigrants rushed to gather it, carrying with them Northern love of liberty; and California became a free State. Mr. Polk, highly gratified with his success, — for he had no doubt that the whole region was to be consecrated to slavery, — presented the treaty to the Senate for its ratification on the 10th of March, 1848.

Justice to Mr. Polk's memory requires that his view of the righteousness and expediency of the war with Mexico should be given. While no one will dissent from the *facts* which have already been presented, there are many who will assert that the reasons which Mr. Polk urges in the following sentences were not the true causes of the war. In his second Annual Message, December, 1846, he says, —

"The existing war with Mexico was neither provoked nor desired by the United States : on the contrary, all honorable means were resorted to to avoid it. After years of endurance of aggravated and unredressed wrongs on our part, Mexico, in violation of solemn treaty stipulations, and of every principle of justice recognized by civilized nations, commenced hostilities, and thus, by her own act, forced the war upon us. Long before the advance of our army to the left bank of the Rio Grande, we had ample cause of war against Mexico. The war has been represented as unjust and unnecessary ; as one of aggression, on our part, on a weak and injured enemy. Such erroneous views, though entertained but by a few, have been widely and extensively circulated, not only at home, but have been spread throughout Mexico and the whole world.

"The wrongs which we have suffered from Mexico almost ever since she became an independent power, and the patient endurance with which we have borne them, are without a parallel in the history of modern civilized nations. Scarcely had Mexico achieved her independence, when she commenced the system of insult and spoliation which she has ever since pursued. Our citizens, engaged in lawful commerce, were imprisoned, their vessels seized, and our flag insulted in her ports. If money was wanted, the lawless seizure and confiscation of our merchant vessels and their cargoes was a ready resource ; and if, to accomplish their purposes, it became necessary to imprison the owners, captain, and crew, it was done. Rulers superseded rulers in Mexico in rapid succession ; but still there was no change in this system of depredation. The government of the United States made repeated reclamations on behalf of its citizens ; but these were answered by the perpetration of new outrages." In this general strain of remark he continues through several closely printed pages, and then says, "Such is the history of the wrongs which we have suffered and patiently endured from Mexico through a long series of years."

"The annexation of Texas," he continues, "constituted no just cause of offense to Mexico." After giving a brief description of the previous history of Texas, and the nature of its union with Mexico, as one of its confederate States, he says, "Emigrants from foreign countries were invited by the colonization laws of the State and of the federal government to settle in Texas. This invitation was accepted by many of our citizens, in the full faith, that, in their new home, they would be governed by laws enacted by representatives elected by themselves; and that their lives, liberty, and property would be protected by constitutional guaranties similar to those which existed in the republic they had left. Under a government thus organized they continued until the year 1835, when a military revolution broke out in the city of Mexico, which entirely subverted the federal and state constitutions, and placed a military dictator at the head of the government.

" The people of Texas were unwilling to submit to this usurpation. Resistance to such tyranny became a high duty. The people of Texas flew to arms. They elected members to a convention, who in the month of March, 1836, issued a formal declaration, that their 'political connection with the Mexican nation has forever ended, and that the people of Texas do now constitute a free, sovereign, and independent republic.' "

He then gives an account of the unsuccessful attempts of Mexico, by her armies, to conquer and reclaim her lost territory. " Upon this plain statement of facts," he continues, " it is absurd for Mexico to allege that Texas is still a part of her territory."

" But there are those," he adds, " who, conceding all this to be true, assume the ground, that the true western boundary of Texas is the Nueces, instead of the Rio Grande; and that, therefore, in marching our army to the east bank of the latter river, we passed the Texan line, and invaded the territory of Mexico." His explanation of this is too long and labored to be inserted here. The substance is, that the Texans claimed the Rio Grande as their boundary; that they had conquered it by the sword; that, as conquerors, they had a right to it; and that the United States government, having annexed Texas to the Union, was under every moral obligation to defend the boundaries which the Texans claimed.

This defense of the policy of the government in the affairs relative to Texas and Mexico gives one a very just idea of the character of Mr. Polk's mind, and of the peculiarity of his abilities. The arguments he presents are plausible rather than convincing. One can scarcely conceive of such a document coming from the pen of Jefferson or of Webster.

On the 3d of March, 1849, Mr. Polk retired from office, having served one term. The next day was Sunday. On the 5th General Taylor was inaugurated as his successor. Mr. Polk rode to the Capitol in the same carriage with General Taylor ; and the same evening, with Mrs. Polk, he commenced his return to Tennessee. Very enthusiastic demonstrations of regard met him as he journeyed through the Southern States. At Wilmington, Charleston, Savannah, and New Orleans, he was honored with splendid ovations. He had previously purchased a beautiful mansion in the heart of the city of Nashville.

He was then but fifty-four years of age. He had ever been strictly temperate in his habits, and his health was good. With an ample fortune, a choice library, a cultivated mind, and domestic ties of the dearest nature, it seemed as though long years of tranquillity and happiness were before him. But the cholera — that fearful scourge — was then sweeping up the valley of the Mississippi. President Polk steamed up the river from New Orleans. On board the boat, he perceived the premonitory symptoms of the dread disease. When he reached his home, his system was much debilitated. A personal friend gives the following account of his last hours : —

" Having reached Nashville, he gave himself up to the improvement of his grounds, and was seen every day about his dwelling, aiding and directing the workmen he had employed, now overlooking a carpenter, now giving instructions to a gardener, often attended by Mrs. Polk, whose exquisite taste constituted the element of every improvement. It is not a fortnight since I saw him on the lawn, directing some men who were removing decaying cedars. I was struck with his erect and healthful bearing, and the active energy of his manner, which gave promise of long life. His flowing gray locks alone made him appear beyond the middle age of life. He seemed in full health. The next day being rainy, he remained within, and began to arrange his large library. The labor of reaching books from the floor, and placing them on the shelves, brought on fatigue and slight fever, which the next day assumed the character of disease in the form of chronic diarrhœa.

" For the first three days his friends felt no alarm ; but the disease baffling the skill of his physicians, Dr. Hay, his brother-in-law, and family physician for twenty years, was sent for from Columbia. But the skill and experience of this gentleman, aided by the highest medical talent, proved of no avail.   Mr. Polk continued gradually to sink from day to day.   The disease was checked upon him for four days before his death ; but his constitution was so weakened that there did not remain recuperative energy enough in the system for healthy reaction.   He sank away so slowly and insensibly that the heavy death-respirations commenced eight hours before he died. He died without a struggle, simply ceasing to breathe, as when deep and quiet sleep falls upon a weary man.   About half an hour preceding his death his venerable mother entered the room and offered up a beautiful prayer to the King of kings and Lord of lords, committing the soul of her son to his holy keeping."

His death occurred on the 15th of June, 1849, in the fifty-fourth year of his age.   His funeral was attended the following day, in Nashville, with every demonstration of respect.   He left no children. As death drew near, he felt, as thousands of others have done, the need of the supports of Christianity, and in that eleventh hour received the rite of baptism at the hands of a Methodist clergyman.

CHAPTER XII.

ZACHARY TAYLOR.

Birth. — Emigration to Kentucky. — Neglected Education. — Enters the Army. — Life on the Frontier. — Battles with the Indians. — Campaign in Florida. — The Mexican War. — Palo Alto. — Resaca de la Palma. — Monterey. — Buena Vista. — Nominated for the Presidency. — Sufferings. — Death.

ZACHARY TAYLOR, the twelfth President of the United States, was born on the 24th of November, 1784, in Orange County, Va.

RESIDENCE OF ZACHARY TAYLOR.

His father, Colonel Richard Taylor, was a Virginian of note, and a distinguished patriot and soldier of the Revolution. When Zachary was an infant, his father, with his wife and two other children, emigrated to Kentucky, where he settled in the pathless wilderness, a few miles out from the present city of Louisville. He was one of the first settlers of that region ; and as such, when the population increased, was honored with many responsible trusts.

In this rude frontier-home, far away from civilization and all its refinements, young Zachary could enjoy but few social or educational advantages. When six years of age he attended a common school, and was then regarded as a bright, active boy, rather remarkable for bluntness, and decision of character. He was strong, fearless, and self-reliant, and manifested an eager desire to enter the army to fight the Indians who were ravaging the frontiers. There is little to be recorded of the uneventful years of his childhood on his father's large but lonely plantation. In 1808 his father succeeded in obtaining for him the commission of lieutenant in the United States army ; and he joined the troops which were stationed at New Orleans under General Wilkinson. Soon after this he married Miss Margaret Smith, a young lady from one of the first families in Maryland.

Our relations with England were, at this time, becoming very threatening, and we were upon the eve of our second war with that power. The English officials in Canada were doing their utmost to rouse the Indians against us. Immediately after the declaration of war in 1812, Captain Taylor (for he had then been promoted to that rank) was put in command of Fort Harrison, on the Wabash, about fifty miles above Vincennes. This fort had been built in the wilderness by General Harrison, on his march to Tippecanoe. It was one of the first points of attack by the Indians, led by Tecumseh. The works consisted simply of a row of log-huts for soldiers' barracks, with a strong block-house at each end. These buildings occupied one side of a square, the other three sides of which were composed of rows of high pickets. Its garrison consisted of a broken company of infantry, numbering fifty men, many of whom were sick.

Early in the autumn of 1812, the Indians, stealthily, and in large numbers, moved upon the fort. Their approach was first indicated by the murder of two soldiers just outside of the stockade. Captain Taylor made every possible preparation to meet the anticipated assault. On the 4th of September a band of about forty painted and plumed savages came to the fort, waving a white flag, and informed Captain Taylor, that, in the morning, their chief would come to have a talk with him. It was evident that their object was merely to ascertain the state of things at the fort; and Captain Taylor, well versed in the wiles of the savages, kept them at a distance.

The sun went down; the savages disappeared; the garrison slept upon their arms. One hour before midnight the war-whoop burst from a thousand lips in the forest around, followed by the discharge of musketry, and the rush of the foe. Every man, sick and well, sprang to his post. Every man knew that defeat was not merely death, but, in case of capture, death by the most agonizing and prolonged torture. No pen can describe, no imagination can conceive, the scene which ensued. The savages succeeded in setting fire to one of the block-houses. There was a large amount of whisky stored in the building; and the sheets of flame, flashing to the clouds, lit up the whole landscape with lurid brilliancy. The forest, the dancing savages, the yells of the assailants, the crackling and glare of the fire, the yelping of the dogs, the shrieks of the women (for there were several in the fort), who had become almost frantic with terror, the shouts of command, the incessant rattle of musketry, — all created a scene of terror which caused the stoutest heart to quail. Of course no one thought of surrender. It was far better to perish by the bullet or the fire than to fall into the hands of the foe. Until six o'clock in the morning this awful conflict continued. The savages then, baffled at every point, and gnashing their teeth with rage, retired. Captain Taylor, for this gallant defense, was promoted to the rank of major by brevet.

Until the termination of the war Major Taylor was placed in such situations that he saw but little more of active service. When the army was reduced at the close of the war, the military board retained him, but assigned to him only the rank of captain. Not relishing this arrangement, Major Taylor resigned his commission, and returned to the peaceful pursuits of agricultural life on his plantation. Soon, however, the influence of friends regained for him his rank of major; and, returning to the army, he was sent far away into the depths of the wilderness, to Fort Crawford, on Fox River, which empties into Green Bay. Here there was but little to be done but to wear away the tedious hours as one best could. There were no books, no society, no intellectual stimulus. Thus with him the uneventful years rolled on. Gradually he rose to the rank of colonel. In the Black Hawk war, which resulted in the capture of that renowned chieftain, Colonel Taylor took a subordinate but a brave and efficient part.

It is related of Colonel Taylor, that, while engaged in this war, he was at one time pursuing Black Hawk with his Indian band, when they came to Rock River, which was then understood to be the northwest boundary of the State of Illinois. He had under his command a pretty large force of volunteers and a few regulars. The volunteers openly declared that they would not cross the river, as they had enlisted only for the defense of the State; and that they were not bound to march beyond the frontier into the Indian country. Colonel Taylor, inclining to the same opinion, encamped upon the banks of the stream. But during the night orders came for him to follow up Black Hawk to the last extremity. The soldiers, hearing of this, assembled on the prairie, in a sort of town meeting, to deliberate respecting what they should do. Colonel Taylor was invited to attend. He was a man of few words, but had already attained some celebrity for his decisive actions.

Very quietly, for a time, he listened to their proceedings. At length it came his turn to speak. " Gentlemen and fellow-citizens," said he, " the word has been passed on to me from Washington to follow Black Hawk, and to take you with me as soldiers. I mean to do both. There are the flat-boats drawn up on the shore; here are Uncle Sam's men drawn up behind you on the prairie."

There was no resisting this argument. In a few hours they were all across the river, in hot pursuit of the foe. For twenty-four years Colonel Taylor was engaged in the defense of the frontiers, in scenes so remote, and in employments so obscure, that his name was unknown beyond the limits of his own immediate acquaintance. In the year 1836 he was sent to Florida to compel the Seminole Indians to vacate that region and retire beyond the Mississippi, as their chiefs, by treaty, had promised they should do. The great mass of the Indians, denying the right of a few chiefs to sell the hunting grounds of their fathers, refused to emigrate: hence the war. Colonel Taylor was sent to capture or destroy them, wherever they might be found.

But little lasting fame can be acquired in fighting undisciplined savages. And still the American Indians were so brave and so cunning, appearing at this moment like a pack of howling wolves in one spot, and the next moment dispersed, no one could tell where, that it required military qualities of a very high character successfully to contend with them. " War," says Napoleon, " is the science of barbarians." Indian warfare has ever been found a very good school in which to acquire the rudiments of that science. It requires constant vigilance, prompt action, patience, versatility of talent, to meet every emergency, and courage of the highest order to face death in its most appalling form.

The war with the Seminoles was long, bloody, and inglorious ; and, with many of the American people, it was considered as, on the part of our government, very unjust. Early in the winter of 1837 Colonel Taylor, with a small army of about one thousand men, commenced a march into the interior to assail a large body of Seminole warriors who were encamped upon the banks of the great inland lake, Okeechobee. Their path, of one hundred and fifty miles, led through an unexplored wilderness, intersected by rivers, vast forests of oak and pine, and immense morasses of gloomy cypress-trees, with almost impenetrable underbrush, and interlacings of vines and pendent moss. There was no path through these vast solitudes, and no food could be gathered on the way for either man or beast.

Upon the northern shore of this lake there was a swamp, in the midst of whose recesses a small island was found. Here seven hundred Seminole warriors, having learned through their runners of the advance of the white man, had stationed themselves to give battle. They were well armed with rifles, and were unerring in their aim. Every man of them stood behind his protecting tree ; and rarely has warfare presented greater peril than the men were exposed to in wading through that swamp in the face of such a foe. The Indians, nimble as deer, could vanish in an hour ; and weeks and months might elapse before they could again be found. Under these circumstances, Colonel Taylor made no reconnoissance, but fell instantly and impetuously upon them.

It was necessary to cross the swamp, three quarters of a mile in breadth, through mud and water knee-deep, impeded by brush and weeds, and tall, coarse, wiry grass, before they could reach the island or hummock where the foe was stationed. As soon as Taylor's advance came within musket-shot, the Indians poured in upon them such a deadly fire that the troops broke and fled in a panic which nothing could check. A second line advanced more cautiously, seeking such protection as the ground could afford, and keeping up a constant discharge of musketry : but the Indians, from their thicket, concentrated upon them such well-aimed shot, that, in a few minutes, every officer was struck down ; and in one company but four men were left untouched.

In the mean time other parties, by other approaches, had gained the hummock, and the Indians broke and fled. For three hours this battle was fought with the utmost desperation on both sides ; but the rout was complete. The Seminoles lost so large a number of their warriors that they never ventured to give battle again. Their forces were afterwards divided into marauding bands, who gradually, crushed in spirit, surrendered, and were removed to the lands allotted to them beyond the Mississippi. General Taylor lost, in killed, about thirty, including many of his most valuable officers. One hundred and twelve were wounded. These unhappy men were carried across the country to Tampa Bay, on litters roughly constructed of poles and hides. This signal victory secured for Colonel Taylor the high appreciation of the government ; and, as a reward, he was elevated to the rank of brigadier-general by brevet ; and soon after, in May, 1838, was appointed to the chief command of the United States troops in Florida. Broken bands of Indians, in a high state of exasperation, were for a long time wandering through the country, requiring the most strenuous exertions on the part of Colonel Taylor to protect the scattered inhabitants.

General Taylor, in his official account of the battle of Okeechobee, says, " The action was a severe one, and continued from half-past twelve until after three in the afternoon ; a part of the time very close and severe. We suffered much. The hostiles probably suffered, all things considered, equally with ourselves ; they having left ten on the ground, besides, doubtless, carrying off many more, as is customary with them when practicable.

" As soon as the enemy were completely broken, I turned my attention to taking care of the wounded, to facilitate their removal to my baggage, where I ordered an encampment to be formed. I directed Captain Taylor to cross over to the spot, and employ every individual whom he might find there in constructing a small footway across the swamp. This, with great exertion, was completed in a short time after dark, when all the dead and wounded were carried over in litters made for that purpose, with one exception, — a private of the Fourth Infantry, who was killed, and could not be found.

" And here, I trust, I may be permitted to say, that I experienced one of the most trying scenes of my life. And he who could have looked on it with indifference, his nerves must have been very differently organized from my own. Besides the killed, there lay one hundred and twelve wounded officers and soldiers, who had accompanied me one hundred and forty-five miles, most of the way through an unexplored wilderness, without guides; who had so gallantly beaten the enemy, under my orders, in his strongest position; and who had to be conveyed back through swamps and hummocks from whence we set out, without any apparent means of doing so.

" This service, however, was encountered and overcome; and they have been conveyed thus far, and proceeded on to Tampa Bay, on rude litters constructed with the axe and knife alone, with poles and dry hides; the latter being found in great abundance at the encampment of the hostiles. The litters were conveyed on the backs of our weak and tottering horses, aided by the residue of the command, with more ease and comfort than I could have supposed, and with as much as they could have been in ambulances of the most improved and modern construction.

" This column, in six weeks, penetrated one hundred and fifty miles into the enemy's country; opened roads, and constructed bridges and causeways, when necessary, on the greater portion of the route; established two depots, and the necessary defenses for the same; and, finally, overtook and beat the enemy in his strongest position. The results of which movements and battle have been the capture of thirty of the hostiles; the coming in and surrendering of more than one hundred and fifty Indians and negroes, mostly of the former, including the chiefs, Oulatoochee, Tustanuggee, and other principal men; the capturing, and driving out of the country, six hundred head of cattle, upwards of one hundred head of horses, besides obtaining a thorough knowledge of the country through which we operated, a greater portion of which was entirely unknown except to the enemy."

After two years of such wearisome employment amidst the everglades of the peninsula, General Taylor obtained, at his own request, a change of command, and was stationed over the Department of the

Southwest. This field embraced Louisiana, Mississippi, Alabama, and Georgia. Establishing his headquarters at Fort Jessup in Louisiana, he removed his family to a plantation which he purchased near Baton Rouge. Here he remained for five years, buried as it were from the world, yet faithfully discharging every duty imposed upon him.

It has been said that bayonets must not think. General Taylor was an officer in the employment of the United States government, and as such was bound, as he supposed, to obey orders. In the spring of 1845 Congress passed a joint resolution for the annexation of Texas, and General Taylor was directed to hold his troops in readiness for action on the Texan frontier. Into the question of the right or wrong of this annexation we have no space to enter. General Taylor's position was, however, embarrassing, as it *appeared* to be the desire of the government (James K. Polk having just entered upon the presidency) that General Taylor should take steps to bring on a collision with Mexico, of which the government wished to avoid the responsibility. He therefore declined acting upon his own responsibility, silently waiting for implicit instructions.

The river Nueces was claimed by Mexico to be the original western boundary of Texas; but Secretary Marcy, in his dispatch to General Taylor, indicated the Rio Grande, nearly two hundred miles farther west, or rather south, as the boundary-line to be defended. He was, however, not ordered, at first, to advance to the Rio Grande; though he was directed to cross the Nueces River and establish his corps of observation at Corpus Christi, on the *western* bank of the river. In August, 1845, he took his position here, with fifteen hundred troops, which in November were increased by reinforcements to four thousand. Although when at Corpus Christi he was on ground which the Mexicans claimed, so long as he remained there there was apparently no danger of collision with the Mexican authorities. He disregarded all the hints which came to him from Washington for a further advance westward, until March, 1846, when there came explicit orders for him to advance to the Rio Grande. He accordingly took up his line of march over the boundless prairies which Mexico claimed as her territory. At the distance of about one hundred miles he came to the waters of the Colorado. Here he found a Mexican force drawn up upon the western bank, but altogether too feeble to attempt to dispute his passage. Still the Mexican commander sent a protest against what he regarded as the invasion of Mexico, and declared that the crossing of the Colorado would be regarded as a declaration of war.

General Taylor, assuming that he was simply bound to obey orders, paid no attention to the warning, and crossed the river in sight of the Mexican detachment, who peaceably withdrew. Continuing his march, he sent a detachment to occupy Point Isabel, on the banks of an inlet opening into the Gulf, which was easily accessible by steamers, and had been fixed upon as the dépôt for army supplies. The main body of the army soon reached the Rio Grande, and commenced throwing up defensive works. Opposite them, upon the western bank, was the Mexican city of Matamoras. This invasion of their country, as the Mexicans deemed it, excited great

GENERAL TAYLOR ON THE RIO GRANDE.

indignation. The Mexican commander, General Ampudia, refused to hold any friendly intercourse with the Americans, and on the 12th of April, by orders from his government, issued a summons to General Taylor to return to the eastern bank of the Nueces, there to await the decision of the two governments, who were discussing the question of the true boundaries of Texas. He added that the refusal to do this must inevitably lead to war. Our government evidently wished to provoke hostilities. General Taylor replied, that, as he was acting in a purely military capacity, his instructions would not allow him to retire to the Nueces ; and that, if war were the only alternative, he accepted it with regret.

General Taylor wrote to the adjutant-general, April 6, 1846, " On our side, a battery, for four eighteen-pounders will be completed, and the guns placed in battery to-day. These guns bear directly upon the public square at Matamoras, and are within good range for demolishing the town. Their object cannot be mistaken by the enemy."

President Polk did not regard this as a hostile measure which the Mexicans had any right to resist. In the mean time, Commodore Sloat was sent to the Pacific with seven ships of war and nearly three thousand men, with secret orders to seize and occupy San Francisco and other Mexican ports on the Pacific as soon as he should hear of the existence of war between Mexico and the United States. Accordingly, on the 7th of July, 1846, hearing of the victories of Palo Alto and Resaca de la Palma, he seized Monterey, in California, without resistance, and " annexed " California ; announcing that " henceforth California will be a portion of the United States."

The whole territory we wrested from Mexico is estimated to be as large as England, Ireland, Scotland, France, Spain, Portugal, Italy, and Germany combined. In Cutt's " Conquest of California " he relates the following anecdote : —

" Just as we were leaving camp to-day, an old Apache chief came in, and harangued the general thus : ' You have taken Santa Fé. Let us go on and take Chihuahua and Sonora. We will go with you. You fight for the soil ; we fight for plunder : so we will agree perfectly. These people are bad Christians : let us give them a good thrashing.' "

This interview between General Kearney and the Indian warrior reminds one of the ancient anecdote of Alexander and the pirate.

The two armed forces upon the Matamoras remained in the presence of each other for a month. For more than two miles along each bank of the river, antagonistic batteries were facing each other, the guns shotted, and the artillery-men on both sides impatient for the order to fire. The situation naturally gave rise to many causes of irritation on both sides. Brazos Santiago, the port of Matamoras, was blockaded by order of General Taylor; and two supply-ships for the Mexican army were ordered off the harbor. No one could deny that this was a hostile act. The deputy quartermaster of the American troops was murdered a short distance from camp. A small party of United States soldiers, in pursuit of the murderers, fell upon a band of Mexicans, fired upon them, and put them to flight, taking possession of their camp. On their return they were fired upon by another Mexican party, and one of their officers was killed. Thus, gradually, hostilities were inaugurated. A Mexican force crossed the Rio Grande above Matamoras. A squadron of United States dragoons, sent to watch their movements, was attacked by the Mexicans, and, after the loss of ten men killed, was captured.

Point Isabel, which, as we have mentioned, was about twelve miles from Matamoras, was threatened by a force of fifteen hundred Mexicans; and General Taylor's connection with his dépôt of supplies was cut off. In order to open his communications, he left a garrison at Fort Brown, as his works opposite Matamoras were called, and with the remainder of his army set out on the 1st of May for Point Isabel. Immediately after his departure the Mexicans opened fire upon Fort Brown from a battery on the western side of the river. The hostile battery was soon silenced; but after the lapse of a day another and more formidable assault was made, the Mexicans having crossed the river, so as to attack the fort both in front and rear. After a spirited bombardment on both sides, night closed the conflict. In the night, by firing his eighteen-pounders at stated intervals, Major Brown, who was in command, signaled General Taylor that he was surrounded. The next morning the Mexicans resumed the assault. Their shells fell with such accuracy into the camp that the garrison was driven into the bomb-proofs. Major Brown was mortally wounded. The command devolved upon Captain Hawkins. He refused the summons to surrender, and endured the terrible bombardment until night again closed the scene. It was the 6th of May.

In the mean time General Taylor, having learned that the Mexicans had crossed the river with six thousand men, and that Fort Brown was surrounded and in great peril, commenced vigorously retracing his steps. The morning of the 8th dawned. The Mexicans opened again their bombardment with new vigor and hope. The thunders of the cannonade floated over the vast prairies, and fell heavily upon the ears of the host advancing to the rescue of their comrades. About noon Taylor's force encountered the Mexicans. Their appearance was very imposing, as three thousand men — infantry, cavalry, and artillery, with waving banners and gleaming armor — were drawn up on the broad prairie, in a line nearly a mile in length. Their right rested upon a dense thicket of chaparral, and their left was protected by a swamp. They had eleven field-pieces in position.

General Taylor had about twenty-two hundred men; and was, on the whole, superior to the Mexicans in artillery, as he had ten guns, two of which were eighteen-pounders. He drew up his army in battle array, about half a mile distant from the Mexicans. The field of Palo Alto, upon which these hostile armies were thus arrayed, was a vast plain with nothing to obstruct the view. When both armies were ready, they stood for twenty minutes looking at each other, each hesitating to begin the work of death. At length a white puff of smoke burst from one of the Mexican guns, and a cannon-ball whistled over the heads of the American troops. This opened the battle. It was mainly an artillery contest on both sides. General Taylor was not a tactician: he was simply a stern, straightforward, indomitable fighter. The combatants kept at quite a distance from each other, throwing their shot and shell often more than three quarters of a mile. Thus the battle raged for five hours, each army being exposed to every shot of its antagonist. The superior skill of the American gunners, and our heavier weight of metal, gave us the advantage; and the loss was far greater on the Mexican side than on ours. The prairie-grass took fire, and sheets of flame rolled along ten feet high. Immense clouds of smoke enveloped the contending hosts. Round shot, grape, and shells tore through the Mexican ranks with great slaughter. Our infantry, generally, threw themselves upon the ground; and most of the enemy's shot either fell short or passed over their heads. Only four Americans were killed, and thirty-two wounded. The Mexican loss was two hundred and sixty-two.

When night came and closed the conflict, neither party knew the effect of the cannonade upon the other. The Mexicans, however, confessed to a defeat, by retiring, under protection of the darkness, to a new position some few miles in their rear. The little garrison at Fort Brown, while repelling the assault which was made upon them, listened with intense anxiety to the booming of the cannon on the field of Palo Alto. Should General Taylor be cut off or driven back, the doom of the garrison was sealed.

The next morning General Taylor, finding that the enemy had disappeared, moved forward to the ground which the Mexicans had occupied. They had left behind them their dead, and many of their wounded. He pressed on in pursuit, and soon found them, at the distance of but about three miles from Fort Brown, formidably posted in a ravine called Resaca de la Palma. Scattered around were dense thickets of dwarf-oaks, almost impenetrable. Here the Mexican general, Arista, had so advantageously posted his forces that it required desperate valor to break through. Again there was a battle. It commenced with artillery, and was followed up with infantry and cavalry. Several charges of great impetuosity were made. The Mexicans fought with great bravery and with disciplined valor. There was but little room for generalship. It was simply hard fighting. The forces were not far from equal on both sides; but the American soldiers, far more intelligent than their foes, fired with much more rapidity and with surer aim, and their victory was complete. Soon the whole Mexican line was seen on the retreat, having lost a thousand of their number in killed, wounded, and missing. The American loss did not exceed a hundred and fifty. The enemy fled across the river, hotly pursued. Enthusiastic were the cheers of the little band in Fort Brown as they saw the stars and stripes advancing so gloriously to their rescue.

The tidings of these victories aroused to an astonishing degree the martial spirit of the country. War was now thoroughly inaugurated. Those who had brought it on were well pleased. " Palo Alto " and " Resaca de la Palma " rang through the land as among the most glorious victories which had ever been achieved. " On to the halls of the Montezumas ! " was the cry ; and the few and feeble voices of remonstrance were drowned in the exultant shout. Congress authorized the President to accept fifty thousand volunteers. The rank of major-general by brevet was conferred on General Taylor. Congressional resolutions complimented him, and the legislatures of several States lavished upon him their honors. These flattering testimonials were received by General Taylor with that unaffected simplicity which was one of his chief characteristics, and which was manifest in all the habits of his life. Though a strict disciplinarian, he could scarcely be distinguished, in his own personal appearance and dress, from any common farmer. These habits secured for him among his troops the *soubriquet* of "Old Rough and Ready."

An incident, which occurred soon after the victories just recorded, amusingly illustrates these traits in his character. After the relief of Fort Brown General Taylor prepared to follow up his victories by the bombardment of Matamoras. Accordingly he went to Point Isabel to arrange for the coöperation of the navy. Commodore Conner, commanding in the Gulf, was as famed for particularity in dress as the general was for negligence in that respect. The commodore sent word that he would pay the general a visit of ceremony. This announcement caused much agitation in the mind of the kind-hearted officer. Without embarrassment, he could have welcomed his guest with a hearty grip of the hand to a seat on the camp-chest, and to a familiar talk over their plans; but that the most carefully-dressed officer in the navy, in command of its finest fleet, should pay him a visit of ceremony, in full uniform, and surrounded by all the retinue and equipments becoming his rank, was an anticipation almost too great for nerves that scarcely trembled in battle. The general, however, decided to receive the commodore, dressed in full uniform, — a sight that his officers, who had been associated with him for years, had never witnessed. Meanwhile, Commodore Conner, quite unconscious of the flutter he had caused in the general's bosom, with the good sense of a gallant and accomplished gentleman, prepared for his interview with the plain old general, whose habits were well known to him.

At the time appointed, habited in plain white drilling, he came ashore, without any parade or any attendants. As soon as it was reported to General Taylor that his visitor had landed, he hastened from some heavy work which he was superintending, rushed into his tent, brought from the bottom of his chest a uniform-coat that for years had been undisturbed, arrayed himself in it, with its standing-collar raised on one side three vacant button-holes above its legitimate height, and, in a very uncomfortable manner, seated himself for the reception. Commodore Conner quietly entered the tent of the commander-in-chief. The distinguished representatives of the army and navy shook hands in mutual astonishment at each other's personal appearance. It is said, that, after that interview, General Taylor took to linen roundabouts, of the largest dimensions, with more pertinacity than ever. It matters little whether this story be accurately true or not: it illustrates the character of the man.

Another amusing anecdote has been told illustrative of this trait of extreme simplicity, and disregard of the ordinary courtesies of life, in the character of General Taylor. A gentleman who had been connected with the army, and was attached to the same regiment with Taylor, and had been intimately acquainted with him, visited Fort Jessup, in Louisiana, while the general was stationed in command at that post. He had not seen his old friend for some time, and was quite disappointed to learn that he was a hundred miles distant, attending a court-martial.

One day the gentleman was walking out from the fort in a morning ramble, when he met " an old country codger " jogging along towards the camp on a donkey. They exchanged salutations, according to the custom in those remote solitudes. But the figure of the donkey-rider, on his diminutive beast, was so comical, that the gentleman could not refrain from turning round, and gazing at him after he had passed. He was dressed in a coarse bombazine frock-coat and drab trousers. The bottoms of his trousers were tucked under his coarse, spattered boots. A black cravat was tied loosely round his neck. He had on a very coarse straw hat, whose broad brim, as he trotted along, flapped up and down; while, from beneath, long, uncombed hair fluttered in the breeze.

The gentleman continued his walk, and, upon returning to the fort, was cordially greeted by this comical-looking donkey-rider, who, to his surprise, he found to be his old friend, General Taylor. In passing neither had recognized the other.

On the 18th of May General Taylor, having obtained pontoons, crossed the Rio Grande unopposed, both above and below Matamoras, and took possession of the city. The request from General Arista, for a suspension of hostilities until the terms of boundary could be amicably arranged by the two governments, was positively refused. For three months General Taylor remained at Matamoras. This was with him a period of great anxiety. His victories had excited unbounded enthusiasm, and both government and people seemed to expect that he would sweep immediately and resistlessly on to the city of Mexico; but this required a march of more than five hundred miles, intersected by rivers easily defended, and mountain-ranges, in whose narrow defiles a small band could resist a host.

President Polk, in transmitting to General Taylor his commission of major-general by brevet, wrote to him as follows : " It gave me sincere pleasure, immediately upon receipt of official intelligence from the scene of your achievements, to confer upon you, by and with the advice and consent of the Senate, this testimonial of the estimate which your government places upon your skill and gallantry. To yourself, and the brave officers and soldiers under your command, the gratitude of the country is justly due. Our army have fully sustained their deservedly high reputation, and added another bright page to the history of American valor and patriotism. They have won new laurels for themselves and for their country.

" The battles of Palo Alto and Resaca de la Palma rank among our most brilliant victories, and will long be remembered by the American people. When all the details of those battles, and of the noble defense of the camp opposite to Matamoras, shall have been received, it will be my pleasure, as it will be my grateful duty, to render to the officers and men under your command suitable testimonials for their conduct in the brilliant victories which a superintending Providence has enabled them to achieve for their country."

It was General Taylor's intention to make Camargo, which was one hundred and forty miles farther up the river, his base of operations in the now contemplated invasion of Mexico. Camargo was nearer to Monterey, his next point of attack. He was, however, delayed for some time by the non-arrival of reinforcements, and by his want of means of transportation. This delay gave the Mexicans time to recover from their panic, and to make preparations for a vigorous resistance. At length, the latter part of July, the army was put in motion. Sixteen hundred mules had been obtained for the transportation. The country through which they marched had long been infested by banditti; and large numbers of crosses were passed, which had been reared by the friends of murdered travelers at the places where they had been slain. These crosses were of wood, about four feet high, some of recent construction, and others hoary and mossy with age. A brief inscription generally told the story. At one place there was quite a cluster of these crosses, in commemoration of a company of men, women, and children, who, on a pleasure-party to Matamoras, were met by a band of savages and all slain. Irreverently our troops tore down these crosses and used them for firewood. Camargo was reached without opposition, and here another delay occurred of six weeks.

Early in September the troops again took up their line of march for Monterey. In the distance there rose sublimely before them the majestic peaks of the mountains, " cutting their outlines against the clear sky like huge masses of indigo." It was generally supposed that the Mexicans would not make any stand at Monterey, and General Taylor was of this opinion. Soon, however, the indications began to multiply that there was trouble to be encountered ahead. The Mexican muleteers shrugged their shoulders ominously. At Marin a very intelligent, honest-looking Mexican was asked if there would be much fighting. " Yes, sir," he replied very decidedly ; " there will be much fighting, and many deaths."

When they reached Seralvo, Mexican cavalry began to appear, hovering in front and upon their flanks, watching every movement. At the village of Ramas quite a skirmish ensued. On the 19th of September the army reached the outskirts of Monterey, and encamped at the Walnut Springs, three miles distant from the city, which was beautifully situated in the valley of the San Juan River, and was surrounded by the lofty ridges of the Sierra Madre. General Taylor was so much deceived, that, two days before, he wrote to the War Department, —

" It is even doubtful whether General Ampudia will attempt to hold Monterey. His regular force is small, say three thousand, eked out, perhaps, to six thousand by volunteers, many of them forced."

Instead of this, there was found in Monterey a garrison of ten thousand soldiers, seven thousand of whom were regular troops. General Taylor had under his command six thousand two hundred and twenty.

The next day after our arrival, Sunday the 20th, the enemy's works were carefully reconnoitred. General Worth was then ordered to make a *détour* to the west of the city, and attack in that direction, and carry the works if possible. To aid him in this endeavor, General Taylor was to make a demonstration on the east. The Mexicans were vigilant, and watched every movement. Promptly they threw out reinforcements to strengthen their western lines. To divert their attention, General Taylor displayed a large force on the east, and, under cover of the darkness of the night, erected a battery of two twenty-four-pounder howitzers, a ten-inch mortar, and four light field-batteries of four guns each. In the night General Worth reached the Saltillo road, and occupied a position just out of the range of the Mexican guns.

Early on the morning of Monday, the 21st, General Taylor received a dispatch from General Worth, dated nine o'clock the evening before, announcing the success of his movement, and urging a strong assault, in his support, upon the eastern portion of the town. About ten o'clock, as these troops were approaching the eastern walls, they were opened upon from masked batteries, with such a storm of iron that they quailed before it. Generals Taylor and Twiggs were both upon the ground. The troops were thrown into confusion; but the indomitable spirit of General Taylor rallied them, and, by an impetuous charge, they captured one fort and an old fortified block-house. Still the scene of confusion was dreadful. Many lives had been lost. General Taylor was in the midst of the *mêlée*, laboring under the most intense excitement.

As night approached, a little order was evolved from the chaos. Garland's brigade held the captured works, and the rest of the troops were sent back to camp. At sunset it began to rain. One of the soldiers writes, —

"That was one of the most miserable nights I ever passed. We had had nothing to eat since the evening before. We had been out all night, and had been fighting all day; nor was it until the next afternoon — making in all about forty-eight hours under arms — that we had even a morsel, except some sugar that had been trampled under foot."

The next day, Tuesday, the 22d, the assault was not renewed. Its hours were mainly devoted to the sad duty of taking care of the wounded, and burying the dead. The enemy kept up a vigorous fire upon any of our troops who came within range. General Worth's division, however, upon the other side of the city, after very hard fighting, succeeded in carrying the bishop's palace, and turned its guns upon the fugitive garrison. General Taylor, having ascertained the fact of this decisive success, felt confident that the Mexicans could not long hold possession of the town.

During the night the enemy evacuated nearly all his defenses on the eastern part of the city, to strengthen those points now so seriously menaced on the west by General Worth. This was reported early in the morning to General Taylor. He says in his report, —

" I immediately sent instructions to that officer, leaving it to his discretion, to enter the city, covering his men by the houses and walls, and to advance as far as he might deem prudent. After ordering the remainder of the troops as a reserve, under the orders of General Twiggs, I repaired to the abandoned works, and discovered that a portion of General Quitman's brigade had entered the town, and were successfully working their way towards the principal plaza. I then ordered up the Second Regiment of Texas mounted volunteers, who entered the city, dismounted, and, under the immediate orders of General Henderson, coöperated with General Quitman's brigade. Captain Bragg's battery was also ordered up, and supported by the Third Infantry; and, after firing for some time at the cathedral, a portion of it was likewise thrown into the city.

" Our troops advanced from house to house, and from square to square, until they reached a street but one square in rear of the principal plaza, in and near which the enemy's force was mainly concentrated. This advance was conducted vigorously, but with due caution, and, although destructive to the enemy, was attended with but small loss upon our part."

In the mean time American batteries were throwing shot and shell into the city, until the fire endangered our own advancing troops. As Quitman's brigade was exceedingly exhausted, and night was drawing on, General Taylor ordered them to withdraw to the safer position of the evacuated works. This was done slowly, and in good order. At eleven o'clock at night he received a note from General Worth, stating that he had penetrated the city almost to the central plaza, and that a mortar which had been forwarded to his division in the morning was doing great execution.

Early in the morning of Thursday, the 24th, General Taylor received a dispatch from the Mexican general, Ampudia, proposing to evacuate the town. This led to a cessation of fire until twelve o'clock. A personal interview took place between the two generals, Taylor and Ampudia, which resulted in a capitulation. The town and its material of war were placed in possession of the victor. The city was found to be very strongly fortified. Its well-constructed works were armed with forty-two pieces of cannon, and well supplied with ammunition. Our loss was very severe. Twelve officers and one hundred and eight men were killed. Thirty-one officers and three hundred and thirty-seven men were wounded. The loss of the enemy is not known ; but it must have been dreadful, as our balls and shells tore through their streets and dwellings.

An eye-witness thus describes the appearance, as our troops were in the distance storming one of the heights : " Each flash looked like an electric spark. The flashes and the white smoke ascended the hillside as steadily as if worked by machinery. The dark space between the apex of the height and the curling smoke of the musketry grew less and less, until the whole became enveloped in smoke, and we knew that our gallant troops had carried it. It was a glorious sight, and quite warmed our cold and chilled bodies."

General Worth's division had left camp with only two days' rations, and much of this was spoiled by the rain ; yet they climbed these cliffs and charged these batteries for forty-eight hours, many of them without any food except raw corn.

General Taylor, consolidating his strength at Monterey, sent out divisions of his army to occupy important posts in the vicinity. Santa Anna was commander-in-chief of the Mexican armies. He collected twenty thousand men at San Luis Potosi, a city of four thousand inhabitants, about two hundred and fifty miles south of Monterey. General Scott was placed in command of all the land-forces in Mexico. As he was preparing to advance upon the city of Mexico by the way of Vera Cruz, nearly all of General Taylor's forces were withdrawn from him. For five months General Taylor remained in Monterey, with merely sufficient men to garrison his defensive works ; but in February, having received reinforcements which raised his army to six thousand men, he commenced a forward movement. When about fifty miles south of Monterey, he learned that Santa Anna was rapidly advancing upon him with twenty thousand men. To meet such a force with but five thousand, it was necessary that General Taylor should have every possible advantage of position. He found a field such as he desired, on a plateau, a

BATTLE OF BUENA VISTA.

PREPARED EXPRESSLY FOR ABBOTT'S LIVES OF THE PRESIDENTS

short distance from the small hamlet of Buena Vista. Having posted his little band to the best possible advantage, General Taylor, with his staff, stood upon an eminence at a little distance, from which he could see the clouds of dust raised by the immense host advancing against him. Onward the vast throng pressed, in numbers which seemed almost countless, until the band of Americans was nearly surrounded. Anxiously his staff looked into the general's face; but no sign of faltering or agitation could be perceived.

Just then a Mexican messenger was seen nearing the outposts with a flag of truce. It was a summons to surrender, with the assurance that twenty thousand Mexicans were in General Taylor's front and rear.

"Were they twice that number," General Taylor quietly remarked to the officers around him, "it would make no difference."

He then returned the modest answer to Santa Anna, "General Taylor never surrenders." As he rode along his ranks, he said to his troops, "Soldiers, I intend to stand here not only so long as a man remains, but so long as a *piece* of a man is left." It was the 22d of February, 1847. The battle soon commenced, — a battle of ten hours' duration. In the midst of one of its most terrible scenes of tumult and carnage, General Taylor rode up to a battery which was dealing destruction in the ranks of the foe, and, in tones as calm as if he were sitting by his camp-fire, said, "A little more grape, Captain Bragg." At the close of the day, over seven hundred of the Americans had been stricken down in killed and wounded, and about two thousand of the Mexicans. Often, during the eventful day, the result of the conflict was extremely doubtful; and, when night closed the scene, it seemed probable, in the American camp, that the dreadful struggle would be renewed on the morrow. The day of the battle was wet and raw. Our exhausted troops, drenched and chilled, bivouacked without fires. It was an anxious night; but in the morning, to their unspeakable relief, they found that the Mexicans had fled. This ended General Taylor's active participation in the Mexican war.

Seldom has a battle been fought in which the troops displayed more gallant conduct than was exhibited by General Taylor's army at the battle of Buena Vista. All of the troops were volunteers, with the exception of about five hundred. But few of them had been with Taylor in his previous victories, and many of them had never been in battle. It is universally admitted that the victory was owing, not merely to the courage and patient endurance of the troops, but also to the military skill of their commander. Three several times during the day, the battle, on our part, seemed hopelessly lost. The Mexicans were so superior in numbers that they could easily concentrate an overpowering force at any point. With most painful interest, General Taylor watched the movements in various parts of the field, as he dispatched reinforcements, now in one direction and now in another, to strengthen his exhausted and wavering lines.

At one time the Second Kentucky Regiment was dispatched to the aid of a column which was slowly giving way before the tremendous pressure of the foe. In hurrying to their relief, the regiment was compelled to pass through a ravine filled with gullies and obstructions. In their eagerness in pressing forward, and surmounting these difficulties they of course became broken, and presented an aspect of confusion and disorder. General Taylor, who was eagerly watching them in the distance, was bitterly disappointed at this apparent failure of troops upon whom he had placed great reliance. Turning sadly to Mr. Crittenden, who stood near, he said, —

"This will not do. This is not the way for Kentuckians to behave themselves."

Mr. Crittenden was also so mortified, and felt so deeply for the honor of his native State, that, for a few moments, he could make no reply. But soon the Kentuckians had crossed the rugged chasm, and were seen ascending the slope to the higher land beyond, shoulder to shoulder, like the veterans of a hundred battles. The general could scarcely restrain his expressions of delight as they moved rapidly on until they reached the crest of the hill. Here they encountered a large body of the Mexicans, rushing onward with shouts of exultation. The Kentuckians leveled their pieces, and poured in their volleys of bullets again and again, with such regularity, precision, and rapidity of fire, that the Mexicans recoiled, staggered, and fled, leaving the ground covered with their dead.

The general, with a throbbing heart and a moistened eye, but in perfect silence, watched this movement so heroic, and its results so decisive. His face was flushed with excitement, and beamed with delight. But when the distant report of the volleys reached his ear, and he saw the Mexicans in wild flight, scattered over the plain, he could no longer restrain his admiration, but shouted, " Hurrah for old Kentucky ! "

A distinguished officer in the army thus describes the appearance of the general toward the close of the conflict : —

" At a time when the fortunes of the day seemed extremely prob-lematical, when many on our side even despaired of success, old Rough and Ready, as he is not inaptly styled (whom you must know, by the by, is short, fat, and dumpy in person, with remarkably short legs), took his position on a commanding height overlooking the two armies. This was about three or perhaps four o'clock in the afternoon. The enemy, who had succeeded in gaining an ad-vantageous position, made a fierce charge upon our column, and fought with a desperation that seemed, for a time, to insure success to their arms. The struggle lasted for some time. All the while General Taylor was a silent spectator; his countenance exhibiting the most anxious solicitude, alternating between hope and despond-ency. His staff, perceiving his perilous situation, — for he was exposed to the fire of the enemy, — approached him and implored him to retire. He heeded them not. His thoughts were intent upon victory or defeat. He knew not at this moment what the result would be. He felt that that engagement was to decide his fate. He had given all his orders and selected his position. If the day went against him he was irretrievably lost; if for him, he could rejoice, in common with his countrymen, at the triumphant success of our arms.

" Such seemed to be his thoughts, his determination ; and when he saw the enemy give way and retreat in the utmost confusion, he gave free vent to his pent-up feelings. His right leg was quickly disengaged from the pommel of the saddle, where it had remained dur-ing the whole of the fierce encounter ; his arms, which were calmly folded over his breast, relaxed their hold; his feet fairly danced in the stirrups ;. and his whole body was in motion. It was a moment of the most exciting and intense interest. His face was suffused with tears. The day was won ; the victory complete ; his little army saved from defeat and disgrace ; and he could not refrain from weeping for joy at what had seemed to so many, but a moment be-fore, as an impossible result."

The tidings of the brilliant victory of Buena Vista spread the

21

wildest enthusiasm over the country.   The name of General Taylor was on every one's lips.   The Whig party decided to take advantage of this wonderful popularity in bringing forward the unpolished, unlettered, honest soldier as their candidate for the presidency. General Taylor was astonished at the announcement, and for a time would not listen to it; declaring that he was not at all qualified for such an office.   So little interest had he taken in politics that, for forty years, he had not cast a vote.   It was not without chagrin that several distinguished statesmen who had been long years in the public service found their claims set aside in behalf of one whose name had never been heard of, save in connection with Palo Alto, Resaca de la Palma, Monterey, and Buena Vista.   It is said that Daniel Webster, in his haste, remarked, "It is a nomination not fit to be made."

General Taylor was not an eloquent speaker or a fine writer.   His friends took possession of him, and prepared such few communications as it was needful should be presented to the public.   The popularity of the successful warrior swept the land.   He was triumphantly elected over two opposing candidates, — General Cass and the ex-President, Martin Van Buren.   Though he selected an excellent Cabinet, the good old man found himself in a very uncongenial position, and was at times sorely perplexed and harassed.   His mental sufferings were very severe, and probably tended to hasten his death. The proslavery party was pushing its claims with tireless energy; expeditions were fitting out to capture Cuba; California was pleading for admission to the Union, while slavery stood at the door to bar her out.   General Taylor found the political conflicts in Washington to be far more trying to the nerves than battles with Mexicans or Indians.

In the midst of all these troubles, General Taylor, after he had occupied the presidential chair but little over a year, took cold, and, after a brief sickness of but five days, died on the 9th of July, 1850. His last words were, "I am not afraid to die.   I am ready.   I have endeavored to do my duty."   He died universally respected and beloved.   An honest, unpretending man, he had been steadily growing in the affections of the people; and the nation bitterly lamented his death.   All assented to the general truthfulness of the following eulogy, pronounced by the Hon. Mr. Marshall: —

"Great, without pride; cautious, without fear; brave, without rashness ; stern, without harshness ; modest, without bashfulness ; apt, without flippancy ; sagacious, without cunning ; benevolent, without ostentation ; sincere and honest as the sun, — the noble old Roman has, at last, laid down his earthly harness : his task is done."

General Scott, who was thoroughly acquainted with General Taylor, gives the following graphic and truthful description of his character : —

" With a good store of common sense, General Taylor's mind had not been enlarged and refreshed by reading, or much converse with the world. Rigidity of ideas was the consequence. The frontiers and small military posts had been his home. Hence he was quite ignorant for his rank, and quite bigoted in his ignorance. His simplicity was child-like, and with innumerable prejudices, amusing and incorrigible, well suited to the tender age. Thus, if a man, however respectable, chanced to wear a coat of an unusual color, or his hat a little on one side of the head, or an officer to leave a corner of his handkerchief dangling from an outside pocket, — in any such case, this critic held the offender to be a coxcomb (perhaps something worse), whom he would not, to use his oft-repeated phrase, ' touch with a pair of tongs.'

" Any allusion to literature beyond good old Dilworth's Spelling-book, on the part of one wearing a sword, was evidence, with the same judge, of utter unfitness for heavy marchings and combats. In short, few men have ever had a more comfortable, labor-saving contempt for learning of every kind. Yet this old soldier and neophyte statesman had the true basis of a great character, — pure, uncorrupted morals, combined with indomitable courage. Kind-hearted, sincere, and hospitable in a plain way, he had no vice but prejudice, many friends, and left behind him not an enemy in the world."

CHAPTER XIII.

MILLARD FILLMORE.

His Lowly Birth. — Struggles with Adversity. — Limited Education. — Eagerness for Intellectual Improvement. — A Clothier. — A Law Student. — Commencement of Practice. — Rapid Rise. — Political Life. — In Congress. — Vice-President. — President. — His Administration. — Retirement. — The Civil War.

MILLARD FILLMORE, the thirteenth President of the United States, was born at Summer Hill, Cayuga County, N. Y., on the 7th of January, 1800. His father was a farmer, and, owing to mis-

RESIDENCE OF MILLARD FILLMORE.

fortune, in humble circumstances. Of his mother, the daughter of Dr. Abiathar Millard of Pittsfield, Mass., it has been said that she possessed an intellect of very high order, united with much personal loveliness, sweetness of disposition, graceful manners, and exquisite sensibilities. She died in 1831 ; having lived to see her son a young man of distinguished promise, though she was not permitted to witness the high dignity which he finally attained.

In consequence of the secluded home and limited means of his father, Millard enjoyed but slender advantages for education in his early years. The common schools, which he occasionally attended, were very imperfect institutions; and books were scarce and expensive. There was nothing then in his character to indicate the brilliant career upon which he was about to enter. He was a plain farmer's boy; intelligent, good-looking, kind-hearted. The sacred influences of home had taught him to revere the Bible, and had laid the foundations of an upright character. When fourteen years of age, his father sent him some hundred miles from home, to the then wilds of Livingston County, to learn the trade of a clothier. Near the mill there was a small village, where some enterprising man had commenced the collection of a village library. This proved an inestimable blessing to young Fillmore. His evenings were spent in reading. Soon every leisure moment was occupied with books. His thirst for knowledge became insatiate ; and the selections which he made were continually more elevating and instructive. He read history, biography, oratory ; and thus gradually there was enkindling in his heart a desire to be something more than a mere worker with his hands ; and he was becoming, almost unknown to himself, a well-informed, educated man.

This intellectual culture of necessity pervaded his whole being. It beamed forth from his countenance; it inspired his words; it placed its impress of dignity and refinement upon his manners. The young clothier had now attained the age of nineteen years, and was of fine personal appearance and of gentlemanly demeanor. It so happened that there was a gentleman in the neighborhood of ample pecuniary means and of benevolence, — Judge Walter Wood, — who was struck with the prepossessing appearance of young Fillmore. He made his acquaintance, and was so much impressed with his ability and attainments, that he advised him to abandon his trade, and devote himself to the study of the law. The young man replied that he had no means of his own, no friends to help him, and that his previous education had been very imperfect. But Judge Wood had so much confidence in him that he kindly offered to take him into his own office, and to loan him such money as he needed. Most gratefully the generous offer was accepted.

There is in many minds a strange delusion about a collegiate education. A young man is supposed to be liberally educated if he has graduated at some college. But many a boy loiters through university halls, and then enters a law office, who is by no means as well prepared to prosecute his legal studies as was Millard Fillmore when he graduated at the clothing-mill at the end of four years of manual labor, during which every leisure moment had been devoted to intense mental culture.

Young Fillmore was now established in the law office. The purity of his character, the ardor of his zeal, his physical health, and his native abilities, all combined to bear him triumphantly forward in his studies. That he might not be burdened with debt, and that he might not bear too heavily on the generosity of his benefactor, he, during the winter months, taught school, and, in various other ways, helped himself along. After spending two years in this retired country village, he went to the city of Buffalo, and entered a law office there, where he could enjoy the highest advantages. Here, for two years more, he pressed onward in his studies with untiring zeal, at the same time supporting himself mainly by teaching.

In 1823, when twenty-three years of age, he was admitted to the Court of Common Pleas. He then went to the beautiful little village of Aurora, situated on the eastern banks of Cayuga Lake, and commenced the practice of the law. In this secluded, peaceful region, his practice, of course, was limited, and there was no opportunity for a sudden rise in fortune or in fame. Here, in the year 1826, he married a lady of great moral worth, and one capable of adorning any station she might be called to fill, — Miss Abigail Powers, daughter of Rev. Lemuel Powers. In this quiet home of rural peace and loveliness, Mr. Fillmore continued to devote himself to juridical studies, and to the fundamental principles of law, as if he had been conscious of the exalted destiny which was before him. Probably no portion of his life was more happy than these serene, untroubled hours.

But true merit cannot long be concealed. His elevation of character, his untiring industry, his legal acquirements, and his skill as an advocate, gradually attracted attention, and he was invited to enter into partnership, under highly advantageous circumstances, with an elder member of the bar in Buffalo. Just before removing to Buffalo, in 1829, he took his seat in the House of Assembly of the State of New York, as representative from Erie County. Though he had never taken a very active part in politics, his vote and his sympathies were with the Whig party. The State was then Democratic, and he found himself in a helpless minority in the legislature ; still the testimony comes from all parties, that his courtesy, ability, and integrity won, to a very unusual degree, the respect of his associates. To the important bill for abolishing imprisonment for debt he gave his earnest and eloquent coöperation, speaking upon the subject with convincing power.

The state Legislature is not unfrequently the entrance-door to the national Congress. After discharging, with great acceptance to his Whig constituents, his responsibilities in the House of Assembly for three years, he was, in the autumn of 1832, elected to a seat in the United States Congress. He entered that troubled arena in some of the most tumultuous hours of our national history. The great conflict respecting the National Bank, and the removal of the deposits, was then raging. Experienced leaders, veterans in congressional battles, led the contending hosts. There was but little opportunity for a new-comer to distinguish himself. In this battle of the giants Mr. Fillmore could do but little more than look on, study the scene, garner wisdom, watch his opportunity, and cast his silent vote.

His term of two years closed, and he returned to his profession, which he pursued with increasing reputation and success. After the lapse of two years he again became a candidate for Congress, was reëlected, and took his seat in 1837. His past experience as a representative gave him strength and confidence. The first term of service in Congress to any man can be but little more than an introduction. He was now prepared for active duty. All his energies were brought to bear upon the public good. Every measure received his impress. The industry and the intensity with which he applied himself to his congressional duties were characteristic of the man, and have, perhaps, never been surpassed.

His reputation now began to be national. The labors which devolved upon him were more arduous than can well be conceived of by one who has not been in the same situation. To draft resolutions in the committee-room, and then to defend them against the most skillful opponents on the floor of the house, requires readiness of mind, mental resources, and skill in debate, such as few possess. Weary with these exhausting labors, and pressed by the claims of his private affairs, Mr. Fillmore, just before the close of the session, wrote a letter to his constituents, declining to be a candidate for re-election. Notwithstanding this communication, his friends met in convention, and unanimously, and by acclamation, renominated him, with the most earnest expression of their desire that he would comply with their wishes. Though greatly gratified by this proof of their appreciation of his labors, he adhered to his resolve ; and, at the close of the term for which he was elected, he returned to his home, rejoicing at his release from the agitating cares of official life.

Mr. Fillmore was now a man of wide repute, and his popularity filled the State. The lines between the two parties, the Whig and Democratic, were strongly drawn ; and the issues involved excited the community to the highest degree. The Whig party brought forward Mr. Fillmore as the strongest candidate whom they could present for the office of governor. The canvass was one of the most exciting which had ever agitated the State, and the Whig party was signally defeated. In the year 1847 he was elected, by a very great majority, to the very important office of comptroller of the State. Many who were not with him in political principles gave him their vote, from their conviction of his eminent fitness for that office.

In entering upon the responsible duties which this situation demanded, it was necessary for him to abandon his profession, and, sundering those social ties which bound him to his numerous friends in Buffalo, to remove to the city of Albany. It was universally admitted that the duties of this office were never more faithfully discharged.

Mr. Fillmore had attained the age of forty-seven years. His labors at the bar, in the Legislature, in Congress, and as comptroller, had given him very considerable fame. The Whigs were casting about to find suitable candidates for President and Vice-President at the approaching election. Far away, on the waters of the Rio Grande, there was a rough old soldier, who had fought one or two successful battles with the Mexicans, which had caused his name to be proclaimed in trumpet-tones all over the land. He was an unpolished, unlettered man, entirely inexperienced in all statesmanlike accomplishments; but he was a man of firmness, of uncompromising integrity, and of sound common sense and practical wisdom. He was an available man; for " Palo Alto " and " Resaca de la Palma " would ring pleasantly upon the popular ear, and catch the popular vote. But it was necessary to associate with him on the same ticket some man of reputation as a statesman, and in whose intellectual powers and varied experience the community might repose confidence.

Under the influence of these considerations, the names of Zachary Taylor and Millard Fillmore became the rallying-cry of the Whigs as their candidates for President and Vice-President. The Whig ticket was signally triumphant. On the 4th of March, 1849, General Taylor was inaugurated President, and Millard Fillmore Vice-President, of the United States. He was admirably adapted for this position. His tall, well-proportioned, manly form, and the natural dignity and grace of his bearing, gave him an imposing presence. His mind, originally of a high order, and disciplined by the laborious culture of years, enabled him promptly and successfully to meet every intellectual emergency. His countenance gave expression to those traits of firmness, gentleness, and conscientiousness which marked his character.

The stormy days of the republic were now at hand. The great question of slavery was permeating every subject which was brought before Congress, shaping the whole legislation of the country, arousing fiery debate, arraying parties in hostile lines in the Senate and in the House, and agitating as with earthquake-throes every city and village in the Union. It was evident that the strength of our institutions was soon to be severely tried. John C. Calhoun, when president of the Senate, had taken the position that he had no power to call a senator to order for words, however intemperate, when spoken in debate. Vice-President Fillmore, upon taking his chair as presiding officer over that august body, announced to the Senate his determination to maintain decorum in that chamber, and that he should promptly call senators to order for any offensive words which might be spoken. The Senate manifested its approval of this decision by unanimously ordering the views thus expressed to be entered upon their journal.

On the 9th of July, 1850, President Taylor, but about one year and four months after his inauguration, was suddenly taken sick, and died. By the Constitution, Vice-President Fillmore thus became President of the United States. He appointed a very able Cabinet, of which the illustrious Daniel Webster was Secretary of State. The agitated condition of the country brought questions of very great delicacy before him. He was bound by his oath of office to execute the laws of the United States. One of those laws was understood to be, that if a slave, escaping from bondage, should

UNITED STATES SENATE.

reach a free State, the United States was bound to help catch him, and return him to his master. Most Christian men loathed this law. President Fillmore felt bound by his oath rigidly to see it enforced. Slavery was organizing armies to invade Cuba, as it had invaded Texas, and annex it to the United States. President Fillmore gave all the influence of his exalted station against the atrocious enterprise. The illustrious Hungarian, Kossuth, visited our shores, and was cordially received by the President, while he frankly informed him that it was the policy of our government to avoid all complications in European affairs.

Mr. Fillmore had very serious difficulties to contend with, since the opposition had a majority in both houses. He did everything in his power to conciliate the South ; but the proslavery party in the South felt the inadequacy of all measures of transient conciliation. The population of the free States was so rapidly increasing over that of the slave States, that it was inevitable that the power of the government should soon pass into the hands of the free States. The famous compromise measures were adopted under Mr. Fillmore's administration, and the Japan Expedition was sent out.

On the 4th of March, 1853, Mr. Fillmore, having served one term, retired from office. He then took a long tour throughout the South, where he met with quite an enthusiastic reception. In a speech at Vicksburg, alluding to the rapid growth of the country, he said, —

" Canada is knocking for admission, and Mexico would be glad to come in ; and, without saying whether it would be right or wrong, we stand with open arms to receive them : for it is the manifest destiny of this government to embrace the whole North American continent."

In 1855 President Fillmore went to Europe, where he was received with those marked attentions which his position and character merited. Returning to this country in 1856, he was nominated for the presidency by the strangely called " Know-Nothing " party. Mr. Buchanan, the Democratic candidate, was the successful competitor for the prize. After that time Mr. Fillmore lived in retirement. During the terrible conflict of the civil war he was mostly silent. It was generally supposed that his sympathies were rather with those who were endeavoring to overthrow our institutions. Edward Everett, who had been a candidate for the vice-presidency, left no one in doubt respecting his abhorrence of the Rebellion, and his devotion to his country's flag. President Fillmore kept aloof from the conflict, without any cordial words of cheer to the one party or the other. He was thus forgotten by both. He died in Buffalo, N. Y., March 8, 1874, aged seventy-five years and two months.

CHAPTER XIV.

FRANKLIN PIERCE.

Character of his Father. — His Promise in Boyhood. — College Life. — Political Views. — Success as a Lawyer. — Entrance upon Public Life. — Service in the Mexican War. — Landing in Mexico. — March through the Country. — Incidents of the March. — Anecdotes. — Nomination for the Presidency. — Election. — Administration. — Retirement.

FRANKLIN PIERCE, the fourteenth President of the United States, was born in Hillsborough, N. H., November 23, 1804. His father

RESIDENCE OF FRANKLIN PIERCE.

was a Revolutionary soldier, who, with his own strong arm, hewed him out a home in the wilderness. He was a man of inflexible integrity; of strong, though uncultivated mind; and an uncompromising Democrat. When, under the administration of John Adams, an effort was made to draw our country into an alliance with England in her war against the French republic, Major Pierce, as his title then was, was offered a high commission in the army which was proposed to be levied.

" No, gentlemen," was his reply. " Poor as I am, and acceptable as would be the position under other circumstances, I would sooner go to yonder mountains, dig me a cave and live on roast potatoes, than be instrumental in promoting the objects for which that army is raised."

His energetic and upright character and commanding abilities gave him great influence in the secluded region where he dwelt, and he occupied nearly every post of honor and emolument which his neighbors could confer upon him. He was for several years in the state Legislature ; was a member of the governor's council, and a general of the militia. He was an independent farmer ; a generous, large-hearted, hospitable man. The mother of Franklin Pierce was all that a son could desire, — an intelligent, prudent, affectionate, Christian woman. Franklin was the sixth of eight children.

Old General Pierce was a politician, ever ready for argument ; and there was ample opportunity for the exercise of his powers in those days of intense political excitement, when, all over the New England States, Federalists and Democrats were arrayed so fiercely against each other. Franklin, as a boy, listened eagerly to the arguments of his father, enforced by strong and ready utterance and earnest gestures. It was in this school that he was led to ally himself with the Democratic party so closely as to be ready to follow wherever it might lead.

Franklin was a very bright and handsome boy, generous, warm-hearted, and brave. He won alike the love of old and young. The boys on the play-ground loved him. His teachers loved him. The neighbors looked upon him with pride and affection. He was by instinct a gentleman ; always speaking kind words, doing kind deeds, with a peculiar unstudied tact which taught him what was agreeable. Without developing any precocity of genius, or any unnatural devotion to books, he was a good scholar ; in body, in mind, in affections, a finely-developed boy.

When sixteen years of age, in the year 1820, he entered Bowdoin College at Brunswick, Me. The writer there became personally acquainted with him.   He was one of the most popular young men in college.   The purity of his moral character, the unvarying courtesy of his demeanor, his rank as a scholar, and his genial nature, rendered him a universal favorite.   There was something very peculiarly winning in his address, and it was evidently not in the slightest degree studied: it was the simple outgushing of his own magnanimous and loving nature.

Upon graduating, in the year 1824, Franklin Pierce commenced the study of law in the office of Judge Woodbury, one of the most distinguished lawyers of the State, and a man of great private worth. The eminent social qualities of the young lawyer, his father's prominence as a public man, and the brilliant political career into which Judge Woodbury was entering, all tended to entice Mr. Pierce into the fascinating yet perilous paths of political life.   With all the ardor of his nature, he espoused the cause of General Jackson for the presidency.   He commenced the practice of law in Hillsborough, and was soon elected to represent the town in the state Legislature. Here he served for four years.   The two last years he was chosen speaker of the house by a very large vote.

In 1833, at the age of twenty-nine, he was elected a member of Congress.   Without taking an active part in the debates, he was faithful and laborious in duty, and ever rising in the estimation of those with whom he was associated.   Strenuously he supported the administration of General Jackson, securing not only the confidence, but the personal friendship, of that extraordinary man.   Mr. Pierce sympathized in the fears of the State-Rights party, that the national government would consolidate so much power as to endanger the liberties of the individual States.   In Congress he warmly allied himself with the Democratic party, being apparently in sympathy with them in all its measures.

In 1837, being then but thirty-three years of age, he was elected to the Senate of the United States, taking his seat just as Mr. Van Buren commenced his administration.   He was the youngest member in the Senate.   The ablest men our country has produced were then among the leaders of the Democracy, — Calhoun, Buchanan, Benton.   Senator Pierce was a remarkably fluent, graceful speaker, always courteous and good-tempered ; and his speeches were listened to by both parties with interest.   In the year 1834 he married Miss Jane Means Appleton, a lady of rare beauty and accomplishments, and one admirably fitted to adorn every station with which her husband was honored. Of three sons who were born to them, all now sleep with their mother in the grave.

In the year 1838, Mr. Pierce, with growing fame, and increasing business as a lawyer, took up his residence in Concord, the capital of New Hampshire. The citizens of his native town, in token of their high esteem, gave him a parting dinner. He devoted himself with new zeal to his duties at the bar, and took his rank at once among the ablest lawyers. His tact, his genial spirit, and his unvarying courtesy, gave him extraordinary power with a jury. It is said that he was never known to insult, browbeat, or endeavor to terrify, a witness.

GENERAL PIERCE LANDING IN MEXICO.

President Polk, upon his accession to office, appointed Mr. Pierce attorney-general of the United States; but the offer was declined, in consequence of numerous professional engagements at home, and the precarious state of Mrs. Pierce's health. He also, about the same time, declined the nomination for governor by the Democratic party. The war with Mexico called Mr. Pierce into the army.

Receiving the appointment of brigadier-general, he embarked, with a portion of his troops, at Newport, R. I., on the 27th of May, 1847.

General Pierce landed upon a sand-beach, at a place called Virgara, on the 28th of June. There was already an encampment of about five hundred men, under the command of Major Lally, at that place. He was ordered to make no delay there, and yet no preparations had been made for his departure. About two thousand wild mules had been collected from the prairies; but a stampede had taken place, in which fifteen hundred had disappeared. He was compelled to remain for several weeks in this encampment, upon sand as smooth as a floor, and so hard that it would scarcely show the footprints of a mule. For three miles the waves dashed magnificently on this extensive beach. Though the mornings were close, and the heat excessive, by eleven o'clock a fine sea-breeze always set in. There were frequent tropical showers, in which the rain fell in floods; and there were peals of thunder such as are rarely heard, and flashes of lightning, such as are, perhaps, never seen, in regions farther north.

Every morning the troops were under drill: they could not bear the exposure to the midday sun. Though they were not far from the city, General Pierce preferred to dwell in his tent upon the beach, rather than to occupy any of the houses. Vigorous measures were adopted to collect mules and mustangs, in preparation for their advance. These animals were generally caught wild upon the prairies, unaccustomed to the harness, and even to the bridle. Much labor was required in taming them, and in breaking them to harness. The troops were kept constantly on the alert, in anticipation of an attack from the Mexicans.

At ten o'clock in the evening of the 7th of July there was an alarm. Musketry-firing was heard in the direction of the advanced pickets. The long-roll was beaten, and the whole command was instantly formed in line of battle. It proved to be a false alarm, or rather was caused by the approach of a small band of guerrillas to the vicinity of the sentinels. The next day, July 9th, Lieutenant Whipple was lured by curiosity to visit the cemetery, near the walls of the city. Imprudently he went unarmed, and accompanied but by a single private. Six guerrillas attacked, overpowered, and seized him; while the private escaped, and informed General Pierce. He immediately dispatched a troop of cavalry in pursuit; but no trace of Lieutenant Whipple could be discovered. In a few days, however, they learned that his life had been spared, but that he was a prisoner about twelve miles from the camp. A detachment was sent by night to surprise the banditti. They took the village; but the guerrillas fled, taking their prisoner with them.

At length, on the 13th of July, after a delay of nearly three weeks, and after great labor and perplexity, General Pierce was able to give orders for an advance. The beautiful beach was covered with wagons, mules, horses, and all the imposing paraphernalia of war.

On the morning of the 14th eighty wagons started, under Captain Wood. They took the Jalapa road for San Juan, twelve miles distant. There they were to await the remainder of the brigade. The heat was so intense that they could not move between the hours of nine in the morning and four in the afternoon. Colonel Ransom accompanied the train with two companies of infantry. Everything being ready, they moved at an early hour, in fine order and spirits. The next day a detachment of six companies was sent off. It was not until the 16th that General Pierce was able to leave. In his journal he writes, —

" After much perplexity and delay, on account of the unbroken and intractable teams, I left the camp this afternoon at five o'clock, with the Fourth Artillery, Watson's marine corps, a detachment of the third dragoons, and about forty wagons. The road was very heavy, the wheels were sinking almost to the hubs in sand, and the untried and untamed teams almost constantly bolting in some part of the train. We were occupied rather in breaking the animals to harness than in performing a march. At ten o'clock at night we bivouacked in the darkness and sand by the wagons in the road, having made but three miles from camp."

The next morning, at four o'clock, they were again on the move. The road was still heavy with sand, leading over short, steep hills. At eight o'clock in the morning they reached Santa Fé, but eight miles from Vera Cruz. The heat of a blazing, torrid sun was now overpowering; and the army remained in camp until four o'clock in the afternoon. Just before starting, two muleteers came in, greatly agitated, bringing the report that five hundred guerrillas, armed to the teeth, were on the Jalapa road, rushing on to attack

22

the camp. The whole force was immediately called to arms, and two pieces of artillery placed in position to command the road. It either proved a false alarm, or the guerrillas, taking counsel of discretion, changed their course.

Resuming their march at four o'clock, the column reached San Juan about nine o'clock in the evening, in a drenching rain. The guerrillas had attempted to retard the march by destroying a bridge over one of the branches of the San Juan River; but the New England men, accustomed to every variety of work, almost without delay repaired the structure. All night, all the next day, and the next night, the rain poured in such floods as are nowhere seen, save in the tropics. The encampment was on low ground, along the margin of the stream. As there was nothing but mud and water to rest in, it was thought best to continue the march.

On the 20th they reached Telema Nueva, twenty-four miles from Vera Cruz. As they were marching along, several musket-shots were fired upon them from an eminence on their left. A few round-shot were thrown in that direction, and a small detachment dashed up the hill; but the enemy had fled. After advancing about a mile farther, quite a number of mounted Mexicans were seen hovering about, evidently reconnoitring parties. As it was supposed that a large force was in the vicinity, all precautionary arrangements were made to repel an attack. Three companies of infantry and a detachment of dragoons were sent to flank our march by advances through a path on the left of the main road. Just as this detachment was returning by the circuitous route to the road along which the main body was passing, the enemy opened a brisk fire upon them.

The foe was in ambush, concealed in the dense chaparral on each side of the road. Our troops met this attack from unseen assailants, and promptly returned the fire. The guns were speedily unlimbered, and a few discharges of canister silenced the fire of the enemy. They fled too rapidly to be caught. We lost six wounded, and seven horses shot. A Mexican paper stated their loss at forty.

"I witnessed," writes General Pierce, "with pleasure, the conduct of that part of my command immediately engaged on this occasion. The first fire of the enemy indicated a pretty formidable force, the precise strength of which could not be ascertained, as they were completely covered by the chaparral. It was the first time on the march that any portion of my command had been fairly under fire. I was at the head of the column, on the main road, and witnessed the whole scene. I saw nothing but coolness and courage on the part of both officers and men."

On the night of the 20th of July the brigade encamped at Paso de Orejas. The rear-guard did not reach the encampment until after dark. As it was descending a slope towards the camp, a band of guerrillas was seen approaching. All the day they had been noticed on the distant hills, watching the advance of our lines. As they approached menacingly within cannon-range, a gun was brought to bear upon them, and a few discharges put them to flight. Paso de Orejas is on the west side of a beautiful stream spanned by a substantial bridge.

At four o'clock on the morning of July 21st they again broke camp, and pursued their course towards Puente Nacionale, anticipating an attack at every exposed point. When they reached the summit of a long hill which descended on the west to the Antigua River, General Pierce halted his command, and with his glass carefully examined the country before them. In the distance could be seen the little village of Puente Nacionale, on the western side of the river. This stream is also crossed by a bridge. A few lancers could be seen in the village, in their gay uniforms, riding rapidly from one position to another, and flourishing their red flags as if in defiance. A strong barricade, defended by a breastwork, was thrown across the bridge. A large body of the enemy was posted on a bluff one hundred and fifty feet high, which commanded the structure over which the little army must pass. It was impossible to turn their position.

General Pierce rode forward to reconnoitre the enemy's works more closely. He then brought forward his artillery, and, by some deadly discharges, swept the bridge, and dispersed the lancers. A few shots were also thrown at the heights, which so distracted the attention of the enemy that Colonel Bonham, with a few companies of picked men, made a rush upon the bridge with a loud battle-cry, leaped the barricade of brush and timber, reached the village, rallied his men under cover of its buildings, and rushed up the steep bluff, to gain its summit just in time to see the bewildered and disorganized foe disappear in the distance. One grand cheer from the victors on the bluff, echoed back by the troops below, greeted this heroic achievement. The remainder of the command followed rapidly, and in good order. A company of dragoons dashed through the village, hoping to cut off the retreat of the fugitives ; but terror had added such wings to their flight, that they had entirely disappeared in the dense chaparral in their rear.

Colonel Bonham's horse was shot, and General Pierce received a musket-ball through the rim of his hat. It is indeed wonderful that so few were hurt, when the bullets, for a short time, rattled so thickly around them ; but the Mexicans on the bluff took poor aim, and most of their balls passed over our heads. Here they encamped for the night, at a distance of thirty miles from Vera Cruz. General Pierce established his headquarters at a large and splended estate which he found here belonging to General Santa Anna.

At four o'clock the next morning, July 22d, the brigade was again in motion. As they moved along, upon all the surrounding heights armed bands of Mexicans were seen watching them. They kept, however, at too great a distance to be reached by bullet or ball. At one point of the march the head of the column was fired upon by a few guerrillas hidden in the chaparral, who succeeded in wounding three horses ; but the skirmishers thrown out in pursuit of them could find no trace even of their ambuscade. At length, on this day's tramp, they came in sight of an old Spanish fort, which commanded both the road, and a bridge that crossed a stream at this point. The bridge was barricaded, with the evident intention of defending it. Here General Pierce expected a stern conflict ; but, to his surprise, he found both fort and barricade silent and solitary. Removing the obstructions, they came to another stream, much broader, also spanned by a bridge.

" It was," writes General Pierce, " a magnificent work of art, combining great strength and beauty, — a work of the old Spaniards (so many of which are found upon this great avenue from the coast), fitted to awaken the admiration and wonder of the traveler. The fact that the main arch, a span of about sixty feet, had been blown up, first burst upon me as I stood upon the brink of the chasm, with a perpendicular descent of nearly a hundred feet to the bed of a rapid stream much swollen by the recent rains. As far as the eye could reach, above and below, the banks on the west side, of vast height, descended precipitously, almost in a perpendicular line, to the water's edge.

" This sudden and unexpected barrier, I need not say, was somewhat withering to the confidence with which I had been animated. The news having extended back along the line, my officers soon crowded around me; and the deep silence that ensued was more significant than anything which could have been spoken. After a few moments' pause, this silence was broken by many short epigrammatical remarks, and more questions. 'We have it before us now,' said Colonel Hebert. 'The destruction of this magnificent and expensive work of a past generation could not have been ordered but upon a deliberate and firm purpose of a stern resistance.' 'This people have destroyed,' said another, ' what they never will rebuild.' "

What to do was now the question. In the mean time a small body of infantry had descended the steep by the aid of trees, rocks, and stumps, and, fording the steam, had taken possession of a stone church on the other side. The line of wagons, brought to a stand, extended back along the road for a distance of a mile and a half. For miles around the growth was dwarfed and scrubby, affording no timber to reconstruct the arch. It was now night; and, weary, and not a little despondent, all sank to repose.

It so happened that there was in the army a Maine lumberman, Captain Bodfish, who had been accustomed to surmount many difficulties of this kind in the logging-swamps of his native state. General Pierce, the next morning, at an early hour, sent for him. With a practiced eye, he examined the ground, and said that he could construct a road over which the train could pass.

" How much time do you need," inquired General Pierce, "to complete the road?"

" That depends," said he, " upon the number of men employed. If you give me five hundred men, I will furnish you a road over which the train can pass safely in four hours."

The detail was immediately ordered, and in *three hours* the trains were in motion. " Bodfish's road," says General Pierce, " unless this nation shall be regenerated, will be the road at that place, for Mexican diligences, for half a century to come." Before the sun went down on the evening of the 23d, every wagon had passed without the slightest accident. There was great glee that night in the camp. Many were the jokes about Mexican stupidity and Yankee cunning. All were now eager to press on; for all felt new assurance in the final success of their bold enterprise.

They were approaching Cerro Gordo. From the heights in that vicinity the Mexicans could easily embarrass the march by a plunging fire. General Pierce himself, with a body of cavalry, set out in the darkness and the rain to occupy the eminences. The darkness was so great that one's hand could scarcely be seen before him, and it soon became impossible to advance. The detachment slept upon their arms until the earliest dawn of the morning, when they pressed on, and succeeded in seizing the important position. A few Mexicans were seen upon one of the heights, who discharged a volley of bullets, harmless from the distance, upon a portion of the train. A six-pounder was brought forward, which threw a few canister-shot into the midst of them, and they scattered in all directions.

They soon reached another of the magnificent estates of Santa Anna, well stocked with fat cattle. General Pierce, in his journal, says very naïvely, " As there was no owner of whom to purchase, I have sent out detachments to supply our wants. The boys had great fun in playing 'hunt buffalo;' and, in the excitement of the chase, some of them wandered to an imprudent distance from the camp. One of them got a bullet-shot through the thigh in consequence. All the night guerrillas were prowling about the camp."

Upon Santa Anna's estate, or *hacienda* as it was called, they found delightful encampment upon a green lawn, gently sloping to a fine stream of clear, pure water. They were then but eight miles from Jalapa.

On the morning of the 24th they left, with regret, their delightful encampment at Encero. The verdant lawn, the sparkling stream rippling over its pebbly bed, and the cultivated region around, reminded all of their New England homes. At noon they reached Jalapa unopposed. Here General Pierce rode to an inn kept by a Frenchman, and dined. At the inn he met several well-dressed, intelligent Mexicans. They were profuse in their commendations of the achievements of the Yankees. The army proceeded about three miles beyond the city, and encamped by another fine stream, " which drives the spindles of Don Garcia, a quarter of a mile below us." He there ascertained, that, beyond doubt, the *gentlemen* with whom he had conversed in the inn at Jalapa were guerrillas in disguise. They were ever hovering around the skirts of the army, ready to murder and to rob as they could find opportunity. That very day a servant who had been sent to water a horse, not six rods from the road, was killed, and his horse stolen.

The next day, the 27th, as they made a short tarry in their encampment just out from Jalapa, several soldiers, who had wandered, in violation of orders, from the camp to the vicinity of the surrounding farms, never returned. It is supposed that they were either killed or captured.

On the morning of the 29th, at seven o'clock, the march was again resumed. The sick-list was increasing, and there were over four hundred on the surgeon's roll. Few inexperienced in such matters can imagine the care and skill requisite to move a body, even of twenty-four hundred men, hundreds of miles, with four hundred sick men in wagons, so that the wants of all shall be attended to, and that every man shall have his regular and proper meals. Fruits were abundant along the line of march, and the soldiers indulged freely. The rain was also falling in torrents, which kept all drenched to the skin, and penetrated the tents, while the flood rushed in torrents through the gullies.

The morning of the 30th found them near the Castle of Perote. "I reached the castle," General Pierce writes, "before dark; and Colonel Windcoop, who was in command of the castle, with Captain Walker's elegant company of mounted riflemen, kindly tendered me his quarters. But I adhered to a rule from which I have never deviated on the march, — to see the rear of the command safely in camp; and where they pitched their tents, to pitch my own. The rear-guard, in consequence of the broken condition of the road, did not arrive until nine o'clock, when our tents were pitched in darkness, and in the sand which surrounds the castle on all sides."

Here they made a halt of two or three days to repair damages, and to refresh the sick and the exhausted. Two hundred of the sick were sent to the hospital in the castle. The next day Captain Ruff arrived with a company of cavalry, having been sent by General Scott to ascertain the whereabouts and condition of General Pierce's command, and to afford him assistance if needed. Soon they resumed their march, and on the 7th of August reached the main body of the army under the commander-in-chief at Puebla. General Pierce had conducted twenty-four hundred men on this arduous march, without the loss of a single wagon.

General Scott had been waiting at Puebla for the arrival of the reinforcement under General Pierce. He was now prepared to move vigorously forward in his attack upon the city of Mexico. Santa Anna had an advance-guard of about seven thousand men at Contreras. General Scott wished to cut off these detached troops from the main body of the Mexican army, and, by destroying their communications with the city, to have them at his mercy. He therefore sent a division of his army, by a circuitous route, to occupy the villages and strong positions in their rear. To hide this movement from the foe, and to distract their attention, General Pierce was ordered, with four thousand men, to make an impetuous assault upon their front.

It was indeed severe service upon which he was thus detached. The enemy had nearly two to his one. They were in their own chosen positions, and were protected by intrenchments, from which, unexposed, they could hurl a storm of shot and shell into the faces of their assailants. The ground over which the charge was to be made was exceedingly rough, bristling with sharp points of rocks, and broken by ridges and gullies. The Mexicans threw out skirmishers, who were posted in great force among the irregularities of this broken ground. As our troops advanced, they were met with a murderous fire of musketry from these concealed riflemen, while the heavy balls from the Mexican batteries shivered the rocks around them. Had the Mexicans been expert gunners, General Pierce's command would have been annihilated; but, fortunately or providentially, most of the shot from the intrenched camp passed over the heads of our troops.

"In the midst of this fire, General Pierce," writes Hawthorne, his eloquent biographer, "being the only officer mounted in the brigade, leaped his horse upon an abrupt eminence, and addressed the colonels and captains of the regiments, as they passed, in a few stirring words, reminding them of the honor of their country, of the victory their steady valor would contribute to achieve. Pressing forward to the head of the column, he had nearly reached the practicable ground that lay beyond, when his horse slipped among the rocks, thrust his foot into a crevice, and fell, breaking his own leg, and crushing his rider heavily beneath him."

The general was stunned by the fall, and almost insensible. His orderly hastened to his assistance, and found him very severely

He declined to do anything, either by voice or pen, to strengthen the hands of the national government. He continued to reside in Concord until the time of his death, which occurred in October, 1869. He was one of the most genial and social of men, an honored communicant of the Episcopal Church, and one of the kindest of neighbors. Generous to a fault, he contributed liberally of his moderate means for the alleviation of suffering and want, and many of his townspeople were often gladdened by his material bounty.

CHAPTER XV.

JAMES BUCHANAN.

His Childhood's Home. — Devotion to Study. — Scholarship, and Purity of Character. — Congressional Career. — Political Views. — Secretary of State. — Minister to the Court of St. James. — Ostend Manifesto. — Elected to the Presidency. — The New Haven Correspondence. — Disasters of his Administration. — Retirement.

JAMES BUCHANAN, the fifteenth President of the United States, was born in a small frontier town, at the foot of the eastern ridge of the Alleghanies, in Franklin County, Pennsylvania, on the 23d of

RESIDENCE OF JAMES BUCHANAN.

April, 1791. The place where the humble cabin of his father stood was called Stony Batter. It was a wild and romantic spot in a gorge of the mountains, with towering summits rising grandly all around.

bruised, and suffering agonizingly from a sprain of the left knee, upon which the horse had fallen. The bullets and balls of the enemy were flying thickly around. As the orderly attempted to assist the wounded general to reach the shelter of a projecting rock, a shell buried itself in the earth at their feet, and, exploding, covered them with stones and sand. "That was a lucky miss," said General Pierce calmly.

Leaving him under shelter of the rock, the orderly went in search of a surgeon. Fortunately, he met Dr. Ritchie near by, who was following the advancing column. He rendered such assistance as the circumstances would permit; and soon General Pierce recovered full conciousness, and became anxious to rejoin his troops. Notwithstanding the surgeon's remonstrances, he leaned upon his orderly's shoulder, and, hobbling along, reached a battery, where he found a horse, whose saddle had just been emptied by a Mexican bullet. He was assisted into the saddle. "You will not be able to keep your seat," said one. "Then you must tie me on," replied the general. Thus bruised and sprained, and agonized with pain, he again rode forward into the hottest of the battle.

Till nightfall the conflict raged unabated. It was eleven at night before General Pierce left his saddle. He had withdrawn his troops from their exposed position, and assembled them in a sheltered spot, where they were to pass the night. The rain was then falling in torrents. It is a curious phenomenon, that it often rains almost immediately after a battle. There were no tents; there was no protection for officers or men : drenched, exhausted, hungry, they threw themselves upon the flooded sods for sleep. General Pierce lay down upon an ammunition-wagon; but the torture of his inflamed and swollen knee would not allow him a moment of repose.

But one hour after midnight of that dark and stormy night had passed, when General Pierce received orders from General Scott to put his brigade in a new position in front of the enemy's works, to be prepared for a new assault with the earliest dawn of the morning. In the midst of the gloom and the storm the movement was made.

As soon as a few glimmers of light were seen in the east these men of invincible resolution and iron sinews were again on the move. General Pierce was again in his saddle, and at the head of his brigade. The Mexican camp was attacked simultaneously in front and rear. In seventeen minutes the "stars and stripes" floated over the ramparts of the foe, and the cheers of the victors proclaimed that the conquest was complete. Many prisoners were taken. Those who escaped fled in wildest disorder towards Cherubusco.

General Pierce almost forgot exhaustion, wounds, and agony, in his eager pursuit of the fugitives. The roads and fields were strewn with the dead and the dying, and every conceivable form of human mutilation and misery. The pursuit continued until one o'clock. The victors then found themselves checked by the strong fortifications of Cherubusco and San Antonio, where Santa Anna was prepared to make another desperate stand. General Scott feared that Santa Anna might escape, and concentrate all his troops within the walls of the city of Mexico. To prevent this, he sent an aide, Colonel Noah E. Smith, to call General Pierce to his presence, that he might give him directions to take a route by which he could assail the foe in their rear. Colonel Smith met the general at the head of his brigade. He writes, —

" General Pierce was exceedingly thin, worn down by the fatigue and pain of the day and night before, and then evidently suffering severely. Still there was a glow in his eye, as the cannon boomed, that showed within him a spirit ready for the conflict."

General Scott was sitting on horseback beneath a tree, issuing orders to his staff, as General Pierce rode up. The commander-in-chief had heard of the accident which had befallen the general, and, as he noticed his aspect of pain and physical exhaustion, said to him, —

" Pierce, my dear fellow, you **are** badly injured. You are not fit to be in the saddle."

" Yes, general," was the reply; "I am, in a case like this."

" You cannot touch your foot to the stirrup," said Scott.

" One I can," answered Pierce.

General Scott looked at him for a moment in silence, and then said in decided tones, " You are rash, General Pierce : we shall lose you, and we cannot spare you. It is my duty to order you back to St. Augustine."

But General Pierce pleaded so earnestly that he might be permitted to remain, and take part in the great battle then imminent, that Scott at last reluctantly consented, and ordered him to advance with his brigade. His path led over a marsh, intersected with ditches filled with water. Over several of these ditches the general leaped his horse. At last he came to one ten feet wide and six feet deep. He was there compelled to leave his horse. He, however, succeeded in getting across the ditch, and was there with his troops under fire. He had now gone to the farthest point of physical endurance. Entirely overcome by sleeplessness, exhaustion, pain, and fatigue, he sank to the ground, fainting, and almost insensible.

Some soldiers hastened to lift him and bear him from the field. He partially revived and, resisting, said, " No, do not carry me off. Let me lie here." There he remained, in the midst of his struggling troops, exposed to the shot of the foe, while the tremendous battle of Cherubusco raged around him. At length the cheers of our men announced their victory. Santa Anna sent a flag of truce, proposing an armistice. General Pierce was appointed one of the commissioners to meet him. He was unable to walk, or to mount his horse without assistance. He was, however, helped into his saddle, and rode to Tacubaya ; and the conference was held at the house of the British consul from late in the afternoon until four o'clock the next morning.

They could not come to satisfactory terms, and military operations were soon renewed. Not long after, on the 8th of September, the sanguinary battle of Molino del Rey, the fiercest conflict of the war, was fought. General Worth, with three thousand men, attacked fourteen thousand Mexicans. General Pierce was ordered to his support. Just as he reached the field, a shell burst almost beneath the feet of his horse, and he narrowly escaped being thrown over a precipice. Again the vanquished enemy fled, and made another stand under protection of the Castle of Chepultepec. In the heroic storming of that castle, on the 13th of September, General Pierce could take no part, though his brigade performed gallant service. But their general had been conveyed to the headquarters of General Worth, where he was taken so extremely ill that he was unable to leave his bed for thirty-six hours. This was the last great struggle. The city of Mexico now fell into the hands of the Americans. General Pierce remained in the captured city until December, when he returned from these strange scenes of violence and blood to the wife and child whom he had left about nine months before among the peaceful hills of New Hampshire.

When General Pierce reached his home in his native State, he was received enthusiastically by the advocates of the Mexican war, and coldly by its opponents. He resumed the exercise of his profession, very frequently taking an active part in political questions, giving his cordial support to the proslavery wing of the Democratic party. The compromise measures met cordially with his approval; and he strenuously advocated the enforcement of the fugitive-slave law, which so shocked the religious sensibilities of the North. He thus became distinguished as a " Northern man with Southern principles." The strong partisans of slavery in the South consequently regarded him as a man whom they could safely trust in office to carry out their plans.

On the 12th of June, 1852, the Democratic convention met in Baltimore to nominate a candidate for the presidency. For four days they continued in session, and in thirty-five ballotings no one had obtained a two thirds vote. Not a vote had thus far been thrown for General Pierce. Then the Virginia delegation brought forward his name. There were fourteen more ballotings, during which General Pierce constantly gained strength, until, at the forty-ninth ballot, he received two hundred and eighty-two votes, and all other candidates eleven. General Winfield Scott was the Whig candidate. General Pierce was chosen with great unanimity. Only four States — Vermont, Massachusetts, Kentucky, and Tennessee — cast their electoral votes against him. On the 4th of March, 1853, he was inaugurated President of the United States.

His administration proved one of the most stormy our country had ever experienced. The controversy between slavery and freedom was then approaching its culminating point. It became evident that there was an "irrepressible conflict " between them, and that this nation could not long exist " half slave and half free." President Pierce, during the whole of his administration, did everything which could be done to conciliate the South ; but it was all in vain. The conflict every year grew more violent, and threats of the dissolution of the Union were borne to the North on every southern breeze.

At the demand of slavery, the Missouri Compromise was repealed, and all the territories of the Union were thrown open to slavery. The Territory of Kansas, west of Missouri, was settled by emigrants mainly from the North. According to law, they were about to meet, and decide whether slavery or freedom should be the law of that realm. It was certain that they would decide for freedom.

Slavery in Missouri and other Southern States rallied her armed legions, marched them in military array into Kansas, took possession of the polls, drove away the citizens, deposited their own votes by handfuls, went through the farce of counting them, and then declared that, by an overwhelming majority, slavery was established in Kansas. These facts nobody denied, and yet President Pierce's administration felt bound to respect the decision obtained by such votes.

This armed mob from other States then chose a legislature of strong proslavery men; convened them in a small town near Missouri, where they could be protected from any opposition from the Free-Soil citizens of the State; and called this band, thus fraudulently elected, the "Legislature of Kansas." No one could deny these facts; and yet President Pierce deemed it his duty to recognize this body as the lawful legislature.

This bogus legislature met, and enacted a code of proslavery laws which would have disgraced savages. Neither freedom of speech nor of the press was allowed, and death was the doom of any one who should speak or write against slavery; and yet President Pierce assumed that these laws were binding upon the community.

The armed mob of invasion consisted of nearly seven thousand men. As they commenced their march, one of their leaders thus addressed them: —

"To those who have qualms of conscience as to violating laws, state or national, the time has come when such impositions must be disregarded, as your rights and property are in danger. I advise you, one and all, to enter every election district in Kansas, and vote at the point of the bowie-knife and revolver. Neither give nor take quarter, as our case demands it. It is enough that the slaveholding interest wills it, from which there is no appeal."

They marched with artillery, banners, music, and mounted horsemen. By such a force, infant Kansas was subjugated, and the most sacred rights of American freemen were trampled in the dust. When the army returned to the city of Independence in Missouri, the "squatter sovereign" of that place said, "They report that not a single antislavery man will be in the Legislature of Kansas."

The citizens of Kansas, the great majority of whom were Free-State men, met in convention, and adopted the following resolve: —

"*Resolved*, That the body of men who, for the past two months, have been passing laws for the people of our Territory, moved, counseled, and dictated to by the demagogues of Missouri, are to us a foreign body, representing only the lawless invaders who elected them, and not the people of the Territory; that we repudiate their action as the monstrous consummation of an act of violence, usurpation, and fraud, unparalleled in the history of the Union."

The Free-State people of Kansas also sent a petition to the general government, imploring its protection. In reply, the President issued a proclamation, declaring that the legislature thus created must be recognized as the legitimate legislature of Kansas, and that its laws were binding upon the people; and that, if necessary, the whole force of the governmental arm would be put forth to enforce those laws.

Such was the condition of affairs when President Pierce approached the close of his four years' term of office. The North had become thoroughly alienated from him. The antislavery sentiment, goaded by these outrages, had been rapidly increasing; and all the intellectual ability and social worth of President Pierce were forgotten in deep reprehension of these administrative acts. The slaveholders of the South also, unmindful of the fidelity with which he had advocated those measures of government which they approved, and perhaps, also, feeling that he had rendered himself so unpopular as no longer to be able acceptably to serve them, ungratefully dropped him, and nominated James Buchanan as the Democratic candidate to succeed him in the presidency. John C. Frémont was the candidate of the Free-Soil party.

James Buchanan was the successful candidate. He had pledged himself to stand upon the same platform which his predecessor had occupied, "lowered never an inch." On the 4th of March, 1857, President Pierce retired to his home in Concord, N. H. Of three children, two had died, and his only surviving child had been killed before his eyes by a railroad accident; and his wife, one of the most estimable and accomplished of ladies, was rapidly sinking in consumption. The hour of dreadful gloom soon came, and he was left alone in the world, without wife or child.

When the terrible Rebellion burst forth, which divided our country into two parties, and two only, Mr. Pierce remained steadfast in the principles which he had always cherished, and gave his sympathies to that proslavery party with which he had ever been allied.

PRESIDENTS

ZACHERY TAYLOR

JOHN TYLER

JAMES K POLK

WILLIAM HENRY HARRISON

MILLARD FILLMORE

FRANKLIN PIERCE

JAMES BUCHANAN

UNITED STATES.

OF THE

His father was a native of the north of Ireland; a poor man, who had emigrated in 1783, with little property save his own strong arms. Five years after his arrival in this country he married Elizabeth Spear, the daughter of a respectable farmer, and, with his young bride, plunged into the wilderness, staked his claim, reared his log-hut, opened a clearing with his axe, and settled down there to perform his obscure part in the drama of life.

In this secluded home, where James was born, he remained for eight years, enjoying but few social or intellectual advantages. His father was industrious, frugal, and prosperous, and was unusually intelligent for a man in his situation. His mother also was a woman of superior character, possessing sound judgment, and a keen appreciation of the beautiful in nature and in art. When James was eight years of age his father removed to the village of Mercersburg, where his son was placed at school, and commenced a course of study in English, Latin, and Greek. His progress was rapid; and, at the age of fourteen, he entered Dickinson College, at Carlisle. Here he developed remarkable talent, and took his stand among the first scholars in the institution. His application to study was intense, and yet his native powers enabled him to master the most abstruse subjects with facility.

In the year 1809 he graduated with the highest honors of his class. He was then eighteen years of age; tall and graceful, vigorous in health, fond of athletic sports, an unerring shot, and enlivened with an exuberant flow of animal spirits. He immediately commenced the study of law in the city of Lancaster, and was admitted to the bar in 1812, when he was but twenty-one years of age. Very rapidly he rose in his profession, and at once took undisputed stand with the ablest lawyers of the State. When but twenty-six years of age, unaided by counsel, he successfully defended before the state Senate one of the judges of the State, who was tried upon articles of impeachment. At the age of thirty, it was generally admitted that he stood at the head of the bar; and there was no lawyer in the State who had a more extensive or a more lucrative practice.

Reluctantly, he then, in 1820, consented to stand a candidate for Congress. He was elected; and, for ten years, he remained a member of the lower house. During the vacations of Congress he occasionally tried some important cause. In 1831 he retired alto-

23

gether from the toils of his profession, having acquired an ample fortune.

In 1812, just after Mr. Buchanan had entered upon the practice of the law, our second war with England occurred. With all his powers, he sustained the government, eloquently urging the vigorous prosecution of the war, and even enlisting as a private soldier to assist in repelling the British, who had sacked Washington, and were threatening Baltimore.

Mr. Buchanan was at that time a Federalist. This term took its rise from those who approved of the federal Constitution, with all the powers which it gave to the national government. The anti-Federalists, who thought that the Constitution gave the central government too much power, and the state governments too little, took the name of Republicans. But, when the Constitution was adopted by both parties, Jefferson truly said, " We are all Federalists; we are all Republicans." Still it was subsequently found that the Constitution allowed some latitude of construction. Consequently, those who approved of a liberal construction, in favor of the general government, still retained the name of Federalists; while those who were in favor of a strict construction, not allowing the central government one hair's breadth more of power than the letter of the Constitution demanded, retained the name of Republicans.

The opposition of the Federal party to the war with England, and the alien and sedition laws of John Adams, brought the party into disrepute; and the name of Federalist became a reproach. Mr. Buchanan, almost immediately upon entering Congress, began to incilne more and more to the policy of the Republicans.

As a member of Congress, Mr. Buchanan was faithful to his duties. He was always in his seat, and took an active part in every important question. The speeches which he made indicated great care in their preparation, and were distinguished for depth of thought and persuasive eloquence. The great question, as to the power of the national government to promote internal improvements, agitated Congress. Mr. Buchanan was in sympathy with the Republicans, and voted against any appropriation to repair the Cumberland Road. The bill, however, passed Congress. President Monroe vetoed it. Mr. Buchanan argued that Congress was not authorized to establish a *protective* tariff; that it was authorized to impose a tariff for revenue only. In an earnest speech upon this subject, he said, —

"If I know myself, I am a politician neither of the East nor of the West, of the North nor of the South. I therefore shall forever avoid any expressions, the direct tendency of which must be to create sectional jealousies, and at length disunion, — that worst and last of all political calamities."

In the stormy presidential election of 1824, in which Jackson, Clay, Crawford, and John Quincy Adams were candidates, Mr. Buchanan espoused the cause of General Jackson, and unrelentingly opposed the administration of Mr. Adams. When our government undertook the singular task of regulating the dress in which our ambassadors should appear in foreign courts, prohibiting the court-costume which most of those monarchs required, Mr. Buchanan supported the measure.

"Imagine," said he, "a grave and venerable statesman, who never attended a militia-training in his life, but who has been elevated to the station of a foreign minister in consequence of his civil attainments, appearing at court, arrayed in this military coat, with a chapeau under his arm, and a small sword dangling at his side! What a ridiculous spectacle would a grave lawyer or judge of sixty years of age present, arrayed in such a costume!"

General Jackson, upon his elevation to the presidency, appointed Mr. Buchanan minister to Russia. The duties of his mission he performed with ability, which gave satisfaction to all parties. Upon his return, in 1833, he was elected to a seat in the United States Senate. He there met, as his associates, Webster, Clay, Wright, and Calhoun. He advocated the measure proposed by President Jackson, of making reprisals against France to enforce the payment of our claims against that country; and defended the course of the President in his unprecedented and wholesale removals from office of those who were not the supporters of his administration. Upon this question he was brought into direct collision with Henry Clay. He also, with voice and vote, advocated *expunging* from the journal of the Senate the vote of censure against General Jackson for removing the deposits. Earnestly he opposed the abolition of slavery in the District of Columbia, and urged the prohibition of the circulation of antislavery documents by the United States mails.

In December, 1835, there was a fire in New York, which consumed property amounting to eighteen millions of dollars. The merchants overwhelmed by this calamity owed the United States the sum of three million six hundred thousand dollars. A bill was introduced for their relief, simply asking for an extension of payment, with ample security. Generously and eloquently Mr. Buchanan advocated the bill. In the discussion of the question respecting the admission of Michigan and Arkansas into the Union, Mr. Buchanan "defined his position" by saying, —

"The older I grow, the more I am inclined to be what is called a State-Rights man."

As to petitions on the subject of slavery, he advocated that they should be respectfully received; and that the reply should be returned, that Congress had no power to legislate upon the subject. "Congress," said he, "might as well undertake to interfere with slavery under a foreign government as in any of the States where it now exists." Many of his speeches developed great ability; all, earnestness and deep conviction; while he invariably treated his opponents in the most courteous manner, never allowing himself to exhibit the slightest irritation.

M. de Tocqueville, in his renowned work upon "Democracy in America," foresaw the trouble which was inevitable from the doctrine of state sovereignty as held by Calhoun and Buchanan. He was convinced that the national government was losing that strength which was essential to its own existence, and that the States were assuming powers which threatened the perpetuity of the Union. Mr. Buchanan reviewed this book in the Senate, and declared the fears of De Tocqueville to be groundless: and yet he lived to sit in the presidential chair, and see State after State, in accordance with his own views of State Rights, breaking from the Union, thus crumbling our republic into ruins; while the unhappy old man folded his arms in despair, declaring that the national Constitution invested him with no power to arrest the destruction.

When Mr. Tyler succeeded President Harrison, and, to the excessive disappointment of the Whigs, vetoed their bank bill, Mr. Buchanan warmly commended his course. In reply to the argument, that Mr. Tyler ought to have signed the bill in fidelity to the party which elected him, he said, —

"If he had approved that bill, he would have deserved to be denounced as a self-destroyer, as false to the whole course of his past life, false to every principle of honor, and false to the sacred obligation of his oath to support the Constitution."

Mr. Buchanan opposed the ratification of the Webster-Ashburton Treaty in reference to our northeastern boundary, and advocated the annexation of Texas, that it might be cut up into slave States, "to afford that security to the Southern and Southwestern slave States which they have a right to demand." Upon Mr. Polk's accession to the presidency, Mr. Buchanan became Secretary of State, and, as such, took his share of the responsibility in the conduct of the Mexican war. Mr. Polk assumed that crossing the Nueces by the American troops into the disputed territory was not wrong, but for the Mexicans to cross the Rio Grande into that territory was a declaration of war. No candid man can read with pleasure the account of the course our government pursued in that movement. At the close of Mr. Polk's administration, Mr. Buchanan retired to private life; but still his intellectual ability, and great experience as a statesman, enabled him to exert a powerful private influence in national affairs.

He identified himself thoroughly and warmly with the party devoted to the perpetuation and extension of slavery, and brought all the energies of his mind to bear against the Wilmot Proviso. He gave his cordial approval to the compromise measures of 1850, which included the fugitive-slave law. Mr. Pierce, upon his election to the presidency, honored Mr. Buchanan with the mission to England. The plan then arose to purchase Cuba. It was feared that Spain might abolish slavery in Cuba, and thus endanger the institution in our Southern States. To consider this important question, Mr. Buchanan, and Messrs. Mason and Soulé, our ministers to France and Spain, met at Ostend. The substance of the result of their deliberations is contained in the following words: —

"After we shall have offered Spain a price for Cuba far beyond its present value, and this shall have been refused, it will then be time to consider the question, 'Does Cuba, in the possession of Spain, seriously endanger our internal peace and the existence of our cherished Union?' Should this question be answered in the affirmative, then by every law, human and divine, we shall be justified in wresting it from Spain, if we possess the power."

This Ostend Manifesto created intense excitement, both in this country and in Europe; but our own internal troubles which soon arose caused it to be forgotten. In the year 1856 a National Democratic Convention nominated Mr. Buchanan for the presidency. In the platform adopted by the convention, it was stated, in connection with other principles to which all parties would assent, "that Congress has no power under the Constitution to interfere with or control the domestic institutions of the several States; that the foregoing proposition covers the whole subject of slavery agitation in Congress; that the Democratic party will adhere to a faithful execution of the compromise measures, the act of reclaiming fugitives from service or labor included; that the Democratic party will resist all attempts at renewing, jn Congress or out of it, the agitation of the slavery question, under whatever shape or color the attempt may be made; and that the American Democracy recognize and adopt the principles of non-interference by Congress with slavery in State and Territory, or in the District of Columbia."

The political conflict was one of the most severe in which our country has ever engaged. All the friends of slavery were on one side; all the advocates of its restriction and final abolition, on the other. Mr. Frémont, the candidate of the enemies of slavery, received 114 electoral votes. Mr. Buchanan received 174, and was elected. The popular vote stood 1,340,618 for Frémont, 1,224,750 for Buchanan. On the 4th of March, 1857, Mr. Buchanan was inaugurated President. The crowd which attended was immense, and the enthusiasm with which he was greeted had never been surpassed. Mr. Buchanan was a man of imposing personal appearance, an accomplished gentleman, endowed with superior abilities improved by the most careful culture, and no word had ever been breathed against the purity of his moral character. His long experience as a legislator, and the exalted offices he had filled at home and abroad, eminently fitted him for the station he was called to fill. Under ordinary circumstances, his administration would probably have been a success.

But such storms arose as the country had never experienced before. Mr. Buchanan was far advanced in life. But four years were wanting to fill up his threescore years and ten. His own friends, those with whom he had been allied in political principles and action for years, were seeking the destruction of the government, that they might rear upon the ruins of our free institutions a nation whose corner-stone should be human slavery. In this emergency, Mr. Buchanan was hopelessly bewildered. He could not, with his long-avowed principles, consistently oppose the State-Rights party in their assumptions. As President of the United States, bound by his oath faithfully to administer the laws, he could not, without perjury of the grossest kind, unite with those endeavoring to overthrow the republic. He therefore did nothing.

In August, 1857, a correspondence took place between a number of gentlemen of distinction in New Haven, Conn., and President Buchanan, which, in consequence of its having been made public by the President, has become historic. As this correspondence de-

INVASION OF KANSAS.

velops very clearly most of the points at issue between President Buchanan and the great Republican party which elected President Lincoln, we shall quote freely from it. Impartiality will be secured by allowing each of the parties to speak in its own language. The circumstances which called forth the correspondence were as follows : —

After the repeal of the Missouri Compromise a struggle began between the supporters of slavery and the advocates of freedom, for the possession of the Territory of Kansas by population and settlement. The more vigorous emigration from the free States, induced by voluntary organizations to favor it, soon resulted in a large excess of population in favor of freedom. To wrest from this majority their proper control in the legislation and regulation of this Territory, large organized and armed mobs repeatedly passed over from the contiguous State of Missouri, and appeared in force at the polls. We have described these occurrences with some particularity in the sketch of President Pierce.

They drove away the regularly constituted inspectors of election, and substituted their own, who received the votes of the mob without scruple. In some instances lists of fictitious votes were returned under feigned names; and representatives of the Missouri mob were thereby furnished by the fraudulent inspectors with regular forms of election. Unfortunately, the territorial governor of Kansas (Reeder), embarrassed by these regular forms, and not knowing how far he would be justified in disputing them, did not, in all instances, withhold his certificates from these fraudulent claimants to seats in the legislature long enough for the people to bring evidence of the fraud. The administrations of both Presidents Pierce and Buchanan, and the supporters of those administrations, strongly proslavery in their sympathies, upheld this iniquitously chosen legislature in its authority and acts.

Governor Walker, who succeeded Governor Reeder, in a public address to the citizens of Kansas, announced that President Buchanan was determined to sustain this legislature, thus mob elected, as the lawful legislature of Kansas; and that its acts would be enforced by executive authority and by the army. This announcement created intense excitement with the advocates of liberty all over the Union.

About forty of the most distinguished gentlemen of New Haven, embracing such names as Benjamin Silliman, A. C. Twining, Nathaniel W. Taylor, Theodore Woolsey, Charles L. English, and Leonard Bacon, sent a memorial to the President upon this subject. It has recently appeared, in the published Life of Professor Silliman, that the paper was from the pen of Professor A. C. Twining, LL. D. It reads as follows: —

" TO HIS EXCELLENCY JAMES BUCHANAN, PRESIDENT OF THE UNITED STATES.

"The undersigned, citizens of the United States, and electors of the State of Connecticut, respectfully offer to your excellency this memorial: —

"The fundamental principle of the Constitution of the United States, and of our political institutions, is, *that the people shall make their own laws, and elect their own rulers.*

"We see with grief, if not with astonishment, that Governor Walker of Kansas openly represents and proclaims that the President of the United States is employing through him an army, one purpose of which is to force the people of Kansas to obey laws not their own, nor of the United States, but laws which it is notorious, and established upon evidence, they never made, and rulers they never elected.

"We represent, therefore, that, by the foregoing, your excellency is openly held up and proclaimed, to the great derogation of our national character, as violating in its most essential particular the solemn *oath* which the President has taken to support the *Constitution of this Union.*

"We call attention further to the fact, that your excellency is in like manner held up to this nation, to all mankind, and to all posterity, in the attitude of levying war against a portion of the United States, by employing arms in Kansas to uphold a body of men, and a code of enactments, purporting to be legislative, but which never had the election nor the sanction nor the consent of the people of of that Territory.

"We earnestly represent to your excellency, that we also have taken the oath to obey the Constitution, and your excellency may be assured that we shall not refrain from the prayer that Almighty God will make your administration an example of justice and beneficence, and, with his terrible majesty, protect our people and our Constitution."

To this, which was called the Silliman Letter, the President returned a very carefully written reply from his own hand, covering seventeen folio pages. As he was well aware that the distinguished character of the memorialists would stamp the memorial with importance, and attract to it national attention, it cannot be doubted that he took counsel in its preparation, and presented those arguments upon which he and his Cabinet wished to rely with posterity in defense of their measures. After some preliminary remarks, which had but little bearing upon the points at issue, he said, —

"When I entered upon the duties of the presidential office, on the 4th of March last, what was the condition of Kansas? This Territory had been organized under the act of Congress of 30th May, 1854, and the government in all its branches was in full operation. A governor, secretary of the Territory, chief justice, two associate justices, a marshal, and district attorney, had been appointed by my predecessor, by and with the advice and consent of the Senate, and were all engaged in discharging their respective duties. A code of laws had been enacted by the territorial Legislature, and the judiciary were employed in expounding and carrying these laws into effect. It is quite true that a controversy had previously arisen respecting the validity of the election of members of the territorial Legislature, and of the laws passed by them, but, at the time I entered upon my official duties, Congress had recognized the Legislature in different forms and by different enactments.

" The delegate elected by the House of Representatives under a territorial law had just completed his term of service on the day previous to my inauguration. In fact, I found the government of Kansas as well established as that of any other Territory.

" Under these circumstances what was my duty? Was it not to sustain this government? to protect it from the violence of lawless men who were determined either to rule or ruin? to prevent it from being overturned by force? in the language of the Constitution, ' to take care that the laws be faithfully executed'? It was for this purpose, and this alone, that I ordered a military force to Kansas, to act as a *posse comitatus* in aiding the civil magistrate to carry the laws into execution.

" The condition of the Territory at the time, which I need not portray, rendered this precaution absolutely necessary. In this state of affairs, would I not have been justly condemned had I left the marshal, and other officers of like character, impotent to execute the process and judgments of courts of justice established by Congress, or by the territorial Legislature under its express authority, and thus have suffered the government itself to become an object of contempt in the eyes of the people? And yet this is what you designate as forcing ' the people of Kansas to obey laws not their own, nor of the United States,' and for doing which you have denounced me as having violated my solemn oath.

" I ask, What else could I have done, or ought I to have done? Would you have desired that I should abandon the territorial government, sanctioned as it had been by Congress, to illegal violence, and thus renew the scenes of civil war and bloodshed which every patriot in the country had deplored? This would have been, indeed, to violate my oath of office, and to fix a damning blot on the character of my administration.

" I most cheerfully admit that the necessity for sending a military force to Kansas to aid in the execution of the civil law reflects no credit upon the character of our country. But let the blame fall upon the heads of the guilty. Whence did this necessity arise? A portion of the people of Kansas, unwilling to trust to the ballot-box, — the certain American remedy for the redress of all grievances, — undertook to create an independent government for themselves. Had this attempt proved successful, it would, of course, have subverted the existing government prescribed and recognized by Congress, and substituted a revolutionary government in its stead.

" This was a usurpation of the same character as it would be for a portion of the people of Connecticut to undertake to establish a separate government within its chartered limits, for the purpose of redressing any grievance, real or imaginary, of which they might have complained against the legitimate state government. Such a principle, if carried into execution, would destroy all lawful authority, and produce universal anarchy.

" I ought to specify more particularly a condition of affairs which I have embraced only in general terms, requiring the presence of a military force in Kansas. The Congress of the United States had most wisely declared it to be ' the true intent and meaning of this act ' (the act organizing the Territory) ' not to legislate slavery into any Territory or State, nor to exclude it therefrom, but to leave the people thereof perfectly free to form and regulate their domestic institutions in their own way, subject only to the Constitution of the United States.'

" As a natural consequence, Congress has also prescribed by the same act, that, when the Territory of Kansas shall be admitted as a State, it ' shall be received into the Union, with or without slavery, as their Constitution may prescribe at the time of their admission.' Slavery existed at that period, and still exists, in Kansas under the Constitution of the United States. This point has at last been finally decided by the highest tribunal known to our laws. How it could ever have been seriously doubted, is to me a mystery. If a confederation of sovereign States acquire a new Territory at the expense of the common blood and treasure, surely one set of the partners can have no right to exclude the other from its enjoyment by prohibiting them from taking into it whatsoever is recognized as property by the common Constitution.

" But when the people,[1] the *bonâ fide* residents of such Territory, proceed to frame a state Constitution, then it is their right to decide the important question for themselves — whether they will continue, modify, or abolish slavery. To them, and to them alone, does this question belong, free from all foreign interference. In the opinion of the territorial Legislature of Kansas, the time had arrived for entering the Union; and they accordingly passed a law to elect delegates for the purpose of framing a state Constitution. This law was fair and just in its provisions. It conferred the right of suffrage on ' every *bonâ fide* inhabitant of the Territory,' [2] and, for the purpose of preventing fraud and the intrusion of citizens of near or distant States, most properly confined this right to those who had resided there three months previous to the election.

"Here a fair opportunity was presented for all the qualified resident citizens of the Territory, to whatever organization they might have previously belonged, to participate in the election, and to express their opinions at the ballot-box on the question of slavery. But numbers of lawless men [3] still continue to resist the regular ter-

---

[1] It is to be observed that President Buchanan limits the term *people* to mean *white* people only. If a man had the slightest tinge of colored blood in his veins, he was not to be considered as one of the *people.* If there were two hundred thousand colored peosons in the State, and one hundred thousand white persons, it was " most wisely declared " that these white persons should be permitted to decide whether these colored persons should work for them, without wages, in lifelong bondage. It most was " wisely declared " that James Buchanan, a *white man,* should be permitted to decide whether Frederick Douglas, a *colored man,* and in no respect his inferior, either morally, intellectually, or physically, should be compelled to black his boots, and groom his horse, from the cradle to the grave ; and *should* James Buchanan thus decide, and *should* Frederick Douglas make any objection to the decision, " illegal, unjustifiable, unconstitutional," then it was fitting that a United States army should be sent under the " stars and the stripes " to compel Frederick Douglas to ply the shoebrush and the curry-comb for James Buchanan. And this was called *democracy,* " equal rights for all ! "

[2] Colored persons, no matter how intelligent, wealthy, or refined, were no more considered *inhabitants* than they were considered *people.* As Mr. Buchanan employs these words with a significance different from that in which they are defined in every English dictionary, it is necessary to explain the sense in which he uses them in order to make his meaning clear.

[3] These " lawless men " were the Free-State men of Kansas, who met in convention,

ritorial government. They refused either to be registered or to vote, and the members of the convention were elected legally and properly without their intervention.

" The convention will soon assemble to perform the solemn duty of framing a Constitution for themselves and their posterity ; and in the state of incipient rebellion [1] which still exists in Kansas, it is my imperative duty to employ the troops of the United States, should this become necessary, in defending the convention against violence while framing the Constitution ; and in protecting the *bonâ fide* inhabitants qualified to vote under the provisions of this instrument in the free exercise of the right of suffrage, when it shall be submitted to them for their approbation or rejection.

" Following the wise example of Mr. Madison towards the Hartford Convention, illegal and dangerous combinations, such as that of the Topeka Convention, will not be disturbed, unless they shall attempt to perform some act which will bring them into actual collision with the Constitution and the laws."

The above contains the whole of Mr. Buchanan's reply bearing upon the points at issue. As this question was so all-absorbing during his administration, and created such intense excitement throughout the whole country, justice to Mr. Buchanan seemed to demand that his views, which were cordially accepted and indorsed by his party, should be fully unfolded. This reply President Buchanan caused to be published, with the memorial ; and it was very widely circulated. By the friends of his administration, it was declared to be triumphant. The rejoinder on the part of the memorialists consisted of an address to the public, also from the pen of Professor Twining. It is too long to be quoted ; but its substance is contained in the following extracts : —

" No man will question that the inhabitants of Kansas, by their Organic Act, became possessed of the same elective privilege with

and passed the resolve, " That the body of men who for the last two months have been passing laws for the people of our Territory, moved, counseled, and dictated to by the demagogues of Missouri, are to us a foreign body, representing only the lawless invaders who elected them, and not the people of the Territory ; that we repudiate their action as the monstrous consummation of an act of violence, usurpation, and fraud, unparalleled in the history of the Union."

[1] These *rebels* were those who objected to the State being ruled by "border-ruffians " from Missouri.

the people of a State, just so far, at least, as that act entitles them to it. Since, therefore, it cannot be denied that the Constitution extends its protection over the elective franchise in that Territory as fully as in any State of the Union, it follows that the employment of troops to compel obedience to a notoriously non-elected and therefore usurping body, would, if performed in a sovereign State, Connecticut for example, be no more fully an unconstitutional act, no more really levying war against a portion of the United States, than if performed in Kansas.

" Are we, inhabitants of the comparatively feeble State of Connecticut, to hold our liberties at so precarious a tenure, that if, hereafter, thousands of armed men from our stronger neighbor in the West shall make an incursion among us, seize our ballot-boxes, deposit their votes, and write certificates for representatives of their own choosing, with the point of the sword, the President of this Union shall assume to compel our obedience ' by the whole power of the government ? ' Could it be expected that even such a menace would drive our citizens to recognize any valid authority in a mere *banditti*, because of their possession of the stolen and empty forms of law and government ?

" It has been denied by the apologists of the Missouri invaders, that what is called the territorial Legislature of Kansas is, in fact, such a non-elected and usurping body as we have just described. How stands this in the President's reply ? Does that reply deny that the body referred to ' never had the election nor sanction nor consent of the people of the Territory ' ? Not at all. In that document, emanating from so high a source, no such denial is made. Nay, we are at liberty to receive it as more ; even as being, under the circumstances, an impressive recognition. And yet, while he does not deny our chief assertion and fact, the President justifies the employment of troops to uphold a body of men and a code of enactments which he has tacitly admitted never had the election nor sanction nor consent of the people of the Territory.

" But the President puts forward a vindication. It rests almost entirely upon two grounds, which we feel called upon briefly to review. The first ground may be sufficiently stated by a single quotation from his document : ' At the time I entered upon my official duties, Congress had recognized this legislature in different forms and by different enactments.'

"What particular forms and enactments are intended, is, with a single exception, left to our conjecture; but by attentively considering that exception, which amounts only to the admission of a delegate to the house after two marked rejections, you will clearly apprehend that there never was any enactment of Congress from which anything more could be derived than some doubtful or imperfect constructive recognition of the territorial body referred to.

"Our first answer, then, to the ground of vindication above stated, is an explicit denial that any joint action of the House and the Senate, not to mention the President, *expressly purporting* to recognize or make valid the body in question, can be found among the statutes of this nation, — anything approaching in solemnity the Organic Act. Again: we assert that the Organic Act stands in all the force of an unrepealed national law. And in this we refer especially to its provisions for an *elective representation of the people.* , No man will dispute us on this point. That great charter of popular representation in Kansas remains unrevoked; and it is undeniable, that the fundamental Organic Act ought to and must control all side-issues. Mere implications cannot be construed to conflict with the unmistakable and express enactments according to which the 'duly elected' legislative assembly shall consist of the persons having the highest number of *legal votes,* and with the intent '*to leave the people thereof* (*i. e.* of the Territory) *free to regulate their domestic institutions in their own way, subject* (not to invaders, but) *only to the Constitution of the United States.*'

"And here we might rest; for here our answer is complete. But we go farther, and deny the propriety even of the implications claimed. The President adduces specifically only the admission of a delegate sent to the house by the supporters of the usurping legislature. Now, it is enough to remark in reply, that, although the admission of a delegate is final as to his seat for a time, it has not even force to oblige a succeeding Congress not to exclude him, much less to oblige a President to subjugate a Territory. But is it on such a knife-edge as this that the franchise of a whole people is made to oscillate and tremble? and is this the logic which guides our statesmen?

"To adduce a meagre vote of a single branch of the government as an act of Congress; to adduce it as such in the face of the repeated adverse action of even that single branch; to do this by ignoring the procedures of that same branch, which, acting as the grand inquest of the nation, had sent forth the details of frauds and the evidence of invalidity, on the strength of which, as contained in the report of their investigating committee, they had *formally voted to abrogate the body for whom their sanction is now claimed!*

"The Organic Act, and, under it, the fundamental principle of our Constitution, stand in full force in Kansas. But, contrary to that act and that principle, a body of men are assuming to legislate, who were never elected or sanctioned by the people. When, therefore, the President offers his oath and his obligation to see the laws faithfully executed, as a plea for supporting that illegal body, he proposes the solecism, that his obligation to the laws binds him to subvert the organic law, and that his oath to preserve and protect the Constitution binds him to contravene the very fundamental element of the Constitution.

"The President's other ground of vindication is embraced in the following extracts: 'I found the government of Kansas as well established as that of any other Territory. A governor, secretary of the Territory, chief justice, two associate justices, a marshal, and district attorney, had been appointed by my predecessor, by and with the advice and consent of the Senate. A code of laws had been enacted by the *territorial Legislature* (mark our italics), and the judiciary were employed in carrying those laws into effect.'

"We assent to the proposition, that if the *bonâ fide* settlers of Kansas have, as a body, given their sanction and consent to the representative authority of the territorial Legislature above referred to, even without having given it their election, and if that authority is of force to execute its enactments in the Territory, it constitutes *de facto*, in union with the federal government and other officers, a valid republican government; but then that sanction, it is obvious, must have been the clear, explicit, unmistakable act of the majority. How, then, does the fact stand in the instance before you?

"So far from such sanction or consent of the majority being in evidence, or even presumable, the President's reply itself supplies distinct proof, in part, to the reverse; and facts notorious to common information supply the rest. 'A portion of the people of Kansas,' you read in the reply, 'undertook to create an independent government for themselves,' 'continued to resist the regular territorial government,' and even 'refused either to be registered or vote.'

"A '*portion of the people*' have always acted out a strong protest. How large a *portion*, the reply does not state; but you are aware, from good authorities, that it is *two thirds* at least, and perhaps *four fifths*, of the entire population."

After showing the conclusive evidence upon which this fact is established, evidence which *no one* now calls in question, the memorialists continue, —

"The emphatic protest of the majority in Kansas, which was expressed by their afore-mentioned refusal to vote, is imputed to them by the President as a political and public wrong. His language is, 'A portion of the people of Kansas, unwilling to trust to the ballot-box, — the certain American remedy for the redress of all grievances, — undertook to create an independent government. Numbers of lawless men continued to resist the territorial Legislature. They refused either to be registered or to vote.'

"The resistance of these *lawless men*, be it observed, was merely a steady refusal to vote, or to recognize the pretended legislature. But were they indeed unwilling to trust the ballot-box? When and how? Was it in November, 1854, when, at the first election for a delegate, they were overpowered by parties of armed intruders, who, obtaining violent possession of the polls, cast about six tenths the entire vote of the Territory? Was it in the following March, when thousands of armed men from Missouri, with tents, provision-wagons, music, and the entire appointments of an invading army, poured into Kansas, occupied every council district, took possession of the ballot-boxes, and excluded all rightful voters whose sentiments were not agreeable to them? Has it been at any subsequent election, every one of which has been controlled by voters from Missouri? Under these circumstances, which are all open to the light of day, the reproachful charge of being 'unwilling to trust to the ballot-box' cannot reach those at whom it is aimed.

"Fellow-citizens, we know not why the President should have introduced to us and to you the exciting subject of slavery, respecting which our memorial was silent. We leave his startling assertions on that subject without any other comment than that our silence is not to be construed into any assent."

The friends of Mr. Buchanan's administration, North and South, were satisfied with his letter. They accepted and adopted the views it expressed as a triumphant defense of the policy which the govern-

24

ment was pursuing. On the other hand, the opponents of the administration accepted and adopted the views contained in the memorial of the New Haven gentlemen, and in their response to the President's letter. It was upon this very platform that the Hon. Stephen A. Douglas planted his feet so firmly, and in defense of which he fought, perhaps, the most heroic battle ever waged in senatorial halls. This was essentially the issue which was presented to the nation in the next presidential election, and which resulted in the choice of Abraham Lincoln by an overwhelming majority of votes.

In the great excitement which this state of things created in the United States, the opponents of Mr. Buchanan's administration nominated Abraham Lincoln as their standard-bearer in the next presidential canvass. The proslavery party declared that if he were elected, and the control of the government were thus taken from their hands, they would secede from the Union, taking with them, as they retired, the national Capitol at Washington, and the lion's share of the territory of the United States.

Mr. Buchanan's sympathy with the proslavery party was such, that he had been willing to offer them far more than they had ventured to claim. All that the South had professed to ask of the North was *non-intervention* upon the subject of slavery. Mr. Buchanan had been ready to offer them the active coöperation of the government to defend and extend the institution. In a " private and confidential letter," addressed to Jefferson Davis in 1850, he wrote, in reference to a letter which he was urged to have published, —

" From a careful examination of the proceedings in Congress, it is clear that *non-intervention* is all that will be required by the South. Under these circumstances, it would be madness in me to publish my letter, and take higher ground for the South than they have taken for themselves. This would be to out-Herod Herod, and to be more Southern than the South. I shall be assailed by fanatics and free-soilers as long as I live for having gone farther in support of the rights of the South than Southern senators and representatives."

As the storm increased in violence, the slaveholders claiming the right to secede, and Mr. Buchanan avowing that Congress had no power to prevent it, one of the most pitiable exhibitions of governmental imbecility was exhibited the world has ever seen. As soon as it was known that Mr. Lincoln was elected, the slaveholding States, drilled to the movement, began to withdraw. Mr. Buchanan had not a word of censure for them. All his rebukes were addressed to those who had wished to prevent the extension of slavery. " The long-continued and intemperate interference," he said, "of the Northern people with the question of slavery in the Southern States, has at length produced its natural effects." He declared that Congress had no power to enforce its laws in any State which had withdrawn, or which was attempting to withdraw, from the Union. This was not the doctrine of Andrew Jackson, when, with his hand upon his sword-hilt, he exclaimed, " The Union must and shall be preserved!" It was an alarming state of things when the supreme executive declared that he had no power " to take care that the laws be faithfully executed."

Innumerable plans of concession were proposed ; but the secessionists did not hesitate to avow their utter contempt for the government of the United States, and to spurn its advances. Mr. Buchanan approached the rebels on his knees. They hastened to avail themselves of his weakness, and to accomplish all their disorganizing measures before his successor should come into power.

South Carolina seceded in December, 1860 ; nearly three months before the inauguration of President Lincoln. Mr. Buchanan looked on in listless despair. The rebel flag was raised in Charleston ; Fort Sumter was besieged ; The Star of the West, in endeavoring to carry food to its famishing garrison, was fired upon ; and still Mr. Buchanan sat in the White House, wringing his hands, and bemoaning his helplessness. Our forts, navy-yards, and arsenals were seized ; our dépôts of military stores were plundered ; and our custom-houses and post-offices were appropriated by the rebels : and all that President Buchanan could do was to send a secret messenger to Charleston to implore the rebels to hold back their hand a little until the close of his administration.[1] Members of his Cabinet began

---

[1] "By the middle of December, Hon. Caleb Cushing of Massachusetts was dispatched to Charleston by President Buchanan as a commissioner or confidential agent of the executive. His errand was a secret one ; but, so far as its object was allowed to transpire, he was understood to be the bearer of a proffer from Mr. Buchanan, that he would not attempt to reinforce Major Anderson, nor initiate any hostilities against the secessionists, provided they would evince a like pacific spirit by respecting the federal authorities down to the close of his administration, now but a few weeks distant." — *The American Conflict*, by Horace Greeley, vol. i. p. 409.

to retire, and join the rebels, after they had scattered the fleet, and robbed the arsenals and the public treasure.

The energy of the rebels, and the imbecility of our executive, were alike marvelous. Before the close of January, the rebels had plundered the nation of millions of property, had occupied and fortified many of the most important strategic points, had chosen their flag, and organized their government; while President Buchanan had not lifted a hand to check them. The nation looked on in agony, waiting for the slow weeks to glide away, and close this administration, so terrible in its weakness.

General Scott, in view of the threatening aspect of affairs, called repeatedly upon President Buchanan, and urged that strong garrisons should be sent to all the imperiled forts. Many of these forts had no garrisons at all, and could at any time be seized and appropriated by the rebels, rendering their reconquest costly in both blood and treasure. Mr. Buchanan would not permit them to be strengthened. General Scott entreated that at least a circular might be sent to the forts where there *were* garrisons, giving them warning of their peril, and urging them to be on the alert. His request was not granted until it was too late to be of avail.

Had General Scott's plan been adopted, it would have placed all the arsenals and forts commanding the Southern rivers and strategic points so firmly in the hands of the national government, that the rebels would scarcely have ventured to attack them. In all probability, it would have prevented the uprising. It would have saved the country four thousand millions of money, and nearly a million of lives. Whatever may have been the motives which influenced Mr. Buchanan, no one can be blind as to the result of his conduct. Probably history may be searched in vain for a parallel case, in which the chief ruler of a great country, the Secretary of War, and the Secretary of the Navy, all seemed to combine to leave the most important fortresses of the nation in as defenseless a condition as possible, when arrogant and armed rebellion was threatening their capture. Was this treachery? Was it imbecility?

It is very evident that for some reason the secessionists had no fear that President Buchanan would place any obstacles in their path. In December, 1860, Hon. L. M. Keitt was serenaded in Columbia, S. C. In response, he made a speech, in which he is reported to have said as follows: —

"South Carolina cannot take one step backwards now without receiving the curses of posterity. South Carolina, single and alone, is bound to go out of this accursed Union. *Mr. Buchanan is pledged to secession, and I mean to hold him to it.* Take your destinies in your own hands, and shatter this accursed Union. South Carolina can do it alone; but, if she cannot, she can at least throw her arms around the pillars of the Constitution, and involve all the States in a common ruin."

When South Carolina, under the leadership of John C. Calhoun, in the days of Andrew Jackson's presidency, was threatening nullification and secession, General Scott received an order from the War Department to hasten to Washington. He arrived in the evening, and immediately had an interview with the President. "The Union must and shall be preserved," said General Jackson, as he inquired of General Scott his views as to the best military measures to be adopted.

General Scott suggested strong garrisons for Fort Moultrie, Castle Pinckney, and for the arsenal at Augusta, which was filled with the *matériel* of war. Fort Sumter was not then built. He also urged that a sloop-of-war and several armed revenue-cutters should be immediately sent to Charleston Harbor.

"Proceed at once," said General Jackson, "and execute those views. I give you *carte blanche* in respect to troops. The vessels shall be there, and written instructions shall follow you."

Under these *persuasives*, nullification and secession soon came to grief. There surely was as great a difference in the treatment of the disease by Jackson and by Buchanan as there was in the results of that treatment.

At length the long looked-for hour of deliverance came, when the sceptre was to fall from the powerless hand of Mr. Buchanan, and to be grasped by another, who would wield it with more of the dignity and energy becoming the chief ruler of one of the most powerful nations on the globe. It was the 4th of March, 1861. Attempts had been made by the rebels to assassinate Abraham Lincoln on his journey to Washington. Very narrowly he escaped. It was deemed necessary to adopt the most careful precautions to secure him from assassination on the day of his inauguration. Mr. Buchanan remained in Washington to see his successor installed, and then retired to his home in Wheatland.

The administration of President Buchanan was certainly the most calamitous our country has experienced. His best friends cannot recall it with pleasure. And still more deplorable it is for his fame, that, in the dreadful conflict which rolled its billows of flame and blood over our whole land, no word came from the lips of President Buchanan to indicate his wish that our country's banner should triumph over the flag of rebellion. He might by a few words have rendered the nation the most signal service; but those words were not spoken. He died at his beautiful Wheatland retreat, June 1, 1868, aged seventy-seven years.

CHAPTER XVI.

ABRAHAM LINCOLN.

Life in a Log-Cabin. — Excellence of Character early developed. — A Day-Laborer. — A Boatman. — A Shopkeeper. — A Student. — A Legislator. — A Lawyer. — A Member of Congress. — A Political Speaker. — The Debate with Douglas. — Eloquence of Mr. Lincoln. — Nominated for the Presidency. — Habits of Temperance. — His Sentiments. — Anecdotes — Acts of his Administration. — His Assassination.

IN the interior of the State of Kentucky there is the county of La Rue. Even now it is but sparsely populated. Seventy-five years

RESIDENCE OF ABRAHAM LINCOLN.

ago it was quite a wilderness, highly picturesque in its streams, its forests, and its prairies; in places, smooth as a floor, and again swelling into gentle undulations like the ocean at the subsidence of a storm. The painted Indian here had free range ; a savage more ferocious than the wild beasts he pursued. Though Daniel Boone had explored this region, and had returned to the other side of the Alleghanies laden with peltry, and with the report that it was an earthly paradise, there were but few who were ready to plunge into the pathless wilderness, leaving all vestiges of civilization hundreds of miles behind them. But Providence, for the sake of peopling this country, seems to have raised up a peculiar class of men who loved hardship and peril and utter loneliness. The Indians were always clustered in villages, but these men, the pioneers of civilization, penetrated the recesses of the forest, and reared their cabins in the most secluded valleys, where they seldom heard the voice or saw the face of their brother man.

About the year 1780, when the war of the Revolution was still raging, one of these men, Abraham Lincoln, left the beautiful valley of the Shenandoah, in Virginia, for the wilds of Kentucky. His wife and one or two children accompanied him. There were no roads ; there were no paths but the trail of the Indian. All their worldly goods they must have carried in packs upon their backs, unless, possibly, they might have been enabled to take with them a horse or a mule. What motive could have induced a civilized man to take such a step it is difficult to imagine, and still, from the earliest settlement of our country until the present day, there have been thousands thus ever crowding into the wilderness. Only two years after this emigration Abraham Lincoln, still a young man, while working one day in his field, was stealthily approached by an Indian and shot dead. His widow was left in the extreme of poverty with five little children. How she struggled along through the terrible years of toil and destitution we are not informed. It was one of those unwritten tragedies of which earth is full.

There were three boys and two girls in the family. Thomas, the youngest of these boys, was four years of age at the time of his father's death. This Thomas was the father of Abraham Lincoln, the President of the United States, whose name must henceforth forever be enrolled amongst the most prominent in the annals of our world. Of course no record has been kept of the life of one so lowly as Thomas Lincoln. He was among the poorest of the poor. His home was a wretched log-cabin ; his food the coarsest and the meanest. Education he had none ; he could never either read or write. As soon as he was able to do anything for himself, he was compelled to leave the cabin of his starving mother, and push out into the world, a friendless, wandering boy, seeking work. He hired himself out, and thus spent the whole of his youth as a laborer in the fields of others.

When twenty-eight years of age he built a log-cabin of his own and married Nancy Hanks, the daughter of another family of poor Kentucky emigrants, who had also come from Virginia. Their second child was Abraham Lincoln, the subject of this sketch. Thomas, his father, was a generous, warm-hearted, good-natured man, with but little efficiency. He greatly deplored his want of education, and was anxious that his children should not suffer in this respect as he had done. The mother of Abraham was a noble woman, gentle, loving, pensive, created to adorn a palace, doomed to toil and pine and die in a hovel. "All that I am, or hope to be," exclaims the grateful son, " I owe to my angel-mother : blessings on her memory ! "

Both the father and mother of Abraham Lincoln were earnest Christians. Their grateful son could ever say, —

> " 'T is not my boast that I deduce my birth
> From loins enthroned, and rulers of the earth ;
> But higher far my proud pretensions rise, —
> The child of parents passed into the skies."

Abraham's mother had received some education, and would often delight her children by reading them some story from the very few books she could command. In that remote region schools were few, and very humble in their character. Abraham, when in his seventh year, was sent to one teacher for about two months, and to another for about three. His zeal was so great, that, in that time, he learned both to read and write. His parents were members of the Baptist Church ; and occasionally an itinerant preacher came along, and gathered the scattered families under a grove or in a cabin for religious service. Good old Parson Elkin gave Abraham his first ideas of public speaking.

When he was eight years of age his father sold his cabin and small farm, and moved to Indiana. Three horses took the family and all their household goods a seven days' journey to their new home. Here kind neighbors helped them in putting up another log-cabin. In a home more cheerless and comfortless than the readers of the present day can easily comprehend, Mrs. Lincoln, with the delicate organization, both of body and mind, of a lady, sank and died beneath the burdens which crushed her. Abraham was then ten years of age. Bitterly he wept as his mother was laid in her humble grave beneath the trees near the cabin. The high esteem in which this noble woman was held may be inferred from the fact that Parson Elkin rode a hundred miles on horseback, through the wilderness, to preach her funeral sermon; and the neighbors, to the number of two hundred, who were scattered in that sparsely-settled region over a distance of twenty miles, assembled to attend the service.

It was a scene for a painter, — the log-cabin, alone in its solitude; the wide-spread prairie, beautiful in the light of the Sabbath morning sun; the grove; the grave; the group seated around upon logs and stumps; the venerable preacher; the mourning family; and Abraham, with his marked figure and countenance, his eyes swimming with tears, gazing upon the scene which was thus honoring the memory of his revered mother.

Abraham had written the letter inviting the pastor to preach the funeral sermon. He soon became the scribe of the uneducated community around him. He could not have had a better school than this to teach him to put thoughts into words. He also became an eager reader. The books he could obtain were few; but these he read and re-read until they were almost committed to memory. The Bible, Æsop's "Fables," and the "Pilgrim's Progress," were his favorites. The Lives of Washington, Franklin, and Clay produced a deep impression upon his sensitive mind. All the events of their varied careers were so stored up in his memory that he could recall them at any time.

An anecdote is related illustrative of that conscientiousness of character which was early developed, and which subsequently gave him the name, throughout the whole breadth of the land, of "Honest Abe." He had borrowed Ramsay's "Life of Washington." By accident, the book was seriously injured by a shower. In consternation at the calamity, he took it back to the owner, and purchased the soiled copy by working for it for three days.

His father soon married again a very worthy woman, who had also several children. Abraham remained at home, toiling upon the farm, and occasionally working as a day-laborer. He had remarkable muscular strength and agility, was exceedingly genial and obliging, and secured to an eminent degree the affection and respect of the lowly community with which he was associated. He was ever ready to make any sacrifice of his own comfort to assist others. Having some considerable mechanical skill, he built a boat to carry the produce of the farm down the Ohio River to a market. One morning, as he was standing by his boat at the landing, two men came down to the shore, and wished to be taken out to a steamer in the river. He sculled them out with their luggage. Each of them tossed a silver half-dollar to him. In telling this story in the day when his income was twenty-five thousand dollars a year, and he had obtained almost world-wide renown, he said, —

"I could scarcely believe my eyes. It was a most important incident in my life. I could scarcely believe that I, a poor boy, had earned a dollar in less than a day. The world seemed wider and fairer before me. I was more hopeful and confident from that time."

When nineteen years of age, a neighbor applied to him to take charge of a flat-boat to float a cargo of produce down the Ohio and the Mississippi to New Orleans, — a distance of more than a thousand miles. A more exciting trip for an adventurous young man can scarcely be imagined. Housed safely in his capacious boat, with food and shelter; floating down the tranquil current of the beautiful Ohio, and swept resistlessly along by the majestic flood of the Father of Waters; passing headlands and forests, huts and villages, the tortuous river bearing the boat in all directions, — north, south, east, west; the stream now compressed within narrow banks, and now expanding to a lake, and almost to an ocean; to be borne along by an insensible motion through such scenes, in the bright morning sunshine or in the serene moonlight, must have enkindled emotions in the bosom of young Lincoln never to be forgotten. With a rifle, and a small boat attached to their floating ark, they could supply themselves with game. Whenever they wished, they could tie their boat to the shore, and visit the cabins of the remote settlers for supplies.

One night, when tied to the shore, they were attacked by seven robbers eager for plunder. Quite a little battle ensued, when the robbers were put to precipitate flight. Having arrived at New Orleans, the cargo was sold, and the boat disposed of for lumber.

Young Lincoln with his companions retraced their passage back to Indiana in a long and weary journey, most of the way on foot.

As the years rolled on, the lot of this lowly family was the usual lot of humanity. There were joys and griefs, weddings and funerals. Abraham's sister Sarah, to whom he was tenderly attached, was married when a child of but fourteen years of age, and soon died. The family was gradually scattered. Mr. Thomas Lincoln, naturally restless, finding his location unhealthy in the almost unbroken wilderness of Spencer County, Indiana, and lured by the accounts which he had heard of the marvelous fertility of Illinois, sold out his squatter's claim in 1830, and emigrated two hundred miles farther northwest, — to Macon County, Illinois. It was a weary spring journey over swollen streams and through roads of mire. The carts, containing the personal effects of the emigrants, were dragged by oxen; and fifteen days were occupied in reaching their new home upon the banks of the Sangamon.

Abraham Lincoln was then twenty-one years of age. With vigorous hands, he aided his father in rearing another log-cabin. It was made of hewn timber. The only tools they had to work with were an axe, a saw, and a draw-knife. A smoke-house and barn were also built, and ten acres of land were fenced in by split rails. Abraham worked diligently at this until he saw the family comfortably settled, and their small lot of inclosed prairie planted with corn, when he announced to his father his intention to leave home, and to go out into the world to seek his fortune. Little did he or his friends imagine how brilliant that fortune was to be. But the elements of greatness were then being developed. He saw the value of education, and was intensely earnest to improve his mind to the utmost of his power. He saw the ruin which ardent spirits were causing, and became strictly temperate; refusing to allow a drop of intoxicating liquor to pass his lips. And he had read in God's word, " Thou shalt not take the name of the Lord thy God in vain;" and a profane expression he was never heard to utter. Religion he revered. His morals were pure, and he was uncontaminated by a single vice.

It is difficult to explain the reason for the fact, that one young man, surrounded by every influence which should elevate, sinks into ruin; and that another, exposed to all the temptations which would naturally tend to degrade, soars to dignity and elevation which render him an honor to his race. Young Abraham worked for a time as a hired laborer among the farmers. Then he went to Springfield, where he was employed in building a large flat-boat. In this he took a herd of swine, floated them down the Sangamon to the Illinois, and thence by the Mississippi to New Orleans. Whatever Abraham Lincoln undertook, he performed so faithfully as to give great satisfaction to his employers. In this adventure his employers were so well pleased, that, upon his return, they placed a store and a mill under his care. A blessing seemed to follow him. Customers were multiplied. His straightforward, determined honesty secured confidence. In settling a bill with a woman, he took six and quarter cents too much. He found it out in his night's reckoning, and immediately, in the dark, walked to her house, two miles and a half distant, to pay it back to her. Just as he was closing the store one night, in the dusk, he weighed out half a pound of tea for a woman. In the morning he found, that, by an accidental defect in the scales, the woman had received scant weight by four ounces. He weighed out the four ounces, shut up the store, and carried them to her ; a long walk before breakfast.

A bully came into the store one day, rioting, blustering, insulting beyond endurance, trying to provoke a fight. " Well, if you must be whipped," said Abraham at last, " I suppose I may as well whip you as any other man." He seized him with his long, powerful arms, threw him upon the ground as though he had been a child, and, gathering in his hand some " smart-weed " which chanced to be near, rubbed it in his face, until the fellow bellowed with pain, and cried for mercy. Abraham, with " malice towards none," helped him up, got some cool water to bathe his burning face, and made him ever after one of his best friends.

He borrowed an English grammar, studied it thoroughly, and completely mastered it. He sought the society of the most intelligent men in that region, joined a debating-club, and took " The Louisville Journal," which he not only read, but carefully pondered all its leading articles. Every leisure moment was devoted to study and thought.

In 1832 the celebrated Indian chief Black Hawk crossed the Mississippi, and, with a large band of savages, was ascending Rock River. Volunteers were called for to resist him. Lincoln, with enough others in his immediate neighborhood to make a company, enlisted. Who should be their captain? There were two candidates, — Mr. Lincoln and a Mr. Kirkpatrick, a man of extensive influence, and who had been a former employer of Mr. Lincoln, but who was so arrogant and overbearing that Mr. Lincoln could not live with him. The mode of election was very simple. The two candidates were placed apart, and each man was told to go to the one whom he preferred. Nearly the whole band was soon found clustered around Lincoln. This was with Mr. Lincoln the proudest hour of his life. The little army of twenty-four hundred ascended Rock River in pursuit of Black Hawk. The savages were attacked, routed, and Black Hawk was taken prisoner. Zachary Taylor was colonel, and Abraham Lincoln captain, in this campaign. Nothing seemed then more improbable than that either of those men should ever become President of the United States.

Upon his return to Sangamon County, he was proposed as a candidate for the state Legislature. He was then twenty-three years of age, and was the political admirer of Henry Clay, and not of General Jackson. The great majority of the county were Jacksonian Democrats: but Mr. Lincoln's personal popularity was such, that he received almost every vote in his own precinct; though, in the general vote, he was defeated. He again tried his hand at storekeeping, and, with a partner, purchased a lot of goods. But his partner proved fickle and dissipated, and the adventure was a failure. He now received from Andrew Jackson the appointment of postmaster for New Salem. The duties were light, and the recompense small, in that wilderness. His only post-office was his hat. All the letters he received he carried there, ready to deliver as he chanced to meet those to whom they were addressed.

That new country was constantly demanding the services of a surveyor. Mr. Lincoln studied the science, and, entering upon the practice of this new profession, followed it vigorously and successfully for more than a year. He was still rapidly acquiring information, and advancing in mental culture. Shakespeare he read and re-read. Burns he could almost repeat by heart. Occasionally he ventured to make a political speech.

In 1834 he again became a candidate for the state Legislature, and was triumpahntly elected. Mr. Stuart of Springfield, an eminent lawyer, advised him to study law; offering to lend him such assistance in money as he needed. He walked from New Salem to

Springfield, borrowed of Mr. Stuart a load of books, carried them upon his back to New Salem, and commenced his legal studies. With earnestness which absorbed every energy of his soul, he entered upon his student-life. He had no pleasant office, no choice library, none of the appliances of literary luxury, to entice him. Much of his time, his study was the shade of an oak-tree. When the Legislature assembled, he trudged on foot, with his pack on his back, one hundred miles to Vandalia, then the capital of the State. He was a silent but studious member, gaining strength and wisdom every day. At the close of the session he walked home, and resumed the study of the law, supporting himself by surveying. These years of thought and study had accomplished their work, and suddenly he flashed forth an orator. It was at a public meeting in Springfield that he electrified the audience, and was at once recognized as one of the most eloquent men in the State.

In 1836 he was reëlected to the state Legislature. Mr. Lincoln was now twenty-seven years of age, and a prominent man in the State of Illinois. It was during this session of the Legislature that Mr. Lincoln first met Stephen A. Douglas, who was then but twenty-three years old. The slavery question was beginning to agitate the country. Both parties were bowing submissive to that great power. Some extreme proslavery resolutions passed the Legislature. There were but two men who ventured to remonstrate. Abraham Lincoln was one. "Slavery," Mr. Lincoln said in his protest, which was entered upon the journal of the house, " is founded on both injustice and bad policy." He was still poor. He walked to Vandalia. He walked home; his only baggage, a bundle in his hand.

Major Stuart of Springfield now proposed that Mr. Lincoln should become his partner in the law; and accordingly, in April, 1839, he removed to Springfield, and commenced the practice of his new profession. In the mean time the capital was removed to Springfield, and Mr. Lincoln, by successive elections, was continued in the Legislature, and was soon recognized as its leading member on the Whig side. In the practice of the law, his success with the jury was so great, that he was engaged in almost every important case in the circuit.

Mr. Lincoln at once took a very high position at the bar. He would never advocate a cause which he did not believe to be a just one, and no amount of odium or unpopularity could dissuade him from espousing a cause where he thought the right was with his client. Few lawyers were at that time willing to undertake the defense of any one who had helped a fugitive slave on his way to Canada. A man who was accused of that crime applied to one of the first lawyers in Springfield as his advocate. The lawyer declined, saying that he should imperil all his political prospects by undertaking the case. He then applied to an earnest antislavery man for advice. " Go," said he, " to Mr. Lincoln. He is not afraid of an unpopular cause. When I go for a lawyer to defend an arrested fugitive slave, other lawyers will refuse me; but if Mr. Lincoln is at home, he will always take my case."

Judge Caton said of him, " His mode of speaking was generally of a plain and unimpassioned character; and yet he was the author of some of the most beautiful and eloquent passages in our language, which, if collected, would form a valuable contribution to American literature."

Judge Breese, speaking of him after his death, said, " For my single self, I have, for a quarter of a century, regarded Mr. Lincoln as the finest lawyer I ever knew, and of a professional bearing so high-toned and honorable, as justly, and without derogating from the claims of others, entitling him to be presented to the profession as a model well worthy the closest imitation."

Judge Drummond's testimony is equally full and emphatic. He says, " With a voice by no means pleasant, and indeed, when excited, in its shrill tones sometimes almost disagreeable; without any of the personal graces of the orator; without much in the outward man indicating superiority of intellect; without quickness of perception, — still his mind was so vigorous, his comprehension so exact and clear, and his judgment so sure, that he easily mastered the intricacies of his profession, and became one of the ablest reasoners and most impressive speakers at our bar. With a probity of character known to all, with an intuitive insight into the human heart, with a clearness of statement which was itself an argument, with uncommon power and felicity of illustration, — often, it is true, of a plain and homely kind, — and with that sincerity and earnestness of manner which carried conviction, he was, perhaps, one of the most successful jury-lawyers we have ever had in the State. He always tried a case fairly and honestly. He never intentionally misrepresented the evidence of a witness or the argument of an opponent. He met both squarely, and if he could not explain the one, or answer the other, substantially admitted it. He never misstated the law according to his own intelligent view of it."

At one time Mr. Lincoln came very near being drawn into a duel very foolishly, but at the same time with a certain kind of characteristic magnanimity. A lady wrote a satirical poem in allusion to a young lawyer in Springfield, which some mischievous person took from her desk, and published in "The Journal." The lawyer, exasperated, called upon the editor, and demanded the name of the author. The editor was perplexed. It would seem ignoble to escape the responsibility by throwing it upon a lady. He consulted Mr. Lincoln, who was a personal friend of the lady. "Inform him," was the prompt reply, "that I assume the responsibility." A challenge was given and accepted. Mr. Lincoln chose broad-swords, intending to act simply on the defensive. Friends interposed; and the silly rencounter, which, had it resulted in the death of Mr. Lincoln, would have proved a great national calamity, was prevented.

In allusion to this event, Mr. Carpenter says, " Mr. Lincoln himself regarded the circumstance with much regret and mortification, and hoped it might be forgotten. In February preceding his death, a distinguished officer of the army called at the White House, and was entertained by the President and Mrs. Lincoln for an hour in the parlor. During the conversation, the gentleman said, turning to Mr. Lincoln, ' Is it true, Mr. President, as I have heard, that you once went out to fight a duel for the sake of the lady by your side?' 'I do not deny it,' replied Mr. Lincoln; ' but, if you desire my friendship, you will never mention the circumstance again.' "

In 1842 Mr. Lincoln married Miss Mary Todd, daughter of Hon. Robert S. Todd, of Lexington, Ky., who had resided several years in Springfield. During the great political contest of 1844 Mr. Lincoln earnestly espoused the cause of his political idol, Henry Clay. In the canvass he acquired much celebrity as an efficient speaker. His chagrin was intense that an intelligent people could prefer Mr. Polk to Mr. Clay. For a time he mistrusted the capacity of the people for self-government, and resolved to have no more to do with politics.

In 1846 Mr. Lincoln was nominated from the Sangamon District for Congress. He was elected by a very great majority, and in

25

December, 1847, took his seat in the thirtieth Congress. During the same session, Stephen A. Douglas took his seat in the Senate. Mr. Douglas was one of the champions of the Democratic party in the Senate. Mr. Lincoln was the warm advocate of Whig principles in the House. He was opposed to the Mexican war, as "unnecessarily and unconstitutionally begun by the President of the United States." A speech which he made on this subject was one of a very high order of ability. His clearness, directness, vigor of style, and oratorical impressiveness, are all remarkable. Speaking of President Polk's apologies for the war, he says, —

"I more than suspect that he is deeply conscious of being in the wrong; that he feels that the blood of this war, like the blood of Abel, is crying to Heaven against him; that he ordered General Taylor into the midst of a peaceful Mexican settlement, purposely to bring on a war; that originally having some strong motive, which I will not stop now to give my opinion concerning, to involve the two nations in a war, and trusting to escape scrutiny by the extreme brightness of military glory, — that attractive rainbow that rises in showers of blood, that serpent's eye that charms to destroy, — he plunged into it and swept on and on, till, disappointed in his calculations of the ease with which Mexico might be subdued, he now finds himself he knows not where."

War and victories were then something new to the American people. General Taylor was nominated in 1848 as the Whig candidate for the presidency. General Cass was the Democratic candidate. General Taylor had said, in accepting the nomination, —

"Upon the subject of the tariff, the currency, the improvement of our great highways, rivers, lakes, and harbors, the will of the people, as expressed through their representatives in Congress, ought to be respected and carried out by the executive."

Mr. Lincoln, pithily and approvingly commenting upon this, said, "The people say to General Taylor, 'If you are elected, shall we have a national bank?' He answers, 'Your will, gentlemen, not mine.' 'What about the tariff?' 'Say yourselves.' 'Shall our rivers and harbors be improved?' 'Just as you please. If you desire a bank, an alteration in the tariff, internal improvements, any or all, I will not hinder you; if you do not desire them, I will not attempt to force them on you. Send up your members to Congress from the various districts, with opinions according to your own; and if they are for these measures, or any of them, I shall have nothing to oppose; if they are not for them, I shall not, by any appliances whatever, attempt to dragoon them into their accomplishment.'

"In a certain sense," Mr. Lincoln continued, "and to a certain extent, the President is a representative of the people. He is elected by them as Congress is. But can he, in the nature of things, know the wants of the people as well as three hundred other men coming from all the various localities of the nation? If so, where is the propriety of having Congress?"

This was the platform upon which Mr. Lincoln ever stood. It was understood that General Taylor was opposed to the Mexican war. He certainly advocated an offensive instead of a defensive attitude. Mr. Lincoln cordially supported him in preference to General Cass, the Democratic candidate. He advocated the Wilmot Proviso, which excluded slavery from the Territories. He prepared a bill which declared that no person *hereafter born* in the District of Columbia should be held a slave, and which also encouraged emancipation. At the same time there is evidence that, while his sympathies were strongly against slavery, he still *then* thought that slaves were recognized as property under the Constitution. Still he *afterwards* denied, in a controversy with Douglas, that the " right of property in a slave is distinctly and expressly affirmed in the Constitution." At the close of his two years' term of service in Washington he returned to Springfield, and assiduously devoted himself to the duties of his profession. He was always ready to advocate the cause of the poor and the oppressed, however small the remuneration, or great the obloquy incurred. The fugitive slave never appealed to him in vain.

In 1854 the proslavery party secured the abrogation of the Missouri Compromise, and thus threw open the whole of the Northwest to the invasion of slavery. This outrage roused the indignation of Mr. Lincoln. He had long and anxiously watched the encroachments of slavery; and he now became convinced that there could be no cessation of the conflict until either slavery or freedom should gain the entire victory. Stephen A. Douglas, with whom Mr. Lincoln had long been more or less intimately associated, was responsible for the bill repealing the Missouri Compromise. It was regarded as his *bid* for Southern votes to secure the presidency.

Mr. Douglas was a man of great intellectual power, and of consummate tact and skill in debate. In October, 1854, he attended a state fair in Springfield, Ill., and addressed a vast assemblage in defense of the Kansas-Nebraska Bill as it was called. The next day Mr. Lincoln replied to him in a speech three hours in length. "The Springfield Republican," in its report, says, —

"He quivered with emotion. The whole house was still as death. He attacked the bill with unusual warmth and energy; and all felt that a man of strength was its enemy, and that he intended to blast it, if he could, by strong and manly efforts. He was most successful; and the house approved the glorious triumph of truth by long and loud continued huzzas. Women waved their handkerchiefs in token of woman's silent but heartfelt consent."

The fundamental principle of the Kansas-Nebraska Bill was, that the *white people* in the Territories had a right to decide whether or not they would enslave the *colored people*. Thus pithily Mr. Lincoln replied to it: —

"My distinguished friend says it is an insult to the emigrants to Kansas and Nebraska to suppose that they are not able to govern themselves. We must not slur over an argument of this kind because it happens to tickle the ear. It must be met and answered. I admit that the emigrant to Kansas and Nebraska is competent to govern *himself;* but I deny his right to *govern any other person without that person's consent.*"

It was the almost universal testimony, that, in this meeting at Springfield, Mr. Douglas was vanquished. Mr. Douglas went to Peoria. Mr. Lincoln followed him. The public excitement drew an immense crowd. Again these able and illustrious men met in the sternest conflict of argument. Mr. Lincoln's speech upon this occasion was fully reported. It was read with admiration all over the Union, and was generally considered an unanswerable refutation of the positions assumed by Mr. Douglas. One portion we will quote, since it has a direct bearing upon one of the questions now deeply exciting the public mind.

Mr. Douglas had assumed that it was a question of no importance whatever to the people of Illinois whether men were enslaved or not in the Territories. "I care not," he said, "whether slavery is voted up or voted down in Kansas."

Mr. Lincoln replied, "By the Constitution, each State has two las had thrown open the Northwest to the slave-power. It was capable of demonstration, that the Lecompton Constitution was not the act of the people of Kansas. Any thoughtful man could have been assured that it would not secure the support of the people of the United States. The Silliman Memorial, to which we have referred, was exerting a wide influence; and conscientious men of all parties were denouncing the fraud. Under these circumstances, Mr. Douglas abandoned the base forgery, and took his stand upon the platform of the Silliman Memorial. The Democratic State Convention of Illinois indorsed his position. Still, Mr. Douglas had not changed his fundamental position. He still advocated the opening of the Territory, which had been consecrated to freedom, to the entrance of slavery; and he still would allow the white inhabitants of the Territory, in their Constitution, to decide whether or not they would perpetuate the enslavement of the colored inhabitants. But he would not support the doings of an armed mob from Missouri, which had invaded Kansas, chosen a legislature, and framed a Constitution. Upon this point he broke away from Mr. Buchanan and his administration.

The Republicans of Illinois were not willing to send back to the Senate one who was the author of the Kansas-Nebraska Bill, but Mr. Douglas was the recognized leader of the Democratic party in Illinois, and they rallied around him. The Republican State Convention met at Springfield on the 16th of June, 1858. Nearly one thousand delegates were present. Mr. Lincoln was unanimously nominated for the Senate in opposition to Mr. Douglas. In the evening he addressed the convention at the State House. The following extracts will give some faint idea of this remarkable speech : —

" 'A house divided against itself cannot stand.' I believe that this government cannot endure permanently half-slave and half-free. I do not expect the Union to be dissolved, I do not expect the house to fall; but I do expect that it will cease to be divided. It will become all one thing, or all another. Either the opponents of slavery will arrest the further spread of it, and place it where the public mind shall rest in the belief that it is in the course of ultimate extinction, or its advocates will push it forward till it shall become alike lawful in all the States, old as well as new, North as well as South.

" In the notable argument of squatter sovereignty, otherwise called 'sacred right of self-government,' this latter phrase, though expressive of the only rightful basis of any government, is so perverted in this attempted use of it as to amount to just this, — that, if any one man choose to enslave another, no third man shall be allowed to object."

The campaign was now fairly opened. After one or two speeches, in which Mr. Douglas and Mr. Lincoln addressed the same audiences, but at different meetings, Mr. Lincoln, on the 24th of July, 1858, sent a proposition to Mr. Douglas that they should make arrangements to speak at the same meetings, dividing the time between them. The proposition was agreed to for seven towns. At the first, Mr. Douglas was to speak for an hour, and Mr. Lincoln for an hour and a half, then Mr. Douglas was to have the closing speech of half an hour. At the next the time occupied was to be reversed. Thus they were to alternate until the close.

The first meeting was at Ottawa. Twelve thousand citizens had assembled. Mr. Douglas had the opening speech. The friends of Mr. Lincoln were roused to the greatest enthusiasm by his triumphant reply upon this occasion, and they almost literally bore him from the stage upon their shoulders. Immense crowds attended every meeting. Both speeches were carefully reported. The whole nation looked on with interest. The Republican party were so well pleased with Mr. Lincoln's success, that they published in one pamphlet the speeches on both sides, and circulated them widely as a campaign document. The verdict of the nation has been that Mr. Lincoln was morally and intellectually the victor.

By an unfair apportionment of the legislative districts Mr. Lincoln was beaten in his contest for a seat in the Senate, but, very unexpectedly to himself, he won a far higher prize. Mr. Lincoln made about sixty speeches during the canvass. When asked how he felt after his defeat, he replied characteristically, " I felt like the boy who had stubbed his toe, — too badly to laugh, and too big to cry."

Mr. Lincoln was now a man of national fame. He was recognized as one of the ablest statesmen and one of the most eloquent men in the nation. He was a good writer, an able debater, a man of well-disciplined mind, and extensive attainments in political science. In years long since past he had helped to split rails to fence in a farm. Unwisely the Republican party introduced this statesman and orator, and man of noble character, to the country as the "rail-splitter."

"It took years," says Mr. Holland, in his admirable "Life of Abraham Lincoln," "for the country to learn that Mr. Lincoln was not a boor. It took them years to unlearn what an unwise and boyish introduction of a great man to the public had taught them. It took years for them to comprehend the fact, that, in Mr. Lincoln, the country had the wisest, truest, gentlest, noblest, most sagacious President who had occupied the chair of state since Washington retired from it."

He visited Kansas, where he was received with boundless enthusiasm. He visited Ohio, and crowds thronged to hear him. His renown was now such, that he was invited to address the citizens of New York at the Cooper Institute. The hall was crowded to its utmost capacity by the most distinguished men of that city of great names. Mr. Lincoln's address was a signal success. All were delighted. Round after round of applause greeted his telling periods. Mr. Bryant, in giving a report in "The Evening Post," said, "For the publication of such words of weight and wisdom as those of Mr. Lincoln, the pages of this journal are indefinitely elastic." The speech was published as a campaign document, and widely circulated. It might be called a scholarly performance. Its logic was faultless. In diction, it presented one of the finest specimens of pure Saxon English. Its illustrations and historic references indicated wide reading.

In New York everybody was charmed with the artlessness, frankness, intelligence, and lovely character of the man. Invitations to speak were crowded upon him. He addressed immense audiences at Hartford, New Haven, Meriden, and Norwich. It was unquestionably greatly through his influence that the State of Connecticut that year gave a Republican majority. The ability which he displayed was very remarkable. A distinguished clergyman said, "I learned more of the art of public speaking in listening to Mr. Lincoln's address last evening, than I could have learned from a whole course of lectures on rhetoric." A professor of rhetoric in Yale College took notes of his speech, and made them the subject of a lecture to his class the next day. He also followed Mr. Lincoln to his next appointment, that he might hear him again. "What was it?" inquired Mr. Lincoln of the Rev. Mr. Gulliver, who was complimenting him upon his speech, " which interested you so much?" The reply was, " It was the clearness of your reasoning, and especially your illustrations, which were romance and pathos, and fun and logic, all welded together."

Alluding to the threats of the proslavery men that they would break up the Union should slavery be excluded from the Territories, he said, —

" In that supposed event, you say you will destroy the Union; and then you say the great crime of having destroyed it will be upon us. That is cool. A highwayman holds a pistol to my ear, and mutters through his teeth, 'Stand and deliver, or I shall kill you, and then you will be a murderer!' To be sure, what the robber demands of me — my money — was my own, and I had a clear right to keep it; but it was no more my own than my vote is my own. And threat of death to me to extort my money, and threat of destruction to the Union to extort my vote, can scarcely be distinguished in principle."

In conversation with Rev. Mr. Gulliver at this time, Mr. Lincoln said, in reply to the question, " What has your education been?" " Well, as to education, the newspapers are correct. I never went to school more than six months in my life. I can say this, — that, among my earliest recollections, I remember how, when a mere child, I used to get irritated when anybody talked to me in a way I could not understand. I don't think I ever got angry at anything else in my life; but that always disturbed my temper, and has ever since. I can remember going to my little bedroom, after hearing the neighbors talk of an evening with my father, and spending no small part of the night walking up and down, and trying to make out what was the exact meaning of some of their, to me, dark sayings.

" I could not sleep, although I often tried to, when I got on such a hunt after an idea, until I had caught it: and, when I thought I had got it, I was not satisfied until I had repeated it over and over; until I had put it in language plain enough, as I thought, for any boy I knew to comprehend. This was a kind of passion with me, and it has stuck by me; for I am never easy now, when I am handling a thought, till I have bounded it north, and bounded it south, and bounded it east, and bounded it west.

" But your question reminds me of a bit of education which I am bound in honesty to mention. In the course of my law reading I constantly came upon the word *demonstrate*. I thought, at first, that I understood its meaning, but soon became satisfied that I did not. I said to myself, 'What do I mean when I *demonstrate*, more than when I *reason* or *prove?* How does *demonstration* differ from any other proof?' I consulted Webster's Dictionary. That told of 'certain proof,' 'proof beyond the possibility of doubt;' but I could form no sort of idea what sort of proof that was. I thought that a great many things were proved beyond the possibility of a doubt, without recourse to any such extraordinary process of reasoning as I understood *demonstration* to be.

"I consulted all the dictionaries and books of reference I could find, but with no better results. You might as well have defined *blue* to a blind man. At last, I said, 'Lincoln, you can never make a lawyer if you do not understand what *demonstrate* means;' and I left my situation in Springfield, went home to my father's house, and stayed there until I could give any proposition in the six books of Euclid at sight. I then found out what *demonstrate* means, and went back to my law studies."

The superintendent of the Five Points' Sabbath-school relates the following incident in reference to Mr. Lincoln during his visit to that city: "One Sunday morning I saw a tall, remarkable looking man enter the room, and take a seat among us. He listened with fixed attention to our exercises; and his countenance expressed such a genuine interest that I approached him, and suggested that he might be willing to say something to the children. He accepted the invitation with evident pleasure, and, coming forward, began a simple address, which at once fascinated every little hearer, and hushed the room into silence. His language was exceedingly beautiful, and his tones musical with intense feeling. The little faces would droop into sad conviction as he uttered sentences of warning, and would brighten into sunshine as he spoke cheerful words of promise. Once or twice he attempted to close his remarks; but the imperative shout of 'Go on! oh, do go on!' would compel him to resume. As I looked upon the gaunt and sinewy frame of the stranger, and marked his powerful head and determined features, now touched into softness by the impressions of the moment, I felt an irrepressible curiosity to learn something more about him; and, while he was quietly leaving the room, I begged to know his name. 'It is Abraham Lincoln, from Illinois.'"

The secessionists had now resolved, at all hazards, to break up the Union. The great object was to find a plausible excuse. The real reason was, that the free States were increasing so rapidly, both in number and population, that the slave States could no longer retain the direction of the government. They at that time had possession of the government, of the army, the navy, the treasury. They scattered the navy, dispersed the army, dismantled the forts and arsenals in the free States, accumulated arms and munitions of war in the slave States, and squandered the money in the treasury. They hoped thus to render the national government impotent.

They declared, that, should the Republican party nominate, and elect to the presidency, a man who was opposed to slavery, they would break up the Union. They then did everything in their power, in a treacherous and underhand way, to secure the election of a Republican President, that they might have this fancied excuse for their revolt. Future ages will scarcely credit these assertions; but no intelligent man at the present time will deny them.

In the spring of 1860 the Democratic party held its National Convention in Charleston, S. C., to nominate its candidate for the presidency. The proslavery men *bolted*, that they might break up the party, and thus secure the election of a Republican candidate. They succeeded. The regular Democratic Convention nominated Stephen A. Douglas. The secession party organized what they called a Constitutional Convention, and nominated John C. Breckenridge, one of the most radical of the proslavery men. A National Union Convention met, and nominated John Bell. This division rendered it almost certain that the Republican nominee, whoever he might be, would be elected. The secessionists were jovial, and pressed on in the preparation for decisive action.

The great Republican Convention met at Chicago on the 16th of June, 1860. The delegates and strangers who crowded the city amounted to twenty-five thousand. An immense building, called "The Wigwam," was reared to accommodate the Convention. There were eleven candidates for whom votes were thrown. William H. Seward, a man whose fame as a statesman had long filled the land, was the most prominent. It was generally supposed that he would be the nominee. On the first ballot Mr. Seward received one hundred and seventy-three and a half votes, and Abraham Lincoln one hundred and two. Nearly all the votes were now concentred upon these two candidates. Upon the second ballot Mr. Seward received one hundred and eighty-four and a half votes, and Mr. Lincoln one hundred and eighty-one. And now came the third ballot, which, it was very evident, would be decisive. Abraham Lincoln received two hundred and thirty-one and a half votes, lacking but one vote and a half of an election. Immediately one of the delegates from Ohio rose, and transferred the four votes of Ohio to Mr. Lincoln. This gave him the nomination. We cannot better describe the scene which ensued than in the language of Mr. Holland : —

" The excitement had culminated. After a moment's pause, like the sudden and breathless stillness that precedes the hurricane, the storm of wild, uncontrollable, and almost insane enthusiasm, descended. The scene surpassed description. During all the ballotings, a man had been standing upon the roof, communicating the results to the outsiders, who, in surging masses, far outnumbered those who were packed into the Wigwam. To this man one of the secretaries shouted, ' Fire the salute ! Abe Lincoln is nominated ! ' Then, as the cheering inside died away, the roar began on the outside, and swelled up from the excited masses, like the voice of many waters. This the insiders heard, and to it they replied. Thus deep called to deep with such a frenzy of sympathetic enthusiasm, that even the thundering salute of cannon was unheard by many on the platform."

When this burst of enthusiasm had expended itself, it was moved that the nomination should be unanimous ; and it was made so. Mr. Lincoln was at this time at Springfield, two hundred miles distant, anxiously awaiting the result of the ballotings. He was in the office of " The Springfield Journal," receiving the telegraphic dispatches. At last a messenger came in with a dispatch in his hand and announced, —

" The Convention has made a nomination, and Mr. Seward is — the second man on the list."

The joyful scene which ensued with Mr. Lincoln's friends must be imagined. When the excitement had a little subsided, he said, " There is a little woman on Eighth Street who has some interest in this matter ; " and, putting the telegram into his pocket, he walked home. Little did he then dream of the weary years of toil and care, and the bloody death, to which that telegram doomed him : and as little did he dream that he was to render services to his country which would fix upon him the eyes of the whole civilized world, and which would give him a place in the affections and reverence of his countrymen, second only, if second, to that of Washington.

The following day a committee of the Convention waited upon him with the announcement of his nomination. As it was known that they were to come, some of Mr. Lincoln's friends sent in several hampers of wine for their entertainment. But he was not only a temperance man, but a " total-abstinence " man. Resolved not to allow that new temptation to induce him to swerve from his principles, he returned the gift with kindest words of gratitude for the favor intended.

Mr. Lincoln received the delegation at the door of his house, and conducted them into his parlor. Governor Morgan of New York, in appropriate phrase, informed him that he had been unanimously nominated by the Convention to the office of President of the United States, and asked permission to report his acceptance. At the close of the ceremony, Mr. Lincoln said, in substance, —

" As a suitable conclusion of an interview so important, courtesy requires that I should treat the committee with something to drink." Then, stepping to the door, he called " Mary, Mary ! " A young girl responded to the call. He said a few words to her in a low tone of voice, and closed the door. In a few moments the girl entered, bringing a large waiter containing a pitcher and several tumblers, which she placed upon a centre-table. Mr. Lincoln then rose, and said, —

" Gentlemen, we must pledge our mutual healths in the most healthy beverage which God has given to man. It is the only beverage I have ever used or allowed in my family ; and I cannot conscientiously depart from it on this occasion. It is pure Adam's ale, from the spring."

Taking a tumbler he touched it to his lips ; and all his guests followed his example. The President subsequently related the following singular incident as having taken place at that time : —

" A very singular occurrence took place the day I was nominated at Chicago, of which I am reminded to-night. In the afternoon of the day, returning home from down town, I went upstairs to Mrs. Lincoln's sitting-room. Feeling somewhat tired, I lay down upon a couch in the room, directly opposite a bureau, upon which was a looking-glass. As I reclined, my eye fell upon the glass, and I saw distinctly *two* images of myself, exactly alike, except that one was a little paler than the other. I arose, and lay down again with the same result. It made me quite uncomfortable for a few moments; but, some friends coming in, the matter passed out of my mind.

"The next day, while walking in the street, I was suddenly reminded of the circumstance; and the disagreeable sensation produced by it returned. I determined to go home, and place myself in the same position; and, if the same effect was produced, I would make up my mind that it was the natural result of some principle of refraction or optics which I did not understand, and dismiss it. I tried the experiment with a like result; and, as I said to myself, accounting for it on some principle unknown to me, it ceased to trouble me.

"But, some time ago, I tried to produce the same effect *here* by arranging a glass and couch in the same position, without effect. My wife was somewhat worried about it. She thought it was a *sign* that I was to be elected to a second term of office, and that the paleness of one of the faces was an omen that I should not see life through the second term."

At the time of his nomination Mr. Lincoln was fifty-two years of age. There was then but little doubt that he would be elected. Crowds flocked to pay their homage to one, who, as President, would soon have so immense a patronage at his disposal. It became necessary that a room should be set apart in the State House for his receptions. From morning till night he was busy. In looking over a book which his friends had prepared, and which contained the result of a careful canvass of the city of Springfield, showing how each man would vote, he was surprised and greatly grieved to find that most of the ministers were against him. As he closed the book, he said sadly, —

"Here are twenty-three ministers of different denominations, and all of them are against me but three. Mr. Bateman, I am not a Christian; God knows, I would be one: but I have carefully read the Bible, and I do not so understand this book. These men well know that I am for freedom in the Territories, freedom everywhere as far as the Constitution and laws will permit; and that my opponents are for slavery. They know this; and yet with this book in their hands, in the light of which human bondage cannot live a moment, they are going to vote against me. I do not understand this."

Then, after a moment's pause, he added, "Does n't it appear strange that men can ignore the moral aspects of this contest? A revelation could not make it plainer to me that slavery or the government must be destroyed. It seems as if God had borne with this slavery until the very teachers of religion have come to defend it from the Bible, and to claim for it a divine character and sanction; and now the cup of iniquity is full, and the vials of wrath will be poured out."

The election day came. Mr. Lincoln received a hundred and eighty electoral votes; Mr. Douglas, twelve; Mr. Breckenridge, seventy-two; Mr. Bell, thirty-nine. The result of the election was known early in November. Nearly four months would transpire before the 4th of March, 1861, when he was to enter upon his term of office.

The spirit manifested by the slaveholders on this occasion is fairly developed in the following article contained in "The Richmond Examiner" of April 23, 1861: —

"The capture of Washington City is perfectly within the power of Virginia and Maryland, if Virginia will only make the effort by her constituted authorities; nor is there a single moment to lose. The entire population pant for the onset. There never was half the unanimity among the people before, nor a tithe of the zeal upon any subject, that is now manifested to take Washington, and drive from it every black Republican who is a dweller there.

"From the mountain-tops and valleys to the shores of the sea, there is one wild shout of fierce resolve to capture Washington City at all and every human hazard. That filthy cage of unclean birds must and will assuredly be purified by fire. The people are determined upon it, and are clamorous for a leader to conduct them to the onslaught. The leader will assuredly arise; ay, and that right speedily.

"It is not to be endured that this flight of abolition harpies shall come down from the black North for their roosts in the heart of the South, to defile and brutalize the land. They come as our enemies. They act as our most deadly foes. They promise us bloodshed and fire; and that is the only promise they have ever redeemed. The fanatical yell for the immediate subjugation of the whole South is going up hourly from the united voices of all the North; and, for the purpose of making their work sure, they have determined to hold Washington City as the point whence to carry on their brutal warfare.

"Our people can take it; they *will* take it; and Scott the arch-traitor, and Lincoln the beast, combined, cannot prevent it. The just indignation of an outraged and deeply-injured people will teach the Illinois ape to repeat his race, and retrace his journey across the border of the free negro States still more rapidly than he came; and Scott the traitor will be given the opportunity at the same time to try the difference between 'Scott's Tactics' and the 'Shanghae Drill' for quick movements.

"Great cleansing and purification are needed, and will be given to that festering sink of iniquity, that wallow of Lincoln and Scott, — the desecrated city of Washington; and many indeed will be the carcasses of dogs and caitiffs that will blacken the air upon the gallows before the great work is accomplished. So let it be!"

One naturally pauses to inquire the cause of all this wrath; and no one can refrain from being amused to find that it was simply that a majority of the nation were opposed to the extension of slavery into the Territories, and that that majority had constitutionally elected as President one of the best and most eminent men in the nation, who was pledged to oppose, so far as he constitutionally could, slavery extension. Again and again Mr. Lincoln had declared, and so had the party which elected him, that he had no right to interfere with slavery in the States; that the compromises of the Constitution left that question with each State; and that he had no power to touch the domestic institutions of the States, except as a war-measure, in the case of war, to save the nation from ruin.

On Mr. Lincoln's journey to Washington he made numerous addresses to the multitudes who thronged to greet him. At Cincinnati a large number of Kentuckians were present. He said to them in a playful way, —

"You perhaps want to know what we will do with you. I will tell you, so far as I am authorized to speak. We mean to treat you, as near as we possibly can, as Washington, Jefferson, and Madison treated you. We mean to leave you alone, and in no way to interfere with your institutions; to abide by all and every compromise of the Constitution; in a word, coming back to the original propo-

26

sition, to treat you, as far as degenerate men (if we have degenerated) may, according to the examples of those noble fathers, Washington, Jefferson, and Madison. We mean to remember that you are as good as we; that there is no difference between us other than the difference of circumstances. We mean to recognize and bear in mind always that you have as good hearts in your bosoms as other people, or as good as we claim to have; and treat you accordingly."

At Buffalo he said, "Your worthy mayor has thought fit to express the hope that I shall be able to relieve the country from the present, or, I should say, the threatened difficulties. I am sure that I bring a heart true to the work. For the ability to perform it, I trust in that Supreme Being who has never forsaken this favored land. Without that assistance I shall surely fail; with it, I cannot fail."

At Philadelphia, where he was received with the greatest enthusiasm, he gave utterance to the following noble sentiments: "I have often inquired of myself what great principle or idea it was that kept this confederacy so long together. It was not the mere matter of the separation of the colonies from the mother-land, but that sentiment in the Declaration of Independence which gave liberty, not alone to the people of this country, but, I hope, to the world for all future time. It was that which gave promise that in due time the weight would be lifted from the shoulders of all men. This was a sentiment embodied in the Declaration of Independence. Now, my friends, can this country be saved on this basis? If it can, I shall consider myself one of the happiest men in the world if I can help save it; if it cannot be saved on that principle, it will be truly awful. But if this country cannot be saved without giving up that principle, I was about to say I would rather be assassinated upon this spot than surrender it. Now, in my view of the present aspect of affairs, there need be no bloodshed or war. There is no necessity for it. I am not in favor of such a course; and I may say in advance, that there will be no bloodshed unless it be forced upon the government, and then it will be compelled to act in self-defense."

At Harrisburg, where there was a large military display, he remarked, "While I am exceedingly gratified to see the manifestation in your streets of the military force here, and exceedingly gratified at your promise here to use that force upon a proper emergency, I desire to repeat, to preclude any possible misconstruction, that I do most sincerely hope that we shall have no use for them ; that it will never become their duty to shed blood, and most especially never to shed fraternal blood. I promise, that so far as I may have wisdom to direct, if so painful a result shall in any wise be brought about, it shall be through no fault of mine."

In South Carolina, four days after the election, a bill was introduced into the Legislature calling out ten thousand volunteers, her two senators in Congress resigned their seats, and a convention was called to pass an act of secession. The rebels had made their preparations for vigorous action. They had nothing to fear from Mr. Buchanan, and their object was to get their strength consolidated before Mr. Lincoln should come into power.

On the 27th of December, 1860, Fort Moultrie and Castle Pinckney were seized, and the revenue-cutter William Aikin taken possession of at Charleston. Three days after the arsenal was seized. On the 2d of January, 1861, Fort Macon in North Carolina, and the arsenal at Fayetteville, fell into the hands of the rebels. On the 3d an armed mob from Georgia took possession of Forts Pulaski and Jackson, and the arsenal at Savannah. The next day, the 4th, Fort Morgan and the arsenal at Mobile were seized by a band of Alabamians. On the 8th Forts Johnson and Caswell, at Smithville, N. C., were captured without a struggle by the rebels. The next day, the 9th, The Star of the West, an unarmed steamer bearing supplies to the garrison in Fort Sumter, was fired upon by a rebel battery and driven back. On the 12th Fort M'Rae, Fort Barrancas, and the navy-yard at Pensacola, in Florida, were taken possession of by the rebels. The day before armed gangs in Louisiana seized Forts Pike, St. Philip, and Jackson, and the arsenal at Baton Rouge.

These United States forts had cost the national government $5,947,000, were pierced for 1,091 guns, and adapted for a war garrison of 5,430 men. Mr. Buchanan did not lift a finger to arrest or to resent these outrages.

On the 17th of December the convention in South Carolina declared the Union dissolved, and that South Carolina was a free, sovereign, and independent State. This act was speedily imitated by several other slave States. The rapidly-recurring scenes of these days of darkness and gloom we have not space here to describe. The air was filled with rumors that President Lincoln was to be assassinated on his journey to Washington. In taking leave of his friends at the depot in Springfield, he said, in a speech full of tenderness and pathos, —

"My friends, no one not in my position can appreciate the sadness I feel at this parting. I know not how soon I shall see you again. A duty devolves upon me which is perhaps greater than that which has devolved upon any other man since the days of Washington. He never would have succeeded except for the aid of Divine Providence, upon which he at all times relied. I feel that I cannot succeed without the same divine aid which sustained him. In the same Almighty Being I place my reliance for support, and I hope that my friends will all pray that I may receive that divine assistance, without which I cannot succeed, but with which success is certain. Again I bid you all an affectionate farewell."

In every city through which he passed he was greeted with enthusiasm perhaps never before equaled in the United States. It was evident, however, that the secessionists were seeking his life. At one time an attempt was made to throw the train off the track. At Cincinnati a hand-grenade was found concealed upon the train. A gang in Baltimore had arranged, upon his arrival, to "get up a row," and, in the confusion, to make sure of his death with revolvers and hand-grenades. A detective unraveled the plot. A secret and special train was provided to take him from Harrisburg, through Baltimore, at an unexpected hour of the night. The train started at half-past ten, and, to prevent any possible communication on the part of the secessionists with their confederate gang in Baltimore, as soon as the train had started the telegraph wires were cut.

Mr. Lincoln took a sleeping-car and passed directly through Baltimore to Washington, where he arrived at half-past six o'clock in the morning. His safe arrival was immediately telegraphed over the country. Great anxiety was felt in reference to the inauguration-day. Washington was full of traitors. Slavery had so debauched the conscience in the slaveholding States, that the assassination of a man who did not believe in slavery was scarce deemed a crime.

The week of the inauguration was one of the greatest peril and anxiety the nation had ever experienced. The air was filled with rumors of conspiracies. It was well known that there were thousands of desperate men resolved by tumult and murder to prevent the inauguration, and then to seize the capital. Multitudes of strange-looking men thronged the streets of Washington, armed with bowie-knives and revolvers.

The morning of the 4th of March dawned serene and beautiful. Even at an early hour Pennsylvania Avenue presented such a mass of human beings as had never crowded it before. At nine o'clock, the procession moved from the White House. It was very imposing. A triumphal car, magnificently draped, emblematic of the Constitution, bore thirty-four very beautiful young girls, picturesquely dressed, as representatives of the several States ; none being recognized as having seceded.

Mr. Buchanan and Mr. Lincoln rode side by side in the same carriage. They ascended the long flight of steps of the Capitol arm-in-arm. It was observed that Mr. Buchanan looked pale and anxious, and that he was nervously excited. Mr. Lincoln's face was slightly flushed, his lips compressed ; and his countenance wore an expression of great firmness and seriousness. General Scott, in his Autobiography, says, —

" The inauguration of President Lincoln was perhaps the most critical and hazardous event with which I have ever been connected. In the preceding two months I had received more than fifty letters, many from points distant from each other, some earnestly dissuading me from being present at the event, and others distinctly threatening assassination if I dared to protect the ceremony by military force."

But for the formidable military display, there would unquestionably have been tumult and assassination. General Scott called out the Washington Volunteers ; brought from a distance two batteries of horse-artillery, with detachments of cavalry and infantry, all regulars. The volunteers escorted the President, while the regulars flanked the movement, marching in parallel streets. A fine company of sappers and miners led the advance. It was under this imposing array of cannon and bayonets that it was necessary to conduct the legally-chosen President of the United States to his inauguration.

Mr. Lincoln took his stand upon the platform of the eastern portico of the Capitol. Thirty thousand persons stood before him. There were many sharpshooters, who, from the distance of nearly a mile, could throw a bullet into his heart. It is hardly too much to say, that the *nation* trembled.   Mr. Lincoln unrolled a manuscript, and in a clear voice, which seemed to penetrate with its distinct articulation the remotest ear, read his inaugural.   We have not space for the whole of this noble document.

"Apprehension," said he, " seems to exist among the people of the Southern States, that, by the accession of a Republican administration, their property and their peace and personal security are to be endangered.   There has never been any reasonable cause for such apprehension.   Indeed, the most ample evidence to the contrary has all the while existed, and been open to their inspection. It is found in nearly all the published speeches of him who now addresses you.   I do but quote from one of those speeches, when I declare that I have no purpose, directly or indirectly, to interfere with the institution of slavery in the States where it exists.   I believe I have no lawful right to do so ; and I have no inclination to do so. Those who nominated and elected me did so with the full knowledge that I had made this and made many similar declarations, and had never recanted them ; and, more than this, they placed in the platform, for my acceptance, and as a law to themselves and to me, the clear and emphatic resolution which I now read : —

" ' *Resolved*, That the maintenance inviolate of the rights of the States, and especially the right of each State to order and control its own domestic institutions according to its own judgment exclusively, is essential to that balance of power on which the perfection and endurance of our political fabric depend ; and we denounce the lawless invasion by armed force of the soil of any State or Territory, no matter under what pretext, as among the gravest of crimes.'

" I now reiterate these sentiments ; and, in doing so, I only press upon the public attention the most conclusive evidence of which the case is susceptible, that the property, peace, and security of no section are to be in any wise endangered by the now incoming administration.

" I add, too, that all the protection which, consistently with the Constitution and the laws, can be given, will be cheerfully given to all the States, when lawfully demanded, for whatever cause, as cheerfully to one section as to another.

" A disruption of the Federal Union, heretofore only menaced, is now formidably attempted.   I hold, that, in the contemplation of universal law and of the Constitution, the union of these States is perpetual. Perpetuity is implied, if not expressed, in the fundamental law of all national governments. It is safe to assert, that no government proper ever had a provision in its organic law for its own termination. Continue to execute all the express provisions of our national Constitution, and the Union will endure forever; it being impossible to destroy it, except by some action not provided for in the instrument itself.

"Again: if the United States be not a government proper, but an association of States in the nature of a contract merely, can it, as a contract, be peaceably unmade by less than all the parties who made it? One party to a contract may violate it, — break it, so to speak; but does it not require all to lawfully rescind it? Descending from these general principles, we find the proposition, that, in legal contemplation, the Union is perpetual, confirmed by the history of the Union itself.

"The Union is much older than the Constitution. It was formed, in fact, by the articles of association, in 1774. It was matured and continued in the Declaration of Independence, in 1776. It was further matured, and the faith of all the then thirteen States expressly plighted and engaged that it should be perpetual, by the articles of the confederation, in 1778; and finally, in 1787, one of the declared objects for ordaining and establishing the Constitution was to form a more perfect union. But, if the destruction of the Union by one or by a part only of the States be lawfully possible, the Union is less perfect than before; the Constitution having lost the vital element of perpetuity.

"It follows from these views, that no State, upon its own mere motion, can lawfully get out of the Union; that resolves and ordinances to that effect are legally void; and that acts of violence within any State or States, against the authority of the United States, are insurrectionary or revolutionary, according to circumstances.

"I therefore consider, that, in view of the Constitution and the laws, the Union is unbroken; and, to the extent of my ability, I shall take care, as the Constitution itself expressly enjoins upon me, that the laws of the Union shall be faithfully executed in all the States. Doing this, which I deem to be only a simple duty on my part, I shall perfectly perform it, so far as is practicable, unless my rightful masters, the American people, shall withhold the requisition, or in some authoritative manner direct the contrary.

"I trust this will not be regarded as a menace, but only as the declared purpose of the Union, that it will constitutionally defend and maintain itself.

"The power confided to me will be used to hold, occupy, and possess the property and places belonging to the government, and collect the duties and imposts; but, beyond what may be necessary for these objects, there will be no invasion, no using of force against or among the people anywhere.

"All the vital rights of minorities and of individuals are so plainly assured to them by affirmations and negations, guaranties and prohibitions, in the Constitution, that controversies never arise concerning them, but no organic law can ever be framed with a provision specifically applicable to every question which may occur in practical administration. No foresight can anticipate, nor any document of reasonable length contain, express provisions for all possible questions. Shall fugitives from labor be surrendered by national, or by state authorities? The Constitution does not expressly say. Must Congress protect slavery in the Territories? The Constitution does not expressly say. From questions of this class spring all our constitutional controversies, and we divide upon them into majorities and minorities.

"If the minority will not acquiesce, the majority must, or the government must cease. There is no alternative for continuing the government but acquiescence on the one side or the other. If a minority in such a case will secede rather than acquiesce, they make a precedent, which, in turn, will ruin and divide them; for a minority of their own will secede from them whenever a majority refuses to be controlled by such a minority: for instance, why not any portion of a new confederacy, a year or two hence, arbitrarily secede again, precisely as portions of the present Union now claim to secede from it? All who cherish disunion sentiments are now being educated to the exact temper of doing this. Is there such perfect identity of interests among the states to compose a new Union as to produce harmony only, and prevent secession? Plainly the central idea of secession is the essence of anarchy.

"One section of our country believes slavery is right, and ought to be extended; while the other believes it is wrong, and ought not to be extended. And this is the only substantial dispute. Physically speaking, we cannot separate; we cannot remove our respective sections from each other, nor build an impassable wall between them. A husband and wife may be divorced, and go out of the presence and beyond the reach of each other ; but the different parts of our country cannot do this. They cannot but remain face to face ; and intercourse, either amicable or hostile, must continue between them. Is it possible, then, to make that intercourse more advantageous or more satisfactory after separation than before ? Can aliens make treaties easier than friends can make laws? Can treaties be more faithfully enforced between aliens than laws can among friends? Suppose you go to war, you cannot fight always ; and when, after much loss on both sides, and no gain on either, you cease fighting, the identical questions as to terms of intercourse are again upon you.

" This country, with its institutions, belongs to the people who inhabit it. Whenever they shall grow weary of the existing government, they can exercise their constitutional right of amending, or their revolutionary right to dismember or overthrow it. I cannot be ignorant of the fact that many worthy and patriotic citizens are desirous of having the national Constitution amended. While I make no recommendation of amendment, I fully recognize the full authority of the people over the whole subject, to be exercised in either of the modes prescribed in the instrument itself; and I should, under existing circumstances, favor rather than oppose a fair opportunity being afforded the people to act upon it.

" My countrymen, one and all, think calmly and well upon this whole subject. Nothing valuable can be lost by taking time.

" If there be an object to hurry any of you in hot haste to a step which you would never take deliberately, that object will be frustrated by taking time ; but no good object can be frustrated by it.

" Such of you as are now dissatisfied still have the old Constitution unimpaired, and, on the sensitive point, the laws of your own framing under it ; while the new administration will have no immediate power, if it would, to change either.

" If it were admitted that you who are dissatisfied hold the right side in the dispute, there is still no single reason for precipitate action. Intelligence, patriotism, Christianity, and a firm reliance on Him who has never yet forsaken this favored land, are still competent to adjust, in the best way, all our present difficulties.

" In your hands, my dissatisfied fellow-countrymen, and not in mine, is the momentous issue of civil war. The government will not assail you.

" You can have no conflict without being yourselves the aggressors. You have no oath registered in heaven to destroy the government ; while I shall have the most solemn one to ' preserve, protect, and defend ' it.

" I am loath to close. We are not enemies, but friends. We must not be enemies. Though passion may have strained, it must not break, our bonds of affection.

" The mystic cords of memory, stretching from every battlefield and patriot grave to every living heart and hearthstone all over this broad land, will yet swell the chorus of the Union, when again touched, as surely they will be, by the better angels of our nature."

At the close of this solemn and imposing scene, Mr. Lincoln was escorted back to the White House, where Mr. Buchanan took leave of him. He was asked if he felt alarmed at any time while reading his address. His reply was, that he had often experienced greater fear in speaking to a dozen Western men on the subject of temperance.

And now commenced his life of care and toil and sorrow, to terminate in a bloody death. Mr. Lincoln's conciliatory words had no softening influence upon the hearts of the secessionists. They knew that it was only by violence and revolution that they could so strengthen the institution of slavery as to make it permanent upon this continent ; and they still believed that the North would yield to their demands, rather than appeal to the dreadful arbitrament of the sword. " The Yankees," said one of their speakers, " are a cowardly race, and I will pledge myself to hold in the hollow of my hand and to drink every drop of blood that will be shed."

The demon of rebellion was unappeased. Treason was everywhere. Openly avowed traitors to the Union were in every department of the government. No step could be taken, and there could be no deliberation, which was not immediately reported to the rebels. Seven States were now in revolt. There were seven other slave States, which it was absolutely necessary the secessionists should secure in order to have any chance of success. On the 12th of April the rebels in Charleston opened fire upon Fort Sumter. This introduced the war.

The rebels were so infatuated as to anticipate an easy victory.

They had already inaugurated their government at Montgomery. Elated with the news of the bombardment and capture of Fort Sumter, Mr. Walker, the rebel Secretary of War, addressing the shouting throng, said, —

" No man can tell where this war, commenced this day, will end; but I will prophesy that the flag which now flaunts the breeze here will float over the dome of the old Capitol at Washington before the 1st of May. Let them try Southern chivalry, and test the extent of Southern resources, and it may float eventually over Faneuil Hall itself."

With wonderful unanimity, the North rallied around the imperiled flag of the nation. The rebels crushed out all opposition to secession within their borders, and forced every available man into the ranks. Mr. Lincoln, three days after the capture of Sumter, issued a proclamation calling for seventy-five thousand troops to defend the national capital, which the rebels threatened to seize; and soon after he declared the ports in the rebellious States under blockade.

In an evil hour Virginia joined the rebels. Terrible was her punishment. Mr. Douglas nobly came forward, and gave all of his strong influence to Mr. Lincoln. As he read the President's proclamation calling for seventy-five thousand men, he said, —

" Mr. President, I cordially concur in every word of that document, except that, in the call for seventy-five thousand men, I would make it two hundred thousand. You do not know the dishonest purposes of those men as well as I do."

"On the 1st of May Senator Douglas addressed an immense gathering in the city of Chicago. Ten thousand persons thronged the Wigwam. The eloquent senator spoke in strains which thrilled the heart of the nation. " I beg you to believe," said he, " that I will not do you or myself the injustice to think that this magnificent ovation is personal to myself. I rejoice to know that it expresses your devotion to the Constitution, the Union, and the flag of our country. I will not conceal my gratification at the incontrovertible test this vast audience presents, — that whatever political differences or party questions may have divided us, yet you all had a conviction, that, when the country should be in danger, my loyalty could be relied on. That the present danger is imminent, no man can conceal. If war must come, if the bayonet must be used to maintain the Constitution, I say before God, my conscience is clean. I have struggled long for a peaceful solution of the difficulty. I have not only tendered those States what was their right, but I have gone to the very extreme of magnanimity.

" The return we receive is war, armies marched upon our capital, obstruction and danger to our navigation, letters of marque to invite pirates to prey upon our commerce, and a concerted movement to blot out the United States of America from the map of the globe. The question is, ' Are we to maintain the country of our fathers, or allow it to be stricken down by those, who, when they can no longer govern, threaten to destroy ? '

" What cause, what excuse, do disunionists give us for breaking up the best government on which the sun of heaven ever shed its rays ? They are dissatisfied with the result of the presidential election. Did they never get beaten before ? Are we to resort to the sword when we get beaten at the ballot-box ? I understand it that the voice of the people, expressed in the mode appointed by the Constitution, must command the obedience of every citizen. They assume, on the election of a particular candidate, that their rights are not safe in the Union. What evidence do they present of this ? I defy any man to show any act on which it is based. What act has been omitted to be done ? I appeal to these assembled thousands, that, so far as the constitutional rights of slave-holders are concerned, nothing has been done, and nothing omitted, of which they can complain.

" There has never been a time, from the day that Washington was inaugurated first President of these United States, when the rights of the Southern States stood firmer under the laws of the land than they do now ; there never was a time when they had not as good cause for disunion as they have to-day. What good cause have they now, which has not existed under every administration ?

" If they say the territorial question, now, for the first time, there is no act of Congress prohibiting slavery anywhere. If it be the non-enforcement of the laws, the only complaints I have heard have been of the too vigorous and faithful fulfillment of the fugitive-slave law. Then what reason have they ? The slavery question is a mere excuse. The election of Lincoln is a mere pretext. The present secession movement is the result of an enormous conspiracy formed more than a year since, formed by leaders in the Southern Confederacy more than twelve mouths ago.

" But this is no time for the detail of causes. The conspiracy is now known. Armies have been raised, war is levied, to accomplish it. There are only two sides to the question. Every man must be for the United States or against it. There can be no neutrals in this war, only *patriots* or *traitors*."

We have no space here to enter into the details of the war which ensued, which cost half a million of lives, and an expenditure of treasure and a destruction of property which cannot be computed. On the 6th of March, 1862, Mr. Lincoln recommended that the United States should coöperate with any State " which may gradually adopt abolishment of slavery, by giving to such State pecuniary aid, to be used at its discretion to compensate for inconveniences, public and private, produced by such changes of system."

The rebels were continually cheered by the hope that all the border States would join them. Mr. Lincoln invited the representatives of those States to a conference with him, in which he said to them, urging them to accept emancipation with compensation, —

" Let the States which are in rebellion see definitely and certainly, that in no event will the States you represent ever join their proposed confederacy, and they cannot much longer maintain the contest. Can you, for your States, do better than take the course I urge ? The incidents of war cannot be avoided. If the war continue long the institution in your States will be extinguished by mere friction and abrasion. It will be gone, and you will have nothing valuable in lieu of it. Much of its value is gone already. How much better for you and your people to take the step which at once shortens the war, and secures substantial compensation for that which is sure to be wholly lost in any other event ! How much better thus to save the money, which else we sink forever in the war ! "

The border-state men were blind and obdurate. Two acts, by Mr. Lincoln's recommendation, were soon passed by Congress. One confiscated the slaves of masters who were in open rebellion ; the other abolished slavery in the District of Columbia.

He was urged to issue a proclamation of emancipation before, in his judgment, the country was prepared for it. He replied, " I do not want to issue a document that the whole world will see must necessarily be inoperative, like the Pope's bull against the comet."

At length he judged that the hour for decisive action had come, and on Monday, September 22, 1862, Mr. Lincoln issued his renowned proclamation, declaring that on the 1st of January, 1863, all the slaves in States then continuing in rebellion should be free.

In cabinet meeting he said to Mr. Chase, " I made a solemn vow before God, that if General Lee should be driven back from Pennsylvania I would crown the result by the declaration of freedom to the slaves."

The excitement which this proclamation created was intense, many applauding, many condemning. In a brief address which he soon made he said, " What I did, I did after a very full deliberation, and under a heavy and solemn sense of responsibility. I can only trust in God that I have made no mistake." Two years after he was enabled to say, " As affairs have turned, it is the central act of my administration, and the great event of the nineteenth century."

President Lincoln gives the following account of the drafting of the proclamation, and the discussion in the Cabinet respecting it : —

" It had got to be midsummer, 1862. Things had gone on from bad to worse, until I felt that we had reached the end of our rope on the plan of operations we had been pursuing, that we had about played our last card, and must change our tactics or lose the game. I now determined upon the adoption of the emancipation policy, and, without consultation with or the knowledge of the Cabinet, I prepared the original draft of the proclamation, and, after much anxious thought, called a cabinet meeting upon the subject. This was the last of July, or the first part of the month of August, 1862.

" This cabinet meeting took place, I think, upon a Saturday. All were present except Mr. Blair, the Postmaster-General, who was absent at the opening of the discussion, but came in subsequently. I said to the Cabinet that I had resolved upon this step, and had not called them together to ask their advice, but to lay the subject-matter of a proclamation before them, suggestions as to which would be in order after they had heard it read.

" Various suggestions were offered. Secretary Chase wished the language stronger in reference to the arming of the blacks. Mr. Blair, after he came in, deprecated the policy, on the ground that it would cost the administration the fall elections. Nothing, however, was offered that I had not already fully anticipated, and settled in my own mind, until Secretary Seward spoke. He said in substance, —

" ' Mr. President, I approve of the proclamation ; but I question the expediency of its issue at this juncture. The depression of the public mind, consequent upon our repeated reverses, is so great, that I fear the effect of so important a step. It may be viewed as the last measure of an exhausted government, — a cry for help ; the government stretching forth her hands to Ethiopia, instead of Ethiopia stretching forth her hands to the government.'

" His idea was," said Mr. Lincoln, " that it would be considered our last shriek on the retreat. ' Now,' continued Mr. Seward, ' while I approve the measure, I suggest, sir, that you postpone its issue until you can give it to the country supported by military success, instead of issuing it, as would be the case now, upon the greatest disasters of the war.'

" The wisdom of the view of the Secretary of State struck me with great force. It was an aspect of the case, that, in all my thought upon the subject, I had entirely overlooked. The result was, that I put the draft of the proclamation aside, waiting for a victory. From time to time, I added or changed a line, touching it up here and there, anxiously watching the progress of events. Well, the next news we had was of Pope's disaster at Bull Run. Things looked darker than ever. Finally came the week of the battle of Antietam. I determined to wait no longer. The news came, I think, on Wednesday, that the advantage was on our side. I was then staying at the Soldiers' Home, three miles out of Washington. Here I finished writing the second draft of the preliminary proclamation ; came up on Saturday ; called the Cabinet together to hear it ; and it was published the following Monday."

At this final meeting, which took place on the 20th of September, as Mr. Lincoln read the words, " And the executive government of the United States, including the military and naval authority thereof, will *recognize* the freedom of such persons," Mr. Seward interrupted him, saying, —

" I think, Mr. President, that you should insert after the word *recognize*, in that sentence, the words *and maintain*."

The President replied, that he had already considered the import of that expression in that connection, but that he had refrained from inserting it, as he did not like to promise that which he was not *sure* that he could perform. " But Mr. Seward," said the President, " insisted ; and the words went in." It so happened that there were just one hundred days between the preliminary proclamation which was issued on the 22d of September, 1862, and the final proclamation which consummated the act of emancipation.

On the 1st of January, 1863, the final proclamation was issued. In his preamble, he alluded to his previous proclamation of promise, and then said, " Now, therefore, I, Abraham Lincoln, President of the United States, by virtue of the power in me invested as commander-in-chief of the army and navy of the United States, in time of actual armed rebellion against the authority and government of the United States, and as a fit and necessary war measure for suppressing said rebellion, do, on this first day of January, in the year of our Lord one thousand eight hundred and sixty-three, and in accordance with my purpose so to do, publicly proclaimed for the full period of one hundred days from the day first above mentioned, order and designate as the States, and parts of States, wherein the people thereof respectively are this day in rebellion against the United States, the following; to wit."

Then follows a list of the States in rebellion. "And by virtue of the power, and for the purpose aforesaid, I do order and declare, that all persons held as slaves within said designated States, and parts of States, are, and henceforth shall be, free; and that the executive government of the United States, including the military and naval authorities thereof, will recognize and maintain the freedom of said persons."

The proclamation is concluded with the following words : "And upon this act, sincerely believed to be an act of justice warranted by the Constitution, upon military necessity, I invoke the considerate judgment of mankind, and the gracious favor of Almighty God."

Of this proclamation "The London Spectator" says, "We cannot read it without a renewed conviction that it is the noblest political document known to history, and should have for the nation, and the statesmen he left behind him, something of a sacred and almost prophetic character. Surely none was ever written under a stronger sense of the reality of God's government; and certainly none written in a period of passionate conflict ever so completely excluded the partiality of victorious faction, and breathed so pure a strain of mingled justice and mercy."

The country abounded with spies and informers ; and, as another measure of military necessity, the writ of *habeas corpus* was suspended. The President issued a circular letter to the army, urging the observance of the Lord's Day, and reverence for the name of God, Sunday desecration and profanity are ever two great evils in an army.

At one time twenty-four deserters were sentenced by court-martial to be shot. Mr. Lincoln refused to sign the warrants for their execution. An officer said to him, " Mr. President, unless these men are made an example of, the army itself is in danger. Mercy to the few is cruelty to the many." Mr. Lincoln replied, " Mr. General, there are already too many weeping widows in the United States. Don't ask me to add to their number, for I will not do it."

A petition was brought to him to pardon a man who had been convicted of being engaged in the slave-trade. He read it carefully, and then said to the one who brought the petition, —

" My friend, that is a very touching appeal to our feelings. You know my weakness is to be, if possible, too easily moved by appeals to mercy. If this man were guilty of the foulest murder that the arm of man could perpetrate, I could forgive him on such an appeal; but the man who could go to Africa and rob her of her children and sell them into interminable bondage, with no other motive than that which is furnished by dollars and cents, is so much worse than the most depraved murderer, that he can never receive pardon at my hands."

A lady, the wife of a captured rebel officer, came to Mr. Lincoln and pleaded tearfully for the release of her husband. In her plea, gushing from a woman's loving heart, she urged that her husband was a very religious man. Mr. Lincoln's feelings were so moved by the grief of the wife, that he released the rebel. He, however, remarked, —

" You say that your husband is a religious man. Tell him that I say that I am not much of a judge of religion; but that, in my opinion, the religion that sets men to rebel and fight against their government because, as they think, that government does not sufficiently help some men to eat their bread in the sweat of other men's faces, is not the sort of religion upon which men can get to heaven."

The fearful trials of his office developed very rapidly Mr. Lincoln's religious nature. " I have been driven," he said, " many

27

times to my knees, by the overwhelming conviction that I had nowhere else to go. My own wisdom and that of all about me seemed insufficient for that day. I should be the most presumptuous blockhead upon this footstool, if I for one day thought that I could discharge the duties which have come upon me since I came into this place, without the aid and enlightenment of One who is wiser and stronger than all others."

Mr. Carpenter, a distinguished artist who spent six months almost constantly in the society of the President, says of him, —

"Absorbed in his papers, he would become unconscious of my presence, while I intently studied every line and shade of expression in that furrowed face. In repose, it was the saddest face I ever knew. There were days when I could scarcely look into it without crying. During the first week of the battles of the Wilderness, he scarcely slept at all. Passing through the main hall of the domestic apartment on one of those days, I met him, clad in a long morning wrapper, pacing back and forth a narrow passage leading to one of the windows, his hands behind him, great black rings under his eyes, his head bent forward upon his breast, — altogether such a picture of the effects of sorrow, care, and anxiety, as would have melted the hearts of the worst of his adversaries. With a sorrow almost divine, he, too, could have said of the rebellious States, ' How often would I have gathered you together even as a hen gathereth her chickens under her wings, and ye would not!' "

The Hon. Mr. Colfax says, "Calling upon the President one morning in the winter of 1863, I found him looking more than usually pale and careworn, and inquired the reason. He replied, that with the bad news he had received at a late hour the previous night, which had not yet been communicated to the press, he had not closed his eyes, or breakfasted; and, with an expression I shall never forget, he exclaimed, ' How willingly would I exchange places to-day with the soldier who sleeps on the ground in the Army of the Potomac!' "

Mr. Frederick Douglas, in the autumn of 1864, visited Washington; and Mr. Lincoln, wishing to converse with him upon some points on which he desired the opinion and advice of that very remarkable man, sent his carriage and an invitation to Mr. Douglas to "come up and take a cup of tea with him." The invitation was accepted. Probably never before was a colored man an honored guest in the White House. Mr. Douglas subsequently remarked, "Mr. Lincoln is one of the few white men I ever passed an hour with, who failed to remind me in some way, before the interview terminated, that I was a negro."

The following is from a correspondent of "The York Independent:" "On New Year's Day, 1865, a memorable incident occurred, of which the like was never before seen at the White House. I had noticed at sundry times, during the summer, the wild fervor and strange enthusiasm which our colored friends always manifested over the name of Abraham Lincoln. His name, with them, seems to be associated with that of his namesake, the father of the faithful. In the great crowds which gather from time to time in front of the White House in honor of the President, none shout so loudly or so wildly, and swing their hats with such utter *abandon*, while their eyes are beaming with the intensest joy, as do these simple minded and grateful people. I have often laughed heartily at these exhibitions.

"But the scene yesterday excited far other emotions. As I entered the door of the President's house, I noticed groups of colored people gathered here and there, who seemed to be watching earnestly the inpouring throng. For nearly two hours they hung around, until the crowd of white visitors began sensibly to diminish. Then they summoned courage, and began timidly to approach the door. Some of them were richly and gayly dressed, some were in tattered garments, and others in the most fanciful and grotesque costumes. All pressed eagerly forward. When they came into the presence of the President, doubting as to their reception, the feelings of the poor creatures overcame them; and here the scene baffles my powers of description.

"For two long hours Mr. Lincoln had been shaking the hands of the 'sovereigns,' and had become excessively weary, and his grasp languid; but his nerves rallied at the unwonted sight, and he welcomed the motley crowd with a heartiness that made them wild with exceeding joy. They laughed and wept, and wept and laughed, exclaiming through their blinding tears, 'God bless you!' 'God bless Abraham Lincoln!' 'God bress Massa Linkum!' Those who witnessed this scene will not soon forget it. For a long distance down the avenue, on my way home, I heard fast young men cursing the President for this act; but all the way the refrain rang in my ears, 'God bless Abraham Lincoln!'"

The telegram one day announced a great battle in progress. Mr. Lincoln paced the floor, pale and haggard, unable to eat, and fearfully apprehensive of a defeat. A lady said to him, " We can at least pray." " Yes," said he; and, taking his Bible, he hastened to his room. The prayer he offered was overheard; and, in the intensity of entreaty and childlike faith, it was such as seldom ascends from human lips. Erelong, a telegram announced a Union victory. He came back to the room he had left, his face beaming with joy, and said, " Good news, good news! The victory is ours, and God is good!" " There is nothing like prayer," the lady responded. " Yes, there is," he replied: " praise, prayer, and praise." It is confidently asserted, that, during the war, Mr. Lincoln found an hour every day for prayer.

There was a peculiarity in the character of this most remarkable man, a peculiarity conspicuous from the cradle to the grave, which no one yet has been successful in satisfactorily explaining. Take the following as an illustration: —

A poor old man from Tennessee went to Washington to plead for the life of his son. He had no friends. Almost by chance, and after much delay, he succeeded in working his way to the President through the crowd of senators, governors, and generals who were impatiently waiting for an audience. Mr. Lincoln looked over his papers, and told the man that he would give him his answer the next day. The anguish-stricken father looked up with swimming eyes, and said, " To-morrow may be too late! My son is under sentence of death! The decision ought to be made now!"

" Wait a bit," said the President, " and I will tell you a story. Colonel Fisk of Missouri raised a regiment, and made every man agree that the colonel should do all the swearing of the regiment. One of his teamsters, John Todd, in driving a mule team over a boggy road, completely lost his patience, and burst into a volley of oaths. The colonel called him to account. ' John,' said he, ' did you not promise to let me do all the swearing of the regiment?' ' Yes, I did, colonel,' he replied: ' but the fact was, the swearing had to be done then, or not at all; and you were n't there to do it.' "

The President laughed at this story most heartily, and even the old man joined him in the laugh. He then, in a few words, wrote a pardon for the boy, and handed it to the father.

Perhaps the most sublime and momentous moment of his life was when he presented to his Cabinet his proclamation, which was to deliver from bondage nearly four millions of human beings then living, and to rescue from that doom uncounted millions yet unborn. He had prepared it without consultation with others, and no one knew the object of the meeting. When all these grave and distinguished men, pressed in body, mind, and heart with the burden of the war, had met in the President's Cabinet, Mr. Lincoln prepared himself to present the proclamation to them by taking down from the shelf "Artemas Ward his Book," and reading an entire chapter of his frivolous drollery, laughing in the mean time with an *abandon* of mirth, as if he had never cherished a serious thought.

Then, with his whole tone and manner suddenly changed, with an expression of countenance and a modulation of voice which indicated that, in every fibre of his soul, he appreciated the grandeur of the occasion, he read that immortal document which, as he afterwards said, was the greatest event of the nineteenth century.

In one of the darkest hours of the war a member of his Cabinet called upon him to confer respecting some weighty matters. The President commenced relating a ludicrous anecdote. " Please, Mr. President," said the secretary remonstratingly, " I did not come here this morning to hear stories. It is too serious a time." The President paused for a moment, and then said, " Sit down, sir. I respect your feelings. You cannot be more anxious than I am constantly. And I say to you now, that if it were not for this occasional vent I should die!"

Mr. Lincoln's literary taste was of a high order. No man more correctly appreciated poetic beauty. The most delicate shades of thought, and the purest sentiments, were those for which his mind had an intuitive affinity. His memory was stored with beautiful fragments of verse, and these were invariably of the highest literary and moral excellence.

" There are," said he on one occasion, "some quaint, queer verses, written, I think, by Oliver Wendell Holmes, entitled ' The Last Leaf,' one of which is to me inexpressibly touching." He then repeated, —

> " The mossy marbles rest
> On the lips that he has pressed
> In their bloom ;

> And the names he loved to hear
> Have been carved for many year
> On the tomb."

He then added, "For pure pathos, in my judgment, there is nothing finer than these six lines in the English language." On another occasion he said, "There is a poem that has been a great favorite with me for years, to which my attention was first called, when a young man, by a friend, and which I afterwards saw and cut from a newspaper, and carried it in my pocket till, by frequent reading, I had it by heart." He then repeated eleven verses of a poem of which we here give the first and last stanzas : —

> "Oh! why should the spirit of mortal be proud?
> Like a swift-fleeting meteor, a fast-flying cloud,
> A flash of the lightning, a break of the wave,
> He passeth from life to the rest of the grave.
>
> 'T is the wink of an eye, 't is the draught of a breath,
> From the blossom of health to the paleness of death,
> From the gilded saloon to the bier and the shroud :
> Oh! why should the spirit of mortal be proud?"

Mr. Lincoln was very remarkable for his fund of anecdote. He always had his little story with which to illustrate any point, and the illustration was often found to contain resistless argument. It has been said that his stories were sometimes coarse. Upon this point Mr. Carpenter says, after six months of the most intimate daily acquaintance, —

"Mr. Lincoln, I am convinced, has been greatly wronged in this respect. Every foul-mouthed man in the country gave currency to the slime and filth of his own imagination by attributing it to the President. It is but simple justice to his memory that I should state that, during the entire period of my stay in Washington, after witnessing his intercourse with nearly all classes of men, embracing governors, senators and members of Congress, officers of the army, and intimate friends, I cannot recollect to have heard him relate a circumstance to any one of them which would have been out of place uttered in a lady's drawing-room.

"And this testimony is not unsupported by that of others well entitled to consideration. Dr. Stone, his family physician, came in one day to see my studies. Sitting in front of that of the President, with whom he did not sympathize politically, he remarked with much feeling, ' It is the province of a physician to probe deeply the interior lives of men, and I affirm that Mr. Lincoln is the purest-hearted man with whom I ever came in contact.' Secretary Seward, who of the cabinet officers was probably the most intimate with the President, expressed the same sentiment in still stronger language. He once said to the Rev. Dr. Bellows, ' Mr. Lincoln is the best man I ever knew.' "

The tact which the President displayed in all his responses to the various kindnesses he received excited universal admiration. On such occasions his awkwardness seemed graceful, and his plain face beautiful. As the President entered one of the rooms of the White House on an occasion when many visitors were present, a lady stepped forward playfully with a beautiful bunch of flowers, and said, " Allow me, Mr. President, to present you with a bouquet." He took the flowers, for a moment looked admiringly on their beauty, and then, fixing his eyes upon the countenance of the lady, which was also radiant with loveliness, said, " Really, madam, if you give them to *me*, and they are *mine*, I think I cannot possibly make so good a *use* of them as to present them to *you* in return."

Upon the betrothal of the Prince of Wales to the Princess Alexandrina, Queen Victoria sent a letter to each of the European sovereigns, and also to President Lincoln, announcing the fact. Lord Lyons, the British ambassador at Washington, who was an unmarried man, sought an audience with the President, that he might communicate this important intelligence. With much formality, he presented himself at the White House, accompanied by Secretary Seward.

" May it please your excellency," said the noble lord, " I hold in my hand an autograph-letter from my royal mistress, Queen Victoria, which I have been commanded to present to your excellency. In it she informs your excellency, that her son, his royal highness the Prince of Wales, is about to contract a matrimonial alliance with her royal highness the Princess Alexandrina of Denmark."

After continuing in this style of stately address for some moments, he placed the letter in the hands of the President. Mr. Lincoln took it, and, with a peculiar twinkle of the eye, simply responded, " Lord Lyons, go thou and do likewise."

Mr. Carpenter, in narrating this incident, adds, " It is doubtful if an English ambassador was ever addressed in this manner before ; and it would be interesting to learn what success he met with in putting the reply in diplomatic language, when he reported it to her majesty."

In conversation at the White House, a gentleman referred to a body of water in Nebraska, which was called by an Indian name signifying *weeping water*. Mr. Lincoln instantly replied, " As *laughing water*, according to Longfellow, is Minnehaha, this, evidently, should be Minneboohoo."

A gentleman who had called upon the President, in the course of conversation inquired of him how many men the rebels had in the field. Promptly and very decidedly he replied, " Twelve hundred thousand." The interrogator, in amazement, exclaimed, " Twelve hundred thousand ! is it possible ? " " Yes, sir," the President replied ; " twelve hundred thousand : there is no doubt of it. You see, all of our generals, when they get whipped, say the enemy outnumbers them from three or five to one. I must believe them. We have four hundred thousand men in the field. Three times four make twelve. Don't you see it ? "

Some gentlemen from the West called one day, with bitter complaints against the administration. The President, as was his wont, listened to them patiently, and then replied, —

" Gentlemen, suppose all the property you were worth was in gold, and you had put it into the hands of Blondin to carry across the Niagara River on a rope, would you shake the cable, or keep shouting out to him, ' Blondin, stand up a little straighter ; Blondin, stoop a little more ; go a little faster ; lean a little more to the north ; lean a little more to the south ? ' No : you would hold your breath as well as your tongue, and keep your hands off until he was safe over. The government are carrying an immense weight. Untold treasures are in their hands. They are doing the very best they can. Don't badger them. Keep silence, and we 'll get you safe across."

" I hope," said a clergyman to him one day, " that the Lord is on our side." " I am not at all concerned about that," was Mr. Lincoln's reply ; " for I know that the Lord is *always* on the side of the *right*. But it is my constant anxiety and prayer that *I* and *this nation* should be on the Lord's side."

As the rebel confederacy was crumbling into ruins, some gentlemen asked Mr. Lincoln what he intended to do with Jeff. Davis. "There was a boy," said he, "in Springfield, who bought a coon, which, after the novelty wore off, became a great nuisance. He was one day leading him through the streets, and had his hands full to keep clear of the little vixen who had torn his clothes half off of him. At length he sat down on the curbstone, completely fagged out. A man, passing, was stopped by the lad's disconsolate appearance, and asked the matter. 'Oh,' was the reply, 'the coon is such a trouble to me!' 'Why don't you get rid of it, then?' said the gentleman. 'Hush!' said the boy. 'Don't you see that he is gnawing his rope off? I am going to let him do it; and then I will go home, and tell the folks *that he got away from me.*'"

On the Monday before his assassination, the President, on his return from Richmond, stopped at City Point. There were very extensive hospitals there, filled with sick and wounded soldiers. Mr. Lincoln told the head surgeon that he wished to visit all the hospitals, that he might shake hands with every soldier. The surgeon endeavored to dissuade him, saying that there were between five and six thousand patients in the hospitals, and that he would find it a severe tax upon his strength to visit all the wards. But Mr. Lincoln persisted, saying, —

"I think that I am equal to the task. At any rate, I will try, and go as far as I can. I shall probably never see the boys again, and I want them to know that I appreciate what they have done for their country."

The surgeon, finding that he could not dissuade Mr. Lincoln, began his rounds, accompanying the President from bed to bed. To every man he extended his hand, and spoke a few words of sympathy. As he passed along, welcomed by all with heartfelt cordiality, he came to a ward where there was a wounded rebel. The unhappy man raised himself upon his elbow in bed as the President approached, and, with tears running down his cheeks, said, " Mr. Lincoln, I have long wanted to see you to ask your forgiveness for ever raising my hand against the old flag."

Tears filled the President's eyes. Warmly he shook the young man's hand, assuring him of his good will and heartfelt sympathy. Several hours were occupied in the tour, when the President returned with the surgeon to his office. They had, however, but just taken their seats, when a messenger came, saying that one of the wards had been missed, and that "the boys" were very anxious to see the President. The surgeon, who was quite tired out, and who knew that Mr. Lincoln must be greatly exhausted, endeavored to dissuade him from going back; but Mr. Lincoln persisted, saying, "The boys will be so disappointed!" He therefore went with the messenger, and did not return until he had visited every bed.

Mr. Lincoln retained at the White House, to a very remarkable degree, the simple habits to which he had been accustomed in his home in Illinois. Mr. Holland relates the following characteristic anecdote: —

"He delighted to see his familiar Western friends, and gave them always a cordial welcome. He met them on the old footing, and fell at once into the accustomed habits of talk and story-telling. An old acquaintance, with his wife, visited Washington. Mr. and Mrs. Lincoln proposed to these friends to ride in the presidential carriage. It should be stated in advance, that the two men had probably never seen each other with gloves on in their lives, unless when they were used as protection from the cold. The question of each — Mr. Lincoln at the White House, and his friend at the hotel — was whether he should wear gloves. Of course the ladies urged gloves; but Mr. Lincoln only put his in his pocket, to be used or not according to circumstances. When the presidential party arrived at the hotel to take in their friends, they found the gentleman, overcome by his wife's persuasions, very handsomely gloved. The moment he took his seat, he began to draw off the clinging kids, while Mr. Lincoln began to draw his on. 'No, no, no!' protested his friend, tugging at his gloves, 'it is none of my doings. Put up your gloves, Mr. Lincoln.' So the two old friends were on even and easy terms, and had their ride after their old fashion."

The Hon. Thaddeus Stevens, on one occasion, called at the White House with an elderly lady who was in great trouble. Her son had been in the army, but for some offense had been court-martialed, and sentenced either to death or imprisonment for a long term at hard labor. There were some extenuating circumstances. The President gave the woman a long and attentive hearing, and then, turning to the representative, said, "Do you think," Mr. Stevens, "that this is a case which will warrant my interference?" "With my knowledge of the facts and parties," was the reply, " I should have no hesitation in granting a pardon." " Then," replied Mr. Lincoln, " I will pardon him." Turning to the table, he wrote the pardon, and handed it to the mother. Her gratitude so overcame her, that for a moment she was speechless, taking the paper in silence ; but, as she was descending the stairs with Mr. Stevens, she turned to him, and said very earnestly, " I knew it was all a copperhead lie." " To what do you refer, madam ? " Mr. Stevens inquired. " Why, they told me," she replied, " that he was an ugly-looking man ; but he is the handsomest man I ever saw in my life."

And surely there was beauty in that furrowed, care-worn, gentle face. A lady connected with the Christian Commission had several interviews with him, consulting him in reference to her humane duties. At the close of one of these interviews, Mr. Lincoln said to her, with that child-like frankness and simplicity so characteristic of him, —

" Madam, I have formed a high opinion of your Christian character ; and now, as we are alone, I have a mind to ask you to give me, in brief, your idea of what constitutes a true Christian."

She replied at some length, stating in substance that, in her judgment, " it consisted of a conviction of one's own sinfulness and weakness, and personal need of a Saviour for strength and support ; that views of mere doctrine might and would differ ; but when one was really brought to feel his need of divine help, and to seek the aid of the Holy Spirit for strength and guidance, it was satisfactory evidence of his having been born again."

With deep emotion he replied, " If what you have told me is really a correct view of this great subject, I think that I can say with sincerity, that I hope that I am a Christian. I had lived, until my boy Willie died, without realizing fully these things. That blow overwhelmed me. It showed me my weakness as I had never felt it before ; and, if I can take what you have stated as a *test*, I think that I can safely say that I know something of that change of which you speak : and I will further add, that it has been my intention for some time, at a suitable opportunity, to make a public religious profession."

" Oh, how hard it is," said he one day, " to die and not leave the world any better for one's little life in it ! "

Four years of civil war passed slowly and sadly away. There

was another presidential election. Those who were opposed to Mr.
Lincoln and the war rallied in great strength ; but Mr. Lincoln was
triumphantly reëlected, receiving two hundred and twelve out of
two hundred and thirty-three electoral votes. The evening of his
election, he said, in reference to this emphatic approval of his administration by the people, —

"I am thankful to God for this approval of the people; but while
deeply grateful for this mark of their confidence in me, if I know
my heart, my gratitude is free from any taint of personal triumph.
I do not impugn the motives of any one opposed to me. It is no
pleasure to me to triumph over any one; but I give thanks to the
Almighty for this evidence of the people's resolution to stand by a
free government and the rights of humanity."

The last hope of the rebels was now gone. It was manifest beyond all controversy that the American people would not submit to
have their government broken up by traitors. Again he said, in response to a delegation which waited upon him with congratulations,
speaking of the election, —

"It has demonstrated that a people's government can sustain a
national election in the midst of a great civil war. Until now, it
has not been known to the world that this was a possibility. It
shows also how strong and sound we still are. It shows also that we
have more men now than when the war began. Gold is good in its
place; but living, brave, and patriotic men are better than gold."

Every month now indicated that the Rebellion was drawing near
to its close. The triumphs of Grant, Sherman, and Sheridan were
striking the hearts of the rebels with dismay, and inspiring all loyal
hearts with hope. The national government had, in the field, armies
amounting to over seven hundred thousand men; and six hundred
and seventy vessels of war were afloat, carrying four thousand six
hundred and ten guns. At President Lincoln's suggestion, Congress
passed an act recommending to the States an *amendment to the Constitution*, prohibiting slavery. This event was generally hailed by
the country with great satisfaction. This settled forever the efficacy
of his proclamation of emancipation. Friends and foes now alike
admitted the great ability of Abraham Lincoln.

An immense and enthusiastic crowd attended his second inauguration. His address on the occasion, characteristic of the man, was
one of the noblest utterances which ever fell from the lips of a ruler

when entering upon office. In allusion to the parties arrayed against each other in the war, he said, —

" Both read the same Bible, and pray to the same God ; and each invokes his aid against the other. It may seem strange that any men should dare to ask a just God's assistance in wringing their bread from the sweat of other men's faces ; but let us judge not, that we be not judged. The prayers of both could not be answered. That of neither has been answered fully. The Almighty has his own purposes. ' Woe unto the world because of offenses ! For it must needs be that offenses come ; but woe to that man by whom the offense cometh ! '

" If we shall suppose that American slavery is one of those offenses, which, in the providence of God, must needs come, but which, having continued through his appointed time, he now wills to remove, and that he gives to both North and South this terrible war as the woe due to those by whom the offense came, shall we discern therein any departure from those divine attributes which the believers in a living God always ascribe to Him ? Fondly do we hope, fervently do we pray, that this mighty scourge of war may soon pass away. Yet if God wills that it continue until all the wealth piled by the bondmen's two hundred and fifty years of unrequited toil shall be sunk, and until every drop of blood drawn with the lash shall be paid with another drawn with the sword, — as was said three thousand years ago, so still it must be said, ' The judgments of the Lord are true and righteous altogether.'

" With malice towards none, with charity for all, with firmness in the right as God gives us to see the right, let us strive on to finish the work we are in ; to bind up the nation's wounds ; to care for him who shall have borne the battle, and for his widow and orphans ; to do all which may achieve and cherish a just and a lasting peace among ourselves and with all nations."

On the morning of the 3d of April, 1865, it was announced by telegraph that the Union army had entered Richmond ; that Lee was in full retreat, pursued by Grant ; and that President Lincoln had gone to the front. No pen can describe the joy with which these tidings were received. The war was over ; slavery was dead ; and the Union, cemented in freedom, was stronger than ever before. Contrary to his own estimate of himself, Mr. Lincoln was one of the most courageous of men. He went directly into the rebel capital, which was then swarming with rebels. Without any guard but the sailors who had rowed him a mile up the river in a boat from the man-of-war in which he ascended the stream, he entered the thronged and tumultuous city, which was then enveloped in flames, the torch having been applied by the retreating foe. He was on foot, leading his little boy " Tad " by the hand.

The rumor of his presence soon spread through the city. The blacks crowded around him, shouting, singing, laughing, praying, and with all other demonstrations of the wildest joy. A poor woman stood in the door-way of her hut, quivering with emotion, exclaiming, as a flood of tears ran down her cheeks, " I thank you, dear Jesus, that I behold President Linkum." Others seemed convulsed with joy as they cried out, " Bless de Lord! bless de Lord! " At last the road became so choked with the multitude, that it was necessary to send soldiers to clear the way.

After visiting the headquarters of General Weitzel, and taking a drive round the city, the President returned to City Point, and again soon after revisited Richmond with Mrs. Lincoln and Vice-President Johnson. On this occasion he had an interview with some of the prominent citizens, by whom he afterwards felt that he had been deceived, and his confidence betrayed. From this trip he returned to Washington, to consecrate his energies to the reconstruction of the nation after these fearful shocks of war.

Mr. Lincoln was a very frank man. He did nothing by guile. No one was left in doubt in respect to his views. The great question of reconstruction now engrossed every thinking mind. In a letter to General Wadsworth, he had written, —

" You desire to know, in the event of our complete success in the field, the same being followed by loyal and cheerful submission on the part of the South, if universal amnesty should not be accompanied with universal suffrage. Since you know my private inclination as to what terms should be granted to the South in the contingency mentioned, I will here add, that should our success thus be realized, followed by such desired results, I cannot see, if universal amnesty is granted, how, under the circumstances, I can avoid exacting, in return, universal suffrage, or at least suffrage on the basis of intelligence and military service."

We have spoken of the attempts which were made to assassinate

ABRAHAM LINCOLN ENTERING RICHMOND, APRIL 3, 1865.

Drawn by L. Hollis

President Lincoln before his inauguration. His life was constantly threatened. His friends urged him to practice caution ; but this was so contrary to his nature, that he could not be persuaded to do so. He walked the streets of Washington unattended, and as freely as any other citizen.

On the 14th of April General Grant was in the city ; and the manager of Ford's Theatre invited the President and the general to witness on his boards the representation, that evening, of "Our American Cousin." To assist in drawing a crowd, it was announced in the play-bills that they would both be present. General Grant left the city. President Lincoln, feeling, with his characteristic kindliness of heart, that it would be a disappointment if he should fail them, very reluctantly consented to go. With his wife and two friends, he reached the theatre a little before nine o'clock ; and they took their seats in a private box reserved for them. The house was full in every part; and the whole audience rose as the President entered, and he was greeted with the greatest enthusiasm.

As the President, having taken his seat, was apparently listening with great interest to the play, a play-actor by the name of John Wilkes Booth worked his way through the crowd, in the rear of the dress-circle, and, reaching the door of the box where the President was seated, presented a pistol within a few inches of his head, and fired a bullet into his brain. Mr. Lincoln, reclining in his chair, instantly lost all consciousness, and did not move. The assassin, brandishing a dagger, leaped upon the stage, and shouting theatrically, "*Sic semper tyrannis !*" rushed across it in the terrible confusion which ensued, mounted a fleet horse at the door, and escaped.

The helpless form of the President, bleeding and unconscious, was borne across the street to a private house. A surgical examination showed that the wound was mortal. It was a sad scene. Upon pillows drenched with blood lay the President, senseless and dying, his brains oozing from his wound. The leading men of the government had speedily gathered, overwhelmed with grief. Staunton and Welles and Sumner and M'Culloch were there ; and tears flooded the eyes of these strong men, while audible sobs burst from their lips. Senator Sumner tenderly held the hand of the sufferer, and wept with uncontrollable emotion. At twenty-two minutes past seven o'clock in the morning, President Lincoln, without recovering consciousness, breathed his last.

It was a widespread conspiracy for the death of the leading officers of the government and of the army. The President, Vice-President Johnson, Secretary Seward, General Grant, and others, were marked for destruction. When Booth was creeping around the dress-circle of the theatre with his pistol, another of the assassins, by the name of Powell, entered the sick-chamber of Secretary Seward, where the illustrious minister was helpless on a bed of suf-

ASSASSINATION OF ABRAHAM LINCOLN.

fering, his jaw being broken, and he being otherwise severely injured, by the accidental overturn of his carriage. The murderer, a man of herculean frame and strength, reached the chamber-door of his victim by asserting that he came with medicine from the physician. With the butt of his pistol he knocked down and stunned Mr. Frederic Seward, the son of the Secretary, who endeavored to arrest his entrance. Then leaping upon the bed, with sinewy arm, three times he plunged his dagger into the throat and neck of Mr. Seward. The wounded man, in the struggle, rolled from his bed upon the floor. An attendant sprang upon the assassin; but the wretch with his dagger cut himself loose, and escaped into the street, after stabbing five persons who attempted to arrest him in his escape. A kind Providence, in various ways, sheltered the others who were marked for destruction.

It was not deemed safe to inform Mr. Seward, in his perilous condition, of the assassination of the President, as it was feared that the shock would be greater than he could bear. Sunday morning, however, he had his bed wheeled round, so that he could see the tops of the trees in the park opposite his chamber. His eye caught sight of the stars and stripes at half-mast over the building of the War Department. For a moment he gazed upon the flag in silence, and then, turning to his attendant, said, " The President is dead!" The attendant, much embarrassed, stammered a reply. " If he had been alive," continued the Secretary, " he would have been the first to call upon me. But he has not been here, nor has he sent to know how I am; and there is the flag at half-mast!" As he said this, tears rolled down his cheeks.

Never before, in the history of the world, was a nation plunged into such deep grief by the death of its ruler. Abraham Lincoln had won the affections of all patriot hearts. Strong men met in the streets, and wept in speechless anguish. It is not too much to say that a nation was in tears. As the awful tidings flew along the wires, funeral-bells were tolled in city and in country, flags everywhere were at half-mast, and groups gathered in silent consternation. It was Saturday morning when the murder was announced. On Sunday all the churches were draped in mourning. The atrocious act was the legitimate result of the vile Rebellion, and was in character with its developed ferocity from the beginning to the end.

The grief of the colored people was sublime in its universality and its intensity. A Northern gentleman, who was in Charleston, S. C., when the tidings of the assassination reached there, writes, —

" I never saw such sad faces or heard such heavy heart-beatings as here in Charleston the day the dreadful news came. The colored people, the native loyalists, were like children bereaved of an only and a loved parent. I saw one old woman going up the street wringing her hands, and saying aloud as she walked, looking straight before her, so absorbed in her grief that she noticed no one, —

"'O Lord, O Lord, O Lord! Massa Sam's dead! Massa Sam's dead! O Lord! Massa Sam's dead!'

28

" ' Who 's dead, aunty ? ' I asked her.

" ' Massa Sam ! ' she said, not looking at me. ' O Lord, O Lord ! Massa Sam 's dead ! '

" ' Who 's Massa Sam ? ' I asked.

" ' Uncle Sam ! ' " she said. ' O Lord, O Lord ! '

" I was not quite sure that she meant the President, and I spoke again. ' Who 's Massa Sam, aunty ? '

" ' Mr. Linkum,' she said, and resumed wringing her hands, and moaning in utter hopelessness of sorrow. The poor creature was too ignorant to comprehend any difference between the very unreal Uncle Sam and the actual President; but her heart told her that he whom Heaven had sent in answer to her prayers was lying in a bloody grave, and that she and her race were left *fatherless.*"

The body of the President was removed to the White House, and placed in a coffin almost buried in flowers, which the affection of a bereaved people supplied. It is estimated that fifty thousand persons went to the White House to take a last look of his loved face. The funeral solemnities were conducted by clergymen of the Presbyterian, Methodist, Episcopal, and Baptist churches. Dr. Gurley, in his noble tribute to the deceased, said, —

" Probably no man, since the days of Washington, was ever so deeply and firmly embedded and enshrined in the hearts of the people as Abraham Lincoln. Nor was it a mistaken confidence and love. He deserved it, deserved it well, deserved it all. He merited it by his character, by his acts, and by the tenor and tone and spirit of his life."

It may be truly said that the funeral-train extended fifteen hundred miles, — from Washington to Springfield, Ill. Groups gathered as mourners at every station, bells were tolled, and bands of music breathed forth their plaintive requiems. In some places the railway, for miles, was lined with a continuous group of men, women, and children, standing in silence, with uncovered heads and swimming eyes, as the solemn pageant swept by. It would require a volume to describe the scenes which were witnessed in the various cities and villages through which the funeral procession passed.

The train reached Springfield, Ill., on the morning of the 3d of May. Bishop Simpson of the Methodist Church, a personal friend of the President, in his funeral address quoted the following words from one of the speeches of Mr. Lincoln in 1859. Speaking of the slave-power, Mr. Lincoln said, —

" Broken by it I, too, may be ; bow to it I never will. The probability that we may fail in the struggle ought not to deter us from the support of a cause which I deem to be just ; and it shall not deter me. If ever I feel the soul within me elevate and expand to those dimensions not wholly unworthy of the almighty Architect, it is when I contemplate the cause of my country, deserted by all the world besides, and I standing up boldly and alone, and hurling defiance at her victorious oppressors. Here, without contemplating consequences, before high Heaven, and in the face of the world, I swear eternal fidelity to the just cause, as I deem it, of the land of my life, my liberty, and my love."

England vied with America in expressions of respect and affection for our martyred President. The statement contained in " The London Spectator " will surely be the verdict of posterity, that Abraham Lincoln was " the best if not the ablest man then ruling over any country in the civilized world." The Queen of England, with her own hand, wrote a letter of condolence to Mrs. Lincoln. The sympathy which was manifested for us by the English, in this our great grief, so touched all loyal hearts, that Americans began to think that it was possible that England and America might yet again be united in the bonds of brotherly love, burying all past grievances in oblivion.

CHAPTER XVII.

ANDREW JOHNSON.

THE early life of Andrew Johnson contains but the record of poverty, destitution, and friendlessness. He was born the 29th of

RESIDENCE OF ANDREW JOHNSON.

December, 1808, in Raleigh, the capital of North Carolina. His parents, belonging to the class of the " poor whites " of the South, were in such circumstances that they could not confer even the slightest advantages of education upon their child. When Andrew was five years of age his father accidentally lost his life while heroically endeavoring to save a friend from drowning. Until ten years of age Andrew was a ragged boy about the streets, supported by the labor of his mother, who obtained her living with her own hands.

He then, having never attended a school one day, and being unable either to read or write, was apprenticed to a tailor in his native town. A benevolent gentleman of Raleigh was in the habit of going to the tailor's shop occasionally, and reading to the boys at work there. He often read from the speeches of distinguished British statesmen. Andrew, who was endowed with a mind of more than ordinary native ability, became much interested in these speeches: his ambition was roused, and he was inspired with a strong desire to learn to read.

He accordingly applied himself to the alphabet, and, with the assistance of some of his fellow-workmen, learned his letters. He then called upon the gentleman to borrow the book of speeches. The owner, pleased with his zeal, not only gave him the book, but assisted him in learning to combine the letters into words. Under such difficulties he pressed onward laboriously, spending usually ten or twelve hours at work in the shop, and then robbing himself of rest and recreation to devote such time as he could to reading.

In 1824, when sixteen years of age, having finished his apprenticeship, he went to Laurens Court House, in South Carolina, and worked as a journeyman tailor for two years. It does not appear, that, during this time, he made much progress in his attempts to learn to read with correctness and fluency. It is said that he became quite interested in a girl of the village, and would have married her but for the objections which her parents made in consequence of his extreme youth.

In 1826 he returned to Raleigh, and, taking his mother with him, removed to Greenville, a small town in East Tennessee, where he resumed his work as a journeyman tailor, and married a young woman of very estimable character, and who was so decidedly in advance of him in point of education, that she became his teacher in reading, writing, and arithmetic. She read to him as he plied the needle on the bench, and in the evenings instructed him in other branches. Rapidly the young mechanic advanced in intelligence. His mental energy gave him influence among the workmen. Words came easily at his bidding, and he knew well how to use all the information he gained. His popularity with the working-classes was such, that, in 1828, he was chosen one of the aldermen in the little town in which he dwelt; which position he held for two years, when, at the age of twenty-two, he was elected mayor. The position which he then occupied in public esteem may be inferred from the fact that he was also appointed, by the county court, one of the trustees of Rhea Academy.

He now began to take a lively interest in political affairs; identifying himself with the working-classes, to which he belonged. His zeal in their behalf, and the ever-increasing ability with which he espoused their cause, won their esteem, and secured for him, with great unanimity, their votes. In 1835 he was elected a member of the House of Representatives in Tennessee. He was then just twenty-seven years of age. He became a very active member of the Legislature, gave his adhesion to the Democratic party, and in 1840 "stumped the State," advocating Martin Van Buren's claims to the presidency, in opposition to those of General Harrison. In this campaign he acquired much readiness as a speaker, and extended and increased his reputation.

In 1841 he was elected state senator from Hawkins and Greene counties. The duties which devolved upon him he discharged with ability, and was universally esteemed as an earnest, honest man, heartily advocating whatever he thought to be right, and denouncing what he thought to be wrong. In 1843 he was elected a member of Congress, and, by successive elections, held that important post for ten years. In 1853 he was elected Governor of Tennessee, and was reëlected in 1855. In all these responsible positions he discharged his duties with distinguished ability, and proved himself the warm friend of the working-classes.

The following characteristic anecdote is related of him when Governor of Tennessee. With his own hands he cut and made a very handsome suit of clothes, and sent them as a present to Governor M'Goffin, of Kentucky, who had been his friend and companion in earlier days. The Kentucky governor had been a blacksmith by trade. He returned the compliment by forging upon the anvil with his own hands, a very neat pair of shovel and tongs, which he sent to Governor Johnson, with the wish that they would help to keep alive the flame of their old friendship.

In 1857 Mr. Johnson was elected, by the Legislature of Tennessee, United States senator for the term of six years. In Congress, both in the Senate and in the House, he adopted, in general, the Democratic policy. He opposed a protective tariff, and advocated the Homestead Bill. He belonged to the strict constructionist class of politicians, fearing lest the national government should have too much power; and he opposed any United States bank, and all schemes of internal improvement by the national government. He also went strongly with the South in its views of the incompetency of Congress to prevent the extension of slavery into the Territories.

Years before, in 1845, he had warmly advocated the annexation of Texas, stating, however, as a reason, that he thought this annexation would probably prove " to be the gateway out of which the sable sons of Africa are to pass from bondage to freedom, and become merged in a population congenial to themselves." In 1850 he also earnestly supported the compromise measures, the two essential features of which were, that the white people of the Territories should be permitted to decide for themselves whether they would enslave the colored population or not, and that the free States of the North should return to the South any persons who should attempt to escape from slavery.

Mr. Johnson was never ashamed of his lowly origin ; on the contrary, he often took pride in avowing that he owed his distinction to his own exertions. " Sir," said he on the floor of the Senate, " I do not forget that I am a mechanic. Neither do I forget that Adam was a tailor and sewed fig-leaves, and that our Saviour was the son of a carpenter."

In the spring of 1858 Senator Hammond of South Carolina made a speech in Congress containing the following sentences : —

" In all social systems there must be a class to do the menial duties, to perform the drudgery of life. Such a class you must have. It constitutes the very mudsill of society and of political government, and you might as well attempt to build a house in the air as to build either the one or the other, except on this mudsill. The man who lives by daily labor, and who has to put out his labor in the market, and take the best he can get for it; in short, your whole class of manual laborers and operatives, as you call them, — are essentially slaves. The difference is, that our slaves are hired for life, yours are hired by the day. Our slaves are black, yours are white; our slaves do not vote, yours vote."

Senator Johnson, in his characteristic reply, said, " Will it do to assume that the man who labors with his hands is a slave? No, sir. I am a laborer with my hands, and I never considered myself a slave."

Mr. Hammond, interrupting him, inquired, " Will the senator define a slave?"

Mr. Johnson replied, " What we understand to be a slave in the South is a person who is held to service during his or her natural life, subject to and under the control of a master, who has the right to appropriate the products of his or her labor to his own use. If we were to follow out the idea that every operative and laborer is a slave, we should find a great many distinguished slaves since the world began. Socrates, who first conceived the idea of the immortality of the soul, pagan as he was, labored with his own hands; yes, wielded the chisel and the mallet, giving polish and finish to the stone. He afterwards turned to be a fashioner and constructor of the mind.

" Paul, the great expounder, himself was a tent-maker, and worked with his own hands. Was he a slave? Archimedes, who declared that, if he had a place on which to rest the fulcrum, with the power of his lever he could move the world, — was he a slave? Adam, our great father and head, the lord of the world, was a tailor by trade. I wonder if he were a slave."

Mr. Johnson was strongly opposed to secession, not however, at first, upon the ground that the slaveholders were not right in their claim that slavery should be nationalized : but, foreseeing the folly of an appeal to arms, he urged them to remain and struggle for the attainment of their ends on the floor of Congress; or, as he expressed it, to "fight for their constitutional rights on the battlements of the Constitution." He said, " We can more successfully resist black republicanism by remaining within the Union than by going out of it." As to Mr. Lincoln, he said on the 19th of December, 1861, " I voted against him, I spoke against him, I spent my money to defeat him."

There was, perhaps, no one in Congress who exposed the absurdity of the doctrine of secession in strains more eloquent and convincing to the popular mind.

"Now let me ask," said he, "can any one believe that, in the creation of this government, its founders intended that it should have the power to acquire territory and form it into States, and then permit them to go out of the Union? Let us take a case. How long has it been since your armies were in Mexico, your brave men exposed to the diseases, the sufferings, incident to a campaign of that kind; many of them falling at the point of the bayonet, consigned to their long, narrow home, with no winding-sheet but their blankets saturated with their blood? What did Mexico cost you? One hundred and twenty million dollars. What did you pay for the country you acquired besides? Fifteen million dollars.

"Peace was made; territory was acquired; and, in a few years, California, from that territory, erected herself into a free and indedent State. Under the provisions of the Constitution, we admitted her as a member of this confederacy. And now, after having expended one hundred and twenty million dollars in the war; after having lost many of our bravest and most gallant men; after having paid fifteen million dollars to Mexico for the territory, and admitted it into the Union as a State, according to this modern doctrine, the national government was just made to let them step in, and then to let them step out! Is it not absurd to say that California, on her own volition, without regard to the consideration paid for her, without regard to the policy which dictated her acquisition by the United States, can walk out, and bid you defiance?

"But we need not stop here. Let us go to Texas. Texas was engaged in a revolution with Mexico. She succeeded in the assertion and establishment of her independence. She applied for admission into this family of States. After she was in, she was oppressed by the debts of the war which had resulted in her separation from Mexico. She was harassed by Indians on her border. There was an extent of territory that lies north, if my memory serves me right, embracing what is now called the Territory of New Mexico. Texas had it not in her power to protect the citizens that were there. It was a dead limb, paralyzed, lifeless.

"The federal government came along as a kind physician, saying, 'We will take this limb, vitalize it by giving protection to the people, and incorporating it into a territorial government; and, in addition to that, we will give you ten million dollars, and you may retain your own public lands.' And the other States were taxed in common to pay this ten million dollars. Now, after all this is done, is Texas to say, ' I will walk out of this Union?' Were there no other parties to this compact? Did we take in California, did we take in Texas, just to benefit themselves?

"Again : take the case of Louisiana. What did we pay for her in 1803? and for what was she wanted? Was it just to let Louisiana into the Union? Was it just for the benefit of that particular locality? Was not the mighty West looked to? Was it not to secure the free navigation of the Mississippi River, the mouth of which was then in the possession of France? Yes: the navigation of that river was wanted. Simply for Louisiana? No, but for all the States. The United States paid fifteen million dollars, and France ceded the country to the United States. It remained in a territorial condition for a while, sustained and protected by the strong arm of the federal government. We acquired the territory and the navigation of the river, and the money was paid for the benefit of all the States, and not of Louisiana exclusively.

" And now that this great valley is filled up ; now that the navigation of the Mississippi is one hundred times more important than it was then ; now, after the United States have paid the money, have acquired the title to Louisiana, and have incorporated her into the confederacy, — it is proposed that she should go out of the Union !

" In 1815, when her shores were invaded ; when her city was about to be sacked ; when her booty and her beauty were about to fall a prey to British aggression, — the brave men of Tennessee and of Kentucky and of the surrounding States rushed into her borders and upon her shores, and, under the lead of her own gallant Jackson, drove the invading forces away. And now, after all this, after the money has been paid, after the free navigation of the river has been obtained, — not for the benefit of Louisiana alone, but for her in common with all the States, — Louisiana says to the other States, —

" ' We will go out of this confederacy. We do not care if you did fight our battles ; we do not care if you did acquire the free navigation of this river from France : we will go out, and constitute ourselves an independent power, and bid defiance to the other States.'

" It may be, that, at this moment, there is not a citizen in the State of Louisiana who would think of obstructing the free navigation of the river. But are not nations controlled by their interests in varying circumstances? And hereafter, when a conflict of interest arises, Louisiana might feel disposed to tax our citizens going down there. It is a power that I am not willing to concede to be exercised at the discretion of any authority outside of this government. So sensitive have been the people of my State upon the free navigation of that river, that as far back as 1796, — now sixty-four years ago, — in their Bill of Rights, before they passed under the jurisdiction of the United States, they declared, —

" ' That an equal participation of the free navigation of the Mississippi is one of the inherent rights of the citizens of this State. It cannot, therefore, be conceded to any prince, potentate, power, person or persons, whatever.'

" This shows the estimate that people fixed on this stream sixty-four years ago; and now we are told that if Louisiana does go out, it is not her intention to tax the people above. Who can tell what may be the intention of Louisiana hereafter? Are we willing to place the rights, the travel, and the commerce of our citizens at the discretion of any power outside of this government? I will not.

" How long is it since Florida lay on our coasts an annoyance to us? And now she has got feverish about being an independent and separate government, while she has not as many qualified voters as there are in one Congressional district of any other State. What condition did Florida occupy in 1811? She was in possession of Spain. What did the United States think about having adjacent territory outside of their jurisdiction? Spain was inimical to the United States; and, in view of the great principles of self-preservation, the Congress of the United States passed a resolution, declaring that, if Spain attempted to transfer Florida into the hands of any other power, the United States would take possession of it. There was the Territory lying upon our border, outside of the jurisdiction of the United States; and we declared, by an act of Congress, that no foreign power should possess it.

" We went still farther, and appropriated one hundred thousand dollars, and authorized the President to enter and take possession of it with the means placed in his hands. Afterwards we negotiated with Spain, and gave six million dollars for the Territory; and we established a territorial government for it. What next? We undertook to drive out the Seminole Indians; and we had a war in which this government lost more than in all the other wars it was engaged in; and we paid the sum of twenty-five million dollars to get the Seminoles out of the swamps, so that the Territory could be inhabited by white men.

"But now that the Territory is paid for, the Indians are driven out, and twenty-five million dollars have been expended, they want no longer the protection of this government, but will go out without consulting the other States; without reference to the remaining parties to the compact. Where will she go? Will she attach herself to Spain again? Will she pass back under the jurisdiction of the Seminoles? After having been nurtured and protected and fostered by all these States, now, without regard to them, is she to be allowed, at her own volition, to withdraw from the Union? I say that she has no constitutional right to do it. When she does it, it is an act of aggression. If she succeeds, it will only be a successful revolution; if she does not succeed, she must take the penalties and terrors of the law.

"I have referred to the acts of Congress for acquiring Florida as setting forth a principle. What is that principle? It is, that from the geographical relations of this Territory to the United States, we authorized the President to expend a hundred thousand dollars to get a foothold there, and especially to take possession of it if it were likely to pass to any foreign power."

In such strains of eloquence and moral demonstration, Senator Johnson exposed the absurdity of the doctrine of secession.

As the secessionists grew more determined in their measures, Mr. Johnson grew more bold in his opposition. The slaveholders became exceedingly exasperated. He was denounced as a traitor to the South, and was threatened with assassination. But he was the last man to be intimidated by menaces. The North looked with admiration upon the moral courage he displayed in thus contending, as it were single-handed, against almost every senator and representative of the South. In this admiration they forgot that Mr. Johnson was, and ever had been, with the South in their claims.

"I am opposed," he said, "to secession. I believe it no remedy for the evils complained of. Instead of acting with that division of my Southern friends who take ground for secession, I shall take other grounds, *while I try to accomplish the same end.* I think that this battle ought to be fought, not outside, but inside, of the Union."

In consequence of this course, the wrath of the secessionists fell bitterly upon him. He was burned in effigy at Memphis ; and on his return to Tennessee in April, 1861, he was insulted repeatedly by mobs, and threatened with lynching. A price even was set upon his head. This did but inspire his zeal, and enable him with more eloquence to plead the Union cause.

Kentucky was now invaded, and the rebels in large armies were ravaging Tennessee, plundering, burning, murdering. Every man who would not espouse their cause was in danger of being hung on the limb of the next tree. Never before was there more ferocity exhibited in a civilized land. A rebel band sacked his home, drove his sick wife and child into the streets, confiscated his slaves (for, with increasing wealth, he had become a slave-owner), and turned his house into a hospital and barracks for the soldiers.

The heroism with which Mr. Johnson opposed the secessionists received a new impulse from these outrages ; and the Union party at the North began to regard him as, in all points, in sympathy with them. Indeed, as he witnessed the violence of the proslavery men, and saw clearly that the institution of slavery was at the foundation of all their treason, his speeches indicated a continually increasing sympathy with the views of the great Republican party which had elected Abraham Lincoln. He had already said, —

" We may as well talk of things as they are ; for, if anything can be *treason*, is not levying war upon the government treason ? Is not the attempt to take the property of the government, and to expel the soldiers therefrom, *treason ?* Is not attempting to resist the collection of the revenue, attempting to exclude the mails, and driving the federal courts from her borders, *treason?* What is it ? It is *treason*, and nothing but *treason*."

This speech, to which reason could make no reply, was met with hisses, reproaches, threats, and a shower of abuse. Growing still bolder, he exclaimed, —

" Does it need any search to find those who are levying war, and giving aid and comfort to enemies against the United States ? And this is treason. Treason ought to be punished, North and South ; and, if there are traitors, they should be entitled to traitors' reward."

Again he said, speaking of the rebels, " Were I the President of the United States, I would do as Thomas Jefferson did in 1806 with Aaron Burr. I would have them arrested and tried for treason ; and, if convicted, by the Eternal God they should suffer the penalty of the law at the hands of the executioner ! Sir, treason must be punished. Its enormity, and the extent and depth of the offense, must be made known."

This was said in the Senate Chamber on the 2d of March, 1861. A few weeks after this, on the 19th of June, in a speech at Cincinnati, he said, speaking in the same impassioned strain, " I repeat, this odious doctrine of secession should be crushed out, destroyed, and totally annihilated. No government can stand, no religious or moral or social organization can stand, where this doctrine is tolerated. It is disintegration, universal dissolution. Therefore I repeat, that this odious and abominable doctrine (you must pardon me for using a strong expression, I do not say it in a profane sense), — but this doctrine I conceive to be hell-born and hell-bound, and one which will carry everything in its train, unless it is arrested, and crushed out from our midst."

Mr. Johnson was a Democrat of the Jacksonian school. Though he had strongly leaned to the doctrine of state sovereignty, and a strict construction of the Constitution, the assumptions of the secessionists were crowding him over into the ranks of those who would increase rather than diminish the power of the central government. Thus upon this point he had abandoned the old Jeffersonian party, and allied himself with the Federalists.

In February, 1862, by the capture of Forts Henry and Donelson, the main body of the rebel army was driven out of Western and Middle Tennessee. President Lincoln, with the approval of the Senate, appointed Andrew Johnson Military Governor of the State. The appointment was received with enthusiasm by nearly all the loyal men in the Union. On the 12th of March he reached Nashville, and commenced his administration with energy, which cheered the hearts of the long-suffering Unionists.

The mayor of Nashville and the city council refused to take the oath of allegiance. He sent them to the penitentiary, and appointed others in their place. The editor of " The Nashville Banner," for uttering treasonable sentiments, was imprisoned, and his paper suppressed. All over the State, guerrilla secessionists were maltreating the Unionists, plundering their homes, and driving their wives and children into the streets, as they had done with Mr. Johnson's family. The difficulty was met in the following proclamation : —

" I, Andrew Johnson, do hereby proclaim, that, in every instance in which a Union man is arrested and maltreated by marauding bands, five or more rebels, from the most prominent in the immediate neighborhood, shall be arrested, imprisoned, and otherwise dealt with as the nature of the case may require ; and further, in all cases where the property of citizens, loyal to the government of the United States, is taken or destroyed, full and ample remuneration shall be made to them out of the property of such rebels in the vicinity as have sympathized with, and given aid, comfort, information, or encouragement to, the parties committing such depredations."

This order was issued on the 9th of May. Early in June another order appeared, declaring that all persons guilty of uttering disloyal sentiments, who should refuse to take the oath of allegiance and give bonds in a thousand dollars for their future good behavior, should be sent South, and treated as spies, that is, hung, if again found within the federal lines. Six clergymen boldly preached treason from their pulpits. As they persisted, after due warning, five were sent to prison, and the sixth paroled in consequence of sickness.

The rebel armies again entered the State. Nashville became isolated, and was in a state of siege. There were many families in Nashville who were starving, their husbands and fathers having joined the rebels. Governor Johnson assessed a tax upon the wealthy rebels in the vicinity for their support. Timid ones began to talk of the necessity of surrender. " I am no military man," he said ; " but any one who talks of surrendering, I will shoot."

There was in the Union army in Tennessee a Methodist clergyman, Colonel Moody, who, in consequence of his patriotic zeal and chivalric bravery, accompanied at the same time with active piety in preaching and in prayer, had acquired the *sobriquet* of the " Fighting Parson." Colonel Moody chanced to be in Washington, and related to President Lincoln the following anecdote respecting Andrew Johnson. General Buell, whose reputation as a determined patriot did not stand very high, being then in command of the Union forces in Tennessee, had evacuated his position in the southern portion of that State, and had fallen back upon Nashville, followed by a rebel army.' He then proposed abandoning the city. As we have mentioned, Governor Johnson would not listen to this: on the contrary, he declared his determination to defend the city to the last extremity, and then to commit it to the flames, rather than surrender it to the rebels.

He was so dissatisfied with General Buell's course, that he wrote a letter to President Lincoln, urging his removal. General Thomas was in cordial sympathy with Governor Johnson, and was placed in command of troops in the city. Soon, however, he took a more important command; and General Negley took charge of the defense. The rebels made several attacks upon the outworks, but were gallantly repulsed. The city was now in a state of siege, provisions were very scarce, and the troops were on half-rations.

Under these circumstances, Colonel Moody had a chance interview with Governor Johnson in Nashville. The governor was in his office, in a state of great excitement, walking the floor, in conversation with two gentlemen. The gentlemen withdrew as the colonel entered, leaving him alone with the governor. After a moment's pause, the governor came up to him, evidently greatly agitated, and said, —

"Moody, we are sold out. Buell is a traitor. He is going to evacuate the city; and, in forty-eight hours, we shall be in the hands of the rebels."

He then commenced rapidly pacing the floor again, wringing his hands, and chafing like a caged tiger, utterly unmindful of his friend's entreaties that he would become calm. Suddenly he stopped, and, turning to the colonel, said, "Moody, can you pray?"

"That is my business, sir," the colonel replied, "as a minister of the gospel."

"Well, Moody," said Governor Johnson, "I wish you would pray;" and, as the colonel knelt, the governor impetuously threw himself upon his knees by his side. A Western Methodist clergyman does not pray in low tones of voice, or with languid utterance. As with increasing fervor the colonel pleaded with God to interpose in their great peril, and save them, the governor threw one of his arms around his neck, and responded heartily, and with the deepest emotion. Closing the prayer with an emphatic "Amen" from each, they arose.

Governor Johnson drew a long breath, seemed somewhat quieted, and said, " Moody, I feel better.   Will you stand by me ? "

" Certainly I will," was the reply.   The governor paced the floor for a moment silently, and then said, " Well, Moody, I can depend on you.   You are one in a hundred thousand."   Again he resumed his rapid walk in silent thoughtfulness; when suddenly he wheeled round, and said, —

" O Moody! I don't want you to think that I have become a religious man because I asked you to pray.   I am sorry to say it; but I am not, and never pretended to be, religious.   No one knows this better than you.   But, Moody, there is one thing about it : I *do* believe in Almighty God ; and I believe, also, in the Bible ; and I say, D—n me if Nashville shall be surrendered ! "

Mr. Lincoln narrated this anecdote to Mr. Carpenter, who, admirably commenting upon it, says, " The incident was given with a thrilling effect, which mentally placed Johnson, for a time, alongside of Luther and Cromwell.   Profanity or irreverence was lost sight of in the fervid utterance of a highly-wrought and great-souled determination, united with a rare exhibition of pathos and self-abnegation."

It was not until October, 1862, that Governor Johnson's family succeeded in reaching him, having passed through scenes of great hardship and peril.   In September Mr. Lincoln recommended an election for members of Congress in several districts in Tennessee which had proved loyal.   In December Governor Johnson issued a proclamation for elections in the ninth and tenth districts.   He was, however, emphatically opposed to allowing any rebel sympathizers to vote on any of the acts necessary to the restoration of the State. It was not enough, in his view, that the representative chosen should be loyal, but he must represent a loyal constituency.   He closed his proclamation in these decisive words : —

" No person will be considered an elector, qualified to vote, who, in addition to the other qualifications required by law, does not give satisfactory evidence, to the judges holding the election, of his loyalty to the government of the United States."

About the same time he imposed a tax of sixty thousand dollars upon the property of the secessionists for the support of the poor, the widows, and the orphans, who had been made such by the war. The current of events had apparently swept him along into entire

29

sympathy with the Republican party.   He was not only opposed to secession, but he was opposed to slavery, its originating cause, and to that senseless and haughty aristocracy which was founded in the oppression of the poor and the helpless.   Although in the presidential canvass he had voted for John C. Breckenridge, he now avowed himself the cordial supporter of the measures of President Lincoln's administration.

In the autumn of 1863 he visited Washington to confer with the President in reference to the restoration of Tennessee to the Union. Our military operations had been so successful that all organized bodies of rebels had been driven from the State.   The people who had been so long under the tyrannic rule of bands of thieves and murderers were rejoiced at their deliverance.   Numerous conventions were held, where Governor Johnson addressed the people with that directness and cogency of utterance which he had so eminently at his command.

"Tennessee," said he, "is not out of the Union, never has been, and never will be.   The bonds of the Constitution and the federal powers will always prevent that.   This government is perpetual. Provision is made for reforming the government and amending the Constitution, and admitting States into the Union, not for letting them out.

"Where are we now?   There is a rebellion.   The rebel army is driven back.   Here lies your State, — a sick man in his bed, emaciated and exhausted, paralyzed in all his powers, and unable to walk alone.   The physician comes.   The United States send an agent or a military governor, whichever you please to call him, to aid you in restoring your government.   Whenever you desire in good faith to restore civil authority, you can do so; and a proclamation for an election will be issued as speedily as it is practicable to hold one. One by one, all the agencies of your state government will be set in motion.   A legislature will be elected.   Judges will be appointed temporarily, until you can elect them at the polls.   And so of sheriffs, county-court judges, justices, and other officers, until the way is fairly open for the people, and all the parts of civil government resume their ordinary functions.   This is no nice, intricate, metaphysical question; it is a plain, common-sense matter; and there is nothing in the way but obstinacy."

Governor Johnson had now so thoroughly identified himself with

the great Republican party, and had so warmly advocated its fundamental principles, that his name began to be spoken of as a candidate for the vice-presidency at the approaching election. Hannibal
Hamlin of Maine now filled that office. He was a gentleman of
high intellectual and moral worth, and discharged his duties to the
full satisfaction of those who elected him. But, for obvious reasons,
it was deemed very important, since President Lincoln was from the
West, to elect a Vice-President from some one of the Southern
States. There was no other name so prominent as that of Andrew
Johnson. The North had learned to admire the man. His bold-
ness, his popular eloquence, his avowed hostility to slavery, his all-
embracing patriotism, and the sufferings he had endured in consequence of his devotion to his country's flag, all endeared him to the
North ; and, with enthusiasm, the Republican party rallied round
him.

At the National Convention assembled in Baltimore on the 6th of
June, 1864, almost by acclamation he was nominated on the same
ticket with Abraham Lincoln, who was renominated for the presidency. Most cordially this nomination was responded to by the
people. When this intelligence reached Nashville, an immense
mass-meeting was assembled to give it their ratification. Governor
Johnson was invited to address them. In the speech which he made
on this occasion, he said, —

" While society is in this disordered state, and we are seeking
security, let us fix the foundations of the government on principles
of eternal justice, which will endure for all time. There are those
in our midst who are for perpetuating the institution of slavery.
Let me say to you, Tennesseeans, and men from the Northern States,
that slavery is dead. It was not murdered by me. I told you long
ago what the result would be if you endeavored to go out of the
Union to save slavery, — that the result would be bloodshed, rapine,
devastated fields, plundered villages and cities ; and therefore I urged
you to remain in the Union. In trying to save slavery, you killed
it, and lost your own freedom. Your slavery is dead ; but I did not
murder it. As Macbeth said to Banquo's bloody ghost, —

'Thou canst not say I did it :
Never shake thy gory locks at me.'

Slavery is dead, but you must pardon me if I do not mourn over its
dead body. You can bury it out of sight. In restoring the State,

leave out that disturbing and dangerous element, and use only those parts of the machinery which will move in harmony.

" Now, in regard to emancipation, I want to say to the blacks, that liberty means liberty to work, and enjoy the fruits of your labor. Idleness is not freedom. I desire that all men shall have a fair start and an equal chance in the race of life: and let him succeed who has the most merit. This, I think, is a principle of Heaven. I am for emancipation, for two reasons: first, because it is right in itself; and, second, because, in the emancipation of the slaves, we break down an odious and dangerous aristocracy. I think that we are freeing more whites than blacks in Tennessee. I want to see slavery broken up; and, when its barriers are thrown down, I want to see industrious, thrifty emigrants pouring in from all parts of the country."

The utterance of such sentiments endeared Governor Johnson very much to all liberty-loving hearts. In a similar strain he wrote, in his letter to the convention accepting the nomination, —

" Before the Southern people assumed a belligerent attitude, and repeatedly since, I took occasion most frankly to declare the views I then entertained in relation to the wicked purposes of the Southern politicians. They have since undergone but little if any change. Time and subsequent events have rather confirmed than diminished my confidence in their correctness.

" At the beginning of this great struggle, I entertained the same opinion of it that I do now. In my place in the Senate, I denounced it as treason, worthy the punishment of death, and warned the government and the people of the impending danger. But my voice was not heard, or my counsel heeded, until it was to late to avert the storm. It still continued to gather over us, without molestation from the authorities at Washington, until at length it broke with all its fury upon the country; and now, if we would save the government from being overwhelmed by it, we must meet it in the true spirit of patriotism, and bring traitors to the punishment due their crimes, and by force of arms crush out and subdue the last vestige of rebel authority in the State.

"I felt then, as now, that the destruction of the government was deliberately determined upon by wicked and designing conspirators, whose lives and fortunes were pledged to carry it out; and that no compromise short of an unconditional recognition of the independence of the Southern States could have been, or could now be proposed, which they would accept. The clamor for ' Southern rights,' as the rebel journals were pleased to designate their rallying-cry, was not to secure their assumed rights *in the Union and under the Constitution,* but to disrupt the government, and establish an independent organization, based upon slavery, which they could at all times control.

" The separation of the government has for years past been the cherished purpose of the Southern leaders. Baffled in 1832 by the stern, patriotic heroism of Andrew Jackson, they sullenly acquiesced, only to mature their diabolical schemes, and await the recurrence of a more favorable opportunity to execute them. Then the pretext was the tariff ; and Jackson, after foiling their schemes of nullification and disunion, with prophetic perspicacity warned the country against the renewal of their efforts to dismember the government.

" In a letter dated May 1, 1833, to the Rev. A. J. Crawford, after demonstrating the heartless insincerity of the Southern nullifiers, he said, ' Therefore the tariff was only a pretext, and disunion and Southern confederacy the real object. The next pretext will be the negro or slavery question.' Time has fully verified this prediction, and we have now not only ' the negro or slavery question ' as the pretext, but the *real cause* of the Rebellion, and both must go down together. It is vain to attempt to reconstruct the Union with the distracting element of slavery in it. Experience has demonstrated its incompatibility with free and republican governments, and it would be unwise and unjust longer to continue it as one of the institutions of our country. While it remained subordinate to the Constitution and laws of the United States I yielded to it my support, but when it became rebellious, and attempted to rise above the government and control its action, I threw my humble influence against it.

" The authority of the government is supreme, and will admit of no rivalry. No institution can rise above it, whether it be slavery or any other organized power. In our happy form of government, all must be subordinate to the will of the people, when reflected through the Constitution and laws made pursuant thereto, state or federal. This great principle lies at the foundation of every government, and cannot be disregarded without the destruction of the government itself.

"In accepting the nomination, I might here close, but I cannot forego the opportunity of saying to my old friends of the Democratic party *proper*, with whom I have so long and pleasantly been associated, that the hour has now come when that great party can vindicate its devotion to true Democratic policy, and measures of expediency. The war is a war of great principles. It involves the supremacy and life of the government itself. If the rebellion triumph, free government, North and South, fails. If, on the other hand, the government is successful, — as I do not doubt that it will be, — its destiny. is fixed, its basis is permanent and enduring, and its career of honor and glory is but just begun. In a great contest like this for the existence of free government, the path of duty is patriotism and principle.

"This is not the hour for strife and division among ourselves. Such differences of opinion only encourage the enemy, prolong the war, and waste the country. Unity of action, and concentration of power, should be our watchword and rallying-cry. This accomplished, the time will rapidly approach when the armies in the field — that great power of the Rebellion — will be broken and crushed by our gallant officers and brave soldiers; and ere long they will return to their homes and firesides, to resume the avocations of peace, with the proud consciousness that they have aided in the noble work of reëstablishing upon a surer and more permanent basis the great temple of American freedom."

These are surely noble truths, nobly uttered. They met with a cordial response in every loyal heart. Every sentence elevated Andrew Johnson in the estimation of the American people. The names of Lincoln and Johnson were not only placed upon the same ticket, but at the fireside and from the church prayers of gratitude ascended to God that he had raised up a Southern man to coöperate with our own noble son of the West in the protection and redemption of our country.

These feelings were increased to enthusiasm by an event which took place a few months after the date of this letter.

On the 24th of October, 1864, Governor Johnson addressed an immense assemblage of the colored people of Nashville in a speech of extraordinary eloquence and power. We give it here, somewhat abbreviated from the admirable report furnished by a correspondent of "The Cincinnati Gazette." Governor Johnson spoke from the steps leading from Cedar Street to the State-House yard. The whole street was packed with the densest mass of human beings, the great proportion of them, men, women, and children, being the dusky-hued sons and daughters of bondage. The State-House yard, and also the great stone wall which separated it from the street, were covered with the multitude. It was in the evening, and many torches threw a weird-like light over the scene. The excitement was so intense that there was almost breathless silence. In tones which the sublimity of the occasion rendered deep and tremulous, the governor began : —

" Colored men of Nashville, you have all heard the President's proclamation, by which he announced to the world that the slaves in a large portion of the seceded States were thenceforth and forever free. For certain reasons which seemed wise to the President, the benefits of that proclamation did not extend to you or to your native State. Many of you were consequently left in bondage. The taskmaster's scourge was not yet broken, and the fetters still galled your limbs. Gradually the iniquity has been passing away ; but the hour has come when the last vestiges of it must be removed.

" Consequently, I too, standing here upon the steps of the Capitol, with the past history of the State to witness, the present condition to guide, and its future to encourage me, — I, Andrew Johnson, do hereby proclaim freedom, full, broad, and unconditional, to every man in Tennessee."

It was one of those moments when the speaker seems inspired, and when his audience, catching the inspiration, rises to his level, and becomes one with him. Strangely as some of the words of this immortal utterance sounded to those uncultivated ears, not one of them was misunderstood. With breathless attention, these sons of bondage hung upon each syllable. Each individual seemed carved in stone until the last word of the grand climax was reached, and then the scene which followed beggars all description. One simultaneous roar of approval and delight burst from three thousand throats. Flags, banners, torches, and transparencies were waved wildly over the throng, or flung aloft in the ecstasy of joy. Drums, fifes, and trumpets added to the uproar ; and the mighty tumult of this great mass of human beings, rejoicing for their race, woke up the slumbering echoes of the Capitol, vibrated through the length and breadth of the city, rolled over the sluggish waters of the Cumberland, and rang out far into the night beyond.

There were in the vicinity of Nashville two slaveholders of immense wealth. Their princely estates spread over thousands of acres, and were tilled by hundreds of unpaid bondmen. The old feudal barons did not wield more despotic power than Cockrill and Harding wielded over their cabined slaves. Both of these men were, of course, intense rebels. Their names were everywhere prominent, and their great wealth gave them vast influence in the State. In allusion to them, Governor Johnson continued : —

" I am no agrarian. I wish to see secured to every man, rich or poor, the fruits of his honest industry, effort, or toil. I want each man to feel that what he has gained by his own skill or talent or exertion is rightfully his, and his alone ; but if, through an iniquitous system, a vast amount of wealth has been accumulated in the hands of one man, or a few men, then that result is wrong ; and the sooner we can right it, the better for all concerned. It is wrong that Mack Cockrill and W. D. Harding, by means of forced and unpaid labor, should have monopolized so large a share of the lands and wealth of Tennessee; and I say, that if their immense plantations were divided up, and parceled out amongst a number of free, industrious, and honest farmers, it would give more good citizens to the Commonwealth, increase the wages of our mechanics, enrich the markets of our city, enliven all the arteries of trade, improve society, and conduce to the greatness and glory of the State.

" The representatives of this corrupt, and, if you will permit me almost to swear a little, this damnable aristocracy, taunt us with our desire to see justice done, and charge us with favoring negro equality. Of all living men, they should be the last to mouth that phrase ; and, even when uttered in their hearing, it should cause their cheeks to tinge, and burn with shame. Negro equality indeed ! Why, pass any day along the sidewalk of High Street, where these aristocrats more particularly dwell, — these aristocrats, whose sons are now in the bands of guerrillas and cut-throats who prowl and rob and murder around our city, — pass by their dwellings, I say, and you will see as many mulatto as negro children, the former bearing an unmistakable resemblance to their aristocratic owners.

" Colored men of Tennessee, this, too, shall cease. Your wives and daughters shall no longer be dragged into a concubinage, compared to which polygamy is a virtue, to satisfy the brutal lusts of slaveholders and overseers. Henceforth the sanctity of God's law of marriage shall be respected in your persons, and the great State of Tennessee shall no more give her sanction to your degradation and your shame."

" Thank God, thank God!" came from the lips of a thousand women, who, in their own persons, had experienced the iniquity of the man-seller's code. " Thank God!" fervently echoed the fathers, husbands, and brothers of these women.

" And if the law protects you," he continued, " in the possession of your wives and children, if the law shields those whom you hold dear from the unlawful grasp of lust, will you endeavor to be true to yourselves, and shun, as it were death itself, the path of lewdness, crime, and vice?"

" We will, we will!" cried the assembled thousands; and, joining in a sublime and tearful enthusiasm, another mighty shout went up to heaven.

"Looking at this vast crowd," the governor continued, "and reflecting through what a storm of persecution and obloquy they are compelled to pass, I am almost induced to wish, that, as in the days of old, a Moses might arise, who should lead them safely to their promised land of freedom and happiness."

" You are our Moses!" shouted several voices; and the exclamation was caught up and cheered until the Capitol rang again.

" God," continued the governor, "no doubt has prepared somewhere an instrument for the great work he designs to perform in behalf of this outraged people; and, in due time, your leader will come forth, your Moses will be revealed to you."

" We want no Moses but you!" again shouted the crowd.

" Well, then," Governor Johnson replied, " humble and unworthy as I am, if no other better shall be found, I will indeed be your Moses, and lead you through the Red Sea of war and bondage to a fairer future of liberty and peace. I speak now as one who feels the world his country, and all who love equal rights his friends. I speak, too, as a citizen of Tennessee. I am here on my own soil; and here I mean to stay, and fight this great battle of truth and justice to a triumphant end. Rebellion and slavery shall, by God's good help, no longer pollute our State. Loyal men, whether white or black, shall alone control her destinies, and, when this strife in which we are all engaged is past, I trust, I know, we shall have a better state of things, and shall all rejoice that honest labor reaps the fruit of its own industry, and that every man has a fair chance in the race of life."

It is impossible to describe the enthusiasm which followed these words. Joy beamed in every countenance. Tears and laughter followed each other in swift succession. The great throng moved and swayed back and forth in the intensity of emotion, and shout after shout rent the air. This was one of those scenes of moral sublimity which few on earth have ever been permitted to witness. The speaker seemed inspired with very unusual power to meet the grandeur of the occasion and the theme. As he descended from the steps of the Capitol in this proudest, holiest hour of his life, the dense throng parted, as by magic, to let him through ; and, all that night long, his name was mingled with the curses and the execrations of the traitor and oppressor, and with the blessings of the oppressed and the poor. General Sherman was then sweeping through the very heart of the rebellious States, and Grant was thundering at the gates of Petersburg and Richmond. Tennessee had returned to her allegiance, revised her Constitution, and abolished slavery.

Mr. Johnson has always been a little boastful of his lowly origin. Certainly it is to his credit that, from a position so extremely obscure, he should have raised himself to stations of so much eminence. In a speech delivered at Nashville soon after his nomination, he said, —

"In accepting the nomination, I shall stand on the principles I here enunciate, let the consequences for good or for evil be what they may. A distinguished Georgian told me in Washington, after the election of Mr. Lincoln, and just before his inauguration, that the people of Georgia would not consent to be governed by a man who had risen from the ranks. It was one of the principal objections of the people of the South to Mr. Lincoln. What will they do now, when they have to take two rulers who have risen from the ranks ? This aristocracy is antagonistic to the principles of free democratic government, and the time has come when it must give up the ghost. The time has come when this rebellious element of aristocracy must be punished.

"The day when they could talk of their three or four thousand acres of land, tilled by their hundreds of negroes, is past; and the hour for the division of these rich lands among the energetic and laboring masses is at hand. The field is to be thrown open; and I now invite the energetic and industrious of the North to come and occupy it, and apply here the same skill and industry which has made the North so rich. I am for putting down the aristocracy, and dividing out their possessions among the worthier laborers of any and all colors."

The election which took place on the 14th of November, 1864, resulted in the choice of Lincoln and Johnson by one of the largest majorities ever given. On the 4th of March, 1865, Mr. Johnson was inaugurated Vice-President of the United States. The clouds of gloom which had so long overhung the land were beginning to break. Grant and Sherman were dealing the armies of Rebellion annihilating blows. On the 3d of April there was a meeting in Washington to rejoice over the glad tidings of the evacuation of Petersburg and Richmond. In the address which Vice-President Johnson made at that meeting, he said, —

" At the time that the traitors in the Senate of the United States plotted against the government and entered into a conspiracy more foul, more execrable, and more odious than that of Catiline against the Romans, I happened to be a member of that body, and, as to loyalty, stood solitary and alone among the senators from the Southern States. I was then and there called upon to know what I would do with such traitors; and I want to repeat my reply here.

" I said, if we had an Andrew Jackson he would hang them as high as Haman. But as he is no more, and sleeps in his grave, in his own beloved State, where traitors and treason have even insulted his tomb and the very earth that covers his remains, humble as I am, when you ask me what I would do, my reply is, I would arrest them; I would try them; I would convict them; and I would hang them.

" Since the world began, there has never been a rebellion of such gigantic proportions, so infamous in character, so diabolical in motive, so entirely disregardful of the laws of civilized war. It has introduced the most savage mode of warfare ever practiced upon earth.

" One word more and I am done. It is this: I am in favor of leniency; but, in my opinion, evil-doers should be punished. Treason is the highest crime known in the catalogue of crimes; and for him that is guilty of it, for him that is willing to lift his impious hand against the authority of the nation, I would say death is too easy a punishment. My notion is, that treason must be made odious, and traitors must be punished and impoverished, their social power broken : they must be made to feel the penalty of their crime. You, my friends, have traitors in your very midst, and treason needs rebuke and punishment here as well as elsewhere. It is not the men in the field who are the greatest traitors : it is the men who have encouraged them to imperil their lives, while they themselves have remained at home, expending their means and exerting all their power to overthrow the government. Hence I say this, ' The halter to intelligent, influential traitors ! '

" To the honest boy, to the deluded man, who has been deceived into the rebel ranks, I would extend leniency; but the leaders I would hang. I hold, too, that wealthy traitors should be made to remunerate those men who have suffered as a consequence of their crime."

The great rebel army under General Lee surrendered on the 9th of April, 1865. Five days after this, on the 14th, while the bells of joy were ringing all over the nation at the utter overthrow of the Rebellion, the bullet of the assassin pierced the brain of President Lincoln. On the morning of the 15th the fearful tidings quivered along the wires, creating almost universal consternation and grief, *Abraham Lincoln died this morning at twenty-two minutes after seven o'clock !*

Immediately upon his death, Hon. James Speed, Attorney-General of the United States, waited upon President Johnson with the following official communication : —

WASHINGTON CITY, *April* 15, 1865.

ANDREW JOHNSON, *Vice-President of the United States.*

Sir, — Abraham Lincoln, President of the United States, was shot by an assassin last evening, at Ford's Theatre, in this city, and died at the hour of twenty-two minutes after seven o'clock this morning. About the same time at which the President was shot, an assassin entered the sick-chamber of Hon. W. H. Seward, Secretary of State, and stabbed him in several places in the throat, neck, and face, severely, if not mortally, wounding him. Other members of the secretary's family were dangerously wounded by the assassin while making his escape.

By the death of President Lincoln, the office of President has devolved, under the Constitution, upon you. The emergency of the government demands that you should immediately qualify yourself according to the requirements of the Constitution, and enter upon the duties of President of the United States. If you will please make known your pleasure, such arrangements as you deem proper will be made.

Your obedient servants,

HUGH M'CULLOCH, *Secretary of the Treasury.*
EDWIN M. STANTON, *Secretary of War.*
GIDEON WELLES, *Secretary of the Navy.*
WILLIAM DENNISON, *Postmaster-General.*
J. P. USHER, *Secretary of the Interior.*
JAMES SPEED, *Attorney-General.*

At ten o'clock, but little more than two and a half hours after the death of the President, a small but august assemblage met at the private apartments of Mr. Johnson, and Chief-Justice Chase administered to him the oath of office. The ceremonies were brief, but invested with unusual solemnity, in consequence of the sad event which rendered them necessary.

When Mr. Johnson was inaugurated Vice-President, an untoward event occurred, which excited great pain and anxiety throughout the nation. It was an event which attracted such universal attention and such severity of comment at the time, that historic fidelity requires that it should be alluded to. Mr. Johnson had been very sick with typhoid fever, and was in a state of extreme debility. He could not walk his chamber-floor without tottering. His physician judged it imprudent for him to attempt to make his appearance at the inauguration; but his anxiety was so great to attend ceremonies in which he was to assume such momentous responsibilities, that, by the reluctant consent of the physician, he went, taking a stimulant to strengthen him for the hour. The stimulant was not a strong one; but, in his weak and fevered state, it so overcame him, that in the Senate Chamber, before the assembled dignitaries of our own and other lands, in his inaugural address, he uttered incoherent thoughts which mantled the cheek of the nation with a blush.

A generous people promptly, gladly, accepted the explanation. The affair, for a moment so humiliating to national pride, was forgiven and forgotten. With confiding trust, Andrew Johnson was received as the worthy successor of Abraham Lincoln, the loved and the lamented. Seldom, if ever, has a President entered upon his office so deeply enshrined in the affections and confidence of the Christian people all over our land as did President Johnson. Two days after he had assumed the duties of his responsible position, a delegation of citizens from Illinois, who were about to accompany the remains of President Lincoln to the burial-ground in Springfield, called upon President Johnson to pay him their respects. Governor Oglesby, in behalf of the delegation, said, —

"I take much pleasure in presenting to you this delegation of the citizens of Illinois, representing almost every portion of the State. We are drawn together by the mournful events of the past few days to give some feeble expression, by appropriate and respectful ceremonies, to the feelings we, in common with the whole nation, realize as pressing us to the earth. We thought it not inappropriate, before we should separate, even in this sad hour, to seek this interview with your excellency, that while the bleeding heart is pouring out its mournful anguish over the death of our beloved late President, the idol of our State and the pride of our whole country, we may earnestly express to you, the living head of this nation, our deliberate, full, and abiding confience in you, as the one who, in these dark hours, must bear upon yourself the mighty responsibility of maintaining, defending, and directing its affairs.

"The record of your whole past life, familiar to all, the splendor of your recent gigantic efforts to stay the hand of treason and assassination, and restore the flag to the uttermost bounds of the Republic, assure that noble State which we represent, and, we believe, the people of the United States, that we may safely trust our destinies in your hands. And to this end we come in the name of the State of Illinois, and, we confidently believe, fully and faithfully expressing the wishes of our people, to present and pledge to you the cordial, earnest, and unremitting purpose of our State to give your administration the strong support we have heretofore given to the administration of our lamented late President, the policy of whom we have heretofore, do now, and shall continue to indorse."

President Johnson, in his reply, said, "I have listened with profound emotion to the kind words you have addressed to me. The visit of this large delegation to speak to me, through you, sir, these words of encouragement, I had not anticipated. In the midst of the saddening circumstances which surround us, and the immense responsibility thrown upon me, an expression of the confidence of individuals, and still more of an influential body like that before me, representing a great commonwealth, cheers and strengthens my heavily-burdened mind. I am at a loss for words to respond. In an hour like this, of deepest sorrow, were it possible to embody in words the feelings of my bosom, I could not command my lips to utter them. Perhaps the best reply I could make, and the one most readily appropriate to your kind assurance of confidence, would be to receive them in silence.

" The throbbings of my heart, since the sad catastrophe which has appalled us, cannot be reduced to words; and oppressed as I am with the new and great responsibility which has devolved upon me, and saddened with grief, I can with difficulty respond to you at all. But I cannot permit such expressions of the confidence reposed in me by the people to pass without acknowledgment. Sprung from the people myself, every pulsation in the popular heart finds an immediate answer in my own. Your words of countenance and encouragement sank deep into my heart; and, were I even a coward, I could not but gather from them strength to carry out my convictions of right. Thus feeling, I shall enter upon the discharge of my great duty firmly, steadfastly, if not with the signal ability exhibited by my predecessor, which is still fresh in our sorrowing minds.

" In what I say on this occasion, I shall indulge in no petty spirit of anger, no feeling of revenge. But we have beheld a notable event in the history of mankind. In the midst of the American people, where every citizen is taught to obey law and observe the rules of Christian conduct, our Chief Magistrate, the beloved of all hearts, has been assassinated; and when we trace this crime to its cause, when we remember the source whence the assassin drew his inspiration, and then look at the result, we stand yet more astounded at this most barbarous, most diabolical assassination. Such a crime as the murder of a great and good man, honored and revered, the beloved and the hope of the people, springs not alone from a solitary individual of ever so desperate wickedness. We can trace its cause through successive steps, without my enumerating them here, back to that source which is the spring of all our woes.

" No one can say that, if the perpetrator of this fiendish deed be arrested, he should not undergo the extremest penalty the law knows for crime. None will say that mercy should interpose. But is he alone guilty? Here, gentlemen, you perhaps expect me to present some indication of my future policy. One thing I will say, Every era teaches its lesson. The times we live in are not without instruction. The American people must be taught, if they do not already feel, that treason is a crime, and must be punished; that the government will not always bear with its enemies; that it is strong, not only to protect, but to punish.

" When we turn to the criminal code, and examine the catalogue of crimes, we find there arson laid down as a crime, with its appropriate penalty; we find there theft and robbery and murder given as crime; and there, too, we find the last and highest of crimes, *treason*. With other and inferior offenses our people are familiar; but, in our peaceful history, *treason* has been almost unknown. The people must understand that it is the blackest of crimes, and that it will be severely punished. I make this allusion, not to excite the already exasperated feelings of the public, but to point out the principles of public justice which should guide our action at this particular juncture, and which accord with sound public morals. Let it be engraven on every heart that treason is a crime, and that traitors shall suffer its penalty.

" While we are appalled, overwhelmed, at the fall of one man in our midst by the hand of a traitor, shall we allow men, I care not by what weapons, to attempt the life of a state with impunity? While we strain our minds to comprehend the enormity of this assassination, shall we allow the nation to be assassinated? I speak in no spirit of unkindness. I do not harbor bitter or revengeful feeling towards any. I know that men love to have their actions spoken of in connection with acts of mercy; and how easy it is to yield to this impulse! But we must not forget that what may be mercy to the individual is cruelty to the state. In the exercise of mercy, there should be no doubt left that this high prerogative is not used to relieve a few at the expense of the many. Be assured that I shall never forget that I am not to consult my own feelings alone, but to give an account to the whole people.

" In regard to my future course, I will now make no professions, no pledges. I have long labored for the amelioration and elevation of the great mass of mankind. I believe that government was made for man, not man for government. This struggle of the people against the most gigantic rebellion the world ever saw has demonstrated that the attachment of the people to their government is the strongest national defense human wisdom can devise. My past life, especially my course during the present unholy rebellion, is before you. I have no principles to retract. I have no professions to offer. I shall not attempt to anticipate the future. As events occur, and it becomes necessary for me to act, I shall dispose of each as it arises."

A nation might well be proud of a ruler with so noble a record, cherishing such sentiments, and capable of expressing them with so much force and eloquence. In conformity with these principles, the very large majority of Congress, both the Senate and the House, began to adopt those measures of reconstruction through which the States which had been in rebellion could be restored to coöperation in the government of the Union. The rebels themselves declared, in the loudest and most defiant tones, that they were conquered only, not subdued; that in heart they were as relentless and determined as ever; and that, having failed upon the bloody field, they would renew the conflict, as of old, upon the floor of Congress. But the patriotic country felt safe in the assurance that we had a President in perfect harmony with the noblest Congress which had ever convened. But, to the surprise and almost the consternation of both Congress and the great mass of the people, it was found that the President, through some inexplicable influence, seemed to have changed his views, and was opposing vehemently, and with mortifying indecorum, those measures which Congress, with the general approval of the loyal population, would adopt, to protect the friends of the government from the vengeance of unrepentant rebels, and to shield our free institutions from renewed assaults.

The change was one of the most sudden and marvelous on record. Almost in an hour, the rebels and their sympathizers, who had been burning President Johnson in effigy, and denouncing him in the strongest language of vituperation which contempt and rage could coin, were shouting his praises, and rushing in from all quarters to greet him with their hosannas. The friends who elected him, who loved him, who leaned upon him for their support, were struck aghast. For a time they were mute in grief. Then came remonstrance and the angry strife. The bitterness of the old days of slavery domination, which we hoped had passed away forever, was

30

revived. It seemed as though all our blood had been shed and our treasure expended in vain. The President urgently advocated measures of reconstruction which, in the judgment of Congress and of the vast majority of the people of the North, would place the government again in the hands of those rebels and their sympathizers who had deluged our land in blood, and swept it with the flames of war, that they might overthrow our free institutions, and establish human bondage forever as the corner-stone of this republic.

The great question upon which this strife arose was, " Shall the United States government extend its protection to all loyal men, without distinction of race, who, during the Rebellion, proved true to the national flag?" President Johnson is understood to assume that we have no such right; that we must leave the nation's defenders, black and white, in the Southern States, to the tender mercies of the rebels; that the rebel States have never been out of the Union, have never forfeited their political rights; and that if they now meet, and elect delegates to Congress, we are bound to receive those delegates upon their oath of loyalty; each house of Congress, of course, having the right to reject or expel any member who is personally obnoxious.

This principle of reconstruction is revolting to the conscience of the great majority of Congress and of the loyal North. Mr. Peter Cooper, whose virtues have given him a national fame, in an admirable letter of respectful yet earnest remonstrance to President Johnson, says, —

" I, with thousands of others who labored to aid the government in putting down the Rebellion, would have rejoiced if Congress could have found all the reports of the continued persecution of Union men throughout the South to be groundless and false.

" The whole Republican party would have rejoiced if Congress could have found it safe to admit the members offered from Southern States at once to a full share in the government.

" This being my wish does not authorize me to denounce the majority in Congress, and accuse them of being radicals and traitors, ' hanging on the skirts of a government which they are trying to destroy.'

" It was said of old, the sin of ingratitude is worse than the sin of witchcraft.

" To my mind, our nation must live in everlasting infamy if we fail to secure a full measure of justice to an unfortunate race of men who were originally hunted down in their own country, and carried off and sold, like beasts, into an abject slavery, with all their posterity.

"This enslaved race has the strongest possible claims for kindness, as well as justice, at the hands of the people and government of the whole country, and more especially from the people of the South. These unfortunate slaves have done a great portion of the labor that has fed and clothed the whites and blacks of the Southern country.

" As true as the laborer is worthy of his hire, so true is it that we, as a nation, cannot withhold justice and equal rights from a race of men that has fought and bled and labored to defend and protect the Union of the States in the hour of our nation's greatest extremity.

" The enemies of our country and government are now trying to persuade the community to believe that a war of races would result from giving the black man the same measure of justice and rights which the white men claim for themselves. This will be found to be a groundless fear. Our national danger will always result from unequal and partial laws. We cannot make laws which will oppress and keep in ignorance the poor without bringing on ourselves and our country the just judgment of a righteous God, who will reward us as a nation according to our works.

"I indulge the hope that you will see, before it is entirely too late, the terrible danger of taking counsel with Northern men in sympathy with the rebels who fought the government with all the energy of desperation to accomplish the destruction of our government, instead of taking counsel with those friends who elected you, — friends who have been and are as desirous as you can possibly be to secure the adoption of every measure calculated to promote the substantial welfare of all parts of our common country."

As to the question whether the national government has the constitutional right to extend its protection to its defenders in the several States, much depends upon the theory which one adopts in reference to the war of the Rebellion. A contest of arms between an established and recognized government and a military force formed by a combination of *individual citizens* is *civil war*. The insurgents, when subdued or captured, are responsible *individually* for their acts, and are consequently amenable to the courts of law on charges of treason and rebellion.

A contest of arms between any government and a military force organized *under the authority of any other government*, exercising an independent sovereignty, is *international war*. The persons engaged in the military operations are not individually responsible for their acts before courts of justice on criminal charges, but, when subdued or captured, can only be treated as prisoners of war. The victorious government is, however, entitled to exercise over the one that is subdued the rights of a conqueror as defined by the laws of war.

The Constitution of the United States is of a twofold character. It establishes a government with sovereign powers in respect to certain specified interests, and, to this extent, is simply a constitution of government framed by a single people. It also at the same time includes a *covenant of union* made by a number of separate governments, each exercising its own independent sovereignty in respect to certain other interests; and to this extent the act is of the nature of a *league* or *treaty*, binding several sovereignties to the fulfillment of certain obligations towards each other.

In case of hostilities arising among the parties of this instrument, the question whether, in a legal point of view, the conflict is to be regarded as a *civil war* or an *international war*, in respect to its character and effects, will depend upon the nature of it in relation to these two different aspects of the instruments; that is, whether the insurgents act in an individual or in a corporate capacity.

If it is a contest between the general government and a force organized by individual citizens, it is an insurrection or civil war. The insurgents may be so numerous and so well organized as to force the government, during the contest, to grant them belligerent rights; but, when vanquished or captured, they are amenable to the courts of law on charges of rebellion or treason.

If, on the other hand, it is admitted by the North to be, what the South claims it to be, a contest between the general government and a force organized by and acting in subordination to any one or more of the state governments, under proceedings regularly taken by the state authorities, in the manner prescribed by law, then it is of the nature of *international war*, in so far as that the governments which inaugurate it assume the responsibility of it, and those acting under their authority are personally released. They can only be treated, when vanquished or captured, as prisoners of war. The victorious governments are entitled to exercise over the States that are vanquished the rights of conquerors, as regulated by the laws of war.

There can be no question that the latter was the view universally taken by those engaged in the Rebellion. They formed a government with its constitution and all its organized officers. They unfurled their flag, and conscripted their soldiers. They raised large armies, and issued letters of marque. They sent their ambassadors to knock at the doors of other governments for admission. In *point of fact*, they sundered all their relations with the national government, and seditiously, illegally, unconstitutionally, but yet *really*, became an independent government, and maintained that independence during a struggle of four years' duration. They were so strong that they compelled the national government to recognize it as *war*, to exchange prisoners, and grant other belligerent rights.

At length they were *conquered*. Their army was crushed; their piratic navy was annihilated. Their constitution and laws vanished. Their flag sank into the dust. Whatever may be their individual responsibility as rebels in organizing this hostile government, there can be no question whatever that they did, *in fact*, sunder their relations with the national government; that they did, *in fact*, assume and exercise the functions of sovereignty; and that, having thus been vanquished, the victors are entitled to exercise over them the rights of conquerors, as regulated by the laws of war.

Within the territorial limits of this rebellious nation there were thousands of patriotic white men who remained true to their country and its flag. In consequence, they were exposed to every conceivable outrage. Multitudes of them were scourged, shot, and hanged. There were some millions of colored men who were patriotic to their hearts' core. The object of the Rebellion was to strengthen the chains which had so long held them in bondage. The result of the Rebellion was to break those chains, and to let the oppressed go free. And now the unrepentant rebels are exceedingly exasperated against those Union white men, and those patriots of African descent whose sympathies were with the national government; and these rebels implore the Northern people to be *magnanimous*, and to interpose no obstacle to their wreaking their vengeance upon the Union people of the South.

This is the great question of *reconstruction* which is now agitating the land. President Johnson is understood to advocate the restoration of the conquered States to the Union, without exacting from them any pledges whatever which will protect from violence the friends of the Union within their borders. He is understood to assume that the Rebellion was merely a series of illegal acts of private individuals; that the States in which the Rebellion took place were, during the Rebellion, completely competent States of the United States as they were before the Rebellion, and were bound by all the obligations which the Constitution imposed, and entitled to all its privileges; and that now, whenever representatives appear from such States and demand admission, there is but one question which we have any right to ask; and that is, " Have these States organized governments which are republican in form ? " It is said that each house of Congress can decide respecting the individual merits of the representative who claims admission to their body, and can receive or reject as it pleases; but, as to the governments which they represent, " how they were formed, under what auspices they were formed, are inquiries with which Congress has no concern. The right of the people to form a government for themselves has never been questioned."

It seems to be assumed, in the first place, that the States have never rebelled : *individuals* only have committed that crime. And then, in the second place, it is assumed that these *individuals* have forfeited nothing by their treason ; that they are entitled to all the rights and privileges which they ever enjoyed ; and that they can send their representatives to Congress, and demand admission for them, with just as much assurance as if they had ever remained loyal. This *unconditional* admission of the rebel States, without securing in advance the imperiled rights of the loyalists, both white and black, is regarded by the great mass of the Northern people as a crime which would justly expose the nation to the scorn of the world.

In September, 1866, there was a large convention in Philadelphia of *loyal men* from all the States which had been in rebellion. In their appeal to their fellow-citizens of the United States, they say, —

" The representatives of eight millions of American citizens appeal for protection and justice to their friends and brothers in the States that have been spared the cruelties of the Rebellion and the direct horrors of civil war. Here, on the spot where freedom was proffered and pledged by the fathers of the republic, we implore your help against a reorganized oppression, whose sole object is to remit the control of our destinies to the contrivers of the Rebellion after they have been vanquished in honorable battle; thus at once to punish us for our devotion to our country, and intrench themselves in the official fortifications of the government."

In illustration of the manner in which the loyal colored population could be oppressed, and, while nominally free, could have burdens imposed upon them more intolerable than they ever bore before, the following statements are made : —

" The laws passed by some of our legislatures provide that all persons engaged in agricultural pursuits, as laborers, shall be required, during the first ten days of the month of January of each year, to make contracts for the ensuing year ; and, in case of failure, such laborer shall be arrested by the civil authorities, and hired out ; and, however much the laborer may be dissatisfied, he dare not leave, under the penalty of being apprehended, and forced to labor upon the public works, without compensation, until he will consent to return to his employer. It is punished with fine and imprisonment to entice or persuade away, feed, harbor, or secrete, any such laborer. In this way they are compelled to contract within a limit of ten days, punished by legal enslavement for violating a simple contract, and prevented from obtaining shelter, food, or employment. By severest penalties, he has been made a serf in the name of freedom, and suffers all the evils of the institution of slavery, without receiving that care which the master, from a sense of his own interest, would give to his bondsmen."

Governor Hamilton of Texas stated, before an immense meeting of the citizens of New Haven, Conn., on the evening of September 15, 1866, that he could testify from his own personal knowledge, that in the single State of Texas, during the last six months, more than one thousand colored men had been brutally and wantonly murdered, — unoffending men, murdered simply because they were colored men and loyalists ; and that not one of their murderers had been arrested. He stated that no Union white man dared to attempt to protect them ; that, should he make the attempt, he would only expose himself to the same fate.

Again: the convention describes the treatment to which the white loyal men are exposed. The massacre in New Orleans was as follows: "On the 30th of July, 1866, in pursuance of a proclamation of Rufus N. Howell, one of the judges of the Supreme Court of Louisiana, the convention of loyal men, which, under the protection of the United States troops, met and framed the organic law under which the civil government of Louisiana was formed, and which adjourned subject to the call of the president, was again convened. The rebel press denounced the convention in the most abusive language, and resorted to every expedient to inflame the minds of the returned rebel soldiers against the convention and its adherents. Public meetings were held, and incendiary speeches made. The mayor of the city declared his intention to disperse the convention if it should attempt to meet within the limits of New Orleans.

"At twelve o'clock of the night before the meeting of the convention, the police were assembled at the station-houses, and each one was armed with a large navy revolver. The convention met at twelve o'clock, at noon, in the Convention Hall, at the corner of Dryades and Canal streets. A large number of Union men were assembled, peaceful, unarmed citizens, in front of the building. At one o'clock, at a signal of the ringing of the bells, the police, joined by hundreds of armed rebel soldiers in citizens' dress, attacked, without the slightest provocation, the people in front of the building. With unrelenting butchery, these men of bloody hands and hearts shot down the loyalists. The street was soon cleared. There were left but pools of blood, and the mangled bodies of the slain.

They then made a dash into the hall of the convention. Paris, during the Reign of Terror, never witnessed a scene more dreadful. The members of the convention were unarmed, and utterly defenseless. At the suggestion of their chaplain, the Rev. Mr. Horton, they quietly took their seats, and thus awaited the storm. Without any attempt at arrest, without encountering any act or word of provocation, these police-officers, with their Union-hating band of rebel soldiers, opened fire with their revolvers upon their helpless victims. Volley succeeded volley. No mercy was shown. White handkerchiefs were waved, as flags of truce, in vain. A deaf ear was turned to every plea. The work of butchery was continued, until every Union man in the room was either killed or wounded, excepting the very few who almost miraculously escaped.

While this scene was being enacted in the hall, bands of murderers were equally active in the streets, for several squares around the building. Every colored man and every known Union man was shot down. The bodies of the slain were mutilated in the most brutal way. In the report which the Southern Union men make of this almost unparalleled outrage, they say, —

"All the circumstances connected with this tragic event, — the expressed intention of the mayor to disperse the convention, the

RIOT AT NEW ORLEANS — SCENE IN MECHANICS' HALL.

withdrawal of the police from their beats in the city, the arming of them with revolvers, the signal given at one o'clock, and the prompt arrival of all the police of the city, including six or seven hundred special policemen sworn in for the occasion, the presence of the mayor during the tumult, the deception practised by the lieutenant-governor to keep troops out of the city, — all clearly prove that the bloody tragedy was, as General Sheridan states, a 'premeditated massacre.'

"And from the brutal manner in which over four hundred Union men were killed or wounded, from the fact that not one single policeman or participant in the murderous affair has been arrested, from the fact that the same men whose hands are yet red with the blood of the patriot soldiers of the Republic, and crimsoned anew in that of the martyrs of the 30th of July, are still retained in office and power in that city, it is clear that there is no security for the lives, the liberty, or the property, of loyal citizens.

" It is a part of the history of this massacre, that indictments were found by the grand jury of the parish, composed of ex-rebel soldiers and their sympathizers, against the survivors of the convention, for having disturbed the peace of the community; and that, to-day, many of them are under heavy bonds to appear and answer the charge. Nor did this seem to satisfy the judge of the criminal court: for the grand jury was brought before him on the following day, and instructed to find bills of indictment against the members of the convention and spectators, *charging them with murder*, giving the principle in law, and applying it in this case, that whosoever is engaged in an unlawful proceeding, from which death ensues to a human being, is guilty of murder; and alleging, that as the convention had no right to meet, and the police had killed many men on the day of its meeting, the survivors were therefore guilty of murder.

" But why continue," these Southern loyalists add, " the recital of this horrible record? We have before us evidences from every portion of the South, proving the extent and the increasing violence of the spirit of intolerance and persecution above set forth. This committee is in possession of information that Union men dare not attend this convention for fear of violence upon their return. Gentlemen of this convention have, since their arrival in this city, received notices warning them not to return home. We have omitted the relation of acts of ferocity and barbarism too horrible to relate. We submit to the impartial judgment of the American people, if these state governments, thus ruled by a disunion oligarchy, and based on the political disfranchisement of three millions of colored citizens, and the social disfranchisement of the entire loyal white citizens, are *republican in form*. Of doubtful legal existence, they are undoubtedly despotic, and despotic in the interests of treason, as we of the South know but too well.

" We affirm that the loyalists of the South look to Congress, with affectionate gratitude and confidence, as the only means to save us from persecution, exile, and death itself. And we also declare that there can be no security for us and our children, there can be no safety for the country, against the fell spirit of slavery, now organized in the form of serfdom, unless the government, by national and appropriate legislation, enforced by national authority, shall confer on every citizen in the States we represent *the American birthright of impartial suffrage, and equality before the law.*

" This is the one all-sufficient remedy. This is our great need and pressing necessity. This is the only policy which will destroy sectionalism, by bringing into effective power a preponderating force on the side of loyalty. It will lead to an enduring pacification, because based on the eternal principles of justice. It is a policy which finally will regenerate the South itself, because it will introduce and establish there a divine principle of moral politics, which, under God's blessing, will, in elevating humanity, absorb and purify the unchristian hate and selfish passions of men."

According to the Constitution, if two thirds of the members of each house of Congress agree upon any amendments, those amendments shall be submitted to the approval of the several States. If three fourths of these accept them, they become a part of the Constitution. The views of a large majority in both houses of Congress were not in harmony with those of the President. Congress took the ground, that, before the rebellious States should be allowed to assume their former privileges in the councils of the nation, certain guaranties should be exacted of them as a protection for the Union men of the South, and to protect the nation from the repetition of so terrible a wrong.

With this view, they presented to the States *Terms of Reconstruction,* to be adopted as constitutional amendments. Whatever may be thought of the policy or the impolicy of these terms, their wonderful leniency no man can deny. The Rebellion was a terrible fact, as terrible as earth has ever known. It cost thousands of millions of money, and hundreds of thousands of lives, and an amount of misery, of life-long destitution and woe, which never can be gauged. A greater crime was never perpetrated. Its responsibility lies somewhere.

If we regard it as merely a combination of *individual citizens,* then these insurgents merit severe punishment on the charge of treason and rebellion. If we regard it as an *international war* between the United States government and independent confederate states, then is the victorious government entitled to the rights of a conqueror as defined by the laws of war. Prussia annihilates the governments of the provinces and the kingdoms she has conquered, and compels them to pay the expenses of the war; and not a cabinet in Europe utters a word of remonstrance.

With magnanimity never before in the history of the world manifested towards a vanquished enemy, the national government calls for no punishment in the dungeon or on the scaffold, for no conscription or exile, for no political or personal servitude depriving states or individuals of any of their rights: it simply requires a few easy terms as a slight security against another war.

These terms are as follows: —

Resolved by the Senate and House of Representatives of the United States of America in Congress assembled (two thirds of both houses concurring), That the following article be proposed to the legislatures of the several States as an amendment to the Constitution of the United States; which, when ratified by three fourths of said legislatures, shall be valid as part of the Constitution; namely: —

ART. 1. SECT. 1. — All persons born or naturalized in the United States, and subject to the jurisdiction thereof, are citizens of the United States and the States wherein they reside. No State shall make or enforce any law which shall abridge the privileges or immunities of citizens of the United States; nor shall any State deprive any person of life, liberty, or happiness, without due process of law, nor deny any person within its jurisdiction the equal protection of the laws.

SECT. 2. — Representatives shall be apportioned among the several States according to their respective numbers, counting the whole number of persons, excluding Indians not taxed. But whenever the right to vote at any election for the choice of electors for President and Vice-President, representatives in Congress, executive and judicial officers, or members of the legislature thereof, is denied to any of the male inhabitants of such State, being twenty-one years of age, and citizens of the United States, or in any way abridged, except for participation in rebellion or other crime, the basis of representation therein shall be reduced in the proportion which the number of such male citizens shall bear to the whole number of male citizens twenty-one years of age in such State.

SECT. 3. — That no person shall be a senator or representative in Congress, or elector of President and Vice-President, or hold any office, civil or military, under the United States, or under any State, who, having previously taken an oath as a member of Congress, or as an officer of the United States, or as a member of any State legislature, or as an executive or judicial officer of any State, to support the Constitution of the United States, shall have engaged in insurrection or rebellion against the same, or given aid and comfort to the enemies thereof. But Congress may, by a vote of two thirds of each house, remove such disabilities.

SECT. 4. — The validity of the public debt of the United States authorized by law, including debts incurred for payment of pensions and bounties for services in suppressing insurrection or rebellion, shall not be questioned. But neither the United States nor any State shall assume or pay any debt or obligation incurred in aid of insurrection or rebellion against the United States, or any claim for the loss or emancipation of any slave; but all such debts, obligations, and claims shall be held illegal and void.

SECT. 5. — The Congress shall have power to enforce by appropriate legislation the provisions of this article.

This amendment allows each State to decide who of its citizens shall enjoy the right to vote; but it declares that those who are not allowed to vote shall not be counted in the basis of representation. If any State chooses to limit the elective franchise to a favored few, it can do so; but that priviledged few are not to have their power augmented by representing large bodies of citizens who are permitted no voice in the selection of their representation. But for this provision, a rebel voter in South Carolina would represent a power in national affairs equal to any two loyal voters in New York. With slavery re-instituted under the guise of serfdom, and with their representation in Congress greatly increased, by counting in their basis of representation each serf as a man, the rebel States would have gained by the conflict in political power.

President Johnson opposed these terms of reconstruction. Congress advocated them. They were cordially approved by an immense majority of the people of the United States. A conflict arose between the President and Congress, which agitated the nation as it has, perhaps, never been agitated before in time of peace. The President availed himself not only of all his constitutional powers, but, as Congress averred, he usurped unconstitutional powers, in his endeavors to thwart the measures which the nation, through its representatives, was endeavoring to enforce. In the progress of this strife, a law was passed by Congress, on the 2d of March, 1867, entitled " The Tenure of Office Act ; " by which it was enacted that all civil officers duly qualified by appointment by the President, with the advice and consent of the Senate, shall be entitled to hold such office until a successor shall have been in like manner appointed and qualified.

The President, who was anxious to remove Mr. Stanton from the office of Secretary of War, and place some one in his position who would act in harmony with his own views, refused to respect this law, declaring it to be unconstitutional. He assumed that he had a right to judge for himself whether or not the laws enacted by Congress were in accordance with the Constitution ; and that if, in his judgment, they were not so, he had a right to refuse to execute them. The distinctly-defined issue which consequently arose was, *may the President annul such laws of the United States, as, in his judgment, he may deem to be unconstitutional?*

The President had a right to veto a bill, which, for any reason, he disapproved ; but a bill thus returned could pass to a law by a two thirds vote, notwithstanding the veto. And again : should the President refuse to return a bill, and retain it for ten days, it then became a law without his signature. It was admitted that the President was not bound to execute an unconstitutional law. But the question of its constitutionality was to be decided, not by the private judgment of the President, but by the solemn decision of the Supreme Court of the United States.

The President, in contravention of the Tenure of Office Act, issued an order removing Secretary Stanton from his office, to which he had been appointed by President Lincoln, and substituting in his place General Lorenzo Thomas. Secretary Stanton, acting in harmony with the advice of Congress, refused to surrender the post which it was endeavored thus illegally to wrest from him. The President, by threats, endeavored to force him to yield. This brought matters to such a crisis, that the impeachment of the President was decided upon. When the President urged the plea, that he violated the law that he might thus bring it before the Supreme Court to test its constitutionality, the reply was, that the President had taken an oath to execute the laws; that he could violate this oath only at his peril, and that peril was, *to be impeached.*

The nation, in general, was in sympathy with Congress. The course which the President had pursued had created intense and widespread exasperation. Those who were in sympathy with the Rebellion applauded him. The loyal community all over the land was incensed. In addition to those articles of impeachment which accused the President of high crimes and misdemeanors in violating the laws, another article was introduced, charging him with attempting to bring into ridicule and contempt the Congress of the United States, and to excite against it the odium of the people. In substantiation of this charge, the following extracts were produced from speeches which he had made on several occasions. To a committee of citizens who called upon him in Washington, on the 18th of August, 1866, he said, in view of the opposition of Congress to *his* mode of reconstructing the rebel States, —

" We have witnessed in one department of the government every endeavor to prevent the restoration of peace, harmony, and union. We have seen hanging upon the verge of the government, as it were, a body called, or which assumes to be, the Congress of the United States; while, in fact, it is a Congress of only part of the States. We have seen this Congress pretend to be for the Union, when its every step and act tended to perpetuate disunion, and make a disruption of the States inevitable. We have seen Congress gradually encroach, step by step, upon constitutional rights, and violate, day after day, and month after month, fundamental principles of the government. We have seen a Congress that seemed to forget that there was a limit to the sphere and scope of legislation. We have seen a Congress in a minority assume to exercise power, which, if allowed to be consummated, would result in despotism, in monarchy itself."

Again: at Cleveland, O., on the 3d of September, 1866, President Johnson, addressing a public assemblage, said, —

"I called upon your Congress, that is trying to break up the government. What has Congress done? Have they done anything to restore the Union of these States? No: on the contrary, they have done everything to prevent it." Again: at St. Louis, Mo., on the 8th of September, the President, addressing a large gathering of the citizens, said, calling several prominent individual members of Congress by name, —

"These are the men that compare themselves with the Saviour; and everybody that differs with them in opinion, and who tries to stay and arrest their diabolical and nefarious policy, is to be denounced as a Judas. Well, let me say to you, if you will stand by me in trying to give the people a fair chance, soldiers and citizens, to participate in these offices, God being willing, I will kick them out: I will kick them out just as fast as I can. Let me say to you, in conclusion, that what I have said I intended to say. I was not provoked into this; and I care not for their menaces, the taunts and the jeers. I care not for threats. I do not intend to be bullied by my enemies, nor overawed by my friends; but, God willing, with your help, I will veto their measures whenever they come to me."

On the 4th of March, at one o'clock P. M., the managers of the impeachment, appointed by the House of Representatives, entered the Senate Chamber, followed by the members of the House. The Chief-Justice of the United States, and the senators, fifty-four in number, formed the court and jury. The people of the United States, through their representatives in the House, entered the prosecution. The President of the United States was the accused at the bar.

The trial was very tedious, continuing for nearly three months. A test-article of the impeachment was at length submitted to the court for its action. It was certain that as the court voted upon that article so it would vote upon all. Thirty-five voices pronounced the President guilty. Nineteen voices declared him not guilty. As a two thirds vote was necessary to his condemnation, he was pronounced acquitted, notwithstanding the very great majority against him. The change of one vote from the *not guilty* side would have sustained the impeachment.

The President, for the remainder of his term, was but little regarded. He continued, though impotently, his conflict with Congress. His own party did not think it expedient to renominate him for the Presidency. The nation rallied, with enthusiasm unparalleled since the days of Washington, around the name of General Grant. Andrew Johnson was forgotten. The bullet of an assassin introduced him to the President's chair. Notwithstanding this, never was there presented to a man a better opportunity to immortalize his name, and to win the gratitude of a nation. He failed utterly. He retired to his home in Greenville, Tenn., taking no very active part in politics until 1875. On January 26th, after an exciting struggle, he was chosen by the Legislature of Tennessee United States Senator in the Forty-fourth Congress, and took his seat in that body at the special session convened by President Grant, on the 5th of March. On the 27th of July, 1875, the ex-President made a visit to his daughter's home, near Carter Station, Tenn. When he started on his journey, he was apparently in his usual vigorous health, but on reaching the the residence of his child the following day was stricken with paralysis, rendering him unconscious. He rallied occasionally, but finally passed away at two A. M., July 31st, aged sixty-seven years. His funeral was attended at Greenville, on the 3d of August, with every demonstration of respect.

CHAPTER XVIII.

ULYSSES S. GRANT.

Birth and Childhood. — Education at West Point. — Life on the Frontiers. — The Mexican War. — Resigns his Commission. — The Civil War. — Returns to the Army. — Battle of Belmont. — Capture of Fort Donelson. — Battles of Shiloh and Pittsburg Landing. — Siege of Vicksburg. — Campaign of Chattanooga. — Public Honors. — Commissioned as Lieutenant-General. — Campaign of the Wilderness. — Capture of Lee's Army. — Chosen President of the United States.

THERE was nothing in the early life of Ulysses S. Grant indicative of a remarkable character. He was an honest-hearted, ener-

RESIDENCE OF GENERAL U. S. GRANT AT GALENA, ILL.

getic, modest, good boy. But for the great Rebellion his name, probably, would never have been known beyond the limits of the small Western town in which he was then engaged in humble commercial life. The war developed in him latent virtues and heroism which have crowned him with renown.

Ulysses was born on the 29th of April, 1822, of Christian parents, in a humble home, at Point Pleasant, on the banks of the Ohio. Soon after his birth his father removed to Georgetown, Brown County, Ohio. In this remote frontier hamlet Ulysses received a common-school education. At the age of seventeen, in the year 1839, he entered the military academy at West Point. Here he was regarded as a solid, sensible young man of fair abilities, and of sturdy, honest character. He took respectable rank as a scholar. In June, 1843, he graduated, about the middle in his class, and was sent as lieutenant of infantry to one of the distant military posts in the Missouri Territory. Two years he passed in these dreary solitudes, watching the vagabond and exasperated Indians.

The war with Mexico came: Lieutenant Grant was sent with his regiment to Corpus Christi. His first battle was at Palo Alto. There was no chance here for the exhibition of either skill or heroism. The two parties stood upon a vast open prairie, with about half a mile of ground between them. For several hours they fired at each other with cannon. Our guns were the heavier and better managed. As night came the Mexicans retreated. They had lost, in killed and wounded, two hundred and sixty-two. The Americans lost four killed and thirty-two wounded.

The foe made another stand, a few miles in the rear, at Resaca de la Palma. Here, in the midst of thickets of dwarf oaks, the battle was fiercer. The Mexicans, having lost a thousand men, retired. General Taylor, who was in command of the United States forces, lost one hundred and fifty. This was Lieutenant Grant's second battle.

The American troops, about six thousand strong, then crossed the Rio Grande, and marched upon Monterey, which was garrisoned by ten thousand Mexicans. After a bloody struggle of several days, the city capitulated on the 24th of September, 1846. This was Lieutenant Grant's third battle. It is said that he here performed a signal service of daring and of skillful horsemanship. His brigade had exhausted its ammunition. A messenger must be sent for more along a route exposed to the bullets of the foe. Lieutenant Grant, adopting an expedient learned of the Indians, grasped the mane of his horse, and, hanging upon one side of the animal, ran the gauntlet in safety.

From Monterey Lieutenant Grant was sent, with the Fourth Infantry, to aid General Scott in the siege of Vera Cruz. Though in the capture of this important place he proved himself an efficient officer, still his rank was too humble to attract any special attention. In preparation for the march to the city of Mexico, he was appointed quartermaster of his regiment. At the battle of Molino del Rey he was promoted to a first lieutenancy, and was brevetted captain at Chapultepec.

At the close of the Mexican war Captain Grant returned with his regiment to New York, and was again sent to one of the military posts on the frontier. The discovery of gold in California causing an immense tide of emigration to flow to the Pacific shores, Captain Grant was sent with a battalion to Fort Dallas, in Oregon, for the protection of the interests of the emigrants. Life was wearisome in those wilds. Captain Grant resigned his commission and returned to the States, and, having married, entered upon the cultivation of a small farm near St. Louis, Mo. He had but little skill as a farmer. Finding his toil not remunerative, he turned to mercantile life, entering into the leather business with a younger brother at Galena, Ill. This was in the year 1860. The integrity of the brothers and their devotion to business gave the firm a high reputation.

On the 12th of April, 1861, the rebels in Charleston, S. C., commenced war against the flag of the United States by opening fire upon Fort Sumter. As the tidings reached the ears of Captain Grant in his counting-room, he said, —

" Uncle Sam has educated me for the army; though I have served him through one war, I do not feel that I have yet repaid the debt. I am still ready to discharge my obligations. I shall therefore buckle on my sword and see Uncle Sam through this war too."

He went into the streets, raised a company of volunteers, and led them as their captain to Springfield, the capital of the State, where their services were offered to Governor Yates. The governor, impressed by the zeal and straightforward executive ability of Captain Grant, gave him a desk in his office to assist in the volunteer organization which was then being formed in the State in behalf of the government. It was soon evident that his military qualities were of so high an order as to demand for him active service in the field. This also was his earnest wish. On the 15th of June, 1861, Captain Grant received a commission as colonel of the Twenty-first Regiment of Illinois Volunteers. This regiment was soon sent across the Mississippi to guard the Hannibal and Hudson Railroad, which ran across the northern portion of Missouri to the Kansas border. There was here no opportunity for distinction. Still, his merits as a West Point graduate, who had served for fifteen years in the regular army, were such, that he was soon promoted to the rank of brigadier-general; and was placed in command at Cairo, where the Ohio and Mississippi rivers meet.

The rebels raised their banner at Paducah, near the mouth of the Tennessee River. Scarcely had its folds appeared in the breeze ere General Grant was there. The rebels fled. Their banner fell, and the stars and stripes were unfurled in their stead. Garrisoning the post, he advanced to Smithland, at the mouth of the Cumberland, which point he also occupied. Subsequent events proved the sagacity which induced him to rear his batteries upon the mouths of these two important streams.

The rebels assembled an armed force on the Kentucky side of the Mississippi, at Columbus, a few miles below Cairo. Here, on a bluff, they fortified themselves with ramparts and batteries. Their heavy guns commanded the river. Twenty thousand men garrisoned the works. On the opposite Missouri shore they were organizing a force at Belmont to invade southwestern Missouri. General Grant had not sufficient strength to attack Columbus; he resolved, however, to attempt the destruction of the camp at Belmont. He knew he could not permanently hold the position, as it was covered by the guns of Columbus.

Early in the evening of the 6th of November, General Grant in person, with about three thousand men on transports, convoyed by two gunboats, commenced the descent of the river. A dark and foggy night favored the enterprise. Early in the morning the troops landed, unopposed, on the west bank of the river, three miles above the batteries of the foe; marched rapidly through the forest, and threw themselves with the utmost impetuosity upon the earthworks at Belmont, which were guarded by nearly twice their own number of men. The rebels were taken by surprise. Bewildered by the desperation of the assault, after a short conflict, they broke and fled in utter rout. The torch was applied to everything that would burn, The stars and stripes were raised over the conquered field; and a shout rose from the lips of the victors which reached the ears of the garrison at Columbus. Their guns were immediately brought to bear upon the audacious assailants, and reinforcements were hurriedly pushed across the river to prevent their retreat. As General Grant commenced the withdrawal of his troops, an aide rode up, exclaiming excitedly, " We are surrounded !"

"Very well," said General Grant, "we must cut our way out as we cut our way in. We have whipped them once, and I think we can do it again."

They did cut their way out, through thirteen regiments of infantry and three squadrons of cavalry. They regained their boats, and returned rejoicing to Cairo. They had destroyed much rebel *materiel* of war, had captured one hundred and fifty prisoners and two guns. Four guns which could not be removed were spiked. The rebels lost, in killed and wounded, six hundred and forty-two men. General Grant's loss in the bold enterprise was also severe; four hundred and eighty-five being numbered among the killed, wounded, and missing.

The rebels constructed two forts; one upon the Tennessee River, and the other upon the Cumberland River, about ninety miles above the mouths of these streams, at a point where these rivers approach within twelve miles of each other. Fort Henry, on the eastern bank of the Tennessee, was garrisoned by twenty-eight hundred men, with seventeen heavy guns. It was a strong fieldwork with bastioned front, supported on the land side by an intrenched camp with an extended line of rifle-pits. An expedition was sent up the river to capture this fort. It consisted of a fleet of seven gunboats, four of which were iron clad, under Commodore Foote; and a land force of seventeen thousand men, under General Grant, which was conveyed in transports. This whole expedition steamed up the river early in February, 1862, and landed the troops about four miles below the fort. Many of the troops disembarked at midnight in a drenching rain. They were to be sent circuitously through the forest to attack the fort in the rear, and to cut off the retreat of the garrison by what was called the Dover Road to Fort Donelson on the Cumberland.

General Grant had a march of eight miles before him, through a wilderness which the rains had converted into a morass, and where he encountered several unbridged streams. The heroic commodore said to General Grant, as he commenced his march, "You must move quickly, or I shall take the fort before you get there." The gallant little fleet opened fire at a mile and a quarter from the fort, and pressed steadily on till within six hundred feet of the muzzles of the foe. The fire of the gunboats was so terrible that soon every gun but four was silenced, and the rebels raised the white flag of surrender.   Nearly all the garrison fled to Donelson, without its being in the power of General Grant to molest them.   General Tilghman, commander of the fort, and sixty-three men, were captured. The fall of Fort Henry opened to our gunboats the great avenue of the Tennessee into the heart of the rebel territory.

Early on the morning of the 12th, General Grant, with his main column, fifteen thousand strong, commenced his march across the country to Fort Donelson.   Commodore Foote descended the Tennessee to repair his gunboats, that he might ascend the Cumberland, and attack Donelson on its water side.   Donelson was a cluster of forts upon a rugged, rocky eminence, which commanded the river for several miles above and below.   A better situation for defense could scarcely be imagined.   Numerous batteries, protected by works which no ball could penetrate, threw thirty-two and sixty-four pound shot.   Ramparts, bastions, rifle-pits, and abatis of felled trees, protected every approach.   Twenty thousand soldiers manned the works, commanded by three prominent rebel generals, — Buckner, Pillow, and Floyd.   The struggle was long, desperate, and bloody, marked by heroism, endurance, and suffering seldom surpassed in the annals of war.   In every sanguinary conflict of the three-days' battle, General Grant gained some important position. Commodore Foote coöperated gallantly with his fleet.   Everything gained was held.

The attack really commenced on the 12th of November, when the rebel pickets were driven in by General Grant's advance.   On the 16th, the fort was surrendered.   As General Grant was preparing to storm the intrenchments with twenty-seven thousand men, two of the rebel generals, with as many of their troops as could escape by steamers, abandoned the fort and ascended the river.   General Buckner sent a bugler to General Grant, with a note asking terms.   " No terms can be accepted," was the reply, " but unconditional surrender.   I propose to move immediately upon your works." There was no choice left to Buckner.   Sixty-five guns, seventeen thousand six hundred small arms, with an immense amount of military stores, fell into the hands of the victors.

The Union loss was about two thousand in killed, wounded, and missing.   General Grant had introduced a new era of hard fighting into the conflict.   The nation was electrified by the victory.   Secretary Stanton recommended the successful general as Major-General of Volunteers. President Lincoln nominated him to the Senate the same day. The Senate at once confirmed the nomination. By the fall of Donelson, which was the first really important success the Union arms had achieved, General Grant was lifted up into national reputation. The new military district of Tennessee was now assigned to him.

Like all able captains, General Grant knew well how to secure the results of victory. Within a week after the fall of Donelson, he sent General C. F. Smith fifty miles farther up the river, with four regiments, to take possession of Clarkesville. He also took military possession of Nashville, a beautiful city of fifteen thousand inhabitants on the same stream, about one hundred and twenty miles from its mouth. Having thus taken command of the Cumberland, he removed his headquarters to Fort Henry, that he might also control the Tennessee River.

The enemy was concentrating a large force at Corinth, just south of the Tennessee line, in the State of Mississippi, preparing to invade Ohio. It was deemed important to break up this rendezvous, and, if possible, to destroy this army. General Grant, with five divisions in fifty-seven transports, convoyed by gunboats, ascended the Tennessee River to Pittsburg Landing. The troops were disembarked on the west side of the stream, twenty miles from Corinth. Here they waited the arrival of General Buell, who, with forty thousand troops, was marching from Nashville to join them. The rebels had seventy thousand men at Corinth. General Grant had thirty-five thousand on the west bank of the Tennessee. General Johnston, in command of the rebel troops, resolved to advance with his whole force, and crush Grant's little band before Buell could arrive.

At five o'clock on the morning of the 6th of April, 1862, the whole rebel army, in three columns, by a secret march from their intrenchments, fell upon our slumbering troops. An awful day of carnage ensued, — a day disastrous to the Union arms. Though our troops fought with desperation, they were driven back nearly three miles with fearful slaughter. Several thousand prisoners were taken by the foe. The field was covered with the dying and the dead. Apparently, the gunboats alone prevented our routed army from being captured, or driven into the river. Night terminated the conflict. The triumphant rebels had no doubt of an easy and entire victory on the morrow. This first day's battle is called the battle of Shiloh, from a church a few miles back from the landing where the battle commenced.

Never was the energy of General Grant more signally displayed than in these hours of disaster. No thought of ultimate defeat seemed to enter his mind. During the night he reorganized his shattered divisions, and formed a new line of battle. Twenty thousand of General Buell's troops, who arrived after dark, were ferried across the stream and placed in battle-array. Relying upon General Buell's remaining troops, fast approaching, for a reserve, every available man was prepared for immediate action. With the earliest dawn the national troops advanced from the right, the centre, and the left, in an impetuous assault upon the astonished foe. Inspired with the confidence of victory, they swept all opposition before them. During the long hours of the day the conflict raged with uninterrupted fury. Considering the numbers engaged, it was one of the bloodiest battles ever fought. A dark and stormy night closed the scene. In utter discomfiture, the rebels retreated to their intrenchments at Corinth, having lost in the two days' campaign nearly twenty thousand men. General Grant lost on these fields of blood over twelve thousand men. No imagination can picture the scene which that plain presented after these two storms of war had swept over it. The battle of Shiloh was a signal defeat; the battle of Pittsburg Landing, as the second day's battle was called, was a still more signal victory.

General Halleck now took command of the troops, and advanced to the siege of Corinth. After the inglorious termination of this siege, by the abandonment of the posts by the rebels, and their escape with all their *materiel* of war, General Halleck was recalled to Washington, and General Grant again assumed command of the army of the Tennessee. Establishing his headquarters at Corinth, he found all his courage and military ability put to the test in warding off the blows of the outnumbering foe who surrounded him. He, however, proved equal to the task. We have not here space to recount the local conflicts which ensued. In the bloody battles of Iuka and Corinth the foe was so thoroughly discomfited as to relieve West Tennessee from all immediate danger.

In the latter part of October large reinforcements were sent to General Grant. Anxious to assume the offensive, he suggested to General Halleck that an attack should be made upon Vicksburg, where the enemy, garrisoned in great strength, commanded the Mississippi River. It was decided to attack the works on the land side by fifty thousand troops; while Commodore Porter, with a fleet of sixty vessels, carrying two hundred and eighty guns and eight hundred men, should attack from the river.

The siege which ensued is one of the most memorable in the annals of war. A volume would be required to give the details of its varied and wondrous undertakings. All the energies of engineering and of battle were called into requisition. The siege of Vicksburg, in reality, spread over countless leagues of territory. For days, weeks, months, there were almost incessant battles. The enterprise may be considered as commencing early in February, 1863. In the progress of the siege, a mine was dug under one of the most important batteries of the enemy, and charged with over two thousand pounds of powder. The explosion of this mine was to be the signal for a simultaneous attack by land and water.

It was the 25th of June, 1863, a delightful summer's day. The match was applied at three o'clock in the afternoon. The whole army, drawn up for an immediate assault, seemed to hold its breath in suspense, awaiting the terrible explosion. A white line of smoke ran along the trench through which the fuse was laid, and the fire crept rapidly towards the buried magazine. Then came an awful underground thundering, as of earthquake throes, a flash, and the upheaving of a mountain into the air. Earth, rocks, timber, guns, and the mangled forms of men, were blended together in that awful volcanic eruption which darkened the skies. Instantly, over a line of twelve miles in length, the tempest of battle immediately burst with the intensest fury. An eye-witness writes, —

"The scene at this time was one of the utmost sublimity. The roar of artillery, the rattle of small arms, the cheers of the men, the flashes of light, the wreaths of pale blue smoke over different parts of the field, the bursting of shells, the fierce whistle of solid shot, the deep boom of the mortars, the broadsides of the ships of war, and, added to all this, the vigorous replies of the enemy, sent up a din which beggars all description."

The defense of Vicksburg was as determined as the assault. When some one asked General Grant if he thought he could take the place, he replied, "Certainly. I cannot tell exactly when I shall take the town; but I mean to stay here till I do, if it takes me thirty years."

On the 1st of July his works were at ten different points, within a few hundred feet of the rebel defenses. The final assault was to take place on the 4th. The rebel general, Pemberton, aware that he could not repel the charge, on the 3d proposed terms of capitulation. General Grant replied, that his only terms were the uncon-

INTERVIEW BETWEEN GRANT AND PEMBERTON.

ditional surrender of the city and garrison. General Pemberton, hoping to obtain more favorable terms, urged a personal interview. The two generals met, each accompanied by several officers of his staff, upon a gentle eminence, beneath an oak-tree, not two hundred feet from the rebel lines. Both armies gazed with interest upon the spectacle. Courteously these leaders of hostile ranks shook hands.   General Grant adhered to his terms of *unconditional surrender*, the officers and soldiers all to be liberated upon their parole.   General Pemberton, conscious that further resistance was hopeless, after conferring with his officers, accepted the terms proposed.   At ten o'clock on the 4th of July, 1863, white flags arose all along the rebel lines, announcing the surrender of the place. General Grant, with his staff, rode at the head of his troops, as they entered the city, and took possession of all the works.   A more signal conquest has seldom been made.   Thirty thousand six hundred prisoners were taken, and one hundred and seventy-two cannon.

The fall of Vicksburg was by far the most terrible blow which the rebels had thus far encountered.   It rendered it necessary for them immediately to evacuate Port Hudson; and thus the Mississippi was thrown open to our gunboats from Cairo to the Gulf.

General Grant was anxious to move immediately upon Mobile. With the force at his command, he could then have easily taken the place; but he received orders from Washington to coöperate with General Banks in a movement upon Texas.   He, accordingly, on the 30th of August, left Vicksburg for New Orleans.   In that city, he was thrown from his horse, receiving injuries which seriously disabled him for several months.   For twenty days he could not leave his bed.   For many weeks afterwards he could only hobble about upon crutches.

General Rosecrans was in East Tennessee, near Chattanooga.   He had fifty-five thousand men under his command.   He was in great peril, far from his base of supplies, and menaced by a rebel force eighty thousand strong.   One of the most terrible battles of the war was fought — the battle of Chickamauga — on the 19th of September, 1863.   The national troops, having lost sixteen thousand in killed, wounded, and missing, were driven back behind their intrenchments at Chattanooga, where they were closely besieged by a rebel force of eighty thousand men.   As their lines of communication were cut off, they were threatened with total destruction. General Grant was sent to their relief.   Seldom before in the history of the world has there been such an illustration of the power of a single man to control events.   On the 19th of October General Grant telegraphed General Thomas, to whose heroism the army was mainly indebted for its salvation in the terrible battle of Chickamauga. " Hold Chattanooga at all hazards. I will be there as soon as possible." The characteristic response of General Thomas was, " I will hold the town till we starve." On the 23d of October, a cold, stormy day, General Grant, chilled, drenched, exhausted, entered Chattanooga in the evening. The gloom of nature seemed in sympathy with the gloom of the army. The energy and the military sagacity immediately displayed by General Grant has perhaps never been surpassed.

First, by a wonderful series of strategic and tactical measures, he opened a sure line of communication, by which his army speedily received reinforcements and abundant supplies. Five days accomplished this. The whole army was inspired with such new life as to double its moral strength. General Sherman, with the Fifteenth Army Corps, was hurried along, by forced marches, from the Valley of the Mississippi. The rebels were alarmed. " The enemy," said their leading organ, " The Richmond Enquirer," " were outfought at Chickamauga ; but the present position of affairs looks as though we had been out-generalled at Chattanooga."

General Sherman, wading through miry roads, bridging flooded streams, and often fighting his way, was painfully delayed, though he manifested heroism and energy which elicited the praises of his superior officer and the admiration of the nation. General Burnside was in imminent danger of being overwhelmed at Knoxville, — a calamity which would have fearfully imperiled the army at Chattanooga. Every energy of General Grant's soul and body was strained to the utmost. At length General Sherman's troops arrived, and were gathered in a concealed camp about two miles west of Chattanooga. General Grant was now ready to assume the offensive. It would require a volume to give the reader any adequate idea of the multiplied evolutions in the terrible battles which ensued, extending over mountains and through forests and valleys for a distance of thirteen miles. At midnight, on the 23d of November, General Sherman's troops crossed the Tennessee River, a few miles above Chattanooga, and took a commanding position to attack the enemy on his right, north of Missionary Ridge. The next day General Hooker magnificently stormed Lookout Mountain, on the enemy's extreme left, driving the rebels in wild rout before him. The next day, the 25th, the whole army rushed upon the foe, upon the right, upon the left, and at the centre. The battle was terrific.

Human valor never has done, never can do more. The main attack was at the centre, from Orchard Knoll, where General Grant took his position.

The scene cannot be described, cannot be imagined. At this point of the line, which extended for many miles, and which along its whole distance was ablaze with the lightnings of battle's tempest, there were thirteen thousand men rushing headlong in the assault, with shouts which blended sublimely with the rattle of musketry and the roar of cannon. Eight thousand rebels opposed them, fighting desperately behind their intrenchments. There were sixty explosions of cannon each minute. The assailants and the assailed were soon blended upon the ramparts and in the trenches. It was a day of blood, anguish, death, to thousands. The Union loss in killed and wounded was four thousand. The rebel loss has never been known. When night came the national banner waved over all the works which the rebels held in the morning, and the panic-stricken foe was retreating in torrents which no commands, entreaties, or threats of their officers could arrest. In the following modest telegram, General Grant announced to the authorities in Washington his glorious victory: —

"Although the battle lasted from early dawn till dark this evening, I believe I am not premature in announcing a complete victory over Bragg. Lookout Mountain top, all the rifle-pits in Chattanooga Valley and Missionary Ridge entire, have been carried, and are now held by us. I have no idea of finding Bragg here to-morrow."

This great achievement pierced the heart of the Rebellion, relieved General Burnside, rescued Kentucky and Tennessee from rebel thralldom, and opened the gate for the triumphant sweep of the national army through Georgia to the Atlantic coast. Vigorously General Grant pushed the routed foe, driving his broken battalions towards Atlanta. The roads along which they had fled were strewed with abandoned guns, muskets, broken wagons, and all the nameless *débris* of a routed, panic-stricken host. The rebels applied the torch to most of the stores which they could not take with them, and destroyed behind them all the bridges, and felled trees into the road to impede the progress of their pursuers. Still their flight had been so precipitate that they had been compelled to leave much behind. Our victorious troops gathered up a pontoon-train of fifteen boats ; forty pieces of artillery, including two sixty-four-pounder rifled cannon ; sixty-nine carriages and caissons ; seven thousand stand of small arms ; sixty thousand rations of corn, fifty thousand of meal, four hundred gallons of molasses, one thousand pounds of bacon, together with a considerable quantity of ordnance stores, artillery and small-arm ammunition, and six thousand one hundred and forty-two prisoners.

In the flight and hot pursuit, the rear guard of the foe occasionally made a stand, and short, fierce conflicts ensued. General Grant gave the fugitive rebels no rest until they were driven fairly out of Tennessee into Georgia. It must be the opinion of all familiar with military affairs, that Grant's campaign of Chattanooga is one of the most memorable in history. He was ably supported by as noble a corps of generals as any commander ever drew around him. Still it was mainly to the skill of the commanding general, in his admirable disposition of his forces, that we were indebted for the result. Without this no human valor could have driven the foe from the almost impregnable post which he occupied. An Indian chieftain, of the Tonawanda tribe, Colonel Parker, in the following terms describes General Grant's conduct in the battle : —

" It has been a matter of universal wonder in this army that General Grant was not killed, for the general was always in the front, and perfectly regardless of the storm of hissing bullets and screaming shells flying around him. His apparent want of sensibility does not arise from heedlessness, heartlessness, or vain military affectation, but from a sense of the responsibility resting upon him when in battle.

" At Ringgold we rode for half a mile, in the face of the enemy, under an incessant fire of cannon and musketry ; nor did we ride fast, but upon an ordinary trot ; and not once, do I believe, did it enter the general's mind that he was in danger. I was by his side, and watched him closely. In riding that distance we were going to the front. I could see that he was studying the positions of the two armies, and, of course, planning how to defeat the enemy, who were making a desperate stand, and slaughtering our men fearfully."

Immediately upon the meeting of Congress after these events, a vote was passed, presenting the thanks of that body to General Grant and the officers and soldiers under his command. A gold medal was also ordered to be struck off, with suitable emblems, to be presented to General Grant. Several of the States also passed resolutions of thanks to Grant and his army.

The energetic general manifested no disposition to rest after the campaign of Chattanooga. He gathered up his strength to push the war with renewed vigor. It was now winter. An immense army was to be housed, clothed, fed. The rebel forces were to be destroyed wherever they could be found in rendezvous. Three armies were under his command, extending over a line a thousand miles in length. Herculean mental energies must be requisite to bear such a burden. General Grant was responsible for all the movements or neglect of action. In a magnificent campaign General Sherman drove the rebels out of Tennessee, subsisting his army upon the stores which he captured. In midwinter, through storms and drifting snows which incumbered the mountain passes, General Grant, on horseback, visited the outposts of his army. At Knoxville, Louisville, Lexington, St. Louis, he was received with the greatest enthusiasm. But no efforts could either flatter him or provoke him into making a speech. He was emphatically a man of deeds, not of words. There was perhaps one exception. He did make a speech at St. Louis. He was serenaded in the evening at his hotel. An immense throng in front of the hotel, in an incessant clamor, shouted "Speech!" "Speech!" After a long delay the general appeared upon the balcony. There was breathless silence. Leaning over the railing the general said slowly, deliberately, firmly, —

"Gentlemen, making speeches is not my business. I never did it in my life, and I never will. I thank you, however, for your attendance here."

He then bowed and retired amidst immense applause. National honors were now lavished upon him. On the 4th of February, 1864, Congress revived the grade of lieutenant-general, and the rank was conferred on General Grant. On the 3d of March he was summoned to Washington to receive his credentials and to enter upon the immense responsibilities of his new office. His fame filled the land. On his rapid journey, at every dépôt crowds were gathered to catch a glimpse of one whose deeds outrivaled those of any other living general. A singular scene of enthusiasm was witnessed upon his arrival in Washington.

With characteristic modesty, arriving unheralded, he quietly repaired to Willard's Hotel, and took a seat at the table in the dining-room. A gentleman at the table recognized him, and, rising, announced to the numerous company that General Ulysses S. Grant was in the room. Simultaneously the whole company sprang to their feet, and cheer after cheer rang through the hall.

In the evening he attended President Lincoln's levee. The enthusiasm his presence excited absorbed universal attention. Such a scene had never before been witnessed in the presidential mansion. The noble President, into whose magnanimous soul an emotion of jealousy never found its way, stood by the side of his illustrious guest, cheering as heartily as any of the company. But General Grant had no taste for such ovations. They were only painful to him. As he retired that night, he said to a friend, —

"I hope to get away from Washington as soon as possible; for I am tired of the show business already."

On the 9th General Grant received in the executive chamber, with impressive solemnities, his commission as lieutenant-general. All the Cabinet, and other distinguished guests, were present. In response to a few hearty words from President Lincoln, General Grant said, —

"Mr. President, I accept this commission with gratitude for the high honor conferred. With the aid of the noble armies who have fought on so many fields for our common country, it will be my earnest endeavor not to disappoint your expectations. I feel the full weight of the responsibility now devolving upon me. I know that, if it is properly met, it will be due to these armies, and, above all, to the favor of that Providence which leads both nations and men."

We were still in the midst of the war. The land was filled with widows and with orphans. Vast armies were still facing each other, gathering their strength for a renewal of the conflict. It was certain that many a bloody battle was yet to be fought, and that many a field was yet to be covered with the mutilated, the dying, and the dead. Some of the ladies in Washington, patriotic and noble women, but without sufficient reflection, proposed a ball in connection with the grand review of the army which was immediately to take place. General Grant replied to them kindly, yet sadly, in terms which endeared him to every soldier and every soldier's friend, —

"Ladies, I am not a cynic. I enjoy rational pleasures as well as any one else. But I would ask you, in all candor and gentleness, if this is a time for music and dancing and feasting among the officers of the army? Is our country in a condition to call for such things at present? Do army balls inspire our troops with courage in the field? Do they soothe our sick and wounded in the hospitals?"

The ladies recognized the propriety of these sentiments, and cheerfully relinquished the plan. All General Grant's energies were now roused anew to terminate the war by the only possible way, the destruction of the enemy's forces. He decided to concentrate the widely-dispersed national troops for an attack upon Richmond, the nominal capital of the Rebellion, and to endeavor there to destroy the rebel armies which would be promptly assembled from all quarters for its defense. The whole continent seemed to tremble beneath the tramp of these majestic armies, rushing to the decisive battlefield. Steamers were crowded with troops. Rail-trains were burdened with the closely packed thousands. All the great roads converging towards Richmond were thronged with the multitudinous host.

General Grant's comprehensive plan involved a series of campaigns. Washington was to be protected from any sudden raid by a force in the valley of the Shenandoah under General Sigel, who, at Pea Ridge, had performed exploits which entitled him to a nation's gratitude. General Butler, a man of wide renown for energy of character and executive ability, which, perhaps, has never been surpassed, with a large force of white and colored troops, was to ascend James River, and take position as near as possible to Richmond on the southeast. General Sherman, the Marshal Ney of our armies, whose signal merits General Grant fully comprehended, and whom the nation was just beginning to appreciate, was intrusted with the conduct of one of the most adventurous campaigns which has ever been recorded in the annals of war.

From Chattanooga, General Sherman was to crowd closely the retreating army of the rebels, so as to prevent their dispatching any reinforcements to Richmond, and to fight his way through the whole length of Georgia to Savannah; destroying the enemy's forces wherever he should meet them, their munitions of war, and everything which could contribute to the support of the rebel armies. Having

32

captured Savannah, to which port ample supplies were to be forwarded to him by water, he was to turn north, sweeping all opposition before him, devastating the country so as to prevent any armies
from the extreme South from following him. He was to capture,
by the way, Charleston, Columbia, and every other military post of
the rebels, and press vigorously on until he should catch sight of the
beleaguering banners gathered around the walls of Richmond. The
conception of the campaign was bold, magnificent. It was executed
by General Sherman with heroism which has elicited the admiration
of the world.

General Meade, one of our most reliable officers, was then in command of the Army of the Potomac, so called. This army consisted
of about one hundred thousand men, encamped among the hills north
of the Rapidan. Here General Grant established his headquarters,
rapidly accumulating strength, so as to attack the rebel general,
Lee, upon the south side of the river, and drive him back behind the
intrenchments of Richmond, when the city would be taken by storm
if possible, if not, by siege.

At midnight of the 3d of May, 1864, General Grant broke camp,
and, with his whole army in light marching order, crossed the Rapidan unopposed, a few miles below the intrenchments of the rebels.
The "sun of Austerlitz" shone upon the rejoicing host, as with
rapid footsteps, all the day, they pressed along, by a flank movement,
to gain the rear of the foe. In three columns this majestic army of
one hundred and fifty thousand men swept through the forest paths
of this wild and rugged region, appropriately called the Wilderness.
The spectacle presented the ensuing night was one of the most brilliant and picturesque in war's pageants. The encampment was in
a region of great beauty. Over a region of eight miles in length,
the hill-sides and the ravines were illuminated with the camp-fires
of the army, and no sounds were heard but those of joy. But, during these warm and peaceful summer hours, the tempest of war was
gathering its bolts.

General Lee, in command of the rebel hosts, was an officer of great
ability. He led troops as desperate in valor as ever shouldered a
musket. Massing his forces in an immense column, he suddenly
emerged from the forest, and fell upon the centre of our extended
line, hoping to cut it in two, and then to destroy each part piece-
meal. The battle was long, terrible, raging hour after hour through-

out the whole day, assault following assault. When night came, six thousand had been struck down on the two sides by war's death-dealing missiles. The night was dark, but mild. The exhausted combatants slept. The dead were buried by the light of "the lantern dimly burning." The dying, on the crimson sod, groaned their lives away. The ambulances dripped with blood as they bore their mutilated burdens over the rough ground. Through all the long hours the surgeons were busy with the mercifully-cruel knife and saw.

With the rising of the next morning's sun the roar of battle was resumed. Both parties had gathered all their strength during the night, again to grapple each other in death's throes. It was a day of terror and of blood. Before the sun went down, ten thousand Union troops were either killed or wounded. Probably an equal number of the rebel host had fallen. But notwithstanding their renewed assaults, striking the line here and there, they had utterly failed to accomplish their purpose.

In the night, General Lee, with his army, retreated to seize upon another important post, previously intrenched near Spottsylvania Court House. The Union army pressed along towards the same point in nearly parallel lines. There were many fierce battles during the day, as portions of the antagonistic hosts, each about one hundred and fifty thousand strong, were brought into contact. This third day's battle of the Wilderness was one of the most singular which ever occurred. The parallel lines were eight or ten miles in length; and there were many sanguinary battles fought where the combatants, concealed by the forest and the underbrush, could scarce catch sight of each other.

The rebels gained the intrenchments during the night of Saturday. Sunday morning General Grant fell upon their works. There was another long day of battle and of blood. The rebels were driven from their first line of intrenchments, with the loss of twenty-five hundred prisoners. The light of Monday morning had scarcely dawned ere General Grant, with all his batteries, again opened fire upon the foe behind his earthworks. All the day the roar of battle was unintermitted. Monday night came and went in silence. Heavy eyelids dropped in sleep, and exhausted arms were nerveless.

Tuesday morning, the 10th of May, roused both armies, invigorated by a few hours of sleep and rest. The rebels were strongly intrenched. The national troops bent around them in a circuit about six miles in extent. With the morning the battle was recommenced, and continued until night. The mightiest billows of war swept incessantly to and fro over the fields. At the close of the day, a simultaneous assault was made upon the entire rebel line. The charge was resistless. They were swept from their outer series of intrenchments, having lost two thousand prisoners. Darkness terminated the awful struggle. Twenty thousand men, ten thousand on either side, were the victims of this day of carnage.

These incessant battles had so exhausted both armies, that for one day there was a partial lull in the conflict. The rebels kept behind their intrenchments, while burial-parties were busy covering the dead. Still General Grant kept up a continual shelling of their lines, and made preparation to attack the sleeping foe by surprise when darkness should come. At midnight, in the midst of a tempest of thunder, lightning, and drenching rain, General Hancock plunged with a strong column upon one division of the foe, and drove them pell-mell before him, capturing seven thousand prisoners and thirty-two guns. This impetuous charge was the signal for another general battle which continued during the remainder of the night, and continued with unintermitted fury, as the sun rose, as noon came and went, until the evening twilight again darkened the scene. A struggle of fourteen hours struck down twenty thousand in dead and wounded. By such carnage both armies would soon have been consumed, were it not that they were both continually receiving reinforcements.

Still General Grant was steadily pressing forward, never relinquishing a foot of ground which he had gained. In the day's conflict he pushed his line forward a full mile, lapping over the left centre of the foe. The night was dark and tempestuous. The rain fell fast, and the dismal storm wailed through the tree-tops as if in sympathy with human woe. Twenty thousand sons, husbands, fathers, wounded and dying! Who can gauge the dimensions of such woe? Who can imagine the anguish the tidings conveyed to thousands of once happy homes? And who is to be held responsible for all this misery, — those who were defending our free institutions, that equal rights for all men might be transmitted to our posterity; or those who had wantonly, with arms in their hands, made war upon the national banner, that they might destroy the government which our fathers have transmitted to us, and erect upon the ruins a new government whose corner-stone should be slavery? There can be no question upon which side the sympathies of Heaven were enlisted.

During this dreadful night of dying groans, of darkness, rain, and wind, the national army marched rapidly and secretly along by another flank movement, and before the dawn had gained the new vantage-ground which they sought. This was a series of ridges two miles beyond Spottsylvania Court House. But the watchful rebels had already manned intrenchments before them, which had previously been prepared to arrest any such march upon Richmond. Sunday morning came, the twelfth day of the campaign. The roads, inundated with rain, had become almost impassable. Both parties were in a state of extreme exhaustion. New supplies of ammunition were needed, and reinforcements to fill up the broken ranks. Intrenchments were thrown up on each side, and positions taken for the renewal of the conflict. Thus passed Monday and Tuesday. At midnight of Tuesday, General Grant put several strong columns in motion to attack the enemy by surprise upon his left: reconnoitring parties had detected some weakness there.

With the early light of Wednesday morning the assault commenced. The roar of another pitched battle, extending for miles, in which several hundred cannon blended their voices, echoed over the hills. The defense was as spirited as the assault. At eleven o'clock in the morning our columns, unable to break a line frowning with rifle-pits, abatis, and ramparts, withdrew, having lost twelve hundred in killed and wounded. As soon, however, as night again came, General Grant sent a cavalry force ten miles forward in a southeast direction to seize Guinea Station, on the Richmond and Fredericksburg Railroad. They seized the position, and in the morning the whole army followed. To meet the wants of the army in this rapid advance, General Grant was continually so changing his base of supplies as to prevent the foe from falling back upon his rear and cutting off his supply-trains.

Many of the intelligent community felt great anxiety lest the foe should turn back, in all his strength, and capture Washington.

The following conversation is reported as having taken place in the tent of the reticent general. A stranger who was present said, —

"General, if you flank Lee, and get between him and Richmond, will you not uncover Washington, and leave it exposed to the enemy?"

"Yes, I reckon so," was the general's quiet reply.

"Do you not think, general," the stranger continued, "that Lee can detach sufficient force to reinforce Beauregard at Richmond, and overwhelm Butler?"

"I have not a doubt of it," Grant replied.

"And is there not danger," the stranger added, "that Johnston may come up and reinforce Lee, so that the latter will swing round, and cut off your communications, and seize your supplies?"

"Very likely," was the unconcerned response.

General Grant had carefully weighed all these possibilities. His military sagacity had taught him that General Lee, pressed as Grant was pressing him, would not attempt any one of them. He had also decided just what to do in case either of these movements should be undertaken. By General Grant's last advance to Guinea Station the rebels were left nearly ten miles in his rear. They made a desperate attack upon the supply-wagons, which were then defiling in a long line from Fredericksburg. The wagons were so well guarded that the attack of the foe was futile. The fierceness of the assault, and the resolution of the defense, may be inferred from the fact that twenty-four hundred men, on the two sides, were killed or wounded in the conflict.

General Lee was thoroughly alarmed. He was not only in danger that his line of communication would be cut off, but also that General Grant might seize the intrenchments around Richmond, and render the capture of the city and the destruction of his army inevitable. Thus, in the greatest haste, he abandoned the strong works he was then occupying, and took another line of defense on the banks of the North Anna River. While on their march, General Grant sent a division to fall upon their rear. Four hundred prisoners were cut off. The rebels were driven across the Ny, leaving the path behind them strewed with their wounded and dying.

Both armies were immersed in the intricacies of hills and ravines densely covered with forests. It was Friday, the 20th of May. The troops on each side were pushing rapidly for Richmond, in nearly parallel lines, but a few miles separated from each other. On Saturday the Union troops reached Bowling Green, having marched thirty-two miles that day.

" The march of the army on Saturday was picturesque and beautiful. It was one of the loveliest days of spring, with a cloudless sky, a bright sun, and an invigorating breeze. The roads were dry and in perfect condition. The scenery was enchanting, with its clear streams, its green meadows, its hills, its groves, its luxuriance, and its bloom. An army of one hundred and fifty thousand men, with their banners, their gleaming weapons, their plumed horsemen, their artillery, their wagons, crowded the roads winding over the hills and through the valleys. Few persons are aware of the magnitude of such an army. General Grant's vast host — artillery, infantry, and baggage-train — would fill, in a continuous line of march, any one road to its utmost capacity, for a distance of nearly one hundred miles. In this march, the immense army crowded the whole region over a breadth of from ten to fifteen miles. All the public roads and wood-paths were traversed. One mind presided supreme over these operations, as day after day, and night after night, through darkness, through forest, through morasses, over streams and rivers, storming intrenchments, and fighting their way against a determined foe of a hundred thousand desperate soldiers, the Union troops pressed resistlessly on." [1]

All day Sunday both armies marched rapidly along. General Lee watched anxiously, but in vain, for an opportunity to break General Grant's line by a flank attack. Several assaults were made, which were promptly repulsed. Monday morning General Grant was within forty miles of Richmond. The rebels attempted to make a stand on the banks of the North Anna. They were driven from their intrenchments, and the Union troops encamped upon both sides of the stream. On Tuesday the whole army, with all its *materiel,* crossed the rapid stream. General Grant was within a day's march of Richmond. His line had a front about four miles in extent, facing west. General Lee, at the distance of a few miles, on a parallel line, was facing east.

A reconnoissance showed that Lee was too strongly intrenched to be attacked. General Grant, concealing his movement by a strong demonstration, re-crossed the river. Marching rapidly down

[1] *Life of General Grant,* by John S. C. Abbott.

its northern bank, he seized Hanover Ferry, on the Pamunkey River, which stream is formed by the union of the North and South Anna. By a new change in his line of communication, all his supplies were brought in transports up the Pamunkey. He was now within fifteen miles of Richmond. The military ability displayed in this march from the Rapidan to the Pamunkey has rarely been surpassed. Apparently, there was perfect harmony between him and his officers. There were no misunderstandings. His words were few. His orders were so distinctly given that they could not be misapprehended.

It is difficult to conceive how the army could have endured such fatigue. It seemed to be General Grant's plan to march all day and fight all night. Waiting at Hanover Ferry for a few hours, to concentrate his troops, the whole army, with its baggage-train, crossed the Pamunkey on Sunday, the 29th. During the day there were many severe skirmishes with the foe. But nothing could retard the advance of the national troops.

On Wednesday morning, June 1st, General Grant's army was at Cold Harbor, within a few miles of Richmond. His troops were posted in a line about eight miles in length, extending northeast and southwest. General Lee vigorously assailed several positions of the line, hoping to break it. He was invariably repulsed. On each side a thousand in killed and wounded were the victims of this day. Lee's army now took position behind the ramparts, bastions, and forts, which had been reared, with the highest attainments of military skill, for the defense of Richmond. These works were manned with the heaviest guns. The garrison in Richmond and Lee's army united crowded them with desperate defenders.

Wednesday night was dark and rainy. Through the dismal hours of the night, and through all the day of Thursday, General Grant was arraying his forces for an attack upon the intrenched foe. The strength of the works could only be ascertained by attacking them. Success would open to him an unobstructed path into Richmond. Should he fail, he had another plan carefully matured. On Thursday, there were several sanguinary conflicts, as the troops were massed for the decisive struggle. At four o'clock, Friday morning, the battle commenced. All the energies of both armies were roused to the utmost. A dreadful day of blood ensued. In charge after charge, the Union troops advanced to the muzzles of the intrenched guns of the foe, which were belching forth storms of canister and grape. Three hundred thousand men were struggling along a line several miles in length, plying, with frantic energy, the most murderous instruments of modern warfare. Clouds of cavalry swept to and fro. Batteries were lost, and batteries were won. There were successful charges and bloody repulses. The battle ceased only with the night. Seven thousand of the national troops had been killed or wounded. Though we had made a decided advance, and gained several important positions, it was manifest that the rebels were so firmly intrenched that they could not be driven from their works.

.Mercy would throw a veil over the horrors of a night succeeding a bloody battle. The burial of the dead, the dying groans, the blood-dripping ambulances, the saw and the knife of the surgeon cutting through quivering nerves, — all this the army must disregard so far as possible, that the troops, in a few hours of sleep, may get strength to renew the struggle on the morrow.

Saturday morning dawned. The hostile forces at many points were within a few yards of each other, rampart frowning upon rampart. Tens of thousands were busy with the spade, while sharpshooters on either side kept up an incessant fire. After dark, the rebels concentrated a heavy force, and threw it upon our extreme left. General Hancock received them without recoil, and threw them back, routed and bleeding. All day Sunday both parties continued at work in the trenches, while shells were vigorously thrown from both sides, and not a head or hand could be exposed but it became the target for many bullets.

The ensuing night was very dark. A chill, dense fog settled down over the whole region. At midnight the rebels made another desperate plunge with a strong column upon a portion in our line, opening at the same time a terrible fire from all the batteries which could be brought to bear upon the point of attack. The veteran national troops, now familiar with all conceivable vicissitudes and horrors of war, stood as firm as the granite cliff against which the surge is dashed and broken. Volley after volley of grape and canister was poured into the advancing ranks. Leaving the ground covered with more than a thousand of the wounded and the slain, they turned and fled. The war-tempest disappeared as suddenly as it had risen.

Tuesday was like Monday. Spades were everywhere busy. The

air was filled with shells. The roar of artillery incessantly shook the hills, and the crackle of rifles from thousands of sharpshooters, ever on the alert, was unintermitted. Again, at midnight, the rebels made an assault upon General Burnside's corps. That gallant officer, who had won renown at Knoxville, repulsed them bloodily. Wednesday came and went. Through all its hours the roar of the bombardment continued, gun answering gun, while ramparts and bastions rose as by magic, facing each other, and often so near that the soldiers interchanged jokes and banter. There was not a strong antagonism between the rank and file of the armies. The leaders of the Rebellion, with power over the unenlightened poor white population of the South scarcely exceeded by that of the feudal despots of the Middle Ages over their serfs, had brought on the war.

Thoughtful men were wondering what object General Grant had in view in the tremendous labors of this week of battle. It was manifest that he could not take by storm the works of the foe frowning before him. The mystery was soon revealed. On Saturday orders were given for the immediate and vigorous change of the base of supplies from the Chickahominy to the James River. Sunday morning, blinding the eyes of the foe with a cloud of skirmishers, General Grant, with the mass of his immense army, commenced another flank movement. Descending the left bank of the Chickahominy, he crossed it unseen, several miles below the enemy's lines, and by a rapid march reached the James River, crossed it on pontoon-bridges, and took a strong position in the rear of Lee's army, south of Richmond. Three days were occupied in this marvelous feat. A more brilliant achievement the war had not witnessed.

In the presence of a foe equal in numbers, whose valor could scarcely be exceeded, led by generals as able as the nineteenth century could furnish, General Grant conducted an army of one hundred and fifty thousand men a distance of fifty-five miles by a flank march, and across two wide rivers, without the loss of a wagon or a gun. It was on Wednesday morning, the 15th of June, that the advance corps crossed James River, and effected a junction with General Butler's encampment at Bermuda Hundred. They then crossed the Appomattox, and, rapidly traversing its southern bank, commenced an attack upon Petersburg.

General Lee was appalled, as he suddenly heard the thunders of

General Grant's artillery fifty miles south of him. With a rush he abandoned his now useless ramparts, and by railroad and turnpike hurried his army, with the utmost possible speed, to man the works which thousands of negro hands had been compelled to rear for the defense of Petersburg. A bird's-eye view of this scene would have presented one of the most picturesque spectacles earth has witnessed. Its beauty, however, would have been lost in contemplation of its horrors, as frenzied men mutilated and destroyed each other, extorting wails of anguish from thousands of distant homes, which, could they have been heard, would almost have drowned the clangor of the battle. Over a space forty miles long and fifteen broad, three hundred thousand men, in martial bands of horse and foot, with all the enginery of war, were sweeping to and fro in apparently inextricable confusion. Wherever the heads of the columns met, a desperate battle ensued. Thundering cannon and mortars hurtled shot and shell through the air. The smoke, the flame, the roar, the turmoil, was as if the region were in volcanic eruption.

Though there were many repulses, and blood flowed freely, the Union troops were steadily gaining. Our soldiers encountered a triple line of intrenchments well manned. The outer line was captured with sixteen guns and three hundred prisoners. Two thousand Union soldiers were struck down in killed and wounded that day. The rebel loss is not known. But little reliance could ever be placed in their statements. The Rebellion commenced in deceit, and was carried on in deceit until its close. The next day, Friday, the battle was renewed, and raged all day long with as much ferocity as human desperation could inspire. Though the enemy contested every foot of ground, step by step General Grant gained upon them, until at night he had obtained a position from which several shells were thrown into the streets of Petersburg.

On Saturday the antagonistic armies again grappled each other in death's throes. Battery answered battery. Charge succeeded charge. The onset of the national troops was so terrible that General Lee was compelled to abandon his second line, and concentrate all his strength for the defense of the inner series of works. This movement he accomplished mainly during Friday night and Saturday. In this three days' battle around the ramparts of Petersburg, we lost over ten thousand men in killed and wounded and missing. As the rebels fought under cover, their loss must have been much less.

Petersburg, with a population of fifteen thousand, is about twenty-five miles south of Richmond. Its defenses were found unexpectedly strong. The city could only be taken by siege. We have not space here to enter into the details of the struggle which ensued. There were never more fearless soldiers, never more able generals, never before such destructive enginery of war. Every day was a battle. The rebels fought with courage which would have elicited admiration had their cause been a good one. But their openly-avowed object was to overthrow the Constitution of the United States, and to erect upon the ruins of our free institutions a government whose corner-stone should be *slavery*.

General Grant gradually extended his lines, fighting for every point he gained, until he had completely invested the city on the south and west, cutting those railroads by which alone supplies could be received directly from the south. His circuitous line soon extended thirty miles in length. It is obvious that General Lee, from his central position, could at his leisure mass an immense force and strike this line upon any point. The skill with which General Grant guarded against this danger, while at the same time he was incessantly attacking the foe and gaining new positions, has placed him, in the estimation of all capable judges, among the most able commanders.

"It is wonderful," writes the army correspondent of "Harper's Weekly," "how entirely the army confides in General Grant. Every soldier's tongue is full of his praises. They will tell you stories of his watchfulness and care; the fearlessness and intrepidity of this man whose plume they delight to follow; how he is everywhere, night and day, looking after the comfort of his men, and quietly prosecuting the strategic work of the campaign; how he rides unexpectedly to the remote outposts, speaking a pleasant word to the pickets if faithfully on duty, and administering reprimands if not vigilant and watchful; how he avoids fuss and show, going often about with only an orderly; how his staff, plain earnest men like himself, get down from their horses that sick and wounded men, struggling hospital-ward, may rest their weariness by riding to their destination; how, in a word, he is a thoughtful, resolute, kind man, sympathizing with the humblest soldier in his ranks, penetrated with a solemn appreciation of the work given him to do, and determined by Heaven's help to do it right on the line he has occupied."

Days, weeks, months ensued, of herculean labors and struggles between the beleaguered and beleaguering hosts. Every day terrific blows were struck by the assailants. Every day these blows were returned by the assailed. Shells of fearful explosive power were thrown by day and by night into the doomed city. Streets were torn up, mutilation and death were scattered widely around, houses were demolished, conflagrations enkindled. The scene at midnight, as viewed from some eminence, was awful in its sublimity. The camp-fires of the slumbering hosts illumining the region for leagues around, the thunders of the heavy siege-guns, the shriek of the shells, the smothered roar of their distant explosion in the streets of Petersburg, the dense volumes of smoke and flame bursting from the city, and the ringing of the alarm-bells borne mournfully to the ear upon the night air, all presented a spectacle as saddening as it was sublime. Terrible as were these woes, they were nothing in comparison with those which would have resulted from the destruction of our free institutions, the breaking up of the Union, and the anarchy and endless wars which would inevitably have ensued. Our nation was born through the throes of the Revolution. In this its second birth, in the purification and regeneration of its institutions, it was the decree of God that the work should be accomplished through the ministration of suffering.

As the weeks of battle and of blood rolled on, General Grant, step by step, was continually approaching nearer the attainment of his one great end. July and August passed rapidly away. Early in September the army was cheered by the news that General Sherman had taken Atlanta, and was preparing for a rapid march through Georgia and the Carolinas to coöperate with the army before the ramparts of Richmond. About this time General Grant said, in one of his official reports to the government, —

" From an early period in the Rebellion, I had been impressed with the idea that active and continuous operations of all the troops that could be brought into the field, regardless of season and weather, were necessary to a speedy termination of the war. From the first, I was firm in the conviction that no peace could be had that would be stable, and conducive to the happiness of the people, both North and South, until the military power of the Rebellion was entirely broken. I therefore determined, first, to use the greatest number of troops practicable against the armed force of the enemy, preventing him from using the same force at different seasons, against first one and then another of our armies, and from the possibility of repose for refitting and producing necessary supplies for carrying on resistance ; second, to hammer continually against the armed force of the enemy, and his resources, until, by mere attrition, if in no other way, there should be nothing left to him but an equal submission, with the loyal section of our common country, to the Constitution and laws of the land."

Still the months rolled on, with bombardments, and exploding mines, and raids, and charges, and fierce battles, each day numbering its multitude of victims. General Grant, in this great struggle, was continually advancing, and seldom losing any position he once had gained. The latter part of December, the cheering tidings reached the army that General Sherman had achieved his sublime march to Savannah. With sixty thousand men, three thousand five hundred baggage-wagons, and thirty-five thousand draft-horses, in addition to his cavalry, he had swept across the State in a path sixty miles wide and three hundred miles long, destroying everything which could assist the rebels in carrying on the war.

In a march of twenty-four days, with a loss of but five hundred and sixty-seven men, General Sherman had routed the foe wherever met, had captured thirteen hundred and thirty-eight rebel soldiers, had taken thirteen thousand head of beef cattle, over nine million pounds of corn, and ten millions of fodder. Foragers in great numbers had been sent out daily to gather from the plantations every variety of supplies for the hungry army, — sheep, swine, turkeys, geese, chickens, and rice. Five thousand horses and four thousand mules were impressed into the service of the troops. Three hundred and twenty miles of railway were destroyed. The ties were burned, the rails twisted, the dépôts laid in ashes. Thus the rebel armies in the southwest were effectually cut off by a barrier of desolation from communication with the troops of Lee in Richmond.

Thus closed the year 1864. The cause of the Rebellion was hopeless. And now General Sherman turned his triumphant columns towards the north. In resistless march he swept through the States of South and North Carolina, driving the rebels before him, and capturing every important place till he met the banners of General Sheridan's cavalry and General Schofield's divisions, sent to Goldsborough to greet him. The two armies were thus united. General Sherman immediately repaired to the headquarters of General Grant. It was the 29th of March, 1865.

General Grant's lines of investment extended forty miles, from the north side of the James to Hatchie's Run. The great fear now was that Lee, with his army, might attempt to escape, and effect a junction with General Johnston, who had an army of infantry and cavalry at Raleigh, N. C., numbering about fifty thousand. These united armies, falling suddenly on Sherman's troops, might crush them. General Grant watched the foe with a sleepless eye, prepared to assail him with his whole force as soon as he should see any indications that he was about to abandon his works.

On Friday, the last day of March, there were decisive indications of a movement. The whole national army was at once hurled upon the rebel lines. For three days the battle raged with determination, on each side, never exceeded during any period of the war. In the night of the 3d of April, Lee, conscious that he could not resist the assault of another day, fled with the bleeding, shattered remnants of his army. As the national troops, in the early dawn of the next morning, rushed into the unoccupied trenches, the joyful tidings ran along the wires through the whole length and breadth of the land, —

"Richmond and Petersburg are ours. A third part of Lee's army is destroyed. For the remainder there is no escape."

The rebels were hotly pursued. The roads along which they fled were strewed with the *débris* of a demoralized and fugitive host. Many prisoners were taken. In anticipation of this flight, General Grant had placed the Fifth Corps in such a position that, by a rapid march, it was thrown in front of the foe, and thus effectually cut off his retreat. The rebel army was now at our mercy. Throughout the whole conflict there had been great sympathy felt in the North for the common soldiers of the rebel army, composed of very ignorant men, who had been deluded or forced into the ranks. Sympathy for them led General Grant magnanimously to make the first advances, and to urge General Lee to spare him the pain of destroying these misguided men. The rebel troops were so surrounded, and so exposed to the fire of many batteries, that a battle-storm of bullets, shot, and shell, would, in a few hours, cover the plain with their corpses. It was the 9th of April, General Grant sent the following dispatch to Lee : —

"The result of the last week must convince you of the hopelessness of further resistance on the part of the Army of Northern Virginia in this struggle. I feel that it is so, and regard it as my duty to shift from myself the responsibility of any further effusion of blood, by asking of you the surrender of that portion of the Confederate Army known as the Army of Northern Virginia."

To General Lee's inquiry, respecting the terms of surrender which would be accepted, General Grant replied, —

"Peace being my first desire, there is but one condition I insist upon, namely, that the men surrendered shall be disqualified for taking up arms against the government of the United States until properly exchanged."

General Lee, assuming that he was not placed in an emergence which required surrender, but that he was still able to carry on the war, proposed an interview, that he and General Grant might talk over the matter of the "restoration of peace." General Grant's prompt reply indicates the clearness of his views respecting the only responsibilities which devolved upon him : —

"As I have no authority," he said, "to treat on the subject of peace, the meeting proposed could lead to no good. I will state, however, general, that I am equally anxious for peace with yourself; and the whole North entertains the same feeling. The terms upon which peace may be had are well understood. By the South laying down their arms, they will hasten that most desirable event, save thousands of human lives, and hundreds of millions of property not yet destroyed. Sincerely hoping that all our difficulties may be settled without the loss of another life, I subscribe myself,

"Very respectfully, your obedient servant,

"U. S. GRANT."

Having dispatched this letter, General Grant lost not a moment in waiting for a reply, but pressed forward his preparations to destroy the army if surrender were refused. General Lee saw clearly that with such a man it was in vain to attempt to parley. He consented to an interview to arrange for a surrender. The terms of General Grant were very simple and decisive. All the rebel officers and men were to give their parole not to serve against the United States until exchanged. All the *materiel* of war was to be given up. The officers could retain their side-arms, horses, and baggage. These terms were signed at half past three in the afternoon of April 9th. The rebel troops were then upon a plain, surrounded by the batteries of the national army. The tidings of the capitulation first reached the ears of the rebels. It was to them deliverance from slaughter. Cheer upon cheer burst from their exhausted ranks. Their shouts conveyed the tidings to our army, and were echoed back in heartfelt hurrahs, till over all the embattled hills and plain the voices of friend and foe blended in the joyful cry. Large bands of the Union army, pressing forward from the rear, one after another caught the shout, and learning its significance, sent it along to those behind in reverberating peals.

It was now certain that the spirit of rebellion was effectually trampled down. Johnston's condition was hopeless. He could be instantly crushed between the armies of Grant and Sherman. He surrendered. All the scattered rebel bands soon did the same, or dispersed. Thousands threw down their arms, and fled to their homes. The number surrendered amounted to 174,223. We had also then on hand rebel prisoners to the amount of 98,802. Jefferson Davis endeavored, with a small cavalry escort, to escape to some southern seaport, whence he hoped to take ship for foreign lands. On the 10th of May he was captured at Irwinsville, in Georgia. The war was ended. The Union was saved. The almost unanimous voice of the nation declared General Grant to be the most prominent instrument in its salvation. The eminent services he had thus rendered the country brought him conspicuously forward as the Republican candidate for the presidential chair.

On the 21st of May, 1868, the Republican Convention, assembled at Chicago, adopted a series of resolutions, a platform, so called, of the principles of the party. The essential points were, that equal civil and political rights should be secured to all; that Congress should guaranty equal suffrage to all loyal men at the South; and that all forms of repudiation were to be denounced as a national crime. The following very important article was also added to their platform: —

" We profoundly deplore the untimely and tragic death of Abraham Lincoln, and regret the accession to the presidency of Andrew Johnson, who has acted treacherously to the people who elected him, and to the cause which he was pledged to support; who has

33

usurped high legislative and judicial functions; who has refused to execute the laws; who has used his high office to induce other officers to ignore and violate the laws; who has employed his executive powers to render insecure the property, the peace, liberty, and life of the citizen; who has abused the pardoning power; who has denounced the national legislature as unconstitutional; who has persistently and corruptly resisted, by every means in his power, every proper attempt at the reconstruction of the States lately in rebellion; who has perverted the public patronage into an engine of wholesale corruption; and who has been justly impeached for high crimes and misdemeanors, and properly pronounced guilty thereof by the vote of thirty-five senators."

This platform having been accepted, ULYSSES S. GRANT was nominated to the Convention as the candidate of the Republican party for the chief magistracy. The vote was taken. In the following terms it was announced: —

" Gentlemen of the Convention, you have six hundred and fifty votes; and you have given six hundred and fifty votes for General ULYSSES S. GRANT."

The enthusiasm inspired by this announcement, in the vast Opera House where the Convention was held, cannot be described. As soon as it had in some degree subsided, the Hon. Schuyler Colfax of Indiana was nominated for the vice-presidency. After a few ballotings, he was unanimously elected.

With this platform, General Grant and Mr. Colfax were submitted to the suffrages of the people of the United States. In accepting the nomination, General Grant, after expressing his cordial approval of the platform, said, —

" If elected to the office of President of the United States, it will be my endeavor to administer all the laws in good faith, with economy, and with the view of giving peace, quiet, and protection everywhere. In times like the present it is impossible, or at least eminently improper, to lay down a policy to be adhered to, right or wrong, through an administration of four years. New political issues, not foreseen, are constantly arising; the views of the public on old ones are constantly changing; and a purely administrative officer should always be left free to execute the will of the people. I always have respected that will, and always shall. Peace and universal prosperity, its sequence, with economy of administration, will lighten the burden of taxation, while it constantly reduces the national debt. Let us have peace."

Governor Horatio Seymour of New York was the candidate of the Democratic party. The election was hotly contested. In the popular vote, there were 5,922,984 votes cast. Of these, Grant received 3,016,353. Seymour received 2,906,631. Grant's majority was 109,722. Thirty-four States cast their votes for electors. Three, unreconstructed, did not vote. Twenty-six of the States gave their electoral votes, numbering 214, for Grant. Eight cast their votes, counting 80, for Seymour. Thus, in accordance with the provisions of the Constitution, it was announced that Ulysses S. Grant was elected President of the United States by a majority of 134 electoral votes.

On the 4th of March, 1869, General Grant entered upon the duties of his office under the most flattering circumstances. The opposing party cordially concurred in the election. All the billows which the tempest of war had raised were rapidly subsiding. The country was in a state of extraordinary prosperity. Nearly all the serious questions which had hitherto divided the parties were settled.

No one can occupy a post of influence and power without exciting obloquy. It is the inevitable penalty of office. None of our presidents have been more fiercely assailed than were George Washington and Thomas Jefferson; and yet there is no candid man now living who will not admit that they were both pure patriots, honestly and earnestly seeking the best good of the country. President Grant took his seat in the presidential chair just after the close of one of the most terrible civil wars which ever, with its earthquake throes, agitated any nation. The difficulties which pressed upon him were greater than any of his predecessors had ever encountered. No mortal wisdom could have marked out any measures which would have met with universal approval.

The Southern States were thrown into a chaotic condition. Their peculiar institutions, which had separated them from the North, had perished forever. To make us a homogeneous republic, where *equal rights for all men* should be universally respected, it was needful that several million illiterate slaves, entirely unaccustomed to self-government, should be elevated to the dignity of citizens. This could not be accomplished without great difficulty. It was one of the most perplexing of political problems. When the passions of the present hour shall have passed away, no candid mind will doubt that President Grant, embracing in his patriotism all sections of the country alike, acted in accordance with his most deliberate judgment for the good of all.

The National Convention of the Republican party, which met at Philadelphia on the 5th of June, 1872, placed General Grant in nomination for a second term by a unanimous vote. The selection was emphatically indorsed by the people five months later, two hundred and ninety-two electoral votes being cast for his reëlection, — the largest number ever given for a presidential candidate.

Soon after the close of his second term General Grant decided to visit the countries of the old world, and started from America, expecting to travel quietly and privately for a year or two. But from the time when he landed at Liverpool until he reached his home at Galena, Ill., his trip was an unceasing ovation. England, France, Germany, Russia, Austria, Switzerland, Belgium, Italy, Turkey, India, and China endeavored each to outdo the other in the heartiness and display of their receptions. In his course, making the complete circuit of the globe, his appearance was the signal for almost unheard-of enthusiasm.

After his return he was again pressed by his ardent admirers to be a candidate for the Presidency of the United States; but party divisions and short-sighted movements on the part of his friends prevented his nomination in the party convention at Chicago. He has since been engaged in various business enterprises, and is at present an active participant in the efforts being made to open an inter-oceanic canal between the Atlantic Ocean and the Pacific Ocean, across the Isthmus of Panama. He is also engaged in the promotion of various railroad enterprises intended for the development of Mexico and the Southwestern Territories of the United States.

Engraved by F.T.Stuart from late Phot?

R. B. Hayes.

CHAPTER XIX.

RUTHERFORD BIRCHARD HAYES.

Birth. — Ancestry. — Childhood. — College Days. — Two Years in the Cambridge Law School. — Practice of the Law. — Cincinnati Literary Club. — City Solicitor. — Military Services, Battles, and Wounds. — Election to Congress. — Three times Governor of Ohio. — Elected President.

RUTHERFORD BIRCHARD HAYES was born in Delaware, O., October 4, 1822, less than three months after the death of his father, Rutherford Hayes. His ancestry, both on the paternal and

PRIVATE RESIDENCE OF R. B. HAYES, FREMONT, O.

maternal side, was of the most honorable character. It can be traced, it is said, as far back as 1280, when Hayes and Rutherford were two Scottish chieftains, fighting side by side with Baliol, William Wallace, and Robert Bruce. Both families belonged to the nobility, owned extensive estates, and had a large following. The Hayes family had for a coat-of-arms, a shield, barred, and surmounted by a flying eagle. There was a circle of stars about the eagle and above the shield, while on a scroll underneath the shield was inscribed the motto, " Recte." Misfortune overtaking the family, George Hayes left Scotland in 1680, and settled in Windsor, Conn. He was an industrious worker in wood and iron, having a mechanical genius and a cultivated mind. His son George was born in Windsor, and remained there during his life. Daniel Hayes, son of the latter, married Sarah Lee, and lived from the time of his marriage until his death in Simsbury, Conn. Ezekiel, son of Daniel, was born in 1724, and was a manufacturer of scythes at Bradford, Conn. Rutherford Hayes, son of Ezekiel and grandfather of President Hayes, was born in New Haven in August, 1756. He was a farmer, blacksmith, and tavern-keeper. He emigrated to Vermont at an unknown date, settling in Brattleborough, where he established a hotel. Here his son Rutherford Hayes, the father of President Hayes, was born. He was married in September, 1813, to Sophia Birchard of Wilmington, Vt., whose ancestors emigrated thither from Connecticut, they having been among the wealthiest and best families of Norwich. Her ancestry on the male side is traced back to 1635, to John Birchard, one of the principal founders of Norwich. Both of her grandfathers were soldiers in the Revolutionary war.

The father of President Hayes was an industrious, frugal, and open-hearted man. He was of a mechanical turn, and could mend a plow, knit a stocking, or do almost anything else that he chose to undertake. As he was a feeble boy, his father procured for him a situation as clerk in a store, and afterwards assisted him to open a store of his own in Brattleborough. He was prosperous in his business, having the confidence and the good-will of all who knew him. He was a member of the church, active in all the benevolent enterprises of the town, and conducted his business on Christian principles. After the close of the war of 1812, for reasons inexplicable to his neighbors, he resolved to emigrate to Ohio. It seemed strange that a man so prosperous should be willing to leave a place where he was enjoying all the social, moral, and religious influences of a well-ordered community, to make his home in a wilderness; but the fever of Western emigration was as potent in that day as it is now, and he yielded to an impulse keenly felt but little understood. The journey from Vermont to Ohio in that day, when there were neither canals, steamers, nor railways, was a very serious affair. A tour of inspection was first made, occupying four months. Mr. Hayes purchased a farm near the present town of Delaware, and, on his return to Brattleborough, announced his intention of removing thither with his family, which consisted then of his wife and two children, and an orphan girl whom he had adopted. Having disposed of his property in Brattleborough, Mr. Hayes and his family, accompanied by Sardis Birchard, a younger brother of Mrs. Hayes, set out upon their Western journey in a covered wagon, in which were stored all the household goods reserved from sale, and nearly all the food they expected to need on the way. They traveled by day, and slept at night in that tented conveyance, passing now through dense forests, now over deep streams, and encountering fierce storms. The orphan girl is the only survivor of the party, and her story of that forty days and nights of travel and peril would furnish materials for a stirring romance.

It was in 1817 that the family arrived at Delaware. Mr. Hayes, instead of settling upon his farm on the Olentangy River, concluded to enter into business in the village. He purchased an interest in a distillery, a business then as respectable as it was profitable. His capital and recognized ability and character insured him the highest social position in the community. His advice was sought in all public affairs; he was one of the first and largest contributors to the fund for the erection of a Presbyterian church, a generous supporter of schools, and active in every movement for the intellectual and moral improvement of society. He died July 22, 1822, a victim of malarial pestilence, less than three months before the birth of the son who filled the office of President of the United States. Mrs. Hayes, in her sore bereavement, found the support she so much needed in her brother Sardis, who had been a member of the household from the day of its departure from Vermont, and in the orphan girl whom she had adopted so long before as an act of charity. Her brother was a noble young man. For five years he had been to her as a son, and had received from her much of that enthusiasm and social education which served him so well in his subsequent remarkable career. And now, in her great sorrow, she was rewarded for her care and devotion. The young man made it the great object of his life to care for his sister and her children; and his aid at this crisis in their history was of the greatest value to them all.

Mrs. Hayes at this period was very weak, and the subject of this sketch was so feeble at birth that he was not expected to live beyond a month or two at most. As the months went by he grew weaker and weaker, so that the neighbors were in the habit of inquiring from time to time "if Mrs. Hayes's baby died last night." On one occasion a neighbor, who was on familiar terms with the family, after alluding to the boy's big head, and the mother's assiduous care of him, said in a bantering way to her, "That's right! Stick to him. You have got him along so far, and I should n't wonder if he would really come to something yet."

"You need not laugh," said Mrs. Hayes. "You wait and see. You can't tell but I shall make him President of the United States yet."

The boy lived in spite of the universal predictions of his speedy death; and when, in 1825, his older brother was drowned, he became, if possible, still dearer to his mother. When the body of her oldest son was borne from the river to the house, and she felt that she had lost the main prop of her widowed life, her heart went out in prayer to God that the feeble little boy, now three years old, and her young daughter, might be spared to her. Her care of these jewels of her heart was anxious and incessant. In her watchfulness she gave herself no rest, and was hardly willing for years that little Rutherford should go beyond her sight.

The boy was seven years old before he went to school. His education, however, was not neglected. He probably learned as much from his mother and sister as he would have done at school. His sports were almost wholly within doors, his playmates being his sister and her associates. These circumstances tended, no doubt, to foster that gentleness of disposition, and that delicate consideration for the feelings of others, which are marked traits of his character. The boys of that period, especially those upon the frontiers of civilization, were too often rude and coarse, though not necessarily lacking in more manly qualities. If young Hayes, on account of his sheltered life, lacked something of the robustness and fiery energy of other boys, he was saved from the little vices and almost brutal habits which too often exhibit themselves at that period of life. At school he was ardently devoted to his studies, obedient to the teacher, and careful to avoid the quarrels in which many of his schoolmates were involved. He was always waiting at the school-house door when it opened in the morning, and never late in returning to his seat at recess. As a playmate he was unselfish and generous, and in all his intercourse with others frank, and without deceit or guile ; and, if teachers praised him as a model boy, his modesty and bashfulness saved him from any false pride on that account. His sister Fannie was his constant companion, and their affection for each other excited the admiration of their friends.

His uncle, Sardis Birchard, took the deepest interest in his education ; and as the boy's health had much improved, and he was making good progress in his studies, he proposed to send him to college. His preparations began with a tutor at home ; but he was afterwards sent for one year to a professor in the Wesleyan University, in Middletown, Conn. He entered Kenyon College in 1838, at the age of sixteen, and was graduated at the head of his class in 1842. His college life was quiet and studious. He was involved in no college "scrapes," but was a favorite with his fellow-students and with the faculty. On one occasion his timely and sensible advice saved a classmate from foolishly provoking expulsion. This classmate had played a practical joke, which gave great offense to the faculty. He was able and brilliant and had much influence with his fellow-students. He was required to make confession of his fault, and ask forgiveness therefor, before the students assembled at prayers. An indignation meeting of his class was held, and resolutions were introduced, and speeches made, extolling the "martyr" who would sacrifice himself to "vindicate his honor." They told him not to yield. Death before such dishonor! The tide was all running one way, when young Hayes had the good sense and the courage to attempt to stem the flood. These, as nearly as his classmates can now recall them, are the words he spoke : —

"Fellows, this is all a mistake. It cannot be that you have stopped to think. Now, I know well what I would do if I had been caught in such a scrape, and had received such a proposition from the faculty : I should not wait a single hour before I went and asked their forgiveness. I tell you, fellows, we have friends at home who care nothing about our codes of honor, but to whom our disgrace would bring great sorrow. I would not put them to shame by refusing to do such a little thing as confessing publicly to the truth. If he did wrong, he ought to confess it. If it was not wrong in itself, but is so held by the faculty, it can do no harm to tell the truth about it, and say he is sorry that he did it.   I tell you, boys, it would be foolish to accept a lasting disgrace rather than acknowledge such a little shortcoming as that.   If he does not do what the professors ask of him, he is a very foolish young man, and will regret it, and his family will regret it, down to his dying day.''

This sensible and courageous speech changed the whole current of opinion in the class ; the inculpated student accepted the advice thus given, and the threatened rebellion was over.   That student is now one of the most honored and distinguished men in Ohio, and a warm friend of President Hayes.

Immediately after his graduation, Hayes began the study of the law in the office of Thomas Sparrow, Esq., in Columbus.   His health was now well established; his figure robust, his muscular and nervous forces strong, his mind vigorous and alert.   Destitute of the showy qualities which so often force young men into a prominence entirely beyond their merits, he was thorough in all his work.   He never was satisfied with a superficial knowledge of anything, but went to the bottom of every question that arose in studying for his chosen profession.   Finding his opportunities for study in Columbus somewhat limited, he determined to enter the Law School at Cambridge, Mass., where he remained two years, pursuing his studies so diligently and quietly that he hardly attracted the notice of his more ambitious fellow-students.

In 1845, after graduating at the Law School, he was admitted to the bar at Marietta, O., and shortly afterward went into practice as an attorney at law with Ralph P. Buckland of Fremont.   Here he remained three years, acquiring but a limited practice, and apparently unambitious of distinction in his profession.   His bachelor uncle, Sardis Birchard, was now a wealthy banker, and it was understood that the young man would be his heir.   It is possible that this expectation may have made Mr. Hayes more indifferent to the attainment of wealth by his own efforts than he would otherwise have been.   But, if his ambition was checked by this means, he was led into no extravagance, still less into any of the vices that so often work the ruin of young men prospectively rich.

In 1849 he removed to Cincinnati, where his ambition found a new stimulus.   For several years, however, his progress was slow.   His diligence, promptness, and accuracy in all matters intrusted to his care, won the confidence of those who employed him, and finally brought him into prominence. Two events, occurring at this period, had a powerful influence upon his subsequent life. One of these was his marriage to Miss Lucy Ware Webb, daughter of Dr. James Webb of Chillicothe ; the other was his introduction to the Cincinnati Literary Club, a body embracing among its members such men as Chief-Justice Salmon P. Chase, General John Pope, Governor Edward F. Noyes, and many others hardly less distinguished in after-life. There is no more powerful stimulus to a young man's ambition than the love of a noble and pure-hearted woman ; and Mr. Hayes, from the moment of his engagement, began to show the sterling stuff of which he was made. The marriage was a fortunate one in every respect, as everybody knows. Not one of all the wives of our Presidents was more universally admired, reverenced, and beloved, than is Mrs. Hayes, and no one has done more than she to reflect honor upon American womanhood. The Literary Club brought Mr. Hayes into constant association with young men of high character and noble aims, and lured him to display the qualities so long hidden by his bashfulness and modesty. His acquaintance was rapidly extended, and he began to take a high position at the bar. Important cases were confided to his care, and his professional business became absorbing and profitable. One of the most noted murder cases ever tried in Ohio was carried through by him in a masterly manner, drawing to him wide attention, and winning for him the applause of some of the most eminent men in the State. He was always ready to undertake the defense of the fugitive slave, or of any other oppressed and friendless person.

In 1856 he was nominated to the office of judge of the Court of Common Pleas ; but he declined to accept the nomination. Two years later, the office of city solicitor becoming vacant, the City Council elected him for the unexpired term. It was only after much urging that he consented to serve. He performed the duties of the office so acceptably that he was chosen for a full term at the next election, running over five hundred votes ahead of his ticket. At the next election he was defeated under circumstances which implied no censure or loss of personal popularity.

In 1861, when the Rebellion broke out, he was at the zenith of a professional life. His rank at the bar was among the first. But the news of the attack on Fort Sumter found him eager to take up arms for the defense of his country. The Cincinnati Literary Club, of which he was now a leading member, organized a military company from its own ranks, giving it the name of the "Burnett Rifles." Thirty-five of the members of this company were lawyers, of whom twenty-three became officers in the Union army, and several of the number generals. Not less than seventy-five commissioned officers were furnished by the club. In all the meetings Mr. Hayes took an active and zealous part. On the 4th of January, 1861, he wrote a letter in which he said, —

"South Carolina has passed a secession ordinance, and federal laws are set at naught in the State. Overt acts enough have been committed, forts and arsenals having been taken, a revenue cutter seized, and Major Anderson besieged at Fort Sumter. Other cotton States are about to follow. Disunion and civil war are at hand ; and yet I fear disunion and war less than compromise. We can recover from them. The free States alone, if we must go on alone, will make a glorious nation. I do not feel gloomy when I look forward. The reality is less frightful than the apprehension which we have all had these many years. Let us be temperate, calm, and just, but firm and resolute. Crittenden's compromise! Windham, speaking of the rumor that Bonaparte was about to invade England, said, ' The danger of invasion is by no means equal to that of peace. A man may escape a pistol, no matter how near his head, but not a dose of poison.' "

When the three months troops were called for, Mr. Hayes thought it a mistake to organize a military force for so short a period, for he foresaw a long and bloody struggle. Soon after the massacre of Massachusetts troops in Baltimore, he enlisted for the whole war, declaring that he should prefer to go into it if he knew he was to die or be killed before the end, rather than to live through and after it without taking any part in it. He and his friend the Hon. Stanley Matthews together tendered their services to Governor Dennison, and were accepted. The governor wished to place each of them in command of a regiment ; but they objected to this, insisting that the colonel should be an experienced officer, who would teach his subordinates their duties. As they did not wish to be separated, Matthews was commissioned as lieutenant-colonel, and Hayes as major, of the Twenty-third Ohio Volunteers, W. S. Rosecrans being appointed colonel. Before the regiment was called into the field, however, Colonel Rosecrans was promoted to a brigadier-general, and another graduate of West Point, Colonel Scammon, was commissioned in his place. The regiment was placed on garrison duty at Clarksburg, W. Va., to protect the Baltimore and Ohio Railroad, and defend the border from raids. General Rosecrans was in command of the post. The Twenty-third was not allowed much ease, being often sent upon expeditions against the raiders and bushwhackers that infested the region. Major Hayes was often connected with these expeditions ; but in the more inactive months of the summer (1861), he served on General Rosecrans' staff as judge-advocate, — a thankless office, the duties of which he fulfilled with such impartiality as to earn the praise of all with whom he had to deal. He rejoined his regiment before the battle of Carnifex Ferry. The regiment, however, did not participate in that battle, though a portion thereof was employed, under the lead of Major Hayes, in making a flank movement to threaten the enemy's rear. In the latter part of September the regiment went into camp with the army at Mount Sewall, in front of Lee ; but the bad weather and worse roads compelled both armies to fall back ; and the Twenty-third took up its quarters at Camp Ewing, near Point Lookout, Va. In October, Lieutenant-Colonel Matthews having been assigned to the post of colonel of the Fifty-first Ohio Regiment, Major Hayes was promoted to the vacancy thus created, and, in consequence of the absence of Colonel Scammon, took command of the Twenty-third. The regiment passed the winter of 1861–62 in scouting over the mountains and raiding into the interior of Virginia. There was more marching than fighting in these expeditions, but Lieutenant-Colonel Hayes had several narrow escapes from death. At one time he fell into an ambuscade, from which he escaped without injury, exhibiting a coolness and bravery under fire that greatly increased his popularity with the regiment. On the 1st of May he led an assault upon the enemy's garrison at Princeton, a point of considerable strategic importance. So unexpected and impetuous was the charge, that the rebels fled at the first fire, leaving their arms and ammunition behind them.

Ten days later Lieutenant-Colonel Hayes had his first experience of manœuvring troops under fire. He was stationed at Giles Court House, and had under his command nine companies of the Twenty-third, five hundred cavalry, and a section of light artillery, when a force of the enemy, numbering nearly four thousand, and commanded by General Heath, made an attack upon the place. It would have been a foolhardy undertaking to defend the unfortified place against so large a force ; to escape capture was the utmost that could be done. Lieutenant-Colonel Hayes comprehended the situation at a glance, and went about his task coolly and deliberately. He was so prompt and unconcerned in his movements that his forces were inspired with courage. The men cheered, and tossed their hats, in their enthusiasm, whenever he passed by. For more than five miles they retreated, keeping the foe at a safe distance by their skirmishers, until at last, with but slight loss, they entered the fortifications of the main army. The men suffered much from hunger and fatigue. Lieutenant-Colonel Hayes was slightly wounded by a piece of shell, and his competency as a commander was thoroughly proved.

On the 13th of July, the Twenty-third, being encamped on Flat Top Mountain, was ordered to report at Green Meadows, on New River; from which place they were hurried, August 15th, to Camp Piatt, on the Kanawha. From this point they were taken in transports to the Ohio, and up that river to Parkersburg, where they took the cars for Washington, arriving there on the 24th. Early in in August, Lieutenant-Colonel Hayes was promoted to be colonel of the Seventy-ninth Ohio Regiment, but he could not bear to leave his comrades of the Twenty-third to go among strangers. It was at this time that Lee crossed into Maryland, and Hayes resolved that he would remain with his regiment until after the impending struggle. The regiment was incorporated in General J. D. Cox's division of Burnside's command, in the Army of the Potomac, and ordered into Maryland.

We cannot tell at length the story of Lee's invasion and of his repulse by the Union forces. The first battle in that great struggle was at South Mountain, in which Lieutenant-Colonel Hayes and his brave little regiment, reduced now to three hundred and ten men, took a courageous and honorable part; and of this we must speak at some length. On the 13th of September, Lee with sixty thousand men crossed the South Mountain range, at Turner's Gap, leaving his rear guard of five brigades, under General Hill, to defend that pass, and hold the top of the mountain until General McLaws could have time to capture Harper's Ferry and join the main army at Hagerstown. The Twenty-third Ohio formed a part of the advance of the Union forces, encamped at Middletown, on whom devolved the duty of making the first movement upon the enemy's stronghold. It was seven o'clock in the morning when the order came to move up the mountain toward Turner's Gap, keeping well out to the right and left of the Boonsborough road, the only highway leading to the Gap. A detachment of Pleasanton's cavalry moved up the road, closely followed by a light battery, and the Twenty-third Ohio, together with several other regiments of Cox's command. It was not long before the clambering troops began to see little whiffs of white smoke in the edge of the woodland above them; then came the hum of bullets high over their heads, closely followed by the reports of muskets, indicating that they were approaching the enemy's skirmish lines. As they drew still nearer, and began to advance in line of battle, over stumps, bowlders, fences, trees, through ravines, and over knolls, the mountain-side became steeper; the cracking of musketry more incessant; while the bursting of shells and hissing of solid shot made the air overhead vocal with hideous, blood-curdling sounds.

The effort of General Cox's division to turn the enemy's flank was resisted by General Garland, with his brigade of veterans; and when that brave Confederate officer was killed, and his troops almost annihilated by the impetuous charges and steady firing of the Union forces, General Longstreet confronted the victors with fresh troops, three lines deep, intrenched behind logs, stone walls, trees, and bowlders. As Colonel Scammon's brigade, in which was the Twenty-third, advanced upon the enemy, the latter opened fire from their artillery, posted on the knolls in the rear of their line of battle; and so close was the range, and so accurate their aim, that the rebel grape, canister, and musket-balls literally stripped the trees of every leaf, and turned up the ground of the advancing soldiers as if it had been systematically plowed. Men could not endure such a torrent. As the Twenty-third clambered over a rising stretch of ground in front of the enemy, a blinding discharge of grape-shot met them full in the face; and, in an instant, more than a hundred of them lay upon the ground, dead or wounded. Five officers were struck by the storm of missiles, and among them Colonel Hayes went down with a broken arm. The brave regiment did not retreat, however, but, obeying the orders of Major Coverly, who now assumed command, advanced upon the enemy. The report that their colonel was killed did not abate their courage. While they paused for reinforcements, a dangerous flank movement of the enemy was discovered; when suddenly Colonel Hayes, with a handkerchief tied around his broken arm, appeared to his men, and, against the protests of friends, again took the lead. His return filled the little remnant of the regiment with great enthusiasm, and they fought like heroes all day. Their flag was torn to tatters, and wounds and death reduced their number to a hundred. Colonel Hayes fought, until, fainting with loss of blood, he was carried from the field. The surgeon, Dr. Webb, his brother-in-law, scarcely hoped to save his life, and the colonel himself had no hope of saving his arm from amputation. There he lay through the eventful days of Antietam, while his decimated regiment was crowning itself with fresh honors.

Mrs. Hayes, on hearing that her husband was wounded, hastened to find him. The task was a difficult one, for the wounded had been carried back from the field, and left indiscriminately in the houses, barns, and sheds for more than twenty miles to the rear. After searching for him in all the hospitals from Washington to Middletown, she found him in the latter place, in an old, dilapidated, two-story brick building. The joy of that meeting may be imagined, not described. Fortunately, it was found unnecessary to amputate the wounded arm; and Colonel Hayes, as he lay there suffering from his wound, said to some Ohio gentlemen who came to see him, " *Tell Governor Tod that I'll be on hand again shortly.*" He suffered, however, severely, and was unable to enter upon active duty for several weeks. Meanwhile, Colonel Scammon having been promoted to a brigadier-general, Governor Dennison revoked the commission of Colonel Hayes, to command the Seventy-ninth, and issued a new commission to him as commander of his own brave Twenty-third. He did not, however, personally command the regiment in any subsequent battles, as he was detached from it soon after his recovery, to act as brigadier-general, and (December 25, 1862) placed in command of the celebrated Kanawha division, to which the Twenty-third was attached. From that time to the next March, Colonel Hayes had a season of quiet, and the soldiers found at Kanawha Falls an opportunity to recuperate their wasted strength.

On the 15th of March the division was ordered to Charleston, W. Va., from which point it made many raids into the Confederacy, destroying stores of salt, ammunition, clothing, and crops, and capturing many prisoners. In June an expedition comprising three brigades, one of them that of Colonel Hayes, was dispatched to Southwestern Virginia, with the view of capturing Saltville, and breaking up the Virginia and Tennessee Railway. After a frightfully hard march the expedition accomplished its object, and, returning by a tedious and difficult route, arrived within fifteen miles of Fayetteville July 23d. The expedition from the first had been cut off from all mail facilities, and therefore knew nothing of the stirring events that had happened in other departments, including the surrender of Vicksburg, the defeat of Lee at Gettysburg, and Morgan's raid in Ohio. Hayes rode forward to Fayetteville to obtain the news. Here he learned that Morgan was on that very day crossing the Scioto at Piketon, and making for Gallipolis, where there was no adequate force to dispute his passage of the Ohio, and protect the supplies that had been gathered there. Colonel Hayes comprehended the situation in a moment, and telegraphed to the quartermaster at Charleston for a couple of steamers to be sent immediately to Fayetteville. Then, jumping into his saddle, he hastened back to camp, — a distance of fifteen miles, — arriving at nightfall. By consent of General Scammon he took two regiments and a section of artillery, and marched to Fayetteville in the darkness of the night. Arriving at early dawn, the steamers sent up from Charleston were found ready; and the men embarked at once for the voyage to Gallipolis, where they arrived at daylight the next morning, and took positions to defend the town. But Morgan had been informed by spies of their approach, and turned his column northward toward Pomeroy. Hayes promptly reëmbarked his force and steamed up the river to overtake him. He arrived in time to dispute the passage of the rebels, who thereupon moved still farther up to Buffington's Island. Here Morgan seized a steamboat, and had ferried over about three hundred of his men, when Colonel Hayes arrived, seized the boat, and put a stop to any further proceedings in that line. Morgan himself had crossed the river, but, seeing that his main body was to be cut off, he recrossed, and remained to share the fortunes of his soldiers. After some fighting, he drew off again, and made for other points up the river, but was at length forced to surrender.

Colonel Hayes returned to Virginia immediately after the capture of Morgan, remaining there until April 29, 1864, when the Kanawha division was ordered to join the forces gathering near Brownston, on the upper Kanawha River, from which point a raid was to be made on the Virginia and Tennessee Railroad, in accord-

34

ance with General Grant's order for a general advance of all our armies. Then began a series of forced marches and hard-fought battles, in which Colonel Hayes appeared in his conspicuous position as brigadier-general. The Union troops in Virginia, under General Crook, of which Colonel Hayes's brigade formed a part, did not exceed sixty-five hundred men. The expedition on which he was sent must have seemed to him of the most desperate character; but of course he did not know that Sigel was moving up the Shenandoah Valley, Sherman forcing his way to Atlanta, Grant moving on Richmond, and almost numberless expeditions starting out to annoy and confuse the rebels, and induce them to scatter their forces. After a hard march over cragged mountains, in snow and ice, wading deep streams, and encountering many other difficulties, General Crook arrived at the last range of hills between himself and the railroad, finding them formidable with fortifications. But there was no other course to pursue than that marked out for him, and consequently that rocky and wooded eminence must be stormed and taken. It fell to Hayes's brigade to lead the desperate assault. The enemy had fortified three crests or spurs of the mountain, one above the other, so that if he should be driven from one he could fall back to the next. Under the mountain was a broad meadow, a deep stream of water, and a rugged ascent, made difficult by fallen trees and hidden pits. Colonel Hayes's brigade formed on the side of the meadow, and, at the word of command, sprang forward at a double-quick pace, while the enemy opened all his batteries and musketry upon them. Colonel Hayes led the brigade, moving about from place to place with such coolness and alacrity that he kept his line steady, and infused into the soldiers the utmost confidence in his ability to lead them to victory. When the meadow was passed, a short halt was made by the stream to dress the line and give such necessary orders as the task before them seemed to demand, and then, with a yell, they rushed into the brush, climbing like squirrels, and as fearless of the shot that riddled the trees as those animals would be of falling acorns. Upward they clambered in such hot haste, and with such an even line, that, before the enemy could ram home the second charge, they were swarming about the rude breastwork, and clubbing their empty muskets to strike down the gunners. Astonished and dismayed the rebels made a hasty retreat, leaving behind them two handsome guns, into one of which a boy in the Twenty-third thrust his cap, to denote that it was his prize, and then rushed on with his comrades to charge and capture the second crest. The movement upon the second position was equally successful, and the enemy fled like sheep to their last stronghold. Here, being reinforced, and knowing that this offered the last means of defense, they met the Union forces in a desperate and heroic contest, — one of the sharpest of the whole war. It continued but a few minutes, when the rebels, discouraged by the death of their leader, fled down the mountain toward the railroad, which had been intrusted to their defense. General Crook, fearing the enemy might attempt to erect new fortifications, hurried his command, and reached the railroad that night, destroying it for eight miles toward Lynchburg, from Dublin Station, and, after a short artillery battle, burned the long bridge over New River, thus completely and specifically obeying his instructions. The men were now foot-sore, bruised, and weak, but it was not safe for so small a force to remain long in the enemy's country, and so the return march was at once begun. The road lay through the most rugged and dangerous regions of the Alleghany Mountains, being a rocky and wild succession of cliffs and chasms, through which meagre roadways had been cut, only to be washed away by the spring freshets, which were then at their height. It rained continually. The mountain torrents raged across their paths; men were drowned at the fords; teams were carried away in the streams; the shoes of the soldiers fell into pieces; their soaked clothing was rent by the least strain; their guns were rusty and unserviceable, and their supply of food exceedingly limited. Sometimes they met the enemy, and had to fight as well as climb. At last they reached their old camping-ground at Meadow Bluff, from which point, after a short rest and obtaining fresh supplies, they marched to Staunton, Va., joining Hunter's army June 8th.

In the attack on Lynchburg, June 18th, and in the retreat that followed, Hayes's brigade bore an honorable part. When the retreat was ordered by General Hunter, Hayes's men had been two days without sleep, and one day without food. The duty of covering the retreat fell upon them, and well was it discharged. On the 19th they marched and fought all day, and at night they had a sharp conflict with a large body of the enemy sent to surprise them, so that another night was passed without sleep; and, as if to test their powers of endurance to the utmost, they had scarcely reached Buford's Gap on the morning of the 20th, before the enemy in great numbers appeared with the evident purpose of securing the heights, and from them shelling the retreating Federals. Hayes drew up his brigade so as to cover the approaches to the gap, and held his position all day. At night, when he knew the army was far beyond the reach of rebel cannon, he collected his men, and hastily retreated. As his column drew near to Salem, a body of rebels managed to outmarch his almost fainting men, and intercept him, while another vigorously pressed him in the rear. It was a situation from which but few leaders could have extricated such a worn, starving, bleeding company of men. But such was Hayes's influence over them, that they enthusiastically obeyed his summons to one more fight, and by a determined charge cleared the way to the camp, where at ten o'clock at night they found their first sleep for nearly four days. They were only half supplied with food until, six days later, they arrived at Big Sewall Mountain. After a short rest at this point, they returned to Charleston, where they arrived July 1st.

We next follow Hayes's brigade into the campaign of the Shenandoah, in which it rendered most valuable service. On the 22d of July, being sent, with two sections of artillery, to reconnoitre the enemy, they were surrounded by two divisions of Confederate cavalry, but fought their way out under their gallant leader, and returned safely to General Crook's division at Winchester on the 23d. On the next day, when Crook was compelled to fall back before Early's whole army, the retreat was covered by Hayes's brigade in a masterly manner.

General Sheridan, not being ready for a general advance, employed his forces in various movements intended to prevent Early from detaching any portion of his force for the assistance of Lee at Richmond. In these movements Hayes's brigade took a conspicuous and valiant part. Often did Colonel Hayes force his way not only through Early's formidable picket lines, but through his main line, compelling him to develop his full strength, and even to seek new positions. So bold and hazardous were these raids, that it was often a matter of grave doubt with officers and men, in setting out, whether the brigade would ever return again to the main body. But it always managed to get back in good fighting trim; and its habitual success greatly increased the confidence of the men in themselves and their leader.

On the 23d of August, at daylight, Early made a sudden attack on Sheridan's outposts at Halltown, when Hayes's brigade sallied out, drove in the enemy's skirmish-line, and captured a lot of prisoners from Kershaw's division. The captured rebels exclaimed in astonishment, "Who the h—— are you-uns?" The next day the brigade made another sortie, capturing sixty officers and one hundred men, all from Kershaw's division. September 3d, Duval's division, including Hayes's brigade, became involved in a serious engagement at Berryville. The fighting was desperate, resulting in victory to neither side.

Sheridan made his grand advance against Early on the 16th of September. The battle of Winchester took place on the 19th. Colonel Hayes's brigade, as a part of General Crook's division, bore a leading part in the conflict. In the course of Crook's advance, it occupied the extreme right of the line, and crossing a swampy stream, reached a position covered by an almost impenetrable growth of cedar. The command pushed on, with Hayes's brigade in front. The brigade advanced rapidly, covered by a light line of skirmishers, driving in the enemy's cavalry. Crossing two or three open fields, exposed to a scattering fire, the brigade reached a slight elevation, where it came into full view of the enemy, who opened upon it a heavy fire of musketry and artillery. Colonel Hayes now started his command forward on the double-quick, and, dashing through a thick fringe of underbrush, came upon a deep slough about fifty yards wide, and stretching nearly the whole front of his brigade. The bottom was treacherous ooze; and the dark water, now churned with flying bullets, was, on the nearer side, about ten feet deep. Just beyond it was a rebel battery, thinly supported, the slough being itself deemed a sufficient protection. Colonel Hayes hesitated not an instant. Catching the situation at a glance, he shouted, "Forward!" and spurred his horse into the horrible ditch. Horse and rider sank nearly out of sight; but the horse swam until he struck the spongy bottom, then gave a plunge or two, and sank helplessly in the mire. Dismounting, Colonel Hayes waded to the farther bank, beckoning with his cap to his soldiers, some of whom succeeded in joining him. Many others, in attempting to follow, were killed or drowned; but enough of them passed to form a nucleus for the brigade; and then, at Colonel Hayes's command, he leading, they climbed the bank, and made for the guns; but the enemy succeeded in withdrawing the battery in time to prevent its capture. Colonel Hayes then reformed his brigade on the farther side of the slough, and resumed the advance. Soon after this General Duval was wounded and carried from the field, and the command of the division devolved upon Colonel Hayes. The battle soon ended in the defeat of Early, who narrowly escaped capture. He fell back to Fisher's Hill, eight miles south of Winchester, where he took up a strong position. But Sheridan followed him up sharply, and, after another hard fight, drove him from the field, his army a disordered mob. In this battle, also, Hayes's division took a conspicuous part, leading successfully one of the most important movements, capturing many guns and hundreds of rebel soldiers.

Nearly a month later, Early had reorganized and reinforced his army, and, taking advantage of Sheridan's brief absence, he attacked the Union forces, flank and rear. Hayes's division was prompt to enter into the conflict, but was soon compelled to choose between retreat and capture. In the face of imminent peril, the division withdrew with steady lines, maintaining its organization perfectly, and losing not so much as a tin plate. Colonel Hayes's superb coolness and courage, in the midst of frightful rout and confusion, acted like magic upon his men; and the example of his division, checking each rebel onset with its firm and steady lines, reanimated the broken regiments, and fired them with its own spirit of resistance. Hayes's division, after its retreat, rallied again, and saved Sheridan's headquarters train from capture. In this onset Hayes's horse fell dead beneath him, and, by the snddenness of its fall while at full speed, threw its rider violently out of the saddle, bruising him and badly wrenching his foot and ankle. For a moment he was thought to be killed; but he soon sprang to his feet, and in the midst of a shower of bullets from the rebels, who were almost upon him, he ran back to his division, which he regained without further injury. The fighting grew more stubborn on the Union side, and soon the rebel advance was checked. It was now that Sheridan appeared upon the scene, riding furiously a magnificent black horse literally flecked with foam. The battle that ensued need not be described here; for everybody knows the story by heart. It is enough to say that the enemy was utterly routed, and that the war in the valley was over from that hour. Colonel Hayes was at once promoted to brigadier-general, " for gallant and meritorious service in the battles of Winchester, Fisher's Hill, and Cedar Creek," to take rank from October 19, 1864. He was also breveted major-general, "for gallant and distinguished services during the campaigns of 1864 in West Virginia, and particularly in the battles of Fisher's Hill and Cedar Creek." In the course of his arduous services, four horses had been shot under him, and he had been wounded four times. His advancement was never sought by himself, but was a spontaneous tribute to his worth and valor. One of his associates pays him this tribute : —

"He proved himself not only a gallant soldier, but a model officer. We had opportunities of close observation of him in Virginia, and found him cool, self-possessed, and as thorough in the discharge of his duties as he was gallant in action. There is probably no position that so thoroughly tries the gentleman as that of the officer in time of war. The despotic power suddenly placed in his hands calls for the higher attributes of manhood to preserve its possession from abuse. To his inferiors in rank General Hayes was ever kind, patient, and considerate. He was, in the first sense of the term, the soldiers' friend. As an officer he was noted not only for his strict loyalty to his superiors, but for gallantry in battle, and activity in the discharge of every duty, however perilous or arduous."

We turn now from the military to the civil and political career of General Hayes. He was first a Whig, and a warm admirer of Daniel Webster, whose speeches and writings he carefully studied. He could not, however, reconcile it to his conscience to follow that great statesman in his course upon the slavery question. He was among the first to unite successively with the Free-Soil and Republican parties, giving to them his earnest support, and laboring with all his might to get before the people the questions which the encroachments of slavery made vital. In the discussion of these questions he evinced a clear comprehension of principles, as well as a mastery of facts. His modesty made him oftener a listener than a speaker; but when he did speak, his tone was judicial, his temper kind, his argument never overstrained, but so manifestly just and candid as to win the confidence even of his opponents. In the campaign of 1860 he was very active, regarding the success of the Republican party as essential to the preservation of the Union; and, when the exciting events which immediately followed the election were agitating the country, he was identified with every movement which favored the overthrow of the slave-power. He had defended too many fugitive slaves, and become too familiar with the barbarities of slavery, to remain neutral in such a crisis. At the grand Union demonstration in Cincinnati, April 16, 1861, he was selected to offer the resolutions which proclaimed the opinion of the citizens, "assembled without distinction of party," that "the authority of the United States, as against the rebellious citizens of the seceding and disloyal States, ought to be asserted and maintained; and that whatever men or means may be necessary to accomplish that object, the patriotic people of the loyal States will promptly and cheerfully produce." From that time until the day of his enlistment in the army, Hayes was unceasingly at work in securing volunteers. His devotion was such as to excite universal admiration; and, when he went to the front, the people of Ohio felt sure that his career as a soldier would do them honor. His movements from the first were closely watched, and as the struggle went on the people became enthusiastic over his achievements in the field.

In 1864 the Republicans of the Second Ohio District besought him to accept a nomination for Congress. He was assured that he was the only man who could carry the district, which had been Democratic by a large majority. He was induced to say that, should the war be closed before the meeting of the Congress to which he was to be chosen, he might take the seat. He was thereupon nominated, and the enthusiasm which followed confirmed the wisdom of his friends. The Democrats nominated a very popular candidate, and the discontent created by the draft made the contest a hard one for the Republicans. General Hayes could not be persuaded to take any part in the canvass. To one of his friends who urged him in strong terms to come home, and personally canvass the district in his own behalf, he wrote this characteristic reply: —

"Yours of —— is received. Thanks: I have other business just now. Any man who would leave the army at this time, to electioneer for Congress, ought to be scalped. Truly yours, R. B. Hayes."

But there was no need of his personal presence in the canvass. His presence in the army was enough. The popular heart was stirred by such mottoes as these on banners and decorations: "Our candidate is stumping the Shenandoah Valley;" "Hayes loves his country, and fights for it;" "Tell Governor Tod I'll be on hand." He was elected by a majority of three thousand and ninety-eight.

After his election, he was importuned to resign his commission in the army; but he firmly declared, " I shall never come to Washington until I can come by the way of Richmond." When, after the close of the war, he took his seat in the house, he displayed the same characteristics which had marked his whole previous course. He was ready for any kind of work, but not in the least inclined to push his way into conspicuous positions. As a new member, the places assigned to him upon committees were not those coveted by ambitious men. But the duties intrusted to him were diligently and faithfully performed, and it was not long before his merits began to be appreciated. As chairman of the House Committee on the Library, he rendered valuable service in superintending the enlargements of the library which at that period were going forward. He also carried through the house an appropriation of one hundred thousand dollars for the purchase of the curious collection of books on America made by Colonel Peter Force, the value of which to future historians will be invaluable. Some attempts to palm off upon the Library Committee some worthless works of art were by him defeated. He also took an active part in securing the passage of the bill prohibiting persons who had been guilty of treason or rebellion from practicing in the United States courts. A gentleman of large influence, who had watched his career, wrote concerning him at this time as follows : —

" Mr. Hayes is a good-sized, well-formed man. He is in every way well made; has a handsome head on a rather handsome body, and a face which would introduce him favorably anywhere. His complexion is light, skin florid, temperament composed of the vital, motive, and mental in almost equal proportions. He is neither too fast nor too slow, excitable nor sluggish; but he is at once energetic, original, comprehensive, dignified, and resolute. He is more profound than showy, and has more application than versatility. He will finish what he begins, and make thorough work. He has a hopeful, happy nature; is eminently social, fond of home and all that belongs thereto, and as hospitable to all as he is thoughtful and considerate. But, to be more specific, this gentleman is comparatively young in years, and younger in spirit. Though he has already accomplished much, he has by no means reached the climax of his fame. He is a rising young man, and, if spared, will in the course of a few years be found in the front rank of the best minds of the nation. We base our predictions on the following points: first, he has a capital constitution, both inherited and acquired, with a cultivated mind, with strong integrity, honor, generosity, hopefulness, sociability, and ambition, and all well guided by practical good sense. At present he may be thought to lack fire and enthusiasm; but age and experience will give him point and emphasis. Mark us, this gentleman will not disappoint the expectations of the most hopeful."

This, if it does not deserve to be called prophecy, was at least pretty good guessing, as General Hayes's subsequent career has fully proved.

In 1866 General Hayes was renominated for Congress, and, for the first time in his life, entered actively into a political canvass. His speeches were marked by careful research, good sense, and sound judgment. If they were not brilliant, they were at least forcible and convincing, and grew constantly better from first to last. There was in them no taint of the coarseness so often exhibited in political discussion, no abuse of his opponents, and no misrepresentation of their acts or opinions. The bold exaggerations so often resorted to by political speakers for present effect were carefully avoided. He appealed always to the reason and good sense, never to the prejudices and passions, of his hearers. If any one supposed that, on this account, his speeches were pointless and dull, a study of them would correct the mistake.

General Hayes was elected the second time by a majority of twenty-five hundred and fifty-six; and he had made his preparations to spend two years more in Washington, when, to his surprise, the State Republican Convention, on June 10, 1867, selected him with great unanimity as its candidate for governor. An amendment to the state Constitution, abolishing the word "white," as a term of discrimination between citizens, was pending; and the Republicans feared that the unpopularity of the measure would doom them to defeat. Hayes was nominated as the only man whose popularity warranted a hope that he could lead them to victory. Hon. Allen G. Thurman, a very strong man, was the Democratic candidate; and General Hayes was expected to answer him on the stump. The contest was very close, General Hayes being elected by a majority of only three thousand; while the Democrats secured a majority in both branches of the Legislature, thus defeating, for the time, the constitutional amendment.

In 1869 General Hayes was again nominated for governor, the Hon. George H. Pendleton being the Democratic candidate. He entered the canvass confident of victory. As chief executive he had won the praises of men of all parties, and incurred the enmity of none; while the Democrats, by their course in the Legislature, had made themselves obnoxious to severe criticism. It was a very heated and exciting contest; but General Hayes, by his courtesy and fairness toward his opponents, passed through it unscathed. His speeches upon the internal affairs of the State were generally admired for their lucidity and force. He was elected this time by a majority of seven thousand five hundred and eighteen votes, while a Republican majority in the Legislature was secured. The Democrats proposed, by a combination with some of the Republicans, to elect him to the United States Senate; but he spurned the bribe, and gave his hearty support to Senator Sherman, who was reëlected.

In 1872 General Hayes was again a candidate for Congress, probably against his own wish, and was defeated by the Liberals and Democrats combined. He now resolved to seek in a retired life the rest and quiet which he and his wife had so much desired. His purpose was to withdraw entirely from the turmoil and strife of politics, as well as from professional labor, and to spend the remainder of his days in the sweet peace of a rural home. His uncle Sardis, now the wealthiest banker in Central Ohio, feeling the infirmities of age, was anxious that he and his family should make their home with him in Fremont; and they went there in compliance with his earnest solicitation.

In January, 1874, Sardis Birchard died, leaving all his large estates and investments to General Hayes. In 1875 the Republicans of Ohio once more besought General Hayes to be their candidate for governor, feeling sure that with him for their leader they could overcome the defeat of the previous year. It was with the greatest reluctance that he accepted the nomination. He had just previously refused to accept the office of Assistant United States Treasurer at Cincinnati, preferring to remain in private life; but when told by his friends that his refusal to run again for governor would probably doom his party to defeat, he was induced to put on the harness once more. During the canvass that ensued, he made the most powerful and eloquent speeches of his whole life. Close study had made him familiar with the questions at issue, while long practice had made him an accomplished platform speaker. His personal popularity drew crowds to hear him, and his powers of persuasion drew a multitude of voters to the Republican standard; and he was elected for the third time.

In 1876 the Republican party was divided upon the question of a candidate for President. Hon. James G. Blaine was most influentially supported; Hon. Roscoe Conkling was the favorite with many; and Hon. Benjamin H. Bristow of Kentucky was warmly supported by those Republicans who were not altogether satisfied with the administration of General Grant. The national convention was held in Cincinnati in June. Governor Hayes had been spoken of in some quarters as a suitable candidate, and as the man likely to be nominated in case of Blaine's and Conkling's defeat. The Ohio delegation was for him from the start, believing him the strongest candidate that could be named. After many ballotings he was nominated. Other candidates had done what they could to secure the prize for themselves, but Governor Hayes had neither spoken a word nor lifted a finger in his own behalf. He treated the nomination with due respect; but it did not fill him with excitement, nor so preoccupy his mind that he could not continue the private business he had in hand when the news came to him. Having written his letter of acceptance, — a document which excited the admiration of the country, — he resigned the office of governor of Ohio, and retired to his home in Fremont, to await the result of the canvass. His fellow-citizens of Fremont, without distinction of party, received him with enthusiasm; and his speech on the occasion was one of the most eloquent and felicitous he ever made.

The result of the election in the States of South Carolina, Louisiana, and Florida, owing to circumstances that need not be recited here, was for a long time in doubt, and complications arose which threatened the peace of the country. The controversy was thrown into Congress, the Senate being Republican, the House Democratic; and the two parties taking opposite views as to the course to be pursued in counting the electoral votes. It was finally agreed that the questions at issue should be referred to a Commission composed of five senators, five representatives, and five judges of the Supreme Court of the United States. Three of the senators were to be Republicans, and two of them Democrats; three of the representatives Democrats, and two of them Republicans. Four judges of the Supreme Court, two of each party, were named by mutual consent; and these four were to name the fifth, who proved to be a Republican, making the Commission stand eight Republicans to seven Democrats. Unfortunately all the questions at issue were decided by party votes, — eight to seven. General Hayes was declared to be elected by one vote over Samuel J. Tilden, the Democratic candidate; and he was inaugurated on Monday, March 5, 1877, as nineteenth President of the United States, for four years.

His administration of the affairs of the government was at first much embarrassed by the fact that many of his political opponents felt that he was not entitled to the office. But in a firm and quiet manner he insisted on the equal rights of all, on the economical management of public affairs, and on the honest and prompt payment of all the obligations of the government, thus winning the respect of all classes, and giving to the nation some of the most peaceable and prosperous years of its political life. The government was carried on so unostentatiously that the people seemed unconscious of the presence of executive power, and felt as if the vast machinery of government had found some means of propelling itself without help. Such is always the feeling under the highest form of political institutions; unconsciousness of its presence, like the absence of pain in a strong human body, indicating the highest degree of health and happiness. With his usual modesty and quietness he laid down the office he had held with such success, and, March 8, 1881, quietly retired to his country home in Ohio, receiving from his old neighbors, of all parties, a most complimentary reception.

CHAPTER XX.

JAMES A. GARFIELD.

Parentage. — Birth. — Wilderness. — Death of his Father. — Youthful Occupations. — Attempts to obtain an Education. — School Life. — College Days. — Marriage. — In State Senate. — Enters the War. — His Campaigns. — His Election to Congress. — His Legislative Career. — Elected to United States Senate. — Nomination for President. — Election. — Inauguration. — Assassination. — Sickness. — Death.

JAMES ABRAM GARFIELD was born November 19, 1831, in the town of Orange, Cuyahoga County, Ohio. His father, Abram Garfield, was a native of Worcester, Otsego County, New York, and was a descendant of the Garfield family of Massachusetts, well known in the days of the American Revolution, and which traces its ancestry to Welsh and English lords in the time of Queen Elizabeth. His mother, Eliza Ballou, was a native of New Hampshire, and a relative of Hosea Ballou, the celebrated preacher and author.

The child's surroundings at the time of his birth and early childhood were as humble and rude as backwoods life could make them. His father and mother lived in a little log cabin, in a small clearing made by cutting away the primitive forest. The front yard was crowded with fresh stumps of giant trees, and the little patch of ground they called "the farm" did not include over two acres open to the sunlight. With scarcely utensils sufficient to cook the most simple food, with rough tables, rude chairs, and an open fire-place, with a floor of rough slabs over one half the small space inclosed by the cabin, with peepholes for windows, logs for doors, and a little brook in the woods for a well, with wild game and wheat or corn cracked in a hand mortar for their meals, his parents struggled on day by day in the close battle for bare life.

James was the youngest of four children, of which the oldest was a boy and two were girls. To care for these children and at the same time clear a farm in that unbroken wilderness required great courage, perseverance, and self-sacrifice on the part of his parents, and necessitated that the baby also should suffer great privation. Thus the opening of his life was most unpromising, and adds another

J.A.Garfield

PRIVATE RESIDENCE OF GEN. GARFIELD.

example to the thousands in the lives of American great men showing that poverty, seclusion, and want in childhood need not prevent growth in goodness or achievements in greatness.

When James was less than two years old his father died, and the extreme lowest point of human need seemed to have been reached by his family. But displaying a vigor and endurance of which they themselves had been ignorant with all their industry and toil, his mother worked on the farm and at the spinning-wheel, while Thomas, the eldest son, although but a youth, entered at once upon the responsibilities and hard labor of manhood.

Amos Boynton, a half-brother of Abram Garfield, lived near by and cheerfully aided them as much as his limited means admitted, while the hardy settlers in the county were generous and sympathetic toward the unfortunate family.

From the outset the life of James was one of work. Compelled by the force of circumstances to run on errands, to do the chores for his mother and for "uncle Amos," he developed that habit of industry and that physical strength which made his after-success possible. Whoever the king of toil has crowned, possesses a patent of nobility no king or parliament can take away.

All his early years until he was twelve years old were spent in cutting brush for fences, watching the cows, digging at the roots of stumps, preparing fire-wood, sowing or harvesting crops, driving cattle and teams with wood to Cleveland, bringing water from the spring, and sometimes for a few weeks attending school in the log school-house erected near his home. His food was cheap, his books few, his clothing coarse and scanty, and his face, hands, and bare feet were brown and rough with exposure and toil in "the boiling of salts," or the burning of charcoal. Yet, like every other boy, he had his desires for sport, his dreams of a grand future, his quarrels with other boys, his mischievous days, and his poetical tendency to make up for human companionship in giving to rocks, apple-trees, dogs, cows, and horses a personality, as boon companions with whom he could converse and for whom he conceived an abiding love.

He was not especially distinguished above other boys during his youthful days, either for his genius as a farmer, woodsman, or herdsman, or for his accomplishments as a debater in the country lyceum, or as a scholar in the schools. Not precocious nor dull as a child, he was regarded as a boy having good common sense and doing his work well. Such a childhood is, as a rule, more prophetic of greatness than astonishing brilliancy or eccentricity.

His youthful years were spent in that unsettled yet industrious manner which has been the lot of many fatherless, poor boys in the early days of pioneer life. If he was distinguished for anything above other boys of his age and neighborhood, it was in the fact that he loved to read, and that as he could not always find employment, he had considerable time to spend in that manner. Like a vast number of other lads, he entertained the wild dreams of exploration, adventure, Indian warfare, voyages of discovery, and hair-breadth escapes, and believed that some day he should be the hero of exploits such as the books of history and of fiction presented to his excitable imagination.

He was often compelled by circumstances to work alone in the woods chopping fuel, and in those lonely hours improved that opportunity to think, plan, and resolve, which a city-bred child can never find or understand. Many a boy, like young James, has likened trees to giants, saplings to armies, and brush to social opposition, and with firm hand and strong determination has attacked them with his axe so successfully as to make his manhood's victories possible and great.

He had, as a youth, an intense longing for a sailor's life, until he met with a rather harsh rebuff one day at the wharf in Cleveland. James had so far determined on a sailor's life as to make a secret visit to Cleveland, where he found a grain vessel lying at the wharf discharging its cargo, and upon which he boldly ventured in search of the captain. But when the besotted, dirty, profane commander of the vessel appeared on deck and with drunken insanity and vile epithets drove him unceremoniously off the vessel as a thieving vagabond, James abandoned his romantic pictures and ambitions concerning a sea-faring life.

There, however, lingered with him a trace of his old purpose to be a sailor, as exhibited in a desire he showed at one time to be a captain of a canal boat. His uncle, Thomas Garfield, was the owner of a boat on the Ohio canal, and employed many workmen in connection with the canal business. So through the kindness of his uncle and cousins young James obtained an opportunity to drive a mule attached to one of the boats used by the owners to transport coal from the mines to Cleveland. He did not remain long in that occu-

35

pation, for one day when his ambition and kindness had led him to attempt to do the captain's work as steersman of the boat, the rudder struck a snag and the tiller in its sudden sweep knocked James overboard into water too deep in which to stand, and in which he had never been trained to swim.   The fright unnerved him, the wetting dangerously chilled him, the laughter of his mates disgusted him, and during the severe fever which followed the accident he gave up all idea of being either a driver, deck-hand, or captain of a canal boat.

His attention appears to have been turned toward literary attainments and the higher ambitions of life, by the kind and earnest advice of a school-teacher and preacher who taught in the town of Orange, and who sometimes officiated as a minister or preacher in the Church of the Disciples, which is a form of the Protestant Baptist Faith, and to which nearly all the Garfield family adhered.   This teacher showed young James the possibility and desirability of becoming a learned and good man.   His representations of the satisfaction there was in the possession of a liberal education and in the increased opportunities of doing good, had great weight with James, and before he had recovered from the fever which brought his kind adviser to his bedside he had firmly and irrevocably resolved that, at whatever sacrifice, he would obtain a college education.

Beginning in the most economical and saving manner, studying evenings and working by day at farm or carpenter work, he obtained sufficent information to venture as a student into the lowest class at the academy or seminary in the adjoining town of Chester.   With the earnings of his vacations and the heroic self-sacrifices of his mother and elder brother, he was able to secure the advantages of several terms at that academy; and it was there in one of the classes that he met Lucretia Rudolph, whom he afterwards married.

From Chester, James went to Hiram College, where he continued his studies until sufficiently advanced in the classics and mathematics to be qualified for admission at Williams College two years in advance.   During his stay at Hiram, Ohio, he was the janitor of the college buildings, and a sort of jack-at-all-trades for the inhabitants who could favor him with employment out of college hours.   To provide himself with the necessary funds to carry him through his college course at Williamstown, Mass., he borrowed five hundred dollars of his uncle Thomas, and worked for the citizens such extra

HIRAM COLLEGE.

hours as he could safely get from his studies. His life at Williams was that of an unostentatious, careful, industrious student seeking no honors but those attached to thoroughness in the prescribed studies, and he seems to have passed through the course creditably but without attracting especial attention by his genius or brilliant acquirements. He was admitted to the college in September, 1854, and graduated in 1856.

On his return to Ohio he was at once engaged as a teacher at Hiram, and was also pressed into the additional work of preaching the gospel. He took a position at once as a leading preacher and most popular teacher, so that he was called to officiate in the largest churches, and within a year was promoted to the presidency of the college at Hiram, where he was the loved and honored friend of rich and poor, great and small. There, in 1858, at her father's house in Hiram, he was married to Miss Rudolph and began a home life of his own.

After his marriage he began the study of law, and giving to it his extra hours he was able in 1860 to pass the necessary examination and was admitted to the bar as an attorney at law. He was attracted to legal studies by his active and patriotic interest in public affairs. He was an Abolitionist, Freesoiler, and Republican, and was always open and bold in the declaration of his political principles, whether in college, church, or caucus. But it appears that he never had any ambition for public office until it was thrust upon him to his surprise. He did hope to be a lawyer and a successful public debater on those public measures which he wished to see successful.

In the autumn of 1859 he was elected to the Ohio State Senate by a sweeping majority, and when he took his seat he was the youngest member of that body, being but twenty-eight years of age.

In the State Senate, during those trying years of 1860 and 1861, he was a very useful and eloquent member of the Legislature. At the opening of the Rebellion in April, 1861, Mr. Garfield was appointed as a member of Governor Dennison's staff to assist in organizing troops for the war. In September, 1861, he was appointed colonel of the Forty-second Ohio Regiment, composed in a great part of his classmates and his students at Hiram College. September, 14, 1861, Colonel Garfield's regiment left Columbus, and on the 18th arrived at Catlettsburgh, Kentucky, where it went into camp during Colonel Garfield's absence at Louisville, to which place he was ordered for the purpose of consulting with General Buell concerning the plans of the campaign in Kentucky.

General Buell was not ignorant of Colonel Garfield's ability, nor of his popularity in Ohio, and hoped to find in the new colonel a vigorous supporter. The campaign in West Virginia had succeeded passably well, and General Buell was in hopes that he might be equally successful in clearing Kentucky of the rebels, and in capturing Nashville. The general was a rather harsh disciplinarian, and did many foolish things with his raw troops. His ideas of military discipline were better adapted to a military empire, or an established and unlimited monarchy, than to the assemblies of free men, who were fighting for themselves and not for a king. However, he was earnest, patriotic, and brave, and recognizing those qualities in Colonel Garfield, he at once confided to him the plan of the Kentucky campaign. Colonel Garfield did not pretend to be a military strategist, but when he looked over the map with General Buell, and heard how many rebel forces were in Eastern Kentucky, and how many in Western Kentucky, he thought it was folly to attempt to march through the centre of the State to Nashville, with such forces on both flanks. The general thought that some movement ought to be made at once, and if the colonel had any doubts about the proposed plan it would be well to think the matter over and consult again about it the next day.

The following morning Colonel Garfield brought in a draft of his plan, which was to move into the State in three columns, leaving no forces behind them, and if either column defeated its opponent, it could readily unite with the centre and move on to Nashville. After some discussion, and after the general had asked the colonel if he would undertake the direction of the eastern column, the plan submitted was adopted so far as it could be without the coöperation of General Halleck's command in Missouri. The general plan was, however, somewhat modified by Zollicoffer's entrance into Kentucky at Cumberland Gap with a rebel army to coöperate with General Humphrey Marshall, who was already in Kentucky near Pound Gap. But General George H. Thomas was sent to drive back Zollicoffer, and Colonel Garfield's orders to attack Humphrey Marshall were not changed.

Thus we find him with a most important campaign on his hands before he had any experience even in drilling a regiment in the manual of arms. The purposed movement was one of such importance, in view of the necessity of keeping Marshall from moving to Zollicoffer's aid and striking General Thomas's forces on the flank, that it is a little surprising that General Buell, with his ideas of military manœuvres, should have intrusted it to a commander so fresh from civil life. Colonel Garfield had never seen a skirmish, nor heard the crack of a single hostile rifle. It therefore seemed somewhat inconsistent with Garfield's well-known character to assume the direction of so important a military movement. It seems probable that he did not know just how important it was, nor appreciate how eagerly the whole field was being watched by President Lincoln and the authorities at Washington for some signs of ultimate victory. It was one of the gloomiest periods of the war; and when the news of the selection of Colonel Garfield for the expedition up the Big Sandy River to meet Marshall was announced to Mr. Lincoln, he sought Secretary Stanton, who was also a native of Ohio, and asked who the man was they were sending " into such dangerously close quarters." The President anxiously awaited General Buell's forward movement toward Bowling Green and Nashville; and seeing how important the defeat of the rebels' flank movements under Marshall and Zollicoffer had become, he followed the movements of Colonel Garfield and General Thomas with the deepest interest.

Colonel Garfield's orders to proceed up the Sandy Valley were delivered to him December 13th or 14th. A few days later he collected the forces intrusted to him at the mouth of the Big Sandy River, and began his march up the valley. His command, which was called a brigade, did not number over twenty-three hundred available men, and consisted of the Fortieth and Forty-second Ohio infantry, the Fourteenth and Twenty-second Kentucky infantry, and eight companies of cavalry. To these he hoped to add a small force then stationed at Paris, and to which he sent orders directing its commander to join him near Paintville.

General Marshall had a force of five thousand men, and was in a country with which he was familiar, while Colonel Garfield was in a strange region, with about one half that number of troops. If there had been any hesitation or delay on the part of the Union forces it would have encouraged Marshall to attack them on their march, for the rebel general was among his friends, and all the people acted as spies and couriers in communicating the advance and condition of the invading forces. But so determinedly and steadily did the troops march on, that it seems to have created a fear of them in advance, which went far toward giving them the victory when the battle came.

All the information which Garfield could gain seemed to locate Marshall near Paintville, and hence he expected a contest at that point. But Marshall retreated to Prestonburg before Garfield arrived, leaving a company of cavalry to hold the place and delay the Union troops. Garfield, finding the enemy, and supposing that the rebel army was immediately in front, notwithstanding the fatigue of his troops, moved immediately forward to attack them.

Directing his cavalry to engage the enemy in front, Garfield made a circuit with his infantry, hoping to reach Marshall's rear.

It is said that when he had given his orders to the cavalry, and had started forward on foot with the infantry, he took off his coat and threw it into a tree, and shouted back to the horsemen so soon to charge, " Give 'em Hail Columbia, boys ! "

But before his troops reached the road in the rear, the vigorous charge of the Union cavalry had sent the enemy flying toward Prestonburg in such haste as to leave their canteens, haversacks, blankets, and dead bodies strewing the highway.

This retreat was quite unexpected to Colonel Garfield, and he had so confidently counted upon a battle at that point, that his brigade was not supplied with provisions for a march farther into the interior. To supply the necessary provisions caused a day's delay, and compelled him to leave a portion of his troops at Paintville, while he pressed on after Marshall. At Paintville, however, he was joined by troops from Paris, numbering about one thousand or twelve hundred.

On the following day, which was the 9th of January, Garfield followed Marshall to Prestonburg, and found that the rebels were posted on a hill in a most advantageous position, with their artillery within a most effective range. Garfield had been misinformed about Marshall's movements, and was compelled to ascertain the enemy's position by skirmishing and feints. While awaiting the troops which he decided to order up from Paintville, his troops were constantly engaged in skirmishing, and the whole command was under fire, many of the men for the first time.

It must have given a much more serious appearance to the art of war to see the line of gray, and hear the shot and shell shriek over their heads. To the colonel, on whose word and judgment hung the lives of so many and, perhaps, the fate of a mighty nation, the feeling of responsibility must have been great, while the peculiar sense of danger and dread of the unforeseen which fills the heart at the opening of the first battle, must have been a trial in his inexperience.

It was nearly dark when the reinforcements arrived, and without delay, and amid the enthusiastic cheering of the men, he ordered an advance, to be followed by a charge upon the enemy's guns. There was a sharp musketry fire for a short time, as the enemy fell slowly back toward their guns, and the artillery of the rebels was handled most skillfully.

When, however, the lines of the Union forces had secured the desired position from which to make their charge, Marshall suddenly sounded a retreat, and left the field under cover of the darkness.

The sudden disappearance of the enemy and the silence which prevailed, together with the uncertainty whether it was an actual retreat or a ruse, made the hour following the disappearance one of great anxiety. The troops, fatigued and hungry, moving cautiously about in the dark woodland and fields, anxiously awaiting developments, were but a counterpart of that other historical picture of the great President at Washington, pacing his room at that very hour, and saying, "I cannot bear this dangerous delay. Have n't we any one who will fight?"

Colonel Garfield's suspense was not long, however, for soon the clouds overhead began to assume an unusual color, and a little later were lit up with the lurid glare of distant fires. The distant mountains stood out prominent in the unnatural light, and pillars of illumined smoke arose along the road toward the gate to Virginia. It was clear, then, that Marshall was retreating out of Kentucky, and was burning his immense military stores.

To pursue the rebels that night was impracticable, and, after a short cavalry reconnoissance, the tired troops used the light of the enemy's burning camps to prepare their meagre supper and hard beds. The time, the circumstances, and the fact that the enemy numbered forty-nine hundred, made the victory an important one, while Colonel Garfield's bravery and ability, displayed in the march and engagement, placed him at once among the experienced and trustworthy soldiers.

The next day the enemy was pursued to the Virginia line, and the order was then given to return to their camps near Piketon with their prisoners. They had killed two hundred and fifty of the enemy and taken forty prisoners, with a loss to the Union troops of only thirty-two men. Colonel Garfield's commission as a brigadier-general was dated so as to take effect from that battle at Prestonburg.

The next day after establishing the brigade camp, a heavy rainstorm came on which laid a large portion of Sandy Valley under water. It was impossible to march or to transport provisions overland. The river became so swollen that the steamboats were detained in the Ohio, and that source of supply was also closed. It was a most alarming condition of affairs, for it was impossible for the army to find sufficient food in the surrounding region, even if they transgressed the strict orders forbidding foraging. When they had rations for two days only the puzzled commander saw no way to save his little army from actual starvation. If the army had been able to march or wade through the mud, it would have been a disobedience of orders to leave the country to be again occupied by the enemy.

In his perplexity he decided to go for provisions himself, thinking that he might find some boat along the river which could be brought up in such an extremity.

But he went as far as the Ohio River before he found one. The great flood was so powerful that no one dared venture into its surges. He found two or three boatmen who said that a boat had once ascended the Big Sandy in a flood like that, but it was a miracle that it escaped destruction.

"Some boat *must* go up," said the general. "My men shall not starve!"

He found a rickety steamboat fastened to the bank of the stream awaiting a subsidence of the flood, and he ordered the captain to take a load of provisions up the river to the camp. The captain refused, saying that it would be as bad as suicide to undertake it. But General Garfield insisted with his revolver in hand, and the captain and men, thinking they might as well be drowned as be shot for disobedience of military orders, allowed the boat, with themselves, to be taken by the general for the dangerous experiment. Finding no one whom he dared to trust to take the wheel, or who was strong enough to manage it in the swift current, the general himself took the wheel, and for two days and the greater part of one night stood at his post. It required the most cautious steering to avoid the projecting banks and trees covered by the flood, and often the boat would graze an obstruction which would have sunk it, if it had struck near the prow.

Once the craft ran aground on a hard sand-bank and refused to back off when the wheel was reversed, and the general tried to induce some of the men to take the small boat and go on shore to fasten a rope so that they might pull the boat off the bank by the aid of the windlass. Not one dared tempt the terrific flood. So the general took the boat and the rope, and at a most hazardous risk of his life, especially so, as the river navigation was new to him, he crossed the stream and fastened the rope.

It was a triumphant hour for him when he saw the crowd of his anxious troops on the river bank awaiting his coming, and one in which he blessed that day on which he learned to steer a canal boat.

The half-famished men, who had descended in despair to the river, believing that no boat could stem the flood, shouted themselves hoarse, and performed all kinds of childish antics, when they saw their general skillfully steering the frail and trembling river steamer. They could scarcely believe their own eyes; and many a night about the camp fires the soldiers afterwards told the story of the general's dangerous trip up the Sandy, with rations for his hungry men.

For three months the Union troops remained at or near Piketon, often making short expeditions to drive out stray bands of rebel marauders.

In the month of March General Garfield determined to drive out the rebels who were posted near Pound Gap, on the Virginia side of the Cumberland Mountains; and with seven hundred men, including two hundred cavalry, he made a forced march of forty miles, and encamped secretly near the enemy's quarters. Early next morning, in a blinding snow-storm, he sent the cavalry through the Gap, while the infantry clambered up by a difficult path to surprise the rebels in the rear. He was completely successful in surprising the post, but the rebels scattered so fast that he captured but few of them. They left valuable stores of ammunition and provisions behind, of which he took possession. The next day he burned the camp and returned to his quarters. A few days later he was ordered to report with the greater part of his command at Louisville.

When General Garfield arrived at Louisville, he found that General Buell was far away in Tennessee hurrying to the assistance of General Grant, at Pittsburg Landing. So General Garfield, obedient to fresh orders, bade a hasty farewell to his comrades, and hurried on after the army. He overtook General Buell at Columbia, Tennessee, and was at once assigned to the command of the Twentieth Brigade, in the division of General T. J. Wood.

This change in his command was a great grief to General Garfield, who had hoped to keep the Fortieth Ohio in his brigade, and thus be with his old friends, scholars, and neighbors throughout the war. But from that time their paths diverged, and never united again during the entire contest.

The army, of which his new command formed a part, made a forced march from Columbia to Savannah, on the Tennessee River, and from that point they were in great haste hurried on by boat to Pittsburg Landing. The battle of Shiloh had been raging for more than a day when these reinforcements arrived. Without rest or time to enter camp they hurried on to the field of battle, and General Garfield's command was under fire during the final contest which gave the victory to the federal troops.

The next day his troops, with other forces under General Sherman, were sent in pursuit of the retreating enemy, and a short but hotly contested battle was fought, in which General Garfield was conspicuously cool and brave.

During that tedious siege of Corinth, which followed, his command was nearly all the time at the outposts, and was engaged often in skirmishes with the rebels, and was with the first column that was ordered forward when the town was evacuated by Beauregard.

In June, 1862, his brigade was sent to repair and protect the Memphis and Charleston Railroad, between Corinth and Decatur, after which he advanced to Huntsville, Alabama, and gained no little credit for his skill in military engineering, connected with the fortifications.

It has been often related of him that while in command of this brigade a fugitive slave came rushing into his camp, with a bloody head, and apparently frightened almost to death. He had scarcely passed the headquarters when a regular bully of a fellow came riding up, and with a volley of oaths began to ask after his "nigger." General Garfield was not present, and he passed on to the division commander. The division commander was a sympathizer with the theory that fugitive slaves should be returned to their masters, and that the Union soldiers should be made the instruments for returning them. He accordingly wrote a mandatory order to General Garfield, in whose command the darkey was supposed to be hiding, telling him to hunt out and deliver over the property of the outraged citizen. General Garfield took the order and deliberately wrote on it the following indorsement: —

"I respectfully but positively decline to allow my command to search for or deliver up any fugitive slaves. I conceive that they are here for quite another purpose. The command is open, and no obstacles will be placed in the way of search."

The indorsement frightened his staff officers, and they expected that, if returned, the result would be that the general would be court-martialed. He simply replied, "The matter may as well be tested first as last. Right is right, and I do not propose to mince matters at all. My soldiers are here for other purposes than hunting and returning fugitive slaves. My people on the Western Reserve of Ohio did not send my boys and myself down here to do that kind of business, and they will back me up in my action." He would not alter the indorsement, and the order was returned. Nothing ever came of the matter further.

June 15th General Garfield was detailed to sit in a trial by court-martial of a lieutenant of the Fifty-eighth Indiana volunteers. His skill in that case, combined with his memory of judicial decisions, caused the officers sitting with him in the court to commend him for his signal ability in such matters. On July 5th he was again detailed to act as president of the important court-martial detailed to try Colonel Turchin of the Nineteenth Illinois. Of that court General Garfield's adjutant-general, Captain P. T. Swaim, acted as judge advocate.

July 30th he was given a leave of absence, owing to the return of the fever and ague, which had not disturbed him until that season, from the spring when he left the canal. For two months he lay at

Hiram, dangerously sick, and several important commands were offered him, which his illness compelled him to decline. It was during this summer that he paid for the small wooden dwelling in Hiram which was afterwards his home.

As soon as he was able to travel he was ordered by the Secretary of War to report to the War Department at Washington. This he did about the 25th of September. His fame as a jurist in martial trials had reached Washington, and he was ordered to sit on the court of inquiry in the case of General McDowell. At one time he was ordered to proceed to South Carolina, with General Hunter, but circumstances intervened to keep them in Washington.

November 25, 1862, he was made a member of the court in the celebrated trial of General Fitz-John Porter for the failure to co-operate with General Pope at the battle of Bull Run. At that trial he had a delicate and important duty to perform, and did his work with such wisdom as to secure the unsolicited compliment from its president that "he must have been a great lawyer in Ohio."

During his engagements at Washington he was called home by the illness and death of his only child. It was a sad blow to a heart so tender as his ; and it is said of him that while he held the body of the sweet little child in his arms, after its death, he remarked how inappropriate to everything about him was his military uniform, and of how little consequence, compared with the love and peace of a happy home, were the honors which men could bestow.

While he was at home, in the months of August and September, as already stated, and confined to his bed, there was no little agitation going on in that congressional district over a successor to the renowned antislavery champion, Joshua R. Giddings. The excitement was caused by the fact that Mr. Giddings had been defeated in the nominating convention, two years before, by some means, and his friends laid all the blame on the successful candidate. They therefore determined upon preventing the renomination of Mr. Giddings's successor. In their canvass for a candidate who would be sure to carry the convention, as there was no hope that the health of Mr. Giddings would admit of his return to Congress, even if he could have left his post as consul-general in Canada, they hit upon General Garfield, who at that time was recovering, but whose return to the malarial districts was considered dangerous. His name was one which was sure to overcome any combination or opposition.

It does not appear that they consulted with General Garfield at all, but very carefully concealed their design, both from him and the opposition. On the presentation of his name to the Republican Congressional Convention in September, it was received with all the enthusiasm that the friends of the measure had expected. He was the single man on the " Western Reserve " against whom it would be a farce to make any opposition.

The movement did not at first meet with General Garfield's approval, and he reserved his decision whether he should refuse the honor, until he could confer with President Lincoln. His pay as a general was much larger than that of a congressman ; he had entered the war to stay, and he disliked to leave it.

On the other hand, his health might break down if he returned to the South, and it was probable that the war would be closed in the year which would intervene between his election and the opening of the Congress to which he would be chosen.

When he visited the President, and told him the circumstances, Mr. Lincoln bluntly remarked that there were generals enough already and plenty more to be had, but the number of congressmen who understood the needs of the country were few, and if the Rebellion continued it was likely to be lessened by the death or enlistment of good men. Members of the Cabinet giving him the same advice, he silently acquiesced in the nomination, and was elected with unheard-of unanimity.

In January he had so far recovered that he was ordered into the field, and directed to report to General Rosecrans at Murfreesborough. Immediately after his arrival he was appointed chief of staff to General Rosecrans, then commanding the Army of the Cumberland.

The writer of the history of the Forty-second Ohio Regiment, whose sources of information were so trustworthy, and whose gifts as a writer were so apparent as to lead to his selection, by that regiment of students, as their historian, wrote, in 1875, of General Garfield's share in the campaigns of the Army of the Cumberland as follows : —

" He was assigned to duty as chief of staff of the army of the Cumberland, in place of the lamented Colonel Garesche, who had been killed in the battle of Stone River. Early in the spring of that year Captain P. T. Swaim, his adjutant-general since the previous April, was directed to organize a Bureau of Military Information. By a system of police and scout reports very full and trustworthy information was obtained of the organization, strength, and position of the enemy's forces.

Early in June the general commanding required each general of a corps and division of the Army of the Cumberland to report his opinions, in writing, in reference to any early or immediate advance against the forces of General Bragg. Seventeen general officers submitted written opinions on that subject. Most of them were adverse to any early movement, and nearly all advised against an immediate advance. General Garfield presented to the commanding general an analysis and review of these opinions, and urged an immediate movement against the enemy. For more than five months the army of Rosecrans had lain inactive at Murfreesborough, while the commanding general had haggled and bandied words with the War Department. As chief of staff, General Garfield did all that adroit diplomacy could do to soften these asperities, and meanwhile gave all his energy to the work of preparing the army for an advance, and ascertaining the strength of the enemy.

His Bureau of Military Information was the most perfect machine of the kind organized in the field during the war. When at last June came, the government and the people demanding an advance, and the seventeen subordinate generals of Rosecrans advising against it, the analysis of the situation drawn up and submitted by General Garfield, met and overthrew them all. Speaking of this letter, Mr. Whitelaw Reid, in his " Ohio in the War," says : " This report we venture to pronounce the ablest military document known to have been submitted by a chief of staff to his superior during the war." This is high praise, but it is history.

Twelve days after it was submitted, the army moved, — against the will and opinion of General Crittenden and nearly all Rosecrans' leading officers. It marched into the Tullahoma campaign, one of the most perfectly planned and ably executed movements of the war. The lateness of the start, caused by the objections which General Garfield's letter finally overcame, alone saved Bragg's army from destruction. There was a certain work to do, which might as well have been begun on the 1st of June as the 24th. Had it been begun on the first of these dates, Bragg's army might, in all probability, have been destroyed. As it was, the heavy rains intervened and saved him from pursuit.

With his military reputation thus strengthened General Garfield went with his chief into the battle of Chickamauga. His influence over Rosecrans had by this time become almost supreme. His clear and comprehensive mind grasped every detail, and his opinions were invariably consulted on all important questions. He wrote many orders upon his own judgment, submitting them to Rosecrans for approval or alteration. On the field of Chickamauga he wrote every order except one, and that one was the fatal order to General Wood, which ruined Rosecrans' right wing and lost the battle. The order from Rosecrans to Wood, as the latter interpreted it, required him to move his command behind another division, leaving a wide gap in the line of McCook's corps, which held the right. Wood says that he knew this move would be fatal, but it was ordered, and he felt compelled to execute it. Longstreet saw the blunder, hurled Hood's division into the gap, and within an hour McCook's corps was broken and streaming, a disorganized mob of men, back to Chattanooga. Trying vainly to check the tide of retreat, General Garfield was swept with his chief back beyond Rossville. But the chief of staff could not concede that defeat had been entire. He heard the roar of Thomas's guns on the left, and gained permission of Rosecrans to go round to that quarter and find the Army of the Cumberland. While the commander busied himself with preparing a refuge at Chattanooga for his routed army, his chief of staff went back accompanied only by a staff officer and a few orderlies, to find whatever part of the army still held its ground, and save what there was left. It was a perilous ride. Long before he reached Thomas one of his orderlies was killed. Almost alone he pushed on over the obstructed road, through pursuers and pursued, found the heroic Thomas encircled by fire, but still firm, told him of the disaster on the right, and explained how he could withdraw his right wing and fix it upon a new line to meet Longstreet's column, which had turned the right of Thomas' position and was marching in heavy column upon his rear. The movement was made just in time; but Thomas's line was too short, it would not reach to the base of the mountain. Longstreet saw the gap, drove his column into it, and would have struck Thomas's line fatally in the rear, but in that critical moment General Gordon Granger came up with Steadman's division, which moved in heavy column, threw itself upon Longstreet, and, after a terrific struggle, drove him back. The dead and wounded lay in heaps where those two columns met, but the army of General Thomas was saved. As night closed in upon the heroic Army of the Cumberland, Generals Garfield and Granger, on foot and enveloped in smoke, directed the loading and pointing of a battery of Napoleon guns, whose flash, as they thundered after the retreating column of the assailants, was the last light that shone upon the battlefield of Chickamauga. The struggle was over, and the rebels retired repulsed. Had the two shattered corps of McCook and Crittenden that night been brought upon the field and enabled Thomas to hold his ground, there might have been a second day to that battle, which would have changed its complexion in history.

The battle of Chickamauga practically closed General Garfield's military career. About four weeks after the engagement he was sent by Rosecrans to Washington to report minutely to the President and the War Department the position, deeds, resources, and capabilities of the army at Chattanooga. He went, had frequent lengthy interviews with the President and Secretary Stanton, and thus, point by point, made a most thorough and satisfactory report. Meanwhile, General Garfield had been promoted to a major-generalship of volunteers " for gallant and meritorious services at the battle of Chickamauga," to take rank from the 19th of September, 1863. Rosecrans had been removed from the command of the army at Chattanooga and General Grant appointed to his place.

General Garfield was then called to a new field of duty. In October of the year previous, while the Forty-second was retreating from Cumberland Gap, the people of the Nineteenth Congressional District of Ohio had elected him as their representative to the Thirty-eighth Congress.

" He was a major-general, young, popular in the army, and in high favor at Washington ; he was poor, and his army pay was double the slender salary of a congressman, but he had been chosen by the people of his district as their representative under circumstances which, in his judgment, would not permit him to decline the trust. General Thomas offered him the command of a corps ; but Lincoln urged him to resign his commission and come to Congress. The President was strenuous, and his advice prevailed. There was no want of major-generals, but there was need of all the zeal, courage, and ability that could be assembled in Congress." So his friends argued, and the sequel proved the wisdom of their demand upon him. Yielding to this, he resigned his commission on the 5th of December, 1863, having served in the army more than a year after his election to Congress, and took his seat on the same day in the House of Representatives, where he served until elected to the United States Senate in 1880, just before his nomination for the presidency.

His election to the Senate was remarkably spontaneous and hearty on the part of the Ohio Legislature, and was a just and reasonable compliment to him for his eminent services through sixteen years of a most active legislative life.

The story of General Garfield's success in the House of Representatives of the American nation is the most interesting and the most remarkable part of the history of his life. We have already seen how his qualities as a young man commended him to the respect and attention of the Senate of Ohio, and we shall see how quickly those same qualities lifted him above the mass of congressmen, and brought him into the notice of the nation.

It must not be considered by the reader that, because General Garfield was known to the President, and to some of the great captains of our army, and was loved and honored by the people of the Western Reserve, that he was known in the House of Representatives. There were hundreds of generals in the field whose names were far better known than that of Rosecrans' chief of staff. There were generals in the House of Representatives who had seen severer service, and whose deeds had been far wider proclaimed. There were old statesmen there whose hairs had grown white in the service of the nation. There were scholars of the highest reputation, and orators whose words had become classic. Not a score of the whole assembly knew him by sight, or could recall his place of residence or past services when his name was called.

It was a new start in life. In Congress, as in the back-woods, he must overcome difficulties and fight his way alone. To win distinction there he must be something more than daring, truthful, and industrious; he must possess that peculiar combination of strong talents and intellectual acuteness to which men somewhat vaguely apply the term "greatness." To be eminently great in a nation of great men, and in a time when especial circumstances combined to develop and disclose human nobility, required masterly talents and incessant watchfulness. To be of unusual service to humanity and of exceptional value to a nation, when twenty-five millions of people were striving at a fever heat to do the same thing, is something of which a man has reason to be proud. Such is General Garfield's record. He entered upon his duties in Congress at a time when there were foes within and foes without; when a strong army threatened the nation in the Southern States, and Great Britain menaced it from the ocean; when the finances of the government were getting into an almost inextricable snarl; when the people were searching for their greatest men for counselors in the nation's peril and distress; and when it required fortitude, wisdom, and patriotism above the common order, to provide securely for the nation's future.

For this work General Garfield was well endowed by nature and education. He was a ready speaker, — apt, elegant, pointed, vehement. He had all the scholarship of the colleges, and more to draw upon. He had the practice of cultured public speaking. He had the experience of war, and a course of extensive reading from which to draw forcible and illuminating illustrations. He had all the physical characteristics of dignity, strength, countenance, and voice, which are so useful in the public forum. Thus he was well equipped for a place in a deliberative assembly. But the growth of a member's influence, under the most favorable circumstances, is slow. He could not be a leader there until he had again and again displayed his ability for the post. He does not appear to have aspired to leadership; but from the first day of the session set himself with stubborn purpose at the task of securing a complete knowledge of the rules and history of Congress.

Then followed a study of the resources of the nation in men and money, and of the history of other countries, whose experience could throw any light, or give any suggestion to statesmen, in the complicated and perplexing trials of the Union. His habits of incessant study served him well, and he always had a book in his hand or in his pocket, for use in any spare moment. His astonishing readiness in congressional debates upon any question of commerce, manufactures, finance, revenue, international law, or whatever came up, can be accounted for by this industrious habit. Never idle himself, and aided by his wife, as only a talented, patient, and affectionate woman of her unusual gifts can help a man of letters, he steadily and heartily favored the measures he thought were wise and good, and earnestly, and sometimes excitedly, opposed those actions which he deemed to be pernicious and wrong.

He was given a place at once, upon his entry into Congress, on the very important committee on military affairs. His colleagues bear testimony to his activity, industry, and efficiency, from the very beginning of his term. His speeches were often models of graceful oratory, and yet have about them none of that objectionable air of conceit which would suggest that the speaker delivered them for any other purpose but to convince.

On the first anniversary of the death of Abraham Lincoln, and during General Garfield's third year of service in the House of Representatives, Congress adjourned for the day as a mark of respect for the martyr President's memory. General Garfield was selected to make the motion to adjourn, and in so doing was selected to make a short address. It was one of the most cultured, thoughtful, and appropriate addresses to be found in the vast collection of patriotic speeches, which remain to this generation from the days of war and reconstruction.

"I desire," said he, "to move that this house do now adjourn. And before the vote upon that motion is taken I desire to say a few words. This day, Mr. Speaker, will be sadly memorable so long as this nation shall endure, which God grant may be ' till the last syllable of recorded time,' when the volume of human history shall be sealed up and delivered to the omnipotent Judge. In all future time, on the recurrence of this day, I doubt not that the citizens of this republic will meet in solemn assembly to reflect on the life and character of Abraham Lincoln, and the awful tragic event of April 14, 1865, — an event unparalleled in the history of nations, certainly unparalleled in our own. It is eminently proper that this house should this day place upon its records a memorial of that event. The last five years have been marked by wonderful developments of individual character. Thousands of our people, before unknown to fame, have taken their places in history, crowned with immortal honors. In thousands of humble homes are dwelling heroes and patriots whose names shall never die. But greatest among all these great developments were the character and fame of Abraham Lincoln whose loss the nation still deplores. His character is aptly described in the words of England's great laureate — written thirty years ago — in which he traces the upward steps of some

"'Divinely gifted man,
Whose life in low estate began,
And on a simple village green;

"'Who breaks his birth's invidious bar,
And grasps the skirts of happy chance,
And breasts the blow of circumstance,
And grapples with his evil star;

"'Who makes by force his merit known,
And lives to clutch the golden keys,
To mold a mighty State's decrees,
And shape the whisper of the throne;

"'And moving up from high to higher,
Becomes on Fortune's crowning slope
The pillar of a People's hope,
The centre of a world's desire.'

"Such a life and character will be treasured forever as the sacred possession of the American people and of mankind. In the great drama of the Rebellion there were two acts. The first was the war with its battles and sieges, victories and defeats, its sufferings and tears.

"That act was closing one year ago to-night, and just as the curtain was lifting on the second and final act, — the restoration of peace and liberty, — just as the curtain was rising upon new characters and new events, the evil spirit of the Rebellion, in the fury of despair, nerved and directed the hand of the assassin to strike down the chief character in both. It was no one man who killed Abraham Lincoln; it was the embodied spirit of treason and slavery, inspired with fearful, despairing hate, that struck him down in the moment of the nation's supremest joy.

"Ah, sir, there are times in the history of men and nations, when they stand so near the veil that separates mortals from the immortals, time from eternity, and men from their God, that they can almost hear the beatings, and feel the pulsations of the heart of the Infinite. Through such a time has this nation passed. When two hundred and fifty thousand brave spirits passed from the field of honor, through that thin veil, to the presence of God; and when at last its parting folds admitted the martyr President to the company of the dead heroes of the republic, the nation stood so near the veil, that the whispers of God were heard by the children of men. Awe-stricken by his voice, the American people knelt in tearful reverence, and made a solemn covenant with him, and with each other, that their nation should be saved from its enemies, that all its glories should be restored, and on the ruins of slavery and treason the temple of freedom and justice should be built, and should survive forever. It remains for us, consecrated by the great event, and under a covenant with God, to keep that faith, to go forward in the great work until it shall be completed. Following the lead of that great man, and obeying the high behests of God, let us remember that, —

> "'He hath sounded forth a trumpet that shall never call retreat;
> He is sifting out the hearts of men before his judgment seat;
> Be swift my soul to answer him; be jubilant my feet;
> For God is marching on.'"

One of the most popular of General Garfield's eulogies, was upon John Winthrop and Samuel Adams, and was delivered December 19, 1876, the house then having under consideration the following resolution : —

IN THE SENATE OF THE UNITED STATES,
December, 19, 1876.

Resolved by the Senate (the House of Representatives concurring). 1. That the statues of John Winthrop and Samuel Adams are accepted in the name of the United States, and that the thanks of Congress are given to the State of Massachusetts for these memorials of two of her eminent citizens, whose names are indissolubly associated with the foundation of the republic.

2. That a copy of these resolutions, engrossed upon parchment and duly authenticated, be transmitted to the governor of Massachusetts.

He said: "Mr. Speaker, I regret that illness has made it impossible for me to keep the promise, which I made a few days since, to offer some reflections appropriate to this very interesting occasion. But I cannot let the moment pass without expressing my great satisfaction with the fitting and instructive choice which the State of Massachusetts has made, and the manner in which her representatives have discharged their duty in presenting these beautiful works of art to the Congress of the nation.

"As, from time to time, our venerable and beautiful hall has been peopled with statues of the elect of the States, it has seemed to me that a third house was being organized within the walls of the Capitol — a house whose members have received their high credentials at the hands of history, and whose term of office will outlast the ages. Year by year, we see the circle of its immortal membership enlarging; year by year, we see the elect of their country, in eloquent silence, taking their places in this American pantheon, bringing within its sacred circle the wealth of those immortal memories, which made their lives illustrious; and, year by year, that august assembly is teaching a deeper and grander lesson to all who serve their brief hour in these more ephemeral Houses of Congress. And now, two places of great honor have just been most nobly filled.

" I can well understand that the State of Massachusetts, embarrassed by her wealth of historic glory, found it difficult to make the selection. And while the distinguished gentleman from Massachusetts (Mr. Hoar) was so fittingly honoring his State, by portraying that happy embarrassment, I was reflecting that the sister State of Virginia will encounter, if possible, a still greater difficulty when she comes to make the selection of her immortals. One name I venture to hope she will not select, — a name too great for the glory of any one State. I trust she will allow us to claim Washington as belonging to all the States, for all time: If she shall pass over the great distance that separates Washington from all others, I can hardly imagine how she will make the choice from her crowded roll. But I have no doubt that she will be able to select two who will represent the great phases of her history, as happily and worthily as Massachusetts is represented, in the choice she has to-day announced. It is difficult to imagine a happier combination of great and beneficent forces, than will be presented by the representative heroes of these two great States.

" Virginia and Massachusetts were the two focal centres from which sprang the life-forces of this republic. These were, in many ways, complements of each other, each supplying what the other lacked, and both uniting to endow the republic with its noblest and most enduring qualities.

" To-day the house has listened with the deepest interest to the statement of those elements of priceless value contributed by the State of Massachusetts. We have been instructed by the clear and masterly analysis of the spirit and character of that Puritan civilization, so fully embodied in the lives of Winthrop and Adams. I will venture to add, that, notwithstanding all the neglect and contempt with which England regarded her Puritans, two hundred years ago, the tendency of thought in modern England is to do justice to that great force which created the Commonwealth, and finally made the British Islands a land of liberty and law. Even the great historian Hume was compelled reluctantly to declare that —

" ' The precious spark of liberty had been kindled and was preserved by the Puritans alone ; and it was to this sect that the English owe the whole freedom of their Constitution.'

" What higher praise can posterity bestow upon any people than to make such a confession ?   Having done so much to save liberty alive in the mother country, the Puritans planted, upon the shores of this New World, that remarkable civilization whose growth is the greatness and glory of our republic.

" Indeed, before Winthrop and his company landed at Salem, the Pilgrims were laying the foundation of civil liberty.   While the Mayflower was passing Cape Cod, and seeking an anchorage, in the midst of the storm, her brave passengers sat down in the little cabin, and drafted and signed a covenant which contains the germ of American liberty.   How familiar to the American habit of mind are these declarations of the Pilgrim covenant of 1620, —

" ' That no act, imposition, law, or ordinance be made or imposed upon us at present, or to come, but such as has been or shall be enacted by the consent of the body of free men or associates, or their representatives, legally assembled.'

" The New England town was the model, the primary cell, from which our republic was evolved.   The town meeting was the germ of all the parliamentary life and habits of Americans.

" John Winthrop brought with him the more formal organization of New England society ; and, in his long and useful life, did more than perhaps any other to direct and strengthen its growth.

" Nothing, therefore, could be more fitting, than for Massachusetts to place in our Memorial Hall the statue of the first of the Puritans, representing him at the moment when he was stepping on shore from the ship that brought him from England, and bearing with him the charter of that first political society which laid the foundations of our country ; and that near him should stand that Puritan embodiment of the logic of the Revolution, Samuel Adams.   I am

glad to see this decisive, though tardy, acknowledgment of his great
and signal services to America. I doubt if any man equaled Samuel
Adams in formulating and uttering the fierce, clear, and inexorable
logic of the Revolution. With our present habits of thought, we
can hardly realize how great were the obstacles to overcome. Not
the least was the religious belief of the fathers — that allegiance to
rulers was obedience to God. The thirteenth chapter of Romans
was to many minds a barrier against revolution stronger than the
battalions of George III., —

"'Let every soul be subject unto the higher powers. For there
is no power but of God; the powers that be are ordained of God.
Whosoever therefore resisteth the power, resisteth the ordinance of
God.'

"And it was not until the people of that religious age were led
to see that they might obey God and still establish liberty, in spite
of kingly despotism, that they were willing to engage in war against
one who called himself 'king by the grace of God.' The men who
pointed out the pathway to freedom by the light of religion as well
as of law, were the foremost promoters of American independence.
And of these, Adams was unquestionably chief.

"It must not be forgotten that, while Samuel Adams was writing
the great argument of liberty in Boston, almost at the same time
Patrick Henry was formulating the same doctrines in Virginia. It
is one of the grandest facts of that grand time that the colonies
were thus brought, by an almost universal consent, to tread the
same pathway, and reach the same great conclusions.

"But most remarkable of all is the fact that, throughout all that
period, filled as it was with the revolutionary spirit, the great men
who guided the storm exhibited the most wonderful power of self-
restraint. If I were to-day to state the single quality that appears
to me most admirable among the fathers of the Revolution, I should
say it was this: that amidst all the passions of war, waged against
a perfidious enemy from beyond the sea, aided by a savage enemy
on our own shores, our fathers exhibited so wonderful a restraint, so
great a care to observe the forms of law, to protect the rights of the
minority, to preserve all those great rights that had come down to
them from the common law, so that when they had achieved their
independence, they were still a law-abiding people.

"In that fiery meeting in the Old South Church, after the Boston massacre, when, as the gentleman from Massachusetts has said, three thousand voices almost lifted the roof from the church, in demanding the removal of the regiments, it is noted by the historian that there was one, solitary, sturdy "nay" in the vast assemblage; and Samuel Adams scrupulously recorded the fact that there was one dissentient. It would have been a mortal offense against his notions of justice and good order, if that one dissentient had not had his place in the record. And, after the regiments had been removed, and after the demand had been acceded to that the soldiers who had fired upon citizens should be delivered over to the civil authorities, to be dealt with according to law, Adams was the first to insist and demand that the best legal talent in the colony should be put forward to defend those murderers; and John Adams and Josiah Quincy were detailed for the purpose of defending them. Men were detailed whose hearts and souls were on fire with the love of the popular cause; but the men of Massachusetts would have despised the two advocates, if they had not given their whole strength to the defense of the soldiers.

"Mr. Speaker, this great lesson of self-restraint is taught in the whole history of the Revolution; and it is this lesson that to-day, more, perhaps, than any other we have seen, we ought to take most to heart. Let us seek liberty and peace, under the law; and, following the pathway of our fathers, preserve the great legacy they have committed to our keeping."

General Garfield was appointed on many important special committees by Congress: he was sent to Louisiana by the President to report upon the political condition of the people with reference to reconstruction, he was chosen one of the High Commission to which was referred the contested presidential election in 1876, and which gave Rutherford B. Hayes the seat.

He delivered many speeches on public occasions in different parts of the United States, and conducted important cases before the Supreme Court of the United States.

His nomination for the presidency by the Republican party at Chicago in June, 1880, was a surprise both to him and to the country. General Garfield was a delegate to the convention, and was an open advocate of the nomination of Hon. John Sherman of Ohio. The party, however, was in danger of a most serious division, in which the adherents of General U. S. Grant and of Hon. James G.

Blaine were the contestants. The friends of each were so strong and so bitter in their opposition to the other, that the only safe measure to adopt was found in the nomination of an unobjectionable man who was allied with neither faction. Hence with great enthusiasm they turned to General Garfield. He was elected by a strong majority both of the people and of the Electoral College, and was inaugurated at Washington, March 4, 1881, amid great rejoicing, the city being crowded with parades, vocal with bands of music, and brilliant with flags, banners, decorations, and pyrotechnics.

But the old theory of the rose and the thorn appears to be as true of the roses of presidential honors as of any other desirable attain-

THE WHITE HOUSE.

ment. As the office was higher than any other which he had held, and as the honor was the greatest the world could give, so the annoyances that accompanied him into his office were more discouraging than any he had experienced, and the dangers which surrounded him the most appalling of any which the world contains. He was set upon by an unusually merciless horde of applicants for political office, who, having heard of his natural goodness of heart, thought that their efforts would be successful if they could succeed in getting their private histories and afflictions within the scope of his personal attention. Many of the seekers after national honor and pay had not restrained themselves sufficiently to await the inauguration ; but at his home in Mentor, in the railway carriages, in hotels, and in private assemblies they had intruded recklessly and remorselessly upon his time and attention. They coaxed, they flattered, they wrote biographical sketches and laudatory poetry; they sent him presents, they filled his rooms with correspondence which it was impossible for him to read, they even cursed and terribly threatened him as he hinted at refusal or stated that several hundred of the applicants for the same office must inevitably be disappointed.

It was a time that tried the metal of the man's character and tested the powers of his mind, as campaigns military and political had failed to do.

Among those who joined that army of office seekers was a man by the name of Charles J. Guiteau, who was a native of Illinois, and who claimed at the time to be a resident of New York. His life had been most erratic, and his ambition most unbounded. He had professed many kinds of religious beliefs, and had unsuccessfully tried to practice law in Chicago and New York. He had attempted to lecture on religious and social themes; but with many another vagabond, he found that to be successful at that he must at least be great in some one direction, to attract or hold the attention of the people. He wrote a book upon his religious hobbies, and cheated the publisher and his landlady in order to get it into print. He had the appearance of a gentleman, and betrayed the confidence of many unsuspecting friends. He was hypocritical, licentious, and cruel. His parents, brother, and wife, after many protests, warnings, and griefs, left him to his natural tastes, and refused to remain in his company.

In the political campaign of 1880 he ingratiated himself into the good-will of some of the Republican committee of New York, and made a few unsuccessful speeches, and on the fact that he had taken part in the contest, he based his claims for a consulship at Marseilles, France, and importuned President Garfield for the appointment.

The President listened patiently at first, but when the man's unfitness became apparent both in his actions and reputation, the refusal was stated promptly and frankly. Guiteau pleaded, but received repeated refusal. Then he boldly threatened vengeance and was forcibly ejected from the White House.

Filled with wrath, shame, and disappointment, he deliberately but firmly resolved to assassinate the President at the first opportunity.

Soon after he formed this resolution a political quarrel arose between the President and Senator Conkling of New York, about the appointment of a collector for the port of New York. The dispute may have been an outburst of the smothered feeling lingering after the defeat of favorite candidates in the Republican Presidential Convention, and may have been connected less remotely with the fact that the President had placed in his Cabinet with William Windom, Wayne MacVeagh, Robert T. Lincoln, William H. Hunt, Samuel J. Kirkwood, and Thomas L. James, Senator James G. Blaine of Maine, who had been one of the candidates opposed in that convention by Senator Conkling.

After endeavoring in vain to prevent the confirmation by the Senate of the President's appointments, and after the President had threateningly but temporarily withdrawn the unconfirmed nominations from before the Senate of some of Senator Conkling's friends, both the senators from New York resigned and went back to their state Legislature, expecting a triumphant reëlection as a rebuke to the President. They failed of their election, and men favoring the President were chosen in their places. The contest created great excitement and awoke much bitter feeling in the nation. It injured the business of the country, created bitter divisions, and encouraged assassination.

Guiteau was so blinded by his desire to kill the President that he drew much encouragement from the quarrel, and expected to find support and defense in his deed from the defeated party. He did not, however, consult with any of them or apprise any man of his intentions.

When the success of the administration party seemed certain, Guiteau purchased a large revolver, and for many days dogged the President's footsteps, seeking a favorable opportunity to kill him. Twice he was on the point of committing the murder, but was prevented first by the accidental turning about of the President, and once later when the President was conveying his sick wife to the railway station, and when the sight of her pale sweet face so stirred his conscience that he could not raise his weapon.

On the morning of July 2d (1881), the President went to the Baltimore station in Washington, expecting to take the train for

New York and make a tour up the Hudson River and through New England with Mrs. Garfield, who was not fully recovered from a prolonged and dangerous illness. Secretary Blaine accompanied him to the railway station, riding in the same carriage, and as they alighted they stood conversing together near the doorway. Guiteau had sought the spot intent upon his murderous purpose, but the constant passing of passengers prevented the accomplishment of his design until the President entered the ladies' room of the station and stood within a very short distance of the assassin. Guiteau, stepping behind his victim, fired two shots into the President's back in quick succession, and amid the alarm and confusion consequent among the people upon such an awful crime, he escaped to the door. But while he was trying to secure a hack to hurry away and while the prostrate and fainting President was being lifted from the floor, he was seized by the bystanders and was soon in the jail.

The wounded man was carried hastily back to the White House, medical attendance called, and his waiting wife at Long Branch summoned by telegraph to meet him at his bedside in Washington, instead of greeting him at New York, as they had planned.

Only one shot had taken dangerous effect in the President's body and that passed through his back from side to side, shattering one rib and a portion of the spine, and lodging in the flesh. It was a wound that must necessarily have proved mortal, and the surgeons who were called, and who represented the most skilled men in the profession, declared that the only expectation of the President's recovery lay in the hope that the wound was not such as it appeared to be.

Then began a season of national humiliation, tears, prayers, and watching such as the world never saw before. Every event of the slightest moment, every mouthful of food, every kind of medicine and treatment, the rise and fall of his temperature and pulse, the words he spoke, waking or in dreams, the heroic watching and fortitude of his wife and children, the sayings of his aged mother, and the opinions of public men, were circulated in the public press and eagerly read and re-read by millions of tearful eyes. A day of fasting and prayer was universally observed by the nation, and men who never prayed before asked earnestly of God that the good man's life might be spared. Day succeeded day, and week followed week, adding hourly to the suspense until the gloom everywhere apparent was saddening and disheartening in the extreme. With a courage and resignation most wonderful, the patient held on to the slender thread of life, and with Christian charity and heroism spoke kindly of his enemies and even of the murderer, and calmly declared to his friends that he did not fear to die.

The heat of the summer came on, and the malaria of the marshes arose to add to the dangers, and after more than two months of suffering in the dreadful heat, the martyr was removed by railway to Long Branch, where for a few days he lingered, looking out upon the sea and holding his wife's hand by day, and dreaming of his boyhood's home and his loved playmates by night. On that little seaside cottage at Long Branch, in the town of Elberon, N. J., was centred the anxious attention of the whole civilized world. Queen Victoria of England, King William of Germany, Emperor Alexander of Russia, President Grévy of France, King Humbert of Italy, Emperor Francis of Austria, the Sultan of Turkey, the Pasha of Egypt, and the rulers of many lesser nations sent frequent inquiries concerning the suffering man. Legislatures, councils, conventions, synods, and colleges in many lands sent words of sympathy. But the simple-hearted man, whose life had been passed among the people, cared much less for all these honorable and official attentions, sincere as they were, than he did for the affectionate hearts whose sympathy had comforted him in his poverty, and whose encouragement had sustained him in previous trials. His wife, his daughter, his aged mother, his cousin Dr. Boynton, his neighbors, his long tried companions in public life, were to him dearer than the notice of kings or queens. No experience recorded of any president so clearly demonstrates the shallowness of political honors and the foolishness of seeking an office for fame or distinction, as the experiences and words of James A. Garfield in his lingering illness. When told by the physicians that it seemed impossible to cure him, he firmly replied, " I am not afraid to die." When told how much the nation had need of him, he said, " Our nation does not depend for its life or prosperity on any one individual." When reminded of the honor to which he had come, he declared that he had " rather be a humble farmer in Mentor than president of the world." When, in his last hours, he did not mention a hope of being again at the head of the nation, or of homage and applause, but simply wished that he might be permitted once more to meet all his family together, he displayed a beautiful trait of character and a wisdom unusual among political leaders. As compared with home, wife, children, and old friends, all offices, honors, praises, and power were not worthy of mention. Unchanging love and faithfulness to wife, children, and neighbors were in him, as in every other noble mind, his highest claim upon the honors and sympathies of a civilized world.

On Monday, September 19th, after eighty days of suffering, the indications were so unfavorable that the physicians warned the attendants and nurses, among whom were several members of his Cabinet, that the hour of death drew very near. All day he lay half dreaming, sometimes asking for his daughter Mollie, sometimes holding the hand of his wife, while the whole nation was weeping and tremblingly awaiting the moment of his death. Late in the evening he seemed to sleep and he was left alone for a while with only one attendant, Major Swaim, of the United States army. Near midnight he awoke and complained of pain in the region of the heart, and after an effort to change his position on his couch, sank into a stupor from which he did not afterwards rally. A half hour later, with his hand clasped by his wife, with his daughter kneeling at the bedside, and surrounded by many of the great men of the nation, the martyred President peacefully drew his last breath. Midnight bells all over the land tolled in gloomy concert, and the grief-stricken people sprinkled their pillows with tears, saying, " Our President is dead."

So swift are the wings of modern communication that before noon of the next day messages of condolence, sympathy, and grief came to the heart-broken widow from all parts of the world. One was from Queen Victoria, and read as follows : —

"BALMORAL, *September* 20*th.*

" To MRS. PRESIDENT GARFIELD, — Words cannot express the deep sympathy I feel with you. May God support and comfort you as He alone can. THE QUEEN."

The history of the President's illness and death, as reported in medical books, was one of the most remarkable events in modern surgery. The *post-mortem* examination revealed to the surgeons for the first time the exact location of the bullet, and showed that it had taken a course entirely different from that which the medical men had supposed. It showed also that such vital portions of the body had been injured that the patient's recovery, from any human standpoint, appeared to have been impossible. The success of the methods adopted in prolonging the President's life in such a wonderful manner, showed a great advance in surgery and medicine within a quarter of a century. Many men during the last war, who were attended by the most skillful surgeons, died within a few hours of wounds apparently less dangerous than this. The immediate cause of death was secondary hæmorrhage from one of the mesenteric arteries adjoining the track of the ball, the blood rupturing the peritoneum, and nearly a pint of blood escaping into the abdominal cavity.

The preparations for the funeral were simple and unostentatious, in accord with the desire of Mrs. Garfield. Funds, which were raised to make the funeral more elaborate, were given by the wealthy donors to the fund of over $350,000, which was presented to Mrs. Garfield as an expression of sympathy.

The coffin was plain and the decorations modest. But the funeral of one so loved by an entire people could not be very private. A desire to see the cottage in which he died, or the funeral train, or the face of the dead, was so great, that every movement of the funeral party was attended by immense assemblies of the people. When the railway train containing the body and the mourners passed through the country on its way from Long Branch to Washington, an almost unending line of weeping people gazed sadly upon it from the road-side. In the large cities tens of thousands crowded about the stations.

The body was placed in the centre of the hall of the Capitol at Washington, under the great central dome, and there for two days lay in state, while many thousand people passed by the casket and looked upon the emaciated features of the dead. On the bier were placed many floral gifts, but chief among them was a beautiful wreath of flowers ordered by the Queen of England. Once during those sad days the multitude was shut out, and for an hour the stricken widow was left alone with her dead, — one of the saddest, sweetest pictures in our nation's history.

The funeral services at the Capitol were very brief and unceremonious, in accordance with the usual customs of the Disciples Church, of which the President had been a member. At 2.40 P. M., said an eye-witness, Colonel Rockwell, Dr. Boynton, Private Secre-

37

tary Brown, and the household of the President entered the rotunda and took seats reserved for them. The members of the House of Representatives filed in through the south door, preceded by the officers of that body and by ex-Speakers Randall and Banks. They were followed by the Senators, Senator Anthony leading, who entered by the north door. At three o'clock the Cabinet and distinguished guests entered in the following order: President Arthur and Secretary Blaine, ex-Presidents Grant and Hayes, Secretary and Mrs. Windom, Secretary and Mrs. Lincoln, Secretary and Mrs. Hunt, Attorney-General and Mrs. MacVeagh, Secretary Kirkwood and Postmaster-General James, and Generals Drum and Beale, the diplomatic corps, and the representatives of the army and navy.

Mrs. Garfield and the children were not present at the ceremonies.

Services were opened by Rev. Dr. Powers promptly at three o'clock. He ascended the dais, and briefly announced the opening hymn, " Asleep in Jesus, blessed sleep," which was rendered by a choir of fifty voices.

Rev. Dr. Rankin then ascended the raised platform at the head of the catafalque, and read in a clear, distinct voice, the scriptural selections. Rev. Dr. Isaac Errett then offered prayer.

As the closing words of the prayer died away, Rev. F. D. Powers, of the Vermont Avenue Christian Church, of which President Garfield was a member, delivered a feeling address.

At the conclusion of Dr. Powers's address Rev. J. G. Butler offered prayer.

This closed the ceremonies, and the vast assemblage, with bowed heads and reverent mien, arose as the casket containing the remains of President Garfield was slowly borne from the building in which he had gained so many laurels and triumphs. The casket was followed by President Arthur, leaning on the arm of Secretary Blaine, and by the members of the Cabinet, and in a quarter of an hour the rotunda was nearly deserted. During the progress of the ceremonies the appearance of the rotunda was solemn and impressive. The chairs, of which there were three hundred in the hall, were completely filled, while many persons remained standing in the aisles. The glitter of the uniforms of the army and the navy, and the court uniforms of the representatives of the diplomatic corps, served to brighten to a certain degree the solemnity of the scene.

Save a little confusion incident upon the seating of the officers of the army and navy, the best of order was preserved throughout, and no incident occurred to interrupt the sad impressiveness of the ceremonies.

Immediately after the close of the services the floral decorations were all removed (Mrs. Garfield having requested that they be sent to her home at Mentor) except the beautiful wreath, the gift of Queen Victoria, which had been placed upon the head of the coffin when the lid was closed, and which, when the coffin was borne to the hearse, remained upon it till the remains were buried. This touching tribute of Queen Victoria greatly moved Mrs. Garfield, as only a woman can feel a woman's sympathy at the time of her greatest earthly sorrow.

The coffin having been placed in the hearse, a single gun was fired from Hanneman's battery, the Second Artillery Band struck up a funeral march, and the procession moved in the following order around the south front of the Capitol to the avenue: Two battalions of District of Columbia militia, ten companies; two companies of United States marines, four companies of the United States Second Artillery, Light Battery Company A, United States Artillery; Grand Army of the Republic, Roscoe Conkling Club, Boys in Blue, Columbia, Washington, and De Molay Commanderies, Knights Templars, of the city, in full regalia; Beausant Commandery Knights Templars of Baltimore. Then came the hearse, drawn by six iron-gray horses, each led by a colored groom; following the hearse came about a hundred carriages, which were occupied by officers of the Executive Mansion and wives, relatives of the late President, ex-Presidents Grant and Hayes, President Arthur, and Secretary Blaine. The other Cabinet ministers and their wives, the diplomatic corps, Chief-Justice Waite, and Associate Justices Harlan, Matthews, and Miller; senators, members of the house, Governors of States and Territories, and Commissioners of the District of Columbia; the Judges of the Court of Claims, the Judiciary of the District of Columbia, and Judges of the United States courts; the Assistant Secretaries of State, Treasury, and Interior Departments; the Assistant Postmaster-General, the Solicitor-General, and the Assistant Attorneys-General. As the procession moved minute guns were fired from the military posts and forts surrounding the city, and the church bells were tolled. At least forty thousand people were gathered about the Capitol to witness the start of the procession, while along the line of march to Sixth Street the crowd was even greater than on the 4th of March. Everywhere it was most orderly and quiet; and as the hearse containing the remains moved along the avenue, from the very door of the Capitol to the entrance of the depot, all heads were uncovered.

On reaching the depot the military were drawn up in line upon the opposite side of the street, facing the Sixth Street entrance. The remains were borne from the hearse upon the shoulders of six soldiers of the Second Artillery and placed in the funeral car. The ten officers from the army and navy, selected as the guard of honor, stood with uncovered heads as the remains were taken from the hearse, and then escorted them to the car.

Again the scenes of the previous Wednesday were repeated, and, as the funeral train proceeded on its way to Cleveland, one almost unbroken line of people, sometimes swelling into great seas of human beings, greeted the sad procession with bare heads, tears, and sad faces.

The funeral train arrived in Cleveland on Saturday, the 24th, and the funeral at that place was held on Monday, the 26th. An eye-witness of the tearful scenes of that day gave the following account: —

All that is mortal of the late President reposes in a tomb in the beautiful Lake View Cemetery of Cleveland. To-day the last funeral rites were celebrated in the open air of the public square, where the body has lain in state since Saturday.

The aged mother, the noble widow, the sons and the daughter, and the other relatives of General Garfield, the members of the household of the White House, the friends who had enjoyed his love and confidence, and the members of the Cabinet and their families, were seated around the coffin under the arched roof of the catafalque, and unseen by the larger company on the platform. The members of the Senate and House of Representatives, governors of States and other official dignitaries and committees, were assembled on the platform in due order, together with the Marine Band and the singing societies who were to take part in the exercises. All faced toward the coffin, resting on its high bier. All around the square, looking on with intense interest, although unable to hear anything but the music, was a dense crowd, completely filling the streets, and numbering from twenty to forty thousand.

Promptly at half-past ten o'clock the ceremonies at the pavilion began. The immediate members of the family and near relatives and friends took seats about the casket, and at each corner was stationed a member of the Cleveland Grays. Dr. J. P. Robinson, president of the ceremonies, announced that the exercises would be opened by singing by the Cleveland Vocal Society of the " Funeral Hymn," by Beethoven ; whereupon the hymn was sung as follows :

> " Thou art gone to the grave, but we will not deplore thee,
> Though sorrow and darkness encompass the tomb ;
> The Saviour has passed through its portals before thee,
> And the lamp of his love is thy light through the gloom."

The Scriptures were read by the Right Rev. Bishop Bedell, of the Episcopal diocese of Ohio.

The Rev. Ross C. Houghton, pastor of the First Methodist Episcopal Church, then offered prayer ; after which the Rev. Isaac Errett of Cincinnati delivered an eloquent address taking for his text the following : —

" And the archers shot King Josiah, and the king said to his servant, ' Have me away, for I am sore wounded.' "

" There was never a mourning in all the world like unto this mourning. I am not speaking extravagantly when I say — for I am told it is the result of calculations carefully made from such data as are in possession — that certainly not less than three hundred millions of the human race share in the sadness and the lamentations and sorrow and mourning that belong to this occasion here to-day. It is a chill shadow of a fearful calamity that has extended itself into every home in all this land and into every heart, and that has projected itself over vast seas and oceans into distant lands, and awakened the sincerest and profoundest sympathy with us in the hearts of the good people of the nations and among all people. . . . He passed all the conditions of virtuous life between the log cabin in Cuyahoga and the White House, and in that wonderful, rich, and varied experience, still moving up from higher to higher, he has touched every heart in all this land at some point or other, and he became the representative of all hearts and lives in this land, and not only the teacher but the interpreter of all virtues ; for he knew their wants and he knew their condition, and he established legitimate ties of brotherhood with every man with whom he came in contact. I take it that this rock on which his whole life rested, followed up by the perpetual and enduring industry that marked his whole career, made him at once the honest and the capable man who invited in every act of his life, and received, the confidence and the love, the unbounded confidence and trust and love, of all that learned to know him. There is yet one other thing that I ought to mention here. There was such an admirable harmony of all his powers ; there was such a beautiful adjustment of the physical, intellectual, and moral in his being ; there was such an equitable distribution of physical, intellectual, and moral forces, that his nature looked out every way to get in sympathy with everything, and found about equal delight in all pursuits and all studies, so that he became, through his industry and honest ambition, really encyclopædic. There was scarce any single chord that you could touch to which he would not respond in a way that made you know that his hands had swept it skillfully long ago ; and there was no topic you could bring before him, there was no object you could present to him, that you did not wonder at the richness and fullness of information somehow gathered ; for his eyes were always open, and his heart was always open, and his brain was ever busy and equally interested in everything. The minute and the vast, the high and the low, in all classes and creeds of men, he gathered up, that immense store and that immense variety of the most valuable and practical knowledge that made him a man not in one department, but in all rounds, everywhere in his whole beautiful and symmetrical life and character.

" But my friends, the solemnity of this hour forbids any further investigation in that line, and further detail of a very remarkable life. For these details you are familiar with, or, if not, they will come before you through various channels hereafter. It is my duty, in the presence of the dead, and in view of all the solemnities that rest upon us now in a solemn burial service, to call your attention to the great lesson taught to you, and by which we ought to become wiser and purer and better men. And I want to say, therefore, that there comes a voice from the dead to this entire nation, and not only to the people, but to those in places of trust, to our legislators, and our governors, and our military men, and our leaders of party, and all classes and creeds in the Union and in the States, as well as to those who dwell in humble life, qualified with the dignities and privileges of citizenship. The great lesson to which I desire to point you can be expressed in few words. James A. Garfield went through his whole public life without surrendering for a single moment his Christian integrity, his moral integrity, or his love for the spiritual. Coming into the exciting conflicts of political life with a nature capable as any of feeling the force of every temptation, with unlawful prizes within his reach, with every inducement to surrender all his religious faith and be known as a successful man of the world, from first to last he has manfully adhered to his religious convictions. . . . I feel just at this point that we need this lesson, this great, wondrous land of ours, this mighty nation in its marvelous upward career, with its ever-increasing power opening its arms to receive from all lands people of all languages, all religions, and all conditions, to blend them with us, to melt them into a common mass, so it becomes like the Corinthian brass, and in one type of manhood thus incorporating all the various nations of the earth in one grand brotherhood, presenting before the nations of the world a spectacle of freedom and strength and prosperity and power beyond anything the world has ever known. . . . And the wife, who began with him in young womanhood, has bravely kept step with him right along through all his wondrous career; and who has been not only his wife, but his friend and his counselor through all their succession of prosperities and this increase of influence and power; and who, when the day of calamity came, was his ministering angel, his prophetess, his priestess, when the circumstances were such as to forbid ministrations from other hands ; speaking to him the words of cheer which sustained him through that long, fearful struggle for life, and watching over him when his dying vision rested on her beloved form, and sought from her eyes an answering gaze that should speak when words could not speak. And the children, who have grown up to a period that they can remember all that belonged to him, left fatherless in a world like this, yet surrounded with a nation's sympathy and with a world's affection, and able to treasure in their hearts the grand lessons of his noble and wondrous life, may be assured that the eyes of the nation are upon them, and that the hearts of the people go out after them. While there is much to support and encourage, it is still a sad thing and calls for our deepest sympathy that they have lost such a father, and are left to make their way through this rough world without his guiding hand or his wise counsels. But that which makes this terrible to them now is just that which, as the years go by, will make very sweet and bright and joyous memories to fill all the lives of the coming years by the very loss which they deplore, and by all the loving actions that bound them in blessed sympathy in the home circle. They will live over again ten thousand times all the sweet life of the past, and though dead he will still live with them, and though his tongue be dumb in the grave he will speak anew to them ten thousand beautiful lessons of love, and righteousness, and truth. May God in his infinite mercy bear them in his arms and bless them as they need in this hour of thick darkness, and bear them safely through what remains of the troubles and sorrows of the pilgrimage unto the everlasting home, where there shall be no more death nor crying, neither shall there be any more pain, for the former things shall have forever passed away. We commit you, beloved friends, to the arms and the care of the everlasting Father, who has promised to be the God of the widow and the father of the fatherless in his holy habitation, and whose sweet promise goes with us through all the dark and stormy paths of life: ' I will never leave thee nor forsake thee.'

" I have discharged now the solemn covenant trust reposed in me many years ago, in harmony with a friendship that has never known a cloud, a confidence that has never trembled, and a love that has never changed. Farewell, my friend and brother! Thou hast fought a good fight. Thou hast finished thy course. Thou hast kept the faith. Henceforth there is laid up for thee a crown of righteousness, which the Lord, the righteous judge, will give to thee in that day; and not unto thee only, but unto all them also who love his appearing."

The Rev. Jabez Hall then read General Garfield's favorite hymn, which was beautifully sung by the Vocal Society, as follows: —

> "Ho! reapers of life's harvest,
>   Why stand with rusted blade
> Until the night draws round thee,
>   And day begins to fade?
> Why stand ye idle, waiting
>   For reapers more to come?
> The golden morn is passing,
>   Why sit ye idle, dumb?"

At 11.45 Dr. Charles S. Pomeroy delivered the final prayer and benediction.

The funeral procession moved from Monumental Park at five minutes before twelve o'clock.

A succession of heavy showers so delayed the funeral procession that the line had to be broken before it reached the cemetery, and forming in files on either side of the avenue for nearly three miles the military and civic societies made way for the funeral car. The state militia were stationed at the entrance to the cemetery, and on either side of the driveways leading to the vault where, at Mrs. Garfield's request, it was decided to place the remains. The steps to the vault were carpeted with flowers, and on either side of the entrance was an anchor of tuberoses and a cross of white smilax and evergreens. Festooned above it a heavy black canopy was stretched over the steps from which the exercises were to be conducted.

At half-past three o'clock the procession entered the gateway, which was arched over with black, with appropriate inscriptions. In the keystone were the words " Come to rest ; " on one side were the words " Lay him to rest whom we have learned to love," on the other " Lay him to rest whom we have learned to trust."

None of the President's family, except two of the boys, left the carriages during the exercises at the tomb, which occupied less than half an hour. Dr. J. P. Robinson, as president of the day, opened the exercises by introducing the Rev. J. H. Jones, chaplain of the Forty-second Ohio Regiment, which General Garfield commanded. Mr. Jones said : —

" Our illustrious chief has completed his journey's end, — a journey that we must all soon make, and that in the near future. Yet when I see the grand surroundings of this occasion, I am led to inquire, Was this man the son of the emperor, of the king, that wore a crown ? For in the history of this great country there has been nothing like this seen. Yet, I thought, perhaps, speaking after the manner of man, that he was a prince, and this was offered in a manner after royalty. But this is not an offering such as is made to earthly kings and emperors, though he was a prince and a freeman, the great commoner of the United States. Only a few miles from where we stand, less than fifty years ago, he was born in the primeval forests of this State and this country, and all he asks of you now is a peaceful grave in the bosom of the land that gave him birth. I cannot speak to you of his wonderful life and works. Time forbids, and history will take care of that, and your children's children will read of this emotion when we have passed away from this earth. . . . You brethren here of the South, I greet you to-day; and you brethren of the North, East, and West. Come, let us lay all our bitternesses up in the coffin of the dear man. Let him carry them with him to the grave in silence. Till the angels disturb the slumbers of the dead let us love each other more, our country better. May God bless you and the dear family; and, as they constitute a great family on earth, I hope they will constitute a great family in the kingdom of God, where I hope to meet you all in the end. Amen."

After an ode by Horace, sung in Latin by the United German Singing Society, Mr. Robinson announced the late President's favorite hymn, "Ho, reapers of life's harvest," which the German vocal societies of Cleveland sang with marked effect. The exercises closed with the benediction by President Hinsdale, of Hiram College, and reëntering their carriages, the mourners drove hurriedly back to the city, to avoid another shower which was threatened. The military and Masonic escort left the cemetery in the same order in which they entered, and kept in line until the catafalque was reached, where they were dismissed.

The following day the sad family of General Garfield returned in gloom to their home in Mentor; there, secluded from the public gaze, to weep with each other, — a precious privilege to lovers of quiet like them, who had been in the focus of the world's gaze for so many terrible weeks.

> "Farewell: the leaf-strown earth enfolds
> Our stay, our pride, our hopes, our fears,
> And autumn's golden sun beholds
> A nation bowed, a world in tears."

CHAPTER XXI.

CHESTER ALAN ARTHUR.

In 1818 a French writer, named Blanché, wrote an article about the government of the United States which was largely copied at the time, to the great annoyance of the French government, and in which he very pointedly and perhaps unjustly said : " In France every man holds himself in readiness to be a slave ; in the United States every man holds himself in readiness to be the President of the nation."

At the time that article was being read for the first time by the people a young lad eighteen or nineteen years of age, named William Arthur, was slowly crossing the Atlantic Ocean in one of the lumbering and uncomfortable packets which plied between the north coast of Ireland and the Canadian ports. He was a descendant of Scotch-English settlers in Ballymena, County of Antrim, Ireland, and had secured through the sacrifices of parents, the kindness of friends, and his own natural perseverance, an unusually practical education, having graduated at the Belfast University. The condition of Ireland during his boyhood had been such as to awaken a spirit of discontent, and the sad losses which the family endured in that terrible civil war of 1798 left many mourners and much financial distress. The tales of successful business enterprises in America, and the encouragement of the English government, induced this youth to seek his fortune in Canada. He was almost penniless and friendless when he landed in America, and penetrated into the woods of Eastern Canada. How utterly unlike the history of royal families with all their vicissitudes, and how illustrative of the French writer's thought is the history of this young man's life ? Unknown, unnoticed, and without political hope or ambition, he makes his home among the rough and hardy backwoodsmen of Upper Mills, Canada, not far from the Vermont line, seemingly a young man the least likely by birth, education, or location, to be the father of a President of the neighboring nation. By nature independent, and by culture a lover of freedom, he followed a course of life so certain to be unpopular, and so separated from political ambitions as to greatly increase the improbability of his being the parent of a political leader. He taught school, he worked with his hands, he was outspoken in his opinions, and soon after his settlement became a dissenter in religion, and adopted the faith of the lowly and often-despised Baptists. After much opposition and an elopement, he married an unusually talented lady, Melvina Stone, who was the daughter of a Methodist preacher. When he entered upon the self-sacrificing profession of a Baptist minister he abandoned the hope of being the companion of the rich, every prospect of political and social preferment, and every probability of either fame or wealth. Yet how great is the number of the successful and great men of America who owe their elevation into political distinction, or into endless fame, wholly to their noble self-sacrificing fidelity to duty in situations where, as far as human eye could see, the path led to oblivion or execration.

William Arthur was neither a great preacher nor a great man, estimated by the standard of the world's great characters, but he was sincere and faithful. Through fifty years of religious labor he worked unflaggingly on for the welfare of others, and too unmindful of his own. A friend to the sorrowing, a companion of the poor, a devoted patriot, and a firm but tender parent, he achieved no remarkable successes and attained no very prominent position as an orator, writer, or theologian.

All his early life was spent on the border of the United States and Canada in most devoted and arduous missionary work.

In 1828 Mr. Arthur was installed as pastor of a small Baptist church, which worshiped in an old barn at Fairfield, Vermont, to which place he removed from Dunham Flats, Canada East. His salary was but $330 per annum, and he was obliged to work in the shop or fields a part of the time in order to defray his expenses. But such work preserved his health both in body and mind, secured to him a long life, and insured to his audience vigorous, practical, common-sense preaching. He was fortunate enough to secure a very comfortable log-cabin with one large room, two small rooms, a porch for a summer-kitchen, and a commodious garret. All the furniture was of rude construction, and consisted of the barest necessities for housekeeping, and many articles were the products of Mr. Arthur's own skill and invention. With a slab for a book-shelf, an old rocker for his easy-chair, the kitchen for his study, and the Bible and two or three " Commentaries from the pen of Antrim's chiefest scholar," for a library, this theologian and student wrought most effective work. The town of Fairfield was then a small village, with one or two country stores and a mill.

In that secluded quarter of the land, just within the sacred precincts of the United States, in a log cabin, and in a rude but happy home, Chester Alan Arthur was born October 5, 1830.

He was the first-born son. But it was an event unknown beyond the gossiping circle of the little hamlet; and even there it was mentioned only as a heavy addition to the poor preacher's heavy burdens. But the same joy that other mothers feel at the birth of their first son, and the same pride which other fathers take in their infant sons, were felt by his parents. It was an experience felt by some parent on our earth again and again, even as often as the beats of a human heart, and could not be regarded as anything unusual or remarkable. Usually with the birth of men who afterwards become noted, there springs up some superstitious story, tradition, or incident, which is believed to have foreshadowed the greatness of the coming man. But in this event not even the aged fortune-tellers seemed interested.

Being a minister's son, and in a New England town, it was a matter of course that he should receive considerable attention from the ladies of the parish, and that he should be flattered and coddled a little more than falls to the lot of other infants. But that was rather to his disadvantage than otherwise.

When the child was one year old, Mr. Arthur moved away to Hinesburg, or to Williston, and for twenty years following was the pastor of many different churches, and made his home in many different places. He was settled as a pastor during those years at Bennington, Hinesburg, North Fairfield, Williston, in Vermont, and at York, Perry, Schenectady, Greenwich, Lansingburg, in New York State ; and after his long pastorate in the Calvary Baptist Church of New York city, he was stationed at Hoosic, West Troy, and Newtonville, in the State of New York. Rev. William Arthur died at Newtonville, N. Y., October 27, 1875.

By most creditable industry and close economy, he accumulated a large library and secured a permanent position among the literary men of his time. He took especial delight in history and biography. He found a pleasant task in unraveling the mysteries which surround the origin and growth of family names, and for twenty years collected facts relating to that subject. At last his material was so varied and important, that he published a book on that subject, to the great satisfaction of all lovers of antiquarian lore. He wrote many articles for the newspapers and magazines of the country, and a large number of his sermons were printed in pamphlet form. He was honored with the degree of " Doctor of Divinity," and was most sincerely and widely mourned at his death.

The boyhood of Chester **Alan** Arthur was spent in attending school in the rude school-houses of that time, in studying with his father at home, and in a great variety of labor. His father being poor, with a family of five for whom to provide, — three girls and two sons, — every child had to bear his share of the household work and earn his share of the income. His mother and his sisters were the most diligent among American women, and to them as much as to his father the young man owed his gratitude for opportunities and encouragement to secure the luxury of a liberal education.

The culture and information which he gained in the conversation and habits of his home were of untold benefit to the boy, who insensibly grew wiser day by day, listening to his father's conversation at meal-time or in the evening, by their log-fire.

When we find him at the age of ten years, 1840, entering at Greenwich, N. Y., upon the difficult studies which shall fit him for college, and wonder that the grammar school at Schenectady, where he is found a year later, furnishes among its many older heads no brighter mind than that of Chester Alan Arthur, we can easily account for it by estimating the power and value of constant association at home with cultivated and interesting people. It saves a child years of school study, and secures a permanent interest in the higher fields of mental culture, if the father selects with care and pleasure those topics of conversation which draw the attention of the family circle to higher and purer things. The home is everywhere a school of immeasurable importance, but to young Arthur it was of unusual potency. He found no teacher more earnest or capable than his father, and with such a parentage he had the advantage of many other boys.

When he was fifteen years of age he entered Union College, Schenectady, and, although so young, was able to compete with the oldest and best, and graduated with more than the average honors, in 1848.

In his college course he was not only very youthful but he was very poor. His father could not, on a salary of $500 per annum, support so large a family and pay the school expenses of so many children. They were all obliged to help themselves, and in that found the most valuable experience of their lives. Chester was obliged to spend a portion of his college years in teaching school in country towns, and while instructing others during the day, to keep up his college studies during the evenings. As the system of compelling the teacher to board a day or two in turn at every scholar's home was then a custom in the country, Chester discovered many uncomfortable boarding-places, and often found his studies wholly interrupted.

During the political campaign preceding the election of 1880, James S. Brisbin published in a sketch of the candidate's life a letter written by Chester in 1846, which gives an instructive and amusing glance at his occupation at that time, when he engaged in teaching at fifteen dollars per month in the most rural of rural districts. He said: —

" The committee-man soon arrived to transfer me to the scene of my future labors. The committee was a puny man, and, as afterward appeared, everything had been spared in his mechanism, ethically as well as corporeally. His principal features were his boots, which, like all Yankees, were blacked only on the frontispiece, he not wishing to invest anything where he could not see the benefit. He had tremendous lurid soles, probably to keep up the equilibrium between his moral and physical system. Just imagine a young man, with hope and expectation beaming on his countenance, with an unruffled mien, in a yellow wagon striped with green, like all down-East vehicles.

" Before me and attached to the concern was a vertebrated quadruped, an amalgamated specimen of comparative anatomy and animal manikinism. From its size it seemed to have been bought by weight, and from its condition its present owner must have had charge of it before the sale, with an eye to its purchase. It seemed to have lived in carnivorous times, for all its flesh had departed and each moment, as it passed, had taken a hair as a memento. But now these mementos were gone, and the wind could only moan a piece to its mane.

"However, under all these circumstances, we at last arrived at an old fabrication on one side of the road, called a house, the only claim to the title being the presence of an immense chimney.

" The animal portion of our establishment had come to a stand-still, and it seemed to be conclusive that this was our destination.

" We entered the domicile. Everything was fixed up, the old trunk was placed in the best room, and the process of getting acquainted commenced. This is very simple; for two little 'quids' climb up on your knee, ask for your knife, and offer to 'swop' at once on terms very disadvantageous to you, as they think you are green. To convince you that there is no gammon, they test the temper of their blades upon all that connects your buttons with your garments. The head of the family talking at the same time, I was convinced that there were some words in the English language that they did not know, and many out of that I did not understand.

" At tea the character of the family was reviewed, and the biographies of individuals were related in the most plain and unequivocal terms.

"The mater-familias had a tongue as glib as a great ant-eater, and it was used to the particular detriment of her neighbors and to the praise of her own domestic arrangements, which certainly needed all.

"I am not an epicure, and if I had been, the peculiar arrangements of the college clubs would have eliminated all such superfluous proclivities. The daily mode of living at the committee's was the antipodes of epicurianism. In my opinion, the diet of the Grahamites was as much superior to it as the feasts of the gods were to the daily meals of the lazarone, Lazarus. It caused me to think how the frugal fare of Zeno, the stoic, would have appeared under the domestic arrangement of the harpies; for their distinct dietetical system was founded more in accordance with the price of corn and the requirements of the law in respect to a peck of dirt than the physical condition of the partakers.

" My examination for a teacher's certificate took place on the night of my arrival, and it was highly interesting to witness the feats of erudition, before unheard of since the dark ages. For they, being untrammeled by most of the customary forms of language, were in a good situation to excite the wonderment of one so unsophisticated.

" On the morrow the hour for commencing the literary instruction came, and with it the scholars. The school-house was an old red fabric, situated at the cross-roads. Just behind could be seen a few birches, — a grove in which the shrine of education is often placed, — and the numberless broken boughs showed that the worship depended very much upon the nature of the surrounding scenery. It was an old building, and had occupied the same position in the community for many years. It had sent forth many enterprising young men as vendors of the multifarious modifications of time, and as itinerant physicians for the vagaries of lunatic time-pieces. It had given a turn to many a youngster's life that had gone with him to the end. Spelling-schools numberless had taken place within its walls; hearts had been lost and won; innumerable 'swoppings' had been transacted; the aromatic bark of the birches had wasted its sweetness on the obdurate back of the inveterate rogue. In the plastering above were the remains of the blank leaves of many books, having been reduced to a pulpy state by a process well known to idle urchins, and then projected with unerring aim to their destined location. Here the weary pedagogue had spent his energies, and counted the dragging hours in pouring knowledge through youthful heads, wondering why the alphabet was not innate as a matter of convenience.

" However, my school commenced. It was composed of motley races of brats. There were nearly all the goddesses, all the saints, and as many of the wise men of antiquity nominally present. There was an African damsel, a score of aspirants for alphabetical mastery, and many a specimen of the Yankee swop-jack-kniver.

" The most prominent object was the oldest boy in school descanting upon the merits of some wooden combs, and endeavoring to negotiate a sale with some small boys. I should be happy to give the experience of the school-room if time and space would permit. There was but one battle, — a strong farmer's boy endeavored to overthrow your humble servant and his authority at the same time; but, thanks to agility and gymnastic practice, there was a triumph for the teacher.

" Beware of trusting to the statistical calculation of committee-

38

men in respect to the number of the scholars, for they are as fallacious as the idea of getting your pay. And when you have over forty youngsters learning the rudiments of an education, do not delude yourself by complying with the direction to hear them four times a day."

After graduating as one of the six best scholars in his class he determined to enter at once upon his studies for the legal profession. The nearest law school was then at Ballston Springs, N. Y., and with some assistance from his father he began his studies at that place. He was obliged, however, again to teach school in order to pay his way at the law school, and in 1849 secured a position in North Pownal, Vermont, as principal of an academy. In 1850 James A. Garfield taught school in the same town.

The salary of young Arthur was then forty-five dollars per month, and with a small additional sum for the private tutorship of private students fitting for college, he was able to pay his way at Ballston Springs, and lay aside a small sum each year for future use. He was naturally economical and careful, and his experience had shown the value of that trait of his character. Few young men would, and perhaps few could, save money under his circumstances, even with the same income.

In 1851 he went to New York, where he obtained permission to enter the office of Hon. E. D. Culver, as a law student. Mr. Culver had been an influential member of Congress from Washington County, N. Y., and had boldly and persistently opposed the extension of slavery. He was an active participant in all the antislavery organizations of New York, and wholly fearless in his denunciations of the crime of human slavery. His feelings and principles were most congenial to young Arthur, and the student soon outstripped his tutor in both zeal and ability, as the defender of the black bondmen. During the two years which he passed in Mr. Culver's office as a student, he took an active part in the political meetings of the Whigs, often managing to throw into the discussions or resolutions some explosive bomb in the shape of a word or thought against slavery.

So close was his application to study, so clear the opinions he expressed upon intricate questions of law, and so frank and manly his demeanor, that before the two years had passed which were necessary to his admission to the bar, Mr. Culver proposed to take him into partnership, and intrusted him with some very difficult and important cases.

At the time when he was admitted to the bar, 1852, he was much interested in a case, now known as the "Lemmon Slave Case," which Mr. Culver had conducted before Judge Paine in New York. Jonathan Lemmon and his wife, from Virginia, arrived in New York with eight colored slaves, and there awaited the departure of a ship for Texas, to which State they were emigrating. A free colored man of New York becoming acquainted with some of the slaves, appeared for them in court, and sued out a writ of *habeas corpus*. Mr. Culver, being well known as an antislavery man, was engaged as counsel for the slaves. Somewhat to the surprise of their own counsel and against the predilections of the judge, they did find themselves so favored by the laws of New York, that they were declared to be free. The rejoicing of the liberated slaves and the excitement of the colored people were genuine and extravagant. The whole nation discussed the case, and the indignant slaveholders of Virginia compelled their state authorities to take an appeal from the decision of Judge Paine. They employed Charles O'Conor, one of the ablest attorneys in the nation, and expected to reverse the decision secured by Mr. Culver. At this time a partnership had been formed under the style of Culver, Partsen, and Arthur, and as Mr. Culver was called to attend to other important matters, the case of the Lemmon slaves was given to Mr. Arthur. He associated with himself William M. Evarts, and the two young men undertook to maintain the cause of the oppressed against public opinion, against precedent, and against Charles O'Conor and Henry L. Clinton. With the eyes of the entire nation upon them, watching every motion, and while condemnation and applause were both profusely bestowed, they fought the slaveholders, through the Supreme Court of the State, and obtaining a victory there, continued the battle in the Supreme Court of the United States. Victory perched upon their banners everywhere. The slaves were not fugitives. Their master had brought them into a free State. The slaves were free. New York was in truth a free State.

The decision awakened the spirit of the Abolitionist party and made the formation of the great Republican party a possibility. It was one of the most important initiatory events in the history of the emancipation of the slaves in the Southern States. In the case, the legislatures of New York and Virginia had by the official employment of counsel taken antagonistic positions. The Northern States were established by it, in their claim to be free States. The States of the South regarded it as a blow aimed at their wealth and rights as citizens of the same nation, and some of them resolved that as the courts "had failed to do righteous judgment and deliberately ignored the Constitution and the law of 1850, the only remaining recourse is to civil war."

It also established Mr. Arthur's reputation as an attorney, and brought to him nearly all the legal business which the colored population of New York had to transact.

But some matters relating to the partnership business being unsatisfactory to Mr. Arthur, who now wished to enter a wider sphere of practice, he withdrew from the partnership with Messrs. Culver and Partsen, and thought of moving into some Western State. With this object in view he formed a partnership with Henry D. Gardner, one of his former room-mates, and they traveled for several months in the West in search of a suitable location for legal practice. They did not find one, and returned to New York, where they began a legal business as the firm of Arthur and Gardner.

In 1855 colored people were not allowed on the street cars of New York. On the Sixth Avenue and one or two other lines, conveyances labeled, "Colored persons allowed in this car," were run at long intervals, but on the Fourth Avenue and other east-side lines not even this provision was made. Under these circumstances Lizzie Jennings, a respectable colored woman, neatly dressed, cleanly and of good appearance, the superintendent of a colored Sunday-school, hailed a Fourth Avenue car and succeeded in obtaining a seat in it. The conductor took her fare, thereby tacitly admitting her right to be a passenger; but hardly had he done so when a drunken white ruffian, who was seated in the car, demanded, "Are you going to let that —— nigger ride in this car?"

"Oh, I guess it won't make any difference," said the conductor.

"Yes, but it will," replied the other; "I have paid my fare and I want a decent ride, and I tell you you 've got to put her out."

Thus appealed to the conductor went to the colored woman and asked her to leave the car. She refused to do so. The car was stopped. The conductor attempted to eject her by force. She resisted bravely, crying all the time, "I have paid my fare and I am entitled to ride."

Her dress was almost torn from her back. Strong men stood by but gave her no assistance. Still she fought bravely for what she believed to be her right. The conductor could not eject her, and was compelled to call for the aid of the police. By their efforts the woman was dragged from the car.

The matter coming to the notice of a number of influential colored people they desired to make it a test case, and applied to Mr. Arthur for advice. He at once espoused their cause and took their case before Justice Rockwell in Brooklyn. When the trial came on, the court room was crowded almost to suffocation; and at one time serious trouble was threatened by those who believed that to seek justice for one of the black race was to do injustice to humanity.

Even the judge seemed to share this opinion, for when the attorney handed him the papers in the case he threw them upon the desk, with the exclamation, —

"Pshaw! do you ask me to try a case against a corporation for the tort [the wrongful act] of its agent?"

In reply to this Mr. Arthur plainly pointed out a portion of the Revised Statutes under which there was an undoubted right of action. After examining it the court concurred cordially with the counsel; the case was tried, and, much to the delight of the colored people, a verdict of $500 was rendered in favor of the plaintiff. The railroad company paid the judgment without further contest, and at once issued orders that thereafter colored people be allowed to ride upon its cars. Similar action was soon after taken by all the city railroad companies. At this there was great rejoicing among all the negroes in New York; the Colored People's Legal Rights Association was established, and for many years afterwards with much ceremony celebrated the anniversary of the trial.

Mr. Arthur was at that time a genial, social young man, loving lively companionship, and a frequenter of social and literary clubs. He took an active interest in militia organizations, and held an office in a New York regiment for several years. But his strongest inclinations were toward political assemblies and political discussions. From early boyhood he had exhibited a precocious interest in national affairs, and followed with eager interest all the details of the antislavery agitation, the Mexican war, the Know-Nothing movement, the Kansas war, and the Free-Soilers' conventions. In the Presidential campaigns which occurred during his youthful days, especially those of 1840, 1844, 1848, and 1852, he was an enthusiastic witness of the unfurling of flags and the mass meetings, and took part as a torch-bearer or color-bearer with the keenest zest. When the Abolition Convention was held at Buffalo in 1852, on the call of James G. Birney, Gerrit Smith, and William Goodell, and nominated the latter as a candidate for President, it was regarded as a fit topic for joking, and the fact that the ticket obtained but seventy-two votes in the entire State shows the insignificance of the movement. But Mr. Arthur is said to have sharply rebuked a friend who ridiculed it, and remarked that we should hear from that party again. In 1856, when the Republican party was so suddenly formed out of the Whig, Free-Soil, Abolition, and Know-Nothing parties, Mr. Arthur was a delegate to the first State Convention, which was held at Saratoga, New York. He was one of the signers, with William M. Evarts and Moses H. Grinnell, of a call for the formation of a Republican Club in New York city. At that time it was not thought by any political leader that the Republican party could secure the vote of a single State. It being right in principle was all he cared to know about it. He was never ambitious to hold an office, and simply followed his natural inclination and did what he could to secure the passage of such political measures as he considered wisest for his State and nation.

In 1860 Mr. Arthur was judge advocate of the Second Brigade of New York militia; and when Hon. E. D. Morgan was elected governor in 1861, he was appointed to the office of engineer-in-chief on the governor's staff. January 27, 1862, Governor Morgan promoted him to the very important office of quartermaster-general, from which time he was known as "General Arthur."

His management of the office of quartermaster-general during the entire term of Governor Morgan's administration was a most remarkable exhibition of practical business ability by a professional man. The contracts for immense quantities of provisions, clothing, arms, ammunition, transportation, and storage, were such as to require millions of money, and most hastily drawn agreements, yet with scarce a mistake, and with such remarkable economy that his accounts at Washington were allowed without dispute in regard to a single item or article. He conducted easily and without flurry the entire business of equipping and feeding the troops of New York. He seems to have been so absorbed in his work for the nation as to be forgetful of himself, and although he had handled such large sums, he found that the increase in his personal expense had been such, that he had grown poorer every day of his public service. Presents were frequently offered him by interested parties, but all gifts were firmly rejected.

His success in arming and provisioning troops was such as to induce the loyal governors of the nation, at their secret meeting at New York, in July, 1862, to call him in as a counselor, an honor extended to no other man. General Arthur served for a time on the staff of Major-General Hunt in the Army of the Potomac as inspector.

At the close of Governor Morgan's term he retired from public life and entered again upon the practice of law. His business, however, took a different course from his previous work, and he devoted himself entirely to suits and claims against the Government and State, and to the preparation of important bills for legislative action. Thus, without holding any public office, and seeking none, his profession led him into constant contact with the public men of the nation and made his professional life for ten years public and prominent.

Mrs. Ella L. Arthur, to whom he was married in 1853, and who died January 12, 1880, was a most excellent example of all that is sweetest and best in the life of American women. She was the daughter of Lieutenant-Commander Herndon, of the United States navy, who was a distinguished officer in the national service, and who died in 1857, at his post on the deck of the Central America, preferring death to the abandonment of his passengers when his ship sank. He was at the time commanding the vessel by permission of the government, and was employed by the Law-Roberts line of California steamers plying between New York and Chagres, Central America. His bravery was made the subject of a special resolution by Congress, a medal was struck at the mint, and a monument at Annapolis erected by the government to his memory. Mrs. Arthur was the mother of two children, a son and a daughter.

In 1871 Hon. Thomas Murphy, who was a firm friend of General Arthur, and who owed his election to the state Senate and perhaps his appointment by General Grant to the active efforts of General Arthur, resigned the office of collector of the port of New York. President Grant then appointed General Arthur to the vacant position. He held the office four years and was reappointed by President Grant for four years more. But in 1878 President Hayes became dissatisfied with the management of the custom house, which under General Arthur's direction seemed to be wielding a great influence on the politics of the State, and after an investigation which disclosed nothing dishonest beyond an inclination to serve his party while making the service efficient and correct, the President removed him during a vacation of Congress. A petition for his retention was signed by every judge of every court in the city, by all the prominent members of the bar, and by nearly every important merchant in the collection district, but this General Arthur himself suppressed.

On his retirement from the custom house, he returned to the practice of law in the firm of Arthur, Phelps, Knevals, and Ransom. But his interest in political questions and his friendship for Senator Conkling and other State and national officials precluded his retirement from active work, and in 1880 he was elected a delegate to the Republican National Convention, which was held in June of that year at Chicago, and which nominated General Garfield for President.

He was selected as a delegate both on account of his personal prominence, and because of his known friendship for General Grant, whose name was prominently before the country as a candidate for a third term in the presidency. General Arthur was also a close and confidential friend of Senator Conkling, who was the acknowledged leader in the movement to nominate General Grant.

The story of the election of delegates throughout the country and the scenes at the convention is one of the most exciting tales of our political history, and has been mentioned in the account of General Garfield's life found in the preceding pages.

So deeply absorbed were the delegates in securing the nomination of their favorites for the first place on the ticket that there was scarce a mention of the second place. The friends of Hon. James G. Blaine and Hon. John Sherman contended against each other, and all against the friends of General Grant, and anxious days and sleepless nights were spent before the convention, and during its session, to win the victory.

But when General Garfield was nominated by the combination of the Blaine and the Sherman forces, while the friends of General

Grant stood firm through all, it was apparent that some compromise must be effected to secure the votes of the Grant men, and thus unite the whole party, or defeat was certain at the polls. The whole convention felt this; and until General Stewart L. Woodford of New York cast his vote for General Arthur for Vice-President, no way out of the dilemma had seemed to suggest itself. But on the suggestion of a name of one who was known to be so close a friend of General Grant and Senator Conkling, the convention, almost with one accord, voted for his nomination. It was done so soon and so unexpectedly that General Arthur could hardly realize the marvelous turn which affairs had taken until long afterward. He could feel the force of Byron's line, " I awoke one morning and found myself famous."

The election resulted in the triumphant choice of Garfield and Arthur, and in March General Arthur took his seat as the presiding officer of the United States Senate, where he won the respect of all the members by his impartiality and courtesy.

But when the quarrel between Senator Conkling and President Garfield disturbed the Senate and the country, General Arthur displayed his friendship for the Senator in an open and vigorous espousal of his cause. It was a contest over political appointments, and reflected no credit on any of the parties concerned in it. It disturbed the business of the country, created many animosities, and gave courage to murderous fanaticism. Senator Conkling's resignation and canvass for reëlection were approved by the Vice-President, and the senator's candidacy before the New York Senate was advocated by the words and personal presence of General Arthur in Albany. Just as the candidacy of Senator Conkling was drawing to a disastrous end, and when the bitterness of political strife was increased by the sense of failure, the bullet of the assassin at Washington called off the combatants to weep at his sickness and grieve at his death.

During the eighty anxious days which the President lived after his assassination, the Vice-President, with sincere grief and most creditable modesty, remained away from the public gaze, and, although entitled legally to the office of President, because of General Garfield's inability to administer the office, refused to do the least act which would disturb or endanger the President's life. His bearing during those days of trial gained him the sympathy and respect of the entire nation.

At his private house in New York, on the morning of the 20th of September, and on the receipt of the news of President Garfield's death, at about three o'clock A. M., General Arthur was sworn by Judge Brady, and with emotion choking his utterance, assumed the great office of President of the United States.

RESIDENCE OF CHESTER A. ARTHUR, 23 LEXINGTON AVENUE, NEW YORK.

CHAPTER XXII.

ONE HUNDRED YEARS' PROGRESS.

A GENTLEMAN connected with the United States government was dining, in London, with a large party of distinguished Englishmen. Some one inquired of him, "How many States are there in the American Union ? "

He calmly replied, " I do not know." There was a pause. Surprise was manifested that he should not be informed upon so vital a point. At length an explanation was called for. He very calmly said, —

"When I left New York for a tour up the Nile, six months ago, there were thirty-four States in the Union. How many have since been added I cannot tell."

Indeed, it is very difficult for any one to bear in mind the number of States over which the stars and stripes now float. It is like remembering the sum of asteroids in our planetary system when a new one is discovered every few months.

Upon the establishment of this government, as an independent power among the nations, there were but thirteen States in the confederacy. Now we count thirty-eight States and ten Territories.

The territory embraced in the thirteen original States covered an area of eight hundred and twenty thousand six hundred and eighty square miles. We have made such vast accessions that, at the present time, the area belonging to the nation embraces three million five hundred and fifty-nine thousand and ninety-one square miles. We have increased fourfold.

The first census was taken in 1790. There were then three million nine hundred and twenty-nine thousand three hundred and twenty-eight inhabitants. Of these six hundred and ninety-seven thousand six hundred and ninety-six were slaves.[1]

At the last census the population numbered fifty million one hundred and fifty-two thousand eight hundred and fifty-six. Not a slave now treads our soil. By an amendment of the Constitution, it has been declared that the right of suffrage shall not be withheld from any citizen of the United States " on account of race, color, or previous condition of servitude."

Our government has passed through as severe an ordeal as it is possible for any nation to be subjected to, and has emerged from it triumphantly. It is not too much to say, that, at the present moment, we have the strongest government on this globe, — a government which gives promise of perpetuity above any other. There is not a throne in Europe which is not menaced with perils far beyond any which we contemplate.

A century ago there were but a few insignificant towns scattered along the coast from Maine to Georgia. Maine was almost an unbroken solitude, with but here and there a hamlet upon her rugged shores. Savages roamed through all the interior of New York. Pittsburgh was but a military post. The largest part of Virginia was an unexplored wilderness, mostly covered with a dense and gloomy forest. It required the laborious journey of twelve days to pass from Baltimore to Pittsburgh. Michigan was deemed a barren waste, utterly worthless. As to the regions beyond the Mississippi, even the imaginations of men had hardly traveled so far.

The great Northwest, now the abode of refinement and culture, and waving with the richest harvests, was then unexplored. St. Louis was a frontier settlement scarcely known. As late as 1803 it was written, —

" The Missouri has been navigated for twenty-five hundred miles. There appears a probability of a communication by this channel with the western ocean."

The planters of Virginia were feudal lords, trampling upon the rights of the industrial classes, who were kept in stolid ignorance. In 1671 Governor Berkeley boasted that Virginia had neither " printing-presses, colleges, nor schools." The land was held by a few

---

[1] *Encyclopædia Americana,* article "United States." Mr. Bancroft estimates that there were less than three millions of inhabitants when the Declaration of Independence was proclaimed.

proprietors. The estate of Lord Fairfax embraced five million acres.

CARPENTERS' HALL.

And yet Virginia, to whom we are indebted for both Washington and Jefferson, coöperated in perfect union with Massachusetts, in resisting the tyranny of the British crown.

At the beginning of the Revolution, the Colonies possessed few public edifices noted for architectural grandeur, or which would bear comparison in historic interest with the famed palaces and castles of the Old World; yet some of the plain structures of those days were hallowed by scenes the memory of which will be cherished as long as the love of freedom lives in the heart of man. Prominent among these honored memorials of the past is Carpenters' Hall in Philadelphia, where assembled the First Continental Congress, and whose walls echoed to the fiery eloquence of Patrick Henry and John Adams. This relic of the past is still preserved with reverential care, and contains interesting mementos of Revolutionary days, which may be seen by visitors.

INDEPENDENCE HALL.

Still more famous is Independence Hall, where the Second Continental Congress held its sittings, where the delegates of the United Colonies discussed the great question upon which hung the destinies of America, and from whose steps was read the Declaration of Independence. The furniture is the same as that used by Congress, portraits of the country's heroes crowd the walls, and relics of our early history are

LIBERTY BELL.

everywhere. In Congress Hall, in the second story, Washington delivered his farewell address. From the steeple a fine panoramic view of the whole city can be had. This hall still attracts the footsteps of pilgrims to the shrines of liberty; and the old bell which rung out a joyful and defiant peal on the 4th of July, 1776, now cracked and useless, but with its grand prophetic motto still intact, finds an honored resting-place within its walls.

While the citizens of Philadelphia proudly cherish Independence Hall, Bostonians look with equal pride upon Faneuil Hall. Hither the citizens of the old Puritan town involuntarily turn their steps in times of national peril; and from its platform go patriotic utterances which stir the heart of the Commonwealth, and find a response in distant States. Here Webster and Everett and Phillips and Sumner held the attention of the critical audiences of the modern Athens, and swayed the multitude at will.

Now stately buildings devoted to religion, to art, and to educa-

FANEUIL HALL.

tion, are rising all over the land; while State vies with State, and city with city, in adorning the edifices devoted to governmental use.

In 1776 we had no navy, no national banner. On the 14th of November of that year, Paul Jones raised our first naval flag, under a salute of thirteen guns. This flag, which consisted of thirteen stripes and a pine-tree with a rattlesnake coiled at the roots, was unfurled at the mast-head of the frigate Alfred, of forty-four guns, lying at anchor off Chestnut Street Wharf in Philadelphia.

> "'T was Jones, Paul Jones, who first o'er Delaware's tide,
> From Alfred's main displayed Columbia's pride;
> The stripes of freedom proudly waved on high,
> While shouts of freedom rang for liberty."

England then had a fleet of a thousand sails. With five small vessels, carrying in all but one hundred guns, we entered upon a naval conflict with that gigantic power.

On the 14th of June, 1777, Congress established our present national flag, with its alternate stripes of red and white and its constellation of stars. It is the most beautiful flag ever unfurled to the breeze. In its folds are enshrined the dearest rights of humanity. Paul Jones was the first to spread that banner from the frigate Ranger.

Triumphantly he bore it across the Atlantic, through battle and through storm, and, with courage which could not have been exceeded, sent dismay through all the cities and towns which lined the British coast.

In February, 1778, France was the first nation to recognize the independence of the United States. On the 22d of February, 1778, the stars and stripes, borne aloft by Paul Jones, were for the first time honored with a national salute by the French fleet in Quiberon Bay.[1]

There is a beautiful lithograph, hanging upon many parlor-walls, which virtually exhibits the whole military power of the United States but about two hundred and fifty years ago. This army consisted of ten men. The lithograph is entitled, —

"THE MARCH OF MILES STANDISH."

"Just in the gray of the dawn, as the mists uprose from the meadows,
  There was a stir and a sound in the slumbering village of Plymouth;
  Clanging and clicking of arms, and the order imperative ' *Forward !* '
  Given in tone suppressed, a tramp of feet, and then silence.
  Figures ten, in the mist, marched slowly out of the village.
  Standish the stalwart it was, with eight of his valorous army,
  Led by their Indian guide, by Hobomok, friend of the white men,
  Northward marching to quell the sudden revolt of the savage." [2]

One hundred years ago the farmers of Lexington and Concord proved that the spirit of Miles Standish still pervaded the land; and the fields won by the fathers in toil and danger were handed down by the sons in title-deeds written in blood. The right of man to defend to the last extreme his life, liberty, and property, was there proclaimed by deeds not to be misunderstood; and the lesson has been slowly winning its way among the nations. To-day, Lex-

[1] *Life of Paul Jones.* Series of Pioneers and Patriots.
[2] Longfellow.

THE BATTLE OF LEXINGTON, APRIL 19, 1775.

ington and Concord are among the most inspiring watchwords of liberty.

Now let foreign invasion venture upon our shores, and our armies would not be numbered by thousands, or hundeds of thousands, but by millions.

It is not too much to say, that there is not another nation upon the globe so capable of repelling invasion as our own. Europe combined could not conquer these United States.

A hundred years ago, New York city had a population of about twenty thousand. Boston had fifteen or eighteen thousand. Philadelphia was what would now be considered an unimportant town of about twenty thousand inhabitants, clinging to the banks of the Delaware. Baltimore was a mere village. There were no large towns farther south.

A stage-coach ran from the Jersey side of the Hudson to Philadelphia in two days. It was ordinarily an eight days' voyage in a sloop from New York to Albany. From Boston to New York, it was a week's journey in the stage-coach.[1] In 1777 Congress met in Baltimore. John Adams, in his diary, gives an account of his fatiguing journey to that " far-away country." It took three weeks of horseback-riding.

A bolder deed was never performed on earth, than when, under these circumstances, fifty-one men met in Philadelphia, in July, 1776, and there, in the name of these thirteen feeble colonies, threw down the gage of battle to the empire of Great Britain, then the most powerful nation upon the globe. As we now contemplate the scene, it seems as though the chances were a hundred to one that the armies and fleets of Great Britain would, in a single campaign, crush out all opposition, and that every signer of the Declaration of Independence would swing upon the gallows.

In the year 1807 Robert Fulton ascended the Hudson in his newly-constructed steamboat, The Clermont, of a hundred and sixty tons' burden. We shall not here enter upon the vexed question of the origin of steamboats. It is sufficient to say, that then and there commenced the era of steamboat navigation in the United States. In 1811 the steamboat Orleans was launched at Pittsburgh, and descended to New Orleans in fourteen days. This was the first steamer which ever floated upon the waters of the Missis-

[1] "First Century of the Republic," *Harper's Magazine* for 1874, p. 874.

sippi. It would be difficult, at the present time, to count our floating palaces, and the thousands who crowd their gorgeous saloons. There is no other nation which can exhibit, in this respect, such a spectacle of prosperity, wealth, and refinement.

The first railway in the United States was constructed in Massachusetts, in the year 1826. It ran from Milton to Quincy, a distance of two miles. The cars were drawn by horses.

The first passenger railway was the Baltimore and Ohio, fifteen miles in length. It was opened in 1830. Its cars were drawn by horses for one year, and then a locomotive was placed upon the track.

The next line was from Albany to Schenectady, sixteen miles in length. This also was first run by horse-power, and then by steam. The number of miles of railroad in the United States is now to be counted by thousands. Every year they are increasing with wonderful rapidity. Our immense continent is embroidered with them. The iron horse, " whose sinews are steel, and whose provender is fire," rushes with undiminished speed, regardless of the Rocky Mountains, from the Atlantic to the Pacific shore.

The fastest time ever as yet made in America was in driving a train over the New York Central, from Rochester to Syracuse, eighty-one miles, in sixty-one minutes.[1] In view of the present condition of railroads, it is amusing to read the following statement in one of the English quarterly reviews of as late date as 1819 : —

" We are not partisans of the fantastic projects relative to established institutions ; and we cannot but laugh at an idea so impracticable as that of a road of iron, upon which one may be conducted by steam. Can anything be more utterly absurd, or more laughable, than a steam-propelled wagon, moving twice as fast as our mail-coaches ? It is much more possible to travel from Woolwich to the Arsenal by the aid of a Congreve rocket."

In the year 1794 Eli Whitney patented the cotton-engine, usually called by abbreviation the cotton-gin. Before that time, cotton was almost worthless in consequence of the difficulty of separating the seed from the fibre. In the cotton-boll there is but about one quarter of fibre. This great invention gave a new impulse to the industry, not only of our own country, but of the civilized world. The annual crop was then but about four thousand pounds. The census of 1859 reported a crop of two thousand million pounds.

[1] *Harper's Magazine*, vol. 1. p. 84.

It would be difficult to compute the number of factories which the cotton crop has reared throughout Christendom, or the hundreds of thousands of busy hands it has employed.

Before the invention of the cotton-gin, cotton was sold at forty cents a pound. It often required the labor of a day to separate one pound of the fibre from the seed.

In the year 1874 it is reported that there were nine million four hundred and fifteen thousand three hundred and eighty-three spindles employed in the United States, and five hundred and sixty-seven million five hundred and eighty-three thousand eight hundred and seventy-three pounds of cotton, were consumed. This made about thirteen and a half pounds for every man, woman, and child.[1]

Many can remember when they first saw a fire built of bituminous or anthracite coal. Little was it imagined, in the days of the Revolution, that beneath the majestic forests which covered the Lehigh Valley and the Mauch Chunk Mountain, mines of richness were stored, beyond all the fabled wealth of Ormuz or of Ind.

It was many years after the independence of our country was achieved, when a solitary hunter, drenched with the rain which was falling in torrents, was returning at night weary to his cabin. He struck his foot against a black stone. Its appearance was so peculiar that he picked it up and carried it to his hut.

An intelligent man happened to call there from Philadelphia. He took the stone to a laboratory. Its true character was ascertained. The mountain was explored, the mines opened; and now more millions of tons are annually consumed than can easily be computed. Coal has become the great motive-*power* of all our physical energies. It is impossible to form an adequate estimate of its value.

In 1776 there was no mode of signalling news, but by beacon-fires, or by arms of wood, swinging from elevated buildings. Abraham could send a letter to Lot on an Arabian charger as rapidly as could Washington, after the lapse of many thousand years, transmit a note from Mount Vernon to Jefferson at Monticello.

In the year 1832 Morse commenced his experiments in telegraphy. He informed the writer that his attention was first drawn to the subject by conversation at the dinner-table, on board a packet as he was crossing the Atlantic. His first patent was obtained in 1840. It was four years before he could inspire the community

[1] "The First Century of the Republic," *Harper's Magazine*, No. 299, p. 715.

with sufficient confidence in his plans to enable him to raise funds to construct a line from Washington to Baltimore.

Professor Morse of course availed himself of scientific discoveries previously made. It was through his own persistent genius that those discoveries were applied to purposes of practical utility. And now the electric telegraph is one of the necessities of the age. Information runs along the insulated wires more rapidly than the earth revolves upon its axis. All Christendom is braided with the electric lines. They rest ten thousand fathoms deep upon the bed of the Atlantic. In our morning papers we read the record of events which occurred the evening before in London and Paris.

In the year 1776 Priestley suggested that India-rubber was an excellent article " for removing pencil-marks from paper." That was all that it was supposed then to be good for. Charles Goodyear, with persistence against discouragements which places him in the front rank of this world's heroes, has made India-rubber one of the necessities of our civilization.

Among the wonderful discoveries of modern times, it is difficult to state what is the most wonderful. But nothing, perhaps, could be more incredible than the statement that a man could be placed in a placid sleep, and thus be subjected, without any conscious pain, to the most terrible surgical operation. The knife can cut through the quivering nerves, and the saw can sever the bones, while the patient sleeps in a dreamless slumber. In the year 1846 Drs. Morton and Jackson of Boston introduced those anæsthetics, now in common use, which have proved one of the greatest blessings ever conferred upon humanity. The amount of suffering they saved in our late civil war no imagination can gauge.

There are but few who can now remember the old-fashioned tinder-box, with its flint, steel, tinder of burnt linen, and splint dipped in brimstone. Lucifer matches are now used throughout the civilized world. They are made by machines which will cut thirty thousand in a minute, and are sold by the hogshead.[1]

A hundred years ago illuminating gas was unknown, save as the result of chemical experiments in the laboratory. It was not until the year 1825 that the streets of New York were lighted by gas. Boston had adopted the improvement three years before. And now it is hardly too much to say, that all our cities and large towns are

[1] *Harper's Magazine*, vol. 1. p. 391.

illumined by the flame of the jet of gas. The extinguishment of that flame would plunge a large portion of our republic into darkness.

The improvements in the printing-press almost surpass credence. The press used by Benjamin Franklin was a clumsy machine of lever power, laboriously worked by hand.

The web perfecting press of Hoe receives upon a cylinder a roll of paper four and a half miles in length. From this roll it cuts and prints on both sides from twelve to fifteen thousand sheets in an hour, amounting to the almost incredible number of more than two hundred a minute, or more than three each second. The machine is twenty feet long, six wide, and seven high. Mr. Hoe, the inventor, is an American. Three of the machines are used by leading printing-offices in London, and five are now in process of being built for offices in the United States, and two for Australia.

Another printing-machine, called the " Victory," will " damp, print, cut, fold, and deliver from six to eight thousand per hour of an eight-page newspaper of fifty inches square." [1]

Many can remember when they first saw a metallic pen. Scarcely the third of a century ago they were regarded as a great novelty, and were sold for fourteen cents each. The metallic pen has now become one of the necessary appliances of civilization ; and those of most perfect manufacture can be purchased at less than a dollar a gross.

In January, 1839, M. Daguerre announced to the world his great discovery. It is very unfair to rob a man of the merit of an invention or discovery, because he avails himself of the experiments of those who have preceded him. As early as 1776, chemists knew that fused chloride of silver is blackened by exposure to the sun's rays. For many years chemists were experimenting upon this subject, and ascertaining new facts.

We have not space even to name the numerous processes by which this most beautiful art is now made effectual. Every year progress is made, and the effects produced are more wonderful and perfect. It is said that the first daguerreotype from life was taken by Professor John W. Draper, of New York, in 1839. It was so announced in the London and Edinburgh Philosophical Magazine of March,

---

[1] " The First Century of the Republic." *Harper's Magazine*, No. 298, p. 534.

1840. Professor Draper also succeeded, in 1840, in obtaining a photograph of the moon.[1]

Almost all inventions are the result of progressive development, rather than of sudden inspiration. This is emphatically true of the sewing-machine. It is generally regarded as an American invention, with which the name of Elias Howe is indissolubly associated. Two thousand patents for sewing-machines have been granted in the United States.

The success of the sewing-machine is to be dated from about the year 1850. It is estimated that forty millions of capital are now employed in their manufacture. In the year 1873 six hundred thousand machines were made and sold. They are now found in almost every dwelling.

As to manufactures in general, there is no array of figures which can convey to the reader an adequate idea of their growth in our country within the last century.

In 1790 it was estimated that the annual value of the manufactures of the United States amounted to twenty million dollars. According to the last census, it is estimated that the value of the manufactures for 1870 amounted to the sum, above finite comprehension, of four thousand eight hundred and thirty-nine million dollars, involving an outlay of capital of two thousand one hundred and eighteen million, two hundred and eight thousand dollars.

Over two and a half million persons, of twenty years of age and upward, were employed in these manufactures. A little over five million were engaged in agriculture, and about one million in trade.[2]

Since the days when an electric current was first used to transmit telegraphic messages, great discoveries have been made in regard to currents of electricity. The speaking telephone combines in its properties a number of very interesting scientific facts. By this instrument the exact words, tone, and pitch of the human voice and all other sounds may be reproduced at a distance, so as to be perfectly understood. The essential principle is a small iron plate which vibrates with the sound, and these vibrations are conducted by an electric current, and reproduced at the other end of the line by means of another iron plate, which vibrates in the same way as the first, and thus speaks to the listening ear. In the talking pho-

---

[1] "First Century of the Republic." *Harper's Magazine*, No. 298, p. 540.
[2] "First Century of the Republic." *Harper's Magazine*, vol. l. p. 121.

AGRICULTURAL BUILDING.

nograph, the invention of Mr. Thomas A. Edison, the vibrations of the sound or voice are impressed on a permanent substance, such as a sheet of tinfoil, and can be reproduced at any time. This is a purely mechanical machine, as no use is made of electricity. One of the latest uses of electricity is for the production of permanent light. Investigations have been made for this purpose; and it has been discovered that the electric current can be divided, and a great number of lights produced by a current of electricity generated from a single source. The cost of maintaining the electric light is much less than that of gas.

It was decided to have an international exhibition in 1876 on a scale of grandeur which the world never before witnessed, in commemoration of the centennial anniversary of the birth of our republic. It was appropriately held in Philadelphia, where the republic was born and cradled.

There then were exhibited, on a scale of unprecedented magnitude, the resources of our own country, and its progress in those arts which elevate and ennoble humanity. Commissioners were appointed from each State and Territory to superintend the plan. The expense, which was estimated at first at ten million dollars, but afterward reduced to about seven million, was easily met; the State of Pennsylvania and city of Philadelphia alone contributing upwards of two and a half millions. All the governments of Europe, and some in Asia, and the other divisions of the world, were invited to coöperate in the celebration by sending commissioners with the richest display of their own manufactures. All products brought into the ports of the United States for this purpose were declared free of duty.

The exhibition continued for six months, from May to November, and every preparation was made for the comfort and convenience of visitors.

The buildings devoted to the exhibition were projected on a magnificent scale, as will be seen from the following description. First in size and importance was

THE MAIN EXHIBITION BUILDING.

This building was in the form of a parallelogram, extending east and west, 1,880 feet in length, and north and south 464 feet in width. The larger portion of the structure was one story in height, the main cornice upon the outside being 45 feet above the ground, and the interior being 70 feet. At the centre of the longer sides were projections 416 feet in length, and in the centre of the shorter sides of the building were projections 216 feet in length. The main entrances were provided with arcades upon the ground floor, and central façades, extending to the height of 90 feet. Upon the corners of the building there were four towers 75 feet in height; and between the towers and the central projections or entrances, a lower roof was introduced, showing a cornice 24 feet above the ground.

MAIN EXHIBITION BUILDING.

In order to obtain a central feature for the building as a whole, the roof over the central part, for 184 feet square, was raised above the surrounding portion, and four towers, 48 feet square, rising to 120 feet in height, were introduced at the corners of the elevated roof.

ART GALLERY.

This is located on a line parallel with and northward of the Main Exhibition Building, on the most commanding portion of the great Lansdowne plateau, and looks southward over the city. Like the Horticultural Building, it is intended that it shall remain in permanence as an ornament of Fairmount Park. The entire structure is in the modern Renaissance; and the materials are granite, glass, and iron. The structure is 365 feet in length, 210 feet in width, and 59 feet in height, over a spacious basement twelve feet in height, surmounted by a dome, the summit of which is 150 feet above the ground. All the galleries and central hall are lighted from the sides. The pavilions and central hall were designed especially for the exhibition of sculpture.

HORTICULTURAL BUILDING.

This is an extremely ornate and commodious building, and was designed to contain specimens of ornamental trees, shrubs, and flowers. It is located a short distance north of the Main Building and Art Gallery, and has a commanding view of the Schuylkill River and the northwestern portion of the city. The main conservatory, the angles of which are adorned with eight ornamental fountains, is 230 by 80 feet, and 55 feet high, surmounted by a lantern 170 feet long, 20 feet wide, and 14 feet high.

ART GALLERY.

AGRICULTURAL BUILDING.

This structure stood north of the Horticultural Building, and was composed of wood and glass. The nave was 820 feet in length by 125 feet in width, with a height of 75 feet from the floor to the point of the arch. The central transept was of the same height, with a breadth of 100 feet, and the two end transepts were 70 feet high and 80 feet wide.

MACHINERY BUILDING.

This structure was located at a distance of 550 feet from the west front of the Main Exhibition Building. The north front was upon the same line as that of the Main Exhibition Building, thus pre-

HORTICULTURAL BUILDING.

senting a frontage of 3,824 feet from the east to the west ends of the exhibition buildings, upon the principal avenue within the grounds. The entire area covered by the building was fourteen acres. It was lit entirely by side-lights, and stood lengthwise nearly east and west.

The following is a summary of the ground covered by the various buildings: Main Building, 21.47 acres; Art Gallery, 1.5 acres; Machinery Hall, 14 acres; Horticultural Hall, 1.5 acres; Agricultural Hall, 10.15 acres; total, 48.62 acres..

TABULATED REVIEW.

The wonderful growth of the United States since this century began cannot be understood or appreciated without great research and close thought. But a partially tabulated statement concerning some of the more important features of the nation's progress will assist the student of our history, and give an outline of our condition to the busy reader who cannot afford the time for a more detailed search.

The territory now occupied by the United States has all been purchased by the inhabitants from some European power, as follows: —

Date.	Acquisition.	Area square miles.	Cost.	Per acre.	From.
1776	13 States..............	421,000	$70,000,000	28 cents.	England.
1803	Louisiana..............	1,172,000	15,000,000	2 cents.	France.
1819	Florida................	60,000	5,000,000	12 cents.	Spain.
1829	Indian Territories.......	123,000	27,500,000	32 cents.	Indians.
1845	Texas.................	376,000	10,000,000	4 cents.	Mexico.
1846	Oregon	280,000	– –	–	England.
1848	California.............	546,000	15,000,000	4 cents.	Mexico.
1853	New Mexico...........	46,000	Acquired.	–	Mexico.
1867	Alaska................	580,000	7,500,000	2 cents.	Russia.
	Total................	3,604,000	$150,000,000		

The territory of the United States is now larger than the whole of Europe.

The population was in —

	White.	Colored.	Total.
1800	4,304,500	1,001,400	5,305,900
1880	43,402,408	6,577,497	50,152,866

Fourteen per cent. of the population are European emigrants, and the sexes are divided as follows, 102 males to every 100 females.

In the war with the Rebellion, 1861 to 1865, 581,000 men were destroyed. The Northern army contained 2,653,000 men, including 186,000 negroes, and the Southern army in 1864 had 549,000 men.

The Indians are steadily diminishing in numbers and soon will be extinct. In 1836 the Indians numbered 333,000, and in 1880 a little less than 300,000.

The United States has a coast line in length equal to half the circumference of the globe, there being 10,300 miles on the Atlantic coast, and 2,300 on the Pacific coast.

At present there are fifty cities of greater magnitude than Philadelphia was eighty years ago.

The criminal statistics show that the highest ratio of criminals to the population was in 1869, then the rate was nearly one to every 800 inhabitants. In 1880 it was nearly one to 1,290 inhabitants, a very marked decrease. Foreigners number only fourteen per cent. of the population, and yet furnish thirty-three per cent. of the criminals.

The agricultural increase of the nation has been enormous since the extension of railroads into the Western States and Territories. From 1875 to 1879, the sales of land by the government averaged 7,000,000 acres annually, and the sales have largely increased since that time. The land grants to railroads in the twenty years, from 1860 to 1880, have averaged about seventeen millions of acres a year. The aggregate of all the lands actually settled and reclaimed from the wilderness, from 1830 to 1880, exceeds in territory the whole of France, Spain, Portugal, and Great Britain. The area still left for settlement is more than twenty times as large as the territory of the British Islands. All of which will doubtless be taken up within twenty years.

The average production of grain is in excess of 58 bushels to every inhabitant of the country. The exportation of grain in 1880 was about 220,000,000 bushels. The grain harvested in 1879 was reported officially as follows: Wheat, 448,756,630 bushels; Indian corn, 1,547,901,790 bushels; oats, 363,761,320 bushels; potatoes, 181,626,400 bushels; hay, 35,493,000 tons; cotton, 2,367,540,900 pounds; tobacco, 391,278,350 pounds. The yearly average value of the crops per acre is about $14.50. The value of land has been greatly enhanced by the railroad competition, which enables a farmer to send his wheat from Chicago or St. Louis to New York or Boston, for eight cents per bushel, and land it in England for twelve cents per bushel.

The cotton fields cover an area as large as the territory of Prussia, and corn and wheat occupy a space equally as large. Great Britain takes about one third of the cotton crop (1880), and one third is manufactured at home. The remaining portion is sent to the European continent. Vineyards are extending rapidly on the Pacific Slope, and in the Mississippi Valley. There are 150,000 acres under vines. The vintage in 1879 was about 21,000,000 gallons.

In 1810 the exports of the United States were 1,000,000 barrels of flour, 90,000 casks of pork, 150,000 tons of cotton, and 120 barrels of rice, which is but the merest item compared with vast shipments now made. The value of the grain exported in 1879 was in excess of $200,000,000. The value of the live stock raised in 1879 was $1,775,000,000. The average number of cattle slaughtered per year, from 1875 to 1881, is nearly 8,000,000 head.

There are about 250,000 head sent yearly to England, having a value of $40,000,000.

The slaughter of hogs is 4,500,000 yearly, of which number one third are killed in Chicago. Sheep raising seems to be on the decline in the number of head, and on the increase in the quantity and value of the wool.

The largest sheep farm is among others nearly its equal, at Albuquerque, New Mexico, where there are 500,000 sheep, and the farm contains 30 square miles. The largest cattle farm is in Texas and contains 4,000,000 acres, and supports 2,225,000 cattle. The largest wheat farms are in California, where one farmer has 90,000 acres under cultivation, the average crop is 13 bushels per acre, which is an average less than one half that per acre of the small farms of Great Britain.

The farms of the United States, with the personal property used on them, are valued at $12,000,000,000. The sum paid yearly for farm wages is in excess of $400,000,000.

The United States at present produces 480,000 tons of butter, and 130,000 tons of cheese. The increase in the number of acres under cultivation is over 3,000,000 per year.

The shipping of the nation is in a sad state of decline, owing to bad legislation. From 1830 to 1860 the ship-building interests were very important, and averaged 40,000 tons annually. Now the foreign trade is nearly all done by foreign steamship lines. The American Marine in 1881 stands 16,830 sailing vessels, 4,717 steam vessels. On the Mississippi and its affluents there are 1,100 steamboats which carry 10,000,000 tons of freight every year.

The total exports of merchandise from June 30, 1879, to June 30, 1880, was $850,866,058. The total imports in that time of merchandise, was $667,954,746.

Until within twenty years nearly all the manufactories of the nation were in New England, and not until as late as 1876 did the manufactories make articles for export. The growth of manufacturing may be seen in the statement of the amount of capital invested at different periods. In 1850 there were $1,020,000,000 invested in mills, etc. In 1860 there were $1,890,000,000. In 1870, $4,230,000,000. In 1880, $5,500,000,000.

The average rate of wages among operatives old and young in the United States is about $455 per year.

The value of cotton goods manufactured in the United States is officially given as follows: Namely, 1831, $40,000,000, 1860, $115,000,000, and in 1877, $200,000,000.

Massachusetts manufactures more cotton goods than all the other States combined; large cities like Lawrence and Lowell have been wholly built up within thirty-five years by this industry.

The woolen manufactories, numbering 2,890, consume annually, 250,000,000 pounds of wool, and produce goods to the value of $180,000,000.

The value of silk goods manufactured in 1880 was $29,983,630.

There are 2,900 breweries in the country, producing annually 400,000,000 gallons of beer, and 3,000 distilleries producing 82,000,000 gallons of spirits. Adding the wine produced we show an enormous production of alcohol.

The manufacture of boots and shoes has grown from $30,000,000 in 1840, to $300,000,000 in 1875. Massachusetts alone makes 120,000,000 pairs of boots and shoes yearly.

The production of lumber in 1840 gave employment to 36,000 men, who manufactured timber worth $11,000,000. In 1879 the value of the lumber produced was $380,000,000. The average of timber felled daily is 24,000 acres.

In 1840 the production of coal was 2,000,000 tons, employing 7,000 miners. In 1879 55,000,000 tons were taken from the mines. The United States coal fields are seventy times as large as the coal fields of Great Britain.

In 1830 there were 29,000 operatives engaged in the iron trade, and the production did not exceed 184,000 tons, but in 1879 it was in excess of 3,070,000 tons. In 1873 it was over 5,500,000 tons.

The production of petroleum, which was discovered in 1859, now amounts to 8,000,000 gallons, with 400,000 gallons wasted daily for lack of storage. The value of the production is $40,000,000 a year.

In 1820 there were no canals, now there are over 4,000 miles.

In 1825 there were no railroads, now there are in use 86,497 miles, of which 4,721 miles were built in 1879.

In 1843 there were no telegraphs; in 1880 there were 200,000 miles in operation.

In 1875 there were no telephone lines; in 1881 there are nearly 80,000 miles of wire in use for that purpose.

In 1850 there were 2,526 newspapers and periodicals published in the United States. In 1881, 10,500 were published.

In 1831 only fifteen per cent. of the population, or about eighty-five per cent. of the school children, attended school; now the average attendance is nineteen per cent. of the population, being over ninety-five per cent. of the school children. The expense of the school system is over $80,000,000 per year.

In 1831 there were but fourteen colleges in the United States. In 1880 there were 364.

There are in the nation 2,851,000 white people and 2,789,689 colored persons who cannot read or write, of whom 777,873 are foreign born.

In 1850 the number of insane persons was 31,397, in 1860, 42,864, in 1870, 61,909, and in 1880 a little in excess of 70,000, averaging one to every 666 inhabitants.

The cost of the last civil war to the national government, not including destruction of property South or loss of revenue uncollected, has already amounted in direct payments to $6,189,929,909.

The total national debt in 1880 was $2,120,415,370.63.

In 1800 there were but 903 post offices. In 1880 there were 42,989.

40

In 1846 the production of gold and silver in the United States scarcely reached $1,300,000. In 1880 it was $73,700,000.

INFLUENCE UPON OTHER NATIONS.

Nations, like individuals, cannot live for themselves alone, neither can they increase in wealth, education, and power without exerting consciously or unconsciously an increased influence upon the institutions of other nations. In this respect the history of the United States has been most remarkable. Sometimes the influence of America in the affairs of the world has been silent and obscure, and at other times open and forcible, but nevertheless ceaseless and potent at all times since its entry into the great family of nations.

The effect of its example and success as a republic has not always been in favor of peace; and it may be that the agitation of the subject of liberty of conscience and freedom of action among the people of the old world, caused by the prosperity attending self-government in America, had much to do with the bloody scenes and startling revolutions of 1789 and 1797.

A glance at the present status of the nations of the earth as we turn the globe eastward under your eyes, will surprise even an American, if he should pause as each country comes up before him and recall those events in their history wherein the United States has had an important share. In the Pacific, midway between America and Asia, is the kingdom of Hawaii, or the Sandwich Islands. In 1820, when the first American missionary stepped on its volcanic shore, the nation was an absolute monarchy of the most rude and barbarous pattern, with a blood-thirsty king and an untamed savage population not wholly free from cannibalism. The beautiful valleys, plains, and mountain slopes were untilled and wild, the villages dirty and irregular, the people naked, and the moral sense in regard to chastity, liberty, and murder almost wholly in abeyance. There was a native acuteness and natural intellectual talent, and an adaptability in their natures, of which the Americans could avail themselves in enlightening and civilizing the people. Carefully and perseveringly cultivating those traits which tended toward moral and intellectual development, and as cautiously eradicating those customs and inclinations which led toward the savage state, the American missionaries steadily and speedily led the people into the light of national, intellectual, and moral freedom. These reformers had all those vices to contend against, which the dissolute sailors persistently introduced, as they swarmed on shore from the sailing ships of every civilized nation.

Yet how wonderful the record as we compare the present with the past! Before Judge Lee went there from America the islands were without form of law other than the will of a savage ruler. Now a perfection of legal proceedings has become national, which is so much admired by the Spanish, Portuguese, and English residents of other Pacific Islands that the same experiment is being tried by many of them. In 1820 the islands were a savage wilderness, in which naked men roamed with the wild beasts. To-day beautiful gardens of flowers, hedged fields of grain, and immense sugar and cotton plantations adorn the charming landscapes. Then none but the most primitive tools or spears were known to the natives ; now all the useful implements for agricultural or household uses, all the ornaments of civilized art, and all the effects of landscape gardening are found as in America. Then there were no manufactories ; now there are many. Then they imported nothing ; now they take merchandise from the United States exceeding in value yearly the sum of $1,100,000. Then the people raised nothing for export ; now the products of their fields and manufactories which they export annually to other countries has a value exceeding $2,200,000. Then they had no written language ; now they have a native literature, and publish books and many newspapers. Then they had no schools ; now the common free school system is universal, and all the people, with scarcely an exception, can read and write. Then they had no national existence among the powers of the world ; now they have their accredited ministers at nearly every national capital. Then they had no churches ; now the religious denominations number an active membership of over 12,000.

The political institutions of the Hawaiian kingdom are modeled after the Constitution of the United States, and the local administration of the law is conducted by the same kind of officials and in the same form as in the United States. So much like the United States are all the institutions of the country, and so closely related to our nation do the population feel, that there have been many popular movements in the islands in favor of reciprocity and free commerce between the two nations, and even for a political union as another State.

The history of the Sandwich Islands seems but a prophecy of what Japan is to be, so far as its political and educational imitation of the United States is concerned. One of the secretaries of the Mikado told the writer in Tokio (Jeddo) in 1870 that thousands of young men were hesitating whether to remain in Japan or to start at once to the United States to secure an education, as the only question then appeared to be only *how soon* they would have the schools and institutions of America in Japan. The progress which the people of Japan have made since 1870 must have astonished even the most expectant men of that empire, and shows what a powerful influence the United States has had in their social and political revolutions. In 1854 Commodore Perry, of the American navy, was sent to secure some treaty with the sealed kingdom of Japan, whereby commerce with the people might be opened. It was a difficult and an apparently hopeless undertaking at the time; for the natives hated all foreigners with religious hatred, and every European who set foot on their shore incurred the penalty of death. The people were not in such a savage state as those of the Sandwich Islands, but their form of government was an absolute monarchy, their religion a low form of idol-worship, and their social relations barbarous and often murderously cruel. They had some knowledge of the culture of rice and tea, and among a favored class writing in Chinese characters was used for correspondence. They were, however, a brave, active, patriotic race, and when once relieved of the superstitions of their religion and the despotism of their government, they become noble, enterprising, honorable freemen.

Commodore Perry met with such success in his interview with the Japanese government that he secured the opening of two ports to the ships of the United States, and the contract was ratified by a solemn treaty. The announcement of that treaty induced many merchants of America to open a trade with Japan, and also drew the attention of the English government to the importance of the Japanese trade. Other nations imitated England in sending fleets and making treaties, so that in a few years an immense trade sprang up between Japan and the civilized world. Soon American missionaries found their way into the ports, and opened schools for children, and translated the Bible into the Japanese language. Then followed the mania among Japanese youth for secreting themselves on foreign vessels and visiting the United States and Europe. Then other ports were opened. Then the young sons of Japanese noblemen were sent to America and Europe to be educated. Then American school-teachers, professors, scientific men, and skilled workmen were invited to take important stations in the kingdom as teachers of the arts and sciences and directors and superintendents of the government's public enterprises; until they now hold influential situations in the Japanese custom houses, national banks, navy, army, government offices at the capitol, post office, public education, and department of agriculture, and are engaged to organize a common-school system after the pattern of the United States, and to connect the large cities of the nation with each other by telegraphs and railroads. Christian churches are being formed and supported by the people in many portions of the empire, and the theory of entire political freedom and universal suffrage as adopted in the United States has the support of the government officials.

Thus, in 1854, Japan was a hidden, unknown land to the enlightened world, and was in a sad state of barbarism. In 1881 it is one of the recognized national powers in the world. With the coinage and national bank system on the American plan which it has adopted, commerce has been greatly simplified and encouraged, until the exports for a single year are in excess of twenty-five millions of dollars, and the imports exceed twenty-eight millions of dollars.

Upon the gigantic empire of China the institutions of the United States are having a strong influence through the agency of the American missionaries, American commerce, Chinese students educated by the thousand in the United States, and through the vast throng of emigrants who ebb and flow in nomadic waves between the Pacific coast and China. Many Americans are employed, in common with Englishmen, in the internal revenue, customs service, treasury department, and diplomatic service of the Chinese nation. Americans have been engaged in the organization of the armies, and have led great armies in time of internal warfare. It is easy to foretell what will some day be the result of American education and experience among American institutions upon the thousands of Chinaman who now visit this country. Not many years hence the people of that land will become civilized and Christian under the influence of the civilized nations which now carry on commerce and otherwise exert an elevating influence upon them.

One of the marvels of this rushing age is found in the progress, within a few years, of the American missions in the work of Christianizing the kingdoms of Farther India. The advance in arts, sciences, agriculture, and religion in the kingdom of Siam, within ten years, has astonished the people who inaugurated the movement to send missionaries there. The success attending the teaching and preaching in Pegu and Burmah has surprised the missionaries themselves, and the aptness and willingness of the people in connection with civilized enterprises has been of late most strikingly displayed. In many places in those heathen countries American school-books, American tools, American machinery, and American teachers, are revolutionizing the whole condition of the people. Their influence is felt in the courts of the rulers, and the way clearly opened for further and greater reforms. The civilizing influences of missionary efforts and commerce seem to go hand in hand. Sometimes the missionaries open a country to commerce, and often commerce opens heathen lands to the missions. But in both commerce and missions the elevating and purifying influence of America is being felt more and more, year by year, in that hitherto benighted land of India.

Even in Mohammedan lands the American nation is becoming known and respected by the colleges and schools, churches and theological seminaries, which Americans are establishing. All along the coast of Palestine and Asia Minor, even into Constantinople, churches and schools proclaim the Americans' desire for the salvation of all men. In Egypt the positions of responsibility which have been hitherto held by Englishmen or Frenchmen are being partly filled with Americans, and the counsels of the oldest empire of the world are being influenced, and its internal policy more or less guided, by men from one of the youngest nations of the world.

The share which America has had in the formation or revival of the ancient Grecian nation will be considered by many as scarcely perceptible. But the outspoken friendship of distinguished Americans for Greece in her day of revolutionary trial, the contributions of money, the active part of American philanthropists, united with the adoption of so many political forms by Greece which were used only in the United States, the presence of enlightened American professors at Athens, and of Grecian professors in American colleges, cannot be lost upon the government or its people.

Italy is again a united, free, and intelligent nation, and no other country in the world has, perhaps, more reason to take pride in her progress in everything valuable to man, than the United States. There were three men whose influence upon the character of the Italian nation was most marked, and who contributed more than kings or queens to the establishment of a united and free nation. Those men were Mazzini, Garibaldi, and Manin. The former was an overzealous and impracticable man in many respects, but it would make a marvelous change in the history of Italy could we rearrange events and leave him out. He was a republican and an earnest student of American liberty. He often used the United States as an example in his speeches and writings in favor of a republic in Italy. He sought the acquaintance of Americans; and in his speeches to the Swiss urged the adoption of the American system of elections. He was also one of the founders of the " Americani," or society of Americans for the liberation of Italy from Austrian rule, and went with the society when it was merged into the " Carbonari."

Garibaldi was, from his earliest youth, an ardent admirer of the American republic, and was one of the few Italians who was well acquainted with the system of government and free institutions of our country. In 1850, after his severe struggle in the great revolution of Italy in 1847–48, he came to New York and became a citizen of the United States. Here he read our books and studied our political proceedings, and copied largely from our laws and constitution in his recommendations concerning the Italian republic which he hoped to see established. Many of the rights and immunities granted to the people at the union of Italy have been the outgrowth of his agitation.

Daniel Manin, the Venetian revolutionist, whose name is perhaps the least known of the trio, nevertheless had the greatest influence upon the policy of Victor Emmanuel and the Italian people in the constitution of the kingdom of Italy, and he was also the most hearty friend and admirer of the United States. His early life was much influenced by American books, as he often declared. He was one of the founders of the " Americani." He favored eloquently and persistently a " United States of Italy." He sent out as an incendiary document the Declaration of Independence, translated verbatim into Italian. He adopted " George Washington " and " Thomas Jefferson " as passwords for his guard, showing his regard for those Americans.

From his exile in Paris, after his almost miraculous heroism and endurance at Venice in the siege of 1848, he continually urged the Italians to take the United States as an example and make a free nation. Thus he, more than any other Italian of his time, prepared the people of Italy for the institutions which they now enjoy under that most limited form of a limited monarchy. He advocated American religious freedom, which was partially adopted. He advocated the adoption of the American school system, which was also partially done. He advocated the establishment of a judiciary and a congress after the plan adopted in America; and loved and honored, and almost worshiped, as he was by many Italians, his words had great influence, and brought about many reforms.

His influence did not die with him in 1857. The potency of his name was seen in 1866, and again in 1870, and should the present king fail to make such a " President " as Manin declared a king should be, if they tolerated one at all, he may reasonably expect to hear the call for his abdication fearlessly spoken as when against the Emperor Ferdinand the people so unanimously shouted " Avremo Manin " (we will have Manin).

The importance which the French people have attached to the example of America has been so often mentioned by French periodicals and French orators, that at times the people have wearied of the cry. The statesman, Gambetta, in a speech made just after the last siege of Paris, exclaimed, " I am accused of quoting ' the United States!' Citizens of France, it is safe to quote the United States!" From the days of Lafayette to the present day the success of the American nation has continued to be a favorite theme with the French in their opposition to tyranny, and the establishment of a republic on the ruins of a monarchy as old as civilization there, could not have been successful had not a mighty nation already tried the experiment successfully and that nation one which was closely united with France in fraternal affection. In the national constitution and laws there are now embodied republican provisions which are taken direct from the state and national constitutions of the United States. Indebted as we are to France for our national existence we rejoice at these opportunities for making some return.

England and the United States are now in such direct commercial competition that the whole internal policy of the British nation is affected by the industry and enterprise of the American people.

With American cotton fabrics securing the markets of the world, with the enormous product of grain, coal, iron, and beef in America, going into her own ports and underbidding the bare cost of production there, the English people are forced to make changes which disturb the tranquillity of the whole empire. Emigration increasing, discontent among the manufacturing population developing into popular political movements, and distress among the farmers causing feuds between landlord and tenant, it may be safely said that the United States is an important factor in shaping the future of England. In addition to these commercial considerations, although somewhat connected with them, the relations which so many of the American people hold to the government of Ireland through ancestry, birth, or sympathy, do influence more or less the policy and history of both nations. The great literary interests which both have in a common language, and the relation to each other being such, that the results of great discoveries or great achievements in literature or science must at once become equally beneficial to both, also shows how great and important our influence over each other's destiny has become.

On the extreme west coast of Africa next south of Senegambia, is a territory over which a republic is gradually but firmly extending its government, and in which will doubtless be seen the head and front of a powerful nation. It is called Liberia. It was founded in 1822 by the American Colonization Society. Its constitution is a copy of that of the United States as far as it could apply to the time and place. Its officers have nearly all been citizens of the United States, and its administration of law and election of officers are conducted in accordance with American custom. It is a foothold upon that vast dark continent similar to that of the English at Cape Colony, and its future appears equally hopeful to its founders.

Over the affairs of the South American nations the United States has exercised but little control, although again and again appealed to by some of them to do so. Yet capitalists of the United States have large sums invested in South American railroads and kindred enterprises, and many citizens of our republic are in the employ of those nations in connection with governmental business.

Upon the principalities of the West India Islands the United States has not used its political influence as much as it clearly ought to have done; and it is clearly the duty of this nation to interfere enough in the government of adjacent countries or islands to secure peace both for them and for itself. For a powerful and wealthy nation to stand carelessly and listlessly by while murder, or human slavery, or useless destruction of property is going on at the next door, is to act the part of a participant in the crimes which it might prevent. Whether the " Monroe Doctrine " is to be upheld or not, it may not so much matter, but whether we are to allow our prestige and power to be wasted, while the oppressed of our continent and its islands cry in vain for succor, is a great matter. The United States would exert a powerful influence on the affairs of the West Indies, if the nation were less selfish   A word of advice would have saved and promoted the civilization of Hayti and San Domingo. A single stroke of diplomatic action would save Cuba from her ceaseless wars and terrible slavery. The United States possesses the necessary influence, but it has not been used.

Upon Mexico, however, the institutions of the United States have made a great and valuable impression. No country in the world, unless it be in Africa, presented a less favorable field for a republic than did Mexico when it declared its independence of Spain in 1821. Ignorant, hasty, and quarrelsome, the Mexican populace had but little fitness for self-government. This was most clearly demonstrated by the ceaseless rebellion and revolution which followed the adoption of a constitution copied almost literally from that of the United States. But yet with the moral influence of the American republic constantly exerted to encourage, enlighten, and caution the Mexican people, they have slowly ascended the scale of self-discipline until the introduction of railroads and telegraphs by the capitalists of the United States appears to be the crowning feature of republican success. Through all these years of internal warfare, election brawls, revolts, deposition of officials, defalcations, betrayals, and discontent, our Great Republic has seized upon the opportunities to calm the fears of officials, to frown down dangerous revolutions among the Mexican people, and by careful diplomacy to keep the nation republican in its form and tending upward in all its institutions. Once, when in the trying days of our civil war, France attempted to get a hold upon Mexico through Maximilian and his companion dupes, the Mexicans looked despairingly toward the United States, and asked a signal of recognition. The reiteration of the " Monroe Doctrine," that no foreign power should be suffered to interfere in the affairs of the New World, by several leading statesmen, was enough to encourage the Mexicans to the greatest resistance, and enough to show the invading nations how useless would be their attempts to gain a permanent footing in America. In the last Mexican civil war in which Juarez was concerned the prompt recognition of him as the rightful president by the United States destroyed all hope of successful rebellion on the part of the insurgents, and peace followed almost immediately. The form of government, the finances, the coin, the banks, the post-offices, the railways, the custom houses, the elections, the militia, the representative assemblies of Mexico, like those of Canada, make a closer and closer imitation of the Great Republic's usages and customs, in every passing year.

Such prestige and position among the nations of the world may be a subject of pride or a subject of humiliation according to the manner in which we use it. It is now time that every citizen of the republic should feel that the nation does not live for itself alone, but that the maintenance of all " its free and enlightening institutions not only insures peace, prosperity, and happiness at home, but also by the powerful force of example hastens the approach of that period when all mankind shall be also blessed with the inestimable boon of civil and religious freedom.

INDEX.
